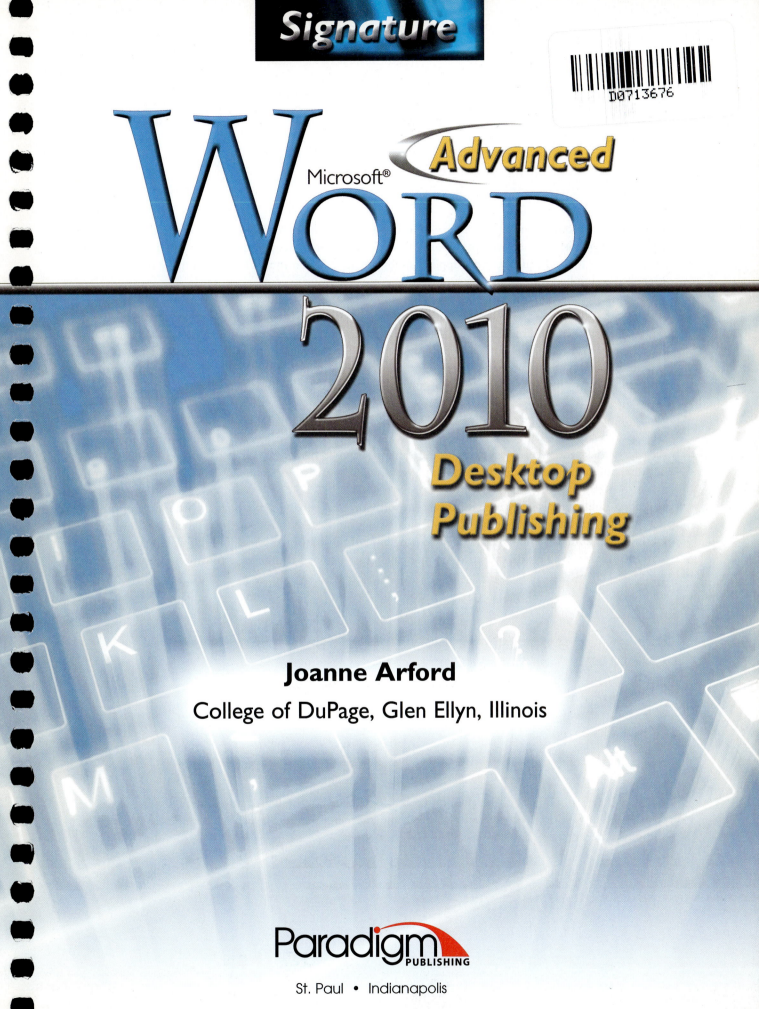

Signature

Microsoft® **Advanced**

WORD 2010

Desktop Publishing

Joanne Arford

College of DuPage, Glen Ellyn, Illinois

Paradigm
PUBLISHING

St. Paul • Indianapolis

Managing Editor: Sonja Brown
Developmental Editor: Spencer Cotkin
Production Editor: Bob Dreas
Cover Designer: Leslie Anderson

Production Specialist: Jack Ross
Proofreader: Julie McNamee
Indexer: Ina Gravitz

Care has been taken to verify the accuracy of information presented in this book. However, the authors, editors, and publisher cannot accept responsibility for Web, email, newsgroup, or chat room subject matter or content, or for consequences from application of the information in this book, and make no warranty, expressed or implied, with respect to its content.

Trademarks: Microsoft is a trademark or registered trademark of Microsoft Corporation in the United States and/or other countries. Some of the product names and company names included in this book have been used for identification purposes only and may be trademarks or registered trade names of their respective manufacturers and sellers. The authors, editors, and publisher disclaim any affiliation, association, or connection with, or sponsorship or endorsement by, such owners.

We have made every effort to trace the ownership of all copyrighted material and to secure permission from copyright holders. In the event of any question arising as to the use of any material, we will be pleased to make the necessary corrections in future printings. Thanks are due to the aforementioned authors, publishers, and agents for permission to use the materials indicated.

Paradigm Publishing is independent from Microsoft Corporation, and not affiliated with Microsoft in any manner. While this publication may be used in assisting individuals to prepare for a Microsoft Business Certification exam, Microsoft, its designated program administrator, and Paradigm Publishing do not warrant that use of this publication will ensure passing a Microsoft Business Certification exam.

ISBN 978-0-76383-888-1 (text)
ISBN 978-0-76383-890-4 (text and CD)

© 2011 by Paradigm Publishing, Inc.
875 Montreal Way
St. Paul, MN 55102
Email: educate@emcp.com
Website: www.emcp.com

Printed in the United States of America

20 19 18 17 16 15 14 13 12 11   3 4 5 6 7 8 9 10

Brief Contents

Contents

Preface

Advanced Microsoft® Word 2010: Desktop Publishing by Joanne Arford focuses on advanced Word 2010 features with an emphasis on desktop publishing concepts and terminology. Word 2010 and other Office 2010 applications, such as PowerPoint and Publisher, allow users to create professional-looking documents with attractive graphics, text effects, and eye-catching design elements. Publishing from the desktop computer greatly reduces production costs, combines the tasks of page design and layout, offers immediate results, and allows control of production from start to finish.

Textbook and Chapter Features

Advanced Microsoft Word 2010: Desktop Publishing is designed for students who are proficient in word processing. This textbook assumes that students are using a custom or full installation of Microsoft Word 2010, in a computer lab or home-study setting.

Course Outcomes

Students who successfully complete a course based on this textbook will have mastered the following competencies:

- Using and applying the design concepts of focus, balance, proportion, contrast, directional flow, consistency, and color
- Evaluating documents for the use of basic design concepts
- Using desktop publishing features of Microsoft Word 2010 to integrate basic layout and design concepts in order to enhance the readability of multiple-page, portrait, or landscape documents such as letterheads, postcards, business cards, certificates, flyers, brochures, online forms, and newsletters
- Producing and enhancing business and personal documents with variable page layouts using standardized type and graphic design techniques while incorporating updated Word 2010 features such as watermarks, Cover Pages, page borders, Themes, Quick Styles, Shapes, WordArt, SmartArt, Quick Parts, Picture Tools, Table Tools, Microsoft Office templates, and Clip art on Office.com
- Managing Word 2010 document files and folders using a Windows 7 operating system
- Publishing Word documents in a variety of formats, including PowerPoint presentations and web pages
- Becoming familiar with the basic features and capabilities of Microsoft Publisher 2010 to produce professional-looking flyers, brochures, and newsletters

Instructional Design

Most of the key desktop publishing concepts addressed in this textbook are presented in Chapter 1. Subsequent chapters reinforce the concepts through instruction and exercises in which students create commercial-quality documents. Exercises are designed not only to build proficiency in the desktop publishing features of Word 2010 but also to develop critical thinking, decision making, and creativity. Many activities reinforce collaborative learning as students work in teams to plan, design, and evaluate business and personal documents for publication. Several exercises incorporate a scenario framework in which basic information for a task is supplied as it might be presented in real-life situations.

Students who wish to build a portfolio of documents for course requirements or job applications should take special note of the exercises identified with a portfolio icon. The final portfolio can be printed and bound in hard copy format, or the documents can be saved in PDF format, organized as a portfolio, and then viewed on a computer monitor.

Emphasis on Visual Learning

Numerous images combined with clearly written instruction offer a highly effective visual learning experience. Screen captures of the entire Word screen highlight ribbon elements and other tools and help students connect concepts with clicks. As students follow the step-by-step practice exercises, they can confirm they are performing the correct actions by comparing their screens with the screen captures displayed. Key steps are labeled on the screen captures to make following the exercise directions as easy as possible. In addition, model answers of these intrachapter exercises are displayed so students can check their completed documents. Sample model answers also are provided for end-of-chapter and end-of-unit assessments.

Chapter Structure

The textbook contains three units with a total of twelve chapters. Each chapter contains the following elements:

- Performance Objectives
- List of desktop publishing terms
- List of Word 2010 features used
- Overview of chapter concepts and features
- Marginal features
  - ○ Definitions of key terms
  - ○ Desktop Publishing (DTP) Pointers, which reinforce concepts
  - ○ Office buttons
- Hands-on exercises with images of model solutions of completed documents
- Chapter Summary
- Commands Review
- Reviewing Key Points (multiple choice, true/false, completion, or short answer review)
- Chapter Assessments

Key terms
Definitions of key terms

DTP POINTERS
Pointers reinforce concepts

Clip Art

In most chapters, the Chapter Assessments include Integrated assessments and Group Project assessments. For Integrated assessments, students incorporate skills learned in the current chapter with techniques and applications discussed in previous chapters and, in places, with features commonly employed in other Office programs. These exercises are identified with an Integrated icon. The Group Project assessments, identified with a Group icon, promote collaborative learning, team building and organization, critical thinking, and individual/group creativity.

At the end of each unit is a Performance Assessments section with problems that evaluate student mastery of both desktop publishing concepts and software skills presented in the unit.

GROUP PROJECT

What's New in Signature Advanced Microsoft® Word 2010: Desktop Publishing

Users familiar with the Advanced Word 2007 book and previous editions will notice the following enhancements to the textbook and software:

- New documents created for event planners and virtual office assistants
- Documents using new Word 2010 typography ligatures and special text effects.
- New challenging Unit Performance Assessments to bring DTP skills to the next level
- New enriched explanations of picture compression, grouping/ungrouping, and cropping
- Documents using new artistic effects: Pencil Sketch, Line Drawing, Watercolor Sponge, Mosaic Bubbles, Glass, Pastels Smooth, Plastic Wrap, Photocopy, and Paint Strokes
- New object alignment technology in Publisher that provides guidance, but keeping you in control of the final placement of any new object such as a graphic or text box
- Dynamic slide transitions in PowerPoint 2010
- PowerPoint 2010 presentations saved as videos

Guidelines for Students on Completing Computer Exercises

Some of the computer exercises in this textbook require students to access and use an existing file (Student Data file). These files are available on the Student Resources CD that accompanies this textbook, as well as on the Internet Resource Center for the book at www.emcp.net/advancedword2010. The files are contained in individual folders for each chapter. A CD icon and folder name is displayed on the opening page of each chapter and each set of unit assessments. Students need to copy the chapter folder from the CD before beginning the chapter activities. Instructions on how to copy and delete folders are provided on the inside back cover of the book.

As you work through the desktop publishing information and exercises, keep the following points in mind:

- All default formatting settings (such as fonts, margin settings, line spacing, and justification), templates, and folders used in this textbook are based on the assumption that none of the original program defaults have been customized after installation.
- Instructions for all features and exercises emphasize using the mouse. Where appropriate, keyboard or function key presses are added as an alternative.
- As you complete the exercises, view the completed figure that follows each exercise to see what the document should look like.
- Be aware that the final appearance of your printed documents depends on the printer you use to complete the exercises. Your printer driver may be different from the printer driver used for the exercises in this textbook. Consequently, you may have to make some minor adjustments when completing the exercises in this book. For example, if you have to select a font different from the one called for in the instructions, you may need to change the type size to complete the exercise in the space allotted. You may also need to adjust the spacing between paragraphs or specific blocks of text. If a Clip art, photograph, or motion clip is not available, please select a similar image. As a result, your documents will look slightly different from what you see in this text. As you will find in the chapters that follow, creating desktop published documents is a constant process of making small adjustments to fine-tune the layout and design.

Student and Instructor Ancillaries

The following resources are available for students and instructors.

Student Resources CD

Packaged with the textbook is a Student Resources CD that contains files required for completing many of the exercises in the book. See the inside back cover for instructions on copying the chapter folders to your storage medium.

Internet Resource Center: Student and Instructor Views

The website for *Signature Advanced Microsoft® Word 2010: Desktop Publishing* is located at www.emcp.net/advancedword2010. For students, the website contains student files, online quizzes, PowerPoint slides, and a variety of tips and links. The password-protected instructor resources include electronic versions of the content in the Instructor's Guide, PowerPoint presentations, supplemental assessments, and additional tests and quizzes.

eBook

For students who prefer studying with an eBook, *Signature Advanced Microsoft® Word 2010: Desktop Publishing* is available in an electronic form. The web-based, password-protected eBook features dynamic navigation tools, Including bookmarking, a linked table of contents, and the ability to jump to a specific page. The eBook format also supports helpful study tools, such as highlighting and note taking.

Printed Instructor's Guide and Instructor's CD

The Instructor's Guide includes course planning resources, such as teaching hints and a sample course syllabus; PowerPoint presentations (on Instructor CD) for each chapter; and assessment resources, including model answers for end-of-chapter and end-of-unit assessments, a grading sheet, and additional exams.

Computerized Test Generator

Instructors can use the **EXAM**VIEW® Assessment Suite and test banks of multiple-choice items to create customized web-based or print tests. The **EXAM**VIEW® Assessment Suite and test banks are provided on the Instructor Resources CD.

Blackboard Cartridge

This set of files allows instructors to create a personalized Blackboard website for their course and provides supplementary content, communication via e-discussions and online group conferences, and testing resources. Content items include a syllabus, assignments, quizzes, exams, and additional course links and study aids.

Blackboard

System Requirements

This interactive text is designed for the student to complete chapter and unit work on a computer running a standard installation of Microsoft Office 2010, Standard or Professional, and the Microsoft Windows 7 operating system. To effectively run this suite and operating system, your computer should be outfitted with the following:

- 1 gigahertz (GHz) processor or faster; 1 gigabyte (GB) of RAM
- DVD drive
- 15 GB of available hard-disk space
- Computer mouse or compatible pointing device

Microsoft Office 2010 will also operate on computers running the Windows XP Service Pack 3 or the Windows Vista operating system.

Screen captures in this book were created using a screen resolution display setting of 1280 × 800. Choose the resolution that best matches your computer; however, be aware that using a resolution other than 1280 × 800 means that your screens may not exactly match the illustrations in this book.

About the Author

Joanne (Marschke) Arford is originally from Berrien Springs, Michigan, lived in South Bend, Indiana, for several years, and has been residing in Naperville, Illinois, for the past 20 years. She and her husband, Frank, are the parents of three grown daughters, Rachel, Lisa, and Kaitlin. Joanne graduated from Western Michigan University in Kalamazoo, where she received her Bachelor's and Master's degrees in Business Education. Joanne is currently an adjunct faculty member at the College of DuPage in Glen Ellyn, Illinois. Her first desktop publishing textbook was co-authored with Nita Rutkosky and Judy Burnside. Since then she has written several editions of the Advanced Word Desktop Publishing textbook. Joanne is a member of the Illinois Business Education Association and has received the Illinois Business Education Association Writer's Hall of Fame awards for all of her textbooks.

Joanne enjoys reading, walking, and traveling. She has visited China, South Africa, Europe, and other destinations with her husband. Joanne also enjoys volunteering at the Loaves and Fishes Community Pantry in Naperville.

Acknowledgments

The author and editors are grateful to the many individuals who provided feedback or contributed ideas and content for various aspects of this project. The following individuals reviewed the previous version of this book and offered valuable suggestions for the 2010 edition:

Teresa Roberts
Wilson Community College
Wilson, North Carolina

Paula Gregory
Yavapai College
Prescott, Arizona

Rhonda Kolbuc
Niagara College
Niagara-on-the-Lake, Ontario

Joanne Davis
Red Deer College
Red Deer, Alberta

Carolyn Clark
Lethbridge College
Lethbridge, Alberta

Kari Phillips
Davis Applied Technology College
Kaysville, Utah

Lynn Dee Eason, MEd
Sault College of Applied Arts & Technology
Sault Ste. Marie, Ontario

Leasa Steadman
Sheridan College
Brampton, Ontario

Lauren LoPresti, MSEd, MA
College of Lake County
Grayslake, Illinois

Margie V. Brunson, MEd
Central Carolina Technical College
Sumter, South Carolina

Tamara Vesselovskaia-Mondadori, MA
Scott Community College
Davenport, Iowa

The author and editors also wish to thank Paula Gregory of Yavapai College, Prescott, Arizona, and Teresa Roberts of Wilson Community College, Wilson, North Carolina, for their valuable contributions as testers of exercises and assessments. Thanks also to Janet Blum of Fanshawe College, London, Ontario, Judy Peterson of Two Harbors, Minnesota, and Jeff Johnson of Minneapolis, Minnesota, and Molly Reavis of Kilgore College, Longview, Texas, for preparing supplements. Finally, we appreciate the academic and technical contributions of Nancy Stanko and Wendy Felder, both of the College of DuPage, Glen Ellyn, Illinois.

Permissions: The following individuals and organizations have generously given permission for use of their materials: Edward Cardiovascular Institute, Naperville, Illinois; Floyd Rogers, Butterfield Gardens, Glen Ellyn, Illinois; Naperville Chamber of Commerce, Naperville, Illinois; Dr. Bradley Kampschroeder and Dr. Michael Halkias, Naper Grove Vision Care, Naperville, Illinois; Barbara Blankenship, Michael Kott, and Terri McCormick, desktop publishing students at the College of DuPage, Glen Ellyn, Illinois; and Jody Bender and Charles McLimans at Loaves and Fishes Community Pantry, Naperville, Illinois.

Unit 1

Creating Business and Personal Documents

Chapter 1

CHAPTER01

Understanding the Desktop Publishing Process

Performance Objectives

Upon successful completion of Chapter 1, you will be able to:

- Define desktop publishing.
- Plan and design documents.
- Create focus, balance, and proportion in documents.
- Achieve contrast, consistency, and directional flow in documents.
- Apply guidelines for color.

- Identify Word 2010 features that promote good desktop publishing design in documents—Text Effects, Quick Styles, Style Sets, WordArt, Pictures, Clip Art, Shapes, Quick Parts, SmartArt, and Themes.
- Use supplemental accessories and programs such as Microsoft Office.com Templates, Microsoft Bing Maps, Microsoft Snipping Tool, and Microsoft Picture Manager.

Desktop Publishing Terms

Alignment	Directional flow	Spread
Asymmetrical design	Focus	Symmetrical design
Balance	Harmony	Theme
Color	Legibility	Thumbnail sketch
Consistency	Proportion	White space
Contrast	Resolution	Z pattern

Word Features Used

Clip Art	File Tab Backstage View	SmartArt
Cover Page	Pictures	Style Sets
Crop	Quick Parts	Templates
Document Themes (Colors, Fonts, and Effects)	Quick Styles	WordArt
	Shapes	

Microsoft Supplemental Accessories and Programs

Microsoft Picture Manager	Microsoft Bing Map	Microsoft Snipping Tool

Defining Desktop Publishing

Since the 1970s, computers have been an integral part of the business environment. Businesses use computers and software packages to perform a variety of tasks. For many years, the three most popular types of software purchased for computers were word processing, spreadsheet, and database programs. The introduction of the laser printer and the inkjet printer, with their abilities to produce high-quality documents in black and white as well as in color, led to the growing popularity of another kind of software called desktop publishing.

Desktop publishing allows the user to produce professional-looking documents for both office and home use. The phrase *desktop publishing*, coined by Aldus Corporation president Paul Brainard in 1984, means that publishing can now literally take place at your desk.

Desktop publishing may involve using dedicated software such as Microsoft Publisher, Adobe InDesign, and QuarkXPress or an advanced word processing program such as Microsoft Word with desktop publishing capabilities. For simpler desktop publishing projects, Word is a good choice; for more complex documents, high-end desktop publishing software may be used. Microsoft Publisher is a mid-range desktop publishing program that provides the user with extensive templates for ease in creating professional-looking documents. Adobe Illustrator and PhotoShop are other software programs that may be used to supplement the advanced digital desktop publishing process.

Until the mid-1980s, graphic design depended almost exclusively on design professionals. However, desktop publishing software changed all that by bringing graphic design into the office and home. Faster microprocessors, larger storage capacity, improved printer capabilities, an increased supply of clip art and photos, the advent of CDs and DVDs, flash drives, and Memory Card Readers, along with access to the Internet continue to expand the role of desktop publishing. Imagine everything from a flyer to a newsletter to a Web page designed, created, and produced at your own computer. Do you remember using a typewriter to type a newsletter? Consider how far desktop publishing has evolved—see Figure 1.1. The past 40 years have seen an evolution from a manual typewriter to an electric typewriter to personal computers and to laptop computers. What will be next?

In traditional publishing, several people may have been involved in completing a publication project, which naturally involved greater costs and time compared with today's desktop publishing. Using desktop publishing software, one person may be able to perform all of the tasks necessary to complete a project, which greatly reduces the costs of publishing documents. The two approaches, however, do have a great deal in common. Both approaches involve planning the project, organizing content, analyzing layout and design, arranging design elements, typesetting, printing, and distributing the project.

Figure 1.1 Producing Documents with a Typewriter, a Personal Computer, and a Laptop Computer

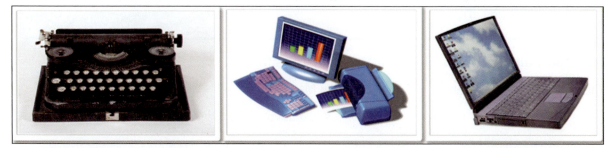

Initiating the desktop publishing process using a typewriter, then a personal computer and inkjet printer, and now a laptop computer. What will be next?

Desktop publishing can be either an individual or a combined effort. As an individual effort, desktop publishing produces immediate results and offers you the ability to control the production from the beginning layout and design to the end result—printing and distribution. However, desktop publishing and traditional publishing work well together. A project may begin on a desktop, where the document is designed and created, but an illustrator may be commissioned to create some artwork, and the piece may be sent to a commercial printer for printing and binding.

Using the new Office 2010 results-oriented interface, along with enhanced desktop features found in Word 2010 and Publisher 2010 with integration of PowerPoint 2010, Excel 2010, and Access 2010, you will find it easier to create, collaborate, manage, review, edit, customize, print, and publish professional-looking publications. The availability of OpenType fonts in Office 2010 also promotes cross-platform sharing between Apple computers and PCs.

When creating desktop applications with publishing and data merge capabilities, you will be able to control and complete your in-house projects that used to be outsourced. Word 2010 and Publisher 2010, along with application-independent file formats (such as PDF, XML, and XPS), allow you to share documents regardless of the computer type and applications used. In addition, you will be able to prepare and send publications more efficiently to professional printers accustomed to sharing PDF and XML file formats. Shared document technology, the Internet, and email provide opportunities for you to collaborate with others outside your home and office, even as you travel.

Note: Comments on how to use this textbook or hints on the exercises will appear in italicized bold type. This book is designed to help those who possess an advanced skill level of Microsoft Word but who have little or no design experience. Today's office support staff are increasingly being required to create more sophisticated documents with little or no background on how to design a visually appealing document that still gets the message across to the reader. Home users are also finding the need to create similar professional-looking documents, whether it is for a home business, an organization, or personal use. In addition to creating documents from scratch, you will learn to use professionally prepared online Office templates, customize them to fit your individual or corporate needs, save them in PDF or XML formats, and print them on a personal printer or send them electronically to a professional printer.

Initiating the Desktop Publishing Process

The process of creating a publication begins with two steps—planning the publication and creating the content. During the planning process, the desktop publisher must decide on the purpose of the publication and identify the intended audience. When creating the content, the desktop publisher must make sure that the reader understands the intended message of the publication.

Planning the Publication

Initial planning is probably one of the most important steps in the desktop publishing process. During this stage, consider the following:

- Clearly identify the purpose of your communication. The more definite you are about your purpose, the easier it will be for you to organize your material into an effective communication. Are you trying to provide information? Are you trying to sell a product? Are you announcing an event?

Desktop Publishing
Use of specific desktop publishing software or high-end word processing software to produce professional-looking documents in which text and graphics enhance the message.

DTP POINTERS
Consider the demographics of your target audience.

- Assess your target audience. Who will read your publication? Are they employees, coworkers, clients, friends, or family? What will your target audience expect from your publication? Will they expect a serious, more conservative approach, or an informal, humorous approach?

- Determine in what form your intended audience will be exposed to your message. Will your message be in a brochure as part of a packet of presentation materials for a company seminar? Or will your message take the form of a newspaper advertisement, surrounded by other advertisements? Will your message be in the form of a business card distributed when making sales calls? Or will your message be tacked on to a bulletin board?

- Decide what you want your readers to do after reading your message. Do you want your readers to ask for more information? Do you want your readers to respond in some way? Do you want your readers to be able to contact you in person or by telephone?

- When planning your project, consider the budget for the entire project. Costs may include paper expenses based on quality, weight, and size; trimming, folding, and binding expenses; number of copies needed; delivery method used; and printing method used—color or black and white.

DTP POINTERS ▶
Pick up design ideas from the works of others.

- Collect examples of effective designs. Keep a design idea folder. Put copies of any designs that impress you into your idea folder. These designs may include flyers, promotional documents, newsletters, graphic images, interesting type arrangements, and the like. Look through your idea folder every time you begin a new project. Let favorite designs serve as a catalyst for developing your own ideas.

Creating the Content

The most important goal in desktop publishing is to get across the message. Design is important because it increases the visual appeal of your document, but content is still the most important consideration. Create a document that communicates the message clearly to your intended audience.

In analyzing your message, identify your purpose, and start organizing your material. Establish a hierarchy of importance among the items in your communication. Consider what items will be the most important to the reader, what will attract the reader's attention, and what will spark enough interest to retain the reader's attention. Begin to think about the format or layout you want to follow. (Check your idea folder!) Clear and organized content combined with an attractive layout and design contributes to the effectiveness of your message.

Designing the Document

DTP POINTERS ▶
Take the time to design!

If the message is the most significant part of a communication, why bother with design? A well-planned and relevant design sets your work apart from others, and it gets people to read your message. Just as people may be judged by their appearance, a publication may be judged by its design. Design also helps organize ideas so the reader can find information quickly and easily. Whether you are creating a business flyer, letterhead, or newsletter, anything you create will look more attractive, more professional, and more convincing if you take a little extra time to design it. As in the planning stages, consider the purpose of the document, the target audience, and the method of distribution. In addition, think about the following factors:

- What feeling does the document elicit?

- What is the most important information, and how can it be emphasized so that the reader can easily identify the purpose of the document?

- What different types of information are presented, and how can these elements be distinguished, yet kept internally consistent?

- How much space is available?

Answering these questions will help you determine the design and layout of your communication.

An important first step in planning your design and layout is to prepare a thumbnail sketch, which is also referred to as *thinking on paper*. A ***thumbnail sketch*** is a miniature draft of the document you are attempting to create. As you can see in Figure 1.2, thumbnail sketches let you experiment with alternative locations for such elements as graphic images, ruled lines (horizontal or vertical lines), columns, and borders.

Thumbnail sketch
A rough sketch used in planning a layout and design.

A good designer continually asks questions, pays attention to details, and makes well-thought-out decisions. Consider examples A and B in Figure 1.3. Which example attracts your attention, entices you to read on, looks convincing, and encourages you to take action?

Overdesigning is one of the most common tendencies of beginning desktop publishers. The temptation to use as many of the desktop publishing features as possible in one document is often difficult to resist. Use design elements to communicate, not decorate. To create a visually attractive and appealing publication, start with the same classic design concepts used as guidelines by professional designers. These concepts include focus, balance, proportion, contrast, directional flow, consistency, and color.

Creating Focus

The ***focus*** or focal point on a page is an element that draws the reader's attention. Focus uses elements that are large, dense, unusual, and/or surrounded by white space.

Focus
An element used to attract the reader's attention.

Two basic design elements used to create focus in a document are:

- text created in larger, bolder, and often contrasting, typefaces; and

- graphic elements such as ruled lines, clip art, photographs, illustrations, watermarks, logos, or images created with a draw program, scanned into the computer, or captured with a digital camera.

Figure 1.2 Thumbnail Sketches: Thinking on Paper

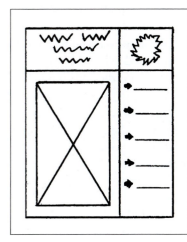
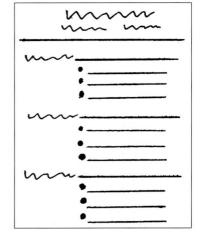

Figure 1.3 Before and After Documents

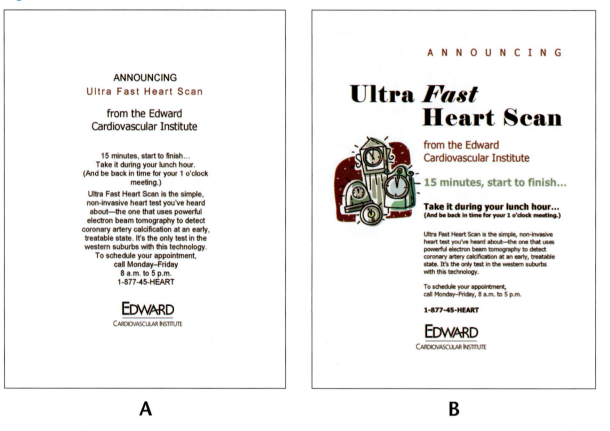

A   B

Creating Focus with Text

You will recognize focus instantly whether the focus is a graphic or text keyed in strong, contrasting fonts. In Word, OpenType fonts and TrueType fonts are available for text formatting. OpenType fonts were created jointly by Microsoft and Adobe in an effort to promote cross-platform compatibility between Macintosh and Windows platforms. A document created on a Macintosh computer might not print in the same way on a Windows-based computer. As OpenType fonts become more common, this difficulty may be corrected. OpenType fonts include exaggerated serif and special ligatures for advanced users working with fine typographic controls (see Chapter 3 for more details). In addition, OpenType fonts also can make multilingual typography easier by including multiple language character sets in one font.

In Word, the majority of fonts are OpenType fonts; however, you will also see a few TrueType fonts still available as well. TrueType fonts were developed by Apple Computer and Microsoft to replace PostScripts fonts that were used in earlier versions of Windows.

Text with weight, contrasting style, text effects (glow, shadow, reflection, and outline), expanded letter-spacing (tracking), varying font sizes, reversed color, rotation, shape (WordArt), and even drop caps can effectively draw the reader's attention. To create a clean-looking document, use the actual fonts from your computer, such as Arial Rounded MT Bold, rather than applying bold or italics to Arial. Organizing similar text, using a consistent strong alignment, and providing generous amounts of white space enhance the appeal of text as focus. *White space* is the background where no text or graphics are located. The amount of white space around a focal element can enhance its appearance and help to balance other design elements on the page. Use color or

White space

Background space with no text or graphics.

Chapter One

white space to emphasize the main message and give the reader's eyes a break from too much text. Consider using a guideline called the ⅓ – ⅔ *Rule*. At least one-third of your publication should consist of white space if the remaining two-thirds contain text and other design elements.

Notice the use of text as a focal point in Figure 1.4 document B. The title "Kids at College" is formatted in Whimsy ICG Heavy, which is a youthful, whimsical font. This formatted text along with a generous amount of white space generates focus in contrast to the unformatted text in document A. Also, notice the impact the reverse text has on the school name.

Creating Focus with Titles, Headlines, and Subheadings

In reports, procedure manuals, newsletters, term papers, tables of contents, titles, headlines, and subheadings, use large or bold type, surrounded by enough white space to contrast with the main text. When creating titles/headlines, keep the following points in mind:

- State your title or headline in a precise, yet easily understood manner.
- Select readable typefaces. *Legibility* is of utmost importance. Readers must be able to clearly see and read the individual letters in the title/headline.
- Size your title or headline in proportion to its importance relative to the surrounding text.
- Set your title or headline in a larger type size so the reader immediately knows the nature of the publication.

DTP POINTERS
One-third of your publication should contain white space.

DTP POINTERS
A well-designed headline attracts the reader's attention.

Legibility
The ease with which individual characters are recognized.

Figure 1.4 Creating Focus with Text

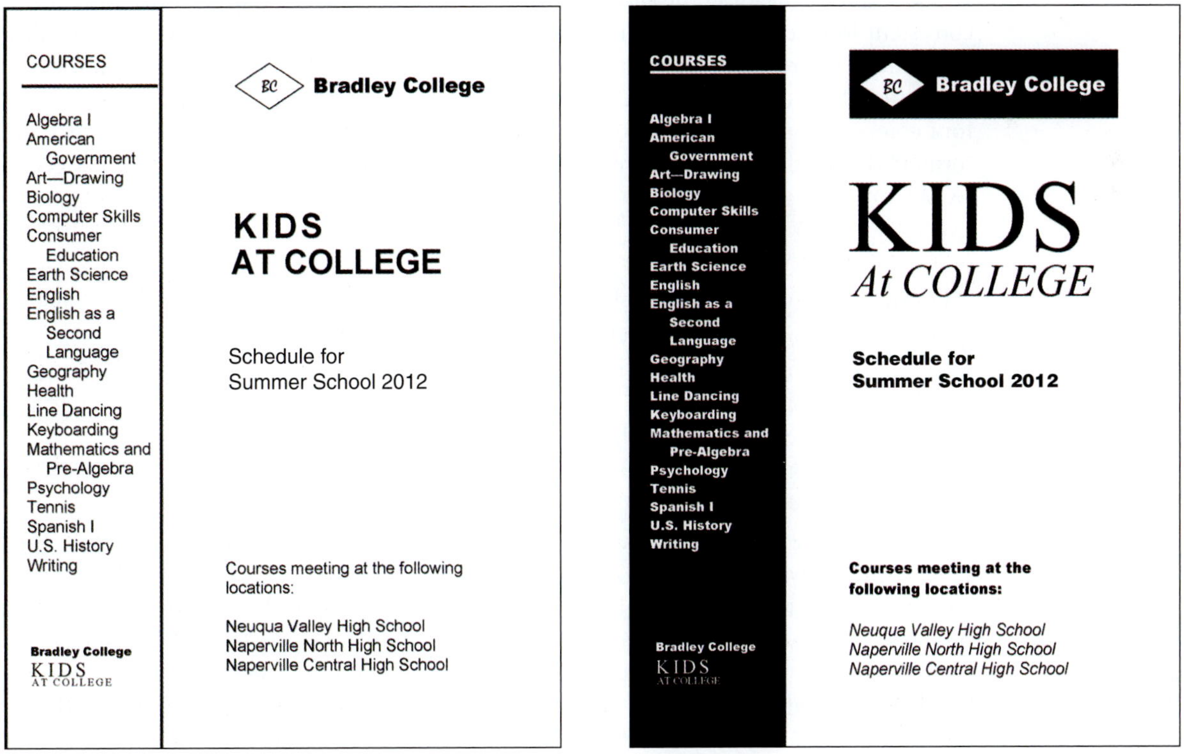

COURSES

Algebra I
American
    Government
Art—Drawing
Biology
Computer Skills
Consumer
    Education
Earth Science
English
English as a
    Second
    Language
Geography
Health
Line Dancing
Keyboarding
Mathematics and
    Pre-Algebra
Psychology
Tennis
Spanish I
U.S. History
Writing

Bradley College
KIDS
AT COLLEGE

BC ◆ **Bradley College**

**KIDS
AT COLLEGE**

Schedule for
Summer School 2012

Courses meeting at the following locations:

Neuqua Valley High School
Naperville North High School
Naperville Central High School

A

COURSES

Algebra I
American
    Government
Art—Drawing
Biology
Computer Skills
Consumer
    Education
Earth Science
English
English as a
    Second
    Language
Geography
Health
Line Dancing
Keyboarding
Mathematics and
    Pre-Algebra
Psychology
Tennis
Spanish I
U.S. History
Writing

Bradley College
KIDS
AT COLLEGE

BC ◆ **Bradley College**

KIDS
At COLLEGE

**Schedule for
Summer School 2012**

**Courses meeting at the
following locations:**

Neuqua Valley High School
Naperville North High School
Naperville Central High School

B

Figure 1.5 **Evaluating the Use of Titles and Subheadings**

A   B   C

In any type of communication—semiannual report, office procedures manual, company newsletter, advertising flyer, or brochure—subheads may provide a secondary focal element. While headlines attract the reader's attention, the subheads may be the key to luring in the reader. Subheads provide order to your text and give the reader further clues about the content of your publication. Include appropriate fonts, line length, line spacing, and alignment. Quick Styles and Style Sets, along with document Themes, make formatting efficient and consistent for any publication or group of similarly designed publications.

Look at document A in Figure 1.5. Does any particular location on the page attract your attention? You might say the title attracts your attention slightly. Now look at document B in the same figure. Do you agree that the bolded text attracts your attention? Now look at document C. Do the title and subheads attract your attention more so than in documents A and B? The title is the primary focal point formatted with the Title style. The subheads, set in a type bolder and larger than the body text but smaller than the heading, provide secondary focal points on the page. Notice how the consistent font selection in all of the subheads makes the document organization readily apparent to the reader. Also, notice that there is more white space before the subheads than after. This spacing connects the subheads to the text that follows. Consistent font colors, font sizes, and effects were created by applying the Decaturthemeto text formatted with the Title, Heading 1, and Heading 2 styles with the Style Set changed to Elegant.

Formatting with Quick Styles

You can apply styles to text by clicking the Quick Styles buttons located in the Styles group in the Home tab. The Styles displayed in the Style Gallery vary with the Theme selected. You can modify fonts, colors, margins, table formatting, and other elements by choosing different Style Sets. In addition, you can save a modified style or new style as a New Quick Style accessible in the Styles gallery.

Using Document Themes

Themes simplify the process of creating professional-looking, matching documents not only within Word 2010 but also within Office PowerPoint 2010 and Excel 2010. The same themes are available in all three applications making it possible to give documents, presentations, and spreadsheets the same *branded* complementary look. With one click, the background, text, graphics, charts, tables, and effects all change to reflect the theme you have selected, ensuring that all parts in your presentation, document, or spreadsheet complement one another. The Angles theme with Franklin Gothic Medium and Franklin Gothic Book fonts were used consistently in the Word itinerary, PowerPoint slide, and Excel spreadsheet shown in Figure 1.6.

DTP POINTERS ▶
Subheads provide order to your text and give the reader further clues about the content of your publication.

DTP POINTERS ▶
Use Themes to consistently format documents created in Word, Excel, and PowerPoint.

DTP POINTERS ▶
Theme Fonts, Theme Colors, and Theme Effects provide opportunities to customize your documents for a professional put together look.

Chapter One

Figure 1.6 Using the Angles Theme in Word, PowerPoint, and Excel

Creating Focus with Graphic Elements

Graphic elements provide focus on a page and can enhance the overall appearance of a publication. Many Word features may be used to create graphical focus in your publications, as shown in Figures 1.7 to 1.10. A SmartArt graphic is a visual representation of information that you can quickly and easily create, choosing from among many different layouts, to effectively communicate your message or ideas. SmartArt located in the Illustrations group on the Insert tab, along with its associated contextual tab, promotes text, shape, and color as it is used to create a focal point in the document shown in Figure 1.7. WordArt, photos, clip art, charts, watermarks, shapes, lines, and text boxes with fill effects were also used in Figures 1.8, 1.9, and 1.10. As you look at each document, ask yourself where its focal point is. What designs on the pages draw you into the document?

Figure 1.7 Using SmartArt for Focus

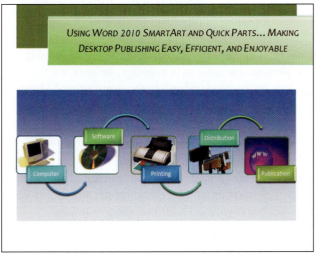

Figure 1.8 Using Photos for Focus

Figure 1.9 Using Clip Art for Focus   **Figure 1.10** Creating a Menu with a Watermark for Focus

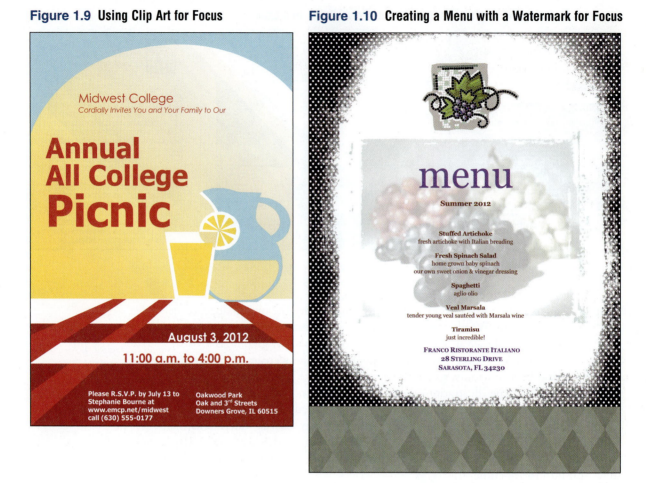

When considering a graphic element as a focal point, remember the following points:

- Legibility is just as important with graphic elements as it is with titles and subheads. Graphic elements should support the message in your text and not interfere with its readability in any way.

- Communicate, do not decorate. Let your message dictate the use of graphic elements. Does the graphic element enhance your message, or does it overshadow your message? Is it relevant, meaningful, and appropriate? Do not use it just for the sake of using it.

- Less is best; keep it simple. One simple, large, and effective graphic image provides more impact than using several smaller images. Too many images create visual confusion for the reader.

- Crop an image if necessary to increase impact. Crop to eliminate unnecessary elements and zoom in on the key parts of an image or crop in unexpected ways to draw attention to the image. See Figure 1.11 for cropping examples.

- Position the graphic to face the text. Graphics or photographs facing away from the text draw the reader's eyes away from the most important part of the document—the content. Compare documents A and B in Figure 1.12. The graphic in document B is a focal point positioned appropriately in the document.

DTP POINTERS
Graphic images should be relevant to your intended message.

DTP POINTERS
Keep your design simple.

DTP POINTERS
Graphics should face the text.

Figure 1.11 Cropping an Image to Increase Impact

Original Image

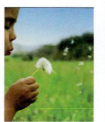

Cropping Using
Aspect Ratio in
Portrait at 4:5

Using the Crop
Tool

Cropping to a Shape

If all other factors are equal, publications containing graphic elements are noticed and perused before text-only publications. The chamber of commerce announcement A shown in Figure 1.13 is not as effective as announcement B. The sun graphic/watermark creates a major focal point. "Good Morning Naperville" stands out as a focal point, but not quite as strong as the image. Varying the type size and type style helps to organize the remaining information and to provide minor focal points on the page.

Figure 1.12 Position Graphics to Face the Text

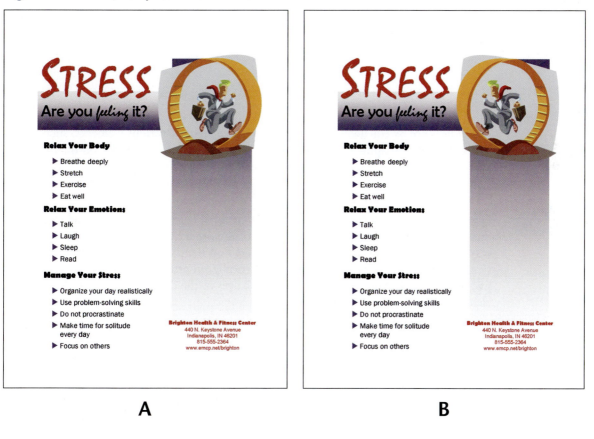

A   B

Figure 1.13 Graphic/Watermark as Focal Point

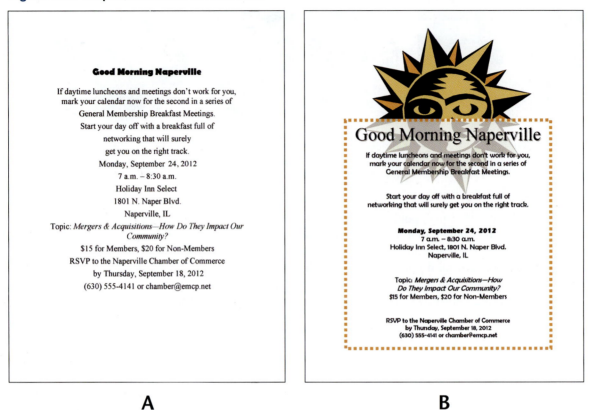

A

B

Creating Balance

Attain *balance* by equally distributing the visual weight of various elements, such as blocks of text, graphic images, headings, ruled lines, and white space on the page. Balance is either symmetrical or asymmetrical.

Symmetrical Balance

A *symmetrical design* contains similar elements of equal proportion or weight on the left and right sides and top and bottom of the page. Symmetrical balance is easy to achieve because all elements are centered on the page. If you were to fold a symmetrically designed document in half vertically (in other words, along its vertical line of symmetry), you would see that both halves of the document contain the same elements.

To better visualize the concept of symmetrical balance, look at the shapes in the top half of Figure 1.14. The squares, representing identical graphic elements, are positioned on the left and right sides of the page. The rectangle, representing a block of text, is centered in between the two squares. Notice the dotted line, representing a vertical line of symmetry, splitting the design in half. It is easy to see that the elements on both sides of the dotted line are equal in weight and proportion because they are the same. Now look at the example of a symmetrically designed letterhead in the bottom half of Figure 1.14. If you were to extend that same line of symmetry down through the sample letterhead, you would see equally distributed design elements on both sides of the page.

Figure 1.14 **Symmetrical Balance**

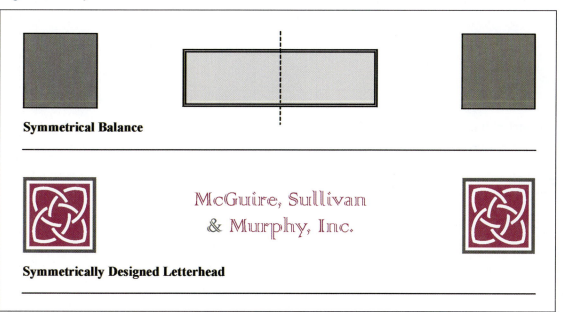

Symmetrical Balance

McGuire, Sullivan & Murphy, Inc.

Symmetrically Designed Letterhead

Rule of Thirds

Try to keep harmony in your design where all the elements on the page work together creating a page that is interesting to look at and easy to read. Design harmony may be accomplished by applying a design guideline called the *Rule of Thirds*. This rule states that pages should be arranged in thirds rather than in halves or fourths. Studies indicate that this basic grid is more appealing to the eye than any other design. Figure 1.15 illustrates a document that is not in harmony and one that is in harmony.

Asymmetrical Balance

Symmetrical balance is easy to identify and to create. However, contemporary design favors asymmetrical balance. An ***asymmetrical design*** uses different design elements of varying weights and/or proportions to achieve balance on a page. Asymmetrical design

◀**DTP POINTERS**
Rule of Thirds -
Design guideline
that states a page
or image designed
in thirds is more
appealing to the eye.

Asymmetrical design
Balancing contrasting
elements on a page.

Figure 1.15 **Applying the Rule of Thirds to Create Harmony in a Document**

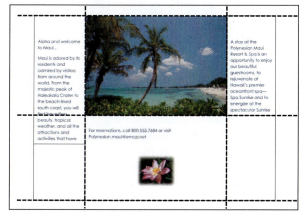

Without Harmony

With Harmony.

Figure 1.16 Symmetrical Balance

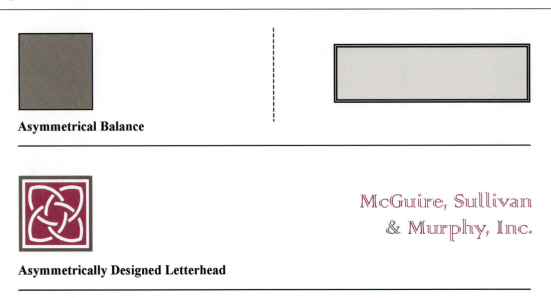

Asymmetrical Balance

Asymmetrically Designed Letterhead

McGuire, Sullivan
& Murphy, Inc.

is more flexible and visually stimulating than symmetrical design. Look at the shapes in the top half of Figure 1.16. Notice the dotted line (the line of vertical symmetry) that divides the page in half. Do both sides match? Are there similar or identical elements on both sides? Even without the dotted line, you can easily see that both sides do not match. Therefore, you know immediately that this is not a symmetrical design. However, just because the design is not symmetrical does not automatically mean that it is asymmetrical.

Remember, the key to asymmetrical design is achieving a visual balance on the page using dissimilar or contrasting elements. Look again at the shapes and the white space surrounding the shapes in Figure 1.16. Even though they are not the same and are not centered, would you agree that a visual balance is achieved on the page? The darker, denser square and its surrounding white space on the left half of the page are balanced by the longer, less dense rectangle and its surrounding white space on the right half of the page. Now look at how those same shapes are converted into the design elements used in the sample letterhead in the bottom half of Figure 1.16. Here, balance is achieved with dissimilar design elements resulting in an effective asymmetrical design.

Multiple-paged documents add another dimension to the challenge of achieving balance. Since balance must be achieved among the elements on more than one page, it is essential that you look at type and graphics in terms of each two-page unit, or *spread*, which is a set of pages facing each other as shown in Figure 1.17. Also, notice that the layout of document A is symmetrical, and the layout of document B is asymmetrical.

Spread
Set of pages facing each other.

Providing Proportion

When designing a communication, think about all of the individual parts as they relate to the document as a whole. Readers tend to view larger elements as more important. Readers also are more likely to read a page where all of the elements are in *proportion* to one another. When incorporating the concept of proportion into your documents, consider the following points:

Proportion
Sizing elements in relation to their relative importance and to each other.

- Size design elements, whether text or graphics, in proportion to their relative importance to the message.

Chapter One

Figure 1.17 Symmetrical and Asymmetrical Newsletters

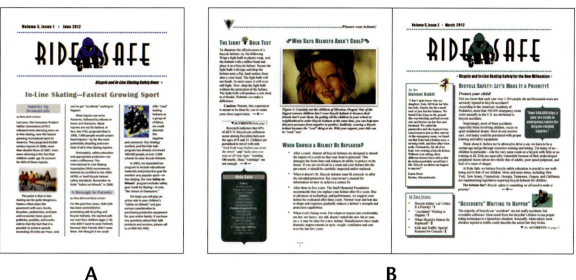

A

Symmetrical Balance

B

Asymmetrical Balance
(Two-Page Spread)

- Size design elements so they are in proportion to each other. However, try not to have everything the same size.

- When pages are split horizontally or vertically, try to divide the design elements at a 60/40 ratio or $^2/_3$ to $^1/_3$ proportions. These proportions have proved to be visually appealing. Text, graphics, and other design elements should take up two-thirds of the document, and at least one-third of the document should be left for white space.

First, decide which elements in your document are the most important in conveying your message. Next, decide which elements are the second most important, and so on. Then proportionally size the visual elements in your publication according to their priority. This way you can make sure your readers see the most important information first. Appropriate typeface and type size for headlines, subheads, and body text can set the proportional standards for a document.

Evaluating Proportion

When viewing the documents in Figure 1.18, look at the headline size in proportion to the body text. Think about this relationship when selecting the type size for titles/headlines and body text. When selecting the type size for subheads, consider how the subhead relates proportionally to the headline and to the body text.

Sizing Graphic Elements to Achieve Proportion

Sizing of graphic elements is also important in maintaining proportion among all of the design elements on a page. For instance, look at illustration A in Figure 1.19. The size of the musical graphic image visually tells the reader that it is the most important item on the page. But should it be? As discussed earlier in this chapter, the message that you want to get across to the reader always takes top priority. The graphic image in illustration A may be relevant, but it is overpowering the message rather than supporting it. The image is definitely out of proportion to its relative importance in the message.

Figure 1.18 Headline Proportions

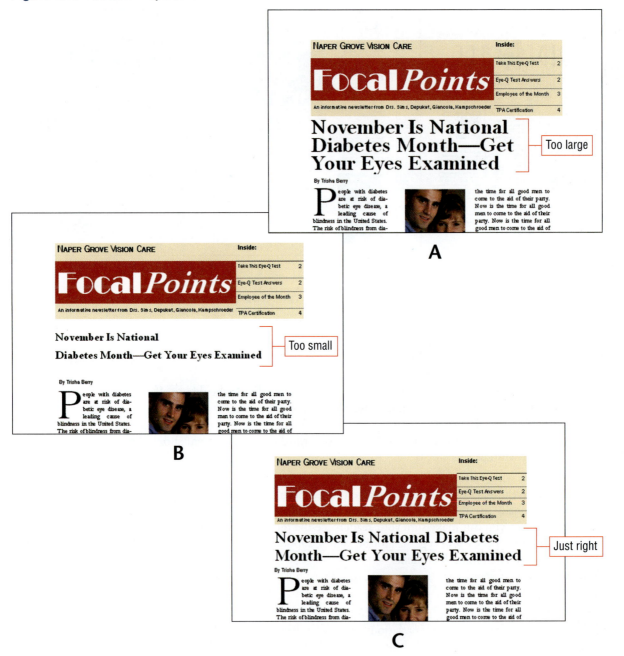

Now look at Figure 1.19B. The musical image is too small to be effective. Looking at the document as a whole, the image is out of proportion to the surrounding elements. What is your reaction to Figure 1.19C? Look at the individual elements as they relate to the whole document. All of the design elements appear to be in proportion to each other and to their ranking of importance in the intended message.

Using White Space

White space is also important in sizing design elements proportionately on your page. Keep the following pointers in mind:

Figure 1.19 Sizing Graphics

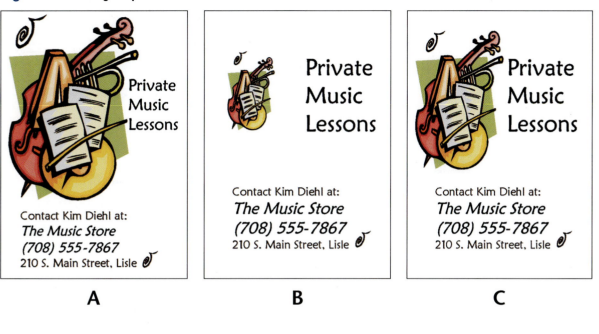

A   B   C

- Narrow margins create a typed line that looks long in relation to the surrounding white space.
- Too much white space between columns makes the line length look short.
- Too little space between columns makes the text harder to read.
- Excess white space between lines of text creates gaps that look out of proportion to the type size.
- Not enough white space between lines of text makes the text hard to read. Achieve proportion consistently throughout your whole project. A whole, integrated, unified look is established when elements are in proportion to one another.

Creating Contrast

Contrast is the difference between different degrees of lightness and darkness on the page. Text with a low level of contrast gives an overall appearance of gray. Consider using strong contrast to achieve some emphasis or focus on your page. A high level of contrast is more visually stimulating and helps to draw your target audience into the document. Use contrast as an organizational aid so that the reader can distinctly identify the organization of the document and easily follow the logical flow of information. Headlines and subheads set in larger and denser type help to create contrast on an otherwise *gray* page as shown in Figure 1.20.

Look at Figure 1.21. Do the documents grab your attention? Why? Contrast was achieved by using a larger type size for "London," reversed text, and bolded text. A black image against a solid white background produces a sharp contrast, as illustrated by the English guard graphic in Figure 1.21A. In addition, look at the program cover for the Brooks University Music Department in Figure 1.21B. A sharp contrast exists between the black background and the white text and piano image, and a not so sharp contrast exists between the light gray text and the watermark notes in the background of the cover.

Contrast

The difference in the degrees of lightness and darkness on a page.

◄ DTP POINTERS
Add contrast by setting headings and subheads in larger, denser type.

◄ DTP POINTERS
Make contrasting elements strong enough to be noticed.

Figure 1.20 Using Contrast in Headlines and Text

A

531 Pineland Avenue
Manchester, MO 63011

Phone (314) 555-5946
Fax (314) 555-9090
E-mail lizm@msn.com

Lisabeth Marchioli

Objective	To work in an Accounting/Business position that offers opportunities for advancement.
Professional experience	2008–Present Patterson Company Manchester, MO Accountant Responsible for accounts receivable. Responsible for all basic accounting functions: coding and distribution of invoices, classifying transactions, and processing orders. Responsible for preparation of tax forms. 2007 Case Foods, Inc. Springfield, MO Accounting Clerk—Cooperative Education Entered data into computer system. Prepared product orders for regional representatives. 2006 Morris Insurance Company St. Louis, MO Accounting Clerk—College Summer Internship Processed billing and receiving payments from multi-state area. Revised and updated accounts. Assisted in telephone survey.
Education	2005–2007 Boston College Brookline, MA Bachelor of Science Degree Major in Accounting Minor in Computer Science 2003–2005 Westlake Community College Manchester, MO Associate Degree Major in Accounting Minor in Computer Information Systems
Awards received	Phi Kappa Phi Honor Society and National Honor Society

B

Lisabeth Marchioli

531 Pineland Avenue, Manchester, MO 63011
Phone (314) 555-5946   Fax (314) 555-9090   E-mail lizm@msn.com

Objective

To work in an Accounting/Business position that offers opportunities for advancement.

Professional Experience

2008–Present   Patterson Company   Manchester, MO
Accountant
Responsible for accounts receivable.
Responsible for all basic accounting functions: coding and distribution of invoices, classifying transactions, and processing orders.
Responsible for preparation of tax forms.

2007   Case Foods, Inc.   Springfield, MO
Accounting Clerk—Cooperative Education
Entered data into computer system.
Prepared product orders for regional representatives.

2006   Morris Insurance Company   St. Louis, MO
Accounting Clerk—College Summer Internship
Processed billing and receiving payments from multi-state area.
Revised and updated accounts.
Assisted in telephone survey.

Education

2005–2007   Boston College   Brookline, MA
Bachelor of Science Degree
Major in Accounting
Minor in Computer Science

2003–2005   Westlake Community College   Manchester, MO
Associate Degree
Major in Accounting
Minor in Computer Information Systems

Awards Received

Phi Kappa Phi Honor Society and National Honor Society

Figure 1.21 Text and Graphic Contrast

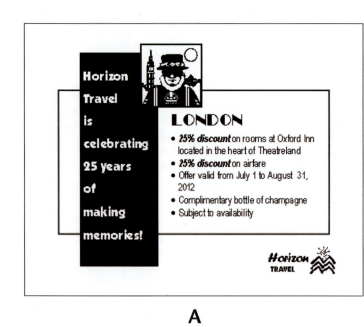

A

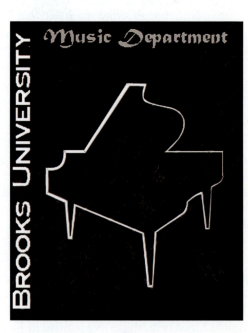

B

Figure 1.22 Contrasting Text

As shown in Figure 1.21 in documents A and B, a graphic image in varying shades of gray or a watermark can produce contrast on a lower level. However, depending on the colors used in the image, a color graphic can also provide great contrast. Warm colors come forward, and cool colors appear to recede.

Text contrast can be accomplished by changing text direction and by using a serif typeface (a small stroke at the end of a character) and a sans serif typeface (without a small stroke); a larger font size and a smaller font size; caps and lowercase; roman (regular font attribute) and italics; thick fonts and thin fonts; and drop caps and normal. See Figure 1.22 for examples. Avoid pairing fonts that are only slightly different from one another, such as Times New Roman and Bell MT. Instead, choose fonts with obvious differences, such as Arial Black (sans serif) and Invitation (serif). Word 2010 Theme Fonts take some of the guesswork out of choosing fonts that complement each other. The font pairs displayed in Figure 1.23 are determined by the Theme selected.

Figure 1.23 Selecting Fonts Based on Themes

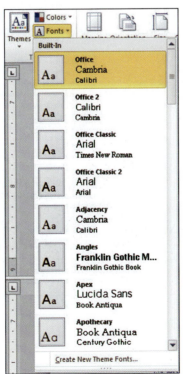

In addition, you have an option to create your own font pairs by clicking *Create New Theme Fonts* at the bottom of the drop-down list of theme fonts, and then save them with a name you provide.

DTP POINTERS ▶

Use bullets to organize information and add visual contrast.

Special characters used as bullets to define a list of important points, such as 👪, 🏖, 👁, 🏺, 💰, 🍽, 📷, and ✒, not only serve as organizational tools but also contribute visual contrast to your page. Placing these special characters in a bolder and larger type size provides a higher level of contrast. Notice the family symbol and the pen bullets used in Figure 1.24.

Achieving Contrast with White Space

DTP POINTERS ▶

Use plenty of white space to convey an open, lighter feeling.

White space is an important tool in achieving contrast. Use more white space on a page to project a more open, lighter feeling. When space is limited, a more closed, darker feeling is projected. Think of white space as the floor space in a room. The more furniture and accessories in the room, the more closed or crowded the room becomes. Rearranging or removing some of the furniture can provide more floor space, which produces an open, lighter feeling. Your page design, like a room, may need to have some elements rearranged or removed to supply some visually contrasting white space. See how too many design elements (accessories) are crowding the white space (floor space) in Figure 1.24A. Notice in illustration 1.24B how eliminating and rearranging some of the design elements to create more white space makes for a more open and lighter design.

Figure 1.24 Adding White Space

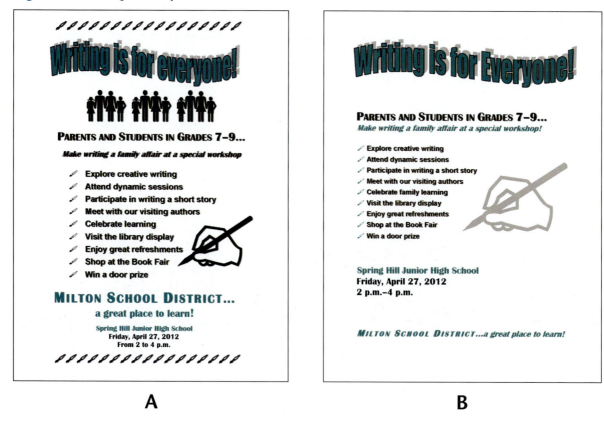

A   B

Figure 1.25 Legibility

A   B

Achieving Contrast with Color

The use of color in a heading, a logo, a graphic image, a ruled line, or as a background can also add to the contrast level on a page. When using more than one color, select colors that provide a pleasing contrast, not colors that provide an unpleasant conflict. In addition, consider whether the color(s) used increases or decreases the legibility of your document. Color may look nice, but it will confuse the reader if there is not enough contrast in the text. Look at the examples in Figure 1.25. In illustration A, the color of the text and the color of the background are not different enough, making the text barely legible. As you can see in Figure 1.25B, the stark contrast between the color of the text and the color of the background makes the text very easy to read. Use high contrast for the best legibility.

Creating Directional Flow

Establish smooth *directional flow* in a document by organizing and positioning elements in such a way that the reader's eyes scan through the text and find particular words or images that the designer wishes to emphasize. By nature, graphics and display type (larger than 14 points) act as focal elements that attract the eye as it scans a page. Focal elements may include a well-designed headline, logo subheads, graphic images, ruled lines, boxes with text inside, charts, reverse text, or a shaded background. When trying to establish the directional flow of your document, you must:

- organize your information into groups of closely related items and then rank the groups in order of importance,
- decide on how to emphasize the most important information,
- place related items close to each other on the page,
- use left or right alignment to establish a stronger visual connection between all of the elements on your page, and
- position elements so that the reader is drawn into the document and then directed through the document.

Organizing Your Information Visually

Organize your information by grouping related items. Place the related items close to each other so the reader views the group as one unit rather than as separate pieces. For example, a subheading should be close to the paragraph that follows it so the reader recognizes the relationship between the two. Dates, times, and locations are frequently grouped close together because of the relationship of when? where? and at what time? Position titles and subtitles close to each other because of their obvious relationship.

What happens when there is little or no organization to the information in a document? Look at Figure 1.26A. Besides being very boring and uninviting to read, do you find it difficult to tell what this is really about, when it is going to take place, at what

Directional flow
Positioning elements to draw the reader's eyes through the document.

◀ **DTP POINTERS**
Rank information according to its importance in conveying the intended message.

◀ **DTP POINTERS**
Position related items close to each other on the page.

time, and so on? Now look at Figure 1.26B. What has changed in 1.26B that did not exist in 1.26A? The Shapes filled with relevant graphics point toward the document content. Therefore, the directional flow directs the reader's eyes from the left side (focal point) to the right side where the grouped content is easy to read. The italicized word *point* reinforces the right-pointing Shapes, and the slant of the text gives a feeling of movement.

The colors you choose should reflect the nature of the business you represent. Someone in an artistic line of work may use bolder, splashier colors than someone creating documents for a business dealing with finance.

Headers and footers, text that appears repetitively at the top or bottom of each page, also contribute to directional flow in a publication. Chapter name, chapter number, report title, and page numbering are common items included in headers or footers. These page identifiers direct the reader to specific locations in a document. Headers and footers may be inserted into a document using the Quick Parts feature in Word 2010.

Figure 1.26 Grouping Related Items and Using Strong Directional Flow

Chapter One

By clicking the Quick Parts button in the Text group in the Insert tab, you may access the Building Blocks Organizer and select an appropriate design for your document. The new Cover Page feature, along with coordinating headers and footers, combine consistent formatting with great design. See Figure 1.27 for an advertising agency protocol manual formatted by using Cover Page, Building Blocks, Quick Styles, and Document Themes.

Figure 1.27 **Creating an Office Protocol Manual Using the Cover Page and Header and Footer Features of Word 2010**

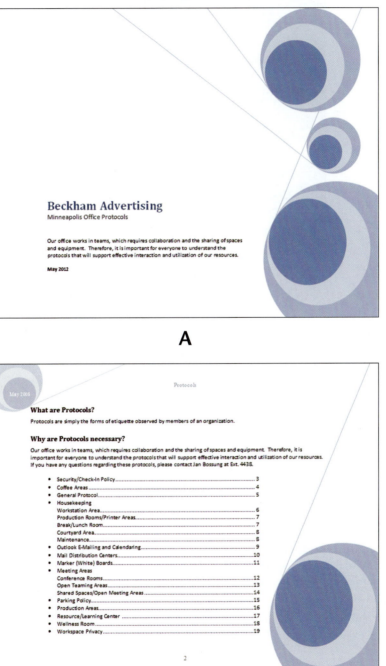

Figure 1.28 Emphasizing Important Information

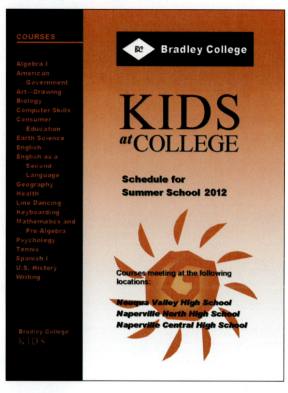

Ranking Elements

After you have organized your information into groups of related items, decide which information plays the most important role in conveying your message and then emphasize that information. For example, the purpose of the flyer in Figure 1.28 is to inform readers of the class schedules for the "Kids at College." The courses and locations offered are important facts to the "kids." Reverse text and larger font sizes emphasize these facts. The gradient fill adds to the overall appeal of the flyer.

Recognizing the Z Pattern

Directional flow in a strictly symmetrical design (all elements centered) is limited to movement down the visual center of the page, producing a static design. On the other hand, an asymmetrical design creates a dynamic directional flow. To accomplish this, think of how your eyes naturally scan a page. When scanning a page, the eyes tend to move in a *Z pattern*. The eyes begin at the upper left corner of the page, move to the right corner, then drop down to the lower left corner, and finally end up in the lower right corner of the page. In text-intensive publications such as magazines, newspapers, and books, visual landmarks are frequently set in these positions. In an advertisement, a company name, address, and phone number often appear in the lower right corner.

Figure 1.29 helps you visualize the Z pattern in this document. Remember that the Z pattern is only a guideline. Some designs may contain modified versions of the Z pattern. However, because there are no hard-and-fast rules, not all designs fit exactly into this pattern.

Choosing Visual Alignment

The way you choose to position and align text and/or graphics on a page greatly influences the directional flow in a document. One of the keys to creating dynamic

Z pattern

When scanning a page, the eyes tend to move in a Z pattern—upper left corner to bottom right corner.

Figure 1.29 Z-Pattern Directional Flow

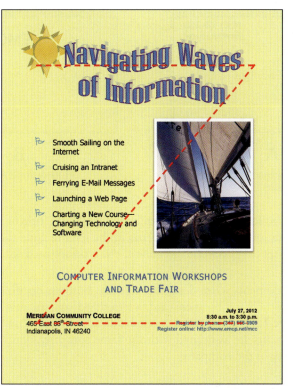

directional flow and producing professional-looking documents is ***alignment***. Center alignment is fine when you are trying to achieve a more formal look, as in a wedding invitation, but tends to be dull and boring in other types of documents. Break away from the center alignment habit! Experiment with using a strong left or right alignment to connect different elements on your page.

Look at Figure 1.30. See what a dramatic difference it made to use a strong right alignment in 1.30B as opposed to 1.30A. The text in business card A is not connected and the reader's eyes tend to jump from one corner to another. Card B uses strong vertical alignment, grouped text, and bolded text to lead the eyes from the top to the bottom and back again.

Establishing Consistency

Uniformity among specific design elements establishes a pattern of ***consistency*** in your document. Inconsistency can confuse and frustrate the reader and can lead to a reduction in your readership. To avoid this, design elements such as margins, columns, typefaces, type sizes, spacing, alignment, and color should remain consistent throughout a document to achieve a degree of unity. In any document, whether single-paged or multiple-paged, consistent elements help to integrate all of the individual parts into a whole unit. Additionally, in multiple-paged publications, such as manuals, reports, or newsletters, consistency provides the connecting element between the pages. Repetitive, consistent elements can also lend identity to your documents and provide the reader with a sense of familiarity.

Consistent elements are evident in many of the figures in this chapter. Consider, for example, the flyer in Figure 1.29. Consistency is achieved by using the same color blue

Alignment
Aligning text and/or graphics on a page.

DTP POINTERS
Save center alignment for formal, conservative documents.

DTP POINTERS
Use a strong left or right alignment to visually connect elements on a page.

Consistency
Uniformity among design elements.

Figure 1.30 Visual Alignment

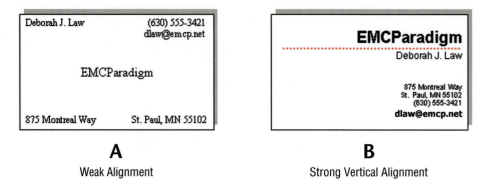

A

Weak Alignment

B

Strong Vertical Alignment

in the heading, the bullets, the sky in the sailboat clip art, the title of the event, and the phone number. Additional consistent elements in the flyer include the left alignment, the flag bullets, the spacing between the bullets, the typeface used for the text, and the margins.

Use consistent elements when designing separate business documents for the same company or person, such as a business card, a letterhead, and an envelope. Look at the documents in Figure 1.31. The consistent elements are obvious. You know immediately that all three documents are associated with the same company, which serves to reinforce the identity of the company.

Evaluating Consistency

Consistency establishes unity not only *within* a section or chapter (or newsletter or advertisement) but also *among* the sections or chapters (or a series of newsletters or advertisements). See how the consistent elements used in the manual pages displayed in Figure 1.32 contribute to the unified appearance of this document. Notice the green color scheme carried throughout the pages of the manual, including the cover page. The same typeface appears in the cover, the headers, the section headings, and the subheadings. A different typeface displays in the body text and remains consistent throughout the document. Additionally, a thin horizontal line appears in the header on every page except the cover.

Figure 1.31 Consistent Documents

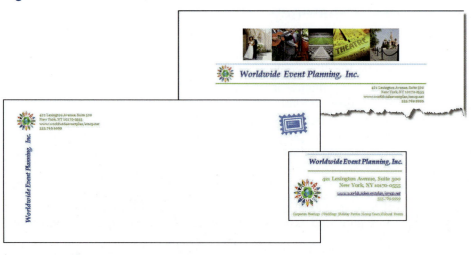

Figure 1.32 Consistent Formatting and Color

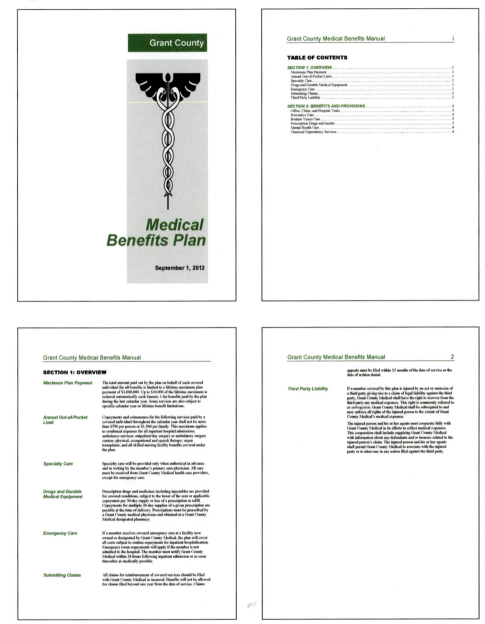

If you plan to insert a graphic image into your document, use the graphic to provide you with some ideas for consistency. For example, the globe/plane/mailbox graphic in the postcard in Figure 1.33 provided the idea for the consistent color scheme used in this document. The arrow pointing to the mailbox slot inspired the use of a dotted line and arrow pointing to the new address. To add consistency and create visual interest, the arrow was repeated in the return address box and in the delivery address section. Did you notice how three rectangles were cleverly arranged to resemble a mailbox in the return address section of the postcard? You, too, can be this creative, given time and lots and lots of practice! One word of advice—because consistent elements are repetitive elements, keep it simple and distinct. Too much of a good thing can be very distracting.

Figure 1.33 **Consistency in a Document**

Using Styles for Consistency

Whether you are creating a newsletter with consistent headings, subheadings, bylines, and headers and footers, or you are creating an office procedure manual with consistent headings and subheadings, styles will make the job of formatting consistent text more time efficient and easier to update. Word 2010 provides a gallery of professionally designed styles, which include preselected combinations of fonts, font sizes, color, and leading before and after paragraphs. In addition, style sets, such as Classic, Elegant, Formal, and Fancy, can be applied to existing styles to completely change the look of your document.

Themes

Applying Document Themes for Consistency

Theme
A set of formatting choices that includes theme colors, fonts, and effects.

Just as styles reinforce consistency, document themes also promote consistency in documents or among documents created in Word, Excel, and PowerPoint. You can quickly and easily format an entire document to give it a professional and modern look by applying a document *theme*. A document theme is a set of formatting choices that includes a set of theme colors, a set of theme fonts (including heading and body text fonts), and a set of theme effects (including lines and fill effects).

Figure 1.34 Using Color to Communicate

Fall
Schedule

Office Technology Information

At a Glance...

MS Word 2010
MS Word 2010 Desktop Publishing
MS Office 2010

MS Word Online Forms
Microsoft Outlook
Voice Recognition Software

Microsoft Office Specialist Review
- PowerPoint Specialist
- Word Specialist
- Word Expert
- Outlook

Using Color

As discussed earlier, *color* may create focus; however, it is also a powerful tool in communicating a message and portraying an image. The colors you choose should reflect the nature of the business you represent. Someone who is trying to attract the attention of a youthful audience may use bolder, splashier colors than someone creating documents for an accounting business. In addition, men and women often respond differently to the same color. Color can even elicit an emotional response from the reader; keep in mind cultural differences and how other cultures interpret the use of color. Always identify your target audience in planning your documents, and think about the impact color will have on your audience.

The colors in the fall leaves in Figure 1.34 reinforce the subject of the text, which is a list of courses offered during the fall semester at a college. Color on a page can help organize ideas and highlight important facts. Publications that use color appropriately have a professional look.

Using Color Graphics and Text Elements

Word provides many ways of inserting color into your documents. You may use graphic pictures, borders, page color, bullets, and lines of a specific design and color. You may also create your own color shapes, lines, borders, text boxes, and text. For instance, look at Figure 1.35. This event invitation uses WordArt to emphasize the event name, the zebra border reinforces the safari theme and attracts attention, the lions facing the grouped text also reinforce the invitation theme (notice the background in the graphic has been removed), and the green gradient fill in the text boxes on the front and back side make you feel like you are with the animals on a green savanna in Africa.

Using Colored Paper

If a color printer is not available, consider using colored paper to complement your publication. Colored paper can match the tone or mood you are creating in your document. Orange paper used for a Halloween flyer, as in Figure 1.36, is an inexpensive alternative to color graphics and text. Your audience will recognize the theme of the flyer by associating the paper color with the event. The colored paper provides contrast and adds vitality and life to the publication.

Color
A powerful tool in communicating a message.

DTP POINTERS
Use color to create focus, organize ideas, and emphasize important elements.

Figure 1.35 Color Graphics and WordArt

Front   **Back**

Using Preprinted Stationery

You may also turn plain white documents into colorful, attention-grabbing documents by purchasing preprinted letterheads, envelopes, brochures, or presentation packets from paper supply companies or your local office supplies store. Achieve color, emphasis, and contrast through an assortment of colorful page borders, patterned and solid color papers, as well as gradient color, marbleized, and speckled papers. Many of these paper suppliers provide free catalogs and offer inexpensive sample paper packets.

Figure 1.37B illustrates a certificate printed on preprinted paper. Word 2010 was used to create the layout and text in Figure 1.37A. The gray fill and green border reinforced the colors used in the paper. Alternatively, a digital signature can be added to a document to verify that the document content has not been changed since it was created. After carefully measuring and adjusting the text boxes, the document was printed on preprinted paper. (Experiment with plain paper first!)

Applying Guidelines for Using Color

Here are a few guidelines to follow when using color in documents:

- Use color sparingly—less is best! Limit your use of colors to two or three, including the color of the paper.
- Color may identify a consistent element.
- Do not let color overpower the words. Color can add emphasis and style, but the message is most important!

DTP POINTERS
Use color sparingly.

Figure 1.36 Colored Paper

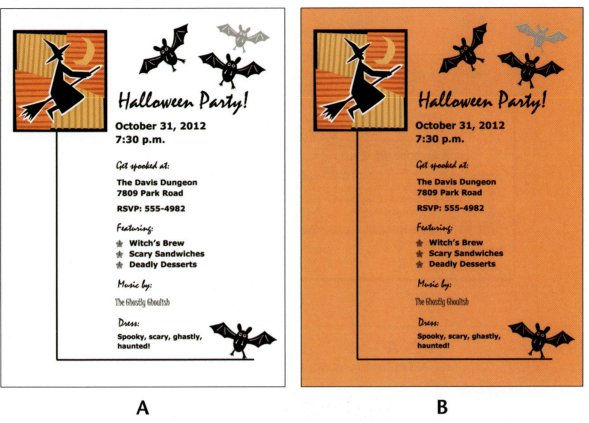

A   B

- Do not set text in light colors—it is too difficult to read. Black text is still the easiest to read.
- Avoid changing all text to one color such as red. It is harder to read, and the whole *color* of the document is changed.
- Use light colors for shaded backgrounds or watermarks.
- Use color to communicate, not decorate!

Printing Options

Even though laser printers have become more affordable, the color laser printer remains rather expensive. A less expensive, but very good, alternative is the inkjet color printer. The printer uses color ink cartridges to produce the color. The copy may be slightly damp when first removed from the printer. Improve the ***resolution*** using specially designed inkjet paper. Some inkjet printers are capable of achieving near-photographic quality with a resolution of 5760 × 1440 dpi (dots per inch) or higher. Learn more about your printer settings by accessing the Print dialog box and clicking the Properties button to view the Advanced Color Settings of your printer. Also consider the margin limitation of an inkjet printer versus a laser printer. Inkjet usually can print up to 0.5" to the edge of the page, while laser printers can print as close as 0.25" depending on the model.

Another option for color is to send your formatted copy to a commercial printer for color printing. You may want to save your documents in PDF format and then send your documents to a commercial printer. You can get almost any color you want from a commercial printer, but it can add significantly to the cost of your project. Always check prices and your budget first!

Resolution
The fineness of detail in an image or text produced by a monitor or printer.

Figure 1.37 Using Preprinted Paper

A

Layout and Text Created in Word

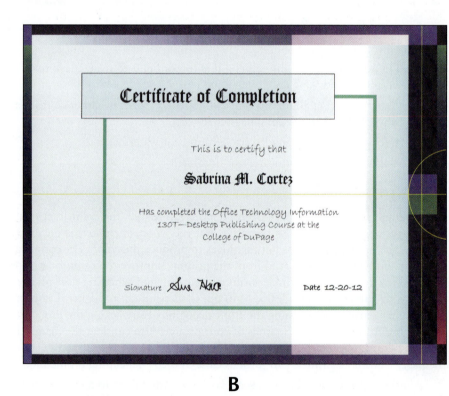

B

Printed on a Paper Style Called *Precision* by Paper Direct®

Keep in mind that documents created in Word 2010 and saved in PDF format cannot be edited in Word. To edit a PDF file, you will need an Adobe program called Adobe Acrobat. If you save your Word documents in PDF format, you may want to save the document first in DOCX format in case editing is required at a later time. You can edit the file and then resave the file again in PDF format. Files saved in PDF format can be viewed using Adobe Reader, which is available free of charge at www.adobe.com.

To save a Word document in PDF format, click the File tab, and then click the Save and Send tab. At the Save and Send tab Backstage view, click the *Create PDF/XPS Document* in the *File Types* section, and then click the Create PDF/XPS button or click the Save As button in the File tab Backstage view, and change the *Save as type* option to *PDF*.

Evaluating Documents Using the Document Analysis Guide

Up to this point, you have learned the importance of carefully planning and designing your publication according to the desktop publishing concepts of focus, balance, proportion, contrast, directional flow, consistency, and color. In Exercise1.1, you will evaluate the document illustrated in Figure 1.38 using a Document Analysis Guide, which can be printed from your student data files. The Document Analysis Guide is a tool used to evaluate design concepts in selected documents. In addition, a Document Evaluation Checklist may be printed from your student data files. This tool serves as a way for you to evaluate your progress during the planning and creation stages of your document and is directed toward the finished product. The Document Evaluation Checklist will be used in Units 2 and 3 in this book. Both forms will be used to analyze your own documents, existing commercial publications, and/or other students' desktop publications.

SAVE! SAVE! SAVE! AND SAVE SOME MORE! Creating desktop published documents involves many steps and, often, a lot of experimentation. Frequently save your work so you always have a recent version to fall back on and to avoid losing it if a power or system failure occurs. Word automatically makes a document recovery file every 10 minutes. You can change this setting by clicking the File tab, clicking the Options button in Backstage view, and then clicking Save in the Word Options dialog box.

Note: In several exercises in each chapter, you will be opening documents from the CD that accompanies this textbook. The files you need for each chapter and for each set of unit assessments are saved in individual folders. Before beginning a chapter, copy the necessary folder from the CD to your storage medium (e.g., a formatted disk, zip disk, CD-RW, or flash drive). Steps on creating a folder, making a folder active, and deleting a folder are presented in the Preface of this textbook and on the inside of the back cover. Remember to substitute for graphics that may no longer be available.

Evaluate the flyer illustrated in Figure 1.38 by completing the following steps:

1. Open **DocumentAnalysisGuide** located in the *Chapter01* folder.
2. Print one copy of the **Document Analysis Guide** or open **DocumentAnalysisGuide** and type your responses.
3. Turn to Figure 1.38 in your textbook.
4. Complete an analysis of the flyer in Figure 1.38 by writing or typing short answers to the questions in the **Document Analysis Guide**. (If you prefer, you may type your answers on the guide, save it with another name, **C01-E01-Evaluate.docx**, and then print.)
5. Close **DocumentAnalysisGuide.docx** without saving your changes.

Using Word 2010 in Desktop Publishing

Word 2010 is a visual word processing program providing an efficient means of editing and manipulating text and graphics to produce professional-looking documents. Word is linear in nature in that every character, picture, and object is part of a line of text. However, Word also contains many desktop publishing features and options that allow you to change linear objects to floating objects that can be moved easily at the document screen.

Learn design by studying well-designed publications and by experimenting. Analyze what makes a specific design and layout visually appealing and unique, and try using the same principles or variations in your publications. Take advantage of the special design and layout features that Word 2010 has to offer. Take time to design. Layout and design is a lengthy process of revising, refining, and making adjustments. Above all else, EXPERIMENT! View each document in terms of focus, balance, proportion, contrast, directional flow, consistency, and use of color. Ask the opinion of your peers, fellow workers, and others, and listen to their feedback. The final judge is the reader, so always try to look at your document from the reader's perspective.

DTP POINTERS
Experiment with different layouts and designs.

The remaining chapters in this book will take you through the steps for creating specific business and personal desktop publishing applications, such as letterheads, business cards, flyers, brochures, postcards, online and hard-copy forms, presentations, and newsletters. In addition to step-by-step directions for completing the applications using Word 2010, each project will introduce guidelines relevant to that document type as well as reinforce the design concepts introduced in this chapter. Remember:

Take the time to design!

Communicate, do not decorate!

Less is always best!

Readability is the key!

Figure 1.38 Exercise 1.1

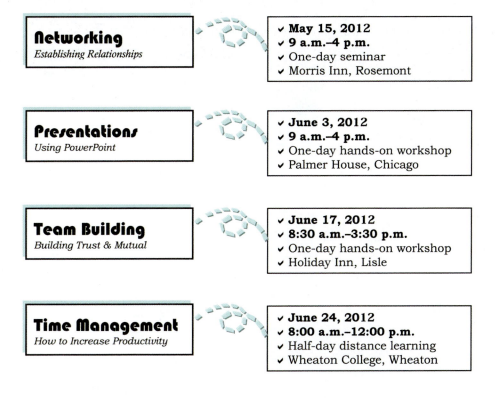

Skyline Communications

305 East Wacker Drive, Chicago, IL 60654
Phone: (312) 555-5647 Fax: (312) 555-6521
Visit us at: www.emcp.net/skyline

For 2012, we are offering three different presentation formats to meet your learning and scheduling needs:

✔ One-day hands-on workshops
✔ One-day seminars
✔ Half-day distance learning seminars

Networking
Establishing Relationships

- ✔ **May 15, 2012**
- ✔ **9 a.m.–4 p.m.**
- ✔ One-day seminar
- ✔ Morris Inn, Rosemont

Presentations
Using PowerPoint

- ✔ **June 3, 2012**
- ✔ **9 a.m.–4 p.m.**
- ✔ One-day hands-on workshop
- ✔ Palmer House, Chicago

Team Building
Building Trust & Mutual

- ✔ **June 17, 2012**
- ✔ **8:30 a.m.–3:30 p.m.**
- ✔ One-day hands-on workshop
- ✔ Holiday Inn, Lisle

Time Management
How to Increase Productivity

- ✔ **June 24, 2012**
- ✔ **8:00 a.m.–12:00 p.m.**
- ✔ Half-day distance learning
- ✔ Wheaton College, Wheaton

Read over the enclosed information for details and fees. Mail or fax the enclosed registration form to the address or fax number listed above or register online at www.emcp.net/skyline.

Begin a *job-hunting* portfolio of the documents you will create in the exercises and assessments throughout this book. Exercises marked with the portfolio icon should be included in your portfolio. These documents have been chosen to show a prospective employer a wide range of your desktop publishing skills. You may also include any additional documents from the chapter and unit assessments. Because the assessments are less structured than the exercises, your creativity can really shine. You will create a title page for your portfolio in the Unit 2 Assessments. As an optional assignment, you may create a table of contents after completing Unit 2. Your instructor will determine a due date and any other specific requirements for your portfolio. If possible, purchase plastic sheet protectors for your documents and a binder to hold them. See Figure 1.39 for sample portfolios. Open **PortfolioRequirements** located in the *Chapter01* folder and then print a copy.

As an alternative, your instructor may request that you prepare an electronic version of your portfolio by saving your cover, divider pages, and a select number of publications in PDF format and then sending them to the instructor as an email attachment. These pages may also be posted to a student's blog, if one has been established. You might also consider preparing your portfolio as a PowerPoint presentation and sending it to your instructor electronically.

Figure 1.39   Photos of Sample Portfolios—Hard Copy and Electronic

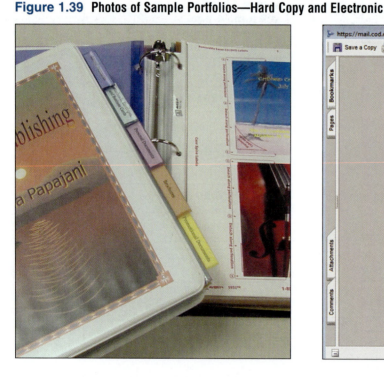

Using the Internet for Templates, Clip Art, and Media

The Internet can provide you with a wealth of information on desktop publishing as well as free Word templates, clip art, tips and tricks, articles, and assistance with new versions of software. For instance, through your preferred browser or search engine, you may type **desktop publishing** in the *Search* text box and access websites on various aspects of the desktop publishing field, which may include reviews on the newest books;

definitions for common terms; discussions on graphics, layout, and design; and facts on career opportunities. You may find hyperlinks to free clip art, fonts, photos, and templates. Besides typing **desktop publishing** in your search, try other keywords such as **clip art**, **free clip art**, **fonts**, **graphics**, **graphic designers**, **Microsoft Word**, **word processing**, **Web design**, **logos**, **digital cameras**, and **scanning** to learn about different techniques and approaches to producing professional-looking documents. ***Note: Words or phrases that are to be typed appear in pink in this book.***

Search engines that provide images and desktop information include www.altavista.com, www.ask.com, www.google.com, www.bing.com, and www.yahoo.com. Be sure that you read the copyright information associated with each collection. Many images are free to use privately, but permission may be needed if the images are used for profit-making endeavors.

You can also download any graphic you may see on the Web by right-clicking on an image and, at the shortcut menu that displays, clicking the option *Save Image As*. A regular Save As dialog box displays where you may choose to name the file and save it to your hard drive or any other location. Again, be especially careful to make sure you have the rights to use the images you select. Most images are copyrighted!

Using Microsoft Office.com Templates

If you have previously used Microsoft Word 2010, you may be familiar with the hundreds of Office templates that are available at the Microsoft Office.com web page. You may access these templates while in Word by clicking the File tab and then clicking the New tab. Microsoft and content experts have collaborated to provide hundreds of professionally designed templates created in Word, Excel, Access, Publisher, PowerPoint, Visio, and One-Note. You may browse by category or initiate a search to find a template. When you find the desired template, click the Download button to send the document to the Office program where you can tailor the template to your exact needs. Many of the templates reinforce integration of the Office programs by using a common theme.

Occasionally , the words *Compatibility Mode* will display in the Title bar next to the document name. *Compatibility Mode* displays to indicate that some new features are disabled to prevent problems when working with previous versions of Office. Converting the file will enable these features but may result in layout changes. To convert the document to Word 2010 format, click the File tab, click Info, and then click the Convert button at the Info tab Backstage view.

Using Microsoft Office Online Images

Besides the media files available in Word at the Clip Art task pane, you may access more image files by clicking the <u>Find more at Office.com</u> hyperlink at the bottom of the Clip Art task pane. This link connects you to the Microsoft Images and more home page as shown in Figure 1.40. Notice the link to image partners and the numerous image categories.

Using Microsoft Resources

In addition to the core applications in Office 2010, which may include Outlook, Word, Excel, PowerPoint, Access, and Publisher (availability is based on version type), Office 2010 also includes access to smaller utility programs, tools, accessories, and links to resources on the Microsoft.com website.

Figure 1.40 Images at www.Office.com

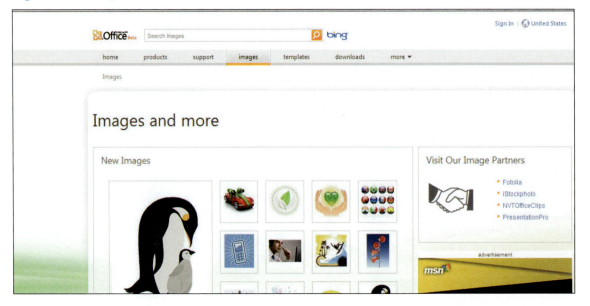

Using Microsoft Office Picture Manager

With this utility, you will be able to organize large collections of image files, convert images to alternative formats, compress images, and edit images using the following tools: Brightness and Contrast, Color, Crop, Rotate and Flip, Red-eye removal, Resize, Save, Save As, and Export. Some of these tools are also available on the Picture Tools Format tab in Word. Notice all the picture editing tools on the Picture Manager as shown in Figure 1.41.

Figure 1.41 Microsoft Office Picture Manager

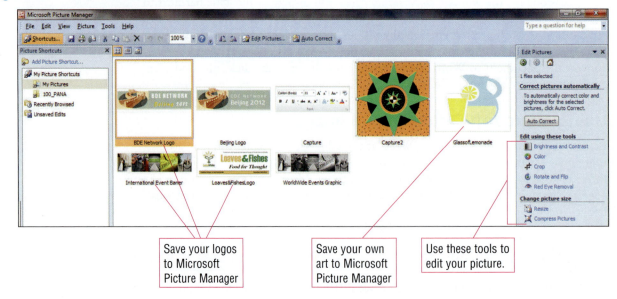

Chapter One

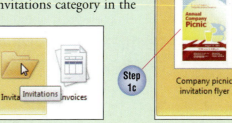

1. At a blank document, create the college picnic invitation shown in Figure 1.42 by completing the following steps:
   a. Click the File tab, and then click the New tab.
   b. At the New tab Backstage view, click the Invitations category in the *Office.com Templates* section.
   c. Click the Business event invitations category, click the *Company picnic invitation flyer* thumbnail, and then click Download. *(If this template is no longer available, open it from your Chapter01 student data folder.)*

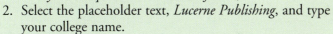

2. Select the placeholder text, *Lucerne Publishing*, and type your college name.
3. Select the placeholder text, *Company*, and type **College**.
4. Select the text box containing the date and time, drag it to the right edge of the flyer as shown in Figure 1.42, select the placeholder date, and then type **August 13, 2012**.

5. Select the placeholder address in the text box below the time and type your college address.
6. Select all the *RSVP* text, and change the text color to Dark Red.
7. Select the text box containing the *RSVP* text, drag it to a position similar to Figure 1.42 (to the left of the glass of lemonade), then select the email placeholder text, and type **bourne@emcp.net**.

8. Save the document by completing the following steps:
   a. Click the File tab, and then click the Info tab.
   b. At the Info tab Backstage view, *do not* click the Convert button in the *Compatibility Mode* section. ***Hint: If you convert this template, which was created in an earlier version of Word, you will lose some of the design elements.***
   c. Click the Save As button.
   d. At the Save As dialog box, click to add a check mark to the *Maintain compatibility with previous versions of Word* check box.
   e. Type the name of the document as **C01-E03-CollegeInvitation**. Click Save.
10. Leave the file open for the next exercise. (Figure 1.42 shows the map that you will insert in the following exercise.)

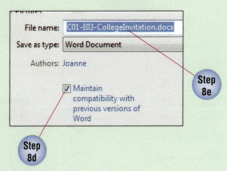

Figure 1.42 Exercises 1.3 and 1.4

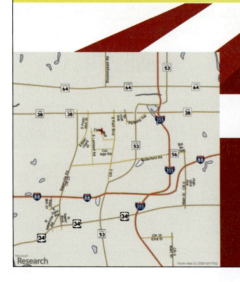

College of DuPage
Cordially Invites You and Your Family to Our

Annual College Picnic

Please R.S.V.P. by July 13 to
Stephanie Bourne at
bourne@emcp.net or
call (242) 555-0177

August 13, 2012

11:00 a.m. to 4:00 p.m.

425 Fawell Blvd.
Glen Ellyn, IL 60137

Figure 1.43 Microsoft Bing Map

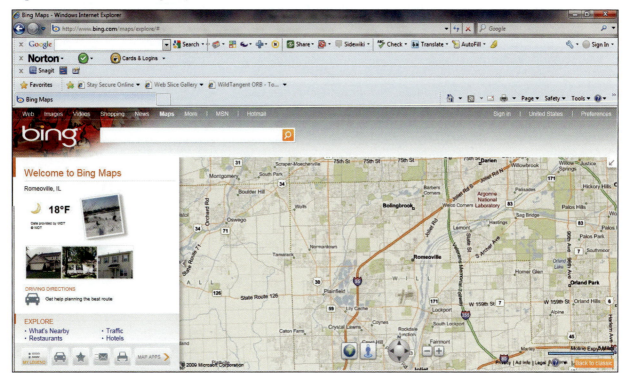

Using Microsoft Bing Map

Have you ever received an invitation to a party and were grateful for the map that was included? For those of you who do not have a GPS device in your car, a map can be very helpful in getting you to an event on time. You may purchase supplemental mapping software to accomplish this task, or you can use a search engine such as Microsoft Bing or Yahoo! to create a map that you can save in a graphic format and insert into your document. To access the mapping tool, type **www.bing.com/map** in your Internet browser, follow the on-screen prompts, save the map in a graphic format, and then insert the image in your document. Figure 1.43 illustrates what the home page may look like (remember, web pages are updated periodically and may not look exactly as shown).

◀ **DTP POINTERS**

In addition to www.bing.com/map, try using www.maps.google.com or www.mapquest.com for creating maps.

In the following exercise, you will use the Bing Map feature to add a map of your college to the invitation created in Exercise 1.3.

Exercise 1.4 Adding a Map to a Document

1. With **C01-E03-CollegeInvitation.docx** open, add a map created in Microsoft Bing Map by completing the following steps:
   a. At your favorite browser, type **www.bing.com/maps** in the URL text box and then press Enter. *Hint: You may have to download and install Bing if it is not available on your computer.*
   b. At the Welcome to Bing Maps home page, click the Map Apps button at the bottom of the left side of the screen.

Step 1b

c. At the Map apps dialog box, click the *Destination Maps* app.

d. At the Destination Maps dialog box, read the text for each step.

e. At the *STEP: 1 Select Destination* section, type the address of your college, click Search, and then click Continue.

f. At the *STEP 2: Set Area of Interest* section, click Continue. **Hint: Drag the sides to adjust the area.**

g. At the *STEP 3: Map Title* section, type the name of your college, and then click Continue. **Hint: You may need to scroll downward to access this option.**

h. At the *Select a map style* section, select *American Style*, and then click the Save/Print button.

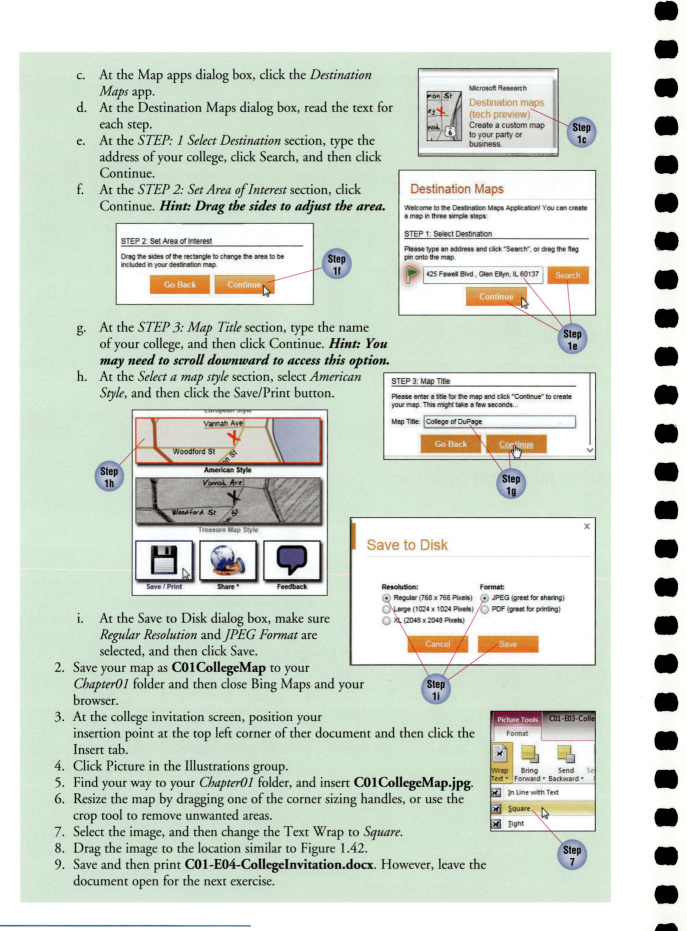

i. At the Save to Disk dialog box, make sure *Regular Resolution* and *JPEG Format* are selected, and then click Save.

2. Save your map as **C01CollegeMap** to your *Chapter01* folder and then close Bing Maps and your browser.

3. At the college invitation screen, position your insertion point at the top left corner of ther document and then click the Insert tab.

4. Click Picture in the Illustrations group.

5. Find your way to your *Chapter01* folder, and insert **C01CollegeMap.jpg**.

6. Resize the map by dragging one of the corner sizing handles, or use the crop tool to remove unwanted areas.

7. Select the image, and then change the Text Wrap to *Square*.

8. Drag the image to the location similar to Figure 1.42.

9. Save and then print **C01-E04-CollegeInvitation.docx**. However, leave the document open for the next exercise.

Figure 1.44 Using the Snipping Tool

Using Windows 7 Snipping Tool

In addition to all of the Office 2010 components, most editions of Office 2010 include an assortment of office tools. Among the office tools, you may want to become familiar with the Snipping Tool. You can use the Snipping Tool to capture a screenshot of, or snip, any object on your screen, and then annotate, save, or share the image. After the image is saved, it may be inserted into your document. Figure 1.44 illustrates the Snipping Tool and a logo that can be saved in JPG format and used in various documents to reinforce the event identity.

Exercise 1.5 Using the Snipping Tool

1. With **C01-E04-CollegeInvitation.docx** open, click the Start button in the bottom left corner of the Taskbar.
2. Click the Snipping Tool icon at the pop-up menu. *Hint: You may need to click All Programs, Accessories, and then Snipping Tool.*
3. At the Snipping Tool dialog box, click the down-pointing arrow at the right of the New button, and then click *Free-form Snip*.

   Step 3

5. With the scissors-shaped tool, draw a free-form shape around the lemonade glass and the pitcher image.
6. Click the File tab, and then click the Save As button. Save the picture as **C01Lemonade.png** to your *Chapter01* folder. *Hint: This image has now been saved in a graphic format, and it may later be inserted into a document.*

   Step 5

7. Close the Snipping Tool program and then close **C01-E04-CollegeInvitation.docx**.

Chapter Summary

➤ When creating a publication, clearly define your purpose, assess your target audience, decide the format in which your audience will see your message, and decide what outcome you are expecting.

➤ Effective design involves planning and organizing content. Decide what items are most important to the reader. Design concepts such as focus, balance, proportion, directional flow, consistency, and the use of color are essential to creating a visually attractive publication that presents information in a logical, organized manner.

➤ Focus can be created by using large and/or bold type, such as for titles and subheads; by using graphic elements, such as ruled lines, clip art, and photographs; and by using color for emphasis.

➤ White space is the background where no text or graphics are located. Use white space to emphasize the main message and give the reader's eyes a break from too much text.

➤ At least one-third of your publication should consist of white space if the remaining two-thirds contain text and other design elements.

➤ Quick Styles and document Themes in Word will make formatting efficient and consistent for any publication or group of similarly designed publications.

➤ A document Theme is a set of formatting choices that include a set of theme colors, a set of theme fonts (including heading and body text fonts), and a set of theme effects (including lines and fill effects).

➤ You can modify fonts, colors, margins, table formatting, and other elements by choosing different style formats from the Quick Styles gallery. You can also change the look of the styles by applying different Style Sets.

➤ Balance on a page is created by equally distributing the weight of elements on a page in either a symmetrical or asymmetrical manner. Symmetrical design (all elements centered) balances similar elements of equal weight and proportion on the left and right sides and the top and bottom of the page. Asymmetrical design balances contrasting elements of unequal proportion and weight on the page.

➤ Design harmony may be accomplished by applying a design guideline called the *Rule of Thirds*. This rule states that pages should be arranged in thirds rather than in halves or fourths. Studies indicate that this basic grid is more appealing to the eye than any other design.

➤ In establishing a proportional relationship among the elements on a page, think about all of the parts as they relate to the total appearance. Proportionally size the visual elements in your publication according to their relative importance to the intended message.

➤ Contrast is the difference between varying degrees of lightness and darkness on the page. A high level of contrast is more visually stimulating and helps to draw your target audience into the document. Contrast is also used as an organizational aid so that the reader can distinctly identify the organization of the document and easily follow the logical flow of information.

➤ Directional flow can be produced by grouping related elements and placing them close to each other on the page, by using a consistent alignment to establish a visual connection between the elements on a page, and by positioning elements in such a way that the reader's eyes are drawn through the text and to particular words or images that the designer wishes to emphasize.

➤ Consistent elements in a document such as margins, columns, typefaces, type sizes, spacing, alignment, and color help to provide a sense of unity within a document or among a series of documents. Repetitive, consistent elements can also lend identity to your documents.

➤ Use color on a page to help organize ideas; emphasize important information; provide focus, contrast, directional flow, and consistency; and establish or reinforce an identity.

➤ By clicking the Quick Parts button in the Text group on the Insert here tab, you access the Building Blocks Organizer and select an appropriate design for your document.

➤ Use the Internet for free clip art, photographs, templates, and helpful newsletters.

➤ Access the Microsoft Office.com templates by clicking the File tab and then clicking the New tab. At the New tab Backstage view, select a template from a category, and then click Download.

➤ Word 2010 is a visual word processing program providing an efficient means of editing and manipulating text and graphics to produce professional-looking documents.

➤ Use Microsoft Office Picture Manager to organize large collections of image files, convert images to alternative formats, compress images, and edit images using the following tools: Brightness and Contrast, Color, Crop, Rotate and Flip, Red-eye removal, Resize, Save, Save As, and Export.

➤ You can use the Snipping Tool to capture a screen shot, or snip, of any object on your screen, and then annotate, save, or share the image.

Commands *Review*

FEATURE	RIBBON TAB, GROUP	BUTTON	KEYBOARD SHORTCUT
Blank Document	File tab, New tab, Blank document, Create		Ctrl + N
Quick Parts	Insert, Text		
Clip Art	Insert, Illustrations		
Picture	Insert, Illustrations		
Microsoft Office Picture Manager	Start, All Programs, Microsoft Office, Microsoft Office 2010 Tools		
Print	File tab, Print tab, Print tab Backstage view		Ctrl + P
Quick Styles	Home, Styles		
Save/Save As	File tab, Save tab or Save As tab		Ctrl + S
SmartArt	Insert, Illustrations		
Snipping Tool	Start, All Programs, Accessories		
Templates	File tab, New tab		
Themes	Page Layout, Themes		

Reviewing Key Points

A. Alignment
B. Asymmetrical
C. Balance
D. Consistency
E. Contrast
F. Color

G. Directional flow
H. Focus
I. Crop
J. Proportion
K. Quick Styles
L. SmartArt

M. Symmetrical
N. Theme
O. Thumbnail sketch
P. White space

Completion: In the space at the left, provide the correct letter or letters from the above list that match each definition.

_____ 1. Areas in a document where no text or graphics appear.

_____ 2. Type of balance achieved by evenly distributing similar elements of equal weight on a page.

_____ 3. A method used to establish a strong visual connection between elements on a page.

_____ 4. Use this design technique to help organize ideas, highlight important information, provide focus and consistency, and reinforce the identity of an organization.

_____ 5. Positioning elements in such a way that the reader's eyes are drawn through the text and to particular words or images that the designer wishes to emphasize.

_____ 6. An element that draws the reader's eye to a particular location in a document.

_____ 7. A preliminary rough draft of the layout and design of a document.

_____ 8. Uniformity among specific design elements in a publication.

_____ 9. The sizing of various elements so that all parts relate to the whole.

_____ 10. To remove unnecessary parts of a graphic.

_____ 11. Contemporary design in which contrasting elements of unequal weight and proportion are positioned on a page to achieve balance.

_____ 12. A graphical representation of information—graphical lists, organizational charts, and process diagrams.

_____ 13. The difference between varying degrees of lightness and darkness on the page.

_____ 14. Word feature that includes sets of unified formatting choices that affect color, fonts, and effects.

_____ 15. A visual representation of your information that you can quickly and easily create, choosing from among many different layouts, to effectively communicate your message or ideas.

Chapter *Assessments*

Assessment 1.1   Creating a Presentation

The purpose of this assignment is to provide you with experience in planning, organizing, creating, and making a class presentation using Microsoft Word or PowerPoint. Specific instructions are provided for you in the document named **Presentation.docx**. To print this document, complete the following steps:

1. Open **Presentation.docx** from your **Chapter01** folder.
2. Print one copy and then close **Presentation.docx**.

Begin researching a topic for your presentation and then give the presentation after completing Chapter 12. You may compose and create a presentation on a desktop publishing or Web publishing article or concept, a Word or PowerPoint desktop publishing or Web publishing feature(s) or process used to create a specific document, or an instructor-approved topic that you would like to share with your class. You may consider using any of the topics presented in this textbook. Include any Word or PowerPoint tips or techniques you may have discovered while creating your presentation. Use any one of the many desktop publishing, Word, and PowerPoint resources available online or at your local library or bookstore. Your instructor will notify you of a scheduled date for your presentation.

Assessment 1.2   Evaluating Documents

The *information highway* is littered with many well-designed and poorly designed documents. Looking critically at as many publications as possible will give you a sense of what works and what does not. In this skill assessment, find two different examples of documents—flyers, newsletters, résumés, brochures, business cards, announcements, certificates, and so on. Evaluate these documents according to the desktop publishing concepts discussed in this chapter using the file, **DocumentAnalysisGuide.docx**. To do this, complete the following steps:

1. Open **DocumentAnalysisGuide.docx**.
2. Print two copies of this form, and then close **DocumentAnalysisGuide.docx**.
3. Complete the evaluation forms, and attach the corresponding form to the front of each example document. Write the exercise number as **C01-A02-AnalysisGuide** along with your name on the front of each form.

Assessment 1.3   Arranging Design Elements in a Flyer

1. Open **HappySummerFlyer**, and save the document with the name **C01-A03-HappySummer**.
2. Apply the design principles discussed in Chapter 1 to create a professional-looking advertisement for the Happy Summer Nursery. Eight design elements have been created and placed randomly on the page. Rearrange the text boxes and graphics displayed on the page in a harmonious design that attracts attention and reinforces the message. Make the following changes:
   a. Click each design element to access the move handle, and then drag the element to a desired location. Make sure the page has good directional flow.
   b. Apply a different theme.
   c. Make sure all of the fonts are consistent and the font sizes are appropriately sized. Use the Format Painter to save time.
3. Save, print, and close **C01-A03-HappySummer.docx**.

Assessment 1.4   Researching the Internet for new Microsoft Word 2010 Desktop Publishing Features

1. Access your favorite search engine, and then search for 10 Word 2010 features that you may consider using to create professional-looking desktop published documents.
2. Working with a group of two or three students, combine your notes into a fact sheet using a table to help organize your findings.
3. Use any Word 2010 features that you are familiar with to enhance the design and layout of your fact sheet. Refer to Figure 1.45 as a guide to the type of information (facts) you may want to include in your document.

4. Below the table, include your resources. If necessary, peruse a current reference manual or the Internet to find the appropriate format for keying your resources appropriately.
5. Save the completed fact sheet, and name it **C01-A04-WordFacts**.
6. Print a copy for each member of your class, and then close the document.

Assessment 1.5   Drawing Thumbnail Sketches for Documents

Create flyers for the situations described below. Draw two thumbnail sketches using lines, boxes, and rough drawings to illustrate the placement of text and graphics on the page. Your group should discuss how to include focus, balance, proportion, contrast, white space, directional flow, and consistency in your thumbnail sketches. Be sure to consider the purpose and target audience for each situation. Designate areas in your sketches for such items as time, date, location, and response information. Label your sketches as **C01-A05-Sketches**. Elect one person on your team to act as a spokesperson for your group explaining how your team used the design elements discussed in Chapter 1 in the creation of your documents.

Situation 1: Volunteer project

Situation 2: Software training seminar

Assessment 1.6   Evaluating a Promotional Document

In this assessment, you will evaluate a poorly designed flyer according to the items listed on the **DocumentAnalysistGuide.docx** located in your *Chapter01* folder.

1. Open **Document AnalysisGuide.docx** in your *Chapter01* folder.
2. Print one copy and then close **DocumentAnalysisGuide.docx**.
3. Open **CleaningFlyer.docx** in your *Chapter01* folder.
4. Print one copy and then close **CleaningFlyer.docx**.
5. Complete the Document Analysis Guide and name the exercise **C01-A06-Evaluate**. List three suggestions for improving the document on the back of the form.

Figure 1.45 Assessment 1.4 Sample Solution

Word 2010 Features
For Desktop Publishing

By: Student Name Here

Quick Tables	Insert a predesigned table at the location of your insertion point. Table Tools Design and Layout tabs will display on the ribbon when a table is created. This is a great way to insert a predesigned calendar.
Screenshots	Insert screenshots to quickly and easily capture and incorporate visual illustrations.
Removing Backgrounds of Images	It's a Photoshop®-like feature that allows you to remove the background of any picture.
Art Effects in Word Art	WordArt has been updated with new colorful art effects. Select the text, click the WordArt button on the Insert tab, and a list of options will appear. You can see how your text will appear when you hover the mouse over the option.
Artist Effects	New artistic effects have been added in Word 2010. Select the image and click on Artistic Effects from the ribbon. You will see options such as Pencil Sketch, Chalk Sketch, Glow Edges, Photocopy, etc.
Ligatures	Most of the fonts in Word 2010 are OpenType fonts. Ligatures are letter combinations such as "fi", "fl", and "vv" that are treated as a single letter joined together.
SmartArt	You can choose from new SmartArt graphics to build impressive diagrams and charts.
Picture-Editing Tools	You can add special picture effects by changing color saturation, temperature, brightness, and contrast to your art.
Backstage View	The Backstage view (File tab) replaces the traditional File menu and the Office button to let you save, share, print, and publish your documents.
Language Translator	You can easily communicate across different languages by using the bilingual dictionary.

Source: *Microsoft Office 2010 Top 10 benefits of Word 2010.* 18 January 2010

Preparing Internal Workplace Documents

Performance Objectives

Upon successful completion of Chapter 2, you will be able to:

- Define basic typography.
- Apply desktop publishing guidelines.
- Apply Themes, Quick Styles, and Style Sets.
- Add symbols and special characters.
- Use the Word Cover Page feature.
- Insert predesigned Building Blocks.
- Use Content Controls.
- Create documents using templates and wizards.
- Insert images and create watermarks.

Desktop Publishing Terms

Ascenders	Ligatures	Serif
Baseline	Luminescence	Swash
Cap height	Monospaced	Template
Cell	Normal.dotm	Typeface (Font)
Descenders	Pitch	Typestyle
Em dash	Point size	Watermark
En dash	Proportional	Wizard
Hue	Readability	x-height
Kerning	Sans serif	
Legible	Saturation	

Word Features Used

Breaks	Live Preview	Tabs
Building Blocks	Picture	Templates
Bullets	Quick Parts	Text boxes
Clear Formatting	Quick Styles	Text Effects
Clip Art	Send to Back	Themes
Cover Page	Size	Washout
Font color	Special Characters	Watermark
Format Painter	Symbol	

Understanding Basic Typography

Typeface *or* Font

A set of characters with a common design and shape.

Baseline

An imaginary horizontal line on which characters rest.

x-Height

Height of the lowercase x of a font.

Cap height

The distance between the baseline and the top of capital letters.

Ascenders

The parts of a lowercase character that rise above the x-height.

Descenders

The parts of a lowercase character that extend below the baseline.

Serif

A small stroke at the end of a character.

Monospaced

Same amount of character spacing for each character in a typeface.

Proportional

Varying amount of space for each character in a typeface.

A document created on a typewriter generally contains uniform characters and spacing. A typeset document may contain characters that vary in typeface, typestyle, and size, and that are laid out on the page with variable spacing. In this chapter, you will produce internal business documents such as a conference sign, company dinner invitation, protocol manual cover, fax cover sheet, memo, and agenda. You will use the Word Templates feature along with producing and formatting your own business documents.

An important element in the creation of internal business documents is the font used to format the text. To choose a font for a document, you need to understand basic typography and the terms that apply. As you learned in Chapter 1, when you plan your document, consider the intent of the document, the audience, the feeling the document is to elicit, and the emphasis on important information. Make sure the headlines, graphics, and the choice of typography work together to support the message.

Before selecting the desired type specifications in a document, a few terms used in desktop publishing need to be defined. Terms that identify the type specifications are typeface, type size, and typestyle.

Defining Typefaces

A *typeface* is a set of characters with a common general design and shape (Word refers to typeface as *font*). One of the most important considerations in establishing a particular mood or feeling in a document is the typeface. For example, choose a decorative typeface for invitations or menus, but choose a simple block-style typeface for headlines or reports. Choose a typeface that reflects the content, your audience expectations, and the image you want to project.

Certain characteristics distinguish one typeface from another. Type characters rest on an imaginary horizontal line called the *baseline*. Parts of type may extend above and below this baseline. Figure 2.1 illustrates the various parts of type.

The *x-height* is the height of the main body of the lowercase characters and is equivalent to the lowercase *x*. The *cap height* is the distance between the baseline and the top of capital letters. *Ascenders* are the parts of lowercase characters that rise above the x-height, and *descenders* are parts of characters that extend below the baseline. *Serifs* are the small strokes at the ends of characters.

Typefaces are either *monospaced* or *proportional*. A monospaced typeface allots the same amount of horizontal space for each character; professional publications rarely use this typeface. Courier is an example of a monospaced typeface. Proportional typefaces allow a varying amount of space for each character. For example, the lowercase letter *i* takes up less space than an uppercase *M*. In addition, different proportional typefaces

Figure 2.1 **Parts of Type**

Chapter Two

Figure 2.2 Serif, Sans Serif, and Monospaced Typefaces

SERIF TYPEFACES	SANS SERIF TYPEFACES	MONOSPACED
Cambria	Calibri	Consolas
Constantia	Candara	QuickType II Mono
Times New Roman	Corbel	OCR A Extended
Bell MT	Agency FB	Courier New
Harrington	Arial	
Bookman Old Style	Tahoma	
Book Antiqua	Impact	

take up different amounts of horizontal space. The same sentence in Times New Roman, for example, takes up less horizontal space when set in the same size Century Gothic.

Proportional typefaces fall into two main categories: serif and sans serif. Traditionally, a serif typeface is more readable (easier to read in blocks of text) and is used with documents that are text-intensive, such as business letters, manuals, or reports. Serifs help move the reader's eyes across the page.

A ***sans serif*** typeface does not have serifs (*sans* is French for *without*). Sans serif typefaces are generally more ***legible*** (higher character recognition) and are often used for headlines and advertisements. In modern designs, sans serif typefaces may also be used for body text, but avoid using more than seven or eight words per line; using bold, italics, outlining, or shadowing; or using a long line length. Figure 2.2 shows examples of serif, sans serif, and monospaced typefaces.

When using a proportional typeface, space once after end-of-sentence punctuation and after a colon. Proportional typeface is set closer together, and extra white space is not needed at the end of a sentence or after a colon. Additionally, since proportional fonts take up varying amounts of horizontal space, you *cannot* use the spacebar to align objects on a page.

Microsoft 2010 includes many typefaces designed for clear, extended on-screen reading, and they are integrated into all the new templates offered as part of Microsoft Office. These typefaces include the default, Calibri, as well as Cambria, Candara, Consolas, Constantia, and Corbel. Calibri, Candara, and Corbel are sans serif typefaces; Cambria and Constantia are serif typefaces; and Consolas is monospaced.

Using OpenType Fonts

OpenType is a font format that was developed jointly by Microsoft and Adobe. OpenTypefonts can potentially contain many thousands of characters. This means that an OpenType font may contain multiple alphabets (such as Latin, Greek, Japanese, and more). This font format provides several advantages over older font technologies, such as TrueType, through better support for international character sets, cross-platform support between Windows and Macintosh computers, support for Postscript and TrueType fonts, and support for advanced typographic features, which include special ligatures (combined characters) and ***swashes*** (exaggerated serifs).

Fonts that Save Ink

Recent studies indicate that different fonts require different amounts of ink to print. Data from www.Printer.com suggests using Century Gothic instead of Arial—Century

DTP POINTERS
To view a list of the fonts that are installed with Office 2010, go to http://support.microsoft.com/kb/2121313.

DTP POINTERS
To view an overview on topics related to typography and free fonts, go to www.microsoft.com/typography/default.mspx.

Sans serif
Without a small stroke at the end of a character.

Legible
Typefaces with higher character recognition.

DTP POINTERS
Use the Find and Replace feature in Word to find ending punctuation with two spaces and replace with one.

DTP POINTERS
Use a sans serif font for headings.

Swash
An exaggerated serif.

Gothic uses about 30 percent less ink than Arial. The amount of ink is determined by the thickness of the font. Choosing a font with "narrow" or "light" in its name is usually more ink efficient than a font with "bold" or "black" in its name. Also, serif fonts tend to use less ink than sans serif fonts.

This research also indicates that the following fonts are most ink efficient in the order given: Century Gothic, Times New Roman, Calibri, Verdana, Arial, and Sans Serif were next, followed by Trebuchet, Tahoma, and Franklin Gothic Medium. However, Century Gothic is a wider font and may extend the text to an additional page.

Applying Advanced Typographical Ligatures

Word 2010 offers advanced OpenType features in the Font dialog box with the Advanced tab selected (see Figure 2.3) that you can use to enhance the visual appeal of your text. The *Ligatures* option is the first option. A ***ligature*** is a combination of characters tied together into a single letter. OpenType fonts support four types of ligatures:

Ligatures

Letters that have been attached to create a single character.

1. The first ligature is the *Standard Only* option. Standard ligatures are designed to enhance readability. For example, if you use the Palatino Linotype font, the standard ligatures "fi", "ff", and "fl" appear as a combined character. Notice that the pair of characters for each Standard Only and Standard and contextual ligature touch each other as shown in Figure 2.4.
2. *Standard and Contextual* ligatures are designed to enhance readability by providing better joining behavior between the characters that make up the ligature as shown in Figure 2.4.

Figure 2.3 OpenType Features at the Font Dialog Box with the Advanced Tab Selected

This standard set of ligatures vary by language, but it contains the ligatures that most typographers use for that language such as the letter "f".

A combination of standard and contextual ligatures that are commonly used for that font.

Click this box to provide fine-tuning of letters based on the surrounding characters.

All ligatures for a font are applied to the text.

Ligatures used for a "period" effect.

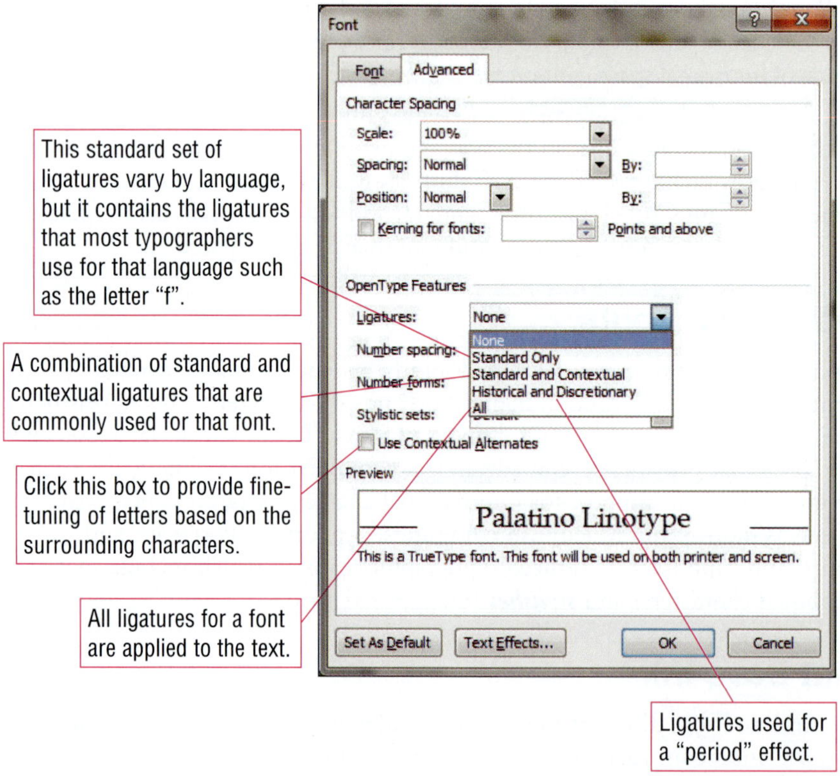

Figure 2.4 **Accessing Ligatures in the Font Dialog Box**

fi fl fitter   fi fl fitter   fi fl fitter

Not using Ligature   Using Ligatures (Standard Only)   Using Ligatures (Standard and Contextual)

3. *Historical and Discretionary* ligatures are designed to be ornamental and are not specifically designed for readability. These ligatures are not commonly used but are available to create a historical or "period" effect.
4. All ligatures allow you to apply all ligature combinations to selected text.

The *Number spacing* option in the *OpenType Features* section is set at *Default*, which means that spacing between numbers is determined by the font designer. You can choose *Proportional*, which spaces numbers with varying widths. Proportional figures treat each numeral as having a different width—"1" is narrower than "5". Three Microsoft fonts—Candara, Constantia, and Corbel—use proportional number spacing by default. Use the *Tabular* option if you want to specify that each number is the same width. This is recommended when typing numbers in columns where you want them to align vertically. The Cambria, Calibri, and Consolas fonts use tabular spacing by default.

The *Number forms* option is also set at *Default*. Change this to *Lining* if you want all numbers to have the same height and not extend below the baseline. The *Lining* option is recommended for numbers displayed in tables and forms. The Cambria, Calibri, and Consolas fonts use *Lining number forms* by default. You may want to choose the *Old Style* option when you want the numbers to flow above and below the baseline. Three fonts that use *Old-style number forms* include Candara, Constantia, and Corbel.

Figure 2.5 shows two proportional figures in the first column and the same two numbers with the widths adjusted by using the *Tabular* option. Notice the difference in width between the numerals "5" and "1".

Figure 2.5 **Using Number Spacing Options**

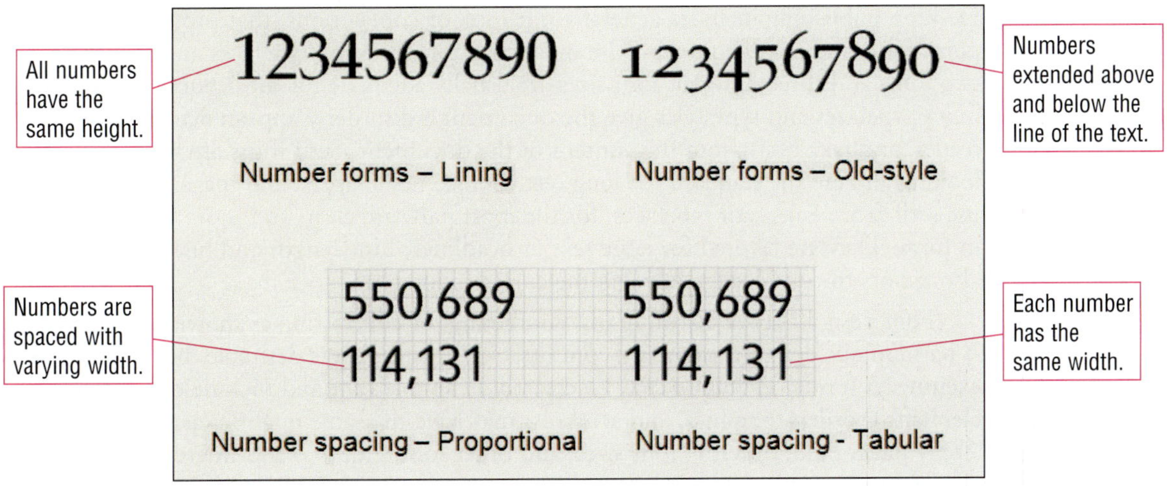

All numbers have the same height.

1234567890   1234567890

Numbers extended above and below the line of the text.

Number forms – Lining   Number forms – Old-style

Numbers are spaced with varying width.

550,689   550,689
114,131   114,131

Each number has the same width.

Number spacing – Proportional   Number spacing - Tabular

Figure 2.6 Applying Stylistic Sets and Contextual Alternates to Text

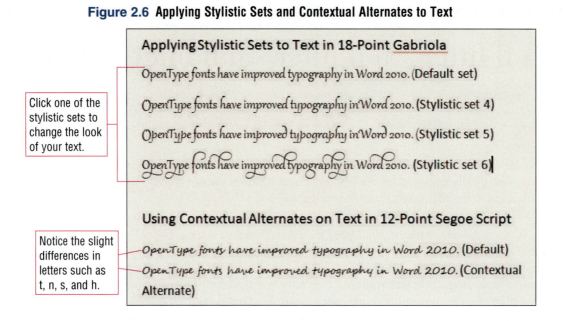

In addition to the previously mentioned OpenType features, you can also apply additional formatting using stylistic sets. Notice the slight variations in characters in the stylistic sets illustrated in Figure 2.6. Another fine-tuned adjustment that may be applied to text is the *Use Contextual Alternates* option. Use this feature to give your script font a more natural and flowing appearance as also shown in Figure 2.6. The text was formatted in 14-point Segoe Script. The first line is the default, and the second line has the *Contextual Alternates* option selected. Notice the slight differences in letters such as *t, n, s,* and *h.*

However, keep in mind that not all fonts contain ligature combinations, number spacing and forms, stylistic sets, or contextual alternates. You will need to experiment with fonts to find the ones that conform to these features.

Applying Desktop Publishing Guidelines

DTP POINTERS▶
Use a serif font for text-intensive documents.

DTP POINTERS▶
Sans serif faces are more readable than serif faces when set in very small point sizes.

DTP POINTERS▶
When using a proportional font, do not use the spacebar to align text; use a tab.

Desktop publishing includes general guidelines, or conventions, that provide a starting point for designing documents. Use moderation in choosing typefaces and type sizes—two fonts and three different font sizes are usually adequate for most publications. Too many typefaces and typestyles give the document a disorderly appearance, confuse the reader, and take away from the content of the document. Serif fonts are more formal looking and are the standard for long text. Books, newspapers, and magazines typically use serif faces. Sans serif typefaces, for the most part, are clean and more contemporary in form. They are favored for large text or headlines. Line length and line spacing are also factors to consider in choosing the correct body type.

Font design may be harmonious, conflicting, or contrasting as shown in Figure 2.7. A harmonious design is calm and comfortable. This design is desirable, but it is not very exciting. A formal invitation may be created using one font and include other design elements (borders, graphics, and symbols) that have the same qualities as the font. Apply italic, bold, differing font sizes, and other font effects to add interest.

Conflicting font design exists when you use two or more typefaces that look too similar. The fonts are different, but not different enough to tell them apart easily. Avoid using conflicting fonts in your documents.

Chapter Two

Figure 2.7 Harmonious, Conflicting, and Contrasting Font Designs

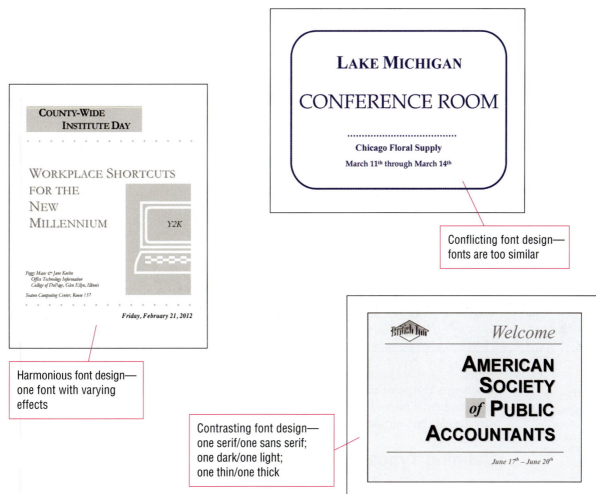

Conflicting font design—
fonts are too similar

Harmonious font design—
one font with varying
effects

Contrasting font design—
one serif/one sans serif;
one dark/one light;
one thin/one thick

Contrasting fonts may create focus and attract the reader's eyes. Achieve contrasting design through varying the font size, weight, appearance, and color. For instance, if one typeface is light and airy, choose a thick black or dark gray font to go with it. If one typeface is small, make the other one large. Avoid creating weak contrasts, such as using a script font with an italic font effect, or a large type size with a slightly larger one.

Additionally, use fonts that complement the message of your document. Figure 2.8 displays fonts that match the mood and tone of your message.

Defining Type Sizes

Type size (font size) is defined by two categories: ***pitch*** and ***point size***. Pitch is a measurement used for monospaced typefaces; it reflects the number of characters that can be printed in 1 horizontal inch. (For some printers, the pitch is referred to as cpi, or characters per inch. For example, the font Courier 10 cpi is the same as 10-pitch Courier.)

Proportional typefaces can be set in different sizes. The size of proportional type is measured vertically in units called points (measured vertically from the top of the ascenders to the bottom of the descenders). A point is approximately $1/72$ of an inch.

Pitch
The number of characters that can be printed in 1 horizontal inch.

Point size
A vertical measurement; a point is approximately $1/72$ of an inch.

Figure 2.8 Matching Fonts to Your Message

Alleycat Seafood Restaurant	Alleycat
CARIBBEAN CRUISE	BERMUDA SOLID
South of the Border	Chilada ICG Uno
Wedding Invitation	Calligrapher
Casper the Ghost	Chiller
Kids on Campus	Curlz MT
Certificate of Completion	Diploma
COMPUTER SEMINAR	NEWTRON ICG
LINE DANCING CLASS	COTTONWOOD
RED PAPERCLIPS	PAPERCLIP
Camp Sandy Feet	KidTYPEPaint
Four Corners Art Gallery	Matura MT Script Capitals

DTP POINTERS
Serif faces printed on textured paper or from 300 dpi or lower-quality printers may lose detail in thin and delicate strokes.

Typestyle
Variations of the basic type design including regular or normal, bold, and italic.

The higher the point size selected, the larger the characters. Figure 2.9 shows Wide Latin and Arial Narrow typefaces in a variety of point sizes. Horizontally, the two fonts vary greatly, but vertically the point size remains the same.

Defining Typestyles

Apply a typestyle to your text by clicking the Bold button and/or the Italic button in the Font group in the Home tab. Alternatively, click the Font launcher button in the bottom right corner of the Font group to access the Font dialog box, where you may select a typestyle to apply regular, italic, bold, or bold italic formatting to a desired font. A ***typestyle*** is a variation of the basic font or typeface that causes the font to display thicker (bold) and/or slanted (italic). Within a typeface, characters may have a varying style. There are four main categories of typestyles: normal (or *light, black, regular,* or *roman*), bold, italic, and bold italic.

Figure 2.9 Varying Point Sizes in Wide Latin and Arial Narrow

8-point Wide Latin	8-point Arial
12-point Wide Latin	12-point Arial
18-point Wide Latin	18-point Arial
24-point Wide Latin	24-point Arial

Figure 2.10 **Substituting Fonts**

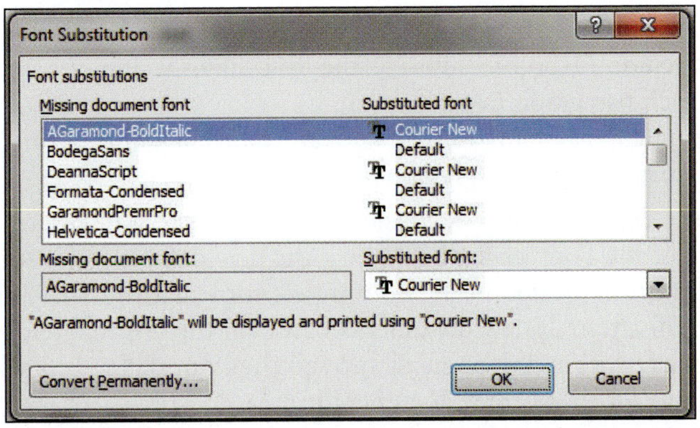

Fonts in Windows 7

The types of fonts you have available with your printer depend on the type of printer you are using, the amount of memory installed with the printer, and the supplemental fonts you have. When software is loaded on your computer, any fonts associated with that software are loaded into Windows 7, possibly resulting in a list of fonts different from the ones in your school computer lab. You can view all the fonts loaded to your computer by clicking Control Panel on the Start pop-up list, clicking the *Appearance and Personalization* category, and then clicking the *Fonts* category.

If your printer does not support a font or size you are using to format your text, Word may substitute the closest possible font and size. You can view the substitution fonts as shown in Figure 2.10 by clicking the File tab, Options button, Advanced tab, and then clicking the Font Substitution button in the Show document content section. ***Note: If the textbook calls for a particular font that is not available on your computer, simply substitute another font.***

Embedding Fonts in Word

Embedding fonts can increase your document's file size and may not work for some commercially restricted fonts, but it is a good way to make sure that your document will look the same on other computers. To embed fonts in Word, click the File tab and then the Options button. Select Save at the Word Options dialog box, and then click to add a check mark next to the embed option that meets your needs as shown in Figure 2.11. For more information about fonts, see the Microsoft.com website.

Figure 2.11 **Embedding Fonts in Word Documents**

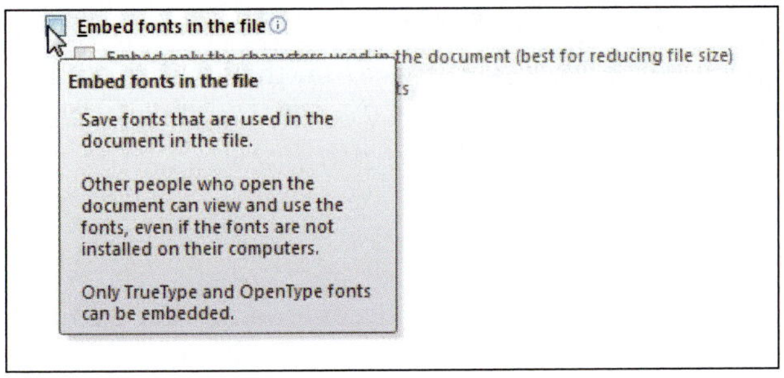

◀ **DTP POINTERS**
Substitute a different font if a particular font is not available.

◀ **DTP POINTERS**
Consider the demographics of your target audience.

Using Default Document Formatting

A Word document is based on a template that applies default formatting. Some of the default formats include 11-point Calibri as the font, line spacing of 1.15, and 10 points of spacing after each paragraph (a press of the Enter key). You can modify the default formatting by manually changing individual features, change formatting by applying styles, or change formatting by applying Quick Styles.

To change the default setting, click the Font dialog box launcher to access the Font dialog box. At the Font dialog box, select the new default you want to use, then click the Default button located in the bottom left corner. At the dialog box stating that the change will affect all new documents based on the Normal template, click Yes. Font selections made within a document through the Font dialog box will override the default font settings for the current document only.

Modifying Font Elements

You can modify text formatted with the default font by changing the font, font size (try clicking the Grow Font and Shrink Font buttons), font style, and text effects; applying a theme; changing theme fonts, changing theme colors, and changing theme effects; using Quick Styles or Quick Style Sets; inserting WordArt, and adjusting character spacing and kerning characters. New to Word 2010, as discussed in an earlier section of this chapter, you may also refine fonts by turning on font ligatures.

Changing Fonts, Font Styles, and Font Sizes

You can select fonts at the *Font* list box in the Font group on the Home tab, at the Font dialog box, or at the Mini toolbar that displays when right-clicking any text in a document. As you drag through the list of fonts displayed in the *Font* list box, the Live Preview feature automatically applies the fonts to the text.

Grow Font

Shrink Font

Font Size

DTP POINTERS▶
Do not use less than 10-point type in large areas of text.

To change a font size at the Font dialog box, select a point size from the *Size* list box or type a specific point size in the *Size* text box. The *Size* list box displays common increments ranging from 8 to 72 points. However, you may type a point size not listed. For instance, to create a font size at 250 points, position the arrow pointer on the number immediately below the *Size* text box, click the left mouse button, and then type **250**.

To change a font size at the Font Size button in the Font Group on the Home tab, type or select a point size from the *Font Size* list box. ***Hint: Press Enter after typing the point size in the Font Size list box—the increment will remain when you move your insertion point back onto the document screen.*** You can also increase or decrease text size by clicking the Grow Font (or press Ctrl + Shift + >) or Shrink Font (Ctrl + Shift + <) buttons located in the Font group. Shortcut key combinations may also be used to decrease the font size by one point by pressing Ctrl + [or Ctrl +] to increase the font size.

At the Font dialog box, select a font style from the list that displays below the *Font style* option box. As you select different typefaces, the list of styles changes in the *Font style* option box.

Selecting Underlining

In desktop publishing, underlining text has become somewhat dated. In place of underlining, consider enhancing your text with italics, bold, a different font size, all caps, or small caps. However, a list of lines is available by clicking the down-pointing

Figure 2.12 Text Effects

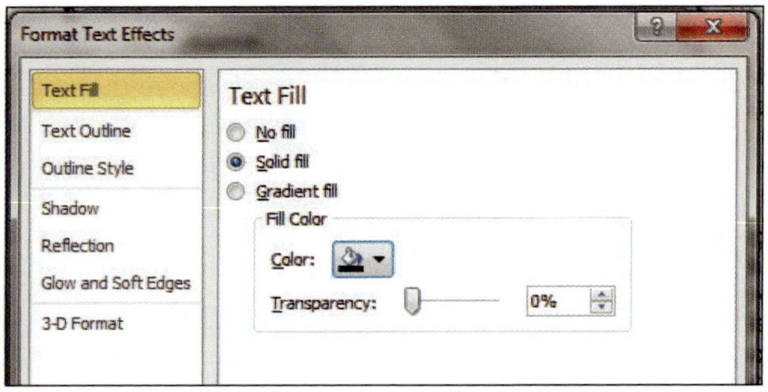

[Format Text Effects dialog box showing Text Fill options: No fill, Solid fill, Gradient fill, with Fill Color section showing Color and Transparency 0%]

arrow at the right of the Underline button in the Font group on the Home tab or by clicking the *Underline Style* option at the Font dialog box where an underline color may also be applied.

Changing Effects

The *Effects* section of the Font dialog box contains a variety of options that can be used to create different character formatting, such as *Strikethrough, Double strikethrough, Superscript, Subscript, Small caps, All caps,* and *Hidden.* To choose an effect, click the desired option. The text in the Preview box will illustrate the change. If the text already exists, select the text before applying these formatting options. At the Font dialog box, you may also click the Text Effects button at the bottom of the dialog box to access additional formatting options located at the Format Text Effects dialog box as shown in Figure 2.12.

You can change the look of your text by changing its fill, changing its outline, or adding effects, such as shadows, reflections, or glows. To add an effect to text, select the text that you want to enhance, and then click the Text Effect button in the Font group on the Home tab. Click the effect that you want as shown in Figure 2.13. The font colors and effects vary with the theme selected. If you want to remove the effect from the text, click the Clear Formatting button in the Font group.

◀DTP POINTERS
Use italics or small caps to emphasize text instead of all caps or underline.

Clear Formatting

Text Effect

Figure 2.13 Text Effects Gallery

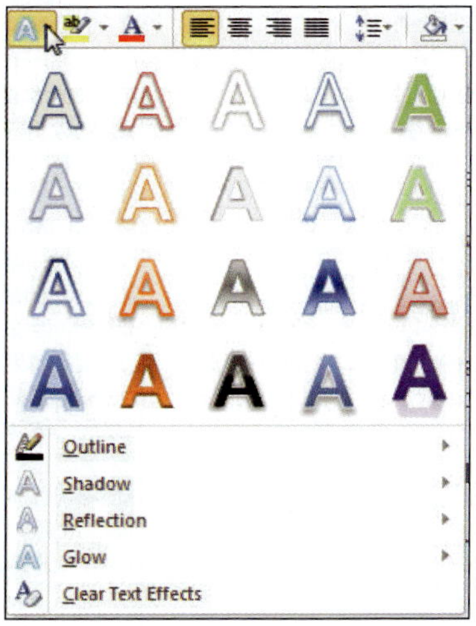

[Text Effects Gallery showing a grid of letter A styles with various fills and outlines, plus menu options: Outline, Shadow, Reflection, Glow, Clear Text Effects]

Themes

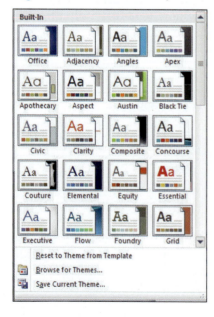

Consider using keyboard shortcut keys for applying font formatting. For instance, press Ctrl + Shift + A for All Caps; press Ctrl + Shift + K for Small Caps; or Shift + F3 for Toggle Capitalization. To access a detailed list of shortcut keys, click the Word Help button (question mark symbol in the upper right corner above the ribbon), and then type **keyboard shortcuts for Word** in the Word Help search text box. Print the list for easy access.

Changing Fonts Using Themes

Colors ▾

Theme Colors

Effects ▾

Theme Effects

A Fonts ▾

Theme Fonts

DTP POINTERS ▸

Select a desired theme, and then create a new color theme and font theme to complement your company logo.

DTP POINTERS ▸

Convert earlier Word documents to the newest format by clicking the Convert button in the *Compatibility Mode* section of the Info tab Backstage view.

In Microsoft Office Word 2010, you can apply a format to selected text, or you can quickly and easily format an entire document to give it a professional and modern look by applying a document theme on the Page Layout tab in the Themes group. A document theme is a set of formatting choices, as shown in Figure 2.14, that can include a color scheme (a set of colors) as shown in Figure 2.15, a font scheme (a set of heading and body text fonts) as shown in Figure 2.16, and an effects scheme (a set of lines and fill effects) as shown in Figure 2.17. The theme defines the major and secondary fonts used in the document, the color palette for the document, and the effects used for shapes, charts, and diagrams inserted into the document. By basing the content of a document on the same theme, you can help ensure a consistent look and make dramatic changes easily when updating the document or reusing the content. Keep in mind that you can customize each of the themes by selecting different color combinations, font combinations, and effects.

The default theme is the Office theme. If the Themes button is grayed and not accessible, you may need to convert the document from compatibility mode to the newest format by clicking the File tab, clicking the Convert button, and then clicking OK at the prompt that displays. In addition, themes are only available if you have applied styles to your document text first. After a style has been applied to text, Live Preview will allow you to see how the themes will vary the look of the document text.

Figure 2.14 Themes Gallery

Figure 2.15 Color Schemes

Figure 2.16 Font Schemes

Figure 2.17 Effects Schemes

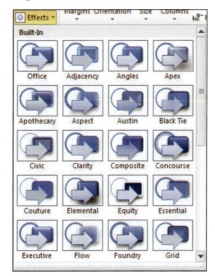

Adding Font Color

In addition, you may apply font colors to text by clicking the Font Color button on the Home tab in the Font group. You are not limited to the 10 colors displayed under Theme Colors or the 50 variations of these colors as they display below the Theme Colors shown in Figure 2.18. You may make additional choices by clicking the More Colors button at the bottom of the color palette or the Gradient button below the More Colors button. After clicking the More Colors button, you may choose the Standard tab where 124 colors are available, as well as 15 shades of gray as shown in Figure 2.19. *Hint: If you*

Font Color

Figure 2.18 Font Color Palette

Figure 2.19 Standard Tab at the Colors Dialog Box

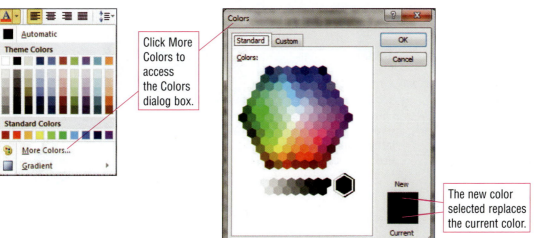

Click More Colors to access the Colors dialog box.

The new color selected replaces the current color.

choose Automatic at the Font Color palette and then change the background to black, the text color changes automatically to white. Also, if you choose the Blue background, white text option at the Options dialog box, the Automatic color choice will enable the text to display in white against the blue background. The Automatic feature works only in Word documents and tables.

At the Custom tab, you may choose from 16 million colors. In addition, you may create your own custom colors by either choosing the RGB or HSL color models shown in Figure 2.20. To create a custom color, click a color in the Colors box, and click the up-pointing arrow or the down-pointing arrow to adjust the **luminescence**, which is the brightness of the color; the **hue**, which is the color itself; and the **saturation**, which is the color's intensity. Alternatively, you may choose the precise three-digit settings in the *Hue, Sat,* and *Lum* text boxes. You may also use the Custom tab to approximately match a color, such as R:65, G:100, B:10 (Red, Green, and Blue). You may copy a color from one object to another using the Format Painter. ***Hint: Matching font colors to custom colors used in graphics will be discussed in Chapter 5.***

Adjusting Character Spacing

Each typeface is designed with a specific amount of space between characters. This character spacing may be changed with options at the Font dialog box with the Advanced tab selected. Use the *Scale* option to stretch or compress text horizontally as a percentage of the current size. You can choose a percentage from 1 to 600 to scale

Figure 2.20 **Customizing Colors Using Color Models**

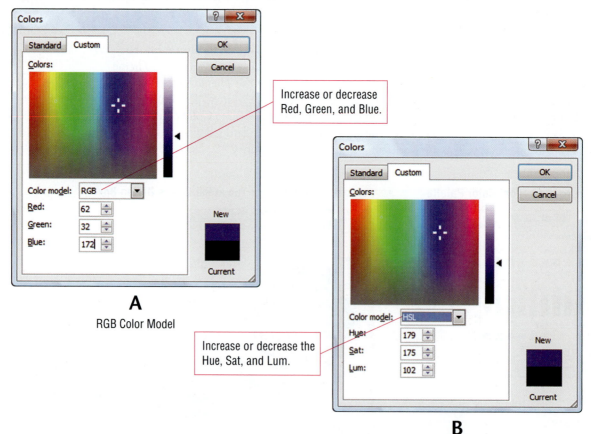

A

RGB Color Model

B

HSL Color Model

Figure 2.21 Adjusting Character Spacing

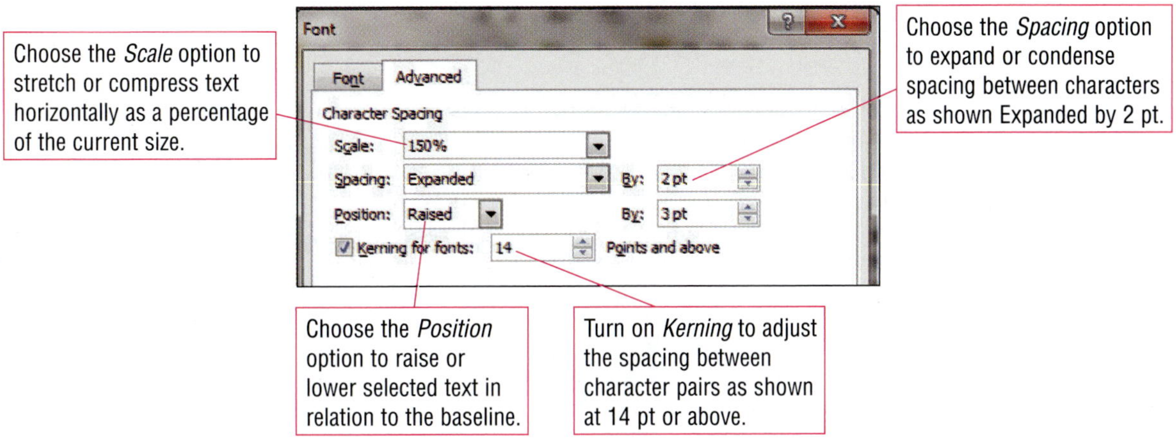

Choose the *Scale* option to stretch or compress text horizontally as a percentage of the current size.

Choose the *Spacing* option to expand or condense spacing between characters as shown Expanded by 2 pt.

Font

Font   Advanced

Character Spacing

Scale: 150%

Spacing: Expanded   By: 2 pt

Position: Raised   By: 3 pt

☑ Kerning for fonts: 14   Points and above

Choose the *Position* option to raise or lower selected text in relation to the baseline.

Turn on *Kerning* to adjust the spacing between character pairs as shown at 14 pt or above.

your text. Expand or condense the spacing between characters with the *Spacing* option. Choose either the *Expanded* or *Condensed* option, and then enter the desired point amount in the *By* text box. Raise or lower selected text in relation to the baseline with the *Position* option. Choose either the *Raised* or *Lowered* option and then enter the point amount in the *By* text box.

You can adjust the spacing between certain characters pairs (referred to as **kerning**) by selecting your text and then inserting a check mark in the *Kerning* check box. Kerning refers to adjusting horizontal space between certain character combinations by positioning two characters closer together to improve readability and help the eye move along the text. Kerned characters include AV, TA, Ty, Vi, and WA. Kerning can be turned on in the Font dialog box, as shown in Figure 2.21.

Kerning
Decreasing or increasing the horizontal space between specific character pairs.

Applying Quick Styles and Style Sets

Besides changing formatting directly, you can apply styles that automatically change formatting. To apply a style from the Quick Styles gallery, select the text to which you want to apply a style, and then click the style that you want in the Styles group on the Home tab as shown in Figure 2.22. Click the More button to expand the Quick Styles gallery. Additionally, you may click the Styles button in the bottom right corner of the Styles group or press Alt + Ctrl + Shift + S to access the *Styles* drop-down list.

If the style that you want does not appear in the Quick Styles gallery, press Ctrl + Shift + S to open the Apply Styles task pane. Under *Style Name*, type the name of the

Figure 2.22 Applying Quick Styles from the Quick Styles Gallery

AaBbCcD   AaBbCc   AaB   AaBbCcI   AaBbCcI   AaBbCcI
No Spacing   Heading 1   Title   Subtitle   Subtle Em...   Emphasis

AaBbCcI   AaBbCcI   AaBbCcL   AaBbCcI   AABBCC   AABBCC
Intense E...   Strong   Quote   Intense Q...   Subtle Ref...   Intense R...

AABBCC   AaBbCcI
Book Title   ¶ List Para...

Save Selection as a New Quick Style...
Clear Formatting
Apply Styles...

Figure 2.23 Applying Style Sets and Changing Colors, Fonts, and Paragraph Spacing

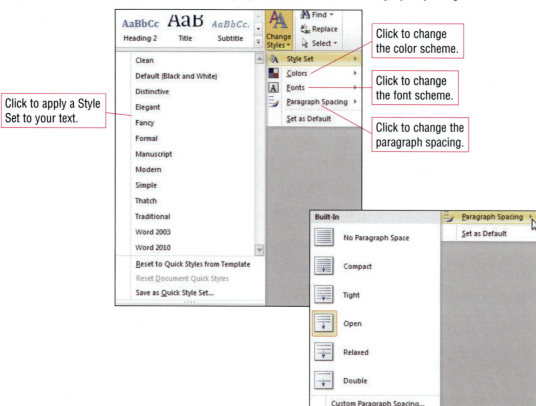

Click to apply a Style Set to your text.

Click to change the color scheme.

Click to change the font scheme.

Click to change the paragraph spacing.

style that you want. The list shows only those styles that you have already used in the document, but you can type the name of any style that is defined for the document.

Click the Change Styles button in the Styles group on the Home tab to access the *Style Set* option. Click *Style Set* to display the list of predesigned styles shown in Figure 2.23. Live Preview enables you to view the results of the style as you point to the desired Style Set. Click to apply the Style Set to your selected text.

In Exercise 2.1, assume you are working at the British Inn, and you are creating a sign welcoming the American Society of Public Accountants to your inn for a conference. Consider printing the sign on 24-lb. bond stock paper and placing it in an acrylic frame or sign stand in the lobby for the conference attendees to see.

Figure 2.24 displays the sign in Exercise 2.1 using two different methods for positioning the text. Both methods include a text box as the container of the text and a textured fill. A right tab aligned all of the text in the first example. Text boxes aligned the text in the second example. The text boxes provide an easy means of positioning text on the screen. Double-click the text box to access the Text Box Tools contextual tab. At the Format tab, click the down-pointing arrow at the right of the Shape Fill button and then click the *No Fill* option. Change the Shape Fill and Shape Outline colors to *No Fill* and *No Outline* so that one box can overlap another. Click the Line button, in the Shapes group in the Insert tab to create the horizontal lines. Otherwise, you may create lines using a graphic border, borderline, or an Art border accessed at the Borders and Shading dialog box.

DTP POINTERS
Use a logo for continuity and recognition.

Notice the font contrast—one thin serif font and one thick sans serif font. Text placed in text boxes facilitates easy movement. The logo, a Shape and WordArt

Figure 2.24 Using Text Boxes or Tabs to Create a Sign

A

Using a Right Tab to Create a Sign

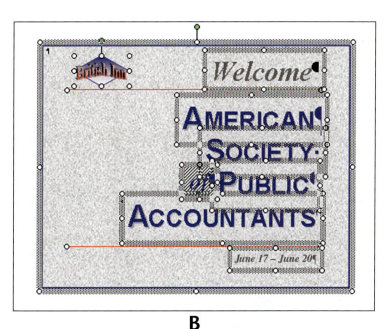

B

Using Text Boxes with No Fill to Create a Sign

combination, reinforces the British Inn's identity. Notice that the address text at the bottom of the sign was enhanced by using Word's new Ligature feature.

*Hint: Copy the Chapter02 data files from your textbook CD to the **Chapter02** folder you have created on your disk, and then make **Chapter02** the active folder. Remember to substitute for graphics that may no longer be available.*

1. Open **Sign** from your *Chapter02* folder. ***Hint: The document has been staged with the text box, logo, and line shape inserted. The line spacing has been changed to single, and the 10 points After setting has been removed.***
2. Save the document and name it **C02-E01-Sign**.
3. Change the theme to Concourse.
4. Make sure the insertion point is located in the upper left corner of the text box. Click the Fonts button in the Themes group, and then select the *Office 2* font theme.
5. Click the Font dialog box launcher, select the Advanced tab, and turn on the features shown (*Kerning* at *14* pts., *Ligatures - All, Proportional, Old-style*). Click OK.
6. Turn on the Show/Hide feature in the Paragraph group in the Home tab.
7. Create a right tab by completing the following steps:
   a. Verify that the insertion point is positioned inside the text box in the upper left corner, and then display the Ruler.
   b. Click the Tab Alignment button until the Right Tab displays.
   c. Position the arrow pointer on 8.5 inches on the Ruler, and then click the mouse to set a tab.
8. Create the sign text in Figure 2.25 by completing the following steps:
   a. With the insertion point in the upper left corner of the text box, press Enter three times.
   b. Press Tab, type **Welcome**, and then press Enter twice.
   c. Press Tab, type **American**, and then press Enter.
   d. Press Tab, type **Society**, and then press Enter.
   e. Press Tab, type **Public**, and then press Enter—you will type **of** later.
   f. Press Tab, type **Accountants**, and then press Enter two times.
   g. Press Tab, type **June 17 – June 19**, and then press Enter two times.

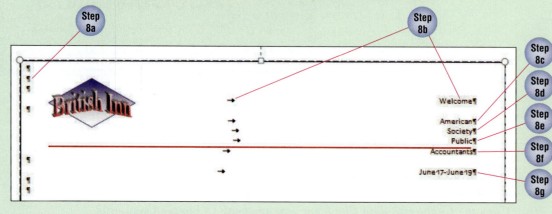

9. Format the sign text by completing the following steps:

   a. Select *Welcome;* (do not select the paragraph symbol) change the font to 60-point Calibri, bold, italic; and add the color *White, Background 1, Darker 35%* in the fifth row and first column of the *Theme Colors* section.

   Step 9a

   b. With *Welcome* selected, display the Font dialog box, select the Advanced tab, and then change the character spacing to *Expanded By* 3 pt in the *Character Spacing* section.

   c. Select *American Society Public Accountants,* and change the font to 65-point Calibri, click the Text Effect button, and then apply the *Gradient Fill - Blue, Accent 4, Reflection* text effect.

   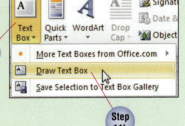
   Step 9c

   d. With the text still selected, change the leading between the lines by accessing the Paragraph dialog box, displaying the Indents and Spacing tab, clicking the down-pointing arrow at the *Line spacing* option box, and selecting *Multiple* from the drop-down list. Type **0.75** in the *At* text box. Click OK.

   Step 9d

   e. Select *June 17 – June 20,* and change the font to 24-point Calibri, bold, italic, and the color to *White, Background 1, Darker 35%.*

10. Select the red horizontal line below *Welcome* and while holding down the Shift and Ctrl keys drag a copy of the line between *Accountants* and *June*. . . **Hint: Release the left mouse button and then the Ctrl key and the Shift key.** You should now have a duplicate of the red line positioned below *Accountants.*

11. Create the text box containing *of* by completing the following steps:

    Step 11a

    Step 11b

    a. Click the Text Box button in the Text group on the Insert tab.

    b. Click the Draw Text Box button at the bottom of the Text Box drop-down list.

    c. Draw a text box that is approximately 1-inch square.

    d. Create an exact measurement for the text box by completing the following steps:

       1) Double-click the border of the text box to display the contextual Drawing Tools Format tab.

       2) Change the height of the text box by typing **1.25** inch in the *Height* text box and **1** inch in the *Width* text box in the Size group.

       Step 11d2

12. Position the insertion point in the text box; change the font to 55-point Book Antiqua, bold italic; and then type **of**.

    Step 13

13. Select *of,* click the Text Effects button in the Font group, and apply the *Fill - Orange, Accent 3, Outline - Text 2* text effect.

14. With the text box still selected, go to the Drawing Tools Format tab, click the down-pointing arrow at the right of the *Shape Outline* option in the Shape Styles group, and click *No Outline.*

15. With the text box still selected, click the down-pointing arrow at the right of the *Shape Fill* option, and click *No Fill.*

16. Click the border of the text box, and when the arrow pointer displays as a four-headed arrow, drag the text box to the left of *Public* as shown in Figure 2.25.
17. Change the color of the border surrounding the sign text by completing the following steps:
    a. Select the border surrounding the sign to display the Drawing Tools Format contextual tab.
    b. Click the More button at the bottom of the Shape Styles gallery, and then click the *Colored Outline - Red, Accent 2* style.

Step 17b

18. Add the textured fill by completing the following steps:
    a. With the text box selected, click the Shape Fill button in the Shape Styles group, and then click Texture.
    b. Click the *Newsprint* texture in the first column in the fourth row.

Step 18b

Newsprint

19. Position the insertion point on the second paragraph symbol below the dates; click the Center button in the Paragraph group; change the font to 14-point Calibri, bold, *Orange, Accent 3* color; and then type **9341 Sam Rittenberg Blvd., Charleston, SC 29412**. *Notice the use of ligatures.*

Step 19

Theme Colors

Orange, Accent 3

20. Save the document again as **C02-E01-Sign.docx**, and then save the document in PDF format by completing the following steps:
    a. Click the File tab, and then click Save As.
    b. At the Save As dialog box, **C02-E01-Sign** should display in the *File name* text box, click the down-pointing arrow at the right of the *Save as type* list box, and then click the *PDF* option at the drop-down list. Click Save.
    c. Click the Print button on the Adobe Reader toolbar, and then close both versions of the document.

Step 20c

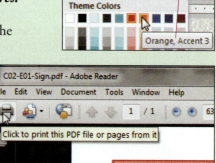

Adding Symbols and Special Characters to a Document

Symbols and special characters add interest and originality to documents. Sometimes, it is the small touches that make a difference, such as adding a symbol (❖) at the end of an article in a newsletter, enlarging a symbol (Υ) and using it as a graphic element on a page, or adding a special character (©) to clarify text. Interesting symbols are found in such fonts as (normal text), Wingdings, Wingdings 2, Wingdings 3, and Webdings. Special characters may include an em dash (—), en dash (–), copyright character (©), registered trademark character (®), ellipses (. . .), or nonbreaking hyphens.

To insert a symbol as shown in Figure 2.26, click the Symbol button in the Symbols group in the Insert tab, and then select one of the symbols displayed on the palette or click the More Symbols button at the bottom of the palette. At the Symbol dialog box, select the Symbols tab, select a desired font, double-click the symbol or click Insert, and then click Close (or press Esc). To insert a special character, follow the same steps except choose the Special Characters tab, and then select a desired character.

Symbol

Figure 2.25 Exercise 2.1

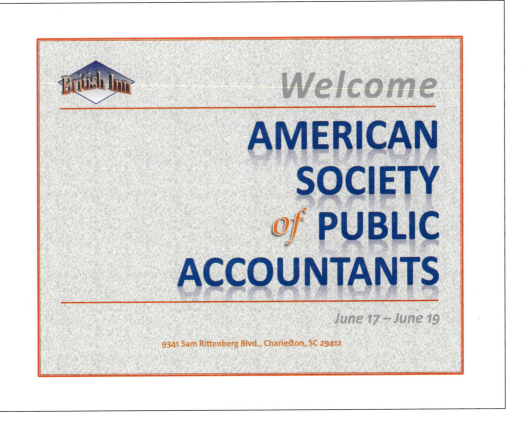

Figure 2.26 Inserting a Symbol

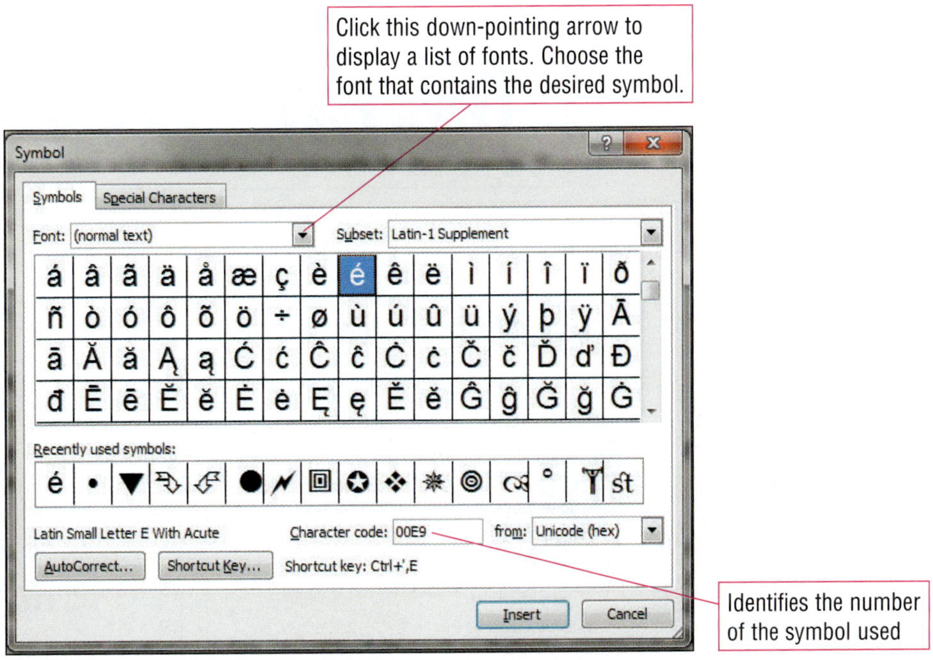

Click this down-pointing arrow to display a list of fonts. Choose the font that contains the desired symbol.

Identifies the number of the symbol used

To find a specific symbol quickly, key the Character code that is given in an exercise in the *Character code* text box that displays toward the bottom of the Symbols tab in the Symbol dialog box.

Creating Em and En Dashes

An *em dash* (—) is as long as the point size of the type used and indicates a pause in speech. An *en dash* (–) indicates a continuation, such as 116–133 or January–March, and is exactly one-half the width of an em dash. Besides inserting em and en dashes using the Symbol dialog box at the Special Characters tab, you may insert an em dash at the keyboard by pressing Alt + Ctrl + Num - or an en dash by pressing Ctrl + Num - . Additionally, the AutoCorrect feature includes an option that will automatically create em and en dashes.

Using Smart Quotes

In typesetting, the *tail* of the punctuation mark extends upward for the open quotation mark and downward for the close quotation mark. In typesetting, the straight quotes are used to indicate inches (") or feet ('). The Smart Quote feature will automatically choose the quote style that is appropriate if it is typed in error. The *Smart Quote* option is turned on or off at the AutoFormat As You Type tab, which is accessed by clicking the File tab, clicking the Options button, clicking the Proofing tab, and then clicking the AutoCorrect Options button.

DTP POINTERS ▶

Use vertical quotation marks only to indicate measurements.

Figure 2.27 Creating Interesting Designs with Fonts (Thick/Thin, Serif/Sans Serif, Contrasting Colors and Sizes)

In addition, symbols and special characters may be added to the AutoCorrect feature, which will automatically insert the desired symbol when using a specific keyboard command. Symbols may also be copied to the Clipboard and pasted when needed.

Using Contrasting Fonts in Design

Consider the designs in Figure 2.27 and the effects these interesting fonts could have on a target audience. The designs incorporate many desktop publishing concepts, such as using contrasting fonts—thin and thick fonts, light and dark font color, serif and sans serif typefaces, ornate and plain appearance; using a variety of colors for focus; and using good directional flow.

◀ DTP POINTERS
Contrasting fonts create interest in a document.

In Exercise 2.2, assume you are working for an international accounting network that will be holding a regional meeting in Istanbul, Turkey and creating an invitation to a dinner as shown in Figure 2.28. The invitation will be created on a 5 × 7 inch-sized document, saved in PDF format, and then sent to a commercial printer to be trimmed and printed on appropriate cardstock. Because you cannot edit your document in PDF format without Adobe Acrobat software, you will need to save the document first in DOCX format for any necessary editing.

◀ DTP POINTERS
If you drag a text box to a wrong location, click the Undo button.

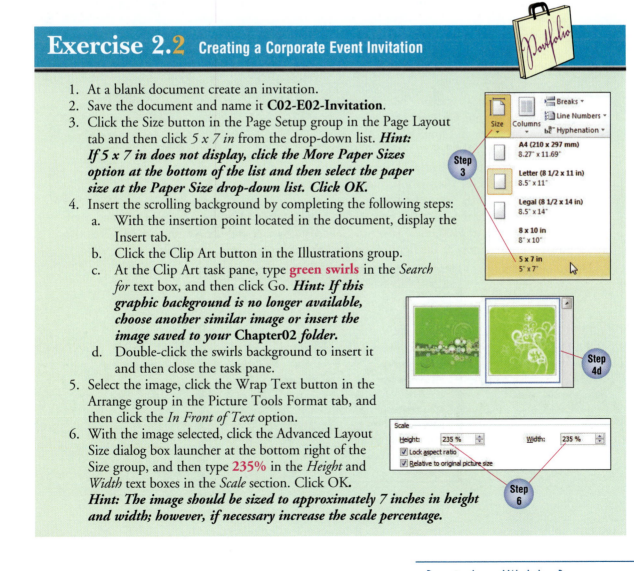

Exercise 2.2   Creating a Corporate Event Invitation

1. At a blank document create an invitation.
2. Save the document and name it **C02-E02-Invitation**.
3. Click the Size button in the Page Setup group in the Page Layout tab and then click *5 x 7 in* from the drop-down list. ***Hint: If 5 x 7 in does not display, click the More Paper Sizes option at the bottom of the list and then select the paper size at the Paper Size drop-down list. Click OK.***
4. Insert the scrolling background by completing the following steps:
   a. With the insertion point located in the document, display the Insert tab.
   b. Click the Clip Art button in the Illustrations group.
   c. At the Clip Art task pane, type **green swirls** in the *Search for* text box, and then click Go. ***Hint: If this graphic background is no longer available, choose another similar image or insert the image saved to your* Chapter02 *folder.***
   d. Double-click the swirls background to insert it and then close the task pane.
5. Select the image, click the Wrap Text button in the Arrange group in the Picture Tools Format tab, and then click the *In Front of Text* option.
6. With the image selected, click the Advanced Layout Size dialog box launcher at the bottom right of the Size group, and then type **235%** in the *Height* and *Width* text boxes in the *Scale* section. Click OK. ***Hint: The image should be sized to approximately 7 inches in height and width; however, if necessary increase the scale percentage.***

7. Drag the swirls background to fit the 5 × 7 inch document. ***Hint: No white space should display around the document. The image will surpass the boundaries of the page.***

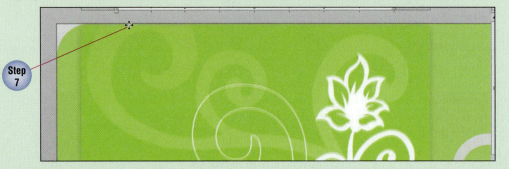

8. Draw a text box that is approximately 3 by 6 inches in width and height.

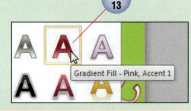

9. Click the down-pointing arrow at the right of the Shape Fill button in the Shape Styles group on the Drawing Tools Format tab, and then click *No Fill*.
10. Click the down-pointing arrow at the right of the Shape Outline button, and then click *No Outline*.
11. Insert the invitation text by completing the following steps:
    a. Position the insertion point inside the text box, click the down-pointing arrow at the right of the Object button in the Text group in the Insert tab, and then click *Text from File*.
    b. At the Insert Text dialog box, insert **InvitationText** located in your *Chapter02* folder.
12. Change the theme to Opulent.
13. Select *European, Middle East, Africa Regional Dinner*, change the font to 28-point Gabriola; click the Text Effects button in the Font group; and then click the *Gradient Fill - Pink, Accent 1* color.
14. With the text selected, click the Font dialog box launcher, click the Advanced tab, and then change the *Scale* to *90%*, the *Spacing* to *Condensed* by *1 pt* and the Kerning to *14*. Click the down-pointing arrow at the right of the *Stylistic sets* list box, and then click *6*. Click OK.

15. Select all the text except for the last two lines, and click the Center button in the Paragraph group. Right align the last two lines.
16. Draw a text box that is approximately 1 inch in height and width.
17. Insert the (&) symbol by completing the following steps:
    a. With the insertion point inside the text box, click the Symbols button in the Symbols group in the Insert tab, and then click More Symbols.
    b. Click the down-pointing arrow at the right of the *Font* list box and then select *Wingdings*.
    c. Type **107** in the *Character code* text box. Click Insert and then Close.

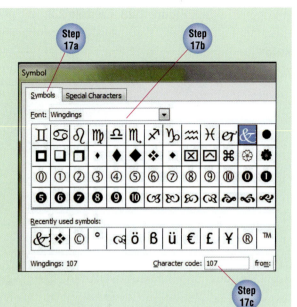

18. Select the (&) symbol, and change the font to 48-point Harrington, click the Text Effects button, and then click the *Fill - White, Gradient Outline - Accent 1* color.

19. Select the text box, and then remove the Shape Fill and the Shape Outline.
20. Drag the text box containing the (&) symbol to a position similar to Figure 2.28.
21. Select the remaining text, and change the font to 11.5-point Papyus.
22. With the text selected, change the line spacing (leading) to *Exactly At 20 pt.*
23. Save **C02-E02-Invitation.docx**. Save the document again as **C02-E02-Invitation.pdf** and then print the document at the Adobe Reader screen. Close both documents. *Hint: You can also save a document in PDF format by clicking the File tab, Save & Send tab, Create PDF/XPS Document button in the File Types section, Create PDF/XPS button, and then Publish. If necessary, download Adobe Reader from the www.adobe.com Web site; this is a free download.*

Figure 2.28 Exercise 2.2

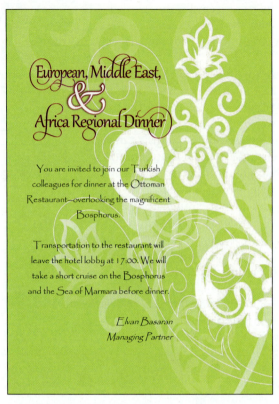

Using the Word Cover Page Feature to Create a Manual Cover

Cover Page

Cover Page is a Word feature that can be used to create title pages for reports, manuals, and any other documents that require a professional-looking cover. Fifteen predesigned Cover Page designs are available; six are displayed in Figure 2.29. At the Insert tab, click the Cover Page button in the Pages group, and then choose a design from the gallery. After inserting a cover page, you can remove it by reopening the Cover Page menu and choosing *Remove Current Cover Page*.

You can customize your cover page by adding your business logo, inserting content controls or Quick Parts, adding a photo, or choosing the color scheme and font style that matches your business brand. Then you can save the cover as a template and reuse it with other reports to give your documents a consistent look and feel.

Inserting Predesigned Building Blocks into a Manual

Quick Parts

Along with the Cover Page feature, you can insert similarly designed headers and footers, sidebars, pull quotes, and other Building Blocks into your documents to coordinate with your cover page. To access these design elements, click the Quick Parts button in the Text group in the Insert tab, and then click the Building Blocks Organizer option. A complete list of reusable pieces of content is available as shown in Figure 2.30. If you have a logo, letterhead, signature line, or mission statement that you want to use again and again, you can save these items as Building Blocks by clicking the *AutoText* option and then clicking *Save Selection to AutoText Gallery*.

Figure 2.29 Inserting Predesigned Cover Pages

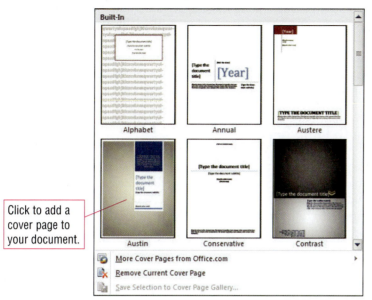

Click to add a cover page to your document.

Figure 2.30 Building Blocks Organizer

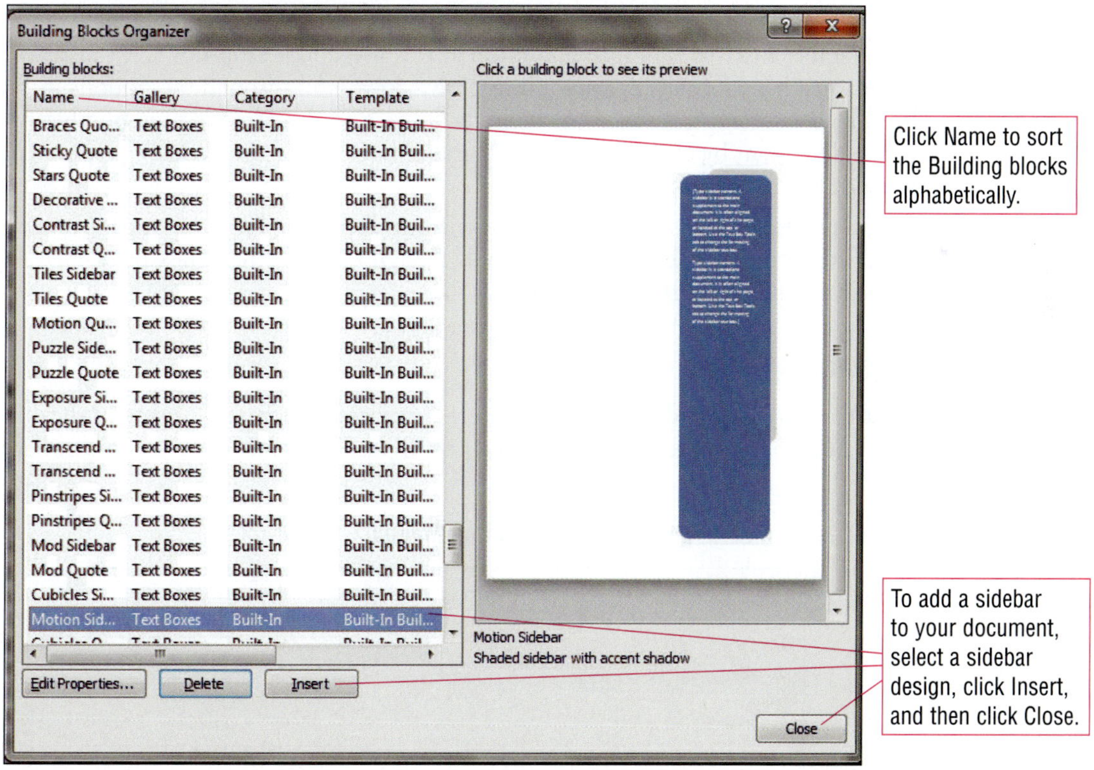

Click Name to sort the Building blocks alphabetically.

To add a sidebar to your document, select a sidebar design, click Insert, and then click Close.

Applying Styles to a Cover Page

Styles reinforce consistency within documents and among similarly designed documents. The Cover Page you select from the Cover Page gallery will most likely contain styles that help to reinforce consistency. In addition, you may add pull quotes and other Quick Parts formatted with similar styles that coordinate with the Cover Page. If you prefer to change the styles or apply other ones, select the text to which you want to apply a style. If you do not see the style that you want, click the More button to expand the Quick Styles gallery. The Quick Styles gallery displays these styles in Live Preview. You may also change the entire look of the document by clicking the Changes Styles button in the Styles group on the Home tab where you can alter the color, fonts, and paragraph spacing.

Working with Long Documents

If you are preparing a cover page for a long document such as a reference manual or a procedures manual, you will want to access the References tab and use the numerous features provided, such as (1) APA, Chicago, MLA, or other style guides; (2) table of contents options; (3) caption options; (4) index features; (5) citations and bibliography formatting options, footnotes, and endnote sections; and (6) even table of authorities' commands.

Inserting Page Numbers

Page Number

Word, by default, does not print page numbers on document pages. If you want to insert page numbers in your manual, as in Exercise 2.3, use the Page Number button in the Header & Footer group in the Insert tab. When you click the Page Number button, a drop-down list displays with options for specifying where on the page you want the page number inserted. Point to an option at this list, and a drop-down list displays of predesigned page formats as shown in Figure 2.31. Scroll through the options in the drop-down list, and then click the desired choice. You can remove page numbering from a document by clicking the Page Number button and then clicking *Remove Page Numbers* at the drop-down list.

To prevent an automatic page number from displaying on the first page or a cover page, display the Header and Footer Tools Design tab, and then click the *Different First Page* check box to insert a check mark.

Inserting Page Breaks

Creating a page break does not really insert a new page; it creates a break at the insertion point. To create a manual page break, position your insertion point where a

Figure 2.31 **Inserting Page Numbering in a Manual**

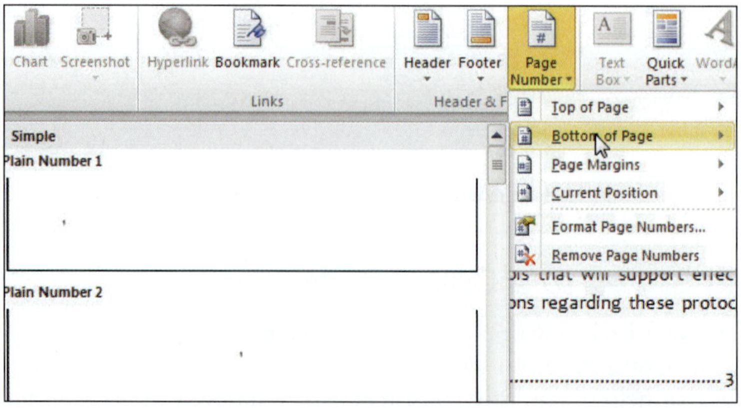

break is desired and then press Ctrl + Enter or click the Page Break button in the Pages group in the Insert tab. However, if text is added or removed from the page, the break may cause an awkward separation in the document. Word 2010 does have a feature that actually inserts a new page: the Blank Page button in the Insert tab. It is the same as if you had created two hard page breaks and then moved the insertion between them.

Page Break

Breaks may also be added to your document by clicking the Breaks button on the Page Setup group in the Page Layout tab. You will use these options in later chapters of this book.

In Exercise 2.3, assume you are creating a protocol manual for an accounting firm. You will use the Cover Page feature to create the cover for the manual, and you will use Quick Styles and Themes to format the document efficiently. You will choose the Contrast cover page design and the Waveform theme for the document formatting. Both designs are conservative and seem to fit the look for this particular type of business. The Waveform theme will influence the styles that are available in the Styles gallery. As you know, styles reinforce consistency, and consistency is important in formatting headings in long documents.

Breaks

Exercise 2.3   Creating a Protocol Manual

1. Open **Protocol** located in your *Chapter02* folder and save it, and then name it **C02-E03-Protocol**.
2. Change the theme to Waveform.
3. Click the Fonts button in the Themes group and then click the *Apothecary* font theme.
4. Click the Change Styles button in the Styles group in the Home tab, click Style Set, and then click the *Distinctive* style set.

Step 4

5. Create the cover page as shown in Figure 2.32 by completing the following steps:
   a. With the insertion point located at the beginning of the document, click the Cover Page button in the Pages group in the Insert tab.
   b. Select the *Contrast* cover design.
   c. Position the insertion point in the upper left corner of the gray text box, and then insert the image shown in Figure 2.32 by clicking the Clip Art button in the Illustrations group. Type **accounting** in the *Search for* text box on the Clip Art pane, and then press Enter. Close the Clip Art task pane.
   d. Select the image and then change the Wrap Text, to *In Front of Text.*
   e. Resize the image by dragging one of the corner sizing handles, and then position the image as shown in Figure 2.32.

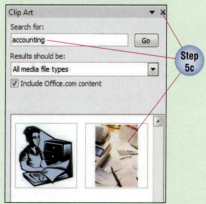

Step 5c

f. With the image selected, click the Corrections button in the Adjust group on the Picture Tools Format tab, and then click *Brightness: 0% (Normal) Contrast: + 20%*.

Step 5f

Brightness: 0% (Normal) Contrast: +20%

g. With the image selected, click the Picture Effects button in the Picture Styles group, click Glow, and then click *Blue, 11 pt glow, Accent color 2*.

h. Click the 3-D Rotation button, and then click *Perspective Heroic Extreme Left*.

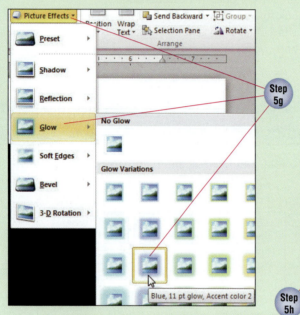

Step 5g

Blue, 11 pt glow, Accent color 2

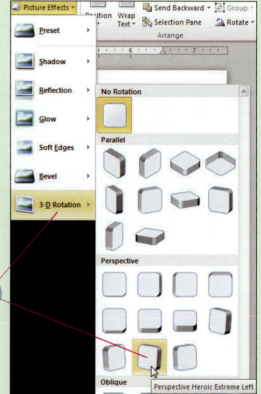

Step 5h

Perspective Heroic Extreme Left

i. Click the Title Content Control, and then type **Winston & McKenzie, LLP**. *Hint: This text may automatically appear in the control.*

j. Select *Winston & McKenzie, LLP*, click the Text Effects button, and then click the *Gradient Fill - Blue, Accent 1* text effect. *Hint: If necessary, click the Align Text Left button in the Paragraph group.*

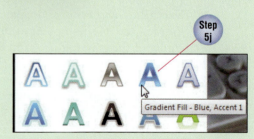

Step 5j

Gradient Fill - Blue, Accent 1

k. Click the Author Content Control (*Your Name Here*) and then type **Minneapolis Office Protocol**. *Hint: Did you see that the styles saved to the template are applied to your text?*

l. Click the Abstract Content Control and then type **Our office works in teams, which requires collaboration and the sharing of spaces and equipment. Therefore, it is important for everyone to understand the Protocols that will support effective interaction and utilization of our resources.**

m. Click the Company Content Control, and type **Winston & McKenzie, LLP**.

n.   Click the Address Content Control and type **5689 Hennepin Avenue**.>>

o.   Click the Phone Content Control and type **612.555.6084**.

p.   Click the Fax Content Control and type **612.555.6060**.

q.   Click the Date Content Control, Calendar icon, and then *Today* to insert the current date.

6. Format the first page of the protocol manual (see Figure 2.32) by completing the following steps:

a.   Position the insertion point anywhere in *What Are Protocols?*, click the More button at the bottom of the Quick Styles gallery in the Styles group, and then click the Title style in the Quick Styles gallery.

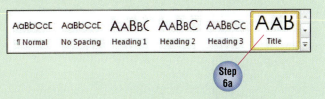

Step 6a

b.   Position the insertion point anywhere in *Why are protocols necessary?*, and click the *Heading 1* style in the Quick Styles gallery.

c.   Select the text beginning with *Security/Check-In Policy* and ending with *Workspace Privacy*, and then type **5** pt in the *After* measurement box in the *Spacing* section in the Paragraph group in the Page Layout tab.

d.   With the text still selected, click the Paragraph dialog box launcher in the Paragraph group in the Home tab, and then click the Tabs button in the lower left corner.

e.   At the Tabs dialog box, type **6.25** in the *Tab stop position* text box, select the *Right* option in the *Alignment* section, and then click the 2 option in the *Leader* section. Click Set and then OK.

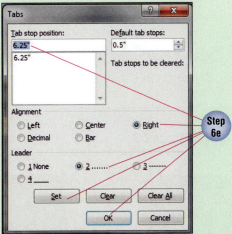

Step 6e

f.   Select *Housekeeping* and while holding down the Ctrl key, select *Meeting Areas* in the tabbed text, apply the Intense Emphasis style, and then click the Center button in the Paragraph group.

7. Format the remaining pages of the manual by completing the following steps:

a.   Position the insertion point to the left of *General Protocol*, and insert another page break by pressing Ctrl + Enter.

b.   Apply the Title style and the Heading 1 style to the headings in the remaining pages.

c.   On page 3 (see Figure 2.32), select all the text in the *Protocol* section, and then click the Bullets button in the Paragraph group in the Home tab.

d.   With the bulleted text selected, click the Paragraph dialog box launcher, remove the check mark at the left of the *Don't add space between paragraphs of the same style* option in the *Spacing* section, and then click OK. **Hint: This applies the 10 points After spacing between the bulleted items making it easier to read the text.**

Step 7d

e.   On page 4 (see Figure 2.32), select all the text in the *Protocol* section except for the last paragraph, and then click the Bullets button again.

f.   With the bulleted text selected, click the Paragraph dialog box launcher, remove the check mark at the left of the *Don't add space between paragraphs of the same style* option in the *Spacing* section, and then click OK.

8. Add page numbering by completing the following steps:
   a. Click the Insert tab.
   b. Click the down-pointing arrow at the right of the Page Number button, and then click Bottom of Page.
   c. Click the *Outline Circle 3* option.

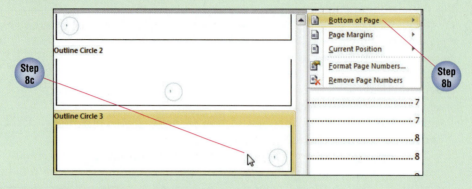

   d. At the Header & Footer Tools Design tab, if necessary click to add a check mark in the check box to the left of the *Different First Page* option, and then click the Close Header & Footer button.

9. Save, print, and then close **C02-E03-Protocol.docx**.

Figure 2.32 Exercise 2.3

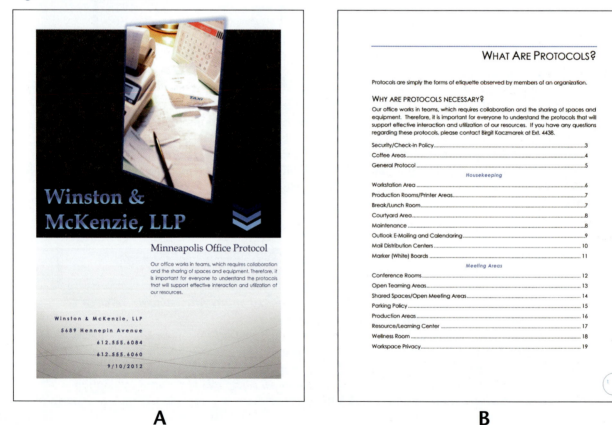

A   B

Figure 2.32 **Exercise 2.3 (continued)**

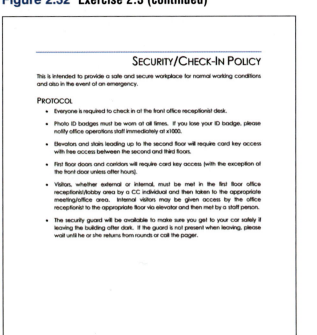

SECURITY/CHECK-IN POLICY

This is intended to provide a safe and secure workplace for normal working conditions and also in the event of an emergency.

PROTOCOL

- Everyone is required to check in at the front office receptionist desk.
- Photo ID badges must be worn at all times. If you lose your ID badge, please notify office operations staff immediately at x1000.
- Elevators and stairs leading up to the second floor will require card key access with free access between the second and third floors.
- First floor doors and corridors will require card key access (with the exception of the front door unless after hours).
- Visitors, whether external or internal, must be met in the first floor office receptionist/lobby area by a CC individual and then taken to the appropriate meeting/office area. Internal visitors may be given access by the office receptionist to the appropriate floor via elevator and then met by a staff person.
- The security guard will be available to make sure you get to your car safely if leaving the building after dark. If the guard is not present when leaving, please wait until he or she returns from rounds or call the pager.

GENERAL PROTOCOL

To create a level of conscious behavior that promotes a work environment where audio and visual distraction is minimized and that promotes the ability to work effectively in the workspace provided.

PROTOCOL

- Headphones are recommended for use with radios, i-pods, CD-players, etc.
- Cell phones and beepers should be set to "vibrate."
- Phone ringers should be set to low, including cell phones.
- Speakerphones should not be used at workstations.
- Conference calls should be held in enclaves or conference rooms so that others around you won't be disrupted.
- Overhead paging will be available. Call the office receptionist to request a page. Overhead paging is intended for urgent requests only. Individual pagers should be tried first before requesting an overhead page.
- Be conscious of noise and other disruptions to adjacent workstation areas. Individuals being disturbed should not hesitate to discuss these distractions with individuals.
- Children in the office must be accompanied by their parent or adult at all times. If at the office for an extended period, they must be in a designated enclave or small conference room that has been reserved for this purpose.
- Please refer to HR Online for protocols on e-mail, voice mail, flex time, and casual business attire.

C   **D**

Creating Documents Using Templates and Wizards

Word includes a number of template documents formatted for specific uses. Each Word document is based on a template document with the *Normal* template the default. Every document created in Word is based on a template. When you create a document as a blank document, you are using the default template. This default template, called the ***Normal.dotm*** template, contains formatting instructions to use 11-point Calibri (Body) as the font, English (U.S.) as the language, left alignment, widow/orphan control, 10 points after, and 1.15 line spacing.

A ***template*** is a document type that creates a copy of itself when you open it. In Office 2010, a template can be a .dotx file or it can be a .dotm file (a .dotm file type allows you to enable macros in the file). With Word templates, you can easily create a variety of documents, such as letters, memos, and brochures, with specialized formatting. Along with templates, Word also includes wizards. ***Wizards*** walk you through a series of steps in which you add or select information to set up formatting, content, and layout of your document.

Templates and wizards are usually accessed at the New tab Backstage view. Click the File tab, and then click the New tab. At the New tab Backstage view as shown in Figure 2.33, click on any of the categories that organize related templates. Other templates may be available on the Internet. Use your favorite search engine to locate these templates.

Normal.dotm
The default template in Word.

Template
A document type that creates a copy of itself when you open it.

Wizard
A feature that walks you through a series of steps in which you add or select information to set up formatting, content, and layout of your document.

Figure 2.33 New Tab Backstage View

Customizing Templates

When customizing a template to meet your specific needs, remember to apply the basic design concepts discussed in Chapter 1. Always begin a document with the end result in mind. Plan your text carefully to achieve your desired results without unnecessary wording or formatting. If you replace the existing fonts in a template, be sure the fonts increase the readability of the text. *Readability* is the ease with which a person can read and understand groups of words.

Templates and wizards can help you create great looking documents. However, if you do not want your documents to look like *one size fits all*, consider the following suggestions:

- Change fonts, font styles, font sizes, font colors, and font effects.
- Use expanded, condensed, lowered, or raised character spacing.
- Use reverse text and/or rotated text.
- Add more or less leading (white space between the lines) and tracking (letter spacing).
- Add fill color and fill effects—gradient, texture, pattern, or picture.
- Add text box shading, shapes, Shadows Effects, or 3-D Effects.
- Apply Quick Styles, Text Box Styles, Themes, Style Sets, SmartArt, Pictures, Clip Art, scanned images, Shapes, Charts, WordArt, Quick Parts, or any of the graphical design enhancement features available in Word 2010.
- Insert special characters and symbols.
- Create unique bullets.
- Add borders and shading.

Readability

The ease with which a person can read and understand groups of words.

DTP POINTERS

You may need to convert the templates you are using to the newest file format (Word 2010). Click the File tab and then the Info tab. Click the Convert button in the *Compatibility Mode* section and then click OK at the Convert to newest format prompt.

- Add Drop Caps.
- Add a company logo.
- Adjust the alignment.
- Create a watermark.
- Use unique column layout and specialized tables.
- Include links to other documents.
- Add form fields that fit your needs.

Basing a New Template on an Existing Document

If your existing document contains many of the features you want to add to a template, you can save time by basing your new template on that document. At the New tab Backstage view, click the New from existing button in the *Available Templates* section. Locate and then select the document you want to use for your template and then click the Open button. The new document is created, with all the same settings and text as the document you chose.

Changing File Locations

By default, Word saves a template document in the *Templates* folder on your hard drive. The templates you save in the *Templates* folder display in *My Templates* located on the New tab Backstage view.

In a setting where more than one person uses the same computer, such as a school or business, consider changing the location where Word saves template documents. (See your instructor about where to save your templates.) For example, in the next exercise, you will create a folder, *DTP Templates*, on your storage device and save templates to this folder. To delete a template in *My Templates*, right-click the template and then click *Delete* from the shortcut menu.

Understanding Content Control in Templates

In Exercise 2.3, you added a Cover Page to a report. Did you notice that the placeholder text on the Cover Page displayed as fields? Did the author placeholder automatically insert a name? The name that possibly appeared automatically was synchronized to the *Properties* section of the document. If you right-click on a document name and then click *Properties* from the pop-up menu, you will find your name or the author's name to the document. When you moved your cursor over the date placeholder, did you see a calendar (date picker) appear automatically? If you saw the calendar, you were looking at another example of a content control. Content controls are usually found in Office templates. They can be added to your document by accessing the Developer tab. You will add content controls to your documents in later chapters.

Faxing Versus Scanning

Facsimiles have been commonplace in offices and homes for many years, possibly even before computers came upon the scene. However, with the availability of saving documents in PDF format, scanning documents at your desktop may be more convenient than faxing them. For instance, suppose you live in one state and sell a home in another state, and the sales agent requests that you sign the sales contract that she has emailed to you as a PDF document. After signing the contract and addendums, initialing

◀DTP POINTERS
Avoid *one size fits all* formatting by customizing to fit your needs.

◀DTP POINTERS
Right-click on the Status bar, and then click *Vertical Page Position* to turn this feature on.

◀DTP POINTERS
Press Shift + Enter to advance the insertion point to the next line without the default 10 points after.

DTP POINTERS

To be able to see table gridlines, click anywhere in a table, and then click View Gridlines in the Table Tools Layout tab.

each page, and convincing a friend or coworker to witness the signatures, you now have to think about the means of transferring the document back to the agent. You have numerous choices—scan, fax, or send through the mail. You may use a Word 2010 fax template as assigned in Exercise 2.4, or you could customize the fax cover sheet to read as an introductory sheet to the scanned document. After the documents are scanned and saved in PDF format, you may use your email account to send them to the agent.

In Exercise 2.4, assume you are working for Butterfield Gardens, a nursery and gardening supply company. To reinforce the identity of your company and save time, you are going to customize a fax cover sheet (include a logo), save it as a template, and reuse it as needed. Observe that in Exercise 2.4, the *Standard and Contextual* ligature, scaling at 100%, and kerning at 12 points were saved to the Word fax template when the Metro theme was selected.

Exercise 2.4   Customizing a Fax Cover Sheet Template

1. Use the Origin Fax template to create a customized fax cover template as shown in Figure 2.34 by completing the following steps:
   a. Click the File tab and then click the New tab.
   b. At the New tab, Backstage view, click the Sample templates category in the *Available Templates* section.
   c. Select the Origin Fax template.
   d. Click the *Template* option above the Create button.
   e. Click the Create button.

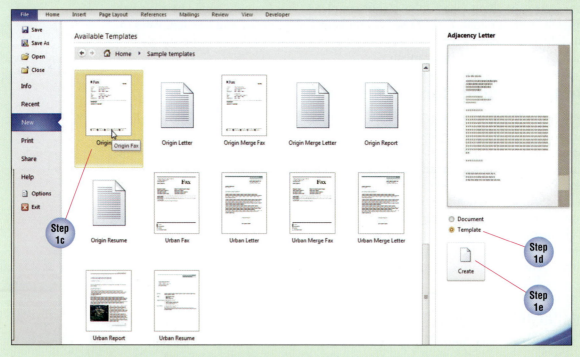

2. Customize the fax design by completing the following steps:
   a. Change the theme to the *Metro* theme.
   b. Type **Your name** in the *From* placeholder.
   c. Type **630.555.1062** in the *Phone* placeholder.

d. Type **630.555.3029** in the *Fax* placeholder.

e. Type **Butterfield Gardens** in the *Company Name* placeholder.

f. Type **29 W 036 Butterfield Road, Warrenville, IL 60555** in the cell below the Company Name, press Enter, and then type **www.emcp.net/grower2you**.

3. Add a logo by completing the following steps:

a. Position the insertion point after *Comments*. **Hint: The insertion point must be outside the table structure.**

b. On the Insert tab, click Picture in the Illustrations group.

c. At the Insert Picture dialog box, make sure the drive where the *Chapter02* student data files are located displays.

d. Double-click **BGLogo** located in your *Chapter02* folder.

e. Resize the image by holding down the Shift key while you click one of the corner sizing handles, and then drag the crosshairs inward. Size the image similar to Figure 2.34.

f. Select the logo to access the Picture Tools Format tab.

g. Click the Wrap Text button in the Arrange group and then click the *Square* option. This permits you to move the image. **Hint: In Word 2010, a clip art image defaults to In line with text; however, this setting can be changed by clicking the File tab and then the Options tab. You can select the Advanced tab and then click the down-pointing arrow at the right of the Insert/paste picture as list box.**

h. With the logo selected, type **1.5** inches in the *Shape Height* measurement box in the Size group. **Hint: The width will automatically display in proportion to the height because the Lock aspect ratio feature is active.**

i.   With the logo selected, click the Color button in the Adjust group, and then click *Green, Accent Color 1 Light* in the *Recolor* section.

j.   Drag and drop the image to the position above the horizontal line at the bottom of the fax cover (see Figure 2.34).

4.   Customize the table inside the template by completing the following steps:

a.   Select the table containing *Fax* and the date content control.

b.   Display the Table Tools Design tab, and then click the More button at the bottom of the Table Styles gallery.

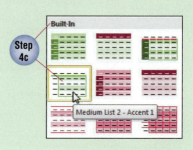

c.   At the Table Styles gallery, click the *Medium List 2 - Accent 1* design in the *Build-In* section.

d.   Select the table below the *Fax* table, and then click the *Medium Grid 3 - Accent 1* design.

e.   Select the table at the bottom of the page, and then click the *Medium Grid 3 - Accent 1* design.

5.   Save the customized template by completing the following steps:

a.   Click the File tab, and then click the Save As tab.

b.   At the Save As dialog box, type **ButterfieldFaxTemplate** in the *File name* text box. Change the location at the left of the dialog box to your *Chapter02* folder where you may want to create a folder named **DTP Templates**. *Hint: Notice that* **Word Template** *displays in the* **Save as type** *list box. By default, this template is being saved to the* **Templates** *folder on the hard drive. You can access the template by clicking My Templates at the New tab Backstage view.*

6.   Open ButterfieldFaxTemplate and then type the text in the bracketed areas below the address as shown in Figure 2.34. Click the *Pick a date* content control in the top right corner of the fax. Click the down-pointing arrow to the right of the date control, and then select *Today*.

7.   Position the insertion point below *Comments*, and then type the text in Figure 2.34.

8.   Save the document, and name it **C02-E04-BGFax.docx**.

9.   Print and then close **C02-E04-BGFax.docx**.

Figure 2.34 Exercise 2.4

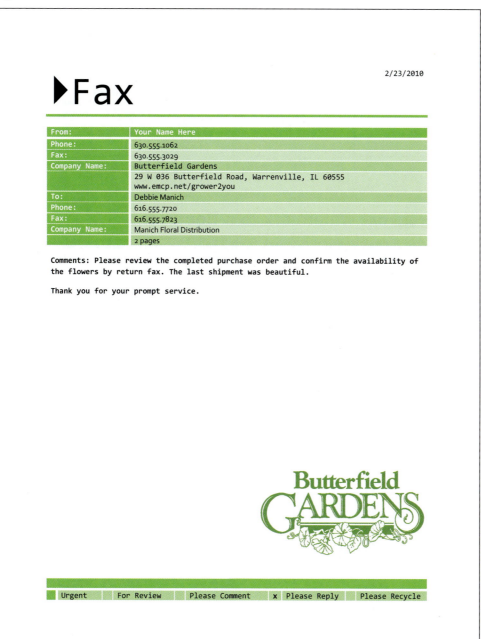

Learning about Watermarks

A *watermark* is a lightened graphic or text that when printed appears either on top of or behind existing document text and adds interest or identifies the document status, such as marking a document with *Sample* as shown in Figure 2.35. Typically, watermarks are intended for printed documents, but they may also be used to identify a protected document posted on a website—similar to a photographer's picture stamped as a Proof. Watermarks can be viewed only in Print Layout and Full Screen Reading views and on the printed page.

Watermark
A lightened graphic or text displayed behind text on a page.

Figure 2.35 **Using Text and Graphics to Create Watermarks**

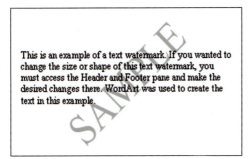

This is an example of a text watermark. If you wanted to change the size or shape of this text watermark, you must access the Header and Footer pane and make the desired changes there. WordArt was used to create the text in this example.

Text Watermark

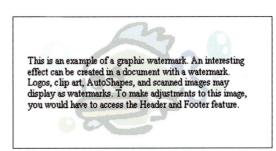

This is an example of a graphic watermark. An interesting effect can be created in a document with a watermark. Logos, clip art, AutoShapes, and scanned images may display as watermarks. To make adjustments to this image, you would have to access the Header and Footer feature.

Graphic Watermark

Adding a Text Watermark to a Document

Watermark

You can insert a predesigned watermark from a gallery of watermark text, or you can insert a watermark with custom text by clicking the Watermark button in the Page Background group on the Page Layout tab. Simply select a predesigned watermark, such as *Confidential*, at the watermark gallery as shown in Figure 2.36, or click More Watermarks, click Text watermark, and then select or type the text that you want. Change the font, size, color, and orientation as desired. Remove a watermark at the text watermark gallery.

Figure 2.36 **Text Watermark Gallery**

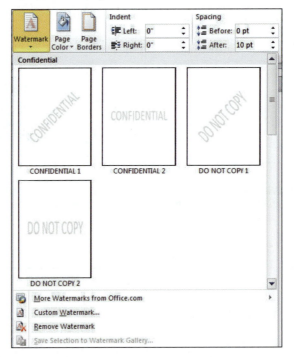

Figure 2.37 Printed Watermark Dialog Box

Click to remove a watermark.

Click to add a picture watermark.

Click to add a text watermark.

This option adjusts the brightness and contrast of an image to improve readability of text.

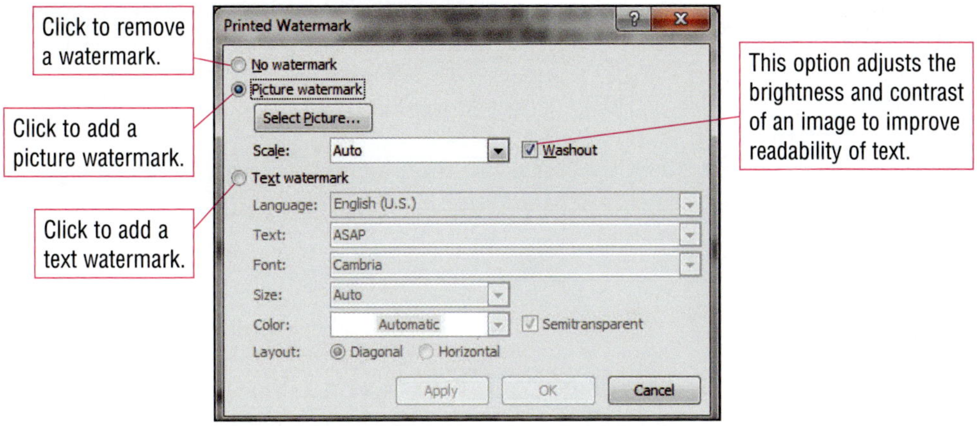

Turning a Picture into a Watermark

You can turn a picture, clip art, logo, or a photo into a watermark that you can use to enhance a document. On the Page Layout tab, in the Page Background group, click the Watermark button, and then click Custom Watermark. At the Printed Watermark dialog box as shown in Figure 2.37, click *Picture watermark*, and then click the Select Picture button. At the Insert Picture dialog box, click the down-pointing arrow at the right of the *Look in* list box, and locate the drive where your graphic files are stored. Select the desired image, and then click Insert.

If you would like to use the Clip Art task pane to search for a particular image, you follow these steps to find the image and then copy it to the Insert Picture dialog box where you can select it and add it to the Printed Watermark dialog box.

1. Click the Clip Art button in the Illustrations group on the Insert tab.
2. Type a keyword for your image search in the *Search for* textbox and then click Go.
3. Right-click on the desired image, and then click *Copy*.
4. Close the Clip Art task pane.
5. Access the Insert Picture dialog box as discussed previously.
6. Right-click anywhere in the white part of the dialog box, and then click *Paste*.
7. At the Insert Picture dialog box, make sure there is a check mark in the *Washout* check box, and then click OK.
8. Select the image, and then click Insert.

Editing a Watermark

Word adds the watermark (graphic or text) to the document's Header & Footer pane, which causes the watermark to appear on every page. If you divide your document into sections, you can remove the watermark from a particular section by choosing Different First Page or Different Odd and Even Pages in the Options group in the Header & Footer Tools Design tab. You will need to deselect Link to Previous in the Navigation group.

To edit a watermark, click the Header button in the Header & Footer group in the Insert tab, and then click Edit Header. Use the buttons on the Header & Footer Tools Design tab to edit the watermark as shown in Figure 2.38. To edit the watermark text, double-click the text, and then use the WordArt tools to change the text.

Figure 2.38 Editing a Watermark Using the Header & Footer Tools Design Tab

Troubleshooting Watermarks

Shape Fill

Shape Outline

If a document contains several text boxes, rectangles, or other shapes, the objects may obstruct the view of the watermark below them. If this should occur, click the down-pointing arrow at the right of the Shape Fill button in the Shapes Styles group in the Drawing Tools Format tab and then select *No Fill*. Also, click the Shape Outline button, and select *No Outline*.

If you use a text box, rectangle, or other shape as a container or border for a document, the graphics you select may fill the entire area of the text box or shape. When using graphics and watermarks in signs or other documents created with a border around them, you may find it helpful to use a page border or a border from the Borders and Shading dialog box to serve as the border around a document or place the image in a text box to control the size of the image.

Using Word Layers in Documents

Besides using the Header & Footer pane to create watermarks, you may also create a watermark by inserting an image or text at the document screen, altering the color of the object, and then sending it behind the text layer. The unique layering aspect of Word allows this to happen. A Word document contains three layers—foreground layer (or drawing layer), text layer, and background layer—as illustrated in the document in Figure 2.39.

The text layer is the one you may be the most accustomed to working with in word processing. In Word 2010, graphics default to *In Line With Text* and anchor to a paragraph in the text layer. At times, you may find it helpful to change this setting to another setting where you can move the image freely about the screen. This is accomplished by clicking the Wrap Text button in the Picture Tools Format tab and then clicking one of the following options: *In Line With Text, Square, Tight, Behind Text, In Front of Text, Top or Bottom, Through*. Shapes, such as lines, ovals, arrows, etc., display in the foreground layer above the text layer and are easy to move. Text or graphics created

Figure 2.39 Word Layers

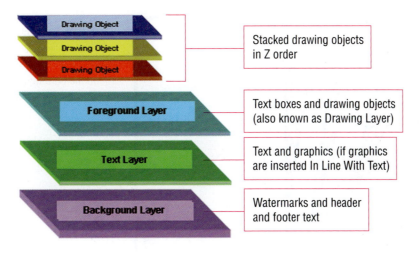

in headers and footers display in the background layer below the text layer. Figure 2.40 illustrates objects and text in various layers in a document.

In addition to these basic layers, Word stacks drawing objects in individual layers in the foreground layer (also known as the *Z order*). Every time you add another object, it is drawn in the layer on top of the previous layer. The stacked objects are similar to the stack of cards in Figure 2.41. You can change the order of the drawing objects by

Figure 2.40 Word Layers in a Document

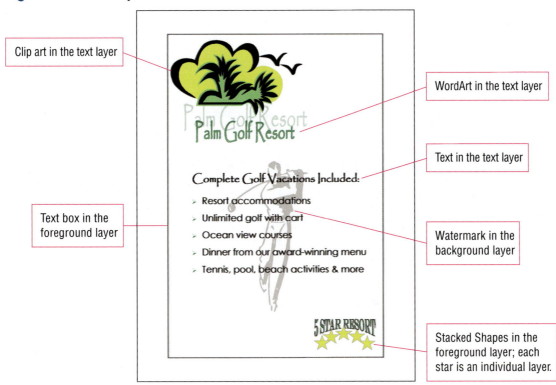

Figure 2.41 Layered Objects—Similar to a Stack of Cards

Objects are stacked in layers like a deck of cards.

The first object created is on the bottom, and the last object is at the top.

Bring Forward ▾
Bring to Front

Send to Back
Send to Back

Bring Forward ▾
Bring Forward

Bring in Front of Text
Bring in Front of Text

Send Backward
Send Backward

Send Behind Text
Send Behind

Selection Pane
Selection Pane

Picture
Picture

Clip Art
Clip Art

clicking the Bring Forward, Bring to Front, Bring in Front of Text, Send Backward, Send to Back, or Send Behind Text buttons in the Arrange group in the Drawing Tools Format tab. You can use the Selection pane to select individual objects and to change their order and visibility.

Inserting Images into a Document

Word 2010 includes a gallery of media images, including clip art, photographs, and movie images, as well as sound clips. To insert an image into a document, click either the Clip Art button or the Picture button in the Illustrations group in the Insert tab. If you click the Clip Art button, the Clip Art task pane as shown in Figure 2.42 will display. To view as many images as possible, make sure *All media file types* and *All collections* display.

Searching for Clip Art and Other Media

In this textbook, you will be instructed to insert an image as shown in the sample document at the end of each exercise. However, if the image is not available, you should replace the image with another similar one. You may use the *Search for* text box at the Clip Art task pane to type the specific file name if you know it, **00442950.jpg**, or to type a name for a category, such as **beach**, and then click Go.

Figure 2.42 Clip Art Task Pane

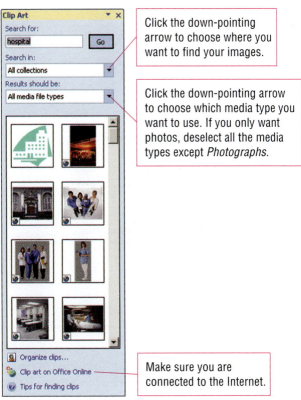

Click the down-pointing arrow to choose where you want to find your images.

Click the down-pointing arrow to choose which media type you want to use. If you only want photos, deselect all the media types except *Photographs*.

Make sure you are connected to the Internet.

Sizing and Moving Images

After an image is inserted in a document, it can be sized using the sizing handles that display around a selected clip art image. To change the size of an image, select it, and position the mouse pointer on a sizing handle until the pointer turns into a double-headed arrow as shown in Figure 2.43. Hold down the *left* mouse button, drag the sizing handle in or out to decrease or increase the size of the image, and then release the mouse button. Use the sizing handles in the corners to change the height and width at the same time and in proportion to each other.

Figure 2.43 Sizing and Moving Images

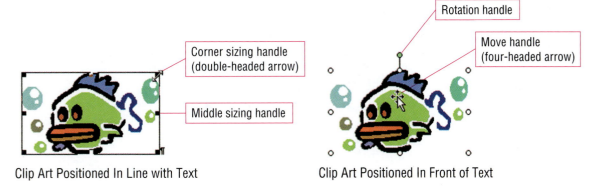

Rotation handle

Move handle (four-headed arrow)

Corner sizing handle (double-headed arrow)

Middle sizing handle

Clip Art Positioned In Line with Text

Clip Art Positioned In Front of Text

Figure 2.44 Adjusting the Size of a Picture at the Size Group in the Picture Tools Format Tab and the Size Dialog Box

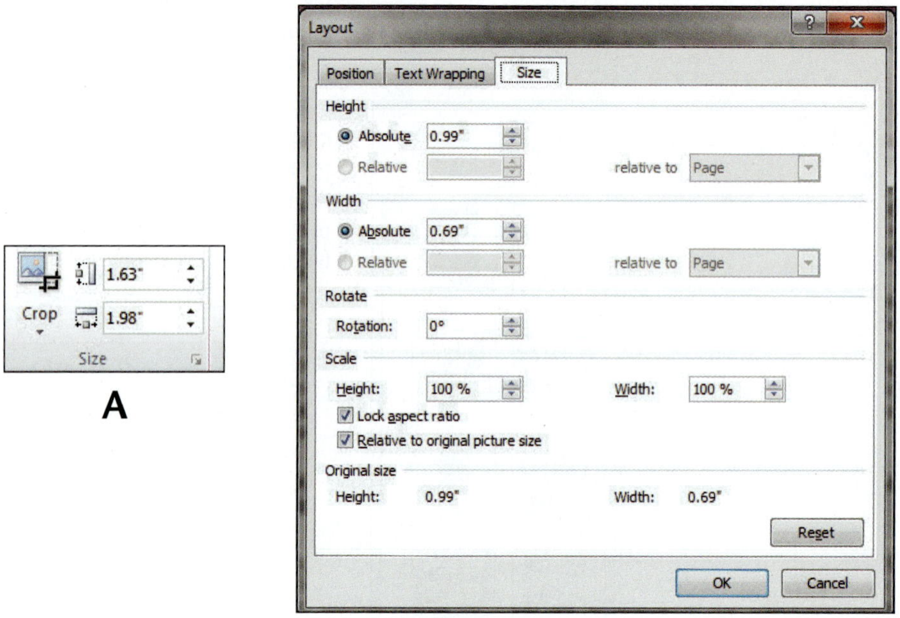

A

B

To move a clip art image, you must first select the image; click the Text Wrapping button; change the wrapping style, such as In Front of Text, In Line With Text, Square, Tight, Through, Top or Bottom, or Behind Text; and then position the mouse pointer inside the image until the pointer turns into a four-headed arrow as shown in Figure 2.43. Hold down the *left* mouse button, drag the image to the desired position, and then release the mouse button. Rotate the image by positioning the mouse pointer on the green, round rotation handle.

You may also size and move an image using the *Height* and *Width* text boxes at the Size group on the Picture Tools Format tab as shown in Figure 2.44A. In addition, you may change the image size by clicking the Size dialog box launcher and then making adjustments at the Size dialog box as shown in Figure 2.44B.

Inserting Bullets

Bullets

Bullets may be inserted in a document by clicking the Bullets arrow button in the Paragraph group in the Home tab. At the Bullet Library dialog box as shown in Figure 2.45, select

Figure 2.45 Bullet Library

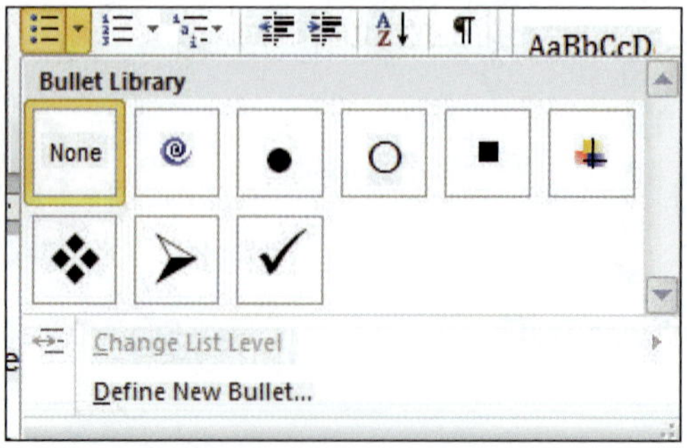

Chapter Two

any one of the bullets displayed, or click the Define New Bullet button. At the Define New Bullet dialog box, change a Symbol, Picture, or Font, and change the Alignment if desired.

When you apply bullets or numbers to existing text, the automatic bullet feature will reduce the leading between the lines in the bulleted or numbered list. You can increase the space between the lines in all of your lists by clearing a check box as discussed here:

1. On the Home tab, in the Styles group, click the More arrow next to the Styles gallery, and then right-click the List Paragraph style.
2. Click *Modify*.
3. In the Modify Style dialog box, click Format, and then click Paragraph.
4. Clear the *Don't add space between paragraphs of the same style* check box. Click OK twice.

You can create a bullet from a clip art image by clicking the Picture button at the Define New Bullet dialog box, clicking Picture, and then selecting an image at the Picture Bullet dialog box, as shown in Figure 2.46A. Also notice how the clip art bullet may be used to reinforce the topic of the text as shown in Figure 2.46B.

In Exercise 2.5, assume you are an employee at Chicago Mercy Hospital. In this exercise, you will customize a memo for the hospital using a watermark. You will also add bullets to help organize the text and add interest as well as add white space to a text-intensive document.

Figure 2.46 **Picture Bullet Dialog Box**

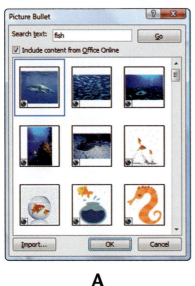

A

Select a clip art image as a bullet.

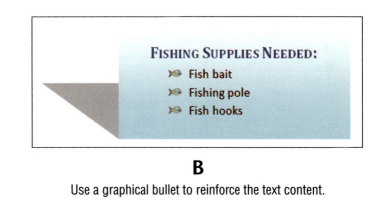

B

Use a graphical bullet to reinforce the text content.

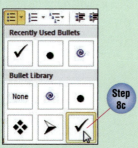

1. Open **MedicalMemo** located in your *Chapter02* folder.
2. Save the document with Save As, and name it **C02-E05A-Watermark**.
3. Change the theme to Verve.
4. Select *Memorandum*, change the font to 26-point Cambria, and then type **Chicago Mercy Hospital**.
5. With Chicago Mercy Hospital selected, click the Text Effects button, and then click the *Gradient Fill - Dark Purple, Accent 4, Reflection* option.

6. Change the line style and color of the line above the memo text by completing the following steps:
   a. Position the insertion point anywhere in the subject line (Re), and then click the Page Borders button in the Page Background group in the Page Layout tab.
   b. At the Borders and Shading dialog box, select the Borders tab.
   c. Scroll downward in the *Style* list box, and select the three line style.
   d. In the *Color* option box, select Purple in the *Standard Colors* section.
   e. Make sure the *Width* option box displays as *1/2 pt*.
   f. Click the bottom line in the Preview box to apply the new line attributes to the paragraph. Click OK.

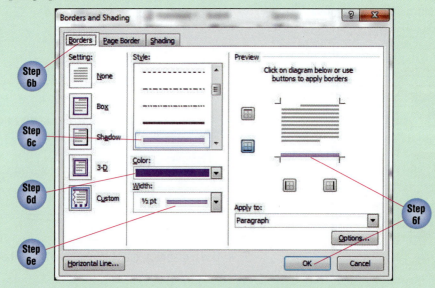

7. Select the gray-shaded circle on the left side of the memo and press Delete. ***Hint: Change the zoom if necessary to see the circle.***
8. Add bullets to the listed text by completing the following steps:
   a. Select the text beginning with *Necessary operative forms* . . . and ending with *Anesthesiologist has reviewed. . . .*
   b. At the Home tab, click the down-pointing arrow to the right of the Bullets button in the Paragraph group.
   c. At the Bullet Library gallery, click the check mark bullet.
   d. Click the Decrease Indent button in the Paragraph group. ***Hint: If necessary, click the Increase Indent button once to properly align the bullets.***

e. Click the Paragraph launcher button. At the Indents and Spacing tab, remove the checkmark next to *Don't add space between paragraphs of same style* option and then click OK.

9. Create the medical watermark in Figure 2.47 by completing the following steps:

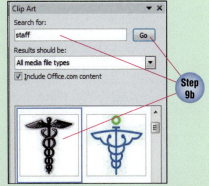

a. At the Insert tab, click the Clip Art button in the Illustrations group.

b. At the Clip Art task pane, type **staff** or **medical staff** in the *Search for* text box, and then click Go or press Enter. ***If this image is not available, substitute a similar image.***

c. Hover over the picture, click the down-pointing arrow to the right of the image, and then click Copy. ***Hint: A copy of the image has been copied to the Office Clipboard.*** Close the task pane.

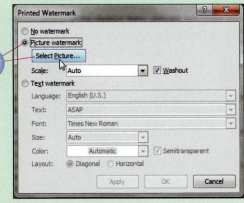

d. At the Page Layout tab, click the Watermark button in the Page Background group, and then click the Custom Watermark button.

e. At the Printed Watermark dialog box, click the *Picture watermark* option, and then click the Select Picture button. (Make sure *Washout* is selected.)

f. At the Insert Picture dialog box, right-click in the white area of the screen, and then click *Paste*. Select the image, click Insert, and then click OK.

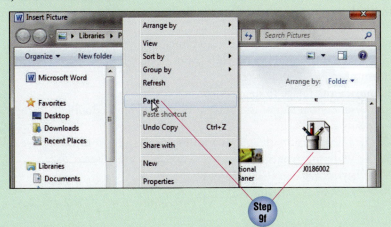

g. At the Insert tab, click the Header button in the Header & Footer group, and then click Edit Header.

h. At the Header & Footer dialog box, select the clip art image, and drag a corner sizing handle to increase or decrease the size so it is similar to Figure 2.47. ***Hint: If you hold down Ctrl as you drag a corner sizing handle, the image will stay centered on the page.***

i. At the Header window, click to select the image and when the four-headed arrow displays, move the image to a position similar to that shown in Figure 2.47.

j. Click the Close button on the Header and Footer toolbar.

10. To demonstrate that the watermark created in the Header & Footer pane will automatically display on following pages, complete the following steps:
    a. Press Ctrl + End to move the insertion point to the end of the document.
    b. On the Insert tab, click the Blank Page button in the Pages group. (The medical staff watermark should display on page 2.)
    c. Click the Undo button to delete the last command. (Did the watermark repeat on the second page?)
11. Save the memo with the same name **C02-E05A-Watermark.docx**.
12. Print **C02-E05A-Watermark.docx**.
13. Remove the watermark created in **C02-E05A-Watermark**, and create another watermark by sending a logo behind the text layer by completing the following steps:
    a. Click the Header button in the Header & Footer group at the Insert tab and then click Edit Header.
    b. At the Header & Footer Tools Design tab, select the medical staff image, and then press the Delete key.
    c. Click the Close Header and Footer button in the Close group.
14. Insert a watermark using a different method:
    a. Position the insertion point at the beginning of the first paragraph of text.
    b. Click the Picture button in the Illustrations group in the Insert tab.
    c. At the Insert Picture dialog box, find the drive where your student data files are located, and open your *Chapter02* folder.
    d. Select **HospitalLogo**, and then click Insert.
    e. Click the Hospital logo to access the Picture Tools Format tab.
    f. Click the down-pointing arrow at the right of the Color button in the Adjust group, and then click *Washout* in the *Recolor* section.
    g. Click the Wrap Text button in the Arrange group in the Picture Tools Format tab, and then click *Behind Text* at the drop-down list.
    h. With the watermark image still selected, increase the size of the image and drag it so it is positioned as shown in Figure 2.48.
    i. Click outside the image to deselect it.

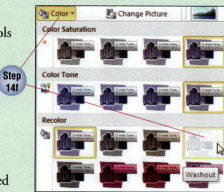

15. Remove the Confidential text at the bottom of the memo by double-clicking *Confidential* and then pressing delete.
16. Add the Surgery text watermark as shown in Figure 2.48 by completing the following steps:
    a. Click the Watermark button on the Page Layout tab.
    b. Click the *Custom Watermark* option.
    c. Click the *Text watermark* option.
    d. Type **Surgery** in the *Text* box in the *Text watermark* section, and then click OK.
17. Save the memo with Save As, and name it **C02-E05B-Watermark**.
18. Save, print, and then close **C02-E05B-Watermark.docx**.

Figure 2.47 Exercise 2.5, Steps 1–12

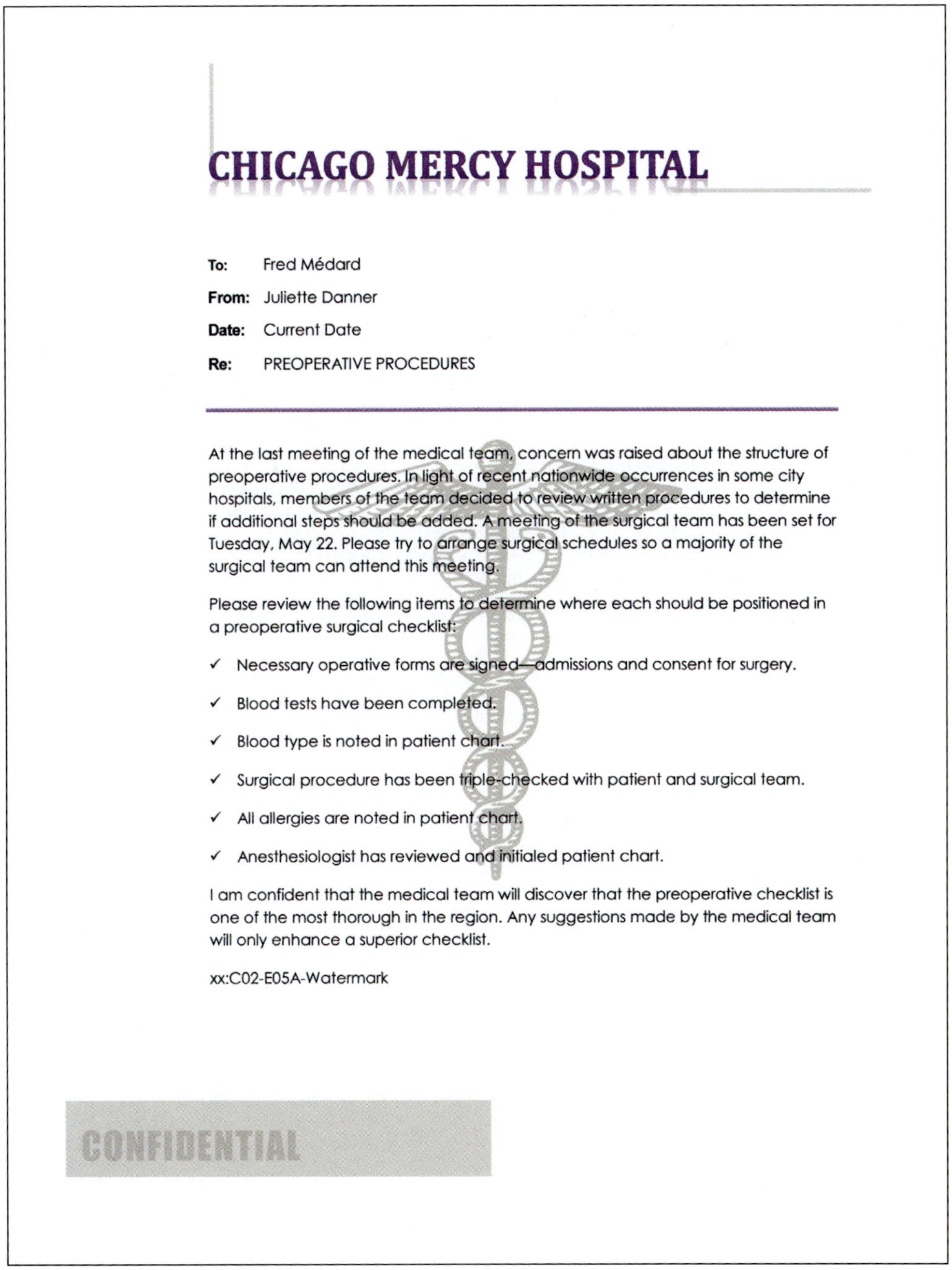

CHICAGO MERCY HOSPITAL

To: Fred Médard

From: Juliette Danner

Date: Current Date

Re: PREOPERATIVE PROCEDURES

At the last meeting of the medical team, concern was raised about the structure of preoperative procedures. In light of recent nationwide occurrences in some city hospitals, members of the team decided to review written procedures to determine if additional steps should be added. A meeting of the surgical team has been set for Tuesday, May 22. Please try to arrange surgical schedules so a majority of the surgical team can attend this meeting.

Please review the following items to determine where each should be positioned in a preoperative surgical checklist:

✓ Necessary operative forms are signed—admissions and consent for surgery.

✓ Blood tests have been completed.

✓ Blood type is noted in patient chart.

✓ Surgical procedure has been triple-checked with patient and surgical team.

✓ All allergies are noted in patient chart.

✓ Anesthesiologist has reviewed and initialed patient chart.

I am confident that the medical team will discover that the preoperative checklist is one of the most thorough in the region. Any suggestions made by the medical team will only enhance a superior checklist.

xx:C02-E05A-Watermark

CONFIDENTIAL

Preparing an Agenda

Before a business meeting, an agenda is generally prepared that includes such information as the name of the group or department holding the meeting; the date, time, and location of the meeting; and the topics to be discussed during the meeting. In Word 2010, you may create an agenda using a table as the underlining structure of the document; using a Word Agenda template; or using an Agenda Wizard. Figure 2.49 shows two customized agendas based on templates found in the Agenda category on the New tab Backstage view.

Figure 2.48 Exercise 2.5, Steps 13-18

CHICAGO MERCY HOSPITAL

To: Fred Médard

From: Juliette Danner

Date: Current Date

Re: PREOPERATIVE PROCEDURES

At the last meeting of the medical team, concern was raised about the structure of preoperative procedures. In light of recent nationwide occurrences in some city hospitals, members of the team decided to review written procedures to determine if additional steps should be added. A meeting of the surgical team has been set for Tuesday, May 22. Please try to arrange surgical schedules so a majority of the surgical team can attend this meeting.

Please review the following items to determine where each should be positioned in a preoperative surgical checklist:

✓   Necessary operative forms are signed—admissions and consent for surgery.

✓   Blood tests have been completed.

✓   Blood type is noted in patient chart.

✓   Surgical procedure has been triple-checked with patient and surgical team.

✓   All allergies are noted in patient chart.

✓   Anesthesiologist has reviewed and initialed patient chart.

I am confident that the medical team will discover that the preoperative checklist is one of the most thorough in the region. Any suggestions made by the medical team will only enhance a superior checklist.

xx:C02-E05B-Watermark

Creating an Agenda Using a Table

Besides using the Agenda template or wizard, an agenda may be prepared at a blank document screen with side-by-side columns, which are similar to parallel columns. Word does not include a parallel column feature, where text displays across a page in rows. However, a table accomplishes the same results. To create a table, click the Table button in the Tables group on the Insert tab. In Exercise 2.6, you will create a table with three columns and seven rows.

Figure 2.49 Customized Agendas from Microsoft Templates

Agenda Template   Customized Template

Entering Text in a Table

Information in a table is typed in cells. A **cell** is the intersection of a row and a column. With the insertion point positioned in a cell, type or edit text as you would normal text. Move the insertion point to other cells with the mouse by positioning the arrow pointer in the desired cell, and then clicking the *left* mouse button. If you are using the keyboard, press Tab to move the insertion point to the next cell, or press Shift + Tab to move the insertion point to the previous cell. If you want to move the insertion point to a tab stop within a cell, press Ctrl + Tab. If the insertion point is located in the last cell of the table, and you press the Tab key, Word adds another row to the table. When all of the information has been entered into the cells, move the insertion point below the table, and, if necessary, continue typing the document, or save the document in the normal manner.

Assume you are an employee at Chicago Mercy Hospital, and you are preparing an agenda for a project meeting. This agenda will be sent as an email attachment to all of the project members. If your class has email access, create the document in Exercise 2.6, and send it to a recipient in your class as an email attachment in PDF format. *Hint: Notice that when typing times, you do not type "00" after times that are on the hour—example: 5 p.m. not 5:00 p.m.*

Cell
The intersection of a row and a column.

Table

1. Open **Agenda** located in your *Chapter02* folder.
2. Save the document with Save As, and name it **C02-E06-Agenda**.
3. Format the heading text by completing the following steps:
   a. Turn on the Show/Hide feature, and then position the insertion point at the right margin (Align Text Right alignment).
   b. Click the Font dialog box launcher button to access the Font dialog box and then turn on *Kerning* at *14* points, select the *Ligatures* setting at *All*, and select the *Number Spacing* at *Proportional*. Click OK.
   c. Change the font to 24-point Harrington (or a similar font), bold, font color *Purple, Accent 4* in the first row of the Theme Colors (Office), type **Chicago Mercy Hospital**, and then press Enter. Turn off bold.
   d. Change the font to 18-point Calibri, font color Black, then type **Quality Care Project**, and then press Enter twice.
   e. Change the font to 14-point Calibri, black, italic, type **Agenda for November 14 Meeting - Conference Room B**, and then press Enter twice.
   f. Change the font to 11-point Calibri.
   g. Change the alignment to Align Text Left and turn off italics.
4. Create a table for the agenda text by completing the following steps:
   a. At the Insert tab, click the Table button, and then click Insert Table.
   b. At the Insert Table dialog box, change the *Number of columns* to *3*.
   c. Change the *Number of rows* to *7*.
5. Format the table by completing the following steps:
   a. With the insertion point inside the table, click the *Light Shading - Accent 4* option in the Table Styles group in the Table Tools Design tab.

b. Show the gridlines by clicking the Table Tools Layout tab and then clicking the View Gridlines button in the Table group.

c. Select the entire table, click the Properties button in the Table group, and then click the Row tab.

d. At the Row tab, click the check box at the left of the *Specify height* option, and then type **0.75"**. Make sure the *Row height is* option shows *At least*.

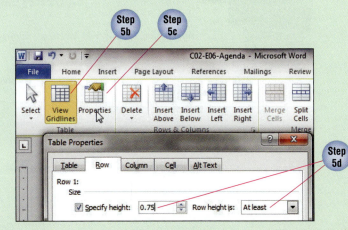

e. Select the Cell tab, and click *Center* in the *Vertical alignment* section.

f. Click OK, or press Enter.

g. Select the first row; change the font to 12-point Calibri, bold, all caps; and change the alignment to *Center*.

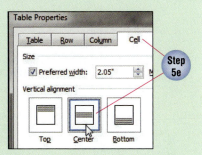

h. Position the insertion point inside the first cell and type **Time**; press Tab and type **Topic**; press Tab and type **Discussion Leaders**; and then press Tab.

i. Select all the rows and columns below the header row, make sure the alignment is set at Align Text Left, and the font is 11-point Calibri. Type **9 a.m. – 9:30 a.m.** in the first cell *(Hint: Type a space, hyphen, and another space—Word will automatically convert the hyphen into an en dash.)*, and then press Tab.

j. With the insertion point positioned in the second cell, type **Call to order and introduction of new project members**, and then press Tab. Continue typing the text and pressing Tab until the agenda is completed as shown in Figure 2.50.

6. Save, print, and then close **C02-E06-Agenda.docx**.

Figure 2.50 Exercise 2.6

Chicago Mercy Hospital
Hospital

Chicago Mercy Hospital
Quality Care Projects

Agenda for November 14 Meeting – Conference Room B

TIME	TOPIC	DISCUSSION LEADERS
9 a.m. – 9:30 a.m.	Call to order and introduction of new project members	Becky Peterson, Chair
9:30 a.m. – 10 a.m.	Presentation of project mission statement	Charles-Etienne Visconti
10 a.m. – 11 a.m.	Determination of project goals and timelines	Katrina O-Dell, Geoffrey Benn, and Wendy Mitaki
11 a.m. – 11:45 a.m.	Brainstorming on public relations activities	Ellen Heitz and Hui Lenzi
11:45 a.m. – 12 Noon	Scheduling of next project meeting	Becky Peterson, Chair
12 Noon	Adjournment	Becky Peterson, Chair

Chapter Two

Chapter Summary

- A font consists of three characteristics: typeface, typestyle, and type size.
- The term typeface refers to the general design and shape of a set of characters.
- The typeface used in a document establishes a particular mood or feeling.
- Characteristics that distinguish one typeface from another include x-height, cap height, height of ascenders, depth of descenders, and serifs.
- A serif is a small stroke on the end of a character. A sans serif typeface does not have serifs.
- Typefaces are either monospaced or proportional. Monospaced typefaces allot the same amount of horizontal space to each character, while proportional typefaces allot a varying amount to each character.
- Point size is a vertical measurement and is approximately $^1/_{72}$ of an inch. The larger the chosen point size, the larger the characters.
- Printer fonts are built-in fonts, and supplemental fonts are available from your printer.
- OpenType fonts support international character sets, cross-platform support between Windows and Macintosh computers, and include advanced typographic features, such as special ligatures (combined characters) and swashes (exaggerated serifs).
- Ligatures are letters that have been attached to create a single character.
- A swash is an exaggerated serif.
- The Font Color feature includes 40 colors on the color palette, 124 colors and 15 shades of gray at the Standard tab, and an option to mix your own colors at the Custom tab of the Colors dialog box.
- At the Custom tab of the Colors dialog box, you can change the *luminescence*, which is the brightness of the color; the *hue*, which is the color itself; and the *saturation*, which is the color intensity. You can also change the values of Red, Green, and Blue.
- Readability is the ease with which a person can read and understand groups of words.
- For text set in a proportional typeface, space once after end-of-sentence punctuation.
- Insert Special symbols by clicking the Symbol button in the Symbols group on the Insert tab, clicking More Symbols, and then choosing the Symbols tab or the Special Characters tab.
- An em dash (—) is as long as the point size of the type and is used in text to indicate a pause in speech.
- An en dash (–) indicates a continuation, such as 116–133 or January–March, and is exactly one-half the width of an em dash.
- Bullets may be inserted in a document by clicking the Bullets button in the Paragraph group in the Home tab. Customize bullets at the Define New Bullet dialog box.
- Quick Styles automatically apply formatting changes to text, SmartArt, and shapes.
- Style Sets are predesigned sets or combinations of styles, colors, and fonts used in a document.
- In typesetting, the open quotation mark is curved upward (") and the close quotation mark is curved downward ("). In typesetting, the straight quotes are used to indicate inches (") or feet (').
- The Clear Formatting command is located at the bottom of the Quick Styles gallery. This command has the same effect as Ctrl + Spacebar.
- Text boxes are often used to move and position text easily in a document. If text boxes overlap, click Shape Fill, and then select *No Fill*. To remove the outline, click Shape Outline, and then click *No Outline*.
- Word provides a number of templates and wizards that can be used to produce a variety of documents. The default template document is *Normal.dotm*.
- Wizards walk you through a series of steps in which you add or select information to set up formatting, content, and layout of your document.

- Insert clip art by clicking the Clip Art button in the Illustrations group on the Insert tab.
- Insert pictures by clicking the Picture button in the Illustrations group on the Insert tab.
- Use the sizing handles around a selected image to size it.
- Move an image by selecting the image and then using the mouse to drag the image to the desired position.
- You may access templates at the New tab Backstage view.
- A watermark is a lightened image or text added to a document to add visual interest.
- Create a watermark by clicking the Watermark button in the Page Background group in the Page Layout tab or by inserting a clip art watermark, changing the image color to Washout, and sending it behind the text layer.
- The *Washout* option adjusts the brightness and contrast of the image to make it less visible behind text.
- Word contains an Agenda template used to prepare an agenda for a meeting. The agenda may be customized and saved as a separate template.
- Tables may be used as the underlining structure for an agenda.

Commands Review

FEATURE	RIBBON TAB, GROUP	BUTTON	KEYBOARD SHORTCUT
Blank Page	Insert, Pages		Ctrl + Enter
Breaks	Page Layout, Page Setup	Breaks ▾	
Bring Forward	Picture Tools Format, Arrange	Bring Forward ▾	
Bring in Front of Text	Picture Tools Format, Arrange	Bring in Front of Text	
Bring to Front	Picture Tools Format, Arrange		
Bullets	Home, Paragraph	☰ ▾	
Clear Formatting	Home, Font		
Change Styles	Home, Styles	AA	
Cover Page	Insert, Pages		
Clip Art	Insert, Illustrations		
Font	Home, Font	Cambria (Body) ▾	Ctrl + Shift + F
Font Color	Home, Font	A ▾	
Font Effects	Home, Font	A ▾	

FEATURE	RIBBON TAB, GROUP	BUTTON	KEYBOARD SHORTCUT
Font Size	Home, Font	11	
Format Painter	Home, Clipboard	Format Painter	Ctrl + Shift + C
Grow Font	Home, Font	A	Ctrl + >
Header & Footer	Insert, Header & Footer		
Increase Indent	Home, Paragraph		
Page Borders	Page Layout, Page Background		
Picture	Insert, Illustrations		
Quick Parts	Insert, Quick Parts		
Send Backward	Picture Tools Format, Arrange	Send Backward	
Send Behind Text	Picture Tools Format, Arrange	Send Behind Text	
Send to Back	Picture Tools Format, Arrange	Send to Back	
Shape Fill	Drawing Tools Format, Shape Styles	Shape Fill	
Shape Outline	Drawing Tools Format, Shape Styles	Shape Outline	
Size	Page Layout, Page Setup		
Shrink Font	Home, Font	A	
Symbol	Insert, Symbols	Ω	
Table	Insert, Tables		
Table Properties	Table Tools Layout, Table		
Theme Colors	Page Layout, Themes	Colors	
Theme Effects	Page Layout, Themes	Effects	
Theme Fonts	Page Layout, Themes	A Fonts	
Themes	Page Layout, Themes	Aa	
View Gridlines	Table Tools Layout, Table		

FEATURE	RIBBON TAB, GROUP	BUTTON	KEYBOARD SHORTCUT
Watermark	Page Layout, Page Setup		
Wrap Text	Page Layout, Arrange		

Reviewing Key Points

A.	Baseline	I.	TrueType	Q.	Ascenders
B.	Template	J.	En dash	R.	Em dash
C.	Serif	K.	Proportional	S.	Content Control
D.	Descenders	L.	PDF format	T.	Table
E.	Pitch	M.	XML format	U.	Theme
F.	Cover Page	N.	Typestyle	V.	OpenType
G.	Cap height	O.	Sans serif	W.	x-height
H.	Point size	P.	Typeface		

Completion: In the space at the left, provide the correct letter or letters from the above list that match each definition.

_____ 1. A set of characters with a common design and shape.

_____ 2. Imaginary horizontal line on which text rests.

_____ 3. A predesigned, fully formatted page.

_____ 4. A set of colors, fonts, and other formatting details that work together to give your documents a stylish, professional design.

_____ 5. Parts of lowercase characters that rise above the x-height.

_____ 6. A special character that is used in durations of time or continuation.

_____ 7. A small stroke at the edge of characters.

_____ 8. Parts of characters that extend below the baseline.

_____ 9. A typeface that does not contain serifs.

_____ 10. Approximately $1/72$ of an inch.

_____ 11. A special symbol that is used to indicate a pause in speech.

_____ 12. This Word feature may be used as an underlining structure to an agenda.

_____ 13. Fonts that were created jointly by Adobe and Microsoft to support cross-platform applications, ligatures, and foreign characters.

_____ 14. This file format is widely used for documents that are sent to commercial printers and sent as email attachments.

_____ 15. You may add this Word 2010 feature to your document to provide the user of the document the ability to select a date from past, present, or future calendars.

Chapter Assessments

Assessment 2.1   Foreign Meeting Agenda

Your company is sponsoring an international conference in the Dominican Republic and you have been asked to prepare a meeting agenda for the participating delegates. Recreate the agenda in Figure 2.51 making the following changes:

1. You may substitute the graphic, use a different color scheme that compliments your graphic, and select other text effects.
2. The basic structure of the agenda is a table. You may choose a different table style.
3. Notice the international time format. ***Hint: To insert a tab within a table cell, press Ctrl + Tab.***
4. Save, print, and then close **C02-A01-DominicanAgenda.docx**.

Figure 2.51 Assessment 2.1 Sample Solution

Assessment 2.2   Company Party Invitation

Your company is holding a fundraiser for a local food pantry, and you have been asked to create an invitation for the event. Include the following specifications:

1. At a blank document, change the paper size to 5 by 7 inches.
2. Turn on kerning, and apply ligatures and number forms.
3. Use a Mardi Gras event theme for your invitation.
4. Support the Mardi Gras theme with an appropriate document theme and coordinating fonts. Vary the size and color of the fonts—use at least one font effect. ***Hint: Do not use more than two or three different fonts.***
5. Use at least one clip art image or photograph, and format it as a watermark.
6. Write appropriate text for the invitation, including the name of a local food pantry, location, time of the event, food and drink options, raffle or silent auction options, and express gratitude for the employees' support.
7. Save, print, and then close **C02-A02-MardiGras.docx**.

Assessment 2.3   Memo with Excel Spreadsheet

In this activity, you will customize a Word memo template and copy and paste a chart from an Excel worksheet into this memo. In addition, you will determine the average monthly cost of gas by inserting a formula into the Excel worksheet and record this amount in the text of the memo. See Figure 2.52 for a model result. Complete the following steps:

1. Select a Word memo template or create your own design.
2. Type the following text to replace the memo heading placeholder text:
   To: **Susan Howard**
   CC: Delete this line.
   From: **Superior Gas**
   Date: **12/21/2012**
   Re: **Superior Gas Budget Plan**
3. Apply a theme and then apply styles to the heading text.
4. Select the body placeholder text, and then insert **BudgetPlan.docx** from your *Chapter02* folder. ***Hint: Do not delete the placeholder text; select it and then insert the file text over it.***
5. Minimize Word and then open Excel.
6. In Excel, open **BudgetPlanChart.xlsx** from your *Chapter02* folder.
7. Position your insertion point in cell B14, and insert this formula to compute the average of the monthly bills: **=Average(B2:B13)**. Press Enter.
8. Select the chart and then click the Copy button.
9. Minimize Excel and then maximize Word.
10. Position the insertion point below the last line of the memo text (increase spacing after) and then click Paste, Paste Special.
11. At the Paste Special dialog box, make sure the *Paste* option is selected, and then select *Microsoft Office Excel Worksheet Chart Object* in the *As* list box. Click OK.
12. Type the average amount that you computed in Excel in place of the text *(insert average cost here)*. ***Hint: You may have to adjust margins or resize the chart to fit on one page.***
13. Save the document and name it **C02-A03-BudgetPlan**.
14. Print and then close **C02-A03-BudgetPlan.docx**.
15. Close **BudgetPlanChart.xlsx**, and then close Excel.

Figure 2.52 **Assessment 2.3**

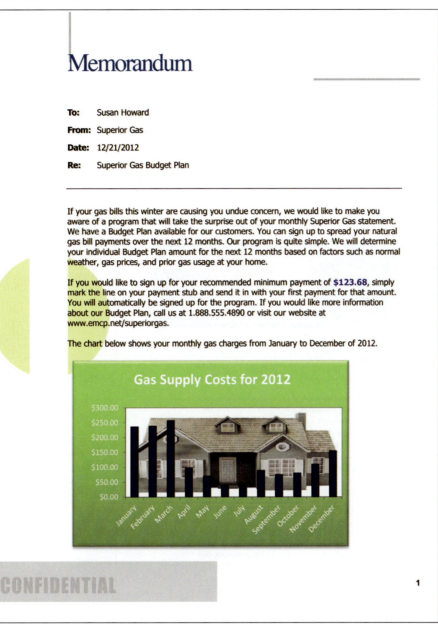

Memorandum

To: Susan Howard

From: Superior Gas

Date: 12/21/2012

Re: Superior Gas Budget Plan

If your gas bills this winter are causing you undue concern, we would like to make you aware of a program that will take the surprise out of your monthly Superior Gas statement. We have a Budget Plan available for our customers. You can sign up to spread your natural gas bill payments over the next 12 months. Our program is quite simple. We will determine your individual Budget Plan amount for the next 12 months based on factors such as normal weather, gas prices, and prior gas usage at your home.

If you would like to sign up for your recommended minimum payment of **$123.68**, simply mark the line on your payment stub and send it in with your first payment for that amount. You will automatically be signed up for the program. If you would like more information about our Budget Plan, call us at 1.888.555.4890 or visit our website at www.emcp.net/superiorgas.

The chart below shows your monthly gas charges from January to December of 2012.

Gas Supply Costs for 2012

CONFIDENTIAL

1

Assessment 2.4 Group Project - International Tipping and Etiquette Fact Sheet

In some countries tipping is considered offensive, in other countries tipping is automatically included in the final cost of the services provided, and yet in other countries standard tipping should be added to the total bill at a percentage that varies depending on where you are. Your company is participating in an international conference being held in a foreign country and in an effort to prepare your conference attendees for cultural differences, you have been asked to prepare a fact sheet summarizing customary tipping and etiquette guidelines. Figure 2.53 shows a sample solution with formatting, including a rotated text box with No Fill and No Outline; a Shape with inserted text, and a logo created with a clip art image and text box containing text. Include the following guidelines:

1. Use an Internet search engine to research the general tipping and etiquette guidelines for a country of your own choosing.
2. Include tipping practices for restaurants, tour guides, hotel personnel, and taxi drivers.
3. Use graphics to add visual appeal and font effects to enhance the text.
4. Include the source of your information.
5. Save the completed fact sheet, and name it **C02-A04-TippingFactSheet**.
6. Print and then close **C02-A04-TippingFactSheet.docx**.

Figure 2.53 Assessment 2.4 Sample Solution

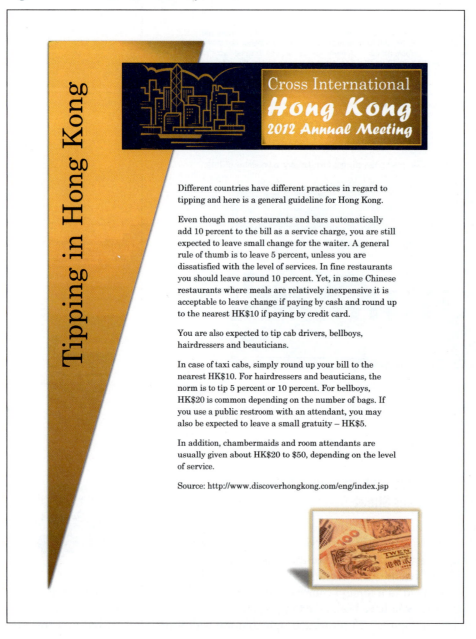

Chapter 3

CHAPTER03

Creating Letterheads, Envelopes, Business Cards, and Press Releases

Performance Objectives

Upon successful completion of Chapter 3, you will be able to:

- Produce letterheads, envelopes, business cards, and press releases using Word features.
- Identify the purpose of a letterhead.
- Customize a Word letterhead template.
- Use the Text Boxes Style Gallery and Change Shapes, Shape Fills, and Shape Outlines.
- Insert WordArt.
- Customize envelopes and labels.
- Create, save, and insert Quick Parts (Building Blocks).
- Kern character pairs.
- Adjust letter spacing (tracking) and line spacing (leading).

Desktop Publishing Terms

Anchor	Line Spacing	Template
Grid	Nudging	Tracking
Kerning	Pixel	
Leading	Ruled lines	

Word Features Used

Anchor	Click and Type	Shapes
Automatic kerning	Envelopes	Text boxes
Borders and shading	Labels	WordArt
Building Blocks (Quick Parts)	Manual kerning	
Character spacing	Office Online Templates	

In this chapter, you will produce business letterheads, envelopes, and business cards using your own design and creative skills as well as the Word features Installed Templates and Office Online Templates. Although Word and Office provide a variety of templates to choose from, they do not meet the needs of all situations. Information on how to customize an existing template and how to create your own design and layout from scratch are presented in this chapter.

Ruled lines, kerning (the spacing between pairs of letters), and tracking (character spacing) are discussed, along with text boxes, envelopes and labels, and Building Blocks (Quick Parts).

Identifying the Purpose of Letterheads

In planning a letterhead design, think about its purpose. While the content of a letter may vary, the purpose of any letterhead is generally the same—to convey information, to establish an identity, and to project an image.

Conveying Information

Consider all of the necessary information you want to include in your letterhead. Also, consider what items your readers expect to find in your letterhead. Although the information provided may vary, letterheads commonly contain the following:

- Name of company or organization
- Logo
- Address
- Shipping or mailing address, if different from street address
- Telephone number, including area code (include actual numbers if your phone number incorporates a catchy word as part of the number; include extra phone numbers, such as a local number and/or an 800 number, if any)
- Fax number, including area code
- Email address
- Internet or Web address
- Marketing statement or company slogan

The information in a letterhead supplies the reader with a means of contacting you by phone, by email, by regular mail, or in person. Omitting an important component in your letterhead projects a careless attitude and can affect your company business.

Establishing an Identity

A business identity is often initiated through written communication. For example, a buyer from one company may write to another company inquiring about a certain product or asking for a price list; a real estate agent may send out a letter explaining his or her services to residents in surrounding communities; or a volunteer organization may send letters to local businesses soliciting their support. Whatever the reason for the letter, a letterhead with a specific design and layout helps to establish the identity of an organization. When readers are exposed to the same pattern of consistent elements in a letterhead over a period of time, they soon begin to establish a certain level of familiarity with the organization name, logo, colors, and so forth. A letterhead is recognizable and identifiable.

You can further emphasize the identity of an organization by using some of the design elements from a letterhead in other business documents. If you do not want to create your own design, many direct-mail paper suppliers offer a whole line of attractively designed color letterheads, along with coordinating envelopes, business cards, fax cover sheets, press release forms, brochures, postcards, note cards, disk labels, and more. All you have to do is plan the layout of the letterhead text to complement the existing design and then print on the preprinted papers. Purchasing a coordinating line of preprinted papers can save on the high costs of professional designing and printing. It also provides a convenient way to establish your identity among your readers. Some paper suppliers offer a sample kit of their papers for purchase at a reasonable price. This is a great opportunity to see and feel the papers and to test some of them in your printer.

Projecting an Image

Along with establishing an identity, think about the image that identity projects to your readers. As mentioned in Chapter 1, assess your target audience. Who are they? What is their background, education, age, and so on? What image do you want your readers to form in their minds about your company, business, or organization? What does their experience tell them to expect?

Look at the two different letterheads in Figure 3.1. Without knowing any other supporting details, what image do you form in your mind about each of these hospitals? The top letterhead projects a fun, casual, somewhat juvenile, not-so-professional image, while the bottom letterhead conveys a serious, businesslike attitude. Even though the projected image may not be an accurate representation of either hospital, it is the image presented to the reader and thus carries a lot of impact. On the other hand, giving your readers what they expect can sometimes lead to boredom. Your challenge is to create a design that gives readers what they expect and, at the same time, sets your letterhead apart from the rest.

Printing your letterhead on high-quality paper may add to the cost, but it certainly presents a more professional image. Off-white, ivory, cream, or gray paper is a better choice than plain white. You may have to go to a commercial printer to purchase this kind of paper. Many print shops let you buy paper by the sheet, along with matching envelopes.

◀ **DTP POINTERS**
Printing on high-quality paper presents a professional image.

Figure 3.1 What Image Does Each of These Letterheads Project?

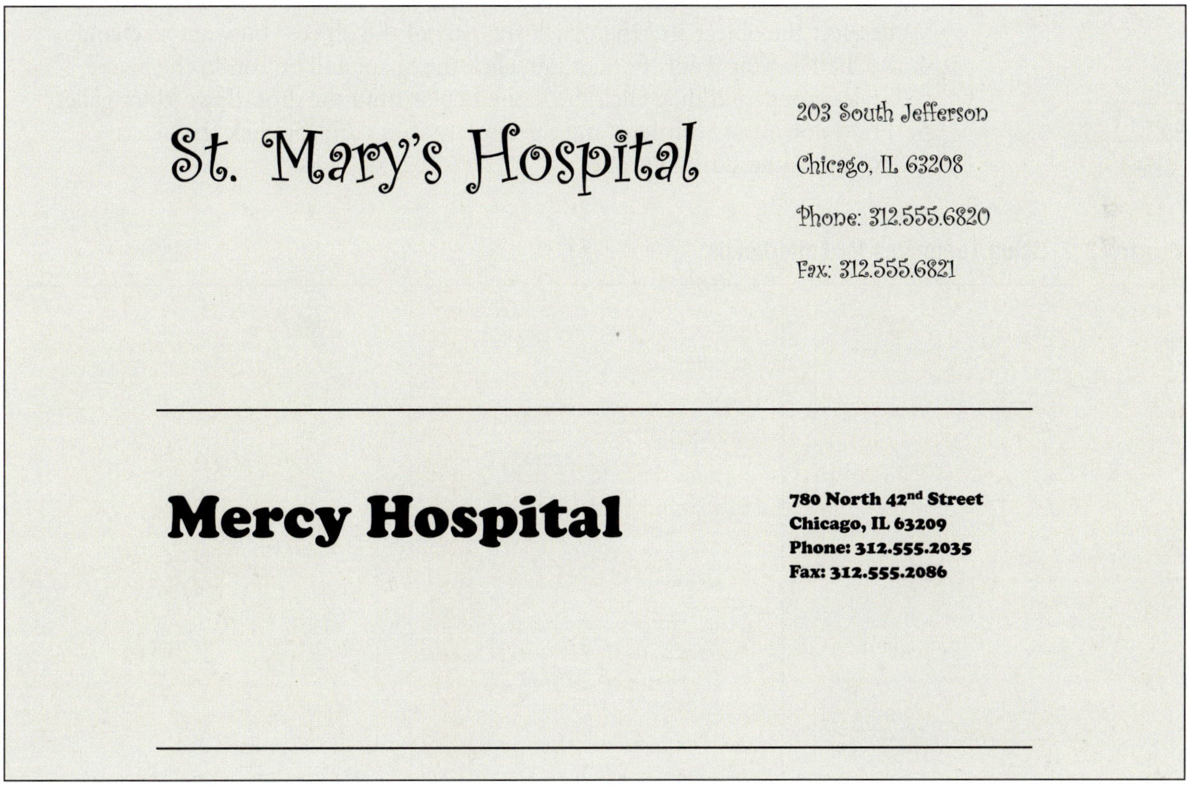

St. Mary's Hospital

203 South Jefferson

Chicago, IL 63208

Phone: 312.555.6820

Fax: 312.555.6821

Mercy Hospital

780 North 42nd Street
Chicago, IL 63209
Phone: 312.555.2035
Fax: 312.555.2086

Using Word Letterhead Templates

As discussed in Chapter 2, Word includes a variety of predesigned ***template*** documents, including letterheads. Click the File tab, and then click the New tab. At the New tab Backstage view, click the Sample Templates category in the *Available* section or the Stationery category in the *Office.com Templates* section, and then click Letterheads. A few sample letterhead templates are shown in Figure 3.2.

The descriptive names of the letterhead templates coordinate with the descriptive names for the memo, fax, report, and resume templates provided by Word. This is an easy way for you to establish identity and consistency between your internal and external business documents.

Visit the Microsoft.com website, http://office.microsoft.com/en-us/templates/default.aspx, and click <u>Avery Dennison</u>, <u>Hewlett-Packard</u>, <u>Inkd</u>, or other links located in the Partner Sites section (see Figure 3.3) for access to other online sites for business and personal templates.

Customizing a Logo Used in a Template

You will customize a grouped object that is used as a logo in Exercise 1. You will need to ungroup the object and change the color to match colors used in your company branding. To ungroup and then regroup an object, you will need to complete the following steps:

1. Right-click on the object, and then click *Edit Picture* at the shortcut menu.
2. At the prompt to convert the picture to a drawing object, click Yes.
3. To change the shape fill color, click in the white area of your document to deselect the object and then click the part of the object you want to change.
4. At the Drawing Tools Format tab, click the Shape Fill button in the Shape Styles group, and then click the desired color from the drop-down color gallery.
5. Hold down the Shift key, and select each object and/or click the Select button in the Editing group.

Select

Figure 3.2 Using Templates for Letterheads

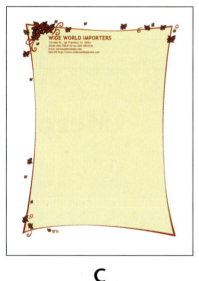

A
Professional Services Letterhead in Microsoft Office Online

B
Oriel Letter in Installed Templates

C
Holiday Letterhead with Poinsettia in Microsoft Office Online, Specialty Paper

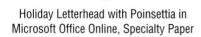

Figure 3.3 Using Other Online Sources for Business Templates

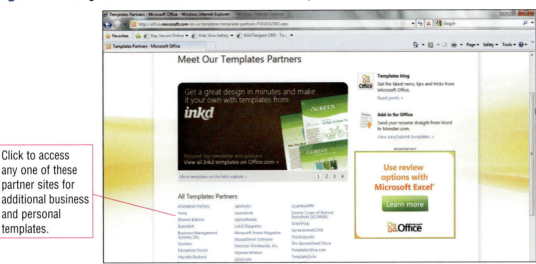

Click to access any one of these partner sites for additional business and personal templates.

6. Click the Group button in the Arrange group on the Page Layout tab, and then click Group.

Using the Selection Pane

You can also use a new Word 2010 feature called the Selection pane, which can make the task of working with layers a little easier. The Selection pane lists each item on a page so you can apply custom effects to just that item, without having to click through the layers on the page itself. To access this feature, click the Select button in the Editing group, and then click *Selection Pane* from the drop-down list. Figure 3.4 shows a document with the Selection Pane active.

In Exercise 1, you will use a professionally designed letterhead template, customize the template, save the new template, and then create a coordinating envelope as shown in Figure 3.6A. Before you can customize the template, you must understand how it was created. If you look at Figure 3.5, you will notice that various shapes and text boxes were used to create design elements on the page. You will leave the template in Compatibility Mode (leaving the previous version options as default settings) as you customize the document and then save it in Word 2010 format.

Hint: Copy the **Chapter03** *folder from the CD that accompanies this textbook to your storage medium, and then make* **Chapter03** *the active folder. Remember to substitute for graphics that may no longer be available.*

Selection Pane

Selection Pane

Figure 3.4 Using the Selection Pane

At the Selection and Visibility task pane, click the desired object from the list in the *Shapes on this Page* section, and at the same time, the object will become selected in the document.

Figure 3.5 Formatting in a Letterhead Template

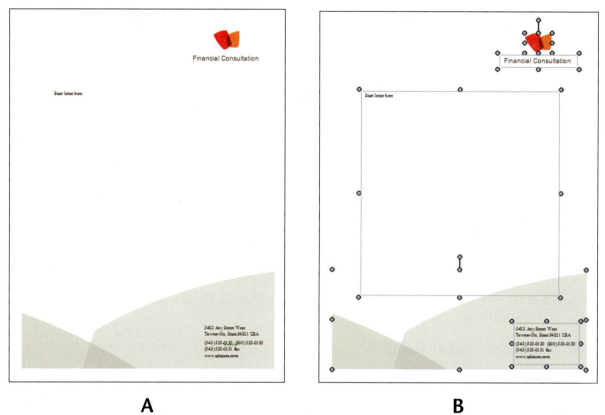

A   B

Exercise 3.1 Creating a Letterhead Using a Template from Microsoft Online

1. At a blank document, create the letterhead in Figure 3.6A by completing the following steps:
   a. Click the File tab, and then click the New tab.
   b. At the New tab Backstage view, click the Letterhead category in the *Office.com Templates* section.
   c. Click the *Professional services business letterhead* template and then click Download. ***Hint: Leave this template in Compatibility Mode for better results with the Group feature.***

d. Click the logo graphic shape in the upper right corner of the letterhead, click the Group button in the Arrange group on the Picture Tools Format tab, and then click *Ungroup*.

e. At the prompt, *Do you want to convert it to a Microsoft Office drawing object?*, click Yes.

f. Deselect the ungrouped drawing object, and then click the red shape of the logo (left shape).

g. At the Drawing Tools Format tab, click the Shape Fill button in the Shape Styles group, and then click Light Green in the *Standard Colors* section.

h. Select the placeholder text, *Financial Consultation*, and type **Graphic Edge**.

i. Select *Graphic Edge* and change the font to 15-point Castellar or a similar font.

j. Click the text box containing *Graphic Edge*, and then at the Text Box Tools Format tab, click the More button at the right of the Text Box Styles gallery. Select *Dashed Outline - Accent 3* in the second row. (Resize the text box if necessary.)

2. Select the text, *Start letter here*, (the text is inside a text box), and insert a text file by completing the following steps:

a. On the Insert tab, in the Text group, click the arrow at the right of Object, and then click the *Text from File* option.

b. At the Insert File dialog box, double-click the **GraphicText.docx** file located in your *Chapter03* folder. ***Hint: If a prompt displays to convert the file to Word 2010, click OK.***

3. Replace the placeholder text at the bottom of the letter with the text in Figure 3.6A. Change the font to 8-point Calibri and right-align the text. Resize the text box if necessary.

4. Add an orange gradient fill and change the shape of the text box containing the address by completing the following steps:

a. Select the text box containing the address information, click the More button (down-pointing arrow at the right of the Text Box Styles gallery), and then click the orange gradient (*Linear Up Gradient - Accent 6*).

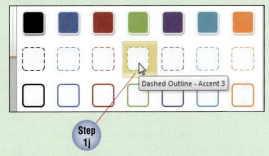

b. With the text box selected, click the Change Shape button in the Text Box Styles group, and then click the *Flowchart: Manual Input* shape in the *Flowchart* section. Resize and reposition the shape as necessary.

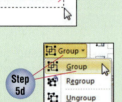

Step 4b

5. Group the logo in the upper right corner by completing the following steps:

a. Click the Select button in the Editing group on the Home tab, and then click the *Select Objects* option.

b. Begin dragging and drawing a dashed rectangle from the top left corner around the logo and the text box below it that contains *Graphic Edge*.

c. Click the *Select Objects* option again to toggle the feature off.

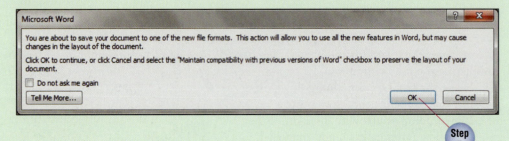

Step 5b

d. At the Page Layout tab, click the Group button in the Arrange group, and then click *Group*.

e. With the grouped logo selected, right-click the logo, and then click Copy. **Hint: A copy of the logo has been sent to the Office Clipboard.**

Step 5d

6. Create a matching envelope by completing the following steps:

a. At the Mailings tab, click the Envelopes button in the Create group.

b. At the Envelopes and Labels dialog box, click the Add to Document button. **Hint: The envelope will appear above the letter.**

c. Position the insertion point inside the envelope, right-click, and then click Paste. If you selected the logo before accessing the envelope feature, a copy of the logo may display in the lower right corner of the envelope. If the logo displays, either disregard the instruction to paste a copy or delete the duplicate logo.

d. Drag the logo to the position shown in Figure 3.6B.

7. Save, print, and then close **C03-E01-GraphicEdge.dotx**. Make sure you change the Save As Type to a Word Template and remove the checkmark from Maintain Compatibility with previous versions of Word. At the prompt to save the file in 2010 format, click OK. *Save this document as a template to your* **DTP Templates** *folder or to your hard drive if desired.*

Step 7

Figure 3.6 Exercise 3.1

August 5, 2012

Mr. Gregory Marshall
400 Rue du Saint-Sacrement
Montréal, Québec H2Y 1X4
CANADA

Dear Mr. Marshall:

It is with great pleasure that I am able to offer you a position at Graphic Edge as a graphic
designer.

After reviewing your portfolio, considering your outstanding grades at Vancouver College, and
discussing your creative contributions during your internship at CDP, I am excited about inviting
you to join our team. In addition to the salary we discussed, you will receive two weeks' paid
vacation every 12 months, a bonus equaling two weeks' salary payable the payday before
Christmas, health benefits, and $75,000 of life insurance. This position is a two-year agreement,
after which it may be renegotiated. Either party may terminate with a two-week notice.

I am very pleased to offer you the position and am sure that you will make a superb addition to
our firm. If you have any questions, please call me at any time.

Sincerely,

Georgiana Forrester
Art Director

ka

GRAPHIC EDGE

10 Bloor Street East, Suite 120
Toronto, Ontario M4W 1A8
CANADA

(416) 555-6011 phone
(416) 555-6012 fax
graphicedge@emcp.net

A

GRAPHIC EDGE

B

Designing Your Own Letterhead

Designing your own letterhead lets you create your own identity and image while cutting costs at the same time. In upcoming exercises, you will have the chance to create a letterhead from scratch and to convert the letterhead into a template.

Incorporating Design Concepts in a Letterhead

When creating thumbnail sketches and, ultimately, your letterhead, think of the following design concepts:

- Focus—create a focal point in the letterhead to draw in your audience.
- Balance—use a symmetrical layout where similar elements are distributed evenly on the page, or use an asymmetrical layout where dissimilar elements are distributed unevenly on the page in such a way as to balance one another.
- Proportion—design elements sized in proportion to their relative importance to the intended message. Your letterhead should not take up any more than 2 inches at the top of the page, preferably less.
- Contrast—use enough contrast to make it noticeable, and make sure there is enough surrounding white space assigned to darker elements on the page.
- Directional flow—group related items close to each other, and establish a visual connection between items on the page by using a strong alignment.
- Consistency—use a typeface consistently in your letterhead even though it may vary in type size, typestyle, or color. Repeat elements that tie the letterhead to subsequent pages, such as a ruled horizontal line that is repeated as a footer on each page.
- Color—use color sparingly to provide emphasis and contrast, and use a color that meets your readers' expectations for the mood, tone, and image of your organization and your message.

Using the Click and Type Feature to Position Design Elements

The Click and Type feature can be used to quickly insert text, graphics, tables, or other items into a blank area of a document in Word. Change to Print Layout view, and then click in a blank area to view the Click and Type pointer as shown in Figure 3.7. The Click and Type pointer displays the alignment formatting that will be applied. Double-click the mouse button to apply the formatting necessary to position the insertion point where you double-clicked the mouse button. If the Click and Type feature does not work, check to see that it is enabled by clicking the File tab, Word Options, Advanced, and then make sure there is a check in the *Enable click and type* check box.

Figure 3.7 Click and Type Alignment

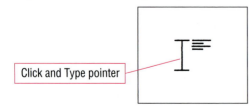

Left Alignment

Center Alignment

Right Alignment

Figure 3.8 Vertical Page Position

Customize Status Bar		
	Formatted Page Number	28
	Section	1
✓	Page Number	28 of 31
✓	Vertical Page Position	9.7"
	Line Number	43
	Column	12

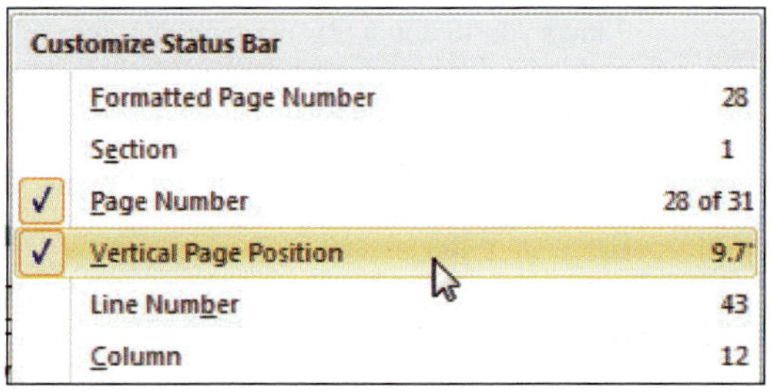

Using the Vertical Page Position Feature

To view the vertical location of your insertion point, position your mouse pointer on the Status bar, right-click, and then click the *Vertical Page Position* option at the Customize Status Bar pop-up menu as shown in Figure 3.8. This feature is helpful when positioning text at an exact inch increment from the top of the page.

◄ **DTP POINTERS**
Turn on the Vertical Page Position feature to view the exact location of your insertion point.

Using Text Boxes in Design

Text boxes are useful in desktop publishing because they can be dragged to any position on the page using the mouse, or exact horizontal and vertical locations can be specified at the Advanced Layout dialog box. Another important feature of a text box is that it is created in the drawing (foreground) layer and is considered a drawing object. Like any other object in Word, a text box may be placed above or below the text layer in a Word document. Text can be wrapped around a text box in a variety of ways, the direction of the text can be changed, and text boxes may also be linked.

Additionally, text boxes, as well as other Word objects, may be formatted by using options on the Drawing Tools Format tab as shown in Figure 3.9. Attributes such as Shape Effects, Insert Shapes, Shadow, Reflection, Glow, Soft Edges, WordArt Styles, Text, Arrange, and Size can be used to alter your text boxes.

Setting Internal Margins in a Text Box

By default, a text box has left and right internal margins of 0.1 inch, and top and bottom internal margins of 0.05 inch. These margins can be adjusted to increase or decrease the distance between the contents of the text box and the text box borders. To do this, click the desired text box to access the Drawing Tools Format tab, and then click the Format Shape dialog box launcher in the Shape Styles group. Notice the internal margins as shown in Figure 3.10.

Figure 3.9 Drawing Tools Format Tab

Figure 3.10 Format Shape Dialog Box

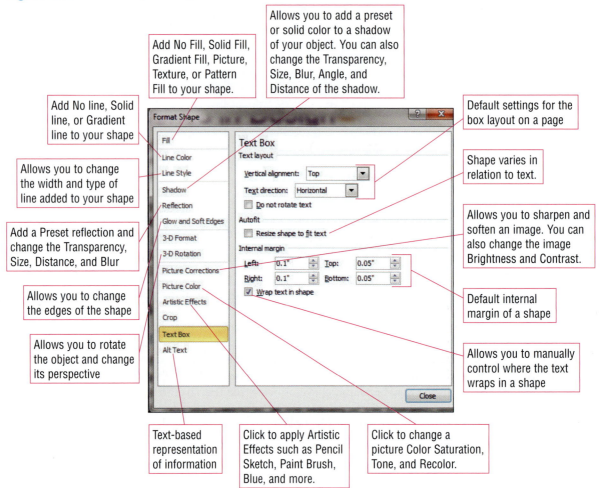

Add No Fill, Solid Fill, Gradient Fill, Picture, Texture, or Pattern Fill to your shape.

Allows you to add a preset or solid color to a shadow of your object. You can also change the Transparency, Size, Blur, Angle, and Distance of the shadow.

Add No line, Solid line, or Gradient line to your shape

Allows you to change the width and type of line added to your shape

Add a Preset reflection and change the Transparency, Size, Distance, and Blur

Allows you to change the edges of the shape

Allows you to rotate the object and change its perspective

Default settings for the box layout on a page

Shape varies in relation to text.

Allows you to sharpen and soften an image. You can also change the image Brightness and Contrast.

Default internal margin of a shape

Allows you to manually control where the text wraps in a shape

Text-based representation of information

Click to apply Artistic Effects such as Pencil Sketch, Paint Brush, Blue, and more.

Click to change a picture Color Saturation, Tone, and Recolor.

Sizing a Text Box

Using the mouse, select the text box (or object) and then position the mouse pointer on a sizing handle until it turns into a double-headed arrow. Hold down the *left* mouse button, drag the outline of the text box toward or away from the center of the object until it is the desired size, and then release the mouse button. To maintain the proportions of the existing text box dimensions, use one of the corner sizing handles to change both the width and the height at the same time. Hold down the Ctrl key as you drag one of the corner sizing handles, and the object will remain centered.

As an alternative, you can type specific measurements in the *Shape Height* and *Shape Width* measurement boxes in the Size group on the Drawing Tools Format tab as shown in Figure 3.11 or click the Format Shapes dialog box launcher and type the desired measurements.

Figure 3.11 Text Box Sizing in the Size Group on the Drawing Tools Format Tab

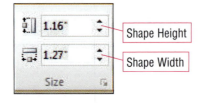

Shape Height

Shape Width

Figure 3.12 **Drawing Grid Dialog Box**

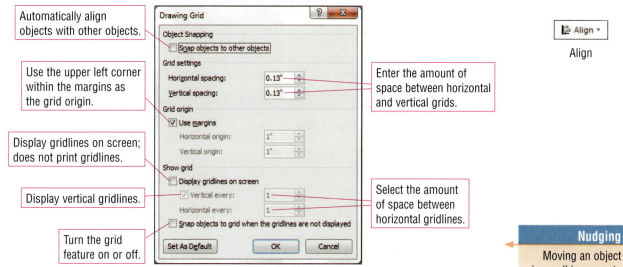

Automatically align objects with other objects.

Use the upper left corner within the margins as the grid origin.

Display gridlines on screen; does not print gridlines.

Display vertical gridlines.

Turn the grid feature on or off.

Enter the amount of space between horizontal and vertical grids.

Select the amount of space between horizontal gridlines.

Align

Positioning a Text Box at an Exact Location on a Page

One of the biggest advantages to using a text box is the ability to position the text box anywhere on the page. Using the move handle (four-headed arrow), hold down the *left* mouse button, drag the outline of the object to the new location, and then release the mouse button.

When using the keyboard, select the text box (or object), and then ***nudge*** or move the shape in small increments by pressing one of the arrow keys (left, right, up, or down). When you nudge a shape, it moves one space over on the ***grid***, which is a set of intersecting lines used to align objects. A grid is not visible in your documents, and the lines do not print. If the *Snap objects to grid* option is turned off at the Drawing Grid dialog box or if you hold the Ctrl key down as you nudge a shape, the shape moves one pixel at a time. A ***pixel*** is a single unit of measurement that your computer monitor uses to paint images on your screen. These units, which often appear as tiny dots, compose the pictures displayed by your screen.

To turn on the grid feature in Word 2010, click the Align button in the Arrange group in the Page Layout tab, and then click the *Grid Settings* option at the bottom of the drop-down menu. At the Drawing Grid dialog box, as shown in Figure 3.12, click the *Snap objects to grid* option to align objects to the nearest intersection of the grid. The grid feature is turned on by default and works even when the grid is not visible. To turn the *Snap objects to grid* option off, remove the check mark from the check box next to this option; to change the grid spacing, change the number in the spacing boxes under *Grid settings*.

Besides moving a text box with the mouse or with the arrow keys on the keyboard, you may position the object on a page using the Position button in the Arrange group on the Drawing Tools Format tab. Click the Position button and then choose the desired location for your text box as shown in Figure 3.13. Notice that each button indicates how the document text will wrap around the text box.

Nudging
Moving an object in small increments using the arrow keys.

Grid
A set of intersecting lines used to align objects.

Pixel
A single unit of measurement that your monitor uses to paint images on your screen.

Figure 3.13 **Positioning a Text Box Using the Position Gallery**

Figure 3.14 **Using the Layout Dialog Box to Precisely Position a Text Box Horizontally and Vertically**

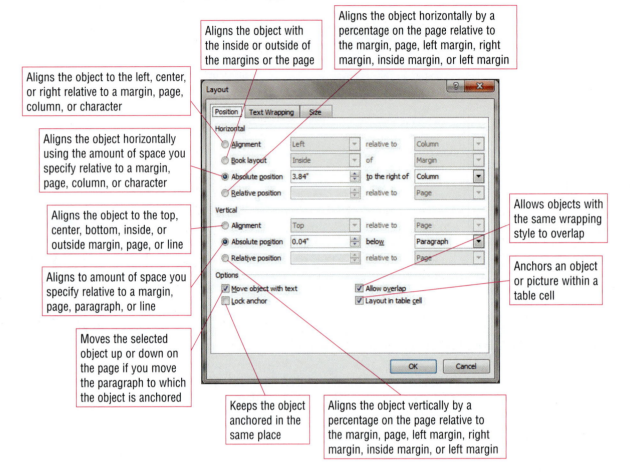

Aligns the object to the left, center, or right relative to a margin, page, column, or character

Aligns the object with the inside or outside of the margins or the page

Aligns the object horizontally by a percentage on the page relative to the margin, page, left margin, right margin, inside margin, or left margin

Aligns the object horizontally using the amount of space you specify relative to a margin, page, column, or character

Aligns the object to the top, center, bottom, inside, or outside margin, page, or line

Aligns to amount of space you specify relative to a margin, page, paragraph, or line

Moves the selected object up or down on the page if you move the paragraph to which the object is anchored

Keeps the object anchored in the same place

Aligns the object vertically by a percentage on the page relative to the margin, page, left margin, right margin, inside margin, or left margin

Allows objects with the same wrapping style to overlap

Anchors an object or picture within a table cell

Position

DTP POINTERS ▶
While holding down the Ctrl key on your keyboard, turn the wheel in the middle of your mouse; the zoom of the print size will get larger or smaller depending on which way you turn the wheel.

In addition, you may position an object precisely on a page by using options on the Layout dialog box. To access this box, first select the text box, click the Position button or the Wrap Text button in the Arrange group in the Page Layout tab or the Drawing Tools Format tab and then click More Layout Options at the bottom of the drop-down menu.

At the Layout dialog box in Figure 3.14, select the Picture Position tab. In the *Horizontal* section, make sure *Absolute position* is selected, and then type the desired measurement in the corresponding text box. In the *to the right of* list box, select the point (*Margin, Page, Column,* or *Character*) from which you want to horizontally position the selected line. Follow the same process with the *Vertical* section. This method allows precise control over the placement of an object.

Copying a Text Box

If you want to make an exact copy of a text box so you can place it in a different location, position the insertion point on the text box border until the I-beam turns into an arrow with a four-headed arrow attached. Hold down the *left* mouse button and press the Ctrl key while dragging a copy of the text box to a new location as shown in Figure 3.15.

Figure 3.15 Dragging and Dropping a Copy of a Text Box   **Figure 3.16** Text Box Anchored to a Paragraph

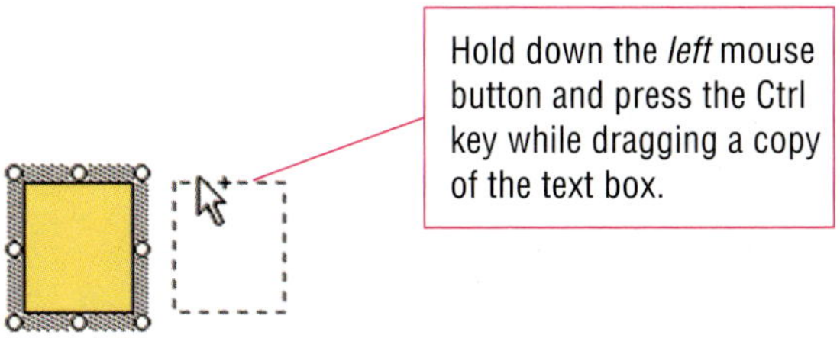

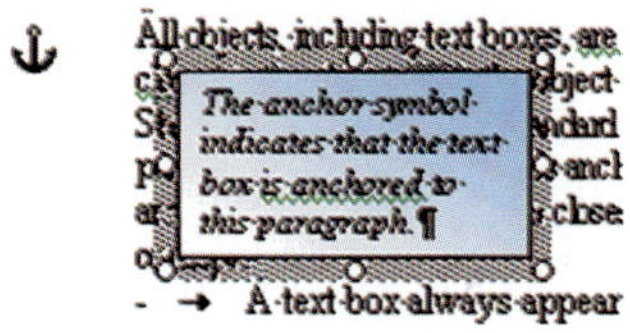

Hold down the *left* mouse button and press the Ctrl key while dragging a copy of the text box.

Anchoring a Text Box

All objects, including text boxes, are automatically anchored or attached to the paragraph closest to the object. With the object selected and nonprinting symbols displayed (click the Show/Hide button in the Paragraph group in the Home tab), an *anchor* symbol will display to the left of the paragraph to which the object is anchored as shown in Figure 3.16.

If a text box is repositioned, the anchor moves to the paragraph closest to the text box. The following points clarify the anchoring concept:

- A text box always appears on the same page as the paragraph to which it is anchored. By default, the text box moves with the paragraph to which it is anchored.
- If you do not want the text box (or object) to move with the paragraph to which it is anchored, access the Layout dialog box, make sure the Picture Position tab is selected, and then remove the check mark from the *Move object with text* check box.
- To always keep the object on the same page as the paragraph to which it is anchored, click the *Lock anchor* check box to insert a check mark. If the paragraph is moved to another page, the object will then be moved to that page also.
- For an object to remain stationary at a specific location on a page regardless of the text that surrounds it, enter specific measurements at the *Absolute position* (*Horizontal* section) and the *Absolute position* (*Vertical* section) options, and make corresponding selections at the *to the right of* and *below* list boxes. Last, remove the check mark from the *Move object with text* check box.

Wrapping Text Around a Text Box

By default, a text box displays in the layer above or *In Front of Text* as illustrated in Figure 3.17. If you want text to wrap around a text box, first select the text box, display the Drawing Tools Format tab, and then click the Wrap Text button in the Arrange group. Several wrapping options are available as explained in Figure 3.17.

Wrap Text

The wrapping styles offered at the Text Wrapping button drop-down menu are summarized in Table 3.1

The *Wrap text* section at the Text Wrapping tab in the Advanced Layout dialog box operates in conjunction with the *Wrapping style* section and offers the options described in Table 3.2.

Figure 3.17 Text Box Wrapping Style Examples

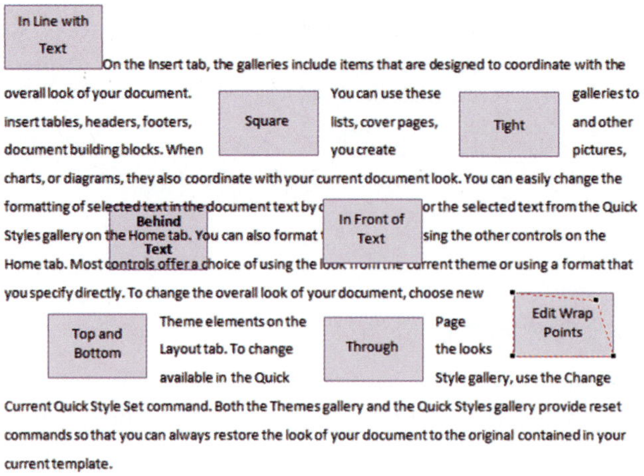

In Line with Text

On the Insert tab, the galleries include items that are designed to coordinate with the overall look of your document. You can use these galleries to insert tables, headers, footers, [Square] lists, cover pages, [Tight] and other document building blocks. When you create pictures, charts, or diagrams, they also coordinate with your current document look. You can easily change the formatting of selected text in the document text by c[...]or the selected text from the Quick Styles gallery on the Home tab. You can also format [In Front of Text] sing the other controls on the Home tab. Most controls offer a choice of using the look from the current theme or using a format that you specify directly. To change the overall look of your document, choose new Theme elements on the [Top and Bottom] Layout tab. To change [Through] the looks available in the Quick Style gallery, use the Change [Edit Wrap Points] Current Quick Style Set command. Both the Themes gallery and the Quick Styles gallery provide reset commands so that you can always restore the look of your document to the original contained in your current template.

Behind Text

Table 3.1 Wrapping Styles

In Line with Text	The object is placed in the text layer at the insertion point in a line of text.	In Line with Text
Square	Text wraps around all four sides of the selected text box or object.	Square
Tight	Text wraps tightly around the shape of an object rather than the box holding the object. (This style is more apparent when applied to a shape other than a square or rectangle.)	Tight
Through	This option is the same as *Tight*. Text not only wraps around the shape of an object, but it also flows through any open areas of the object box. This option may produce a visible change with certain graphic images, but no changes will occur when applied to a text box.	Through
Top and Bottom	Text wraps around the top and bottom of the text box (object) but not on both sides. Text stops at the top of the text box (object) and restarts on the line below the object.	Top and Bottom
Behind Text	Text wrapping is removed, and the text box (object) is placed behind the text layer in the document.	Behind Text
In Front of Text	Text wrapping is removed, and the text box (object) is placed in front of the text. This is a default setting.	In Front of Text
Edit Wrap Points	This option allows you to wrap text closer to the object.	Edit Wrap Points

Table 3.2 Advanced Wrapping Styles

Both sides	Text wraps on both sides of the text box.
Left only	Text wraps along the left side of the text box but not on the right side.
Right only	Text wraps along the right side of the text box but not on the left side.
Largest only	Text wraps along the largest side of the object. This does not produce any changes when applied to a text box.

Customizing Text Boxes and Other Shapes

By default, a text box has a black single-line border around all sides and contains white background fill. However, a text box can be customized in a variety of ways, including changing border style and color and changing the background fill color.

Changing Text Box and Shape Attributes

The following methods, along with some creativity, can be used to customize the border of a text box or other shapes as shown in Figure 3.18:

- **To add, remove, or change the color, weight, or style of a text box border:** Select the text box and then click the Shape Outline button in the Shape Styles group on the Drawing Tools Format tab. At the Shape Outline drop-down palette, select a color from the *Theme Colors* or *Standard Colors* sections, or select the *More Outline Colors* option to pick from an extended selection of standard colors or to create your own custom colors. Select Weight or Dashes to add various widths or dashed styles to the text box border. Choose No Outline to remove a border from a text box (shape). By clicking the shape borders illustrated in the Shape Styles gallery, you can add colored borders based on the theme selected as shown in Figure 3.19.

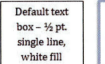

Shape Outline

As discussed earlier, you may also click the Format Shape dialog box launcher at the bottom of the Shape Styles group to access border options.

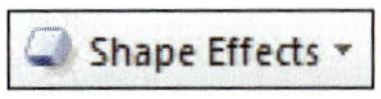

- **To add Shape Effects to a text box:** Select the text box (or other shape), click the Shape Effects button in the Shape Styles group, and then select Preset, Shadow, Reflection, Glow, Soft Edges, Effects, Bevel, or 3-D Rotation as shown in Figure 3.20.

Shape Effects

Figure 3.18 Text Box and Shape Borders

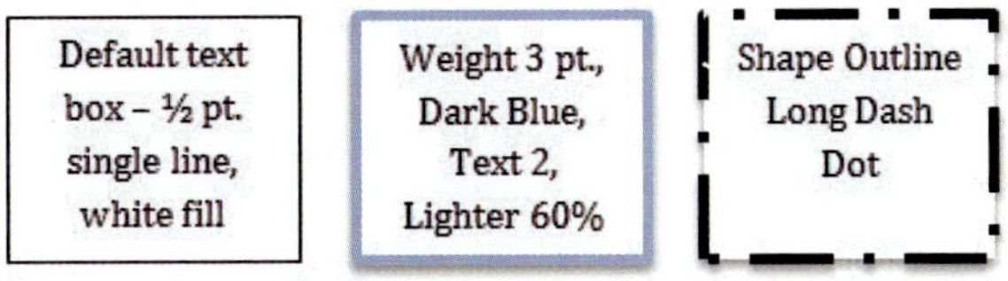

Default text box – ½ pt. single line, white fill	Weight 3 pt., Dark Blue, Text 2, Lighter 60%	Shape Outline Long Dash Dot

Figure 3.19 Applying Shape Style Borders to Text Boxes (Shapes)

Figure 3.20 Applying Shape Effects to Text Boxes (Shapes)

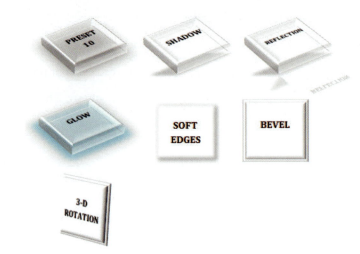

Changing Text Box Fill

Shape Fill

After you have selected your text box or object, you may click the Shape Fill button in the Shape Styles group on the Drawing Tools Format tab and then make choices to customize the fill of your text box. Your choices will include Theme Colors, Standard Colors, No Fill, More Fill Colors, Picture, Gradient, and Texture as illustrated in Figure 3.21.

You may also add text box (Shape) fills by selecting color fills based on the theme selected by clicking the Shape Styles More button and then selecting a desired fill from the Shape Styles gallery as shown in Figure 3.22.

A transparent effect can be added to the shape fill color of a text box or an object by clicking the *More Fill Colors* option and then dragging the slider in the *Transparency* option as shown in Figure 3.23. The *Transparency* option makes the selected color partially transparent. Drag the slider to the right to increase transparency.

Figure 3.21 Shape Fill Options

Figure 3.22 Applying Fills from the Shape Styles Gallery

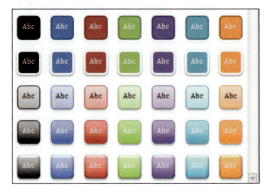

Figure 3.23 Adding Transparency to a Color

Figure 3.24 Built-In Text Boxes (Pull Quotes and Sidebars)

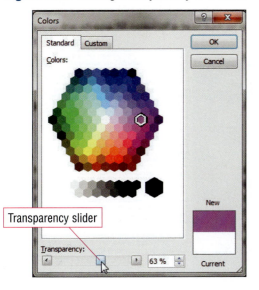

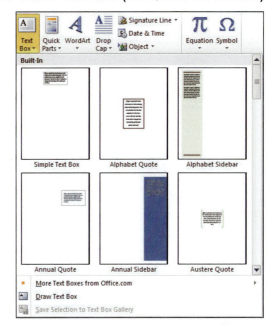

Inserting Preformatted Text Boxes

Word 2010 includes several preformatted text boxes that may be used as pull quotes or sidebars. However, do not let your imagination stop there. Use these professionally designed boxes for other purposes in your documents. Simply insert the text box and then replace the placeholder text with a picture, graphic, or attention-getting text. To access these decorative text boxes, click the Text Box button in the Text group on the Insert tab as shown in Figure 3.24. Scroll up or down to select the desired design. The accompanying text next to the design will help you decide where you may be able to use it. Figure 3.25 illustrates a few uses for this feature.

Using Linked Text Boxes

An additional characteristic of a text box is that two or more text boxes may be linked to each other, and text that does not fit in one box may be poured into another linked box as shown in Figure 3.26. This feature is particularly useful when formatting a newsletter. To link text boxes, you must first create two or more text boxes. To create a link between the two text boxes, complete the following steps:

1. Click the text box that is to be the first text box in the chain of linked boxes.
2. Display the Drawing Tools Format tab.
3. Click the Create Link button in the Text group. The mouse displays as a small upright pitcher.
4. Position the pitcher in the text box to be linked. The pitcher appears tipped with letters spilling out of it. Click once to complete the task.
5. To create a link from the second text box to a third text box, click the second text box, and then repeat steps 3 and 4.

Figure 3.25 Using Predesigned Text Boxes

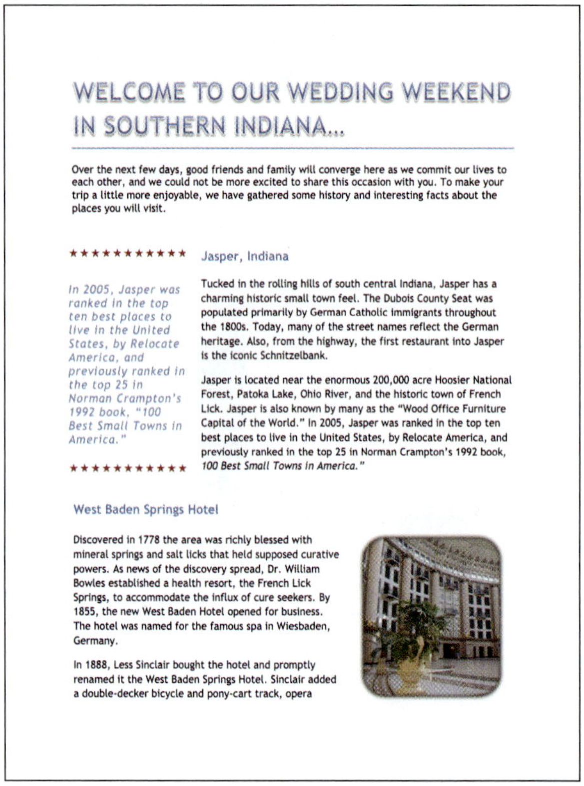

WELCOME TO OUR WEDDING WEEKEND IN SOUTHERN INDIANA...

Over the next few days, good friends and family will converge here as we commit our lives to each other, and we could not be more excited to share this occasion with you. To make your trip a little more enjoyable, we have gathered some history and interesting facts about the places you will visit.

★ ★ ★ ★ ★ ★ ★ ★ ★ ★   Jasper, Indiana

In 2005, Jasper was ranked in the top ten best places to live in the United States, by Relocate America, and previously ranked in the top 25 in Norman Crampton's 1992 book, "100 Best Small Towns in America."

Tucked in the rolling hills of south central Indiana, Jasper has a charming historic small town feel. The Dubois County Seat was populated primarily by German Catholic immigrants throughout the 1800s. Today, many of the street names reflect the German heritage. Also, from the highway, the first restaurant into Jasper is the iconic Schnitzelbank.

Jasper is located near the enormous 200,000 acre Hoosier National Forest, Patoka Lake, Ohio River, and the historic town of French Lick. Jasper is also known by many as the "Wood Office Furniture Capital of the World." In 2005, Jasper was ranked in the top ten best places to live in the United States, by Relocate America, and previously ranked in the top 25 in Norman Crampton's 1992 book, *100 Best Small Towns in America."*

★ ★ ★ ★ ★ ★ ★ ★ ★ ★

West Baden Springs Hotel

Discovered in 1778 the area was richly blessed with mineral springs and salt licks that held supposed curative powers. As news of the discovery spread, Dr. William Bowles established a health resort, the French Lick Springs, to accommodate the influx of cure seekers. By 1855, the new West Baden Hotel opened for business. The hotel was named for the famous spa in Wiesbaden, Germany.

In 1888, Less Sinclair bought the hotel and promptly renamed it the West Baden Springs Hotel. Sinclair added a double-decker bicycle and pony-cart track, opera

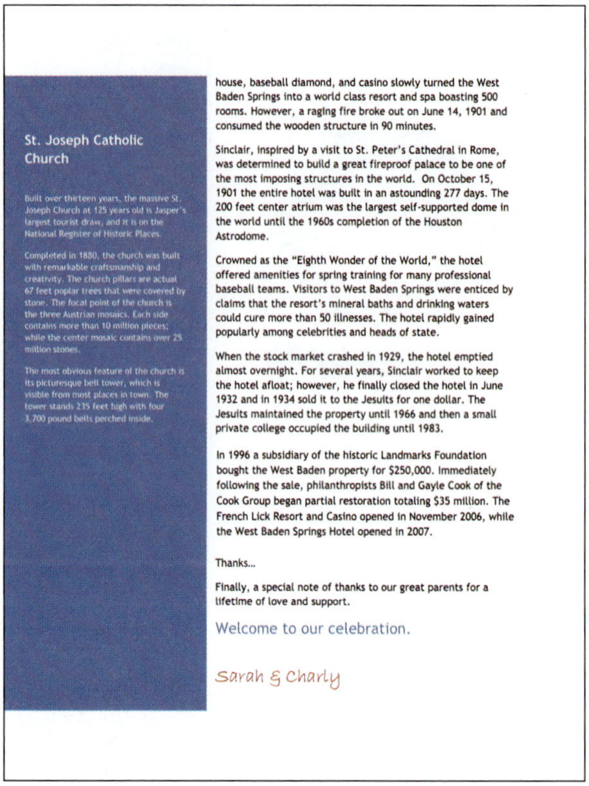

St. Joseph Catholic Church

Built over thirteen years, the massive St. Joseph Church at 125 years old is Jasper's largest tourist draw, and it is on the National Register of Historic Places.

Completed in 1880, the church was built with remarkable craftsmanship and creativity. The church pillars are actual 67 feet poplar trees that were covered by stone. The focal point of the church is the three Austrian mosaics. Each side contains more than 10 million pieces; while the center mosaic contains over 25 million stones.

The most obvious feature of the church is its picturesque bell tower, which is visible from most places in town. The tower stands 235 feet high with four 3,700 pound bells perched inside.

house, baseball diamond, and casino slowly turned the West Baden Springs into a world class resort and spa boasting 500 rooms. However, a raging fire broke out on June 14, 1901 and consumed the wooden structure in 90 minutes.

Sinclair, inspired by a visit to St. Peter's Cathedral in Rome, was determined to build a great fireproof palace to be one of the most imposing structures in the world. On October 15, 1901 the entire hotel was built in an astounding 277 days. The 200 feet center atrium was the largest self-supported dome in the world until the 1960s completion of the Houston Astrodome.

Crowned as the "Eighth Wonder of the World," the hotel offered amenities for spring training for many professional baseball teams. Visitors to West Baden Springs were enticed by claims that the resort's mineral baths and drinking waters could cure more than 50 illnesses. The hotel rapidly gained popularity among celebrities and heads of state.

When the stock market crashed in 1929, the hotel emptied almost overnight. For several years, Sinclair worked to keep the hotel afloat; however, he finally closed the hotel in June 1932 and in 1934 sold it to the Jesuits for one dollar. The Jesuits maintained the property until 1966 and then a small private college occupied the building until 1983.

In 1996 a subsidiary of the historic Landmarks Foundation bought the West Baden property for $250,000. Immediately following the sale, philanthropists Bill and Gayle Cook of the Cook Group began partial restoration totaling $35 million. The French Lick Resort and Casino opened in November 2006, while the West Baden Springs Hotel opened in 2007.

Thanks...

Finally, a special note of thanks to our great parents for a lifetime of love and support.

Welcome to our celebration.

Sarah & Charly

Creating Horizontal and Vertical Ruled Lines

In Word 2010, you may create horizontal and/or vertical lines anywhere on a page using the Line buttons in the Shapes drop-down gallery or using paragraph/cell borders by clicking the Borders button in the Paragraph group in the Home tab. You can create freeform lines, curvy lines, straight lines, or even arched lines. As with text boxes, you can adjust the weight, length, position, color, and shading of the lines created with either method. In typesetting, these horizontal and vertical lines are called ***ruled lines***, *rules*, or *ruling lines* to distinguish them from lines of type.

Figure 3.26 Linked Text Boxes

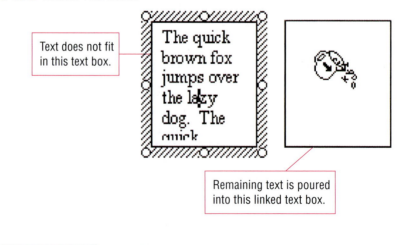

Text does not fit in this text box.

The quick brown fox jumps over the lazy dog. The quick

Remaining text is poured into this linked text box.

Figure 3.27 Applying Line Shape Styles

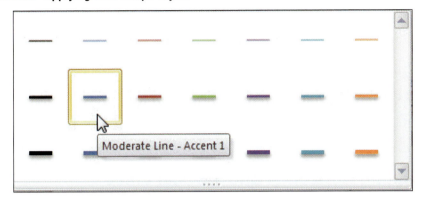

Click the Shape Styles More button to display the Shape Styles gallery as shown in Figure 3.27. These line colors will change with the theme selected.

Horizontal and vertical ruled lines are used to guide a reader's eyes across and down the page, to separate one section of text from another, to separate columns of text, or to add visual interest. Remember that ruled lines act as boundaries to the surrounding text. A thicker line serves as more of a barrier than a thinner line. Place ruled lines above the heading rather than below the heading. This way, the reader definitely knows that the heading belongs to the text that follows it. In addition, when using ruled lines, be consistent in their purpose and their appearance.

Drawing Horizontal and Vertical Lines

To insert a horizontal or vertical line using the Shapes drop-down gallery, select the Line shape, and then position the crosshairs where you want the line to begin. To create a straight horizontal or vertical line, hold down the Shift key and the *left* mouse button, drag the mouse horizontally or vertically to the location where you want the line to end, and then release the mouse button and the Shift key. (Ragged or imperfect lines are created when the Shift key is not pressed during the drawing process.) To create horizontal or vertical arrow lines, follow the same basic procedure, but click the Arrow Shape.

Line

Changing Line Colors, Size, Weight, and Style

Sizing a line created with the Line shape in the Drawing Tools Format tab is similar to sizing a text box. Select the line to be sized, position the mouse pointer on either sizing handle until it turns into crosshairs (hold down the Shift key if you want a straight line), drag the crosshairs in the appropriate direction until the line is the desired length, and then release the *left* mouse button. For precise measurements, select the line (or object) and then double-click the *left* mouse button. In the *Shape Width* text box in the Size group, enter the exact line length desired.

You can select different styles and weights of solid lines, such as those shown in Figure 3.28, from the Shape Outline drop-down gallery that displays when you click the Shape Outline button in the Shape Styles group on the Drawing Tools Format tab. Select a color to add to the line, or click *No Outline, More Outline Colors, Weight, Dashes,* and *Arrows* from a variety of options at the drop-down gallery.

Shapes

Figure 3.28 Customizing Lines

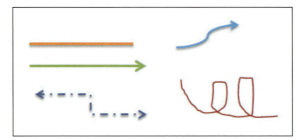

Positioning Horizontal and Vertical Lines

Horizontal and vertical lines may be positioned in the same way a text box is positioned. Select the line, and then use the mouse, the arrow keys on the keyboard, options in the Drawing Tools Format tab, or options in the Layout dialog box.

Creating Horizontal Lines Using Paragraph Borders

The Borders feature in Word may be used to add horizontal or vertical lines in headers and footers, as well as to any other text. Every paragraph you create in Word contains an invisible frame. (Remember that a paragraph may contain text, or it may consist of only a hard return.) To create a border on the top or sides of your paragraph, you may use the Border button in the Paragraph group in the Home tab. The Border button icon changes according to the most recent border position selected. To change the position of the border, click the down-pointing arrow at the right of the Border button, and then select the desired border location.

Border

You can further customize lines created with the Border button by clicking Borders and Shading at the drop-down gallery. At the Borders and Shading dialog box (see Figure 3.29), options exist to change the border settings, the border line style, the border line color, the border line width, the border location, and the distance between any border and text.

Figure 3.29 Borders and Shading Dialog Box - Borders Tab

Choose a border style, color, and width with options in this dialog box.

Click the sides, top, or bottom of this preview area to insert or remove a border.

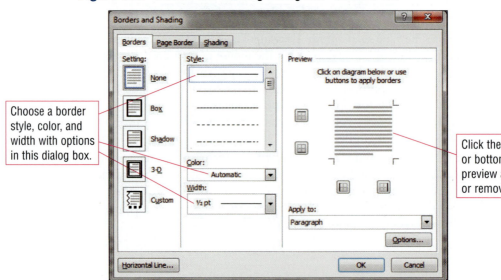

In Exercise 2, you will create a letterhead for an event planning firm. You will use grouped images, text boxes, graphic lines, and text effects.

1. Open **EventPlanLetterhead**, save the document, and name it **C03-02-EventLetterhead**. *Hint: Make sure the Office theme has been selected.*
2. Arrange the pictures to create the letterhead as shown in Figure 3.30 by completing the following steps:
   a. Click each picture and drag each image to form a straight, tight line of pictures. *Hint: The images have already been sized appropriately and their wrap changed to Tight.*

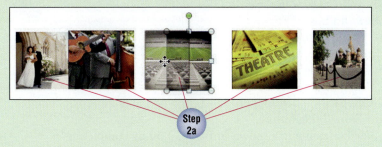

Step 2a

   b. Hold down the Shift key and select each image.

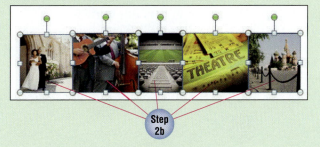

Step 2b

   c. With each image selected (sizing handles displayed), click the down-pointing arrow at the right of the Align button in the Arrange group on the Picture Tools Format tab, and then click the *Align Top* option.

Step 2c

   d. With the images still selected, click the down-pointing arrow at the right of the Group button in the Arrange group, and then click *Group*.

3. Position the grouped image by completing the following steps:
   a. Select the grouped image and then click the Position button in the Arrange group on the Picture Tools Format tab.
   b. Click the *More Layout Options* button at the bottom of the drop-down gallery.
   c. Select the Position tab, select the *Alignment* option in the *Horizontal* section, and then select *Page* in the *relative to* list box and *Centered* in the *Alignment* list box.
   d. In the *Vertical* section, select the *Absolute position* option, click the down-pointing arrow at the right of the *below* list box and select Page. Type **0.5** in the *Absolute position* text box. Click OK.

4. Turn on the Show/Hide feature.
5. Draw the blue horizontal line shown in Figure 3.30 by completing the following steps:

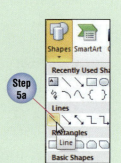

   a. Click the Shapes button in the Illustrations group on the Insert tab and then click the *Line* option in the *Lines* section.
   b. Hold down the Shift key as you drag the line crosshairs to create a horizontal line approximately 6 inches long.
   c. Select the line and then click the second line style in the Shape Styles gallery.
   d. With the image selected, type **6.5** in the Shape Width measurement box.

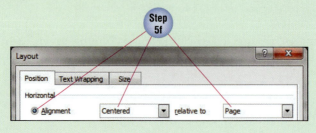

   e. Drag the line close to the grouped image as shown in Figure 3.30.
   f. Select the line, click the Position button in the Arrange group, click the More Layout Options button at the bottom of the drop-down list, and then select *Centered* relative to *Page* in the *Alignment* section. Click OK.

6. Insert the globe Clip Art image by completing the following steps:

Step 6b

   a. Position the insertion point on the third paragraph symbol from the bottom, and then click the Clip Art button in the Illustrations group on the Insert tab.
   b. Type **international** in the *Search for* text box, search for the globe image as shown in Figure 3.30 and insert it. ***Hint: If the globe image is not available, you may find it in your* Chapter03 *folder.***
   c. Size the image to approximately 0.5 inches.
   d. Select the image and type **0.5"** in the Shape Height measurement box in the Size group on the Picture Tools Format tab. ***Hint: Word will automatically size the Shape Width to 0.5".***

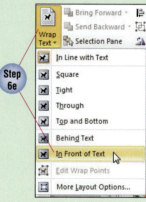

Step 6e

   e. Change the Wrap Text to *In Front of Text*, and then drag the image similar to the location shown in Figure 3.30.
7. Create the *Worldwide* text by completing the following steps:
   a. Click the Text Box button in the Text group in the Insert tab, and then click Draw Text Box.
   b. Drag the text box crosshairs to create a rectangular shape that is approximately 4.0 inches by 0.5 inches.
   c. Position the insertion point inside the text box, and then type **Wordwide Event Planning, Inc.**.
   d. Select the text and then apply the *Gradient Fill - Blue, Accent 1* option from the Text Effects gallery. ***Hint: The default Office theme should be selected.***
   e. Change the font to 18-pt. Palatino Linotype, bold, and italics.
   f. Display the Font dialog box and turn on *Kerning* at *12* points, *Ligatures* at *All*, and *Number forms* at *Old-style*. Click OK.
8. Customize the text box by completing the following steps:
   a. Click the Shape Fill button in the Shape Styles group on the Drawing Tools Format tab and then click *No Fill*.

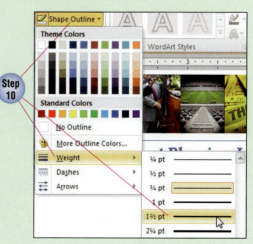

Step 10

   b. Click the Shape Outline button, and click *No Outline*.
   c. Drag the text box similar to Figure 3.30.
9. Select the blue line previously created, and then while holding down the Ctrl key and the Shift key drag a copy of the line below the *Worldwide* text.
10. With the second line selected, click the Shape Outline button, click *Weight*, and then click $1^1/_2$ pt from the drop-down gallery.
11. Click the Shape Outline button again and then click the *Olive Green, Accent 3* color in the *Theme Colors* section.

12. Select the line and drag it into the position similar to Figure 3.30. *Hint: With the line selected, use the arrow keys on your keyboard to nudge the line into correct position. Select each line and then use the Align command to vertically align them properly.*

13. Select the text box containing the address and drag it to a position similar to Figure 3.30.
14. Click on the last paragraph mark below the heading, change the font to 11-pt. Calibri, change the line spacing back to the default 1.15 line spacing, and then add 10 points after (default settings).
15. Save, print, and then close **C03-E02-EventLetterhead.docx**.

Figure 3.30 Exercise 3.2

Worldwide Event Planning, Inc.

421 Lexington Avenue, Suite 500
New York, NY 10170-0555
www.worldwideeventplan/emcp.net
555.769.9999

Corporate Meetings | Weddings | Holiday Parties | Group Tours | Cultural Events

Creating Envelopes

Let your company letterhead be the starting point for the design of your other business documents. An envelope designed in coordination with a letterhead is another way of establishing your identity with your target audience. Using some of the same design elements in the envelope as in the letterhead contributes to continuity and consistency among your documents. These same elements can be carried over into memos, faxes, business cards, invoices, and brochures.

Designing Your Own Envelope

When planning your design, remember that the envelope design does not have to be an exact replica of the letterhead. Select enough common elements to establish a visual link between the two documents. For example, using the same typeface and typestyles in a smaller type size and repeating a graphic element on a smaller scale may be just enough to establish that link.

Changing the Text Direction

You can change the direction of your text within a text box by clicking the Text Direction button in the Text group on the Drawing Tools Format tab. Rotating the text at 90 degrees or 270 degrees can add focus and contrast to your text. Figure 3.31 shows these interesting text options.

Using the Word Envelope Feature

The Word envelope feature makes creating professional-looking envelopes easy and inexpensive. You can create a blank envelope that already contains appropriate formatting for margins and a text box in the mailing address position. First, you must add a blank envelope to a document, then add your own design and return address. To create a customized envelope, complete the following steps:

1. At the Mailings tab, click the Envelopes button in the Create group.
2. At the Envelopes and Labels dialog box, select the Envelope tab.
3. Click the Options button, and make sure the desired envelope displays at the *Envelope size* list box. If not, select the desired size. (If the size you want is not listed, click *Custom size* from the drop-down list, and then enter the dimensions of your envelope.) Select a desired font for the Delivery address and the Return address. View the Printing Options, and then click OK.
4. Click the Add to Document button.

Figure 3.31 **Using the Text Direction Feature**

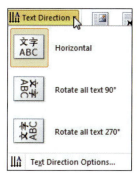

DTP POINTERS
Use your company letterhead as the starting point for the design of your business documents.

Envelopes

DTP POINTERS
Consider the actual size of the design area.

DTP POINTERS
Use consistent elements to establish a visual connection between your envelope and letterhead.

Text Direction

Figure 3.32 Choosing Envelope Printing Options

Envelope Options

Envelope Options | Printing Options

Printer: Epson Stylus NX510(Network)

Feed method

○ Face up   ○ Face down

☑ Clockwise rotation

5. Position the insertion point inside the envelope, insert a logo, and then drag to position the logo.

Word adds the envelope to the beginning of the current active document (which is usually a blank document). Word numbers the envelope as page 1 and the blank page as page 2. When you print your envelope, print the current page only to avoid sending a blank piece of paper through the printer.

The Word envelope feature also includes an option to add electronic postage to envelopes and labels. However, you need to install electronic postage software before you can use this feature. The Microsoft Office website provides information about electronic postage add-ins.

Checking Printing Options

Word determines the feed method for envelopes and the feed form that is best suited to your printer in the *Feed* section of the Envelopes and Labels dialog box (with the Envelopes tab selected). If this method does not work for your printer, choose the correct feed method and feed form at the Envelope Options dialog box with the Printing Options tab selected. Feed methods are visually displayed at this dialog box. You can also determine if the envelope is fed into the printer face up, as shown in Figure 3.32, or face down.

Exercise 3.3   Designing a Coordinating Envelope

1. Create an envelope design to coordinate with the Worldwide Event Planning letterhead created in Exercises 3.2 by completing the following steps:
    a.   Open **C03-E02-EventLetterhead.docx**.
    b.   Display the Mailings tab, and then click the Envelopes button in the Create group.
    c.   At the Envelopes and Labels dialog box, delete any text that displays in the *Delivery address* text box. If a default address appears in the *Return address* text box, click the *Omit* check box to insert a check mark.
    d.   Make sure a business-sized envelope appears in the *Preview* box, and then click Add to Document to insert a blank envelope form in your document.
    e.   Display the Insert tab, click the Text Box button in the Text group, and then draw a text box, that will contain the company name, on the left side of the envelope that is approximately the same size and in the same location as that shown in Figure 3.33.

2. Customize the text box by completing the following steps:
   a. Display the Drawing Tools Format tab and then verify that the text box measures 3" in height by 0.5" in width.

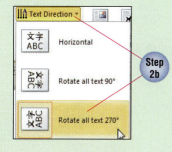

   b. Select the text box, click the Text Direction button in the Text group, and then click the *Rotate all text 270°* option.
   c. Position the insertion point inside the text box, type **Worldwide Event Planning, Inc.**, apply the *Gradient Fill - Blue, Accent 1* text effect, and change the font to 14-pt. Palatino Linotype, bold, italics.

   d. At the Font dialog box, turn on *Kerning* at *12* points, and select *Standard and Contextual* in the *Ligatures* section. Click OK.
   e. Remove the Shape Fill and the Shape Outline.
3. Insert the globe image by completing the following steps:
   a. Select the global image in the Worldwide Event Planning, Inc. letterhead, and click Copy or press Ctrl + C.
   b. Position the insertion point in the envelope, and then click Paste.
   c. Size and position the global image as shown on the envelope in Figure 3.33.
4. Insert the return address text by completing the following steps:
   a. Select the text box containing the Worldwide Event Planning, Inc. address in the letterhead and then click Copy.
   b. Position the insertion point in the envelope, and then click Paste.
   c. Select the address text and then change the horizontal alignment to Align Left Text.
   d. Drag the return address text box to a location similar to Figure 3.33.
5. Position the insertion point in the text box in the middle of the envelope, and type **[Type address here.]**
6. Save your envelope/letter as a template by completing the following steps:
   a. Click the File, tab and then click the Save & Send tab.
   b. At the Save & Send Backstage view, click the Change File Type tab in the *File Types* section, click the *Template* option in the *Change File Type* section, and then click the Save As button.

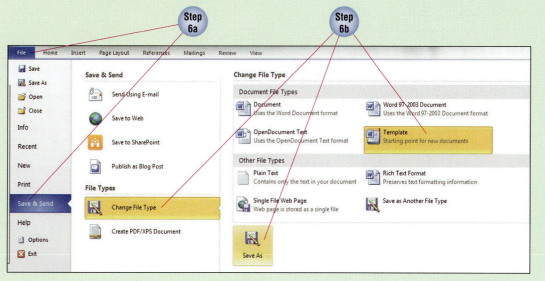

c. Type **C03-E03-EventLetter&Env** in the *File name* text box and change the folder
    location to the template folder that you created in Chapter 2 (most likely the location is
    DTP Templates) or save to the *Templates* folder in the Navigation pane.
d. Close **C03-E03-WorldwideLetter&Env.dotx**.

Figure 3.33 Exercise 3.3

Figure 3.34 Saving a Logo with Quick Parts

Figure 3.35 Creating a New Building Block

Using Quick Parts to Store and Reuse Text and Graphics

In earlier versions of Word, you used the AutoText feature to quickly and easily store and reuse commonly used text and/or graphics, including any associated formatting, and inserted them into documents whenever you needed them. The AutoText feature is not available in Word 2010; however, Quick Parts (Building Blocks) function similarly. Quick Parts are reusable pieces of content, such as the logo shown in Figure 3.34, or other document parts that are stored in galleries. You can access and reuse Quick Parts (Building Blocks) at any time. You can also save Building Blocks and distribute them within templates. Each selection of text or graphics is stored as Quick Parts and then stored in the Building Blocks Organizer and assigned a unique name that makes it easy for you to find the content when you want to use it as shown in Figures 3.35 and 3.36.

Quick Parts

Creating Business Cards

A business card is one of your best marketing opportunities. A business card usually includes your name, title, company or organization name, address, telephone number, fax number, email address, and if appropriate the URL of your website. You can also include a one-sentence description of your business, business philosophy, or slogan. To establish your identity and to stay consistent with other business documents such as letterheads, envelopes, and so on, include the same company logo or symbol in reduced size. Also, continue to use the same typefaces and colors that are in your other business documents.

Most business cards are created with sans serif typefaces because the characters are easier to read. The type sizes vary from 12 to 14 points for key words and 8 to 10 points for telephone and fax numbers. Vary the appearance by using bold, italics, small

◀ **DTP POINTERS**
Keep your business card design simple. Simplicity is elegant.

◀ **DTP POINTERS**
Avoid large pictures in the background of your business card. Avoid images of men shaking hands, landscapes, or any other large image.

Figure 3.36 Storing a Logo in the Building Blocks Organizer

Building blocks:				Click a building block to see its preview
Name	Gallery	Category	Template	
Loaves & Fi...	Quick Parts	General	Building Blo...	
Manual Table	Table of C...	Built-In	Built-In Buil...	
Automatic ...	Table of C...	Built-In	Built-In Buil...	
Automatic ...	Table of C...	Built-In	Built-In Buil...	
Calendar 4	Tables	Built-In	Built-In Buil...	

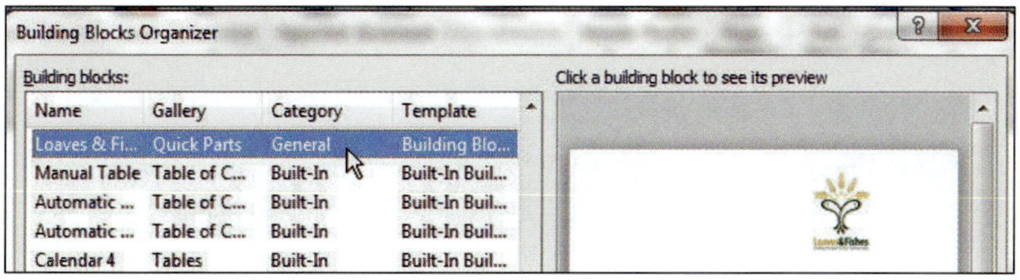

Figure 3.37 Business Card Design

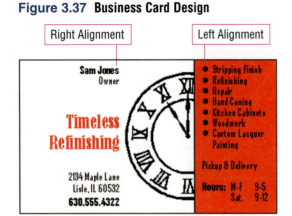

Right Alignment — Left Alignment

Right Alignment — Right Alignment

caps, or text effects. Figure 3.37 illustrates two similar business cards that include all of the necessary information but are slightly different in design. The one on the right is the best choice as it reinforces a consistent strong right alignment. The photograph adds an updated, professional feel over the clip art image used in the first example.

Business cards should be printed on high-quality cover stock paper. Specially designed full-color papers and forms for creating business cards more easily and professionally are available at office supply stores and paper companies. Printing your own business cards saves you the expense of having to place a large minimum order with an outside printer. This is especially helpful to a new small business. You may decide to design your own card and then take it to a professional printer to be printed in large quantities or contact an online printing source for convenient, efficient printing. Be sure to contact the printer first to confirm whether your Word file saved in PDF format will be acceptable or if a hard copy will suffice.

Using the Word Labels Feature to Create Business Cards

Labels

You can use the Word business card label definition to design and create your own business cards such as the ones in Figure 3.38. You can also use the business card label definition to create membership cards, name tags, coupons, placeholders, or friendly reminders. Most label definitions will produce 10 business cards—two columns of labels with five rows in each column. The columns and rows are set up automatically in a Word table. Each label is actually a cell in the table.

Figure 3.38 Creating Your Own Business Cards

When creating business cards, use the label definition that matches the labels you have purchased. A common label is the Avery standard 5371 or 8371 Business Card label definition. The only difference between these two label product numbers occurs in the actual product when you purchase these brand-name items at an office supply store—the 5371 is made to be used in a laser printer and the 8371 is made to be used in an inkjet printer. In both cases, the business card will be 3 inches by 2 inches and the sheet containing the business cards will be 8 inches by 11 inches.

Using the Microsoft Office Online Templates for Business Cards

As an alternative to designing business cards, you may use an array of professionally designed business card templates at the Microsoft Online templates as shown in Figure 3.39. To access these templates, complete the following steps:

◀ DTP POINTERS
Do not use more than 2-3 fonts in the business card design; one is preferable. Change the font size and other font effects for interest.

◀ DTP POINTERS
Use a generous amount of white space.

Figure 3.39 **Using Microsoft Online Business Card Templates**

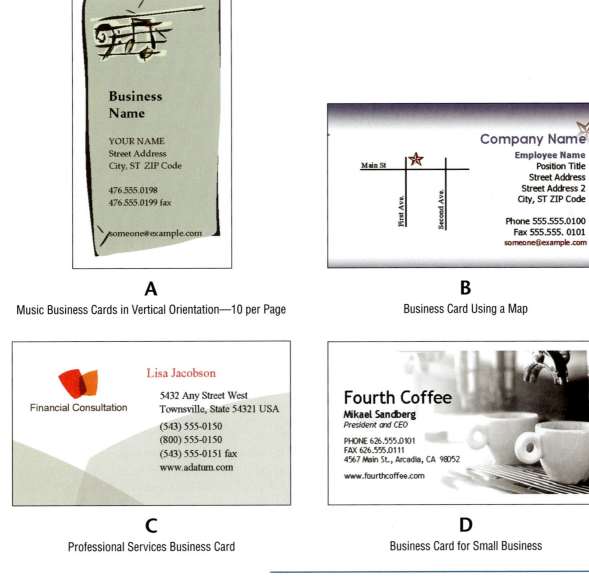

A

Music Business Cards in Vertical Orientation—10 per Page

B

Business Card Using a Map

C

Professional Services Business Card

D

Business Card for Small Business

1. Click the File tab, and then click the New tab.
2. At the New tab Backstage view, click the Business cards category in the *Office. com Templates* section.
3. Select the desired template and then click Download.
4. Customize the downloaded document by replacing the placeholder text with your own text.

When the card templates are edited in Word, they will display as a full sheet of formatted labels. To customize this sheet of cards (labels), you may use one of the following two methods:

Method 1—Using Quick Parts to Customize Business Cards Based on a Template

1. After selecting and then downloading the desired business card template, delete all of the cards in the template except for the card in the upper left corner of the template, and then modify the remaining business card to meet your needs. ***Note: Do not delete the table cells containing the cards.***
2. Hold down the Shift key and select each text box, picture, or object in the formatted card. ***Note: The text box you inserted may obscure other objects or text boxes in the card. If that is the case, right-click the text box, point to Order, and then click Send to Back so that other objects can be viewed and selected.*** Click the Group button in the Arrange group in the Drawing Tools Format tab, and then click *Group*.
3. With the grouped objects selected as one unit, click the Quick Parts button in the Text group in the Insert tab and then click the *Save Selection to Quick Parts Gallery* option (Building Blocks).
4. Give your entry a short name at the Create New Building Block dialog box. Click OK.
5. At a clear document screen, display the Mailings tab and then click the Labels button in the Create group.
6. At the Envelopes and Labels dialog box with the Labels tab selected, click the Options button. At the Label Options dialog box, select a label definition that corresponds with the label definition you noted when you downloaded the business card template from the Microsoft Office Online templates (e.g., Avery 5371, 8371, etc.). Click the OK button.
7. Type your Quick Parts entry name in the *Address* text box and then press F3. Make sure that the *Full page of the same label* option is selected and then click the New Document button.
8. Your customized business cards should display as a full sheet of cards.

Method 2—Using Copy and Paste to Customize Business Cards

1. Delete all of the business cards *except* the first row of formatted cards. ***Note: Do not delete the table structure.***
2. Customize the remaining two business cards.
3. Select the two business cards (select them as a row in a table).
4. Click Copy in the Clipboard group in the Home tab.
5. Position the insertion point in the first cell of the second row of the table, click the Paste button in the Clipboard group in the Home tab. ***Hint: If the table gridlines do not display, click the Show Gridlines button in the Table group in the Table Tools Layout tab.***
6. Press F4 to repeat copying the rows.
7. Select and then delete any blank rows at the end of the copied rows.

Exercise 3.4 Creating Business Cards Using the Word Envelopes and Labels Feature and AutoText Feature

1. At a blank document, create the business cards shown in Figure 3.40 by completing the following steps:

   a. Click the Labels button in the Create group in the Mailings tab.

   b. At the Envelopes and Labels dialog box, click the Labels tab, and then click the Options button.

   c. At the Label Options dialog box, change the *Label vendor* to *Avery US Letter*, select *8371 Business Cards* in the *Product number* list box, and then click OK.

   d. Delete any text that may appear in the *Address* list box, and then click the New Document button.

   e. If the table gridlines do not display, click the Table Tools Layout tab, and then click the Show Gridlines button in the Table group.

2. Create the blue line above *Worldwide* by completing the following steps:

   a. Position the insertion point in the first cell, click the Shapes button in the Illustrations group in the Insert tab, and then click the first line shape in the *Line* section. **Hint: Make sure the Office theme has been selected.**

   b. Hold down the Shift key while dragging the crosshairs to draw a line that is approximately 2.75 inches in length. Verify the length at the Shape Width measurement box in the Size group.

   c. If necessary, select the line and change the style to *Subtle Line - Accent 1* style at the Shape Style gallery.

   d. Click the Shape Outline button and change the color to *Light Blue* in the *Standard Colors* section.

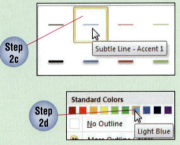

3. Create a text box that will contain the company name by completing the following steps:

   a. At the Insert tab, click the Text Box button in the Text group, and then click the *Draw Text Box* option.

   b. Position the crosshairs in the first label (cell) and draw a text box that is approximately the same size and in the same location as the *Worldwide Event Planning, Inc.* text box shown in Figure 3.40.

   c. Select the text box, and verify that the height is 0.4 inches and the width is 3 inches.

   d. Remove the Shape Outline and the Shape Fill.

   e. Change the font to 14-point Palatino Linotype, bold, italics, and then apply the *Gradient Fill - Blue, Accent 1* style in the Text Effects gallery. Type **Worldwide Event Planning, Inc.** and then right align the text within the text box. **Hint: Create a style if you are going to repeat this formatting often.**

   f. Select the text, and then at the Font dialog box, turn on *Kerning* at *12* points and select *Standard and Contextual* in the *Ligatures* section. Click OK.

g. Select the blue line, hold down the Shift key and Ctrl key and then drag a copy of the line below the text box containing the Worldwide text. ***Hint: Make sure the two lines align vertically over the Worldwide Event Planning text.***

Step 3g

g. Change the color of the line to *Olive Green, Accent 3* in the first line of the *Theme Colors* section, and then change the weight to $1^1/_2$ pt.

4. Create another text box to contain the address text by completing the following steps:
   a. Draw a text box that measures approximately 1 inch in height by 2.75 inches in width.
   b. Remove the Shape Outline and the Shape Fill.
   c. Click the Align Text Right button to right align the text.
   d. Type the following text:

      421 Lexington Avenue, Suite 500 (Press Shift + Enter)
      New York, NY 10170-0555 (Press Enter)
      www.worldwideeventplan/emcp.net (Press Shift + Enter)
      555.769.9999 (The text may not fit until you change the font size below.)

   e. Select *421 Lexington…0555*; change the font to 10-pt. Georgia, bold; and change the font color to *Olive Green, Accent 3.*
   f. Select *www…9999*; change the font to 8-pt. Georgia, italics; and change the font color to *Olive Green, Accent 3.*
   g. Drag the text box in a position similar to Figure 3.40.

5. Create another text box to contain Corporate Meetings, etc. as shown in Figure 3.40 by completing the following steps:
   a. Draw a text box that measures approximately 0.25 inch by 3.5 inches.
   b. Remove the Shape Outline and the Shape Fill.
   c. Center align the text.
   d. Change the font to 7-point Calibri in the *Olive Green, Accent 3* color and then type the following text:

      Corporate Meetings | Weddings | Holiday Parties | Group Tours | Cultural Events (Press the spacebar before and after each bar character.)

   e. Drag the text box in a position similar to Figure 3.40.

6. Position the insertion point in the upper left corner of the cell (not in a text box), and then insert the person/globe clip art image.

7. Size the image to approximately 0.70 inches, apply Text Wrap of *In Front of Text*, and then drag it into a position similar to Figure 3.40.

8. To save the business card as a Quick Part (Building Block) entry, the objects in the business card must be grouped together so they can be treated as one unit. Group the objects, and create a Quick Part entry by completing the following steps:

Step 8b

   a. Select the text box that contains the company name.
   b. Hold down the Shift key and select the remaining text boxes and lines. (All six objects should be selected.)
   c. Click the Group button in the Arrange group in the Drawing Tools Format tab and then click *Group*. (Sizing handles should display on all four sides of the business card.)

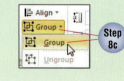

Step 8c

d. Click the Quick Parts button in the Text group on the Insert tab.
e. Click the *Save Selection to Quick Part Gallery* option.
f. At the Create New Building Block dialog box, type **Worldwide** in the *Name* text box. Click OK.

9. Create a full sheet of business cards using your Quick Part entry by completing the following steps:
    a. At the Mailings tab, click the Labels button in the Create group. Make sure the *Avery US Letter* vendor and the product number *8371 Business Cards* have been selected.
    b. At the Envelopes and Labels dialog box with the Labels tab selected, delete any text that may appear in the *Address* list box, type **Worldwide**, and then press F3.
    c. At the same dialog box, make sure *Full page of the same label* is selected, and then click New Document. A full sheet of business cards will display on your screen.

10. Save the full sheet of business cards with the name **C03-E04-BusCards**.

11. Print and then close **C03-E04-BusCards.docx**. Printing the business cards on a sheet of business cards made especially for your type of printer is preferable. If you print the business cards on plain paper, you may want to print the table gridlines as shown in Figure 3.40. (To print the gridlines, display the Table Tools Design tab and then click the Table Grid button in the Table Style gallery.)

12. Close the document that you used for creating the sample label.

Figure 3.40 Exercise 3.4

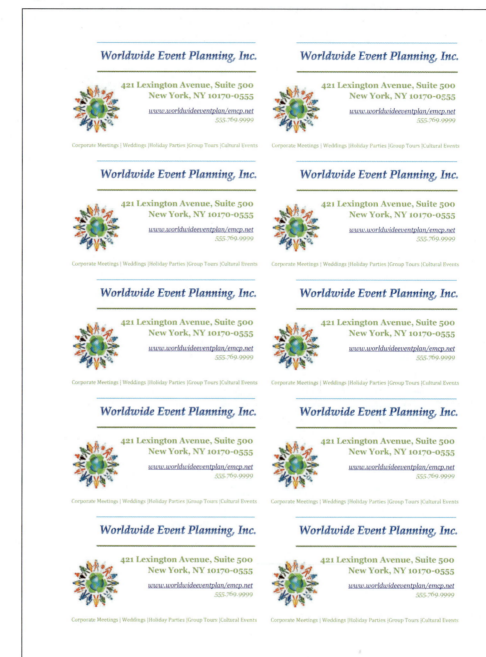

Using WordArt for Interesting Text Effects

You can create compelling text effects with WordArt. WordArt can distort or modify text to conform to a variety of shapes. This is useful for creating company logos and headings and can be easily incorporated into a company letterhead. It is also especially useful for headlines in flyers and announcements. The shapes can exaggerate the text to create an interesting focal point.

Figure 3.41 WordArt Text Effects

Using WordArt in a letterhead is one way to project a particular image and to establish an identity with your target audience. ***Hint: Type*** logos ***at the*** **Search** ***text box at the Clip Art task pane to view shapes that may be used to create logos as shown in Figure 3.41. Add your company name, formatted in WordArt, to any one of these images to create a simple logo. In addition, view the various Signs and Symbols clips by clicking the*** <u>Find more at Office.com</u> ***link at the bottom of the Clip Art task pane.***

Creating a WordArt Object

As stated earlier, with the WordArt feature, you can distort or modify text to conform to a variety of shapes. This is useful for creating company logos, letterhead, flyer titles, or headings. To insert WordArt in a document, click the Insert tab and then click the WordArt button in the Text group. This displays the WordArt gallery shown in Figure 3.42. Select the desired option at the gallery, and a WordArt text box is inserted in the document containing the words *Your text here* with the Drawing Tools Format tab active. Type the desired WordArt text and then format the WordArt with options in the Drawing Tools Format tab. The WordArt styles that display at the gallery are based on the theme selected.

Formatting WordArt Text

Figure 3.42 WordArt Gallery

With options in the WordArt Styles group in the Drawing Tools Format tab, you can apply formatting to the WordArt text. You can apply a predesigned WordArt style, change the WordArt text color and text outline color, and apply a text effect such as shadow, reflection, glow, bevel, 3-D rotation, and transform. With the transform option, you can mold the WordArt text to a specific shape. To do this, click the Text Effects button, point to Transform, and then click the desired shape at the drop-down gallery. Use options in the Arrange group to specify the position, alignment, and rotation of the WordArt text, and specify the size of the WordArt with options in the Size group.

Formatting the WordArt Text Box

WordArt text is inserted in a text box, and this text box can be customized with options in the Shape Styles group in the Drawing

Figure 3.43 Examples of Character Pair Kerning

WA (kerned)	Ta (kerned)
WA (not kerned)	Ta (not kerned)
Ty (kerned)	Vi (kerned)
Ty (not kerned)	Vi (not kerned)

WordArt

Tools Format tab. Use options in this group to apply a predesigned style to the WordArt text box, change the text box fill color and outline color, and apply an effect to the WordArt text box such as shadow, reflection, glow, soft edges, bevel, and 3-D rotation. Click the Rotate button, and then click *Rotate Left 90°* at the drop-down list.

Refining Letter and Word Spacing

Leading
The vertical spacing between lines of type.

Certain refinements such as kerning and tracking make your documents look more professional by fine-tuning the spacing between characters. *Leading* adjusts the vertical space between lines of type.

Kerning Character Pairs

Kerning
The process of decreasing or increasing the white space between specific character pairs.

The process of decreasing or increasing the white space between specific character pairs is called *kerning*. Generally, the horizontal spacing of typefaces is designed to optimize body text sizes (9- to 13-point). At larger sizes, the same relative horizontal space appears *loose*, especially when uppercase and lowercase letters are combined. Kerning visually equalizes the space between specific characters and generally is used only on headlines and other blocks of large type (14-point and larger). Figure 3.43 illustrates common character pairs that are affected by using the kerning feature.

Using Automatic or Manual Kerning

In Word, kerning can be accomplished automatically, or character pairs may be selected and kerned manually.

Figure 3.44 Turning on Automatic Kerning

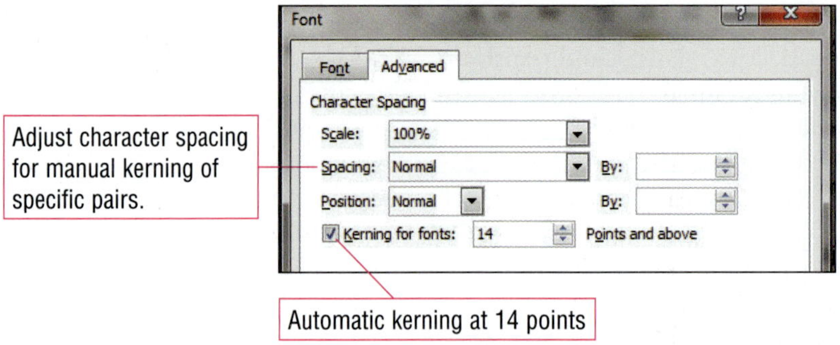

Adjust character spacing for manual kerning of specific pairs.

Font

Font | Advanced

Character Spacing

Scale: 100%

Spacing: Normal | By:

Position: Normal | By:

☑ Kerning for fonts: 14 | Points and above

Automatic kerning at 14 points

Automatic Kerning

When automatic kerning is turned on, Word adjusts the space between certain pairs of letters above a specific point size. Not all character pairs are affected with automatic kerning. Some common character pairs that may be automatically kerned are *Ta, To, Ty, Vi,* and *WA*. The amount of space that is adjusted for specific character pairs is defined in a kerning table, which is part of the printer definition. The printer definition is a preprogrammed set of instructions that tells the printer how to perform various features.

To turn on automatic kerning, click the Font dialog box launcher in the Font group on the Home tab, and then select the Advanced tab as displayed in Figure 3.44. Click the check box to the left of the *Kerning for fonts* option to insert a check mark. In the *Points and above* text box, use the up and down arrows to specify the minimum point size for kerning to take effect, or type the desired point size.

Manual Kerning

If you choose to kern letters manually, you make the decision as to which letters to kern. Manual kerning is especially helpful if you need to increase or decrease space between letters to improve legibility, to create a special effect, or to fit text in a specific amount of space. As a word of caution, do not sacrifice legibility when making kerning adjustments. To manually kern a pair of letters, select the pair of characters you want to kern, and then access the Font dialog box, Advanced tab. Click the *Spacing* list box, and then select *Expanded* (if you want to increase the spacing between the selected character pair) or *Condensed* (if you want to decrease the spacing). In the *By* list box, click the up or down arrows to specify the amount of space the selected character pair is to be increased or decreased. Manual kerning can provide accurate results; however, it can be very tedious. For example, compare the normal text to the manually kerned text in Figure 3.45. The *S* and the *A* were selected, and the character spacing was condensed. This then led to minor character spacing adjustments between some of the other letters and several printings to achieve the desired result.

Figure 3.45 Normal and Manually Kerned Text

RIDE SAFE, INC. (normal)

RIDE SAFE, INC. (manually kerned)

DTP POINTERS
Do not sacrifice legibility when kerning text.

Tracking Text

In traditional typesetting, equally reducing or increasing the horizontal space between all characters in a block of text is called ***tracking***. Tracking affects all characters, while automatic kerning affects only specific character pairs. The purpose of tracking is the same as kerning: to produce more attractive, easy-to-read type. In addition, you can use tracking to create unusual spacing for a specific design effect or to fit text into a certain amount of space.

In Word, tracking is virtually the same as manual kerning because both processes involve condensing or expanding character spacing at the Font dialog box. Whereas manually kerning involves adjusting the character spacing of selected character pairs, tracking involves adjusting the character spacing of a selected block of text, such as a heading, a subheading, a phrase, and so on. Adjust character spacing by expanding or condensing text at the Font dialog box as shown in Figure 3.46.

Tracking
Equally reducing or increasing the horizontal space between all characters in a selected block of text.

Figure 3.46 Adjusting Character Spacing

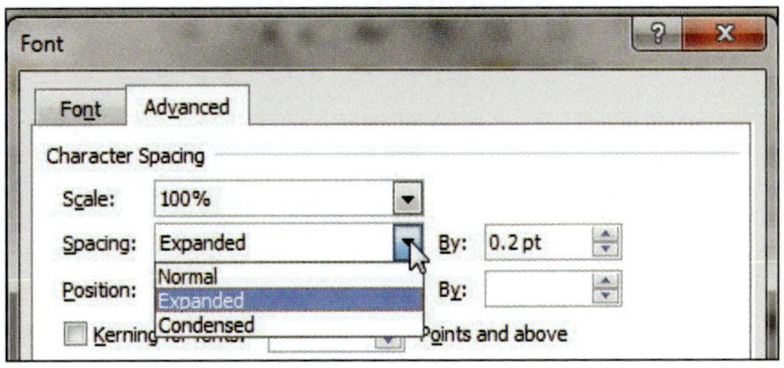

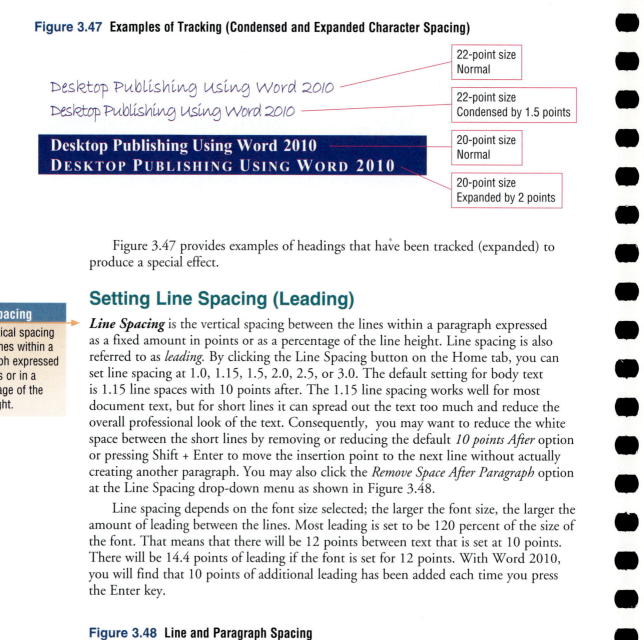

Figure 3.47 provides examples of headings that have been tracked (expanded) to produce a special effect.

Setting Line Spacing (Leading)

Line Spacing

The vertical spacing of the lines within a paragraph expressed in points or in a percentage of the line height.

Line Spacing is the vertical spacing between the lines within a paragraph expressed as a fixed amount in points or as a percentage of the line height. Line spacing is also referred to as *leading.* By clicking the Line Spacing button on the Home tab, you can set line spacing at 1.0, 1.15, 1.5, 2.0, 2.5, or 3.0. The default setting for body text is 1.15 line spaces with 10 points after. The 1.15 line spacing works well for most document text, but for short lines it can spread out the text too much and reduce the overall professional look of the text. Consequently, you may want to reduce the white space between the short lines by removing or reducing the default *10 points After* option or pressing Shift + Enter to move the insertion point to the next line without actually creating another paragraph. You may also click the *Remove Space After Paragraph* option at the Line Spacing drop-down menu as shown in Figure 3.48.

Line spacing depends on the font size selected; the larger the font size, the larger the amount of leading between the lines. Most leading is set to be 120 percent of the size of the font. That means that there will be 12 points between text that is set at 10 points. There will be 14.4 points of leading if the font is set for 12 points. With Word 2010, you will find that 10 points of additional leading has been added each time you press the Enter key.

Figure 3.48 Line and Paragraph Spacing

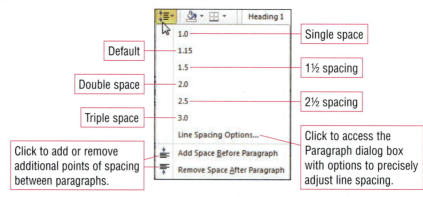

Table 3.3 Line Spacing Options at the Paragraph Dialog Box

Single	No extra space between lines.
1.5 Lines	An extra half-height blank line between each printed line of the paragraph.
Double	An extra blank line between each printed line of the paragraph.
At Least	A minimum line height that you specify in point value.
Exactly	A precise line height that you specify. If you specify a size that is smaller than the largest font size used in the paragraph, the large letter will be truncated on top.
Multiple	Enter **3** for triple spacing, **2** for double, **1** for single spacing. You can enter any value from 0 to 132, in decimal increments of 0.01. This is how the default 1.15 is created. For instance, to tighten the leading between lines typed with the default 1.15 line spacing, you can type 0.75 line spacing in the *Multiple* text box.

Setting Precise Line-Spacing

The Line Spacing drop-down list in the Paragraph dialog box offers the choices shown in Table 3.3 to adjust leading as shown in Figure 3.49.

In Word, you cannot specifically set leading. However, the *At Least* and *Exactly* settings are the closest thing to it. Both these settings express values that are in total line height, not blank space height. For instance, if you set the *Exactly* setting to 16 pt, when used on a paragraph that has 12-point text, this would result in a 4-points of leading between lines. If you used the same setting with a 20-point text, there would be no leading, and the tops of the larger letters would be cut off. You will need to experiment with using the *At Least* and *Exactly* settings. Any extra space that you add to a line of text is added below the text.

Figure 3.49 Line Spacing Drop-Down List

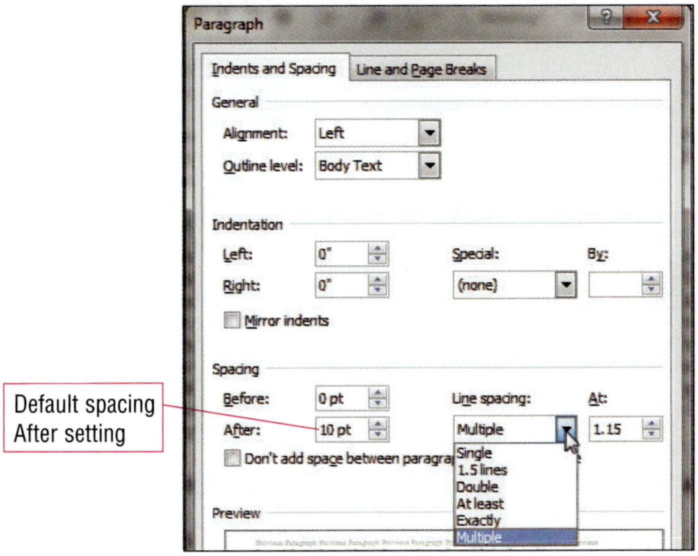

Setting Spacing Before or After a Paragraph

Line Spacing

The best way to add space before or after a paragraph is to choose Add Space Before Paragraph or Remove Space After Paragraph from the Line Spacing button menu on the Home tab. The Page Layout tab also has *Before* and *After* boxes that work the same as their counterparts in the Paragraph dialog box. Of course, you can add line spacing between paragraphs by pressing the Enter key, but each Enter is considered a paragraph in itself, which becomes inflexible when trying to apply styles to paragraphs of text. By adding line spacing before or after, you make the line spacing an integral part of the paragraph associated with the spacing.

Paragraph spacing may also be adjusted by clicking the Change Styles button in the Styles group in the Home tab. At the drop-down list, click the Paragraph Spacing option, and then select one of these options: *No Paragraph Space, Compact, Tight, Open, Relaxed, Double,* or *Custom Paragraph Spacing.*

DTP POINTERS

Press Shift + Enter (line break) to start a new line within the same paragraph. A line break forces the insertion point to the next line without 10 Points After.

In Exercise 3.5, you will create a press release, which is a written or recorded communication directed to the news media for the purpose of announcing something claimed as having news value. Typically, press releases are mailed, faxed, or emailed to newspapers, radio stations, and television stations; they may also be posted on the Internet. Press releases can announce a range of news items such as scheduled events, personal promotions, awards, news products and services, sales and other financial data, accomplishments, or new office or store openings.

You will incorporate the WordArt feature in the press release design in addition to using the Snipping Tool to create a graphic file from a grouped object.

Exercise 3.5 Creating a Press Release Document with WordArt

1. Open **C03-E02-EventLetterhead.docx**.
2. Save the grouped image in the letterhead as a graphic file in JPG format by completing the following steps:
   a. Click the Start button on the Taskbar, and then click the Snipping Tool at the Start Menu. ***Hint: If the Snipping Tool is not on the Start menu, click All Programs, Accessories, and then Snipping Tools.***
   b. Click the down-pointing arrow at the right of the New button at the Snipping Tools dialog box and make sure the *Rectangular Snip* option is selected. Click the New button.

Step 2b

   c. Drag the crosshairs around the grouped image in the letterhead.

Step 2c

   d. At the Snipping Tool dialog box, click File and then Save As.
   e. At the Save As dialog box, type **EventGraphic** in the *File name* text box.
   f. Click the down-pointing arrow at the right of the *Save as type* list box, and select *JPEG* file.

g. Save the graphic file to your *Chapter03* folder on your storage device.
h. Close the Snipping Tool dialog box.
i. Close **C03-E02A-EventLetterhead.docx**.
3. Open **PressRelease.docx** from your *Chapter03* folder.
4. Select the text in the upper left cell of the table at the top of the page, and then change the font to 7.5-point Century Gothic. Select *Contact: Margo Hamel* and apply bold.
5. Position the insertion point in the cell to the right of the contact information, and complete the following steps: *Hint: Display the table gridlines.*
   a. Click the WordArt button in the Text group in the Insert tab and select the *Fill - White, Drop Shadow* option in the first row and third column.

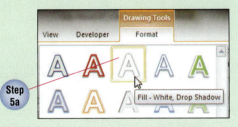

   b. Drag the *Your text here* text box to the center of the cell.
   c. Select *Your text here*, and then type **Worldwide Event Planning, Inc**.
   d. Change the font to 18-point Palatino Linotype, bold, italics.
   e. Select the text, and then at the Font dialog box, turn on *Kerning* at *12* points and select *Standard and Contextual* in the *Ligatures* section. Click OK.
   f. Select *Worldwide Event Planning, Inc.*, click the Text Effect button in the WordArt Styles group, and then click Transform.
   g. Click the *Chevron Down* option in the *Wrap* section.

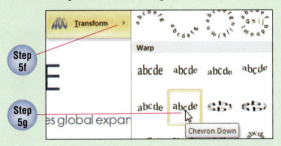

   h. Using the mouse, drag the corner sizing handles to increase the size of the WordArt object to fill the cell.

   i. Click the Shape Fill button in the Shape Styles group in the Drawing Tools Format tab, click the *Picture* option, and then insert the **EventGraphic.jpg** image located in your *Chapter03* folder on your storage device.
6. Press Ctrl + End to position the insertion point at the bottom of the table, and then press Enter.

7. Make sure the Office theme has been selected.
8. Type **PRESS RELEASE**, and then press Enter.
9. Select *Press Release*, change the font to 42-pt. Century Gothic in all caps and then change the font color by completing the following steps:
   a. With *Press Release* selected, click the down-pointing arrow at the right of the Font Color button in the Font group, and then click the *More Colors* option.
   b. Select the Custom tab.
   c. Select the *RGB* Color Model and then type **42** in the *Red* section, **90** in the *Green* section, and **120** in the *Blue* section. Click OK.

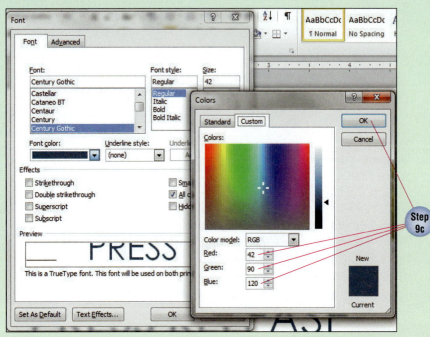

   d. Select *PRESS RELEASE* and then click the Font dialog box launcher, select the Advanced tab, change the *Character Spacing* to *Condensed* at *0.25 pt.* and turn on *Kerning* at *14* pts. Click OK.
10. Press the Down Arrow key once, type **Worldwide Event Planning, Inc. Announces Global Expansion**, and then press Shift + Enter.
11. Type **London will serve Eastern European region.** Press Enter twice.
12. Select *Worldwide Event Planning, Inc.* and change the font to 14-pt. Century Gothic, and apply the blue color in step 9c.
13. Select *London will serve Eastern European region,* and change the font to 11-pt. Century Gothic in the same blue color.
14. Press Ctrl + End.
15. Type the text shown in the Press Release in Figure 3.50 and then change the font to 9-pt. Century Gothic.
16. Insert the footer text in Figure 3.50 by completing the following steps:
    a. Click the Footer button in the Header & Footer group in the Insert tab.

b. Click the *Contrast (Even Page)* option in the *Build-In* section of the drop-down list.
c. With the insertion point positioned in the footer pane, change the font to 9-pt. Century Gothic, and then type **For Release 9 a.m. EST, July 23, 2012, USA - 14:00 p.m., U.K.**
d. Click the date picker in the left margin, and select July 23, 2012.
e. Click the Close Header and Footer button.

17. Save, print, and then close **C03-E05-PressRelease.docx**.

Figure 3.50 **Exercise 3.5**

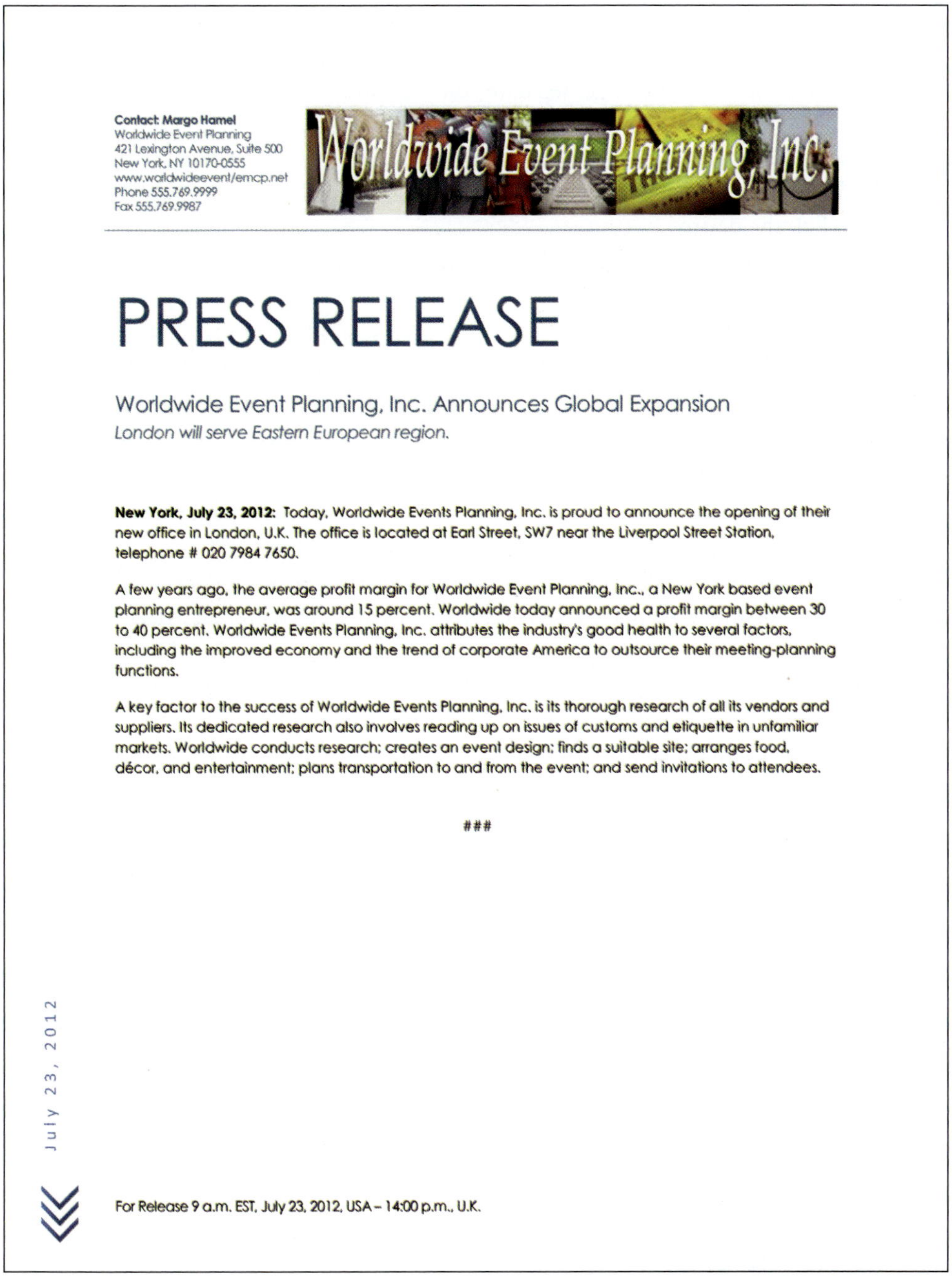

Contact: Margo Hamel
Worldwide Event Planning
421 Lexington Avenue, Suite 500
New York, NY 10170-0555
www.worldwideevent/emcp.net
Phone 555.769.9999
Fax 555.769.9987

Worldwide Event Planning, Inc.

PRESS RELEASE

Worldwide Event Planning, Inc. Announces Global Expansion
London will serve Eastern European region.

New York, July 23, 2012: Today, Worldwide Events Planning, Inc. is proud to announce the opening of their new office in London, U.K. The office is located at Earl Street, SW7 near the Liverpool Street Station, telephone # 020 7984 7650.

A few years ago, the average profit margin for Worldwide Event Planning, Inc., a New York based event planning entrepreneur, was around 15 percent. Worldwide today announced a profit margin between 30 to 40 percent. Worldwide Events Planning, Inc. attributes the industry's good health to several factors, including the improved economy and the trend of corporate America to outsource their meeting-planning functions.

A key factor to the success of Worldwide Events Planning, Inc. is its thorough research of all its vendors and suppliers. Its dedicated research also involves reading up on issues of customs and etiquette in unfamiliar markets. Worldwide conducts research; creates an event design; finds a suitable site; arranges food, décor, and entertainment; plans transportation to and from the event; and send invitations to attendees.

###

July 23, 2012

For Release 9 a.m. EST, July 23, 2012, USA – 14:00 p.m., U.K.

Chapter Summary

➤ A letterhead contains a design and layout that helps establish an identity for your organization with a target audience. Designing and producing your own letterhead can be a less costly alternative to having it designed and produced through a professional printer.

➤ A number of letter templates are available, including Contemporary, Elegant, Professional, Technology, Urban, Oriel, Level, Origin, Academic, and many more.

➤ A text box is used as a container for text and graphics. Text boxes are extremely useful in desktop publishing because text and graphics can be placed at exact horizontal and vertical locations on the page. They can also serve as placeholders for items such as illustrations and photos.

➤ Ruled lines act as boundaries to the surrounding text. Ruled lines can be used in a document to create a focal point, draw the eye across or down the page, separate columns and sections, or add visual appeal.

➤ Lines can be created using the Line button in the Shapes group in the Insert tab. To create a straight line, hold down the Shift key as you drag the crosshairs to draw the line. To create lines around a paragraph, click the down-pointing arrow at the right of the Border button in the Paragraph group in the Home tab, and then click the desired button.

➤ In typesetting, the thickness of a line, called its *weight*, is measured in points. Word defaults to a line thickness of 0.75 point.

➤ Use options in the Drawing Tools Format tab to customize shapes by applying a Shape Style; changing the Shape Fill and Outline Fill; adding a Shadow, Reflection, Glow, Soft Edges, Bevel, and 3-D Rotation; and arranging the shape by positioning, aligning, grouping, and rotating.

➤ By using Quick Styles and document Themes, you can quickly change the appearance of text, tables, and graphics throughout your document to match your preferred style or color scheme.

➤ You may position an object precisely on a page by using options on the Position tab at the Layout dialog box.

➤ An existing template document can be customized after it is displayed at the document screen. Any changes made affect only the document displayed on the screen, leaving the template available in its original format.

➤ All objects, including text boxes, are automatically anchored or attached to the paragraph closest to the object.

➤ Insert symbols by clicking the Symbol button in the Symbols group on the Insert tab.

➤ Objects can be grouped, ungrouped, and regrouped by selecting each object and then clicking the Group button in the Arrange group on the Page Layout tab.

➤ To view the vertical location of your insertion point, position your mouse pointer on the Status bar, right click, and then click the *Vertical Page Position* option at the Customize Status Bar pop-up menu.

➤ Nudging is moving an object in small increments using the arrow keys.

➤ A grid is a set of intersecting lines used to align objects.

➤ A pixel is a single unit of measurement that your monitor uses to paint images on your screen.

➤ Spacing adjustments can be made to text by adding points before or after at the *Spacing* section in the Paragraph group in the Page Layout tab.

➤ A new template can be created from any existing Word document. Saving documents, such as letterheads or envelopes, as template documents ensures that they are always available to use over again and thus increases efficiency and productivity.

➤ Kerning is the process of decreasing or increasing the white space between specific character pairs and is used on headlines and other blocks of large type.

- ➤ Adjust the leading (line spacing) by clicking the Paragraph dialog box launcher and adjusting the line spacing by typing a point increment.
- ➤ After you have selected your text box or object, you may click the Shape Fill button in the Shape Styles group in the Drawing Tools Format tab and then make choices to customize the fill of your text box.
- ➤ In traditional typesetting, equally reducing or increasing the horizontal space between all characters in a block of text is called *tracking*. Tracking affects all characters, while automatic kerning affects only specific character pairs. Tracking is the equal reduction or enlargement of the horizontal space between all characters in a block of text.
- ➤ With the WordArt feature, you can distort or modify text to conform to a variety of shapes. Use options in the WordArt Styles group on the Drawing Tools Format tab to customize your WordArt text. Themes also affect the colors, fonts, and text effects available to you when using the WordArt feature.
- ➤ When creating a design for an envelope, select enough common elements so that a link is established in the viewer's mind between the letterhead and the envelope.
- ➤ Press Shift + Enter (line break) to start a new line within the same paragraph. A line break forces the insertion point to the next line without 10 Points After.
- ➤ Use the Quick Parts (Building Blocks) feature to save and insert frequently used text and graphics.
- ➤ Business cards are another way to establish identity among a target audience. Establish an identifying connection between a business card and a letterhead by repeating some of the design elements from the letterhead.
- ➤ A press release is a written or recorded communication directed to the news media to announce something claimed as having news value. Create a press release to inform the public of scheduled events, personal promotions, awards, news products and services, sales and other financial data, accomplishments, or new office or store openings.

Commands Review

FEATURE	RIBBON TAB, GROUP	BUTTON	KEYBOARD SHORTCUT
Envelopes	Mailings, Create		
Group	Page Layout, Arrange	Group ▾	
Kerning	Home, Font, Advanced, Character Spacing		
Labels	Mailings, Create		
Line	Insert, Shapes, Line		
Line Spacing	Home, Paragraph		
Picture	Insert, Illustrations		
Position	Drawing Tools Format, Arrange		

FEATURE	RIBBON TAB, GROUP	BUTTON	KEYBOARD SHORTCUT
Quick Parts	Insert, Text		
Quick Styles	Home, Styles		Ctrl + Shift + S
Select	Home, Editing	Select ▾	
Selection Pane	Drawing Tools Format, Arrange	Selection Pane	
Shape Effects	Drawing Tools Format, Shape Styles	Shape Effects ▾	
Shape Fill	Drawing Tools Format, Shape Styles	Shape Fill ▾	
Shape Outline	Drawing Tools Format, Shape Styles	Shape Outline ▾	
Shapes	Insert, Illustrations		
Size	Drawing Tools Format		
Symbol	Insert, Symbols	Ω	
Templates	File tab, New	New	
Text Box	Insert, Text	A	
Text from File	Insert, Text, Object	Text from File...	
Tracking	Home, Font, Advanced, Character Spacing		
View Gridlines	Table Tools Layout, Table		
WordArt	Insert, Text	A	

Reviewing Key Points

Multiple Choice: Fill in the blanks with the correct term from the choices listed below each question.

_____ 1. The term that refers to the decreasing or increasing of white space between specific character pairs is _____.
a. tracking b. leading c. kerning
d. nudging

_____ 2. In typesetting, the thickness of a line is called its weight and is measured in _____.
a. points b. pixels c. dots per inch
d. inches

3. Press the _____ key while drawing a line with the Line Shape to create a straight line.
   a. Ctrl   b. Shift   c. Alt
   d. Spacebar

4. To transform the shape of WordArt text, click this button on the Drawing Tools Format tab.
   a. Text Outline   b. Text Effects   c. Transform
   d. Text Fill

5. Which feature is used to save and insert frequently used text and/or graphics?
   a. Click and Type   b. Smart Tags   c. Quick Parts
   d. Quick Styles

6. Which feature is used to distort or modify text to create a variety of shapes?
   a. Clip Art   b. Shapes   c. Picture
   d. WordArt

7. Which feature is used to position the insertion point in a blank area of the document or to change paragraph alignment for text to be typed?
   a. Click and Type   b. AutoText   c. Smart Tags
   d. AutoFormat

8. Equally reducing or increasing the horizontal space between all characters in a selected block of text is called _____.
   a. kerning   b. nudging   c. tracking
   d. aligning

9. You may position an object precisely on a page by using options in which dialog box?
   a. Layout   b. Drawing Tools Format   c. Paragraph
   d. Styles

10. To add a shadow effect to a text box, click the _____ button in the ShapeStyles group on the Drawing Tools Format tab.
    a. Shadow   b. Position   c. Shape Fill
    d. Shape Effects

Chapter Assessments

Assessment 3.1   Creating a Restaurant Letterhead

1. You have decided to open your own restaurant. Design a letterhead and envelope for your business that will be used for a mailing to introduce it to the community and for all of your future business correspondence. Include the following information:

Company Name: You decide on the name depending on the picture/graphic that you incorporate into your design.

Name of Owner: Use your own name and include *Owner* or *Proprietor* as your title.

Slogan: You choose a slogan.

Address: 250 San Miguel Boulevard
Mission Viejo, CA 92691
Phone: 714.555.8191   Fax: 714.555.8196
Website: www.ChiliVine@emcp.net

2. Create thumbnail sketches of your restaurant letterhead by incorporating the following elements:
   a. Create an asymmetrically balanced design.
   b. Use appropriate fonts, type sizes, and text effects.
   c. Turn on kerning, and use tracking (condensing or expanding character spacing), if necessary, for a desired effect.
   d. Incorporate some of these suggestions for graphics and layout:
      1) Include a clip art image; possible search keywords may include *food, southwest, coffee, dining,* or *restaurant.* Use the image to inspire a theme and a color scheme. (You may use any other relevant clip art that is available to you.)
      2) Create a restaurant logo using WordArt and/or Shapes.
      3) Include a ruled horizontal or vertical line.
      4) Include consistent elements such as typeface, color, alignment, repetitive symbol, graphic element, and so on.
      5) Group related items close to each other.
      6) Use color (sparingly) if a color printer is available.
      7) Make sure your letterhead is not too large.
      8) Use special characters, if appropriate.
3. Design an envelope to be used with your letterhead. Include some consistent elements that demonstrate continuity from the letterhead to the envelope.
4. Save the document and name it **C03-A01-RestaurantLtrhd.docx**.
5. Print **C03-A01-RestaurantLtrhd.docx. Optional:** Print a map of the restaurant location. Use Bing Maps as discussed in Chapter 1 or any other mapping website or software.
6. Save your letterhead as a document template in your DTP *Templates* folder on your desired storage device.
7. As a self-check for your design, print a copy of **DocumentAnalysisGuide.docx** located in your *Chapter03* folder, name it **C03-A01-DAGRestaurant.docx** (if typed), and then answer the questions on the form.
8. Attach the **DocumentAnalysisGuide.docx** to the hard copy of the letterhead.

Assessment 3.2   Creating Restaurant Business Cards

1. Create a page of business cards to coordinate with the restaurant letterhead and envelope created in Assessment 3.1. Even though a business card does not have to be an exact replica of your letterhead, include some consistent identifying elements that link the two documents together. Include the following specifications when creating the business cards:
   a. Create thumbnail sketches of your proposed business card design and layout.
   b. Use the Labels feature and the Avery 5371 (or 8371) business card label definition.
   c. Create a Quick Part entry that will work easily in the Envelopes and Labels feature. If you have difficulty using the Quick Part entry in the Envelopes and Labels feature, you may have to add a blank sheet of label forms to a clear document screen, create the business card in the first label form, and then copy it to the rest of the labels. You may have to reapply the theme you originally chose for the business card design.
2. Save and name the business cards as **C03-02-Restaurantbuscard**.
3. Print and then close **C03-A02-Restaurantbuscard.docx**.

Assessment 3.3   Creating a Menu

1. Create a menu for a restaurant of your own choosing.
2. Use a design that reinforces the type of restaurant you have chosen—Italian, Tapas, Sushi, Chinese, and so on.
3. Include a photograph or a clip art image. Enhance the image by using options on the Picture Tools Format tab. Use at least two enhancements—Artistic Effects, Corrections, Colors, or Picture Styles.

4. Use the Internet to research different menus for menu offerings, prices, and design ideas.
5. Use an Internet search engine to find a tip calculator and then print your findings, or go to the Microsoft Office Online Templates website and download the Excel Tip Calculator Template, and print the Excel worksheet.
6. Save your document as **C03-A03-Menu.docx** and then in PDF format. Send a copy of the menu as an email attachment to each of the members of your class. Print the document for your instructor. Figure 3.51 displays a sample menu; however, use your own designs for your menu.

Figure 3.51 Assessment 3.3 Sample Solution

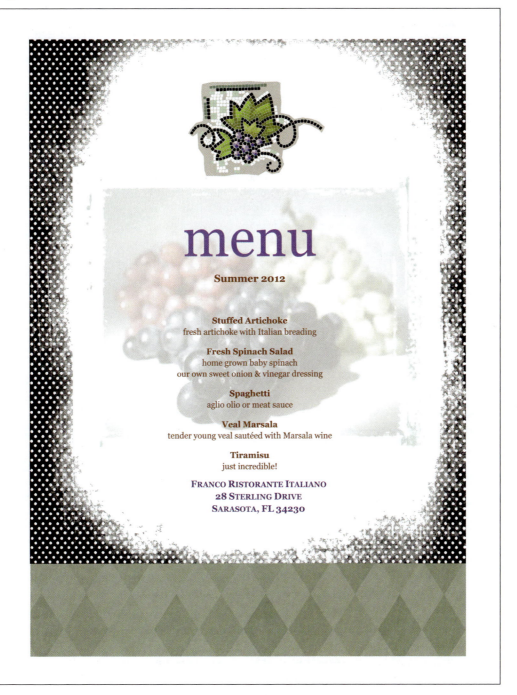

Assessment 3.4   Creating a Letterhead for a Foreign Hotel

1. As an employee of the Isar Hotel in Munich, Germany, create a letter welcoming guests to the hotel, and include the following specifications:
   a. Design a simple but appropriate letterhead design for the Isar Hotel Munich located at Wilenmayerstraße 10, 80335 München GERMANY, TEL +49 (0) 89 55544 0, FAX + A49 (0) 89 555544 1000, www.isarhotel@emcp.net. *Note: The umlaut symbol, above the "u," is located in Symbols on the Insert tab; the character code 00FC, and the ß symbol is character code 03B2.*
   b. Insert a graphic in the design of your letterhead.
   c. Use a text color that coordinates with the graphic and use at least two text effects.
   d. Insert **GermanLetter.docx**.
   e. Refer to a current reference guide for appropriate formatting for a block-style letter includes an international address.
   f. Using the Translation feature in Word, select *Welcome to the Isar Hotel Munich* located above the dateline and translate the text into German. Also select the Greeting and Complimentary Close text, and translate the phrases from English to German. *Hint: The translation may vary.*

Figure 3.52 Assessment 3.4 Sample Solution

2. Design an envelope to complement the letterhead.
3. Save the document, and name it **C03-A04-LtrGerman.docx**.
4. Print and then close the document and envelope. Figure 3.52 displays a sample solution.

Assessment 3.5 Group Project - Event Planning

As a group project, select tasks for each of the members of your group. The tasks may include researching a wedding reception and location, hotel, wedding ceremony; collaborating to create an overall design; and assigning job roles. You have several out-of-town guests attending your daughter's wedding. To welcome your guests to the hotel where you have reserved a block of rooms, you prepare gift bags containing water bottles, a small package of aspirin, energy bars, a wedding rehearsal dinner invitation, and a theme-related small gift. In addition, you include an itinerary for the weekend activities and a brief history or information sheet on the location of your daughter's wedding or on a place of interest in your city (see Figure 3.53).

Include the following information for the itinerary:

- Include a SmartArt graphic showing the progression of the day or use clip art depicting the church, synagogue, mosque, and so on., where the wedding will take place; the transportation (bus, limo, trolley, etc.); the reception hall; and the hotel for the final destination.
- Use two contrasting fonts or an appropriate font theme.
- Include appropriate times for these intended activities.
- Include names and addresses for each destination in case your guests want to drive on their own.
- Save the document as **C03-A05-WedItin.docx**.
- Print on colored paper for added interest.

Include the following for the information sheet:

- Research the Internet for information about the reception hall, historic church, public garden, river walk or nature trails, or any other significant place of interest. (Example: Research the West Baden Springs Hotel, "Eighth Wonder of the World," in French Lick, Indiana, or the Seven Sacred Pools in Hana on the island of Maui in Hawaii for a destination wedding.)
- Include a sidebar or pull quote from the new Word feature Quick Parts.
- Format the text in two contrasting fonts, or use an appropriate font theme.
- Include at least one photograph of the featured area.
- Print on colored paper or include color in the formatting of your document.
- Print and save the document as **C03-A05-WedInfo.docx**.
- *Optional:* Roll the information sheet, tie a ribbon around it, and include it in each guest bag.

Figure 3.53 Assessment 3.5 Sample Solutions

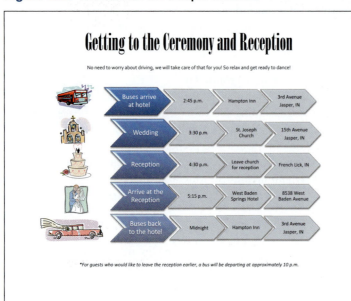

Getting to the Ceremony and Reception

No need to worry about driving, we will take care of that for you! So relax and get ready to dance!

Buses arrive at hotel	2:45 p.m.	Hampton Inn	3rd Avenue Jasper, IN
Wedding	3:30 p.m.	St. Joseph Church	15th Avenue Jasper, IN
Reception	4:30 p.m.	Leave church for reception	French Lick, IN
Arrive at the Reception	5:15 p.m.	West Baden Springs Hotel	8538 West Baden Avenue
Buses back to the hotel	Midnight	Hampton Inn	3rd Avenue Jasper, IN

*For guests who would like to leave the reception earlier, a bus will be departing at approximately 10 p.m.

WELCOME TO OUR WEDDING WEEKEND IN SOUTHERN INDIANA...

Over the next few days, good friends and family will converge here as we commit our lives to each other and we could not be more excited to share this occasion with you. To make your trip a little more enjoyable, we have gathered some history and interesting facts about the places you will visit.

★★★★★★★★★★ Jasper, Indiana

In 2005, Jasper was ranked in the top ten best places to live in the United States, by Relocate America, and previously ranked in the top 25 in Norman Crampton's 1992 book, "100 Best Small Towns in America."

★★★★★★★★★★

Tucked in the rolling hills of south central Indiana, Jasper has a charming historic small town feel. The Dubois County Seat was populated primarily by German Catholic immigrants throughout the 1800s. Today, many of the street names reflect the German heritage. Also, from the highway, the first restaurant into Jasper is the iconic Schnitzelbank.

Jasper is located near the enormous 200,000 acre Hoosier National Forest, Patoka Lake, Ohio River, and the historic town of French Lick. Jasper is also known by many as the "Wood Office Furniture Capital of the World." In 2005, Jasper was ranked in the top ten best places to live in the United States, by Relocate America, and previously ranked in the top 25 in Norman Crampton's 1992 book, *100 Best Small Towns in America."*

West Baden Springs Hotel

Discovered in 1778 the area was richly blessed with mineral springs and salt licks that held supposed curative powers. As news of the discovery spread, Dr. William Bowles established a health resort, the French Lick Springs, to accommodate the influx of cure seekers. By 1855, the new West Baden Hotel opened for business. The hotel was named for the famous spa in Wiesbaden, Germany.

In 1888, Less Sinclair bought the hotel and promptly renamed it the West Baden Springs Hotel. Sinclair added a double-decker bicycle and pony-cart track, opera

St. Joseph Catholic Church

Built over thirteen years, the massive St. Joseph Church at 125 years old is Jasper's largest tourist draw, and it is on the National Register of Historic Places.

Completed in 1880, the church was built with remarkable craftsmanship and creativity. The church pillars are actual 67 feet poplar trees that were covered by stone. The focal point of the church is the three Austrian mosaics. Each side contains more than 10 million pieces; while the center mosaic contains over 25 million stones.

The most obvious feature of the church is its picturesque bell tower, which is visible from most places in town. The tower stands 235 feet high with four 1,700 pound bells perched inside.

house, baseball diamond, and casino slowly turned the West Baden Springs into a world class resort and spa boasting 500 rooms. However, a raging fire broke out on June 14, 1901 and consumed the wooden structure in 90 minutes.

Sinclair, inspired by a visit to St. Peter's Cathedral in Rome, was determined to build a great fireproof palace to be one of the most imposing structures in the world. On October 15, 1901 the entire hotel was built in an astounding 277 days. The 200 feet center atrium was the largest self-supported dome in the world until the 1960's completion of the Houston Astrodome.

Crowned as the "Eighth Wonder of the World," the hotel offered amenities for spring training for many professional baseball teams. Visitors to West Baden Springs were enticed by claims that the resort's mineral baths and drinking waters could cure more than 50 illnesses. The hotel rapidly gained popularly amongst celebrities and heads of state.

When the stock market crashed in 1929, the hotel emptied almost overnight. For several years, Sinclair worked to keep the hotel afloat; however, he finally closed the hotel in June 1932 and in 1934 sold it to the Jesuits for one dollar. The Jesuits maintained the property until 1966 and then a small private college occupied the building until 1983.

In 1996 a subsidiary of the historic Landmarks Foundation bought the West Baden property for $250,000. Immediately following the sale, philanthropists Bill and Gayle Cook of the Cook Group began partial restoration totaling $35 million. The French Lick Resort and Casino opened in November 2006 and the West Baden Springs Hotel opened in July 2007.

Thanks...

Finally, a special note of thanks to our great parents for a lifetime of love and support.

Welcome to our celebration.

Sarah & Charly

Chapter 4

CHAPTER04

Creating Personal Documents

Performance Objectives

Upon successful completion of Chapter 4, you will be able to:

- Group objects.
- Customize labels.
- Crop pictures.
- Save text as Quick Parts.

- Access the Developer tab.
- Insert a date picker content control.
- Protect documents.
- Create documents on odd-sized paper.

Desktop Publishing Terms

Bleed	Form	Placeholder
Content controls	Form field	Stacking
Crop	Grouping	Unprintable zone

Word Features Used

Bring to Front	Group and Ungroup	Shape Fill
Calendar Wizard	Object Orientation	Shape Outline
Clip Art	Office.com Templates	Shapes
Clipboard	Page Borders	Tables
Content controls	Picture	Tabs
Date Picker	Protect Documents	Templates
Design mode	Quick Parts	Text Box Styles
Developer tab	Quick Styles	Text fields
Drawing canvas	Rotate	Text Wrapping
Drawing grid	Scribble	Themes
Envelopes and Labels	Send to Back	Watermark
Form fields	Shadow Effects	WordArt

In this chapter, you will produce create, and format, personal documents using Word templates and wizards. You will use other Word features such as tables, text boxes, and labels to produce compact disc covers, calendars, address labels, certificates, change of address postcards, and hanging name tags. In addition, you will apply basic desktop publishing concepts of planning document content, maintaining consistency, and achieving balance through pictures, symbols, text, lines, color, and borders.

While you are creating the documents in this chapter, consider how you can apply what you have learned to create other personal documents such as invitations, greeting cards, tickets, bookmarks, recipe cards, bookplates, change-of-address cards, thank-you cards, personal note cards, and even birth announcements. Several sample personal documents are shown Figure 4.1.

Figure 4.1 Sample Personal Documents

CD Face Label

CD Case Cover

Graduation Invitation

Nutrition Log

Personalized Calendar

Place Cards

Bookplates

Invitation

Change-of-Address Card

Gift Tags

Recipe Card

Personal Note Cards

Creating a Compact Disc Label

Standard disk labels and compact disc labels are used to catalog the contents of a disk/disc. If you were to purchase a new computer today, you may have the option to purchase a CD-ROM, CD-R, CD-RW, DVD-ROM, DVD-R, DVD-RW, and flash drive.

Most of these storage devices are associated with a particular label and/or additional elements to identify the contents. Word 2010 offers more label vendors and product numbers than previously available. Some of the new vendors include Microsoft, Compulabel, Ace Label, A-ONE, Formtec, and Office Depot. A list of vendors is available by clicking the down-pointing arrow at the right of the *Label vendors* option at the Label Options dialog box in the *Label information* section.

The CD-ROM and rewritable CD-RW discs measure approximately 4¾ inches in diameter and may be identified using a label on the disc cover (sometimes called a *jewel case*). Word includes Avery label definition (#8955) for a CD front and back label measuring 4¾ by 4¾ inches. However, this label does not include a spine, which identifies the disc when stored on edge. Avery US Letter – CD/DVD Labeling System - Slim Line Jewel Case is identified as product number 8965, measures 4.63 inches by 4.73 inches, and is suggested for storing single CDs in a slim clear plastic case.

In Exercise 4.1, you will use a commonly used Avery label. Assume you recently purchased a computer with a CD-RW disk drive and as a student in a desktop publishing class, you will prepare a jewel case cover for a CD that will contain your completed documents. Figure 4.2 illustrates several CD case templates from the Office. com Templates Web page. As you look over these examples, think of how you would customize any one of them to fit your personal needs.

Figure 4.2 Examples of CD/DVD Case Labels

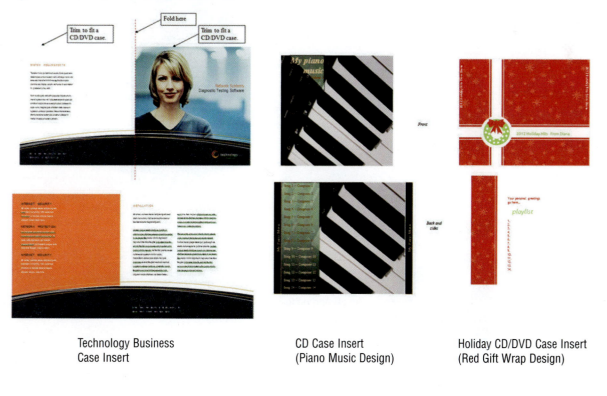

Technology Business
Case Insert

CD Case Insert
(Piano Music Design)

Holiday CD/DVD Case Insert
(Red Gift Wrap Design)

Working with Placeholders in Labels Templates

A *placeholder* is a reserved area on a page where an object, image, or text is entered later. Templates contain various placeholders (also called *boilerplates*) in the form of text boxes containing formatted sample text or pictures; drawing objects in specific sizes, shapes, and colors; and sample images. The placeholder text or objects may be replaced and customized with text, objects, pictures, and formatting that you choose to use. Generally, you do not delete the selected text, but instead replace it with your text, keeping the formatting in place. The placeholder objects save a great deal of time because they are already sized and formatted to fit properly in the template. Many times, the placeholder text will give you tips on how to use the template.

At times you may need to resize and *crop* an image. Cropping involves trimming horizontal or vertical edges. Images may have to be resized or cropped in order to fit a placeholder, especially if the desired image originated in a shape other than the placeholder shape. For instance, the image may be rectangular and the placeholder may be square as in Figure 4.3, in which case you may resize the image by dragging a corner sizing handle to fit the parameter of the placeholder. The image may extend into other areas; however, after cropping, resizing, and moving the image, it should fit properly.

Figure 4.3 **Resizing and Then Cropping an Image**

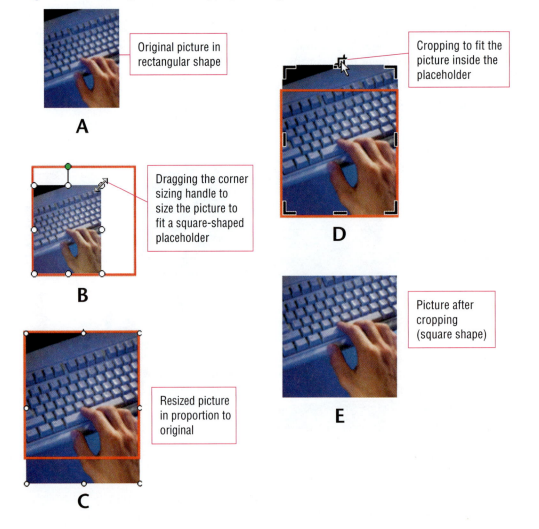

Original picture in rectangular shape

A

Cropping to fit the picture inside the placeholder

D

Dragging the corner sizing handle to size the picture to fit a square-shaped placeholder

B

Picture after cropping (square shape)

E

Resized picture in proportion to original

C

Figure 4.4 Using Enhanced Cropping Options

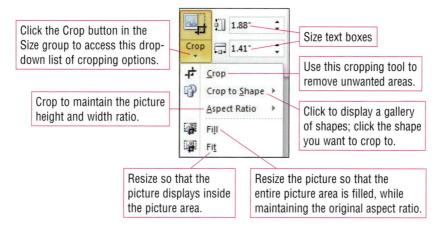

Click the Crop button in the Size group to access this drop-down list of cropping options.

Size text boxes

Use this cropping tool to remove unwanted areas.

Crop to maintain the picture height and width ratio.

Click to display a gallery of shapes; click the shape you want to crop to.

Resize so that the picture displays inside the picture area.

Resize the picture so that the entire picture area is filled, while maintaining the original aspect ratio.

Cropping a Picture

Cropping is often used to hide or trim a part of a picture, either for emphasis or to remove unwanted portions.

The cropping feature has been enhanced so that you can now easily crop to a specific shape, crop to fit or fill a shape, or crop to a common picture aspect ratio. To access the cropping tools displayed in Figure 4.4, select the picture, click the Cropping button in the Size group on the Picture Tools Format tab, and then click the selected option.

Crop

Cropping suggestions:

- To crop one side, drag the center cropping handle on that side inward.
- To crop equally on two sides at the same time, press and hold CTRL while you drag the center cropping handle on either side inward.
- To crop equally on all four sides at the same time, press and hold CTRL while you drag a corner cropping handle inward.
- To crop the picture to exact dimensions, right-click the picture, and then on the shortcut menu, click *Format Picture*. On the Crop pane, under Picture position, enter the numbers that you want in the *Width* and *Height* boxes.
- To outcrop or add a margin around a picture, drag the cropping handles away from the center of the picture.

Figure 4.5 illustrates the use of the new cropping options. Experiment with these tools to learn how they can be used to emphasize certain parts of your image.

Deleting Cropped Areas of a Picture

Even after you crop parts of a picture, the cropped parts remain as part of the picture file. You can reduce the file size by removing croppings from the picture file. It is also a good idea to do this to help prevent other people from viewing the parts of the picture that you have removed. ***Hint: This cannot be undone. Therefore, you should only do this after you are sure that you have made all the crops and changes that you want.***

Compress Pictures

Compress Picture

To delete cropped areas from a picture, do the following:

1. Click the picture or pictures that you want to discard unwanted information from.
2. Click the Compress Pictures button in the Adjust group on the Picture Tools Format tab.
3. Select the *Delete cropped areas of pictures* check box in the *Compression Options* section as shown in Figure 4.6.

Figure 4.5 Applying Cropping Options to a Picture

Cropping and Applying the Reflected Perspective Right Picture

Cropping to Fit a Shape

Cropping using Aspect Ratio in Portrait at 2:3

Cropping Using Fit - to resize so that the entire picture displays inside the picture area while maintaining the original aspect ratio.

4. Click OK to close the dialog box.

*Hint: Before completing computer exercises, copy the folder from the CD that accompanies this textbook to the **Chapter04** folder on your storage medium and then make **Chapter04** the active folder. Remember to substitute graphics that may no longer be available.*

In Exercise 4.1, you will create a universal Avery brand CD label that may be used for a CD/DVD Jewel case or for a Trim Line CD/DVD case. The label is formatted in a table with the first cell used for the cover, the second cell for the spine (if one is used), and the third cell for the back side of the cover. You may separate the different parts by using the perforations (if available) or by trimming along the borders of the cells. A spine was not specifically defined in this label definition—typing in the area between the cover and back cells is a way to improvise the spine.

Figure 4.6 Compressing a Picture

Compress Pictures

Compression options:
- ☑ Apply only to this picture
- ☑ Delete cropped areas of pictures

Target output:
- ○ Print (220 ppi): excellent quality on most printers and screens
- ○ Screen (150 ppi): good for Web pages and projectors
- ○ E-mail (96 ppi): minimize document size for sharing
- ● Use document resolution

OK   Cancel

Exercise 4.1 Creating CD/DVD Labels

1. Create the CD/DVD case label in Figure 4.7 by completing the following steps:
   a. At a blank document, click the Labels button in the Create group in the Mailings tab.
   b. Select the Labels tab and then click the Options button.
   c. At the Label Options dialog box, select *Avery US Letter* by clicking the down-pointing arrow at the right of the *Label vendors* list box in the *Label Information* section.

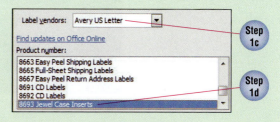

   d. At the *Product number* list box, select *8693 Jewel Case Inserts*, and then click OK.
   e. Click the New Document button at the Envelopes and Labels dialog box.
2. Add a picture to the label by completing the following steps:
   a. Position the insertion point inside the first label (cell of a table).
   b. Click the Cell Margins button in the Alignment group in the Table Tools Layout tab, and change the cell margins to 0 inch. Click OK.
   c. Click the Clip Art button in the Illustrations group in the Insert tab.
   d. Type **computer (or woman)** in the *Search for* text box at the Insert Clip Art task pane.

   e. Click to insert the computer image as shown in Figure 4.7 or select a similar image if this image is not available.
   f. Close the Clip Art task pane.
3. Notice that the image does not fill the label (cell). Crop the image to fit the cell properly by completing the following steps:
   a. Drag the bottom left corner sizing handle outward to the bottom dashed border of the cell.
   b. When you release the mouse, the image will shift to the right and only part of the woman will display. With the image selected,

   click the down-pointing arrow at the bottom of the Crop button in the Size group on the Picture Tools Format tab.
   c. At the Crop drop-down list, click the *Aspect Ratio* option and then click *1:1* in the *Square* section.

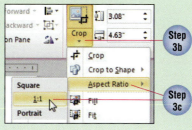

Step
3d

d. With the picture selected (gray areas should display to the left and right of the image), click the Compress Pictures button in the Adjust group.

e. At the Compress Pictures dialog box, make sure a check mark displays next to the Apply only to this picture option and next to the *Delete cropped areas of the pictures* option. Click OK.

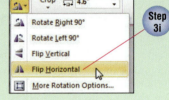

Step
3e

f. Select the image, click the Wrap Text button in the Arrange group and then click Square.

g. Select the image and then click the Copy button.

h. Position the insertion point inside the bottom label (cell) and then click Paste.

i. With the image in the bottom cell selected, click the Rotate button on the Picture Tools Format tab, and then click the *Flip Horizontal* option.

Step
3i

4. Add the text to the labels by completing the following steps:

a. Click to select the image in the cell, and then change the theme to the Verve and the font theme to Flow.

b. Draw a text box measuring 3.75" height and 2.5" width in the first cell.

Step
4e

c. Remove the shape fill and the shape outline.

d. Position the text box as shown in Figure 4.7.

e. Position the insertion point inside the text box and type the following: ***Hint: Make sure the Verve theme is selected and remove the 10 points After option.***

   OFTI 1218 (or your course name and #) (Press Enter at the end of each line unless directed otherwise.)
   Advanced Word 2010 DTP
   Data Files & Exercises
   Fall 2012 (Press Enter twice.)
   Your name (Type your name.)
   Your email address (Type your email address and then press Enter twice.)
   Your college name
   College address
   City, State and ZIP

f. Selec*t OFTI 1218* and apply the Title style from the Quick Styles gallery.

g. Select *Advanced Word 2010. . . Fall 2012* and apply the Intense Emphasis style from the Quick Styles gallery.

h. Select *Your Name, Your college. . . City, State and Zip*, and apply the Subtle Emphasis style from the Quick Styles gallery.

5. Format the back of the CD case label by completing the following steps. ***Hint: The back text is actually typed on a separate label, but it could be printed on the back of the cover label if desired.***

a. Create another text box, as completed earlier in Step 4, in the bottom cell and position this text box as shown in Figure 4.7.

b. Type the following inside the text box: ***Hint: Make sure you have removed the 10 points After option.***

> **Documents created:** (Press Enter and then change the font size to 9 points.)
> **Signs** (Press Enter after each of the following entries.)
> **Report covers**
> **Procedures manuals**
> **Fax covers**
> **Agendas**
> **Letterheads & envelopes**
> **Business cards**
> **CD case covers**
> **Calendars**
> **Merged postcards**
> **Certificates**
> **Flyers & announcements**
> **Brochures & booklets**
> **Cards**
> **Forms**
> **PowerPoint presentations**
> **Newsletters**

c. Select *Documents created:*, apply the Subtitle style from the Styles drop-down gallery, and then change the alignment to Align Text Right.

d. Select the text from *Signs. . . Newsletters*, and change the alignment to Align Text Right.

e. Position the insertion point inside the cell separating the top and bottom cells, change the alignment to Center, and then type **OFTI 1218: Advanced Word 2010 DTP** (or the name and number of your own course) as shown in Figure 4.7. This row may be cut and used in the spine of the CD/DVD jewel case.

f. Select the cell, and add a black fill by clicking the Shading button in the Table Styles group in the Table Tools Design tab and then clicking the *Black* color in the *Theme Colors* section. ***Hint: The text color will automatically convert to white.***

g. Select the reversed text, click the Paragraph dialog box launcher In the Paragraph group in the Home tab, and then type **3** pt in the *Before* text box in the *Spacing* section. Click OK.

6. Save the document as **C04-E01-CDCaseLabel.docx**.

7. Print and then close **C04-E01-CDCaseLabel.docx**. ***Hint: Print the cover and back text on a sheet of Avery labels, product number 8693 or on 50# paper.***

Figure 4.7 Exercise 4.1

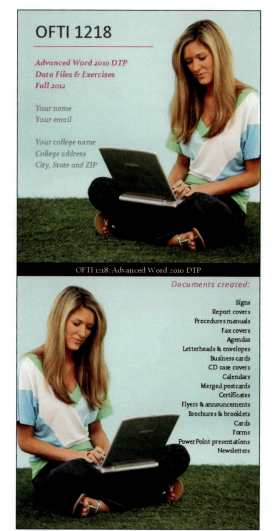

Creating a CD Face Label Using a CD Face Label Template

In Exercise 4.2, you will create a CD face label from a Microsoft Office Online CD label template. Buying the right CD for your specific needs can be complicated. You may be asking yourself if you should buy a CD, CD-RW, CD-R, or DVD. A rewritable compact disc (CD-RW) is capable of storing data. The RW stands for ReWritable, so data can be saved and resaved on this disc. You must have a CD burner (informal name for a CD Rewriter) on your computer to use this kind of disc. CD-R is an abbreviation for compact disc, recordable and it allows one-time recording of sound files. It is not possible to delete files and then reuse the space.

Word includes several CD face label templates in the Labels category at the New tab Backstage view. Samples of CD label templates from the *Office.com Templates* section are shown in Figure 4.8. If you have purchased labels, make sure that you select a label to match the product number (if generic, match the disc label sizes) to the template you are using. Print a hard copy of your disk label before printing on an actual sticky-backed label, and hold the sample to your disk to evaluate the fit. When

Figure 4.8 Sample CD Label Templates

Holiday CD/DVD Label
(works with Avery 5692, 5931, 8692, 8694, and 8965)

Data Backup CD Face Labels

you use the templates, you will be able to format vivid color pictures and text that print to the edge. In both traditional publishing and desktop publishing, printing to an edge is known as a ***bleed***. A bleed may also extend beyond the trim edge, leave no margin, and it may affect one or more sides. Generally, you need a printer that will allow you to print to the edge of the paper. However, you may simulate a bleed by selecting a paper size larger than your document.

Bleed

When an element on a page prints to the edge of the page, extends beyond the trim edge, and leaves no margin.

Exercise 4.2 Customizing a CD Face Label from a Template

Portfolio

1. At a blank document, create a CD Face label by completing the following steps:
   a. Click the File tab and then click the New tab.
   b. At the New tab Backstage view, click the *Labels* category in the *Office.com Templates* section.
   c. Click the Media labels category, click the *CD or DVD labels (works with Avery label 5824)* template, and then click Download.
   d. Click the File tab, and then click the Convert button in the *Compatibility Mode* section of the Info tab Backstage view.
   e. Click OK at the prompt to convert to the newest format.
2. Use the Clip Art task pane search feature to find a travel photo that could be used on the label by completing the following steps:
   a. At the Insert tab, click the Clip Art button in the Illustrations group.
   b. At the Clip Art task pane, type **Africa** in the *Search for* text box, and then click Go or press Enter.

Office.com Templates

Step 1c

CD or DVD labels (works with Avery labels 5824)

Holiday music CD face labels (works with Avery 5931, 8692, 8694, and 8931)

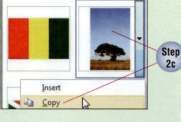

c. Right-click the photo, click Copy, and the close the ClipArt task pane. ***Hint: You are copying the desired photo to the Office Clipboard for use later.***

d. Click the outside rim of the CD label to access the Drawing Tools Format tab.

e. Click the Shape Fill button in the Shape Styles group.

f. At the Shape Fill drop-down menu, click Picture.

g. At the Insert Picture dialog box, right-click in any white area in the file list section of the dialog box, and then click *Paste*. With the photo selected, click Insert.

3. Format the text on the label as shown in Figure 4.9A by completing the following steps:

a. Select the placeholder text, *CD Title, Date*, and type **Photos of our safari at Kruger National Park, South Africa Fall 2012**. ***Hint: Increase the size of the text box if necessary.***

b. Select the text change the font color to White, and turn off bold.

c. Remove the Shape Fill and Shape Outline.

d. Position the insertion point after *This CD Contains:*. Change the font size to 9-point Tahoma, and then type **Lion Sands River Lodge, Sabi Sands Reserve, African cultural village excursion, helicopter trip, hot air trip, animals**. ***Hint: Increase the size of the text box if necessary.***

e. Select the text in step 3d, and change the font color to White.

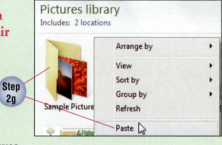

4. Format the blank CD label below the label created in this exercise with text and an image of your choosing. The sample CD shown in Figure 4.9B was created for exercising.

5. Save, print, and then close **C04-E02-CDLabels.docx**. ***Hint: Print on plain paper, on Avery 5824 labels, or a similar-sized label.***

Figure 4.9 Exercise 4.2

Figure 4.10 Sample Calendar Templates from Microsoft Office Online

Excel Calendar Template

Publisher Calendar Template

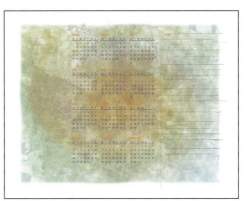

Word Calendar Template

PowerPoint Calendar Template

Creating a Personal Calendar

A calendar can be one of the most basic tools of organization in your everyday life. No desk at home or at work is complete without a calendar to schedule appointments, plan activities, and serve as a reminder of important dates and events.

A calendar may also be used as a marketing tool in promoting a service, product, or program. For example, a schedule of upcoming events may be typed on a calendar to serve as a reminder to all of the volunteers working for a charitable organization, or the calendar may be sent to prospective donors to serve as a daily reminder of the organization.

In Exercise 4.3, you will create your own calendar design using photos, borders, text boxes, and a 2012 calendar template for the date formatting. As you look at Figure 4.16 later in this chapter, notice the use of the photo as a watermark and again as a focal point in the design. When you are thinking about different ways to customize your calendar, you may want to view the numerous predesigned templates available in Office 2010. In addition to Word, you will notice that PowerPoint, Publisher, and Excel include professionally prepared calendar designs, as shown in Figure 4.10.

Figure 4.11 Calendar Wizard Template Types

Boxes & Borders

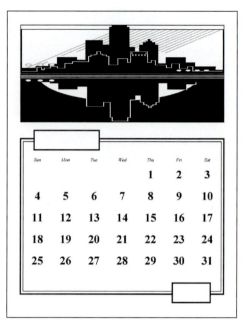

Banners

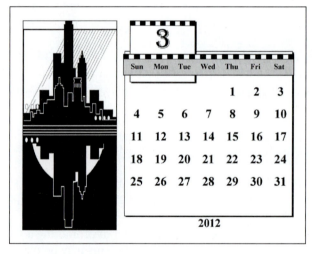

Jazzy

Using a Calendar Wizard

The Calendar Wizard helps you create monthly calendars. Three styles of calendars are available: Boxes & Borders, Banners, and Jazzy (as shown in Figure 4.11). The Calendar Wizard provides options to change the orientation, add a picture, and choose starting and ending months.

To access the Calendar Wizard, click the File tab and then the New tab. At the New tab Backstage view, click the Calendar category, the Other calendars category, and then the Calendar wizard category. Click the Download button to insert the calendar into Word. Follow the prompts within the wizard to customize your calendar.

Figure 4.12 Calendar Building Blocks

Building Blocks Organizer

Building blocks:

Name	Gallery	Category	Template
Dots	Page Num...	Plain Number	Built-In Buil...
Circle	Page Num...	With Shapes	Built-In Buil...
Brackets 2	Page Num...	Plain Number	Built-In Buil...
Brackets 1	Page Num...	Plain Number	Built-In Buil...
Bold Numb...	Page Num...	Page X of Y	Built-In Buil...
Bold Numb...	Page Num...	Page X of Y	Built-In Buil...
Bold Numb...	Page Num...	Page X of Y	Built-In Buil...
Accent Bar 2	Page Num...	Page X	Built-In Buil...
Accent Bar 1	Page Num...	Page X	Built-In Buil...
LoavesFront	Quick Parts	General	Building Blo...
LoavesBC	Quick Parts	General	Building Blo...
Worldwide	Quick Parts	General	Building Blo...
Ride Safe P...	Quick Parts	General	Building Blo...
LoavesBack	Quick Parts	General	Building Blo...
Jump line	Quick Parts	General	Building Blo...
Manual Table	Table of C...	Built-In	Built-In Buil...
Automatic ...	Table of C...	Built-In	Built-In Buil...
Automatic ...	Table of C...	Built-In	Built-In Buil...
Calendar 4	Tables	Built-In	Built-In Buil...
Calendar 3	Tables	Built-In	Built-In Buil...
Calendar 2	Tables	Built-In	Built-In Buil...

Click a building block to see its preview

Calendar 4
Vertical calendar with large month name and dark background

Edit Properties...   Delete   Insert

Close

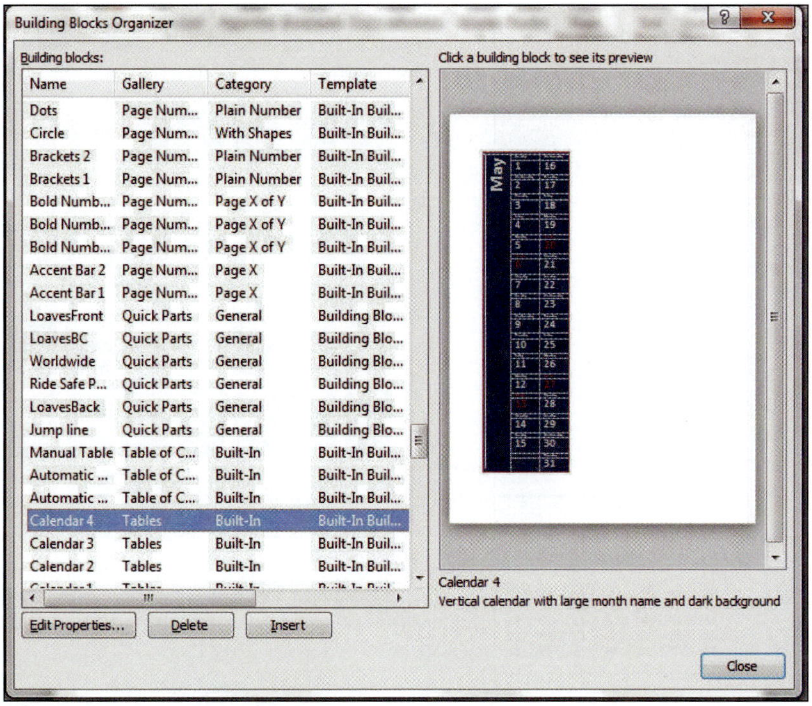

Inserting Calendar Quick Parts

Quick Parts (Building Blocks) are reusable pieces of content or other document parts that are stored in galleries. You can access and reuse these building blocks at any time. You can also save Quick Parts and distribute them with templates. Calendar 4, as shown in Figure 4.12, is an example of a calendar building block (Quick Parts). This calendar is formatted in a table and may be customized using options in the Table Tools Design tab and the Table Tools Layout tab. In addition, you may insert predesigned calendars by clicking the Table button in the Illustrations group on the Insert tab as shown in Figure 4.13. Consider inserting calendar building blocks into a newsletter, travel itinerary, flyer, pamphlet, or many other business or personal documents.

Adding, Removing, or Replacing a Picture in a Calendar

Many calendar templates include a picture placeholder. You may decide to delete the picture placeholder, or you may replace the image by either clicking the Picture button or the Clip Art button in the Illustrations group in the Insert tab. (A photo would look great!)

If you want to add a watermark, complete steps similar to above; click the Color button in the Adjust group on the Picture Tools Format tab: click *Washout* in the *Recolor* section; click the Wrap Text button in the Arrange group; and click Behind Text or insert the recolored image into a header or footer. Alternatively, you may add a watermark by clicking the Watermark button in the Page Background group in the Page Layout tab.

The Color feature in Word 2010 offers you many opportunities for design creativity. You can adjust the color intensity (saturation) and color tone (temperature) of a picture, recolor it, or change the transparency of one of its colors. You can also apply multiple color effects to your picture. In the following exercise, you will use the

Table

Quick Parts

Watermark

◀ **DTP POINTERS**
When adjusting the Temperature, the higher the temperature number, the more orange added to your picture. The lower the number, the more blue added to your picture.

Figure 4.13 **Quick Tables**

1. Click the Table button in the Table group in the Insert tab.

2. Click Quick Tables.

3. Select a predesigned calendar from the Built-In Calendar gallery.

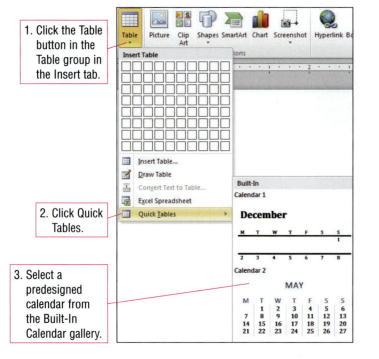

Figure 4.14 **Washout Option in the Color Gallery**

Recolor gallery to apply a *Washout* effect to the image used in the calendar. Figure 4.14 illustrates the *Washout* option in *Recolor* section of the Color gallery.

The following are some helpful tips for working with the *Recolor* options:

1. You can move your mouse pointer over any of the effects, and use Live Preview to see what your picture will look like with that effect applied before you click the one that you want.

2. To use additional colors including variations of colors on the Standard tab, or custom colors, click More Variations. The *Recolor* effect will be applied using the color variation.

3. To remove a *Recolor* effect but keep any other changes you have made to the picture, click the first effect, *No Recolor*.

Adding a Shape to a Calendar

If you want to draw attention to your calendar, use a predesigned shape as an attention-getter, which may include text, color, and other special effects. One of the star shapes (Explosion 1) is used in Exercise 4.3 to emphasize the name of the company that issued the calendar. Text will be added to the shape by selecting the star shape, right-clicking the mouse, and then clicking the *Add Text* option, as shown in Figure 4.15.

In Exercise 4.3, assume that a friend of yours owns a small real estate office in your hometown and you occasionally volunteer your time to help with desktop publishing projects. Create a calendar that will be given to the real estate agents.

Figure 4.15 **Adding Text to a Shape**

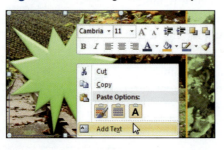

Exercise 4.3 Creating a Calendar

1. At a blank document create a calendar.
2. Display the Insert tab, click the Clip Art button, insert the image shown in Figure 4.16 by searching for **autumn vineyards** in the *Search for* text box and then insert the image or a similar one if desired.
3. Click the Size dialog box launcher in the Size group in the Picture Tools Format tab.
4. At the Size tab of the Layout dialog box, remove the check mark at the left of the *Lock aspect ratio* option and then type **9.25"** in the *Absolute* text box in the *Height* section and **7"** in the *Absolute* text box in the *Width* section. Click OK.

5. With the image selected, customize the image by completing the following steps:
   a. Click the Color button in the Adjust group, and then click the *Olive Green, Accent color 3 Dark* effect in the *Recolor* section.
   b. Click the Color button again, and then click the *Temperature: 7200 K* effect in the *Color Tone* section.

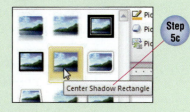

   c. Click the Picture Style More button to display the Picture Style drop-down gallery, and then click the *Center Shadow Rectangle* style in the second row.
   d. With the image selected, click the Position button in the Arrange group, and then click the *Position in Middle Center with Square Text Wrapping* option.

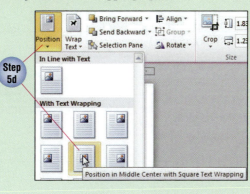

e. Deselect the image, and then insert the same image again. The image will display below the watermark image. Select the second image, click the Wrap Text button in the Arrange group and then click the *In Front of Text* option. Move the picture up so it covers the first picture.

f. Change the width of the picture to 5.75", click the Crop button in the Size group, and crop from the top and bottom of the image until the image height measures 4.15".

g. Drag to a position similar to Figure 4.16.

h. Add an orange border around the image by displaying the Picture Tools Format tab. Click the Picture Border button in the Picture Styles group, select *Orange* in the *Standard Colors* section, click the *Weight* option, and select 2¼ pt.

6. Save the document and name it **C04-E03-Calendar**. *Hint: Keep this document open.*

7. Insert a predesigned calendar below the image by completing the following steps:
   a. Open a blank document.
   b. Click the File tab and then click the New tab.
   c. At the New tab Backstage view, click the *Calendars* category in the *Office.com Templates* section.
   d. Click the *2010 calendars* category or a current year category.
   e. Click the *2010 calendar (Basic design, Mon-Sun)* template icon, and then click Download.
   f. Scroll to locate the calendar for September 2010. The calendar is formatted as a table. Select the calendar (table) and change the size of the table by completing the following steps:
      1) Select the table. At the Table Tools Layout tab, click the Properties button in the Table group. At the Table Properties dialog box, select the Table tab and then change the Preferred width to 5.75". Click OK. *Hint: Add a check mark to the check box preceding Preferred width.*
      2) Select the five rows containing the dates, display the Table Properties dialog box again and then select the Row tab. Change *Specify height* to *0.6"*. Click OK, or press Enter.

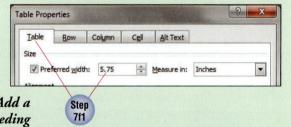

3) With the calendar (table) selected, copy it to the Office Clipboard. Close the document and then go back to the exercise document screen.

g. Click the Text Box button in the Text group in the Insert tab and then click the *Draw Text Box* option. Position the crosshairs below the Vineyard photo, and then drag and draw a text box that measures 4.2" height and 5.75" width in the Size group in the Drawing Tools Format tab. Click the Shape Fill button in the Shape Styles group and click the *Orange* color in the *Standard Colors* section.

h. Position the insertion point inside the text box and then click the Paste button in the Clipboard group in the Home tab to copy the calendar. ***Hint: Alternatively, right-click and paste from the clipboard.***

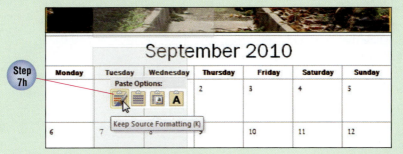

i. Resize and position the fall photo and the calendar as shown in Figure 4.16. ***Hint: Select the objects you want to move and then press the arrow keys on your keyboard to help you position the objects precisely.***

j. With the table selected and the Table Tools Design tab displayed, click the Shading button in the Table Styles group, and then select the *Orange* color in the *Standard Colors* section.

8. Add the text to the dates shown in Figure 4.16. ***Hint: Reduce the point size if necessary and press Shift + Enter after positioning your insertion point to the right of the date in each designated cell.***

9. Create a style for the text in the date cells by completing the following steps:

a. Select the text in one of the dates, change the font color to the *Olive Green, Accent 3, Darker 25%* color, and then click the More button at the Styles gallery in the Styles group in the Home tab.

b. Click the *Save Selection as a New Quick Style* option.

c. At the Create New Style from Formatting dialog box, type **Events** in the *Name* text box. Click OK.

d. Apply the Events style to all the dates that include text.

e. Change the text color and update the style… did the style change all occurrences of the text in the dates?

10. Add the star-burst attention-getter to the calendar as shown in Figure 4.16 by completing the following steps:

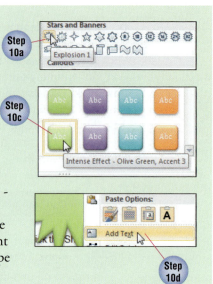

Step 10a

Step 10c

Step 10d

   a. Click the Shapes button in the Illustrations group on the Insert tab, and then click *Explosion 1* in the *Stars and Banners* section of the Shape gallery.
   b. In the bottom left corner of the Vineyard picture, drag and draw a star that is approximately 1.6" in diameter.
   c. Select the star shape (attention-getter), click the Shape Styles More arrow, and then click *Intense Effects - Olive Green, Accent 3*.
   d. Right-click the attention-getter, click Add Text, change the font to 12-pt. Berlin Sans FB, change the alignment to Center, change the font color to Black, and then type **Forecast Realty #1!**. Resize the star if necessary.
11. Save, print, and then close **C04-E03-Calendar.docx**.

Figure 4.16 **Exercise 4.3**

Arranging Drawing Objects to Enhance Personal Documents

Drawing objects include shapes, diagrams, flow charts, curves, lines, and WordArt. These objects are part of your Word document. You can change and enhance these objects with colors, patterns, borders, and other effects. A drawing in Word refers to a drawing object or a group of drawing objects. For example, a drawing object that is made up of shapes and lines is a drawing.

Moving and Placing Objects Precisely

To move a shape, click the shape that you want to move (to move multiple shapes, click the first shape, and then press and hold the Shift key while you click the additional shapes), and then drag the shape to its new location or press the Up Arrow, Down Arrow, Right Arrow, or Left Arrow keys to move the shape in the direction that you want; this is called nudging. To nudge an object at smaller increments, make sure the Text Wrap for the object has been changed to any setting other than *In Line with Text* and the *Snap objects to grid when the gridlines are not displayed* has not been checked.

In addition, you can select the object or objects, and then click the Align button in the Arrange group on the Page Layout tab or on the Drawing Tools Format tab to position the objects precisely on the page or in relation to each other. The align options are shown in Figure 4.17.

Using the Drawing Canvas to Align Drawing Objects

When you insert a drawing object in Word, you can place it in a drawing canvas. The drawing canvas helps you arrange a drawing in your document and provides a frame-like boundary between your drawing and the rest of your document. By default, the canvas has no border or background, but you can apply formatting to the drawing canvas as you would any drawing object. This feature also helps you keep parts of your drawing together, which is especially helpful if your drawing consists of several shapes. The best practice is to insert a drawing canvas if you plan to include more than one shape in your illustration. For example, if you want to create a flow chart, you start with a drawing canvas and then add the shapes and lines for your chart. In Word 2010, the drawing canvas is turned off by default. The lasso works only in the drawing canvas; this tool allows you to draw a dashed border around the objects you want to group together.

To turn on the drawing canvas, click in your document where you want to create the drawing, display the Insert tab, click the Shapes button in the Illustrations group, and then click *New Drawing Canvas*. A drawing canvas is inserted into your document.

Right-click anywhere in the drawing canvas and then click Fit, Expand, or Scale Drawing, or click the *Format Drawing Canvas* option to display the dialog box. Click the *Fit* option at the pop-up menu to compress the area around the drawing objects as shown in Figure 4.18. Notice that the drawing canvas adjusts to fit all three objects into one tight area. If you change the wrapping style of the drawing canvas to *In Front of Text* and drag the canvas, all three items will move in unison.

Figure 4.17 **Aligning Options**

Align

◀ **DTP POINTERS**

You can duplicate an object and align the objects at the same time by holding down the Shift key as you hold down the Ctrl key and drag and drop the copy.

◀ **DTP POINTERS**

If you are having difficulties grouping objects, you may want to use the drawing canvas to select the objects and then group them into one unit.

◀ **DTP POINTERS**

Layering drawn shapes works only if you are NOT using a drawing canvas.

Figure 4.18 Adjusting the Drawing Canvas to Fit the Contents

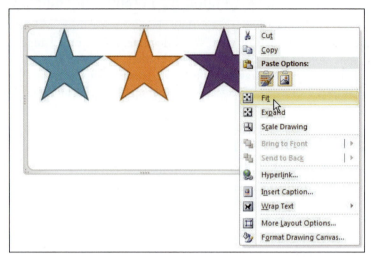

Stacking Objects

When you draw one object on top of another, you create an overlapping stack. This is known as *stacking*. Objects automatically stack in individual layers as you add them to a document. You see the stacking order when objects overlap. The top object covers a portion of objects beneath it, as discussed in Chapter 2.

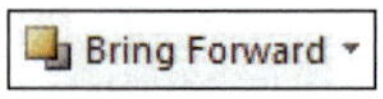

You may overlap as many drawing objects as you want and then rearrange them in the stack by clicking the down-pointing arrow at the right of the Bring to Front button in the Arrange group in the Drawing Tools Format tab and then choose *Bring to Front, Bring Forward,* or *Bring in Front of Text* as shown in Figure 4.19. As you can see, the shapes are layered on top of each other.

Alternatively, you may send the object backward by clicking the down-pointing arrow at the right of the Send to Back button in the Arrange group and then choose *Send to Back, Send Backward*, or *Send Behind Text* as shown in Figure 4.20. If you lose an object in a stack that has been grouped together, you can press Tab to cycle forward or Shift + Tab to cycle backward through the objects until it is selected.

Bring Forward ▼

Bring Forward

Send Backward ▼

Send Backward

Figure 4.19 Rearranging Objects by Bringing to Front at the Drawing Tools Format Tab

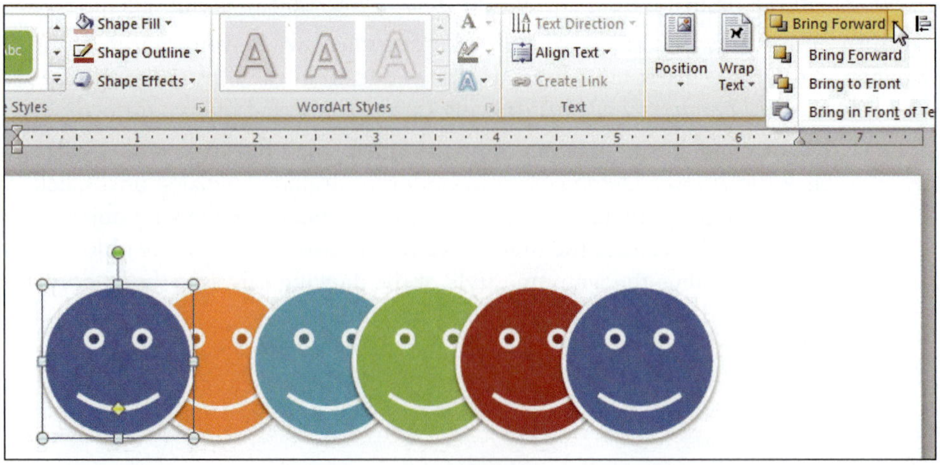

Figure 4.20 Rearranging Objects by Sending to Back at the Drawing Tools Format Tab

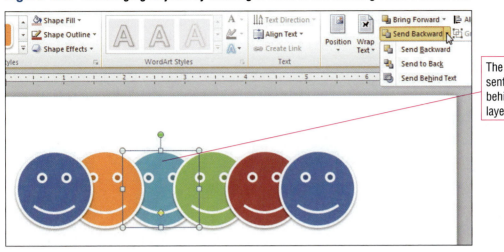

The shape was sent backward behind all the other layered objects.

Grouping Objects

Grouping objects combines the objects as a single unit. To group drawing objects, hold down the Shift key as you click each object, click the down-pointing arrow at the right of the Group button in the Arrange group in the Drawing Tools Format tab, and then click *Group* or *Ungroup* as shown in Figure 4.21. When objects have been grouped, sizing handles should appear around the new unit and not around each individual object.

Rotating and Flipping Objects

To rotate or flip objects, select the object or grouped objects, click the down-pointing arrow at the right of the Rotate button in the Arrange group in the Drawing Tools Format tab, and then click the option that corresponds with the direction you want to point the object as shown in Figure 4.22. Click the More Rotation Options button at the bottom of the *Rotate* drop-down list to access an additional option to rotate an object or picture. You may also use the Free Rotate button on the selected object as shown in Figure 4.23. Generally, you can rotate, align, and distribute pictures in Word.

Grouping
Combining objects as a single unit.

Group

Rotate

DTP POINTERS
Always position your graphics to face the document text.

Figure 4.21 Grouping and Ungrouping Objects

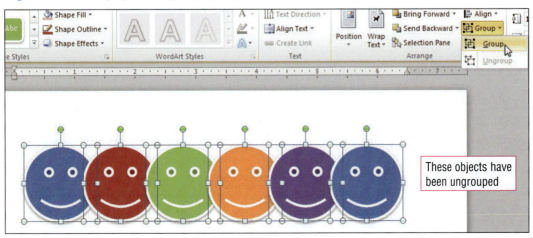

These objects have been ungrouped

Figure 4.22 Rotating an Object

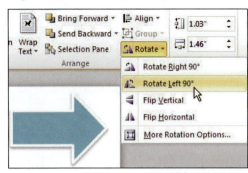

Figure 4.23 Rotating an Object Using the Free Rotate Button

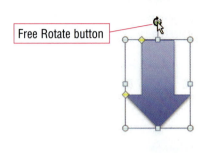

Free Rotate button

Creating Personal Return Address Labels

DTP POINTERS▶

If the Group feature in Word 2010 does not work properly, you may have to change the Wrap Text option for the object, or use the Drawing Canvas to group the objects together as one unit.

Return address labels are convenient and cost efficient to use at home as well as at the office. Whether you are paying a huge stack of bills, addressing holiday cards, or volunteering to mail a hundred PTA newsletters, the convenience of having preprinted return and address labels is worth the little time it takes to create them. You can create your own labels using the Word label feature. Word includes a variety of predefined label definitions that coordinate with labels that may be purchased at office supply stores.

When purchasing labels, be careful to select the appropriate labels for your specific printer. Labels are available in sheets for laser and inkjet printers. Carefully follow the directions given with your printer to insert the forms properly into the printer.

Return labels may be created using two different methods—creating labels individually using the label feature and copying them, or creating labels using a data source and the merge feature. In Exercise 4.4, you will create labels that include a picture and use the label definition Avery 5160 that results in a label measuring 1 inch by 2.63 inches. You may choose to use smaller-sized labels for your own personal return labels, such as Avery 8167, which measures ½ inch by 1¾ inches. Merging to labels will be discussed in Chapter 7.

Exercise 4.4 Creating Personal Return Address Labels with a Graphic

1. At a blank document create address labels.
2. Click the Labels button in the Create group on the Mailings tab.
3. At the Envelopes and Labels dialog box, choose the Labels tab, and then click the Options button.
4. At the Label Options dialog box, select *Avery US Letter* at the *Label vendors* drop-down list, and then select 5160 in the *Product number* list box. Click OK.
5. At the Envelopes and Labels dialog box, click the New Document button.
6. If gridlines of the labels (cells) do not display, click the View Gridlines button in the Table group on the Table Tools Layout tab.

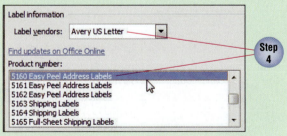

Step 4

7. With the insertion point positioned in the first cell, click the Clip Art button in the Illustrations group on the Insert tab. In the Clip Art task pane, type **tropical** in the *Search for* text box, and then click the Go button or press Enter. ***Note: You may insert a clip art of your own choosing and insert your own name and address instead of the name and address given in the following steps.***

8. Select the image, change the text wrap to Square, and then resize and position the image as shown in Figure 4.24.

9. Draw a text box that measures approximately 0.8" height and 1.6" in width at the right of the clip art image. Verify the sizes in the *Shape Height* and *Shape Width* text boxes in the Size group in the Drawing Tools Format tab. ***Hint: Adjust the size of the text box if necessary.***

10. Click the Shape Styles dialog box launcher, select the Text Box, and then change all internal margins to 0". Click Close.

11. Remove the Shape Fill and the Shape Outline.

12. Position the insertion point inside the text box, and click the Align Text Right button in the Paragraph group in the Home tab.

13. Change the font to 11-point Calligraph 412 BT or similar font, and then type the following (you may substitute your own name and address):

        Joan & John Kane (Press Shift + Enter.)
        55 Pine Island Road (Press Shift + Enter.)
        Myrtle Beach, SC 29472

14. Select *Joan & John Kane*; click the Text Effects button in the Font group; click the *Gradient Fill - Orange, Accent 6, Inner Shadow* style; and then change the font size to 13 points.

15. Select the text box containing the address and change the Wrap Text to Square.

16. Resize and position the address text box if necessary.

17. Group the two text boxes by completing the following steps:
    a. Click the picture, hold down the Shift key, and then click the text box containing the address.
    b. Click the down-pointing arrow at the right of the Group button in the Arrange group in the Drawing Tools Format tab, and then click Group.

18. Create a Quick Parts object (Building Blocks) by completing the following steps:
    a. Select the first label.
    b. Click the Quick Parts button in the Text group in the Insert tab, and then click *Save Selection to Quick Part Gallery* option.
    c. Type **address** in the *Name* text box in the Create New Building Block dialog box, and then click OK or press Enter. Close the document screen.
    d. At a blank document, display the Mailings tab, click the Labels button, select the Labels tab at the Envelopes and Labels dialog box, and then make sure the product number selected is *Avery 5160*.
    e. Position the insertion point in the *Address* text box, type **address**, press F3, and then click New Document.

19. Save the document and name it **C04-E04-Address.docx**.

20. Print and then close **C04-E04-Address.docx**.

Figure 4.24 **Exercise 4.4**

Creating a Certificate Using Certificate Templates

Certificates are generally used to show recognition and promote excellence. Some other suggested uses for certificates include diplomas, coupons, warranties, special event awards, program completion awards, and special-offer documents.

When printing your certificate, consider using an appropriate choice of high-quality 24-lb. uncoated bond stock or parchment paper in conservative colors, such as natural, cream, off-white, light gray, or any light marbleized color. In addition, consider using preprinted borders, ribbons, seals, and jackets, which are generally available through many mail-order catalogs and office supply stores.

The Microsoft Office Online Templates Web page provides several certificate templates created in either PowerPoint or Word. Certificate templates are available at http://office.microsoft.com/en-us/templates/default.aspx. Figure 4.25 illustrates three sample certificate templates edited in PowerPoint and in Word.

DTP POINTERS
View information on how to use labels and access additional templates at www. averylabels.com.

Figure 4.25 **Certificate Templates in PowerPoint and Word**

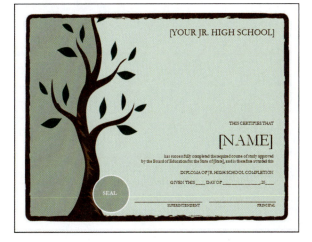

Adding Borders

In Word 2010, borders can add interest and emphasis to various parts of your document. You can add borders to pages, text, tables and table cells, graphic objects, and pictures. You can add a border to any or all sides of each page in a document, to pages in a section, to the first page only, or to all pages except the first. You can add page borders in many line styles and colors, as well as a variety of graphical borders. You can add borders to drawing objects and pictures. You can change or format the border of an object in the same way that you change or format a line.

Adding Borders to Tables

Borders

To apply a border to specific table cells, select the cells, including the end-of-cell marks. On the Table Tools Design tab, select a predesigned table style with professionally designed borders and shading or click the Borders button in the Tables Styles group and then select a desired border. You can customize the border by changing the border style, color, and width at the Borders and Shading dialog box accessed by clicking the *Borders and Shading* option at the bottom of the *Borders* drop-down list as shown in Figure 4.26.

Adding Borders to Pages

In addition to tables, you can add borders to pages by clicking the Page Borders button in the Page Background group on the Page Layout tab. By clicking the Page Borders button, you are accessing the Borders and Shading dialog box. Select the Page Borders tab and then click one of the border options under Settings. Select the style, color, and width of the border. To specify an artistic border, such as trees, select an option in the Art box as shown in Figure 4.27. To place borders only on particular sides of the selected area, click Custom under Setting. Under Preview, click the diagram sides, or click the buttons to apply and remove borders. To specify a particular page or section in which you want the border to appear, click the desired option under Apply to.

Figure 4.26 **Borders Options on the Table Tools Design Tab**

Chapter Four

Figure 4.27 Selecting an Artistic Page Border at the Borders and Shading Dialog Box

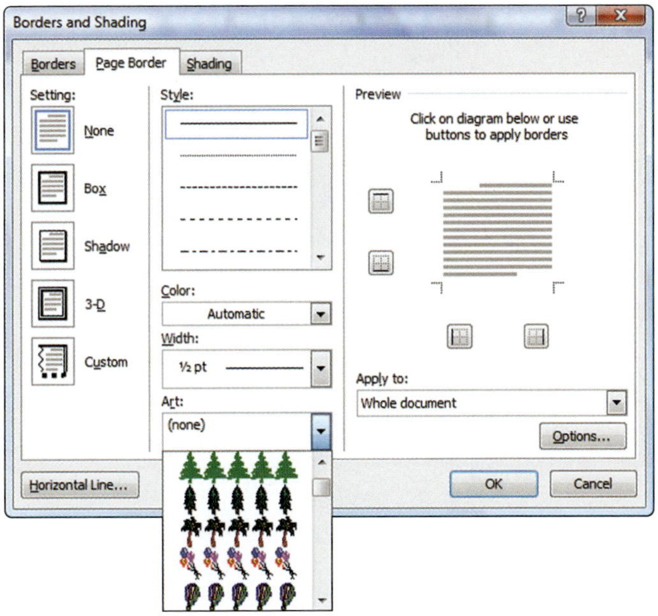

To specify the exact position of the border on the page, click Options, and then select the options that you want. To remove a border from a page, display the Page Layout tab, and click Page Borders in the Page Background group. Make sure you are on the Page Border tab in the Borders and Shading dialog box. Under *Setting*, click *None*.

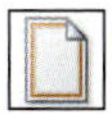

Page Border

Changing Page Border Margins

Most printers cannot print to the edge of a page, especially at the bottom of the page (check your printer *Properties* options). If a page border does not print, click the down-pointing arrow at the right of the *Measure from* list box in the Border and Shading Options dialog box, and select *Text* as shown in Figure 4.28. Also, experiment with changing your document margins.

If the bottom line of your document does not print, you may have to make adjustments to your document to compensate for the ***unprintable zone*** of your particular printer. The unprintable zone is an area where text will not print; this area varies with each printer.

DTP POINTERS
Inkjet printers usually can print up to 0.5" to the edge of the paper, while laser printers can print as close as 0.25" depending on the model.

Unprintable zone
An area where text will not print.

Adding Borders to Paragraphs

To specify the exact position of a paragraph border relative to the text, click Paragraph in the *Apply to* list box, click Options, and then select the options that you want. To specify a cell or table in which you want the border to appear, click the option that applies to that selection in the *Apply to* list box.

Inserting Text Fields

Whether creating a client survey form for the marketing and research department of your company or creating an award certificate for volunteers at your local hospital, using form fields in your templates saves time and effort. In Word, a ***form*** is a protected document that includes fields where information is entered. A form document contains

Form
A protected document that includes fields where information is entered.

Figure 4.28 Border and Shading Options

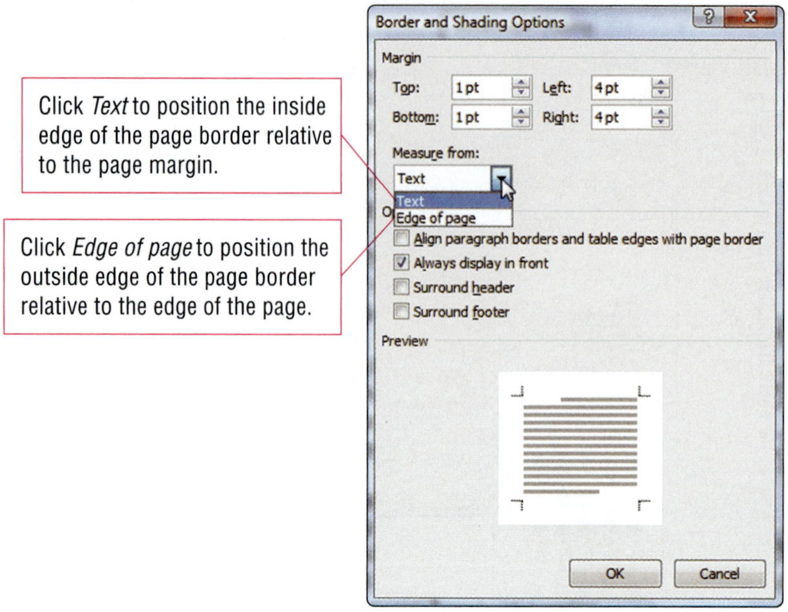
Border and Shading Options
Margin
Top: 1 pt
Left: 4 pt
Bottom: 1 pt
Right: 4 pt
Measure from:
Text
Text
Edge of page
Align paragraph borders and table edges with page border
Always display in front
Surround header
Surround footer
Preview
OK
Cancel
Click *Text* to position the inside edge of the page border relative to the page margin.
Click *Edge of page* to position the outside edge of the page border relative to the edge of the page.

> **Form field**
> Location in a document where text is entered, a check box is turned on or off, or a drop-down list is accessed.

form fields that are locations in the document where one of three things is performed: text is entered (text field), a check box is turned on or off, or information is selected from a drop-down list. Complete the following three steps to create a form template:

1. Design the form by sketching a layout first, or use an existing form as a guide, and then enter the text that will appear in your document or template.
2. Starting with a template, you can add content controls and instructional text to quickly and easily create a form or you can insert form fields prompting the user to insert information at the keyboard. In an advanced scenario, any content controls that you add to a form can also be linked to data.
3. Save the document as a protected document or template.

In Exercise 4.5, assume you are a volunteer at Edward Hospital and have offered to create an award certificate template. To create this document, you will need to display the Developer tab as shown in Figure 4.29 and then insert content controls to make it easy to insert recipients' names and dates.

> **Content controls**
> Individual controls that you can add and customize for use in templates, forms, and documents.

Inserting Content Controls

Content controls are individual controls that you can add and customize for use in templates, forms, and documents. For example, many online forms are designed with a drop-down list control that provides a restricted set of choices for the user of the form. Content controls can provide instructional text for users, and you can set controls to disappear when users type in their own text, which you will do in Exercise 4.5. You can

Figure 4.29 Using the Developer Tab to Create Forms

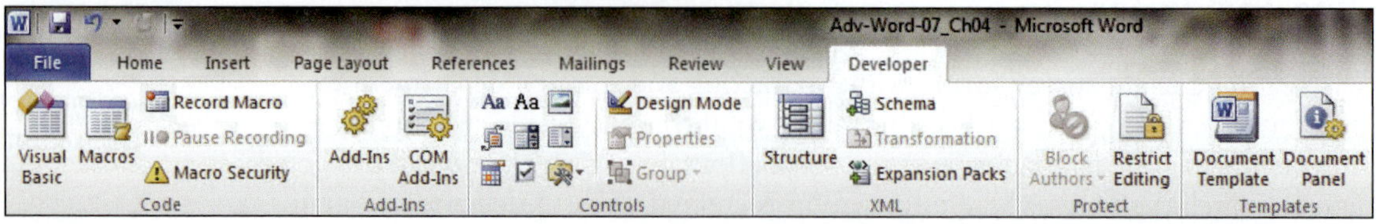
Adv-Word-07_Ch04 - Microsoft Word
File
Home
Insert
Page Layout
References
Mailings
Review
View
Developer
Visual Basic
Macros
Record Macro
Pause Recording
Macro Security
Code
Add-Ins
COM Add-Ins
Add-Ins
Design Mode
Properties
Group
Controls
Structure
Schema
Transformation
Expansion Packs
XML
Block Authors
Restrict Editing
Protect
Document Template
Document Panel
Templates

reuse and distribute your customized content controls, as well as create your own building blocks to include in a content control. The content controls as shown in Figure 4.30 can be found in the Developer tab. Complete the following steps to add the Developer tab to the Ribbon:

Figure 4.30 **Showing the Developer Tab**

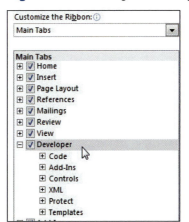

1. Click the File tab and then click the Options button.
2. Click Customize Ribbon.
3. Under Customize the Ribbon, select the *Developer* check box. Click OK. ***Note: If content controls are not available, you may have opened a document created in an earlier version of Microsoft Office Word. To use content controls, you must convert the document to the Word 2010 file format by clicking the File tab and then clicking the Convert button in the*** Compatibility Mode ***section. Click OK.***

Inserting a Date Picker Content Control

The certificate in Exercise 4.5 will be saved as a template to be used over and over. A date picker content control will be added to the document so that the user can select a date from the calendar control.

Date Picker

Adding Instructional Text to a Template

Sometimes it is helpful to add placeholder text instructing the user how to fill out a particular content control that you have added to a template. The instructions are replaced by content when someone uses the template. To add instructional text, complete the following steps:

1. On the Developer tab, in the Controls group, click Design mode.
2. If you haven't already added a content control to your document, click where you want the control to appear. Add the content control.
3. With the content control selected, click Properties in the Controls group, type a title, apply a specific style, and add protection if desired.
4. Click the Design mode again to turn off the feature.

Design Mode

Design

Creating a Signature Line

You can also create a signature in a document by using a shape, scanning a signature, or inserting a Microsoft digital signature.

Creating a Shape Signature

To create a signature using a shape, click the Shapes button in the Illustrations group in the Insert tab, and then select the Scribble tool in the *Lines* section. The Scribble tool is the last line in the *Lines* section. The mouse pointer will display as a pen. Write your name by dragging the pen. Save the signature as part of the document.

Using a Scanner to Create a Signature

If you have access to a scanner, write your name on a blank sheet of paper using a thick black ink pen or black marker. Scan the signature, save it in TIF for PNG format, and then insert the file at the Insert Picture dialog box. If you need to remove any unnecessary white space, use the cropping tool. With the object selected, change the wrap to *In Front of Text*. Copy and paste the signature wherever you want to use it in a document. In addition, you may select the signature object and then save it as a Quick Parts.

Inserting a Microsoft Signature Line

A signature line resembles a typical signature placeholder that might appear in a printed document. However, it works differently. When a signature line is inserted into an Office file, the author can specify information about the intended signer and instructions for the signer. When an electronic copy of the file is sent to the intended signer, this person sees the signature line and a notification that his or her signature is requested. The signer can type a signature, select a signature digital image, or write a signature by using the inking feature of the Tablet PC.

To insert a signature line, click the Signature Line button in the Text group in the Insert tab. Click the *Microsoft Office Signature Line* option, and then click OK at the next prompt. Type your name, title, and email address at the Signature Setup dialog box.

Exercise 4.5 Creating an Award Certificate

1. At a blank document create an award certificate.
2. Create the blue text box in the certificate shown in Figure 4.31 by completing the following steps:
   a. Click the File tab, and then click the Save & Send tab.
   b. At the Save & Send tab Backstage view, click Change File Type in the *File Types* section.
   c. Click *Template* at the *Document File Types* section, and then click the Save As button.
   d. Type **C04-E05-AwardTemplate** in the *File name* text box. Select the *DTP Template* folder, or specify a folder of your own choosing. Click Save.
   e. Change the orientation to Landscape.
   f. Change all the margins to 0.75".
   g. Click the Page Borders button in the Page Background group and then select the diamond shape border in the *Art* drop-down list.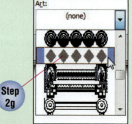
   h. Click the Options button. At the Border and Shading Options dialog box, click the down-pointing arrow at the right of the *Measure from* list box, and select *Text*. Type **4 pt** in each of the four margin text boxes. Click OK twice.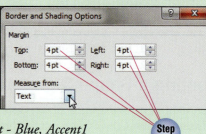
   i. Create a text box inside the border in a position similar to Figure 4.31 that measures 6.67" in height and 5.86" in width in the Size group in the Drawing Tools Format tab.
   j. With the text box selected, click the Shape Styles More button, and then select the *Subtle Effect - Blue, Accent1* style. ***Hint: Make sure the Office theme is selected.***

k. With the text box selected, click the Shape Fill button and then Gradient. At the Gradient gallery, click the *From Center* pattern in the *Variations* section.

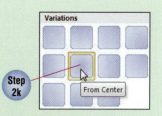

Step 2k

l. Click the Shape Outline button in the Shape Styles group, and then the click *Blue, Accent 1, Lighter 60%* color in the *Theme Colors* section.

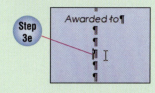

Step 2l

m. With the insertion point positioned inside the text box, click the down arrow next to the Object button in the Text group on the Insert tab, click Text from File, click the **Award** file located in your *Chapter04* folder, and then click Insert.

3. Display the Developer tab on the ribbon by completing the following steps:

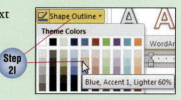

Step 3e

   a. Click the File tab and then click the Options button.
   b. Click Customize Ribbon.
   c. In the *Customize the Ribbon* section, select the *Developer* check box. Click OK.
   d. Click the Show/Hide button in the Paragraph group on the Home tab to turn on this feature.
   e. Position the insertion point on the third paragraph symbol below *Awarded to*, and then display the Developer tab.

Step 3f

   f. Click the Design Mode button in the Controls group (this toggles the feature on), and then click the Plain Text Content Control button in the Controls group.
   g. Mouse over and then select the text control in the document by clicking the three dots at the left of *Click here to enter text.*, and then click the Properties button in the Controls group.
   h. At the Content Control Properties dialog box, type **Insert recipient's name** in the *Title* text box, click to add a check mark in the check box at the left of the *Use a style to format contents* option. Click the down-arrow at the right of the *Style* list box, and then click the *Heading 1* style. Click OK.

Step 3h

   i. Position the insertion point on the blank line, not the paragraph symbol, below *Ameeta Singh, M.D.*, click the Date Picker button in the Controls group on the Developer tab, select the control in the document, and then click the Properties button in the Controls group.

Step 3i

j. At the Content Control Properties dialog box, type **Select award date**, select the third date format from the list, click OK, and then click the Design Mode button to toggle this feature off. You may have to turn on the Design Mode button first and then toggle it off.

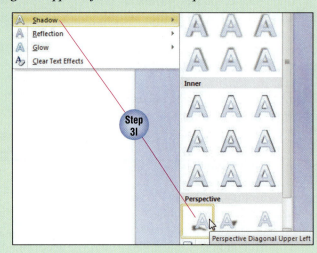

Step 3j

k. To insert a date control below *Diane Gohlke, R.N.,* position the insertion point next to the paragraph symbol at the end of the line, and then repeat steps 3i and 3j. **Hint: You may drag and drop a copy of the date picker control while holding down the Ctrl key instead of repeating the steps.**

l. Select *Community Service Award,* change the font to 32-point Broadway, click the Text Effects button, click the Shadow option from the drop-down list, and then click the *Perspective Diagonal Upper Left* effect in the *Perspective* section.

Step 3l

4. Draw the signature lines in the award by completing the following steps:
   a. Click the Shapes button in the Illustrations group on the Insert tab. Click the Line shape in the Shapes gallery and then drag the crosshairs while holding down the Shift key to draw a line above *Ameeta Singh, M.D.* The line should be approximately 2.5" width. **Hint: Select the line and then verify the correct width at the Shape Width** *text box in the Size group in the Drawing Tools Format tab.*

Step 4a

   b. Select the line created in step 4a, and hold down the Ctrl key and the Shift key while dragging and dropping a copy of this line above *Diane Gohlke, R.N.* as shown in Figure 4.31.

5. Insert a photo and a logo by completing the following steps:
   a. Position the insertion point in the upper left corner within the gray diamond border. Click the Clip Art button in the Illustrations group in the Insert tab.
   b. At the Clip Art task pane, type **health** in the *Search for* text box. Click the image to insert it into your document. Close the task pane.

   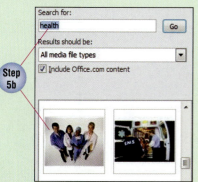

   c. Select the image, click the Wrap Text button, and then change the wrap to *In Front of Text*.
   d. Resize the image by either dragging a corner sizing handle while holding down the Shift key or by verifying the height and width at the Size group. The measurement for the shape height should be 3.5", and the shape width should be approximately 3.5".
   e. Apply the *Drop Shadow Rectangle* Picture style found on the Picture Tools Format tab in the Picture Styles group, and then position the image as shown in Figure 4.31.

   f. Add the logo by clicking the Picture button in the Illustrations group on the Insert tab, browse to locate your *Chapter04* folder, and then insert the logo, **EdwardCardio.tif**.
   g. Click the Wrap Text button, and then click *In Front of Text* option.
   h. Size and position the image similar to Figure 4.31.
6. Save and name the template **C04-E05-AwardTemplate.dotx**. (Ask your instructor if you should save the template to the *DTP Templates* folder.) Close the template.
7. Open the award template, and create a document based on the template by completing the following steps:
   a. Click the File tab and then the New tab.
   b. Click the *New from existing* category in the *Available Templates* section.
   c. Locate **C04-E05-AwardTemplate.dotx**, and then click Create New.
8. Click the placeholder text, *Click here to enter text.*, and type **Kathleen Sinnamon**. Press Tab, click the down arrow on the calendar control, and select any date. Press Tab, and then select the same date.
9. Save the document as **C04-E05-CompletedAward.docx**. *Hint: Do not save over the template; save the certificate as a Word document. If you have any difficulty printing this document, you may want to resave it in PDF format and then print.*
10. *Optional:* You may choose one of the methods discussed in this chapter to create a signature for each of the individuals responsible for signing the certificate.
11. Print and then close **C04-E05-CompletedAward.docx**.

Figure 4.31 Exercise 4.5

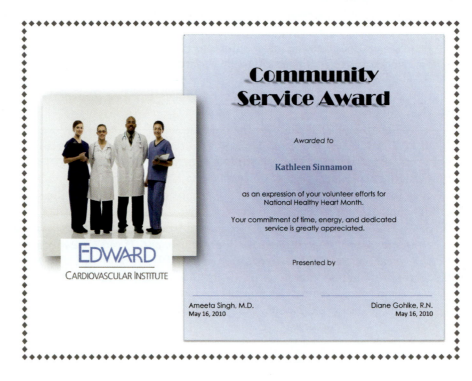

Chapter Summary

➤ Fill effects are added to documents for impact and focus.

➤ Word provides a Calendar Wizard that guides you through the steps of creating monthly calendars in either portrait (narrow) or landscape (wide) orientation.

➤ A placeholder is a reserved area on a page where an object, image, or text is entered later.

➤ Crop to trim horizontal and vertical edges off an image. Crop to maximize impact from an image.

➤ Watermarks, pictures, special characters, shading, and text may be added to a calendar to enhance its appearance and add to its effectiveness. You may adjust the Color Saturation, adjust the Color Tone (Temperature), or Recolor the image to improve the design as well as the readability of the document text.

➤ Shapes are added to documents to emphasize important facts. Shape Fill, Shape Outline, Shape Styles, Text, and other effects may be added to a shape.

➤ The unprintable zone is an area where text will not print; this area varies with each printer. Adjustments may be necessary in the size and position of document elements to compensate for the unprintable zone of a particular printer.

➤ Content controls are added to documents or templates to allow the user to efficiently insert data into templates, forms, and documents.

➤ You may move objects precisely by pressing an arrow key on the keyboard. This method is called nudging.

➤ Press the F4 key on your keyboard to repeat the last command you initiated in Word.

➤ Objects automatically stack in individual layers as you add them to a document. You see the stacking order when objects overlap—the top object covers a portion of the objects beneath it.

➤ To display the drawing canvas, click the Shapes button in the Illustrations group on the Insert tab, and then click New Drawing Canvas at the bottom of the drop-down list. The drawing canvas helps you keep parts of your drawing together, which is especially helpful if your drawing consists of several shapes.

➤ Grouping objects combines the objects into a single unit.

➤ A date picker content control will be added to the document so that the user can select a date from the calendar control.

➤ You can align two or more drawing objects relative to each other by their left, right, top, or bottom edges, or align them horizontally or vertically by their centers.

➤ Selecting a predefined label definition at the Envelopes and Labels dialog box creates personal return labels, shipping labels, address labels, CD labels, place cards, tent cards, and many more useful labels.

➤ Return labels may be duplicated on a sheet of labels by saving a formatted label as a Building Block to the Quick Parts gallery where it can be named, saved, and reused.

➤ A page border can be added to any or all sides of a page.

➤ Signatures may also be created using the Shapes Scribble tool.

➤ Signature objects may also be created by using a scanner to scan your handwritten signature. After the signature is scanned, it may be inserted into a document and then copied and pasted to other locations or documents. This signature may also be saved as a Quick Parts entry.

➤ A Signature Lines may be added to a document where the signer may type a signature, select a signature digital image, or write a signature by using the inking feature of the Tablet PC.

Commands Review

FEATURE	RIBBON TAB, GROUP	BUTTON
Align	Page Layout, Align	Align ▾
Bring Forward	Page Layout, Arrange	Bring Forward ▾
Colors	Picture Tools Layout, Adjust	Color ▾
Compress Picture	Picture Tools Layout, Adjust	Compress Pictures
Date Picker	Developer, Controls	
Envelopes	Mailings, Create	
Group	Drawing Tools Format, Arrange	Group ▾
Labels	Mailings, Create	
Line	Insert, Shapes	
Page Border	Page Layout, Page Background	
Picture	Insert, Illustrations	
Portrait/Landscape	Page Layout, Page Setup	
Quick Parts	Insert, Text	
Rotate	Picture Tools Format, Arrange	Rotate ▾
Scribble	Insert, Shapes	
Send Backward	Page Layout, Arrange	Send Backward ▾
Text box	Insert, Text	A
Text Content Control	Developer, Controls	Aa
View Gridlines	Table Tools Layout, Table	
Watermark	Page Layout, Page Background	
WordArt	Insert, Text	A

Reviewing Key Points

True or False: Select the correct answer by circling T or F.

1. Content controls are individual controls that you can add and customize for use in templates, forms, and documents.

   T   F

2. You can align two or more drawing objects relative to each other by their left, right, top, or bottom edges, or align them horizontally or vertically by their centers.

   T   F

3. An existing template document cannot be customized after it is displayed at the document screen.

   T   F

4. You may nudge a selected object in a document by pressing the plus and minus keys on the keyboard.

   T   F

5. Return labels may be duplicated on a sheet of labels by using the Quick Parts feature, copying and pasting, or pressing the F5 key to repeat the last command as many times as necessary to fill a sheet.

   T   F

6. Grouping objects combines all the objects into a single unit with eight sizing handles.

   T   F

7. The Crop button is located on the Page Layout tab.

   T   F

8. A date picker content control will be added to the document so that the user can select a date from the calendar control.

   T   F

9. Hold down the Ctrl key as you select each object you want to group.

   T   F

10. To constrain an object so that it moves only horizontally or vertically, press and hold Shift while you drag the object.

    T   F

11. A text field is a form field where the user is prompted to enter text.

    T   F

12. A page border can be added to any or all sides of a page.

    T   F

13. You must use the Drawing Canvas to stack objects in a document.

    T   F

14. A text box is not a Shape.

    T   F

15. You can insert merge codes into a certificate of completion.

    T   F

Chapter *Assessments*

Assessment 4.1   Change-of-Address Postcard

1. Create the change-of-address postcard in Figure 4.32 by following the specifications in the boxes; however, use your name and address and send the postcard to a friend.
2. Access the Labels feature and choose the postcard definition *Avery US Letter 5389 Postcards*, which measures 4 inches by 6 inches.
3. Insert a clip art image that is similar to the one shown in Figure 4.32. Find the clip art displayed by typing the keyword **stamps** or **postage** in the *Search for* text box at the Clip Art task pane. ***Hint: If the image in the sample document is no longer available, select a different image, and change the text box fill colors to complement the image.***
4. Use the Papyrus font or a similar font if this one is not available.
5. The triangle-shaped object is a Shape located in the *Flowchart* section of the Shapes gallery.
6. Use shapes in your document to reinforce a consistent color or to draw the reader's eyes through the document.
7. Group any related objects.
8. Save the document as **C04-A01-AddressChange**.
9. Print and then close **C04-A01-AddressChange.docx**.

Assessment 4.2   Volunteer Invitation in a Brown Bag

1. As a volunteer for a community food pantry, create an invitation that will be sent to the donors of the organization. Because the food and personal items are sorted and packaged in brown paper grocery bags for distribution, you will use the paper bag theme as the envelope for your invitation. You will size the invitation to fit into a brown lunch bag that measures approximately 5½ inches by 10½ inches. Include the following specifications:
   a. To change the size of the invitation, display the Page Layout tab, click the Size button, and then select More Paper Sizes. At the Page Setup dialog box, select the Paper tab, click the down-pointing arrow near Paper size, and then select Custom size. Type **5"** in the *Width* text box and **11"** in the *Height* text box.
   b. Refer to Figure 4.33 for the text for your invitation. Figure 4.33 is a sample document; you may use it for reference, but use your own ideas and creativity in designing your invitation.
   c. Insert the **Loaves&FishesBW** logo located in your *Chapter04* folder.
2. Save the document as **C04-A02-Volunteer.docx**.

Figure 4.32 Assessment 4.1

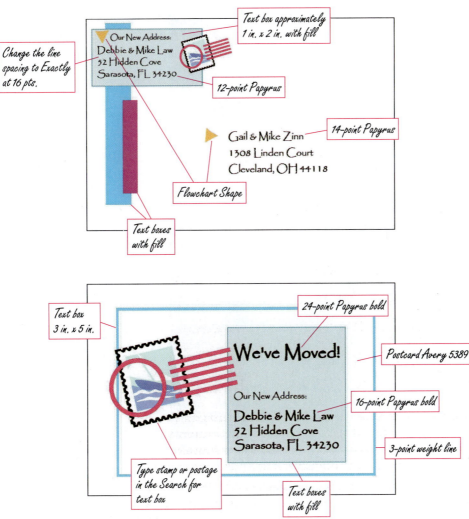

3. Print the invitation and trim the excess paper. ***Hint: Print the invitation on card stock, or save the file in PDF format, and send it to a commercial printer.***

4. ***Optional:*** Insert the invitation into a brown paper lunch bag and then create a label to attach to the front of the bag. The label should include the text *You're invited! Look inside. . . .* Include the **grocerybag** graphic located in your *Chapter04* folder.

Assessment 4.3   Course Certificate of Completion

1. Create a certificate of completion for the course you are currently taking. Refer to the sample certificate shown in Figure 1.37 in Chapter 1. You may create the certificate at a blank document or you may use a predesigned template.

2. Include your name, the course name and number, and the course completion date.

3. Include a signature line for your instructor.

4. Print the certificate on preprinted paper. Paper Direct® is a possible source for predesigned papers or print the certificate on marbleized or speckled papers—visit the website at www.paperdirect.com.

5. Save the certificate as **C04-A03-ClassCertificate**.

6. Print and then close **C04-A03-ClassCertificate.docx**.

Figure 4.33 Assessment 4.2 Sample Solution

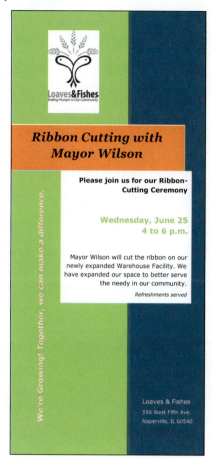

Assessment 4.4   Hanging Name Tag/Agenda

As a virtual event planner, you run your business from your home. One of your clients, *Global Network,* is a network of accounting firms with members from all over the world. You are organizing an annual meeting for this group in Beijing in 2013. You have already prepared a template for the hanging name tags that the attendees will wear to all the activities. Along with the attendee's name, city, and country, the tag will include the conference agenda. Complete the following steps to complete the hanging name tag and agenda as shown in Figure 4.34 and 4.35.

1. You will want to open the template as a document. To do this, complete the following:
    a. Click the File tab, and then click New.
    b. Click the New from existing category in the *Available Templates* section.
    c. Insert the **HangingNameTagTemplate** from your *Chapter04* folder.
    d. Save the document as **C04-A04-HangingNameTag**.
2. Type the text as shown in Figure 4.34 according to the specifications given. You may use text boxes with the fill and outline removed, or you may type the text adjusting the line spacing by pressing the Enter key and setting point increments at the *Spacing Before* and *After* text boxes at the Paragraph dialog box. You may also want to adjust the line spacing setting from the default *1.15* to *Single* or type increments in the *Multiple*, *Exactly*, or *At least* text boxes at the Paragraph dialog box.
3. Select the logo on the cover, click *Copy*, and then paste the copy to the back side of the tag.
4. Type the agenda text in the table cells of the template.
5. Use the tab settings as shown in Figure 4.34.

Figure 4.34 Assessment 4.4

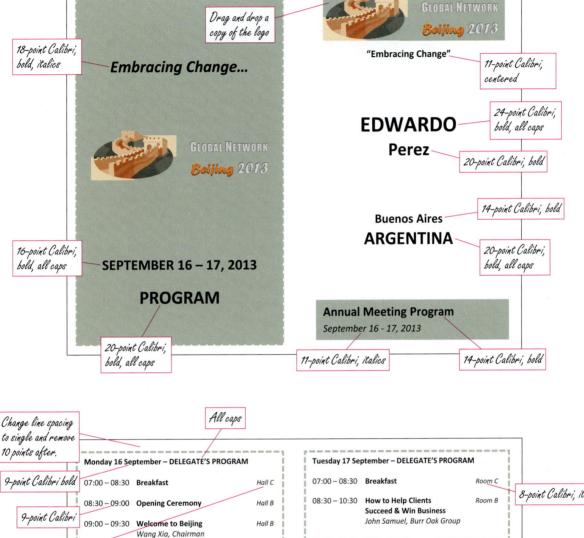

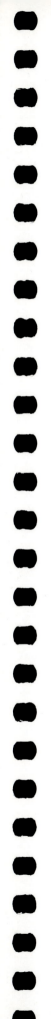

Figure 4.35 Sample Hanging Name Tag in Holder (Front and Back)

6. Type an en dash in the time durations. Word will automatically change the hyphen to an en dash when you type a space before and after each hyphen (AutoCorrect feature).
7. Save the document as **C04-A04-HangingNameTag.docx**. *Hint: You may want to create a data source and merge names to the name tag.*
8. Print one side of the document, reload the document into your printer, and then print the other side.
9. Trim the tag and fold it to fit into a clear plastic holder. The tag would be more durable if it were printed on 80# or 100# text stock paper (consult a professional printer).

Assessment 4.5   Group Marketing Plan Project

1. Using the SmartArt feature, create an attention-getting document describing a new marketing plan your team has developed for the spring promotion for a new line of products of your choosing. Please include styles; an appropriate theme; a background color, gradient, picture, texture, etc.; and print a copy of this document for each member of your class. Elect one person on your team to act as a spokesperson explaining how your team came up with the product, plan, and document using new Word features. Consider using an Excel spreadsheet to prepare a schedule of assignments for each team member.
2. Save your document as **C04-A05-SpringPromotion.docx**.

Performance Assessments

UNIT 1

Creating Business and Personal Documents

ASSESSING PROFICIENCIES

In this unit, you have learned to plan and design documents based on design principles that include focus, balance, proportion, contrast, color, directional flow, and consistency.

Note: Before completing the computer exercises, copy the **Unit02** *folder from the CD that accompanies this textbook storage medium and then make* **Unit02** *the active folder. If necessary, substitute any graphics that are not available with similar graphics.*

Assessment U1.1   Letterhead & Envelope

1. At a clear document screen, create the letterhead illustrated in Figure U1.1. Use the following list of specifications to help you in the creation process:
   a. Complete a search for the keyword **eagles** at the Clip Art task pane.
   b. Insert the image shown in Figure U1.1 and size it similarly to this figure.
   c. Select a theme that reinforces the colors in the graphic.
   d. Use a WordArt style for the text **Blue Eagle Airlines**.
   e. Type **On the Wings of Eagles** in 13-point Book Antiqua italics, expand the text by 1.5 points, and then turn on kerning. Change the font color to a color that coordinates with the eagle clip art. Add any text effects desired.
   f. Create the blue dashed arrow extending from the graphic image to the text box containing *On the Wings of Eagles*. ***Hint: Hold down the Shift key as you draw the arrow.***
   g. Create a text box that contains the address information in 9-point Book Antiqua (substitute a different font if necessary). Adjust the line spacing, color, and font sizes as desired. Type the following data, aligned at right:

   > **Dallas Love Field**
   > **22 Mockingbird Lane**
   > **Dallas, TX 75235**
   > **www.emcp.net/beair**
   > **214.555.6073**
   > **1.800.555.6033**
   > **214.555.6077 (Fax)**

   h. Create another arrow that extends from *Eagles* to the text box containing the address as shown in Figure U1.1. Use the same arrow style and color used in the figure.
2. Create a coordinating envelope using the company name, address, and contact information as shown in Figure U1.1. To add the envelope to the top of the letterhead, open the Envelopes and Labels dialog box, and click the Add to Document button. Copy the letterhead graphics to the envelope by copying and pasting, and then resize the graphics as necessary to fit the envelope.
3. Save the completed letterhead and envelope, and name it **U1-PA01-Airlines**.
4. Print and then close **U1-PA01-Airlines.docx**.

5. Access the Internet and use a search engine to locate the website for Dallas Love Field Airport. After you have located the website, print a map of the airport and a one-page information sheet from the website's home page. Attach the map and information sheet to your letterhead.

Assessment U1.2 Virtual Travel Agent Flyer

1. Your community college is offering a course in its Travel & Tourism department for the virtual travel agent. Prepare a flyer promoting this new course. Save the document in PDF format as it will be sent to all the faculty members as an email attachment. The flyer will also be sent to a professional printer for duplication.

Figure U1.2 Performance Assessment U1.2 Sample Solution

Are you a virtual travel agent?

Enroll today!

Do you make all the travel arrangements and decisions for your family and friends? Do you spend endless hours researching travel sites online? Take our new **Virtual Travel** course at Midwest College and discover the tricks of the trade. *Call* Registration at 630.555.1188 or *register* online at www.emcp.net/midwest for TRAV-1121-001.

2. Include the following specifications and use Figure U1.2 as a guide in providing the necessary text:
   a. Use the Word 2010 default settings.
   b. Use at least one style.
   c. Select a theme that supports the graphics and the overall look of the flyer.
   d. Use at least two graphics and at least two new Word 2010 picture effects.
   e. Use the text provided in Figure U1.2, and include your college name and contact information.
   f. Add an attention-getting shape.
3. Save the document as **U01-PA02-VirtualAgent**.

4. Conduct a document inspection by completing the following steps:
   a. Click the File tab and then at the Info tab Backstage view, click the Check for Issues button in *the Prepare for Sharing* section.
   b. Click *Inspect Document* from the drop-down list.
   c. At the Document Inspector dialog box, click Inspect.
   d. Click the Remove All button in the *Document Properties and Personal Information* section, and then click Close.
5. Print **U1-PA02-VirtualAgent.docx**, save it again as a PDF file, and then send a copy to your instructor as an email attachment.
6. Close **U1-PA02-VirtualAgent.pdf** and **U1-PA02-VirtualAgent.docx**.

Assessment U1.3   Business Card

1. As a volunteer at the Loaves & Fishes Community Pantry, you have been asked to use your creative talents to create a business card for the community relations coordinator. Loaves & Fishes is a community-based, not-for-profit organization established to provide food and personal care essentials to Naperville residents in need. Include the following specifications:
   a. Create a business card with text on the front and back sides.
   b. The slogan for the agency is "Together we can make a difference."
   c. The Loaves & Fishes logos are provided for you in your *Unit01* folder. Consider adding the *Be a Part of It* logo (**Loaves&FishesBeAPart.png**) to the backside of the business card.
   d. Be sure to include at least three of these Word 2010 features: Picture Styles, Quick Parts, WordArt, Quick Styles, Shapes, Text Boxes, leading and tracking, and font enhancements. The following information may be used in the documents. *Hint: When inserting several drawing objects into a cell in a table (label), you may have difficulties grouping all of the objects into one unit. If you encounter difficulty with grouping, you may want to select each object while holding down the Shift key and then create a Quick Part without first grouping the objects into a single unit.*

   Jody Bender, Coordinator
   Community Relations
   Loaves & Fishes
   Community Food Pantry
   556 W. Fifth Avenue
   Naperville, IL 60563
   630.555.3663
   loaves@emcp.net
   Together we can make a difference.

2. Save your documents as **U1-PA03-LoavesBCFront** and **U1-PA03-LoavesBCBack**.
3. Print and then close **U1-PA03-LoavesBCFront.docx**, reinsert the page in your printer, and then print and close **U1-PA03-LoavesBCBack.docx**.
4. Evaluate your documents using the **DocumentAnalysisGuide.docx** located in your *Unit01* folder.

Assessment U1.4   Procedural Manual

In this assessment, you will format a procedural manual using Word's Cover Page, Quick Parts, and Quick Styles.

1. Open **PoliciesandProceduresManual** located in your *Unit01* folder.
2. Save the document as **U1-PA04-Manual**.
3. Position the insertion point at the beginning of the document and then insert an appropriate Cover Page design. If necessary, substitute the template graphic with a college theme photograph or graphic.
4. Change the theme to a theme of your own choosing.
5. Change the font theme to a theme of your own choosing—customize the font theme if you desire.
6. Change the color theme to a theme of your own choosing—customize the color theme if you desire.
7. Apply a Style Set of your own choosing.
8. Adjust any line spacing if necessary.
9. At the *Title* placeholder in the cover, type **Policies and Procedures Manual**.
10. At the *Subtitle* placeholder, type **For Instructors at Midwest Community College**.
11. At the *Abstract* placeholder, type **To familiarize instructors with policies and procedures for successful employment at Midwest Community College.**
12. Type **your name** and the **current date** and apply a Text Effect of your own choosing.
13. Apply the Title Style to the title on the first page (not the cover page).
14. Apply Heading 1 to all the paragraph headings in the text.
15. Click the Page Number button in the Header & Footer group in the Insert tab and choose a page number style that complements the design of the manual. *(Hint: Make sure **Different First Page** is selected at the Header & Footer Tools Design tab.)*
16. Select the telephone text, click the Table button in the Insert tab, and then click Convert Text to Table. Apply an appropriate Table style.
17. Insert a SmartArt object near one of the paragraphs. Insert appropriate text.
18. Save the document again as **U1-PA04-Manual**.
19. Print and then close **U1-PA04-Manual.docx**.

Assessment U1.5   Excel Calendar

In this assessment, you will customize an Excel calendar template as shown in Figure U1.5 by completing the following steps: *Hint: You may use a Word calendar template if one is available for your desired year. At the current time, one is not available for the year needed.*

1. Open Excel 2010.
2. Click the File tab, and then click the New tab.
3. At the New tab Backstage view, click the Calendars category in the *Office.com Templates* section.
4. Click the Other calendars category in the *Available Templates* section.
5. Click the Calendar (any year) thumbnail, and then click Download.
6. Click the right-pointing arrow at the right of the calendar year. Continue clicking until 2012 displays in the title.
7. Change the theme to Slipstream.
8. Click the Orientation button in the Page Setup group in the Page Layout tab, and then click Landscape.

9   Select cells AI, AJ, and AK in the first row and then click the Merge & Center button in the Alignment group in the Home tab. Type **RENTAL SEASONS**.

10. Select *Rental Seasons*, and then change the font to 10-point Arial Black in the Blue, Accent 1 color in the first row and fifth column in the *Theme Colors* section.

11. Select cells AI, AJ, and AK in the fourth row, click the Merge & Center button, type **SPRING - March 15 - June 1**.

12. Select *SPRING –March 15 – June 1*, change the font to 9-point Arial in Black, click the Fill Color button in the Font group in the Home tab, and then click the *Yellow* color in the *Standard Colors* section.

13. Select cells AI, AJ, and AK in the sixth row, click the Merge & Center button, type **EASTER – April 5 – 15**.

14. Select *EASTER – April 5 – 15,* change the font to 9-point Arial in Black, click the Fill Color button, and then click *Green, Accent 3* in the *Theme Colors* section.

15. Type the remaining seasons and apply the fill colors as shown in Figure U1.5.

16. Position the insertion point in any cell below the last season in Step 14, click the Picture button in the Illustrations group in the Insert tab, locate the **BeachTime.bmp** logo in your *Unit01* folder, insert the logo, and then position the image as shown in Figure U1.5.

17. Using Figure U1.5 as your guide, select the cells (dates) that correspond to the rental seasons, and apply the same fill color.

18. Align the rental seasons merged cells with the *Rental Seasons* title cells by clicking the borderline at the right of the AK cell in Row 1 and dragging to align properly. Drag the borderline at the right of the A cell in Row 1 to reduce the width of the A column. Resizing the A column will allow the calendar to print horizontally centered. *(Hint: View the spreadsheet at the Print tab Backstage view to determine if it is positioned properly on the page.)*

19. Save the document as **U1-PA05-IntegratedCalendar**.

20. Click the File tab, and then click the Print tab. At the Print tab Backstage view, click the down arrow at the right of the Normal Margins setting and then click *Narrow Margins*. Click the down arrow at the right of No Scaling and then click Fit Sheet on One Page. Click Print and then close **U01-PA05-IntegratedCalendar.xlsx**. *Hint: In Excel, you can use a picture as a sheet background for display purposes only. A sheet background is not printed, and it is not retained in an individual worksheet or in an item that you save as a Web page.*

21. Close Excel.

DTP CHALLENGE

Take your skills to the next level by completing this more challenging assessment.

Assessment U1.6   Researching and Creating a Travel Itinerary

1. Create an itinerary for an upcoming trip. Search the Internet for a vacation of your own choosing. Locate a hotel or condo, fictitious airplane reservation, limousine or taxi reservation, car rental, one fictitious sightseeing event, and all return-to-home arrangements. Format the itinerary with creativity by including color, font effects, themes, and styles. Consider formatting your itinerary in a table format. Refer to a current Reference Manual for tips on formatting an itinerary.
2. Organize your itinerary by dates and activities. Include all pertinent times, addresses, and telephone numbers. Include flight information - airline name, flight number, departure time, arrival time, departure and arrival terminals, and seat number. Hotel information - hotel name, confirmation number, phone number, fax number, check-in date and time, check-out date and time. Transportation information - rental car, taxi, or limousine name, telephone number, confirmation number, pick-up date and time, and return pick-up date and time.
3. Include any tours if relevant. Include tour company name, destination, pick-up date and time, and telephone number. Include any other pertinent information for your trip.
4. Save the document as **U01-CA06-ItineraryChallenge**.
5. Print and then close **U01-CA06-ItineraryChallenge.docx**.

Figure U1.5 **Performance Assessment U1.5. Sample Solution**

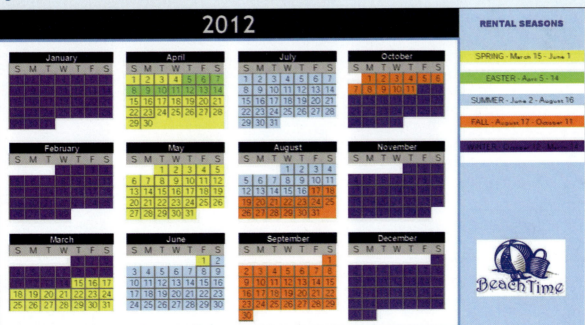

Unit 2

Preparing Promotional Documents and Newsletters

Chapter 5

CHAPTER05

Creating Promotional Documents–
Flyers and Announcements

Performance Objectives

Upon successful completion of Chapter 5, you will be able to:

- Produce promotional documents such as flyers and announcements.
- Review and apply design concepts.
- Use page color and change page orientation.
- Adjust letter spacing (tracking) and line spacing (leading).
- Use the Word tables feature to guide the layout of design elements.
- Apply Picture Effects—Shadow, Reflection, Glow, Soft Edges, Bevel, and 3-D Rotation.

- Adjust Brightness and Contrast.
- Adjust Color Saturation, Color Tone, Recolor, and Transparent Color.
- Apply Artistic Effects - Marker, Pencil Grayscale, Line Drawing, Paint Brush, and more.
- Remove Backgrounds from Pictures.
- Understand graphic formats and color terminology.
- Use Shapes and SmartArt objects in documents.

Desktop Publishing Terms

Announcement	Contrast	HSL	Thumbnail sketch
Bitmapped graphics	Crop	Pixel	Transparency
Bleed	Crop marks	Raster graphics	Unprintable zone
Brightness	Grid	RGB	Vector graphics
Color Saturation	Fill	Resolution	
Color Tone	Flyer	Scanning	

Word Features Used

Align	Drawing grid	Picture Effects	Shape Outline
Artistic Effects	Gradient	Picture Styles	Shape Styles
Aspect Ratio	Group/Ungroup	Position	SmartArt
Brightness	Line Spacing (Leading)	Recolor	Tables
Compress Pictures	Microsoft Office Picture	Remove Background	Text Boundaries
Contrast	Manager	Rotate	WordArt
Corrections	Page Color	Shape Effects	Wrap Text
Crop to Shape	Picture Border	Shape Fill	

In this chapter, you will produce flyers and announcements for advertising products, services, events, and classes using your own design and layout ideas with Word desktop features. First, you will review basic desktop publishing concepts for planning and designing promotional documents. Next, you will integrate fonts, graphics, borders, and objects into your documents to increase their appeal. Finally, you will use more complex and powerful features such as Picture and Clip Art Corrections, Color Adjustments, and Artistic Effects; WordArt; drawing grid; SmartArt, Shapes, Quick Parts, Quick Styles, Tables, and Page Borders.

Creating Flyers and Announcements

Flyers generally advertise a product or service that is available for a limited amount of time. Frequently, you may find flyers stuffed in a grocery bag; attached to a mailbox, door handle, or windshield; placed in a bin near an entrance; or placed on a countertop for customers to carry away. The basic goal of a flyer is to communicate a message at a glance, so the message should be brief and to the point. For the flyer to be effective, the basic layout and design should be free of clutter, without too much text or too many graphics. Use white space generously to set off an image or text and to help promote good directional flow.

An *announcement* informs an audience of an upcoming event. An announcement may create interest in an event but does not necessarily promote a product or service. For instance, you may have received an announcement for course offerings at your local community college or an announcement of an upcoming community event, sporting event, concert, race, contest, raffle, or a new store opening that informs and creates interest but does not promote the event.

Planning and Designing Promotional Documents

As stated in Chapter 1, planning your document is a basic desktop publishing concept that applies to flyers and announcements as well as to other publications. Most important, always prepare a *thumbnail sketch*, which is like thinking on paper, before beginning a project. Clearly define your purpose, and assess your target audience. For instance, consider your audience when choosing type sizes; the older your audience, the larger the print might need to be. Besides assessing your needs and your approach, consider your budget as well. Generally, producing flyers and announcements is one of the least expensive means of advertising.

Successful promotional documents attract the reader's attention and keep it. Consider how you can attract the reader's eyes by using eye-catching headlines, displaying graphics that create impact, or using color for emphasis or attention. People generally look at the graphics first, then they read the headline, and finally they look at the logo for company identity. The logo may be placed low on the page to anchor the message.

Using a Table for Layout

Use a thumbnail sketch as a tool to guide you in creating documents. In addition, you may draw a table to block off areas of the page to reflect the layout you have sketched in your thumbnail. Figure 5.1 shows how a table can serve as a framework for an announcement.

Figure 5.1 **Using a Table to Create an Announcement**

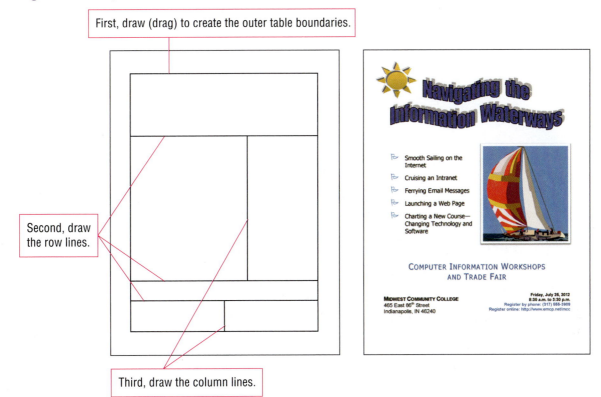

First, draw (drag) to create the outer table boundaries.

Second, draw the row lines.

Third, draw the column lines.

Tables provide an efficient means for aligning text and objects using options on the Table Tools Layout tab as shown in Figure 5.2. These options include *Align Top Left*, *Align Top Center, Align Top Right, Align Center Left, Align Center, Align Center Right, Align Bottom Left, Align Bottom Center,* and *Align Bottom Right.* Table designs are shown in Figure 5.3. You will learn how to create an announcement in a table in Exercise 5.1.

Figure 5.2 **Table Tools Layout Tab**

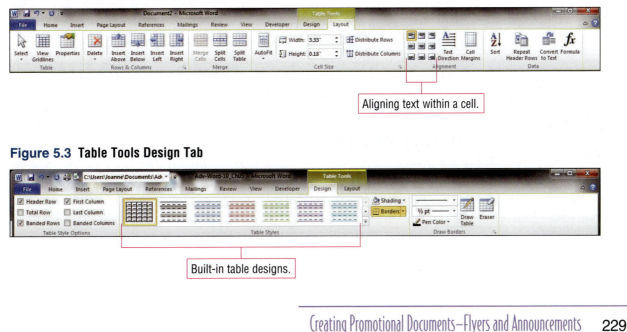

Aligning text within a cell.

Figure 5.3 **Table Tools Design Tab**

Built-in table designs.

Figure 5.4 No Borders in a Table

Table

Draw Table

Eraser

Table Move Handle

Properties

To create a table for the announcement in Figure 5.1, complete the following steps:

1. On the Insert tab, click the Table button in the Tables group, and then click Draw Table (the arrow pointer will display as a pen).
2. Position the pen in the upper left corner of your screen and then drag from the left corner to the bottom right corner to create a table.
3. Draw lines by clicking and dragging. To erase lines, click the Eraser button on the Table Tools Design tab in the Draw Borders group (see Figure 5.3). Drag the eraser along the line you want to erase. Remember to turn off the Eraser when you are done.
4. If you do not want borders on your table, click the down-pointing arrow at the right of the Borders button in the Table Styles group on the Table Tools Design tab, and then click the *No Border* option at the drop-down list (see Figure 5.4).
5. If you want to change the cell width or length, drag the boundary you want to change. (Position the insertion point on the boundary line you want to change; when the insertion point displays as either two horizontal or two vertical lines with up-/down- or left-/right-pointing arrows, drag the line to a new location.) Alternatively, drag the Move Column markers on the Ruler, or change the column widths at the Table Properties dialog box.
6. By clicking and dragging the Table Move Handle icon in the upper left corner of the table (it displays as a four-pointed arrow), you can move the table to a new location or you can click the Properties button in the Table group in the Table Tools Layout tab, and then change the Alignment at the Table tab of the Table Properties dialog box as shown in Figure 5.5.

Using Text for Focus

Flyers and announcements provide tremendous opportunities for you to be creative. To grab attention, consider using large graphics, uncommon typefaces, asymmetrical design, and plenty of white space. Use color or white space to emphasize the main message and give the eye a break from too much text. Keep in mind the ¹/₃ - ²/₃ Rule discussed in Chapter 1: ¹/₃ of the document should be white space; ²/₃ of the document may be text and/or design objects. Do not use more than three fonts or three colors. An inexpensive alternative is to use colored paper or preprinted paper. Figure 5.6 illustrates a flyer that attracts attention with varying fonts and font attributes.

Figure 5.5 **Center Alignment Option at the Table Properties Dialog Box**

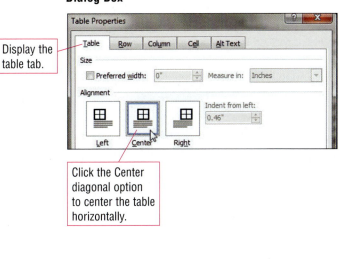

Display the table tab.

Click the Center diagonal option to center the table horizontally.

Figure 5.6 **Sample Flyer (All Text)**

After you have finished a document, look at the document from a distance to make sure that the important information is dominant. Also, look through a newspaper or magazine to find ads that grab your attention and prompt you to act. Study the designs, and apply what you have learned to your own documents.

Using Graphics for Emphasis

Graphics can add excitement to a publication and generate enthusiasm. A well-placed graphic can transform a plain document into a compelling visual document as shown in Figure 5.7. However, it is effective only if the image relates to the subject of the document. Before selecting a graphic, decide what your theme or text will be. If you are deciding among many graphics, select the simplest. A simple graphic demands more attention and has more impact; graphics that are too complicated can cause clutter and confusion. Use a graphic to aid in directional flow. Also, use a generous amount of white space around a graphic. Use a thumbnail sketch as a tool to help you make decisions on position, size, and design.

Consider using clip art and/or photographs as a basis for your own creations. Combine clip art images with other clip art images, and then crop, size, or color different areas of the combined image to create a unique look. Alternatively, you may include photographs in your flyers or announcements. Photographs tend to add a professional, polished appeal to document design. In addition, people are generally drawn to another person's face.

Easy access to the Internet through Word also provides opportunities to locate additional graphics as shown in the Clip Art task pane. Have you wondered what the small star means? The small star in the lower right corner indicates that the graphic is a motion clip. To ensure that the greatest number of graphics are available at the Clip Art task pane, click the down-pointing arrow at the right of the *Search in* list box and make sure that *All collections* is selected. Also, make sure that *Selected media file types* displays in the *Results should be* list box. To narrow your search for a particular type of graphic— for example, photographs—click to remove the check mark next to *All media types* and then click to add a check mark next to *Photographs*. Make sure that the *Include Office. com content* option has been checked to include online selections.

> **DTP POINTERS**
> Choose images that relate to the message.

> **DTP POINTERS**
> Leave plenty of white space around a graphic.

> **DTP POINTERS**
> Do not overuse clip art; use one main visual element per page.

> **DTP POINTERS**
> To search for all available clip art, photographs, movies, and sounds, make sure *All collections* displays in the *Search in* list box and *All media file types* displays in the *Results should be* list box at the Clip Art task pane.

Figure 5.7 Using Graphics for Emphasis in a Document

Downloading Graphics from the Web

If you have access to the Internet, you can add to your clip art, photographs, videos, and sound clips collection by downloading images and clips from Office.com or any other clip art websites. For instance, assume you want to insert a beach clip art into your document; you may want to begin by accessing the Clip Art task pane and then typing **beaches** in the *Search for* text box. If you know the file name, such as 00407451.jpg, you can type it in the *Search for* text box, click Go, and then insert the image after it displays. However, remember that if you are already connected to the Internet, you will be able to view the same online images when you conduct your search at the Clip Art task pane.

To download images from Office.com complete the following steps:

1. Display the Clip Art task pane.
2. At the Clip Art task pane, click the <u>Find more at Office.com</u> hyperlink as shown in Figure 5.8.
3. The first screen that displays is the Microsoft Office Images Web page, as shown in Figure 5.9. Type the desired search topic (**beaches**) in the *Search for* text box to the left of Bing, and then click the Search button to execute the search.
4. Figure 5.10 shows the screen that may display after initiating the search. To download an image, mouse over the image and then click one of these options: *Copy to Clipboard, See Similar Images,* or *Add to Basket.* If you click the *Add to Basket* option, you will see an option to Download the image as shown in Figure 5.11.

Figure 5.8 Accessing More Clip Art at Office.com

Figure 5.9 Microsoft Office.com Web Page

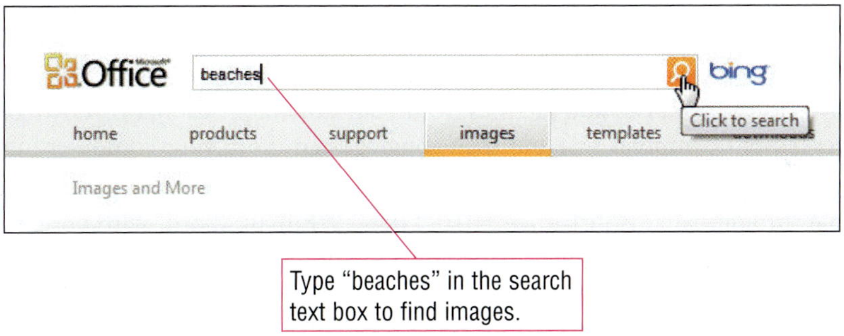

Type "beaches" in the search text box to find images.

Figure 5.10 Results of a Search

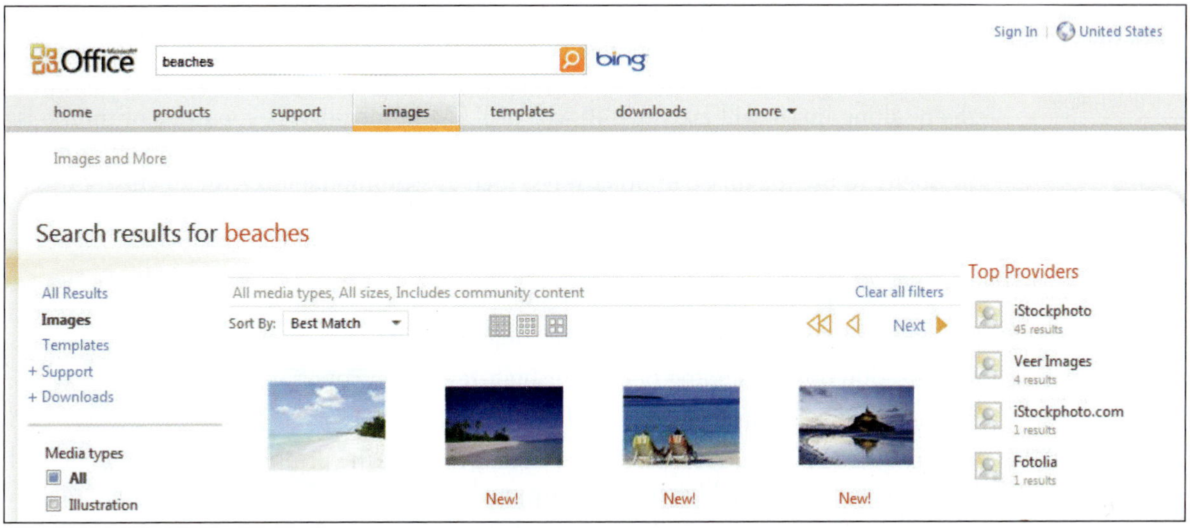

Figure 5.11 Adding and Downloading an Image from the Selection Basket at www.Microsoft Office.com

Inserting Images from a Scanner or Digital Camera

The *From Scanner or Camera* option for adding pictures to a document, which was available in previous versions of Word, is not available in any of the tabs in the ribbon in Word 2010. Instead, you can add pictures from your camera or scanner by downloading the pictures to your computer first and then copying them from your computer into Word.

You can also scan images and store them in the Microsoft Clip Organizer, which is accessible through Microsoft Office 2010 Tools. While in Word, with your scanner ready and the image on the scanner glass, you can click the Start button, All Programs, Microsoft Office, Microsoft Office 2010 Tools, and then Microsoft Clip Organizer. At the Microsoft Clip Organizer dialog box, click File, click *Add Clips to Organizer*, and then click *From Scanner or Camera* as shown in Figure 5.12.

Choosing Scanner Resolution

dpi

The resolution of an image is determined by the number of dots per inch (dpi).

One of the most common mistakes in scanning is over scanning. Most scanners are capable of scanning up to 1200 dots per inch (*dpi*) or more, so it may be tempting to scan at the highest resolution. However, if you scan a 5" × 7" inch image at 1200 dpi, the resulting image will take up 140 MB of RAM in memory. A good rule of thumb is to scan your images at 300 dpi. This produces a file of reasonable size and gives you the flexibility to use the image in other ways, such as sending the image in an email or using it in a Web page layout.

Hewlett-Packard recommends these settings:

72 dpi – Scanning images for email or online

150 dpi – Scanning photos for inkjet printing

300 dpi – Scanning photos for high-resolution copies of your photos

Above 300 dpi – Scanning slides or negatives for prints 5" × 7" or larger

For photographs, 600 dpi is more resolution than the printer requires, and you will not see any noticeable difference in print quality. However, if you are scanning line art and color drawings, you may want to scan at 600 dpi for a sharper picture. Many cameras and scanners produce pictures with resolutions from 300 dpi to 2400 dpi. For displaying images on a website, the optimal resolution is 96 dpi. Most computer monitors have a screen resolution of 96 dpi. A photograph with higher or lower resolution may appear blurry on a monitor at 96 dpi. A photograph saved at 96 dpi will download 10 times faster than an image saved at 1200 dpi. Therefore, for publishing images on a website, save your photographs at 96 dpi.

Figure 5.12 Adding Images from a Scanner or Digital Camera

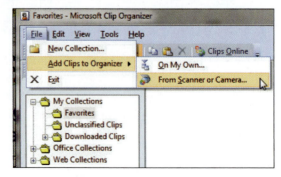

Choosing Scanner and Digital Camera File Formats

After you scan an image, you can save it in several different file formats. The most common types of formats are JPEG (Joint Photographic Experts Group), TIFF (Tagged Image File Format), GIF (Graphics Interchange Format), PNG (Portable Network Graphics), and BMP (Bitmap Image). Choosing the right format depends on how you will use your image.

When choosing an appropriate format, consider that the GIF format allows only 256 colors (8-bit), so it may not be as desirable as TIFF or JPEG formats where more colors may be needed—12-bit or 24-bit. The PNG format is the successor to GIF, and it supports True Color (16 million colors). The PNG and GIF formats are typically used for online viewing. The general rule is to use JPEG for photographic images, and GIF or PNG for images that have text, sharp lines, or large areas of solid colors.

Understanding Graphic File Formats

Basically, there are two major graphic file formats. A map (or **raster**) image is one of the two major graphic types (the other being **vector**). Bitmap-based images are comprised of pixels in a grid. Each pixel or "bit" in the image contains information about the color to be displayed. Bitmap images have a fixed resolution and cannot be resized without losing image quality. Common bitmap-based formats are JPEG, GIF, TIFF, PNG, and BMP. Most bitmap images can be converted to other bitmap-based formats very easily. Bitmap images tend to have much larger file sizes than vector graphics, and they are often compressed to reduce their size.

Bitmapped graphics use individual pixels of color that can be edited one by one or as a group. A **pixel** is each individual dot or square of color in a picture or bitmapped graphic. An enlarged bitmapped image appears jagged around the edges as shown in Figure 5.13. If the software program has the words *draw* or *illustrate* in its name, it is a vector graphics program. An enlarged **vector graphic** looks smooth around the edges because the shapes are mathematically defined as shown in Figure 5.13 You can size a vector graphic by dragging the sizing handles surrounding the image.

Using Color in Promotional Documents

Color is a powerful tool in communicating information. Choose one or two colors for a document and stick with them to give your page a unified look. Add "spot color" in your document by using color only in specific areas of the page. Also, pick up a color from your graphic and apply it to your text.

Raster graphics
Images that are displayed on a monitor and are made up of dots of black, white, or another color.

Vector graphics
Images made up of mathematically defined lines and curves.

Bitmapped graphics
Images that use individual pixels of color that can be edited one by one or as a group.

Pixel
Short for picture element; a pixel is each individual dot or square of color in a picture or bitmapped graphic.

Figure 5.13 Raster (Bitmapped) Image and Vector (Line Art) Image

Raster

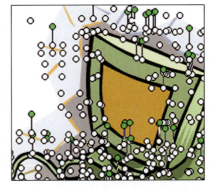

Vector

Many flyers and announcements are printed on either white or color paper and duplicated on a copy machine to help keep down costs. A color printer or color copier adds to the cost but can help the appeal of the document. If you are using a color printer, limit the color to small areas so it attracts attention but does not create visual confusion.

As an inexpensive alternative to printing in color, use color paper or specialty papers to help get your message across, as discussed in Chapter 1. Specialty papers are predesigned papers used for brochures, letterheads, postcards, business cards, and certificates and they can be purchased through most office supply stores or catalog paper supply companies. Be sure to choose a color that complements your message and matches the theme of your document.

Understanding Desktop Publishing Color Terms

When working in desktop publishing and using Word 2010, you may encounter terms used to explain color. Here is a list of color terms along with definitions:

- *Balance* is the amount of light and dark in a picture.
- *Brightness* or value is the amount of light in a color.
- *Contrast* is the amount of gray in a color.
- *CYMK* is an acronym for cyan, yellow, magenta, and black. A color printer combines these colors to create different colors.
- *Gradient* is a gradual varying of color.
- *Grayscale* is a range of shades from black to white.
- *Hue* is a variation of a primary color, such as green-blue.
- *Luminescence* is the brightness of a color, that is, of the amount of black or white added to a color. The larger the luminosity number, the lighter the color.
- *Pixel* is each individual dot or square of color in a picture or bitmapped (or raster) graphic.
- *Resolution* is the number of dots that make up an image on a screen or printer—the higher the resolution, the denser the number of dots and "higher resolution" of the print. Typical monitors display images in 96 dpi and inkjet and laser printers print from 150 dpi to 600 dpi. However, some photo-quality printers can print at 5760 × 1440 dpi in black and white as well as in color.
- *RGB* is an acronym for red, green, and blue. Each pixel on your computer monitor is made up of these three colors.
- *Saturation* is the purity of a color. A color is completely pure, or saturated, when it is not diluted with white. Red, for example, has a high saturation.

Adding Color to an Entire Page

Page Color

Word 2010 offers a feature that allows you to color entire printed pages (as well as pages that display on a monitor). You can click the Page Color button in the Page Background group in the Page Layout tab to add color as the background of a page as shown in Figure 5.14. Color choices consist of Theme Colors, Standard Colors, No Color, More Colors, or Fill Effects.

Printing a Page Color

If you choose to add a page color to your document and want to print this background color, you will need to verify that an option to print background colors has been

Figure 5.14 Adding a Page Color   **Figure 5.15** Printing Background Colors

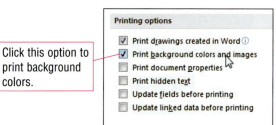

Click this option to print background colors.

selected. To do so, click the File tab and then click the Options button. At the Word Options dialog box, click Display, and then make sure a check mark has been added to the check box next to *Print background colors and images* in the *Printing options* section as shown in Figure 5.15.

Even though you have applied a background to the entire page, your document may—depending on your printer—print with a white border along the edge of your paper. This border may measure approximately 0.25 inch. If your printer allows you to print to the edge of the page, this is known as a **bleed**. However, most inkjet printers do not allow printing to the edge of the page. You may want to print to a slightly larger paper size to compensate for your printer. The width of the unprintable area on your page is determined by your print driver; this white area is referred to as the **unprintable zone**. Determine the nonprintable region of your desktop printer by setting the left, right, top, and bottom margins to zero. The margins will be reset automatically to the minimum margin that is supported by the printer.

Showing Text Boundaries and Crop Marks

Word includes an option that allows you to view the margin boundaries of your document. These boundaries cannot be printed. To show the boundaries, click the File tab and then click the Options button. At the Word Options dialog box, select Advanced, and then click to add a check mark in the check box next to *Show text boundaries* in the *Show document content* section as shown in Figure 5.16. Click OK. You may use this feature to position design elements on the page in a manner similar to using page layout guides and ruler guides in Microsoft Publisher and other desktop publishing and design software.

Crop marks show where a publication page will be trimmed. In Word, these marks display on the screen when the *Show crop marks* option at the Word Options dialog box has been selected (see Figure 5.16). Crop marks show only on a printed page when the page has been printed to a paper size that is larger than the page.

As an employee of Midwest Community College, you are responsible for preparing advertisements for new courses and workshops sponsored by the college. You will create the announcement in a table format to simulate creating a document using layout guides and rules as found in many design software programs, turn on the text boundaries feature, add page color, and then print the page in color.

Hint: Copy the **Chapter05** *folder from the CD that accompanies this textbook to your storage medium, and then make* **Chapter05** *the active folder. Remember to substitute for graphics that may no longer be available.*

Bleed
Printing to the edge of a page.

Unprintable zone
The width of the unprintable area on your page.

◀**DTP POINTERS**
Add approximately 0.125" (1/8") to your document margins for a bleed that will be trimmed away.

◀**DTP POINTERS**
Be careful that your text does not come too close to the bleed; this text may be in danger of being trimmed.

Crop marks
Marks that show where a publication page will be trimmed.

Figure 5.16 Showing Boundaries and Crop Marks

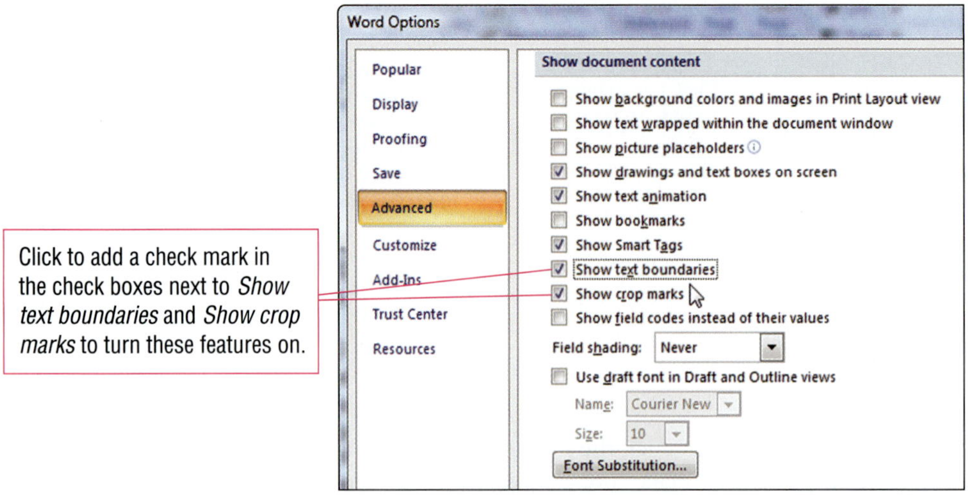

Click to add a check mark in the check boxes next to *Show text boundaries* and *Show crop marks* to turn these features on.

Exercise 5.1   Creating an Announcement Using a Table

1. At a blank document create the announcement shown in Figure 5.17. By completing the following steps you will create a table that is the basis for Figure 5.1:
   a. Change all of the margins to 0.75 inch.
   b. Change the theme to Oriel.
   c. Display text boundaries to help you visualize where to draw a table for the underlining structure of this announcement by completing the following steps:
      1) Click the File tab and then click the Options button.
      2) At the Word Options dialog box, click *Advanced* at the left of the screen.
      3) Click to add a check mark in the check box near *Show text boundaries* in the *Show document content* section. Click OK.

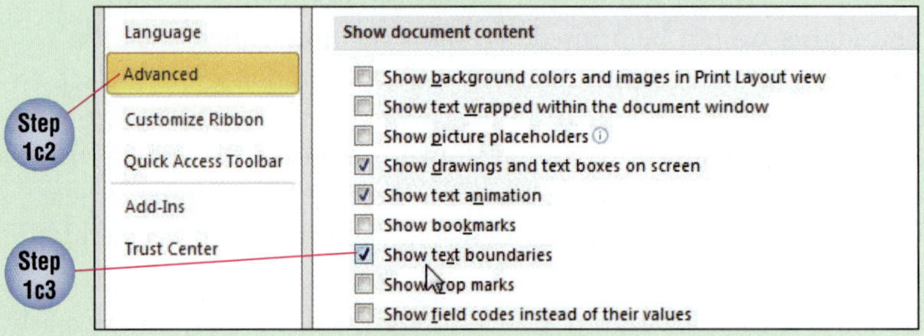

Step 1c2

Step 1c3

   d. Click the Table button in the Tables group in the Insert tab and then click Draw Table from the drop-down list. ***Hint: The arrow pointer will display as a pen.***
   e. Position the pen inside the text boundaries that you turned on in Step 1c3. Drag to create the outer boundary lines of a table, dragging from the upper left corner to the bottom right corner of the page. The lines should be similar to the illustration on the next page. ***Hint: Use your horizontal and vertical ruler bars to guide you. If the bottom line causes another page to display, drag the line upward away from the text boundary.***
   f. Position the pen approximately 2 inches below the top boundary line of the table and draw a horizontal line by clicking and dragging.

g. Position the pen approximately 2 inches above the bottom boundary line of the table and draw another horizontal line by clicking and dragging.

h. Position the pen approximately 0.75 inch below the line created in step 1g, and then draw another horizontal line by clicking and dragging.

i. In the center section, position the pen approximately 2.5 inches from the right boundary line and draw a vertical line by clicking and dragging.

j. In the bottom section, position the pen at the approximate center of the last row, and then draw a vertical line by clicking and dragging.

k. Turn the Draw Table feature off by clicking the Draw Table button in the Draw Borders group on the Table Tools Design tab.

l. Turn off the text boundaries feature by removing the check mark next to *Show text boundaries.*

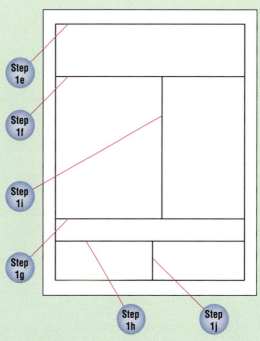

2. Insert the announcement text by completing the following steps:

a. Position the insertion point in the first cell, click the down arrow next to the Object button in the Text group on the Insert tab, and then click *Text From File.* Insert the **Navigating** file located in your *Chapter05* folder.

b. Double-click the WordArt text to open the WordArt Tools Format tab, click the Position button in the Arrange group, and then click the Center button in the drop-down gallery.

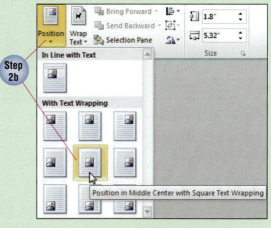

c. Position the insertion point in the first cell of the second row of the table and insert the **Sailing.docx** text file located in your *Chapter05* folder. In the Table Tools Layout tab, click the Align Center Left button in the Alignment group.

d. Position the insertion point in the second cell in the second row of the table, and insert a sailing photograph by typing **Sailboat** in the *Search for* text box at the Clip Art task pane. Size the image similar to the photo in Figure 5.17 and rotate the image to face the bulleted text if necessary.

e. Select the image, click the Wrap Text button in the Arrange group, click Square from the drop-down gallery, and then drag the image to the center of the cell.

f. With the picture selected, click the *Simple Frame, White* picture style in the first row of the Picture Styles gallery in the Picture Styles group in the Picture Tools Format tab.

g. Position the insertion point in the cell in the third row of the table, and then insert **TradeFair.docx** located in your *Chapter05* folder. Make sure that the text is centered horizontally and vertically. Resize the row if necessary.

h. Position the insertion point in the first cell in the fourth row and insert **Midwest.docx** located in your *Chapter05* folder. Align the text at the left and center it vertically.

i. Position the insertion point in the second cell in the fourth row and insert **Register.docx** located in your *Chapter05* folder. Align the text at the right and center it vertically.

3. Create the sun shape shown in Figure 5.17 by completing the following steps:

a. Position the insertion point inside the first cell and then display the Insert tab. Click the Shapes button in the Illustrations group. Select the sun shape in the third row in the *Basic Shapes* section.

b. Drag and draw the sun shape in the upper left corner of the table. Size and position it similar to the sun in Figure 5.17.

c. Select the sun shape to open the Drawing Tools Format tab. Click the More button in the Shape Styles group, and then click the *Colored Fill - Gold, Accent 4* fill style.

d. With the sun shape still selected, click the Shape Effects button in the Shape Styles group, click Shadow, and then click the *Perspective Diagonal Upper Left* option in the *Perspective* section.

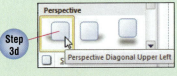

e. Click the Wrap Text button in the Arrange group and then click *Behind Text*.

4. Add a page color by displaying the Page Layout tab, clicking the Page Color button, and then clicking the *Light Yellow, Background 2* color in the *Theme Colors* section.

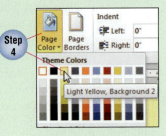

5. View your announcement at the Print tab Backstage view (Ctrl + F2). If any of the cells are not sized to where the items are postioned as shown in Figure 5.17, drag any boundary line in the table to its correct position. ***Hint: When you click a line in a table, the arrow pointer should display as two vertical bars with two arrows pointing to the left and right or as two horizontal bars pointing to top and bottom; drag to move the line, and then release the left mouse button when you are satisfied with the position.*** If the flyer displays too high or low on the page, change the top and/or bottom margins to help center the flyer vertically on the page. Adjust the position of the sun shape and WordArt if necessary. Close Print Preview by clicking the Home tab.

6. Select the table, click the down-pointing arrow at the right of the Borders button in the Table Styles group in the Table Tools Design tab, and then click *No Border*. ***Hint: Light gray gridlines may display if the View Gridlines button was selected in the Table group in the Table Tools Layout tab. These gridlines do not print.***

7. Save, print, and then close **C05-E01-Sailing.docx**. ***Hint: Review the chapter text on printing Background colors. Turn off the Show text boundaries option.***

Figure 5.17 Exercise 5.1

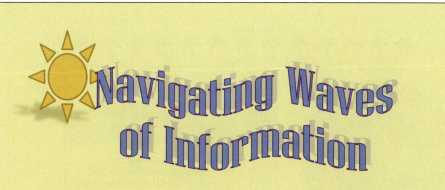

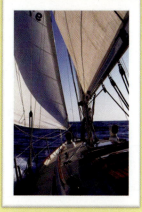

☞ Smooth Sailing on the Internet

☞ Cruising an Intranet

☞ Ferrying Email Messages

☞ Launching a Web Page

☞ Charting a New Course—
Changing Technology and
Software

**Computer Information Workshops
and Trade Fair**

MIDWEST COMMUNITY COLLEGE
465 East 86th Street
Indianapolis, IN 46240

July 25, 2012
8:30 a.m. to 3:30 p.m.
Register by phone: (317) 555-3909
Register online: http://www.emcp.net/mcc

Adding Lines, Borders, and Special Effects to Text, Objects, and Pictures

As discussed in Chapter 3, ruled lines can be used in a document to create a focal point, draw the eye across or down the page, separate columns and sections, or add visual appeal. Borders are generally used to frame text or an image with more than one side. Shading can be added to the background of a table, a paragraph, or selected text, or used as fill in a drawing object. Examples of lines, borders, shading, shadow, and 3-D effects are displayed in Figure 5.18.

Figure 5.18 Samples Lines, Borders, Shading, Shadow, and 3-D Effects

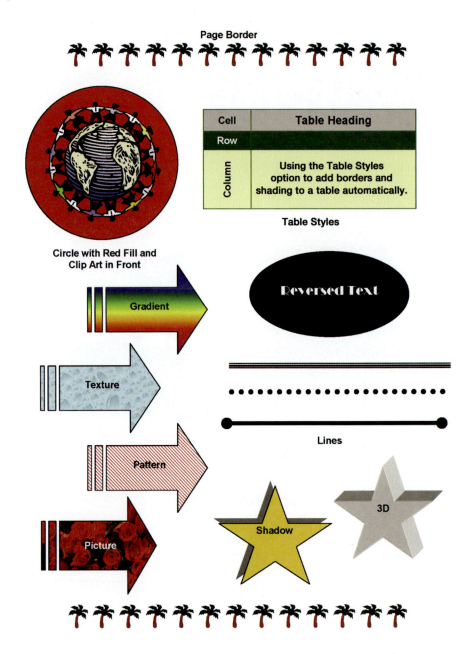

Adding Lines, Borders, and Frames to Images

You can add a border to any or all sides of a table, a paragraph, or selected text in a document. You can add a page border or an art border (such as a row of trees) to any or all sides of each page or section in a document. You can also add borders to text boxes, pictures, and imported pictures using tools on each associated tab. Rules and/or borders can be drawn using the Line button or the Rectangle button at the Shapes drop-down gallery, using lines in a table, inserting preformatted lines/borders in Quick Parts, clicking the Page Borders button in the Page Background group in the Page Layout tab, and accessing options at the Borders and Shading dialog box. In addition, graphic borders are available in Word 2010 and accessed as any other clip art.

Page Borders

Creating Automatic Lines

You can create automatic lines in Word 2010 by using any one of the following methods:

- Type three or more hyphens (-), and then press Enter to create a thin bottom border.
- Type three or more underscores (_), and then press Enter to create a thick bottom border.
- Type three or more equal signs (=), and then press Enter to create a double bottom line.
- Type three or more pound symbols (#), and then press Enter to create a thin/thick/thin bottom border.
- Type three or more tildes (~), and then press Enter to create a wavy bottom border.
- Type three or more asterisks (*), and then press Enter to create a thick dotted bottom border.

To turn off the automatic lines created using the methods discussed above, hover over the automatic line, and then click the down arrow at the right of the AutoCorrect Options Smart Tag. From the shortcut menu that displays, click *Undo Border Line, Stop Automatically Creating Border Lines,* or *Control AutoFormat Options.* The *AutoFormat* option allows you to adjust settings for automatic borders, bulleted lists, built-in Heading styles, automatic numbering, smart quotes ("), ordinals, fractions, and more. You may also simply click the Undo button on the Quick Access toolbar to undo the lines you created and do not want to use.

Adding Lines and Borders to Tables

All tables default to a single ½-point black solid-line border that prints. To add a line or customized border to a table, display the Tables and Borders dialog box and choose options to create lines around, within, beside, or below a table, or click the Horizontal button to add predesigned lines to your table. Alternatively, select predesigned formats from the Table Styles group in the Table Tools Design tab. Select the cells where you want the line or border to appear and then click any one or more of the options at the Border button drop-down list. If you prefer drawing the line or border, use the Draw Table button.

Adding a Page Border

Word provides page borders that range from simple to highly ornate. Choose the art border that best complements the content of your document. Refer to Chapter 4 for additional information on the *Page Border* option in the Borders and Shading dialog box. Click the Page Borders button in the Page Background group on the Page Layout tab to access the Borders and Shading dialog box.

Adding Fill to Design Elements

You can add shading to the background of a table, a paragraph, or selected text, shapes, SmartArt, charts, text boxes, and some graphics. You can fill drawing objects with solid or gradient (shaded) colors, a pattern, a texture, or a picture. Photographs or clip art may even be added to shapes to create an interesting focal point. As instructed in Exercise 5.2, you will add a picture to an arrow shape as a means of reinforcing the theme of the document—pointing to a healthy lifestyle. To add a picture as *fill,* insert a shape, click the Shape Fill button, click Picture, locate and select the desired picture, and then click Insert.

Fill
Shading added to drawing objects.

Figure 5.19 Picture Conforming to a Shape

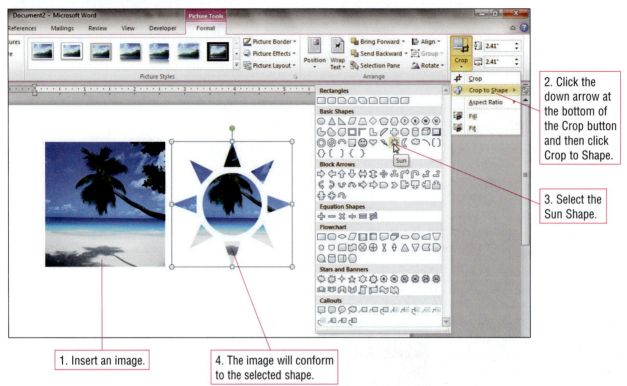

1. Insert an image.

2. Click the down arrow at the bottom of the Crop button and then click Crop to Shape.

3. Select the Sun Shape.

4. The image will conform to the selected shape.

DTP POINTERS
To find the graphic file number assigned to an image, right-click on a picture at the Clip Art task pane, click Preview/Properties, and then write the file number down.

DTP POINTERS
Press Ctrl+D to create duplicate objects.

Grid Settings

DTP POINTERS
Pick up design ideas from the works of others.

To help you locate the desired image for the shape fill, you may want to use the *Search* option at the Clip Art task pane. After you have located the desired image, right-click the image, and then click *Copy* from the shortcut menu, which sends the image to the Clipboard. At the Select Picture dialog box, paste the image at a white area of the screen.

The above mentioned approach is just one method of filling a shape with a picture. Alternatively, you may insert the picture first, select the picture, click the Crop button in the Size group in the Picture Tools Format tab, and then click the desired shape. The picture will conform to the design shape as shown in Figure 5.19.

Using the Drawing Gridlines

The Word drawing grid is a network of lines that help you align drawing objects, such as Shapes, Text Boxes, Clip Art, and Pictures. As you drag or draw an object, Word pulls it into alignment with the nearest intersection of gridlines or other objects. By default, gridlines are not visible, but you may choose to display gridlines on the screen at the Drawing Grid dialog box. The horizontal and vertical spacing between the gridlines defaults to 0.13 inch, but you may change this setting. You also have the option to change the starting point or origin for the gridlines from the default 0 (zero) inch to any increments you choose from the margins as shown in Figure 5.20. To override settings for the gridlines temporarily, press the Alt key as you drag or draw an object.

Assume you are working part time at the Brighton Health & Fitness Center while attending classes at a local community college. Prepare an announcement promoting a new summer program. Keep the theme of the flyer in mind as you decide on photos to use in the document.

Figure 5.20 Customizing the Drawing Grid

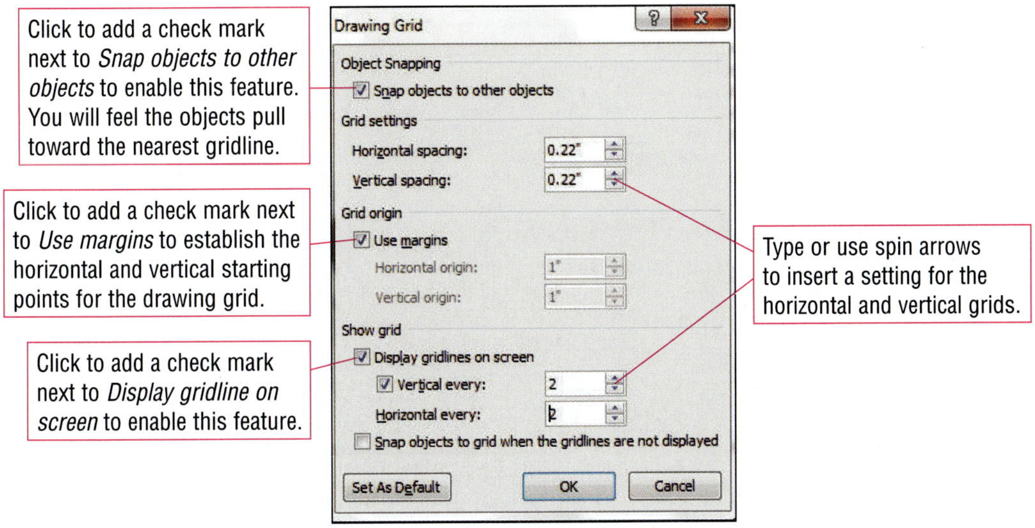
Click to add a check mark next to *Snap objects to other objects* to enable this feature. You will feel the objects pull toward the nearest gridline.
Click to add a check mark next to *Use margins* to establish the horizontal and vertical starting points for the drawing grid.
Click to add a check mark next to *Display gridline on screen* to enable this feature.
Type or use spin arrows to insert a setting for the horizontal and vertical grids.
Drawing Grid
Object Snapping
Snap objects to other objects
Grid settings
Horizontal spacing:
0.22"
Vertical spacing:
0.22"
Grid origin
Use margins
Horizontal origin:
1"
Vertical origin:
1"
Show grid
Display gridlines on screen
Vertical every:
2
Horizontal every:
2
Snap objects to grid when the gridlines are not displayed
Set As Default
OK
Cancel

Exercise 5.2 Creating an Announcement with Shapes and Picture Fill Using the Drawing Grid

Portfolio

1. Create the announcement in Figure 5.21 by completing the following steps:
   a. Open **Health** located in your *Chapter05* folder.
   b. Save the document, and name it **C05-E02-Health.**
   c. Turn on the Show/Hide feature.
   d. Select *Healthy choices point to healthy lives. . .*, change the font to 36-point Papyrus in bold, select both occurrences of *healthy,* and apply a green color of your choosing. ***Hint: Click on the first occurrence of healthy and then hold down the Ctrl key and select the other occurrence. Apply the formatting change.*** Select *point*, and apply italics. Turn on kerning at 14 points. Change the Shape Fill to No Fill in this text box.
   e. Position the insertion point in the text box below *Healthy choices. . .*, and insert **Cardio.docx** located in your *Chapter05* folder.
   f. Select all of the *Cardio* text, right-align the text, and then change the font to 14-point Arial; select *Summer Cardio Mix,* change the point size to 18-point Bauhaus 93, and apply the same green color used in Step 1d. Apply italics to all the text except the *Summer Cardio Mix.*
   g. Change the Shape Outline to No Outline to remove the border around the text box containing the *Cardio* text, and change the Shape Fill to No Fill.
   h. Select the text in the text box below *Summer Cardio Mix* and then change the alignment to center. (The text box contains the text *Brighton Health. . ..*)
   i. Select *Brighton Health & Fitness Center,* and change the font to 16-point Bauhaus 93 in the same green used earlier.
   j. Select the address and change the font to 10-point Arial in the same green.
   k. Select the text box containing *Brighton. . .*, and change the Shape Fill to No Fill and the Shape Outline to No Outline.

l. Position the insertion point in the text box behind the *Brighton* text, and insert the symbol (logo) in Figure 5.21 by completing the following steps:

Step 1l

1) Display the Insert tab, and then click the Symbol button in the Symbols group.
2) Click More Symbols, choose the Symbols tab, select the Webdings font, and then select the symbol (Webdings: 134) located seventh from the left in the seventh row. **Hint: Type 134 in the Character code *text box.***
3) Click Insert and then Close.
4) Select the symbol, change the point size to 115 points, and change the font color to a light gray of your choosing.
5) Position the text box as shown in Figure 5.21.
6) Change the Shape Fill to No Fill and the Shape Outline to No Outline.

Step 1l2

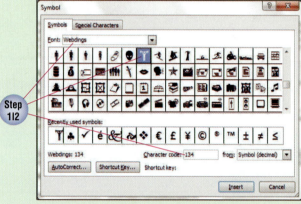

2. Create an underlining grid to help in aligning the arrow shapes shown in Figure 5.21 by completing the following steps:
   a. Click the Align button in the Arrange group in the Page Layout tab, and then click Grid Settings.
   b. At the Drawing Grid dialog box, make sure a check mark displays in the *Snap objects to other objects* check box.
   c. In the *Grid settings* section, type **0.22"** in the *Horizontal spacing* and *Vertical spacing* text boxes.
   d. In the *Grid origin* section, make sure a check mark displays in the *Use margins* check box.
   e. Make sure a check mark displays in the *Display gridlines on screen* check box. Also, make sure a check mark displays in the *Vertical every* check box, and type **2** in the *Vertical every* and *Horizontal every* text boxes. Click OK.

3. Create the arrows by completing the following steps:
   a. At the Insert tab, click the Shapes button and then click the Striped Right Arrow located in the *Block Arrows* section.

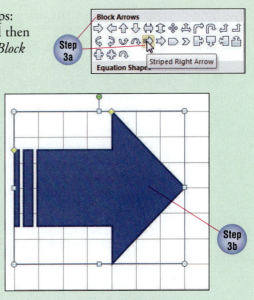

   b. Drag the crosshairs to create an arrow similar to Figure 5.21. Select the arrow shape to access the Drawing Tools Format tab. Change the *Shape Height* measurement to *2.64"* and the *Shape Width* measurement to *3.08"* in the Size group.
   c. Select the shape, click the Shape Effects button in the Shape Styles group, click Shadow from the drop-down list, and then click the *Perspective Diagonal Upper Left* option in the *Perspective* section. Position the object as shown in Figure 5.21.

   d. Hold down the Ctrl key as you select the arrow shape and drag a copy below the first shape as shown at the right. The drawing grid will pull your arrow shape to the closest gridline.
   e. Copy another arrow shape below the last one and position it as shown in Figure 5.21.

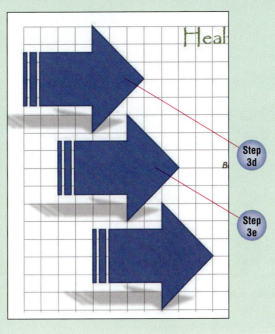

4. Add the photo picture fill by completing the following steps:

   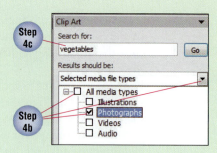

   a. Display the Clip Art task pane.
   b. Click the down-pointing arrow at the *Results should be* option box and then remove the check marks from the *All media types* check boxes, with the exception of that for *Photographs*, which should be checked.
   c. Type **vegetables** in the *Search for* text box, and then click Go.
   d. Locate a vegetable photograph similar to Figure 5.21 or a different photograph of your choosing.
   e. Right-click the photograph and then click *Copy* at the shortcut menu.
   f. Select the first arrow shape, click the Shape Fill button in the Shape Styles group in the Drawing Tools Format tab, and then click Picture.

   g. At the Select Picture dialog box, right-click in the white area of the dialog box, and then click *Paste*.
   h. Select the photograph and then click Insert.
   i. Complete similar steps to insert a fruit (citrus) photograph in the second arrow shape.
   j. Complete similar steps to insert an exercise photograph in the third arrow shape.
   k. Click the down-pointing arrow at the *Results should be* option box in the Clip Art task pane, and add a check mark to the *All media types* check box.
   l. Select each shape and change the Shape Outline to the *Olive Green, Accent 3, Darker 25%* color.

5. Remove the check mark from the *Display gridlines on screen* options at the Drawing Grid dialog box.
6. Save, print, and then close **C05-E02-Health.docx**.

Figure 5.21 Exercise 5.2

Matching Colors

To make your document look even more professional, match a color from an image used in your document to your font color as shown in Figure 5.22. To match colors, ungroup the clip art image, *Hint: you can ungroup graphics saved in WMF format, but not when saved in PNG, JPG, or GIF formats*, select a segment that contains the color you want to use, and then write down the values for Red, Green, and Blue (*RGB*), or click the down-pointing arrow at the right of the Color model and record the values for Hue, Saturation, and Luminescence (*HSL*). The RGB and HSL settings are on the Custom tab of the Colors dialog box. Use the same values to color your fonts and other drawing objects.

RGB
Stands for the colors Red, Green, and Blue.

HSL
Stands for Hue, Saturation, and Luminescence.

Figure 5.22 Matching Colors

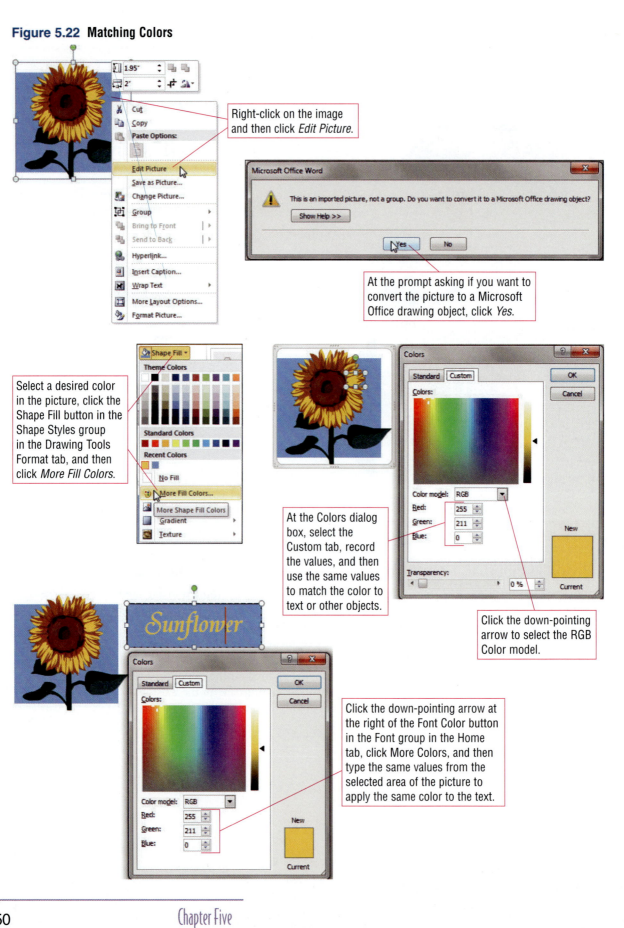

Right-click on the image and then click *Edit Picture*.

At the prompt asking if you want to convert the picture to a Microsoft Office drawing object, click *Yes*.

Select a desired color in the picture, click the Shape Fill button in the Shape Styles group in the Drawing Tools Format tab, and then click *More Fill Colors*.

At the Colors dialog box, select the Custom tab, record the values, and then use the same values to match the color to text or other objects.

Click the down-pointing arrow to select the RGB Color model.

Click the down-pointing arrow at the right of the Font Color button in the Font group in the Home tab, click More Colors, and then type the same values from the selected area of the picture to apply the same color to the text.

Chapter Five

Figure 5.23 Picture Effects

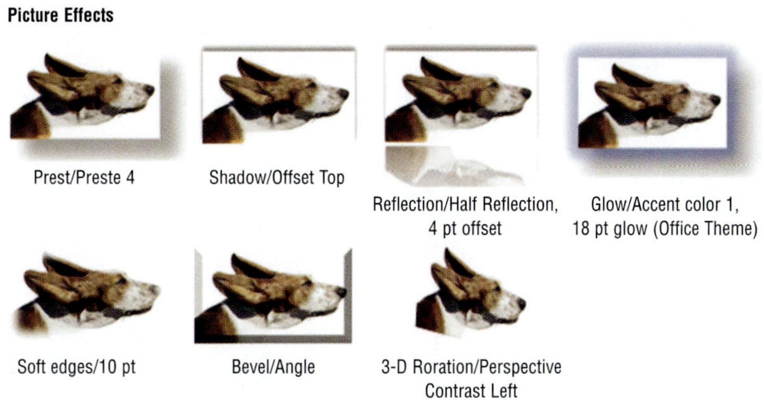

Picture Effects
Prest/Preste 4
Shadow/Offset Top
Reflection/Half Reflection, 4 pt offset
Glow/Accent color 1, 18 pt glow (Office Theme)
Soft edges/10 pt
Bevel/Angle
3-D Roration/Perspective Contrast Left

Adding Special Effects

Picture Effects

Picture Effects

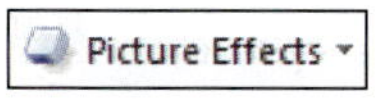

You can add depth to lines, text boxes, drawing objects, and some pictures by using either Shape Effects or Picture Effects as shown in Figure 5.23. Many of these features have been discussed in earlier chapters. Take time to experiment with each of these features to see what results you can accomplish. However, remember that a basic rule in design is to keep the design simple…do not over design.

In addition to all the Picture Effects options shown above, you may also use the Format Picture dialog box to select even more options to customize your object or image. The Format Picture dialog box is shown in Figure 5.24.

Figure 5.24 Format Picture Dialog Box

Format Picture
Fill
Line Color
Line Style
Shadow
Reflection
Glow and Soft Edges
3-D Format
3-D Rotation
Picture Corrections
Picture Color
Artistic Effects
Crop
Text Box
Alt Text
3-D Format
Bevel
Top:
Width: 0 pt
Height: 0 pt
Bottom:
Width: 0 pt
Height: 0 pt
Depth
Color:
Depth: 0 pt
Contour
Color:
Size: 0 pt
Surface
Material:
Lighting:
Angle: 0°
Reset
Close

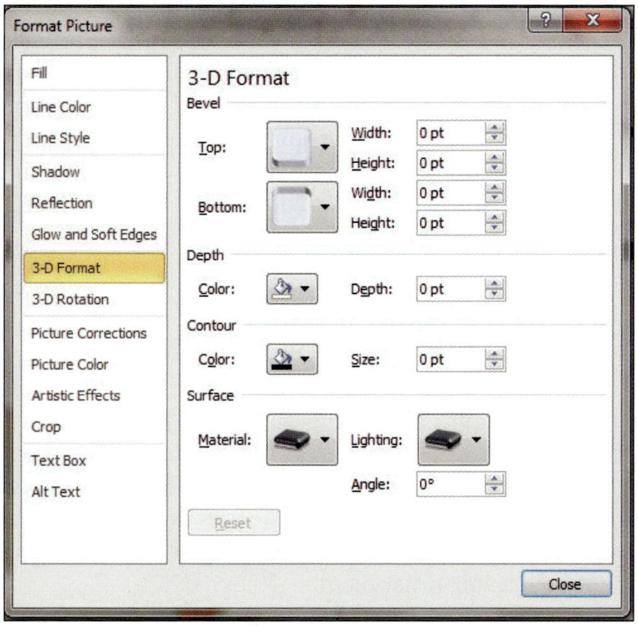

Figure 5.25 Microsoft Office Picture Manager

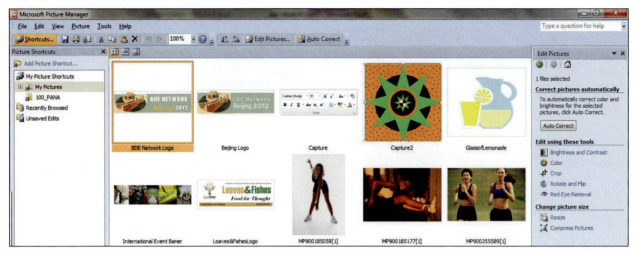

Editing Pictures

Microsoft Picture Manager, as shown in Figure 5.25, is located in the Microsoft Office 2010 Tools group in the All Programs menu. It lets you organize collections of image files from disks, shared network folders, and SharePoint websites. You can also compress and resize images and perform image-editing tasks, such as removing "red-eye" from photographs. In addition, you can convert images to alternative formats (for instance, from bitmap format to JPEG, PNG, or GIF format).

Editing Pictures Using Microsoft Office Word

DTP POINTERS
You may not be able to ungroup all images.

Microsoft Picture Manager is a graphic editor available within Word. You can invoke the editor by right-clicking the selected image and then clicking *Edit Picture* from the shortcut menu. The object has become ungrouped and you may click on any part of the object and use the tools on the Drawing Tools Format tab to alter the image as shown in Figure 5.26. You will need to make sure the image is *In line with Text*, which is the default setting. In addition, you may have difficulty ungrouping images saved in formats other than the WMF format. You cannot use the editor in Word to ungroup graphics saved in PNG, JPG, or GIF formats.

Creating a Flyer Using a Graphic Border

In Exercise 5.3, you will create a flyer using a Word graphic border and insert text inside the border. Compare Figure 5.27 to Figure 5.28. Which flyer attracts your attention and pulls you in to read the text? Of course, Figure 5.28 communicates more effectively because of the relevant graphic border and the varied typefaces, typestyles, and type sizes. How many typefaces can you find in this document? (There are only two typefaces used in this flyer—Gabriola and Calligraph421 BT). A graphic border is inserted into a document like any other picture.

Figure 5.26 Ungrouping, Altering, and Regrouping a Picture

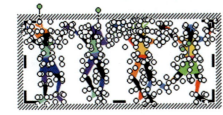

Ungrouping an image

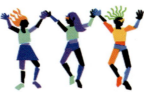

Altering an image

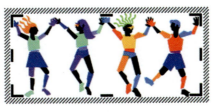

Regrouping an image

Figure 5.27 Flyer Before

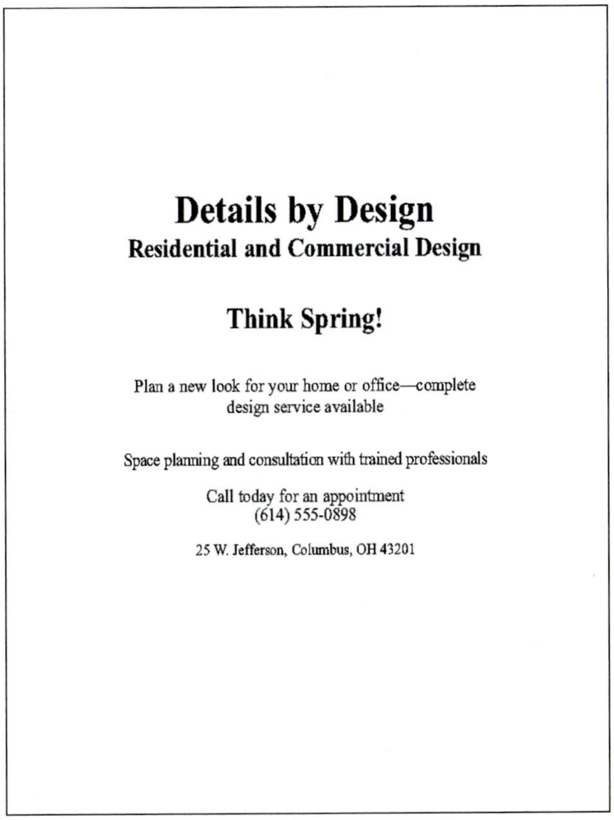

Details by Design

Residential and Commercial Design

Think Spring!

Plan a new look for your home or office—complete design service available

Space planning and consultation with trained professionals

Call today for an appointment
(614) 555-0898

25 W. Jefferson, Columbus, OH 43201

Figure 5.28 Flyer After (Exercise 5.3)

Details by Design

RESIDENTIAL AND

COMMERCIAL DESIGN

Think spring!

Plan a new look for your home or office—complete design service available. We provide space planning and consultations with trained professionals.

Call today for an appointment.

614-555-0898

25 W. Jefferson • Columbus, OH • 43201

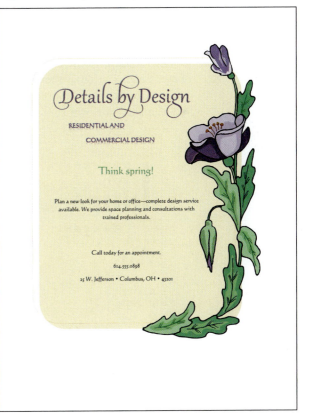

Create the flyer in Figure 5.28 by completing the following steps:

1. At a blank document, create a flyer with a graphic border.
2. Insert the graphic border shown in Figure 5.28 by typing **flower border** in the *Search for* text box at the Clip Art task pane. Close the task pane. ***Hint: If this border is no longer available, you may locate it in your* Chapter05 *folder.***

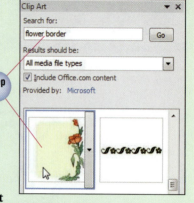

3. Save the document, and name it **C05-E03-Design**.
4. Customize the graphic border by completing the following steps:
   a. Select the graphic border to access the Picture Tools Format tab. In the Size group, type **8"** in the *Height* text box, and the width will automatically display (approximately 6.5"). ***Hint: By default, the* Lock aspect ratio *option and the* Relative to original picture *option are selected at the Size dialog box.***
   b. Select the graphic, right-click, and then click *Edit Picture* at the shortcut menu. Click the *Yes* option at the prompt to convert the image to a drawing object.

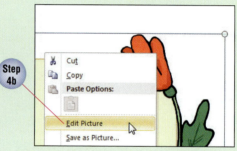

   c. Make sure the Office theme is selected, click each segment of the flowers and apply a variation of the purple color in the *Theme Colors* section at the Shape Fill color palette. Use Figure 5.28 is a guide, but feel free to make your own choices.

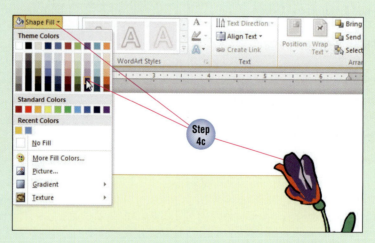

5. Create a text box inside the graphic border, and add text by completing the following steps:
   a. Click the Text Box button in the Text group in the Insert tab, and then click the Draw Text Box button.
   b. Drag the crosshairs inside the graphic border, and draw a box near the inside edge of the graphic border.
   c. Remove the Shape Outline around the text box. Remove the Shape Fill.

d. Position the insertion point inside the text box, and insert **Design.docx** located in your *Chapter05* folder.

e. Select all the text and then change the font to 11-point Calligraph421 BT or Lucida Calligraphy if Calligraph421 BT is not available.

6. Format *Details by Design* by completing the following steps:

a. Select *Details by Design*, change the font to 48-point Gabriola; the font color to the *Purple, Accent 4, Darker 25%* color in the Font Color palette, and then center the text horizontally. ***Hint: Make sure the left edge of "Details" is not cut off; if it does not display entirely, increase the size of the text box.***

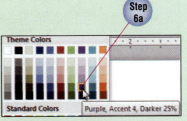

b. With *Details by Design* selected, click the Font dialog box launcher, and then select the Advanced tab.

c. Expand the text by 0.5 pt., turn on *Kerning* at *14* points, select the *Standard and Contextual* option at the *Ligature* list box, and then select 6 in the *Stylistic sets* list box. Click OK.

d. Position the insertion point in front of *Residential*, and press the Tab key.

e. Position the insertion point in front of *Commercial Design*, and press the Tab key twice.

f. Select *Residential and Commercial Design*, click the Text Effects button in the Font group, and then click the *Gradient Fill - Purple, Accent 4, Reflection* effect.

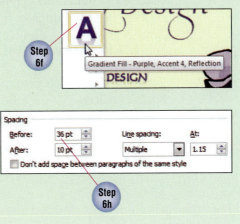

g. Position the insertion point in front of *Think spring!* and press Ctrl + Shift + End to select from the insertion point to the end of the document. Click the Center button in the Paragraph group in the Home tab.

h. Position the insertion point before *Think spring!*, click the Paragraph dialog box launcher, and then type **36 pt** in the *Before* text box in the *Spacing* section. Click OK.

i. Select *Think spring!*, change the font to 20-point Calligraph421 BT, click the Font color button in the Font group, click More Colors, and then change the Font color to the green color in some of the leaves. Type **51** in the *Red* text box, **153** in the *Green* text box, and **102** in the *Blue* text box in the Custom tab in the Colors dialog box. Click OK.

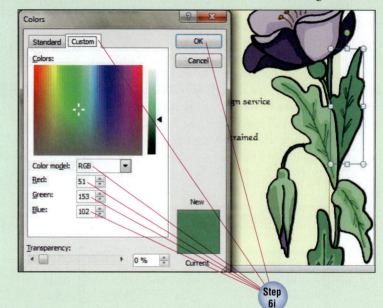

Step 6i

j. Position the insertion point in front of *Plan a new look…,* and type **36 pt** in the *Before* text box in the *Spacing* section of the Paragraph dialog box.

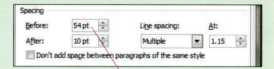

Step 6k

k. Position the insertion point in front of *Call today for an appointment. . .* and then type **54 pt** in the *Before* text box in the *Spacing* section of the Paragraph dialog box.

l. Resize the text box, and make any other needed adjustments.

m. Select the flower border graphic, click the Position button in the Arrange group in the Picture Tools Format tab and then click the *Position in Middle Center with Square Text Wrapping* option from the Position gallery.

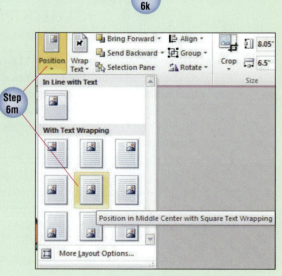

Step 6m

7. Save, print, and then close **C05-E03-Design.docx**.

Figure 5.29 Adjusting Brightness and Contrast

Original Picture

Brightness: +20% Contrast: -20%

Brightness: -20% Contrast: +20%

Adjusting Pictures

On the Picture Tools Format tab, you will find numerous options for customizing pictures. Whether adjusting the brightness and/or contrast of a picture, applying distinctive picture styles with depth and dimension, or selecting unique picture effects, you will be amazed by all of these new Word creative opportunities. Be sure to experiment.

Many of the features on the Picture Tools Format tab have been discussed earlier. The following sections highlight features not previously discussed and other advanced features new to Word 2010.

Adjusting Brightness, Contrast, and Blurriness in Pictures

You can adjust the relative lightness (brightness) of a picture, the difference between its darkest and lightest areas of a picture (contrast), and the blurriness of the picture by clicking the Corrections button in the Adjust group in the Picture Tools Format tab. Select a thumbnail that represents the changing you want to make as shown in Figure 5.29. To enhance photo details, you can sharpen the picture or removed any unwanted marks on the picture by using a soften effect. To fine-tune the amount of brightness or contrast, move the *Brightness* slider (or *Contrast* slider) or type a number in the box next to the slider at the Format Picture dialog box.

Corrections
Corrections

Adjust the image clarity by choosing a thumbnail that corresponds with your needs in the *Sharpen and Soften* section. The image in Figure 5.30 was sharpened by 50 percent.

Figure 5.30 Sharpening an Image

Original Picture

Sharpen: 50%

Figure 5.31 Saturation, Color Tone, and Recolor at the Color Gallery

Original Picture

Color Saturation: 33%

Color Tone Temperature: 11200 K

Recolor Black and White: 50%

Recolor Olive, Green Accent
color 3 Dark

Adjusting Color Saturation, Color Tone, and Recolor

Saturation is the intensity of the color. A higher saturation makes a picture look more vivid, whereas a lower saturation turns the colors toward gray. When color temperatures are not measured correctly by a camera, a color cast can show on the picture making the picture look too orange or too blue. You can adjust this by increasing or decreasing the color temperature to enhance the details of the picture and make the picture look better. The higher the temperature number, the more orange is added. The lower the number, the more blue is added. Choose the *Recolor* thumbnails to apply built-in stylized effects to your picture. Figure 5.31 illustrates a sample of the Color gallery effects applied to a picture.

If you click the Picture Color Options button at the bottom of the Color gallery, you will access the Format Picture dialog box with the Picture Color tab displayed. To choose the most common *Saturation, Color Tone,* and *Recolor* effects, click the *Presets* options in each of these categories as shown in Figure 5.32.

Color

Making a Picture Transparent

You can make part of a picture transparent to better show any text that is layered on top of it, to layer pictures on top of each other, or to remove or hide parts of a picture for emphasis. You cannot make more than one color in a picture transparent. However, you can make more than one color transparent in another image editing program, save the picture in a format that preserves transparency information, such as Portable Network Graphics (PNG), and then insert the file into your office document. Select the picture, click *Set Transparent Color* option, and then click the color in the picture you want to make transparent. See Figure 5.33 for an example of the transparency feature.

Figure 5.32 Most Common Preset Color Effects

Select a desired Recolor Preset
thumbnail such as Grayscale.

Select a desired Color Saturation Preset
thumbnail such as Saturation: 200%.

Select a desired Color Tone Preset
thumbnail such as Temperature: 8800 K.

Figure 5.33 Using the Transparency Tool

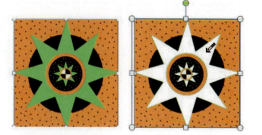

Original Graphic   **Transparency Applied to Graphic**

Applying Artistic Effects to Pictures

Artistic Effects

You can apply artistic effects to a picture or a picture fill to make the picture look more like a sketch, drawing, or painting. You can apply only one artistic effect at a time to a picture, so applying a different artistic effect will remove the previously applied artistic effect. Figure 5.34 shows the effects of applying the Photocopy and Pencil Grayscale effects to a picture.

Compressing Pictures

Compressing a picture to reduce the size of the file changes the amount of detail retained in the original picture. This means that after compression, the picture can look different than before it was compressed. You should compress your picture and save the file before you apply any of the artistic effects. It is a good idea to compress a picture after cropping to remove any unwanted areas.

Using Pictures Styles

The Live Preview feature in Word 2010 is intuitive and efficient when determining which Picture Styles you may want to apply to your picture. As shown in Figure 5.35, there are approximately 30 creative borders and effects that can be added to a picture to enhance the appeal of the image.

Figure 5.34 Applying Artistic Effects

Original Picture   **Photocopy Effect**   **Pencil Grayscale Effect**

Figure 5.35 **Examples of Picture Styles**

Simple Frame, White

Beveled Matte, White

Metal Frame

Drop Shadow Rectangle

Reflected Rounded Rectangle

Soft Edge Rectangle

Double Frame, Black

Thick Matte, Black

Simple Frame, Black

Beveled Oval, Black

Compound Frame, Black

Moderate Frame, Black

Center Shadow Rectangle

Rounded Diagonal Corner, White

Snip Diagonal Corner, White

Moderate Frame, White

Rotated White

Perspective Shadow, White

Relaxed Perspective, White

Soft Edge Oval

Bevel Rectangle

Bevel Perspective

Reflected Perspective Right

Reflected Perspective Left, White

Reflected Bevel, Black

Reflected Bevel, White

Metal Rounded Rectangle

Metal Oval

Figure 5.36 **Removing the Background of a Picture**

Original Picture   Choosing the Area to Remove   Remove Background

Using the Remove Background Feature

Remove Background

The Remove Background option in the Adjust group automatically removes unwanted portions of the picture. If you select an image and then click the Remove Background button, the Background Removal tab will display with three options in the Refine group and two options in the Close group (Figure 5.36). Click the Mark Areas to Keep button to draw lines to mark areas to keep in your picture. Click the Mark Areas to Remove button to draw lines to mark areas to remove from the picture. The Delete Mark button may be used to delete lines you have drawn to change areas to keep or remove. The Discard all Changes button allows you to close Background Removal and discard all changes. Finally, the Keep Changes option allows you to close Background Removal and keep all changes.

In Exercise 5.4, you will create an announcement that will promote an auction to benefit a local zoo. The document will be trimmed to a 5" by 7" size page. You will insert several photographs and a graphic border that reinforces the overall theme of the document. You will use several adjustment features, remove the background of an image, and then group all the objects before saving it.

Exercise 5.4   Safari Ball Announcement with Front Side

1. At a blank document create the announcement in Figure 5.37.
2. Insert the graphic border shown in Figure 5.37 by typing **zebra** in the *Search for* text box at the Clip Art task pane. Click to insert the zebra border. ***Hint: If the zebra border is no longer available, you may find the image in your* Chapter05 *folder.***
3. Save the document, and name it **C05-C04-SafariBall**.

Step 2

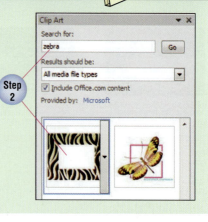

4. Customize the graphic border by completing the following steps:
   a. Double-click the graphic border to access the Picture Tools Format tab. Click the Size Layout dialog box launcher in the Size group, and then click to remove the check marks next to the *Lock aspect ratio* option and the *Relative to original picture size* option in the Scale section.
   b. In the *Height* section, click the *Absolute* option, and then type **5.1"** in the *Height* text box.
   c. Click the *Absolute* option in the *Width* section, and then click in the *Width* text box and type **7.1"**. Click OK.

   d. Select the border, click the down-pointing arrow at the right of the Rotate button in the *Arrange* group, and then click the *Rotate Right 90°* option.
   e. With the border selected, click the Position button, and then click the *Position in Middle Center with Square Text Wrapping* option.
5. Create a text box containing the document text as shown in Figure 5.37 by completing the following steps:
   a. Drag and draw a text box inside the zebra border.
   b. Select the text box, type **5.5"** in the *Shape Height* text box, and type **3.5"** in the *Shape Width* text box in the Size group.
   c. Position the text box as shown in Figure 5.37, and then insert the **SafariText.docx** file located in your *Chapter05* folder.
   d. Change the theme to the *Austin* theme.
   e. Select the text and change the font to 10-point Century Gothic and the alignment to Center.
   f. Apply bold and italics to the text as shown in Figure 5.37.
   g. Position your insertion point on the third paragraph symbol below *Please join us for the*. **Hint: Turn on the Show/Hide feature.**
   h. Click the WordArt button in the Text group on the Insert tab and then click the *Fill - Green, Accent 1, Metal Bevel, Reflection* style.
   i. Select *YOUR TEXT HERE*, type **Sixth Annual**, press Shift + Enter, and type **Safari Ball**. **Hint: Resize the WordArt text box if necessary.**
   j. Select *Sixth Annual Safari Ball* and change the font to 28-point Century Gothic and the alignment to Center.

k. Click the Paragraph dialog box launcher and type **0 pt** in the *After* text box in the *Spacing* section. Click the down-pointing arrow at the right of the *Line Spacing* list box, select the *Multiple* option from the drop-down list, and then type **0.75"** in the *At* list box. Click OK.

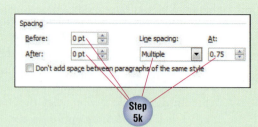

Step 5k

l. Select the text box containing the document text, click the More button in the Shape Styles group, and then click the *Subtle Effect - Green, Accent 1* style.

Step 5l

Subtle Effect - Green, Accent 1

6. Insert the picture shown in Figure 5.37 by completing the following steps:

a. Type **safari** in the *Search for* text box at the Clip Art task pane. Click to insert the lion picture shown at the right, and then close the task pane. ***Hint: Click outside the text box before inserting the image.***

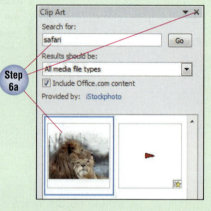

Step 6a

b. Select the image, change the Wrap Text to *In Front of Text*, and then click the Remove Background button in the Adjust group. If the lion's mane displays in purple (marked to be deleted), drag the middle sizing handle outward to remove the purple fill. Click the middle sizing handle at the bottom of the picture if the purple fill includes the lion's chin and drag down to remove the purple fill.

c. Click the Keep Changes button in the Background Removal tab.

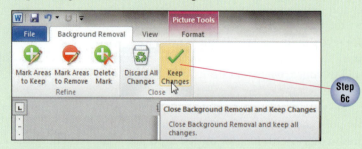

Step 6c

Close Background Removal and Keep Changes

Close Background Removal and keep all changes.

d. Resize the image and then drag and drop it as shown in Figure 5.37.

e. Select the image, click the Rotate button in the Arrange group, and then click the *Flip Horizontal* option. ***Hint: The image should face the text.***

7. Save, print, and then close **C05-E04-SafariBall.docx**.

Figure 5.37 Exercise 5.4

Exercise 5.5 Safari Ball Announcement Back Side

1. At a blank document create the back side of the announcement.
2. Save the document as **C05-E05-SafariBall**.
3. Create a text box and then size the text box to measure 7.1" in the *Shape Height* text box and and 5.1" in the *Shape Width* text box.
4. Change the theme to the *Austin* theme.
5. Select the text box, click the Position button in the Arrange group in the Drawing Tools Format tab, and then click the *Position in Middle Center with Square Text Wrapping* option.
6. Click the More button in the Shape Styles group and then click the *Subtle Effect - Green, Accent 1* style.
7. Position the insertion point inside the text box, and insert the **SafariText2.docx** file location in your *Chapter05* folder.
8. Create the WordArt text, at the top of the page, as instructed in Exercise 5.4 steps 5h - 5k.
9. Select the text from *Chicago White Sox...Candleabras*, and then click the Bullets button in the Paragraph group.
10. Select the bulleted text, click the Paragraph dialog box launcher, and then click to remove the check mark to the left of the *Don't add space between paragraphs of the same style* option. Click OK.

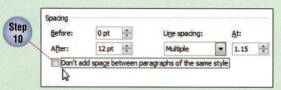

11. Insert two safari images of your own choosing, apply at least two picture effects to the images, and then size and position the images similar to Figure 5.38.
12. Insert the paws graphic at the bottom of the page by searching for **paws** at the Clip Art task pane. Size and then position the paws similar to Figure 5.38.

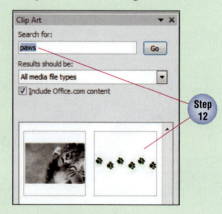

13. Save, print, and then close **C05-E05-SafariBall.docx**. Print the document on the back of **C05-E04-SafariBall.docx**. Trim the page to 5" by 7". You may consider sending the document to a commercial printer and having the document printed on 45# paper and professionally trimmed. You should save the document in PDF format before sending it to a commercial printer.

Figure 5.38 Exercise 5.5

LIVE AUCTION ITEMS:

- Chicago White Sox Home Game Package for Two

- Hacienda del Mar, Puerto Rico Vacation Package for Four

- Wisconsin Dells Family Vacation

- Ocean Course – Kiawah Island, South Carolina Golf Vacation Package for Four (Parkside Villa)

- Theatre Tickets and Dinner in Chicago

- Northern Michigan Vacation Package for Two (Old Mission Peninsula)

- Outdoor Tree Candelabras

And more...

Invitation design and printing underwritten by: Your name

Figure 5.39 Using SmartArt Types

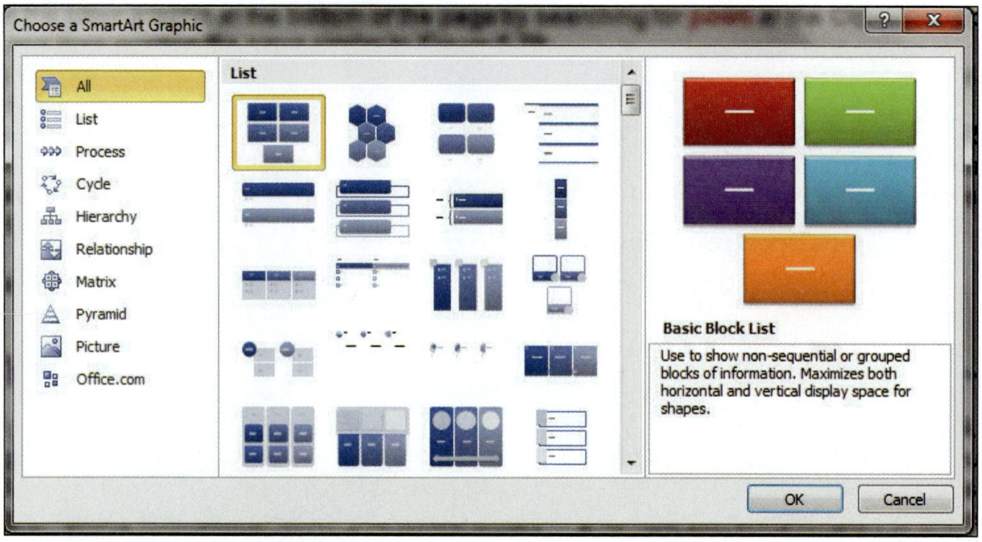

Learning About SmartArt Graphics

A SmartArt graphic is a visual representation of your information and ideas. You can create SmartArt graphics by choosing from many different SmartArt layouts, options, colors, and designs to creatively communicate your message. With SmartArt graphics and other Word 2010 features such as Themes and Quick Styles, you can create designer-quality illustrations. When you create SmartArt graphics, you are prompted to choose a type such *as List, Process, Cycle, Hierarchy, Relationship, Matrix,* or *Pyramid* as shown in Figure 5.39.

Smart Art

The information in Table 5.1 will help you decide on the type of SmartArt that will serve your needs.

Table 5.1 Using SmartArt Types

Use this type of SmartArt	*To do this. . .*
List	Show nonsequential information.
Process	Show steps in a process or timeline.
Cycle	Show a continual process.
Hierarchy	Create an organizational chart or decision tree.
Relationship	Illustrate connections.
Matrix	Show how parts relate to a whole.
Pyramid	Show proportional relationships with the largest component on the top or bottom.

Figure 5.40 Using the Text Pane

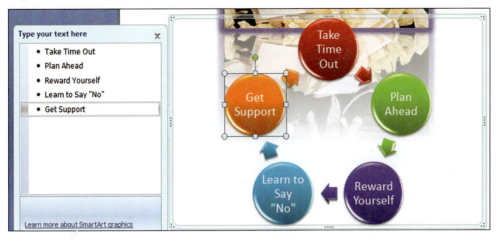

Using the Text Pane

The Text pane is used to enter and edit the text that appears in your SmartArt graphic. The Text pane displays at the left of your SmartArt graphic. When you create a SmartArt graphic, placeholder text displays in the Text pane as well as the SmartArt object as shown in Figure 5.40. As you type the text, the SmartArt object is automatically updated.

Using the SmartArt Tools Design Tab

A quick and easy way to add professional effects to your SmartArt graphic is to apply a SmartArt Style. SmartArt Styles include shape fills, edges, shadows, line styles, gradients, and 3-D perspectives as shown in Figure 5.41. To apply additional colors, shapes, and effects, click the Change Colors button in the SmartArt Styles group and the Add Shape button in the Create Graphic group. When you insert a SmartArt graphic into your document, it will match the rest of the content in your document. If you change the theme of the document, the look of the SmartArt graphic is updated automatically.

Using the SmartArt Tools Format Tab

Further customizations can be applied to your SmartArt graphic by accessing options on the SmartArt Tools Format tab as shown in Figure 5.42. You can change the look of your SmartArt graphic by changing the fill of its shape or text; by adding effects, such as shadows, reflections, glows, or soft edges; or by adding 3-D effects, such as bevels or rotations. WordArt formatting choices and preformatted Shape Styles are also available on this tab.

Figure 5.41 SmartArt Tools Design Tab

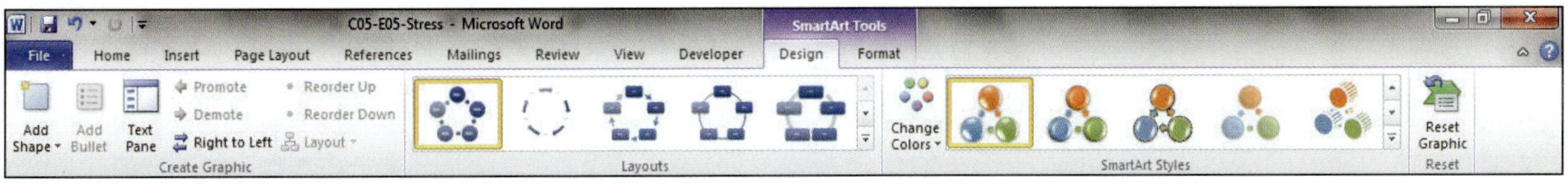

Figure 5.42 SmartArt Tools Format Tab

[Screenshot of Microsoft Word ribbon showing the SmartArt Tools Format Tab with Shapes, Shape Styles, WordArt Styles, and Arrange groups]

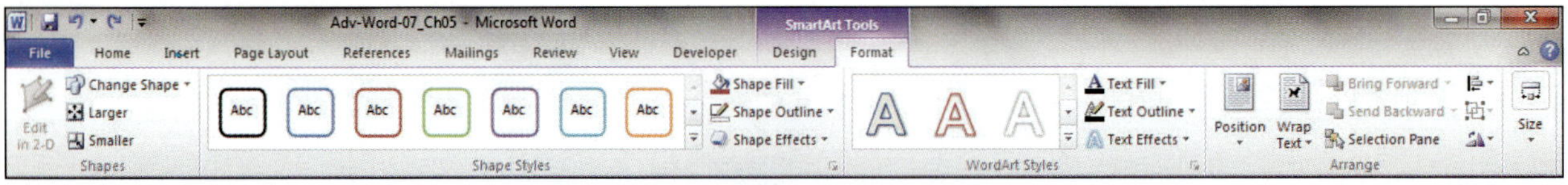

Exercise 5.6 Using Picture Styles, Border Enhancements, and WordArt in a Flyer

1. Create the announcement in Figure 5.43 by completing the following steps:
   a. Open **Stress.docx** located in your *Chapter05* folder.
   b. Save the document as **C05-E06-Stress**.
   c. Change the theme to the *Sketchbook* theme in the *From Office.com* section.
   d. Turn on the Show/Hide feature, select *Five Ways to De-Stress* (do not select the Paragraph symbol), and then click the WordArt button in the Text group in the Insert tab.

   Step 1e

   [Image showing WordArt style gallery with letter A styles; tooltip "Gradient Fill - Blue, Accent 4, Reflection"]

   e. Click the *Gradient Fill - Blue, Accent 4, Reflection* style. 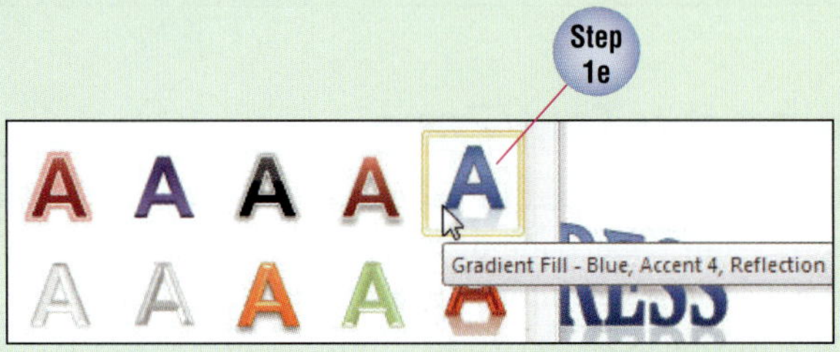
   f. Click the Text Effects button in the WordArt Styles group, click Transform, and then click the *Triangle Up* style in the *Warp* section.

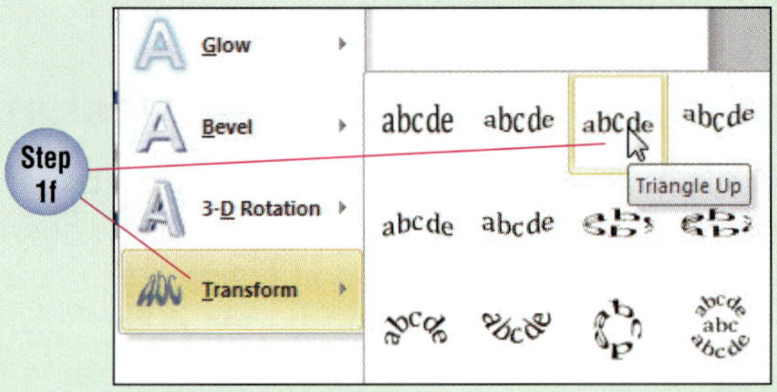

   Step 1f

   [Image showing Text Effects menu with Glow, Bevel, 3-D Rotation, Transform options and Transform gallery; tooltip "Triangle Up"]

   g. Click the Text Effects button, click Shadow, and then click the *Perspective Diagonal Upper Right* style in the *Perspective* section. 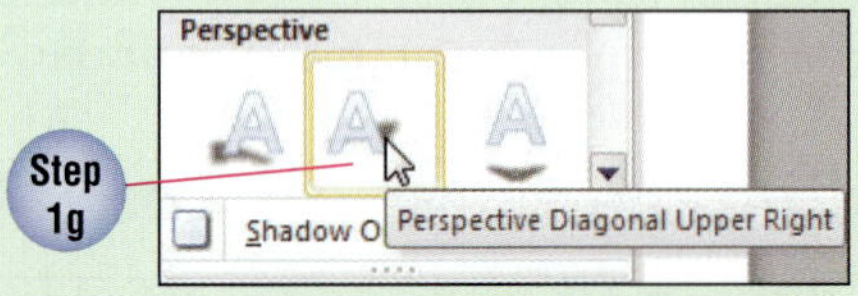
   h. Drag the WordArt object upward to within approximately 0.5 from the edge of the page and drag it to the horizontal center between the margins.

   Step 1g

   [Image showing Perspective shadow options; tooltip "Perspective Diagonal Upper Right"]

2. Position your insertion point below the WordArt object, click the Insert tab, and then click the Clip Art button in the Illustrations group.
   a. At the Clip Art task pane, type **stress** in the *Search for* text box. You may substitute another photograph of your own choosing. Click to insert it and then close the task pane.
   b. Select the image, size the image similar to Figure 5.43, and then change the wrap to *Behind Text*.
   c. Drag the picture to the horizontal center of the page and below *Five Ways to De-Stress* as shown in Figure 5.43.
   d. Select the image and then click the Picture Effects button in the Picture Styles group. Select *Reflection* from the drop-down list, and then click *Full Reflection, 4pt offset*.

   Step 2d

e. With the image selected, click the Picture Effects button again, click *Glow* from the drop-down list, and then click Glow Options at the bottom of the Glow Variations gallery.

f. Click the down-pointing arrow at the right of the *Color* option, and then click the *Indigo, Accent 5* color in the *Theme Colors* section.

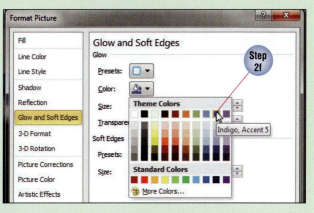

g. Type **30%** in the *Transparency* section, and then click Close.

h. Click the Artistic Effects button at the left of the Format Picture dialog box, click the down-pointing arrow at the right of the Artistic Effect button, and then click the *Film Grain* style. Click Close.

3. Create the SmartArt object below the photograph as shown in Figure 5.43 by completing the following steps:

   a. With the insertion point positioned at the top of the document below the WordArt object, click the SmartArt button in the Illustrations group in the Insert tab.

   b. At the Choose a SmartArt Graphic dialog box, select *Cycle*.

   c. Click Basic Cycle in the gallery, and then click OK.
   Hint: Do not be concerned that the SmartArt object may push the picture downward on the screen.

   d. At the SmartArt Tools Design tab with the Text pane displayed (if the Text pane does not automatically display, click the left-/right-pointing arrows at the left of the SmartArt object), type the text shown in Figure 5.43 (in the cycle shape) or as shown below. Close the Text pane.

   e. With the SmartArt object selected, click the SmartArt Tools Format tab, click the Wrap Text button in the Arrange group, click *In Front of Text*, and then drag the SmartArt graphic below the photograph as shown in Figure 5.43.

   f. Display the SmartArt Tools Design tab, click the Change Colors button in the SmartArt Styles group, and click *Colorful - Accent Colors* in the *Colorful* section. ***Hint: Experiment with choosing other color combinations in the Change Color gallery.***

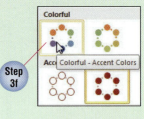

   g. Click the More button at the bottom right of the SmartArt Styles gallery and then click *Polished* in the *3-D* section.

4. Apply Quick Styles to the text at the bottom of the document by completing the following steps:

   a. Position the insertion point anywhere in the text *Help is on the way!* located in the text box at the bottom of the document.

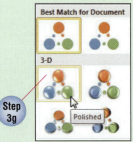

b. In the Home tab, click the More button in the bottom right corner of the Styles gallery, and then click the Intense Quote style to apply it.

   c. Select the remaining text in the text box, *Join the Anxiety. . .*, apply the Strong style, and then right-align the selected text.

5. Hold down the Shift key as you click to select each object in the document, click the Group button in the Arrange group, and then click Group.

6. Save, print, and then close **C05-E06-Stress.docx**.

7. *Optional:* Experiment with changing the Themes, Colors, Fonts, and Effects settings used in this document. Display the Page Layout tab, and then click the Themes button in the Themes group. Experiment with changing the Colors, Fonts, and Effects. Did you notice how the Effects change the depth and design of the SmartArt object? Did you notice that the font and font color changed in the text at the bottom of the document? Figure 5.43B shows the document after the Sketchbook theme was changed to the Thatch theme.

Figure 5.43 Exercise 5.6

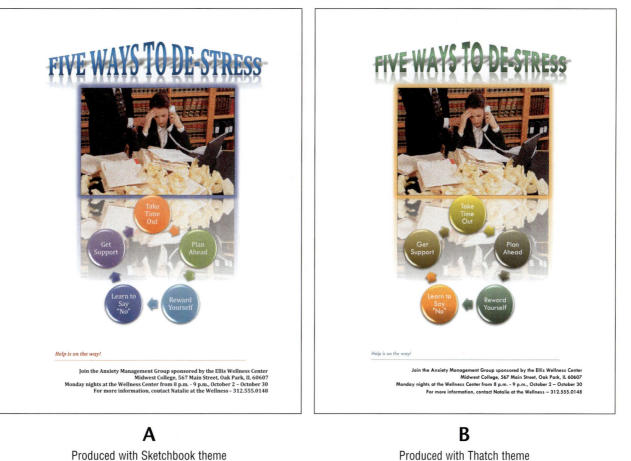

A
Produced with Sketchbook theme

B
Produced with Thatch theme

Chapter Summary

- Flyers and announcements are considered among the least expensive means of advertising.
- A flyer advertises a product or service that is available for a limited amount of time. An announcement informs an audience of an upcoming event.
- When creating headlines for flyers or announcements, select typefaces that match the tone of the document and type sizes that stress important information.
- Graphics added to a flyer or announcement can add excitement and generate enthusiasm for the publication. A simple graphic demands more attention and has more impact than a complex one.
- Use color in a publication to elicit a particular feeling, emphasize important text, attract attention, organize data, or create a pattern in a document. Limit the color to small areas so it attracts attention but does not create visual confusion.
- In planning a flyer or announcement, use a table to organize text, graphics, and other design elements on the page.
- Borders and lines added to a document aid directional flow, add color, and organize text to produce professional-looking results.
- Alter a clip art image by right-clicking on the image and selecting Edit Picture from the shortcut menu that displays, and then customize the image using buttons on the Drawing Tools Format tab.
- By default, pictures and clip art are inserted with the *In Line with Text* text wrapping style applied.
- You can use the Picture Tools Format tab to access options that Sharpen and Soften an image, Brightness and Contrast picture elements, alter Color Saturation and Color Tone, offer Recolor options, and add Transparency.
- The higher the saturation the more vivid the picture; the lower the saturation the more gray the colors become.
- You can remove a background from a picture to accent or highlight the subject of the picture or to remove distracting details.
- Add Artistic Effects to your images to make them interesting and unique.
- You can compress a picture to reduce the size of the file and the time it takes to download a file or view an image online. Use picture compression to remove cropped areas from an altered image.
- Apply Picture Styles, Picture Borders, Picture Effects, and Picture Layouts to enhance images for more visual appeal.
- You can crop an image to conform to a selected shape.
- To nudge an object is to move it in small increments (pixels) by pressing the arrow keys on the keyboard.
- The drawing canvas also helps you to arrange drawing objects and pictures and to move them as a single unit.
- The Microsoft Office Picture Manager is an Office utility that can compress and resize images and perform image-editing tasks, such as removing "red-eye" from photographs.
- Download clip art from the Office.com Web page.
- The Microsoft Clip Organizer may be used to organize images from scanners and digital cameras.
- When you scan a picture, consider the destination for the picture, the output resolution, and the file format needed.
- With the drawing grid turned on, an object is pulled into alignment with the nearest intersection of gridlines or to other objects.
- A raster image is a bitmapped image where pixels of color create the image.

- A vector image is created using mathematical equations. Line art is an example of a vector image.
- A common graphic file format is the bitmap format.
- You cannot ungroup bitmapped graphics.
- You can ungroup an image, discover the formula for a color used in the image, and then apply the color formula to text.
- RGB stands for Red, Green, and Blue; HSL stands for Hue, Saturation, and Luminescence.
- Use WordArt to distort or modify text to create a variety of shapes.
- Logos may be added to flyers and announcements to reinforce company identity or promote product recognition. The logo may be placed low on the page to anchor the message.
- A SmartArt graphic is a visual representative of your information and ideas.
- When you create a SmartArt graphic, you are prompted to choose a type such as List, Process, Cycle, Hierarchy, Relationship, Matrix, or Pyramid.
- You can use the SmartArt Tools Design tab and the SmartArt Tools Format tab to access options to create and customize a SmartArt graphic using the SmartArt Styles gallery (in Live Preview) and the SmartArt Layout gallery.
- The Text pane is the pane that you can use to enter and edit the text that appears in your SmartArt graphic.

Commands *Review*

FEATURE	RIBBON TAB, GROUP	BUTTON
Artistic Effects	Picture Tools Format, Adjust	Artistic Effects ▾
Color	Picture Tools Format, Adjust	Color ▾
Corrections	Picture Tools Format, Adjust	Corrections ▾
Draw Table	Table Tools Layout, Draw Borders	
Drawing Grid	Page Layout, Arrange	Grid Settings...
Eraser	Table Tools Design, Draw Borders	
Page Borders	Page Layout, Page Background	
Page Color	Page Layout, Page Background	
Picture Effects	Picture Tools Format, Picture Styles	Picture Effects ▾
Properties	Table Tools Layout, Table	
SmartArt	Insert, Illustrations	
Table	Insert, Tables	

Reviewing Key Points

True or False: Select the correct answer by circling T or F:

1. A complex graphic has more impact than a simple graphic.

    T   F

2. Flyers and announcements are considered among the least expensive means of advertising.

    T   F

3. You can ungroup an image, discover the formula for a color used in the image, and then apply the color formula to text.

    T   F

4. A grouped picture or object functions as a single unit.

    T   F

5. You can crop an image to conform to a selected shape.

    T   F

6. To copy a picture, hold down the Shift key, select the picture, and then drag and drop the picture to another location.

    T   F

7. The Microsoft Clip Organizer is an Office utility that can compress and resize images and perform image-editing tasks, such as removing "red-eye" from photographs.

    T   F

8. By default, pictures and clip art are inserted with the *In Front of Text* wrap text style applied.

    T   F

9. With the drawing grid turned on, an object is pulled into alignment with the nearest intersection of gridlines or to other objects.

    T   F

10. You can remove a background from a picture to accent or highlight the subject of the picture or to remove distracting details.

    T   F

11. When you create a SmartArt graphic, you are prompted to choose a type such as *List, Process, Cycle, Hierarchy, Relationship, Matrix,* or *Pyramid.*

    T   F

12. When a picture is inserted into a document, you can add a Glow effect to the image by clicking the Picture Effects button on the Insert tab.

    T   F

Chapter Assessments

Assessment 5.1   Creating a Community Flyer

1. At a blank document create the flyer in Figure 5.44 by completing the following steps:
   a. Complete a search for a sun graphic (sun face) similar to the one used in Figure 5.44, and then insert the image.
   b. Select your sun image, change the text wrap so you can move it easily, and then position and size the image as shown in Figure 5.44.
   c. Copy the image to the Clipboard.
   d. Crop off the bottom half of the image.
   e. Display the Clipboard task pane and paste a copy of the original image into your document. *Hint: Click the Clipboard launcher button at the right of the Clipboard group on the Home tab.*
   f. Crop the top section of the image to the point where you cropped the bottom section.
   g. With the image selected (the bottom half), click the Color button in the Adjust group, and then click the Washout thumbnail in the *Recolor* section. Make any adjustments that you feel are necessary to brighten or sharpen the image.
   h. Change the text wrap to match that chosen for the top graphic, drag the lightened part of the image to the colored part of the image, and then match the two halves. *Hint: Use the drawing canvas to group the halves of the image if you are having difficulty grouping the halves.*
   i. Drag the image to the horizontal center of the page as shown in Figure 5.44.
   j. Draw a text box that measures approximately 6.75 inches in height and 6.25 inches in width. Position the text box with the top of the text box even with the top of the lightened part of the image. *Hint: It looks like the sun is peeking over the text box.*
   k. Remove the Shape Fill from the text box.
   l. Add a dotted orange border to the text box and increase the thickness to match Figure 5.44.
   m. With the insertion point positioned in the text box, insert **GoodMorning.docx** from your *Chapter05* folder.
   n. Select the entire document (Ctrl + A) and change the horizontal alignment to Center, and turn on kerning.
   o. Select the title *Good Morning Naperville*, and change the font to 40-point Bradley Hand ITC Bold or a font of your choice. Position the insertion point before the line beginning *If daytime luncheons. . .*, press Ctrl + Shift + End (to select from the insertion point to the end of the document), and then change the font to a font of your choice change the font size, and add any desired text effects.
   p. Select the date and apply a text effect. *Hint: Experiment with different themes and different text effects.*
   q. Select *Mergers & Acquisitions—How Do They Impact Our Community?*, and apply italics.
2. Save the document, and name it **C05-A01-GoodMorning**.
3. Insert white space between groups of text as shown in Figure 5.44. *Hint: Adjust the spacing using specific line spacing options or insert additional spacing before and after each paragraph at the Spacing Before and After text boxes in the Paragraph group on the Page Layout tab.*
4. View the document at Print tab Backstage view. Make any necessary adjustments.
5. Save, print, and then close **C05-A01-GoodMorning.docx**.

Figure 5.44 Assessment 5.1

Assessment 5.2 Creating a Good Health Flyer

1. Create a flyer promoting better heart health through avoidance of certain risk factors by completing the following steps:
   a. At a new document screen, make sure the Office theme has been selected, and change the orientation to Landscape.
   b. Insert the Continuous Picture List SmartArt graphic found in the List category at the Choose a SmartArt Graphic dialog box.

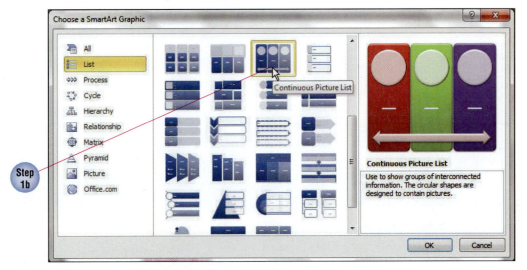

   c. At the SmartArt Tools Design tab, make sure the Text pane is displayed.
   d. Apply the *Metallic Scene* SmartArt Style in the *3D* section or another style of your own choosing.
   e. Apply a color of your own choosing (click the Change Color button in the SmartArt Styles group on the SmartArt Tools Design tab).
   f. Click the border of the SmartArt graphic to select it, then at the SmartArt Tools Format tab, click the Wrap Text button in the Arrange group and then select *In Front of Text*. Size and position the SmartArt graphic as shown in Figure 5.45. **Hint: Drag a corner sizing handle.**
   g. At the Text pane, type the following text: **Hint: Each bulleted item will produce another colorful shape.**
      Smoking
      Gender
      Age
      Stress
      Alcohol/Drug Abuse
      Family History
      High Cholesterol
      Obesity
      Hypertension
   h. Insert appropriate photos to represent each risk factor. **Hint: You may want to use the Clip Art task pane to search for the art, and then copy the image into the Insert Picture dialog box, where you can select and insert the image into the picture placeholder in the SmartArt graphic.**
   i. Position your insertion point at the top of the document and type **Heart Attack Risk Factors**. Format the text with appropriate fonts and font sizes. You may insert a graphic such as the one shown in Figure 5.45 by searching for **lightning** at the Clip Art task pane. This image was edited, recolored, and then sent behind the text.

Figure 5.45 Assessment 5.2

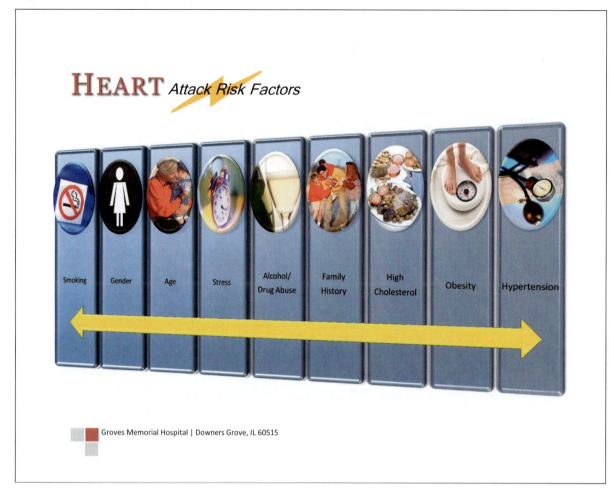

j.   Insert *Puzzle (Even Page) Footer* from the Building Blocks Organizer by clicking the Quick Parts button in the Text group on the Insert tab. Replace the placeholder text with the following: **Groves Memorial Hospital | Downers Grove, IL 60515**. ***Hint: To type the | vertical bar, hold down the Shift key and press the backslash key on your keyboard.***

2. Save your document as **C05-A02-Heart**.
3. Print and then close **C05-A02-Heart.docx**.

Assessment 5.3   College Flyer

Create a flyer promoting the spring session of classes at Midwest College in Oak Park, Illinois. Create a college logo in WordArt or find one on the Internet. Customize the sale flyer to accommodate the text given below. Figure 5.46 shows a sample of the college flyer. You may want to walk the halls of your local community college and pick up sample flyers and announcement for your idea folder. Possibly you will find some inspiration.

1. At a blank document create a flyer similar to the sample in Figure 5.46. Use text boxes, shapes, photographs, WordArt, and any other graphic adjustment techniques that you have learned in the chapters already covered. ***Hint: You may use an appropriate template, but customize it.***
2. Type **SUMMER 2012 Midwest** in text boxes. ***Hint: You may have to layer your design objects, and change the text wrap.***
3. Include the following text in the flyer.

Midwest College, 567 Main Street, Oak Park, IL 60607-5019 or use the name and address of your college.
Dates to note: Summer Session, May 27 to July 25, Call 312.555.0148 or Register Online. www.emcp.net/midwest/summer.
Summer is a chance to: Learn new skills. Complete a prerequisite course. Take one course at a time. Have time to work while taking a class.

4. Use font ligatures, text effects, leading, and kerning.
5. Insert photographs of college scenes by accessing the Clip Art task pane, typing **college** or **door** in the *Search for* text box. ***Hint: You may want to crop the image and resize it appropriately.***
6. Use at least one of each of the following adjustments: Correction, Color, and Artistic Effects.
7. Create a logo for Midwest College using WordArt.
8. Save the document, and name it **C05-A03-College**.
9. Print and then close **C05-A03-College.docx**.

Figure 5.46 Assessment 5.3 Sample Solution

Assessment 5.4   Promoting Island Rentals

1. Create a flyer advertising an island rental program for vacation condominiums, and embed an Excel table containing information on yearly temperatures. Include the following text and specifications. A sample document has been prepared in Figure 5.47. Use your own design ideas for the flyer.
   a. The name of the rental company is **BeachTime Rentals, Inc.**
   b. Prepare a logo with WordArt and possibly a clip art image. Group the design elements, or use the one provided in your *Chapter05* folder.
   c. Insert an appropriate number of beach scene photographs.
   d. Include this text: **Vacation at the celebrated Lowcountry islands of Kiawah and Seabrook near historic Charleston, South Carolina. BeachTime Rentals, Inc. offers a variety of unique condos, villas, and homes on Kiawah and on Seabrook. For more information on our short- and/or long-term rental programs, call 843.555.1234 or 1.800.555.4321. Office hours are 9-5 Monday through Friday and 9-6 Saturday seasonally. Visit us online at www.emcp.net/beachtime/rentals.**
2. To embed the Excel table, open Excel and then open **Temperatures** from your *Chapter05* folder.
   a. Select cells A1:D17 and then copy the table to the Office Clipboard.

Figure 5.47 Assessment 5.4 Sample Solution

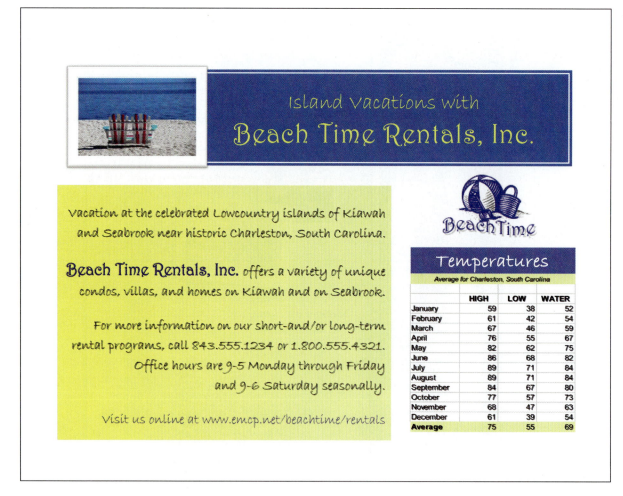

b. In Word, click the down-pointing arrow below the Paste button in the Clipboard group in the Home tab, and then click Paste Special. At the Paste Special dialog box, select *Microsoft Office Excel Worksheet Object* in the *As* list box. Make sure that the *Paste* option is selected, and then click OK.
  c. Right-click on the temperature table, click Format Object, select the Layout tab, and then click *In front of text* in the *Wrapping style* section. Click OK.
  d. Drag the table below your logo.
3. Close Excel.
4. Save the document, and name it **C05-A04-Rentals**.
5. Print and then close **C05-A04-Rentals.docx**.

Assessment 5.5   Hospital Organizational Chart Group Project

1. Create an organizational chart using SmartArt showing a hospital administrative structure. Your team may visit a local hospital to obtain this information or view the hospital Web site if one is available on the Internet. Your team should include the board of directors, president and CEO, vice presidents, manager, directors, liaison personnel, volunteer coordinators, and any other relevant divisions or levels. Include at least one photograph of the hospital and/or personnel and hospital activities. As a group, assign individual responsibilities, which may include defining the purpose of the document, thumbnail sketches, layout and design objectives, collection of images, and the creation of a logo. Review the numerous SmartArt features available on the SmartArt Tools Format tab and the SmartArt Tools Design tab. Your team may complete a Google search for a hospital organizational chart and any relevant data that will enhance the purpose of your document. Your team may use Quick Styles, Themes, or Quick Parts along with picture enhancements such as Picture Styles, Picture Effects, and Recolor.
2. Save and then print **C05-A05-Organizational.docx**.

Chapter 6

Creating Brochures and Booklets

CHAPTER06

Performance Objectives

Upon successful completion of Chapter 6, you will be able to:

- Produce promotional documents such as a letter-fold (trifold) brochure, single-fold brochure, and book fold membership directory.
- Review and apply design concepts.
- Evaluate folds.
- Use columns, text boxes, tables, book fold and 2 pages per sheet features as underlying design.

- Change and save a custom Quick Style set.
- Print on both sides using a manual or automatic duplex option (printer dependent).
- Insert a chart and SmartArt object into a brochure.

Desktop Publishing Terms

Book fold	Letter fold	Parallel folds
Character style	List style	Reverse text
Draft view	Map fold *of* gate fold	Right-angle folds
Drop cap	Newspaper columns	Style
Dummy	Normal style	Table style
Duplex printing	Panels	2 pages per sheet
Gutter	Paragraph style	

Word Features Used

Book fold	Orientation	Style Sets
Breaks	Paper size	Tables
Bullets and numbering	Picture Effects	Tabs
Columns	Picture Shape	Text Effects
Drop caps	Picture Styles	2 pages per sheet
Headers and Footers	Quick Styles	
Manual duplex	Styles	

In this chapter, you will be introduced to different methods for creating your own brochures and booklets. You will use text boxes and columns to create trifold brochures; 2 pages per sheet, 2 pages per sheet and tables to create single-fold brochures; and book fold to create a membership directory, which you will then print using the Word manual duplex feature. Purpose, content, paper selection, brochure folds, page layout, design considerations, and desktop publishing concepts will be discussed.

Planning Brochures and Booklets

Clearly defining the purpose of your communication is a very important step in initiating the desktop publishing process. We will explore this step first and then turn our attention to other aspects of producing brochures and booklets.

Defining the Purpose

The purpose of a brochure or booklet can be to inform, educate, promote, or sell. Identify the purpose in the following examples:

- A city agency mails brochures to the community explaining a local recycling program.
- A doctor displays brochures on childhood immunizations in the patient waiting room.
- A car salesperson hands out a brochure on a current model to a potential buyer.
- A new management consulting firm sends out brochures introducing its services.
- A professional organization mails booklets to its members listing membership information—addresses, telephone numbers, fax numbers, email addresses, and so on.
- A homeowners association prepares a directory of names, addresses, and services provided by residents (babysitting, pet sitting, garage cleaning, and so on).
- Volunteers for a local theater prepare a playbill (formatted as a booklet) for distribution during theatrical production.

If you found yourself thinking that some brochures and booklets have more than one purpose, you are correct. As examples, the goals of a brochure on childhood immunizations may be to inform and educate; the goals of a brochure about a car model may be to inform and promote the sale of the car. Alternatively, the goals of a playbill (booklet) may be to inform an audience of facts about a play, introduce people who are playing the roles, and promote publicity for organizations supporting the community theater.

In addition, using a brochure or booklet may be another means of establishing your organization's identity and image. Incorporating design elements from your other business documents into the design of your brochure reinforces your image and identity among your readers.

Determining the Content

Before creating the actual layout and design of your brochure or booklet, determine what the content will be. Try to look at the content from a reader's point of view. The content should include the following items:

- A clearly stated description of the topic, product, service, or organization
- A description of the people or company doing the informing, educating, promoting, or selling
- A description of how the reader will benefit from this information, product, service, or organization
- A clear indication of what action you want your audience to take after reading the brochure or booklet
- An easy way for readers to respond to the desired action, such as a phone number to call, a detachable postcard to request more information, or a form to fill in (i.e. request to be added to a mailing list, make a contribution, order a product, or subscribe to a membership).

Creating Brochures

Before you actually start typing the copy for your brochure, a number of decisions need to be made, including determining the size and type of paper, deciding on the brochure page layout, setting the brochure margins, and determining the brochure panel widths.

Determining the Size and Type of Paper

Brochures are usually printed on both sides of the page on an assortment of paper stocks. The paper stock may vary in size, weight, color, and texture, and it can also have defined folding lines.

Brochures can be folded in a number of different ways. The manner in which a brochure is folded determines the order in which the panels are set on the page and read by the recipient. The most common brochure fold is called a *letter fold*. It is also known as a trifold or three-panel brochure. The letter fold and other common folds, as shown in Figure 6.1, are referred to as *parallel folds* because all of the folds run in the same direction. *Right-angle folds* are created by pages that are folded at right angles to each other, such as the folds in a greeting card. Standard-size 8½ by 11-inch (landscape orientation) paper stock can easily accommodate a letter fold, accordion fold, and single fold. Standard legal-size paper that is 8½ by 14 inches can be used to create a brochure with a *map fold* or a *gate fold*. Different paper sizes can be used to create variations of these folds. In addition, folds do not always have to create equal panel sizes. Offsetting a fold can produce an interesting effect.

The type of paper selected for a brochure affects the total production cost.

When selecting the paper stock for a brochure, consider the following cost factors:

- Standard-size brochures, such as a three-panel brochure created from 8½ by 11-inch paper stock or a four-panel brochure created from 8½ by 14-inch paper stock, are easily enclosed in a #10 business envelope.
- Standard-size brochures designed as self-mailers satisfy postal regulations and are, therefore, less costly to mail.
- Nonstandard-size paper stock may be more expensive to purchase and to mail.
- Heavier weight papers are more costly to mail.
- Higher-quality paper stocks are more expensive to purchase.
- Color paper is more costly than standard white, ivory, cream, or gray.
- Predesigned paper stock is more expensive than plain paper stock.

Letter fold
Also known as a trifold or three-panel brochure.

Parallel folds
All folds run in the same direction.

Right-angle folds
Pages folded at right angles to each other.

Map fold *or* gate fold
Folds requiring Legal-sized paper.

Figure 6.1 Brochure Folds

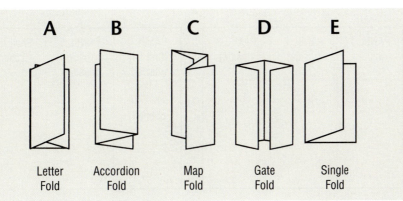

A   Letter Fold   B   Accordion Fold   C   Map Fold   D   Gate Fold   E   Single Fold

Although cost is an important issue when choosing paper stock, you should also take into account how the brochure will be distributed, how often it will be handled, and the image you want to project. If you plan to design the brochure as a self-mailer, take a sample of the paper stock to the post office to see if it meets USPS mailing regulations.

If you expect your target audience to keep your brochure for a period of time or to handle it often, plan to purchase a higher-quality, heavier paper stock. Similarly, choose a paper within your budget that enhances the image you want to leave in the reader's mind.

If you intend to print the brochure yourself, run a sample of the paper you intend to use through your printer. Some papers are better suited for laser and inkjet printers than others. If you are unsure about what type of paper to purchase, take a master copy of your brochure to a printer for advice on the best type of paper for the situation. You can also take your printed brochure to a print shop and have it folded on commercial folding equipment.

Deciding on Brochure Page Layout

Panels

Sections separated by folds in a brochure page layout.

A brochure page (defined by the dimensions of the paper stock) is divided into sections called *panels*. At least one fold separates each panel. Folds create distinct sections to place specific blocks of text. For example, a three-panel or letter-fold brochure layout actually has six panels available for text—three panels on one side of the paper and three more panels on the other side. The way a brochure is folded determines the order in which the panels are read by the recipient. The correct placement of text depends on understanding this order. Look how the panels are labeled in the letter-fold page layout illustrated in Figure 6.2. Panels 1, 2, and 3 are located on the inside of the brochure, counting left to right. Panel 4 is the page you see when the cover is opened. Panel 5 is the back of the folded brochure, which may be used for mailing purposes, if desired. Panel 6 is the cover of the brochure. The main content of the brochure is focused in panels 1, 2, and 3.

Dummy

A mockup that is positioned, folded, trimmed, and/or labeled as the actual publication.

To avoid confusion about the brochure page layout and the panel reference numbers, create a mockup or *dummy* of your brochure. A dummy is folded in the same manner as the actual brochure and is particularly useful because brochures can be folded in a number of different ways. A dummy can be as simple or as detailed as you would like. If you need only a visual guide to make sure you are placing the correct text in the correct panel, make a simple dummy using the number of columns desired and label each panel as in Figure 6.2. If you need to visualize the placement of text within each panel, the margins, and the white space between columns, make a more detailed dummy that includes very specific margin settings, column width settings, and settings for the spacing between columns.

Figure 6.2 Letter-Fold Panel Layout

PANEL 1 (inside)	PANEL 2 (inside)	PANEL 3 (inside)		PANEL 4 (first flap viewed when cover is opened)	PANEL 5 (back/ mailing)	PANEL 6 (cover)

A brochure or a dummy can be created using Word's Columns, Table, Text Box, or 2 pages per sheet feature (applicable only to single-fold brochures). For example, for a standard-size three-panel brochure, the actual page size is 8½ by 11 inches positioned in landscape orientation. The page is divided into three columns using the Columns feature or into three columns and one row using the Table feature. Alternatively, three text boxes can be sized and positioned on the page to represent three panels.

Setting Brochure Margins

The left and right margins for a brochure page are usually considerably less than those for standard business documents. Many printers will only allow a minimum of a 0.5-inch left or right side margin (depending on page orientation) because a certain amount of space is needed for the printer to grab the paper and eject it from the printer. If you set margins less than the minimum, Word prompts you with the following message: *One or more margins are set outside the printable area of the page. Choose the Fix button to increase the appropriate margins.* Click Fix to set the margins to the printer's minimum setting. Check the new margin setting by clicking the Margins button in the Page Setup group on the Page Layout tab. If landscape is the selected paper orientation, the right margin will be the only margin "fixed" by Word because that is the side of the paper the printer grabs to eject the paper from the printer.

When creating a brochure, adjust the opposite side margin to match the margin adjusted by Word. For example, the printer used to create the brochure exercises in this chapter will only allow a minimum of 0.5 inch for the right margin with landscape chosen as the paper orientation. Hence, you are directed to set the left and right margins at 0.5 inch using the *Narrow margin* option at the Margin drop-down list. Alternately, the printer imposes minimum margin settings when portrait is the selected paper orientation. The bottom margin setting is affected the most because it is the last side of the paper to come out of the printer.

If you click Ignore as a response to Word's prompt to "fix" the margins, the program will ignore the printer's minimum requirement and accept whatever margins you have set. However, the printer will not print anything in its defined unprintable area, which will result in text that is cut off. Use the Print tab Backstage view to view the results of setting margins that are less than the printer's minimum requirements.

Determining Panel Widths

The widths of the panels in most brochures cannot all be equal. If equal panel sizes are used, the margins on some of the panels will appear uneven and the brochure folds will not fall properly in relation to the text. In addition, the thickness of the paper stock affects the amount of space taken up by the fold. To solve this problem, individually size the text boxes for each panel to accommodate the appropriate placement of the text and the folds to achieve the desired result. You will have to experiment somewhat and make adjustments to find the appropriate widths. ***Hint: These suggestions give you a starting point from which to work, but experiment by printing and folding the brochure and then fine-tuning any measurements.***

Several methods can be used in creating pamphlets. You will use columns, text boxes, the book fold feature, and the 2 pages per sheet feature in the chapter exercises. Text boxes are often used in Microsoft brochure templates. The trifold brochure template shown in Figure 6.3 uses the columns feature. Most of the brochure templates accessed through Office.com use text boxes to accommodate the panels in a trifold brochure as shown in Figure 6.4. In addition, a table may be used as the underlining structure of a brochure; however, this method was not used in any of the templates. After each method is introduced, it will be up to you to choose which method is the easiest to use.

Figure 6.3 Using Word's Brochure Template (Formatted in Columns)

This brochure is formatted in columns.

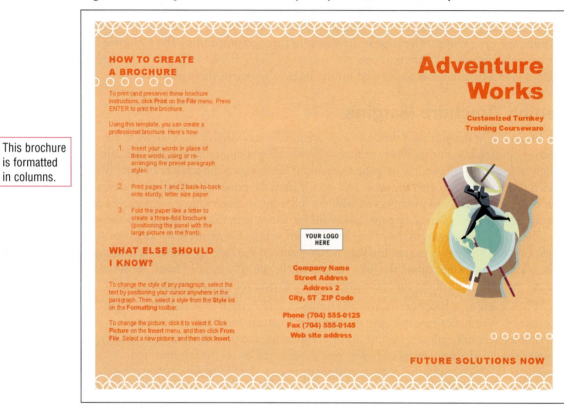

Figure 6.4 Office.com Template—Real Estate Agent Brochure
(tri-fold A4, 8½ x 11, letter fold, 2 pages)

This brochure is formatted in text boxes.

Using panels 1, 2, and 3 of a letter-fold brochure as an example in Figure 6.5, consider the following steps for determining panel widths and the space between columns or text boxes:

1. One way to determine the approximate width of each panel is to fold the brochure paper stock into the desired brochure fold configuration, which, in this example, is a letter-fold brochure. Measure the width of each panel. The width obtained will be approximate because a ruler cannot measure hundredths of an inch, but it will be a good starting point.

2. Establish the left and right margins for the whole page. One-half inch margin settings, or something close to that, are common. (See the previous section on setting brochure margins.)

3. For panel 1, the left margin for the whole brochure page is also the left margin for the panel. Therefore, subtract the left margin setting from the total width of panel 1. From the remaining amount, estimate how much of that space is needed to allow for an appropriate column or text box width for the text and for an appropriate amount of white space on the right side of the panel. For example, if panel 1 measures approximately 3.7 inches, and the left page margin is 0.55 inch, subtract 0.55 inch from 3.7 inches. From the 3.15 inches that remain, estimate how much of that space will be occupied by text and how much needs to be allotted for the right margin of panel 1 (i.e., the white space before the fold).

Figure 6.5 Panel Width Guide for a Letter-Fold Brochure

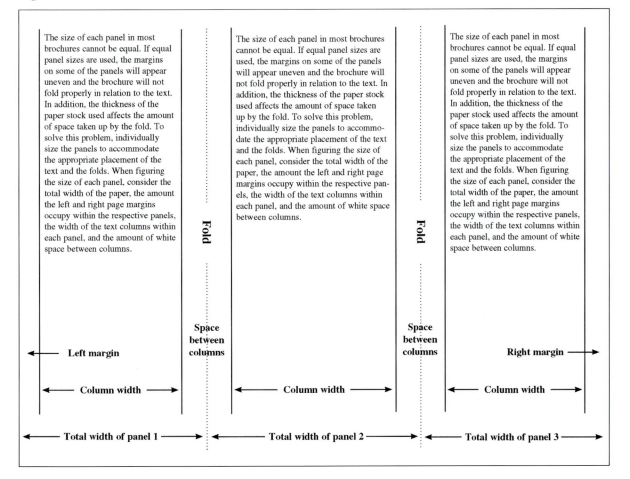

4. For panel 2, use the whole panel width to estimate an appropriate column width or text box width for the text and an appropriate amount of white space on the left and right sides of the panel. The column width in panel 2 will be wider than the widths in panels 1 and 3.

5. For panel 3, the right margin for the whole brochure page is also the right margin for the panel. Therefore, subtract the amount of the right margin setting from the total width of the panel. From the remaining amount, determine an appropriate width for the text and an appropriate amount of white space on the left side of the panel.

6. After establishing text column widths and the amount of white space in between for panels 1, 2, and 3, reverse the measurements for panels 4, 5, and 6. For example, panels 1 and 6 will be the same measurement, panels 2 and 5 will be the same, and panels 3 and 4 will be the same. *Hint: If you are using the Columns feature, you will need to insert a section break to vary the column formatting on the second page. See the section "Varying Column Formatting within the Same Document" later in this chapter for more information. If you are using the Table feature, you will have to create another table for the second page of the brochure reversing the column measurements from panels 1, 2, and 3. If you are using the Text Box feature, remember to reverse the order as stated previously.*

7. Refer to Figure 6.5 to see that the space between panels is actually divided by the fold, allowing white space on either side of the fold. In other words, the space between columns serves as the margins for two different panels. For example, the space between columns surrounding the first fold in Figure 6.5 provides the white space (or margin) for the right side of panel 1 and the left side of panel 2.

8. Use the previous suggestions to create a dummy. Insert random text in every panel and print. *Hint: To insert random text, type* =rand() *and then press Enter.* Fold the page as you would the brochure, and check the amount of space between columns. Is the text positioned correctly within each panel? If not, adjust the space between columns and/or the column width settings, and then print again.

The method used to create the white space between columns depends on the method used to create the columns, as explained in Figure 6.6.

Figure 6.6 Methods Used to Create Spacing between Columns

Method Used to Create Columns	Method Used to Create Spacing between Columns
Columns feature	At the Columns dialog box in the *Width and spacing* section, adjust the amount in the *Spacing* text box.
Table feature	Create blank columns in between the columns that contain the text for each panel.
Text Box feature	Size and position the text boxes containing the text for each panel, leaving the desired amount of white space between text boxes.
2 pages per sheet feature	Applicable only to single-fold brochures, white space is achieved by adjusting the margin settings.
Book Fold feature	White space is achieved by adjusting the margin settings and the gutter space.

Figure 6.7 Newspaper Columns

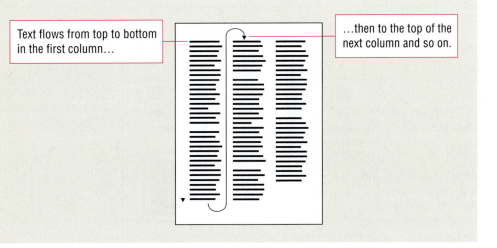

Text flows from top to bottom in the first column...

...then to the top of the next column and so on.

Understanding Newspaper Columns

The types of columns created by using the Columns feature are commonly referred to as *newspaper columns*. Newspaper columns are used for text in newspapers, newsletters, brochures, and magazines. Text in these types of columns flows continuously from the bottom of one column to the top of the next column, as shown in Figure 6.7. When the first column on the page is filled with text, the insertion point moves to the top of the next column on the same page, and so on. When the last column on the page is filled with text, the insertion point moves to the beginning of the first column on the next page.

By default, all Word documents are automatically set up in a one-column format. However, a document can include as many columns as there is room for on the page. Word determines how many columns can be included based on the page width, the margin settings, the size of the columns, and the spacing between columns. Column formatting can be assigned to a document before the text is typed, or it can be applied to existing text.

Newspaper columns
Text flows from the bottom of one column to the top of the next column.

Columns

Creating Newspaper Columns for Use in Brochures

Click the Columns button in the Page Setup group in the Page Layout tab to easily split text into newspaper columns of equal or unequal width as shown in Figure 6.8. From the Columns drop-down list, you can select preset column designs for One, Two, Three, Left, and Right column configurations. When you select one of these designs, the column feature is applied to the whole document, unless section breaks have been inserted into the document at predetermined locations.

Figure 6.8 Preset Column Designs

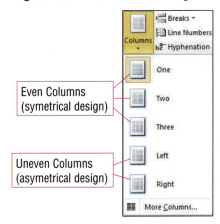

Even Columns (symetrical design)

Uneven Columns (asymetrical design)

Using the Columns Dialog Box

To maintain more control over customizing columns, such as selecting the number of columns and entering the desired column

Figure 6.9 Columns Dialog Box

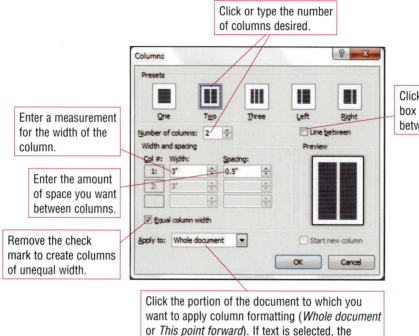

Click or type the number of columns desired.
Enter a measurement for the width of the column.
Enter the amount of space you want between columns.
Remove the check mark to create columns of unequal width.
Click inside the check box to add a vertical line between the columns.
Click the portion of the document to which you want to apply column formatting (*Whole document* or *This point forward*). If text is selected, the choices will be *Selected text* or *Whole document*.
Columns
Presets
One
Two
Three
Left
Right
Number of columns: 2
Line between
Width and spacing
Preview
Col #: Width: Spacing:
1: 3" 0.5"
2: 3"
Equal column width
Apply to: Whole document
Start new column
OK
Cancel

width and spacing between the columns, click *More Columns* at the bottom of the Columns drop-down list to display the Columns dialog box as shown in Figure 6.9. Experiment with changing the width between columns so you can see how the changes affect the text in each panel. For example, in a letter-fold brochure column layout, increasing the space between columns 1 and 2 will cause the text in panel 2 to be shifted to the right, whereas decreasing the space between columns 1 and 2 will cause the text in panel 2 to shift to the left.

Using the Horizontal Ruler to Adjust Column Settings

After columns have been created, the width of the columns or the spacing between columns may be changed with the column markers on the horizontal Ruler (Figure 6.10). To do this, make sure the horizontal Ruler is displayed (click the *Ruler* option in the Show/Hide group on the View tab). Position the arrow pointer in the middle of the left or right margin column marker on the horizontal Ruler until it turns into a double-headed arrow pointing left and right. Hold down the *left* mouse button, drag the column marker to the left or right to make the column narrower or wider, and then release the mouse button. Hold down the Alt key as you drag the column marker to view exact measurements on the ruler.

Figure 6.10 Adjusting Column Widths on the Horizontal Ruler

Move Column

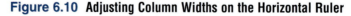

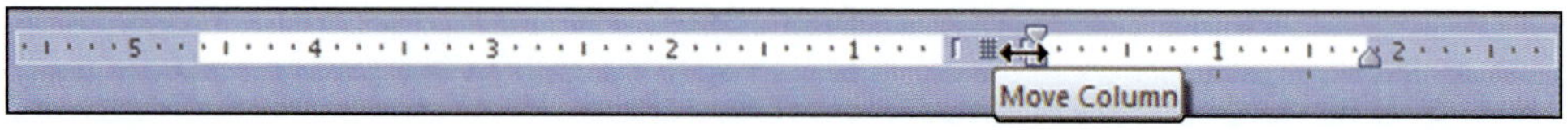

Varying Column Formatting within the Same Document

By default, any column formatting you select is applied to the whole document. If you want to create different numbers or styles of columns within the same document, the document must be divided into sections. For example, if a document contains a title, you may want the title to span the top of all of the columns rather than be included within the column formatting. To span a title across the tops of columns, type and format the title. Position the insertion point at the left margin of the first line of text to be formatted into columns, click the Breaks button in the Page Setup group in the Page Layout tab, and then choose a section break as shown in Figure 6.11.

Additionally, you may use the Columns dialog box to apply a section break automatically from the location of the insertion point to the end of the document or until other column formatting is encountered by changing the *Apply to* option at the bottom of the Columns dialog box from *Whole document* to *This point forward*.

Section breaks are used to create layout or formatting changes in a portion of a document. Use them for changes to margins, paper size or orientation, paper source for a printer, page borders, headers and footers, columns, page numbering, line numbering, and footnotes and endnotes.

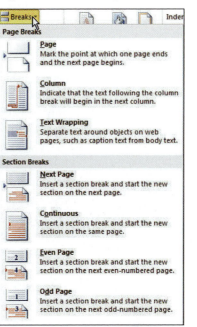

Figure 6.11 **Inserting Section Breaks**

◀ **DTP POINTERS**
Be consistent when varying column widths within a document.

Removing a Section Break

When you delete a section break, you also delete the section formatting for the text before the break. The text becomes part of the following section, and it assumes the formatting of that section. Make sure you are in **Draft view** so that you can see the doubled dotted line section break. Select the section break that you want to delete, and then press Delete.

Draft view
A view that shows text formatting and a simplified page layout.

Removing Column Formatting

To remove column formatting, position the insertion point in the section containing columns and change the column format to one column either at the Columns drop-down list or at the Columns dialog box.

Inserting a Column Break

When formatting text into columns, Word automatically breaks the columns to fit the page. At times, text may wrap from one column to another in an undesirable location or you may want a column to break in a different location. For example, a heading may appear at the bottom of the column, while the text that follows the heading begins at the top of the next column. You can insert a column break into a document to control where columns end and begin on the page.

To insert a column break, position the insertion point where you want the new column to begin and then press Ctrl + Shift + Enter, or click the Breaks button in the Page Setup group on the Page Layout tab and click *Column* in the *Page Breaks* section. If you insert a column break in the last column on a page, the column continues on the next page. If you want any other column on the page that is not the last column to continue on the next page, insert a page break.

◀ **DTP POINTERS**
Make sure all column breaks are in appropriate locations.

If you want to "even out" or balance the text in columns, insert a continuous section break at the end of the last column. Any text that follows the section break will start at the top of the next column.

To familiarize yourself with the layout of panels in a letter-fold (or three-panel) brochure, you will create a simple dummy (three even columns with default spacing between the columns) in the following exercise. Measuring the panels and creating unequal column widths is not necessary in this case because you will use the dummy only as a guide to placing text in the correct panels. Remember, you can always make a more detailed dummy if necessary.

You can use a procedure similar to Exercise 6.1 to create a dummy using a table. Insert a table with five columns and one row—three columns for the panels and two columns for the space between the columns. Label the panels, and then print the dummy.

A dummy can also be created with pencil and paper. Take a piece of the paper stock to be used and position it correctly (portrait or landscape). Fold the paper as the brochure will be folded and label each panel as shown earlier in Figure 6.2.

Hint: Copy the **Chapter06** *folder from the CD that accompanies this textbook to your storage medium, and then make* **Chapter06** *the active folder. Remember to substitute graphics that may no longer be available.*

Exercise 6.1   Creating a Dummy of a Three-Panel Brochure Using Text Boxes

1. At a blank document create a dummy similar to the one illustrated in Figure 6.2 by completing the following steps:
   a. Change the paper orientation to landscape.
   b. Change the left and right margins to 0.55 inch.
   c. Change to a three-column format by clicking the Columns button in the Page Setup group in the Page Layout tab. Click *Three* at the Columns drop-down preset list.
   d. Insert the panel labels by completing the following steps:
      1) Change the paragraph alignment to Center.
      2) Type **PANEL 1**, press Enter, and then type **(inside)** in the first panel (column 1).
      3) At the Page Layout tab, click the Breaks button in the Page Setup group, and then click Column in the *Page Breaks* section.
      4) Using Figure 6.2 as a guide, repeat steps 1d1 through 1d3 until all six panels are labeled. *Hint: Press Ctrl + Shift + Enter to insert a column break.*
   e. Print the three-panel brochure dummy by completing the following steps:
      1) Position the insertion point on the first page (panels 1, 2, and 3) by pressing Ctrl + Home.
      2) Click the File tab, and then click the Print tab.
      3) At the Print tab Backstage view, click the down-pointing arrow at the right of Print All Pages in the *Settings* section, and then click the *Print Current Page* option. Click the Print button.

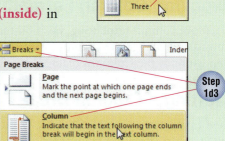

4) Put the first printed page back in the printer so the second page can be printed on the back of the first page. (Experiment with your printer to position the paper correctly.)
5) Position the insertion point on the second page (panels 4, 5, and 6), and print the current page.
   f. Fold the dummy as you would the real brochure, and refer to the panel labels when creating the actual brochure to avoid confusion on the placement of text.
2. Save the dummy brochure and name it **C06-E01-Dummy**.
3. Close **C06-E01-Dummy.docx**. (Your brochure should look similar to the panel layout illustrated in Figure 6.2.)
4. *Optional:* Open **SingleFoldLandscape.docx**, **GateFold.docx**, **SingleFoldPortrait.docx**, **AccordionFold.docx**, **LetterFold.docx**, and **MapFold.docx** from your *SampleBrochures* folder in the *Chapter06* folder, print, and then practice folding the different folds. You may want to print some of the sample folds on legal-sized paper.

Using Reverse Text as a Design Element

Reverse text usually refers to white text set against a solid background (such as 100% black), as shown in the first example in Figure 6.12. Reversing text is most effective with single words, short phrases such as headings, or special characters set in a large type size. Impact is also achieved by using screens (shading with lighter shades of gray or color) for the background fill. Solid areas of black, white, and varying shades of gray on a page give the visual effect of color, creating a dramatic effect with the use of only one color. In addition, interesting effects are achieved by reversing color text out of a solid, screened, gradient, or textured colored background fill and/or by varying the shape that contains the reverse text. As shown in Figure 6.12, many different variations of reverse

Reverse text
White text set against a solid background.

◀ **DTP POINTERS**
Brochures involve many steps, so save often as you work.

Text Box

Figure 6.12 Reverse Text Examples

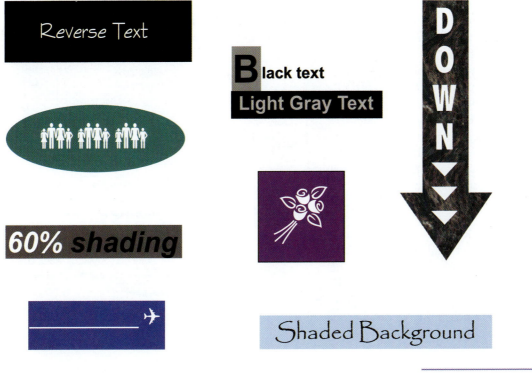

type can be created. Keep these examples in mind when you are trying to provide focus, balance, contrast, and directional flow in a document.

One of the easiest ways to create reverse text is to use the Text Box feature. To create traditional reverse text (solid black background with white text) using a text box, simply create a text box, change the fill to black, change the text color to Automatic or White, and then type the desired text. Or, you can create a reverse text effect using a Shape by selecting Shape, adding text, and then adding background fill.

DTP POINTERS ▶

Select Automatic at the Font Color gallery, and the text will automatically change to white when a black fill is added.

In the chapter exercises, you will have the opportunity to create a letter-fold (or three-panel) brochure using three uneven newspaper columns and other formatting features such as text boxes to create reverse text, color, and bulleted lists. Remember to save often! Creating even a simple brochure involves many steps. Also, view your document frequently to assess the overall layout and design. Adjustments often need to be made that can affect other parts of the document not visible in the document window.

Exercise 6.2 Creating Panels 1, 2, and 3 of a Letter-Fold Brochure Using Columns and Reverse Text

1. Keep the dummy created in Exercise 6.1 on hand to visually guide you in the correct placement of text (or create a new dummy following the directions in Exercise 6.1).
2. At a blank document create an informational brochure on a safari similar to the one illustrated in Figure 6.13 by completing the following steps:
   a. Change the page orientation to *landscape*.
   b. Change the margins to *Narrow* (top, bottom, left, and right at 0.5 inch).
   c. Change the theme to the Solstice theme.
   d. With the insertion point positioned at the top of the page, insert **SafariIntro** from your *Chapter06* folder.
   e. On the Home tab, click the Change Styles button in the Styles group, point to Style Set, and then select *Formal*.
   f. Position your insertion point anywhere in *What are the Big 5?*, and apply the Heading 2 style from the Quick Styles gallery. Change the spacing before to **0 pt** and the spacing after to **10 pt** in the *Spacing* section of the Paragraph group on the Page Layout tab.
   g. Select the paragraph that begins *The "Big 5" refers to . . .*, and apply the Intense Reference style from the Quick Styles gallery.
   h. Position the insertion point at the end of the previously mentioned paragraph, press the Enter key twice, and then click the No Spacing style in the Quick Styles gallery. Make sure bold and italics is turned off.

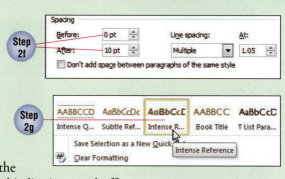

i. Change to a three-column format by completing the following steps:
1) Click the Columns button in the Page Setup group in the Page Layout tab. Click the More Columns button at the bottom of the Columns drop-down list.
2) At the Columns dialog box, click *Three* in the *Presets* section, and change the column *Width* to **2.47"** and the *Spacing* to **1.30"**. ***Hint: The spacing may display as 1.29".***
3) Make sure the setting for *Apply to* is *This point forward*. Click OK. ***Hint: This point forward inserts a section break.***

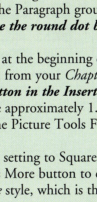

j. With the insertion point positioned below the "Big 5" paragraph, insert **Safari1** from your *Chapter06* folder.
k. Select the text beginning with *Large, robust . . .* and then click the Bullets button in the Paragraph group on the Home tab. ***Hint: Make sure the round dot bullet styles has been selected.***
l. Position the insertion point at the beginning of *Lion* and insert the graphic file, **Lion**, from your *Chapter06* folder. ***Hint: Click the Picture button in the Insert tab.***
m. Resize the image to measure approximately 1.8" by 2.4".
n. Select the image to access the Picture Tools Format tab, and then make the following adjustments:
1) Change the Wrap Text setting to Square.
2) Click the Picture Styles More button to display the Picture Styles gallery and then click the *Rotated, White* style, which is the third style in the third row.

o. Position the insertion point in *Lion* and apply the Heading 1 style from the Styles gallery. ***Hint: The color and formatting included in this style is determined by the Solstice theme and the Formal Style Set selected.***
p. Make any necessary adjustments to the image or text to make the document look similar to Figure 6.13. ***Hint: You may have to add or delete Enters before and/or after the image or add additional points of space Before or After so the headings will align horizontally as shown. Display Show/Hide.***
q. Position the insertion point at the end of the text in the first column and then insert a column break by either clicking the Breaks button arrow in the Page Setup group in the Page Layout tab or by pressing Ctrl + Shift + Enter.

r. Complete steps similar to those above to insert the following text files and photographs (then apply the following Picture Styles). ***Hint: You could use the Format Painter to copy the bullets to panel text. Remember to insert a column break after formatting each panel! Resize the images to approximately 1.8" by 2.4". After changing the Wrap Text to Square, you may have to drag the image to a position similar to Figure 6.13 to make sure that the animal names line up horizontally.***

Text File	Graphic File	Picture Style
Panel 2: **Safari2**	**Leopard**	Beveled Matte, White
Panel 3: **Safari3**	**Rhino**	Bevel Perspective Left, White

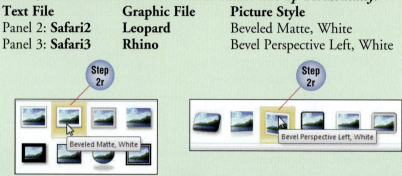

3. Insert the safari graphic at the bottom of the page as shown in Figure 6.13 by completing the following steps:

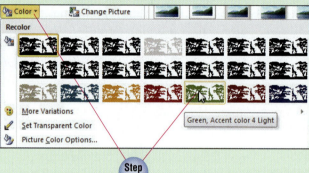

   a. Position the insertion point at the top of the document (display Show/Hide).
   b. Click the Picture button in the Illustrations group and then insert the **SafariBorder** graphic file from your *Chapter06* folder.
   c. Select the image, click the Color button, and then click the *Green, Accent color 4 Light* thumbnail in the *Recolor* section.
   d. Select the image, click the Corrections button in the Adjust group on the Picture Tools Format tab, and click the *Brightness: +40% Contrast -40%* option in the first row of the *Brightness and Contrast* section.

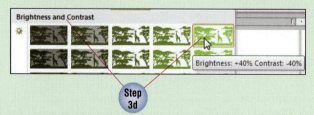

   e. Resize the safari image to measure approximately 2.96" × 11".
   f. Change the Wrap Text to the *Behind Text* option to enable you to move the image toward the bottom of the page.
   g. Make any necessary adjustments to make the document look like Figure 6.13. ***Hint: Add any additional points before or after (or Enters) to keep the Lion, Leopard, and Rhino text consistently aligned.***

4. Save the brochure and name it **C06-E02-Panels1,2,3**.
5. Keep **C06-E02-Panels1,2,3.docx** open if you are going to continue with Exercise 6.3 now; otherwise, close **C06-E02-Panels1,2,3.docx**.

Figure 6.13 Exercise 6.2

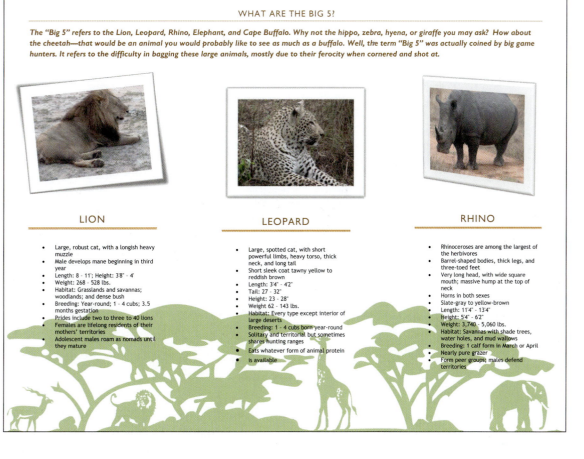

WHAT ARE THE BIG 5?

The "Big 5" refers to the Lion, Leopard, Rhino, Elephant, and Cape Buffalo. Why not the hippo, zebra, hyena, or giraffe you may ask? How about the cheetah—that would be an animal you would probably like to see as much as a buffalo. Well, the term "Big 5" was actually coined by big game hunters. It refers to the difficulty in bagging these large animals, mostly due to their ferocity when cornered and shot at.

LION

- Large, robust cat, with a longish heavy muzzle
- Male develops mane beginning in third year
- Length: 8 - 11'; Height: 3'8" - 4'
- Weight: 268 - 528 lbs.
- Habitat: Grasslands and savannas; woodlands; and dense bush
- Breeding: Year-round; 1 - 4 cubs; 3.5 months gestation
- Prides include two to three to 40 lions
- Females are lifelong residents of their mothers' territories
- Adolescent males roam as nomads until they mature

LEOPARD

- Large, spotted cat, with short powerful limbs, heavy torso, thick neck, and long tail
- Short sleek coat tawny yellow to reddish brown
- Length: 3'4" - 4'2"
- Tail: 27 - 32"
- Height: 23 - 28"
- Weight 62 - 143 lbs.
- Habitat: Every type except interior of large deserts
- Breeding: 1 - 4 cubs born year-round
- Solitary and territorial but sometimes shares hunting ranges
- Eats whatever form of animal protein is available

RHINO

- Rhinoceroses are among the largest of the herbivores
- Barrel-shaped bodies, thick legs, and three-toed feet
- Very long head, with wide square mouth; massive hump at the top of neck
- Horns in both sexes
- Slate-gray to yellow-brown
- Length: 11'4" - 13'4"
- Height: 5'4" - 6'2"
- Weight: 3,740 - 5,060 lbs.
- Habitat: Savannas with shade trees, water holes, and mud wallows
- Breeding: 1 calf form in March or April
- Nearly pure grazer
- Form peer groups; males defend territories

Printing on Both Sides of the Paper

Some printers offer the option of automatically printing on both sides of a sheet of paper (automatic ***duplex printing***). Other printers provide instructions so that you can manually reinsert pages to print the second side (manual duplex printing). Some printers do not support duplex printing at all. To determine whether a specific printer supports *duplex printing*, check your printer manual or review the options in the *Settings* section of the Print tab Backstage view. If your printer does not support automatic duplex printing, you can select the *Manually Print on Both Sides* option in the *Settings* section as shown in Figure 6.14. Microsoft Office will print all of the pages that appear on one side of the paper and then prompt you to turn the stack over and feed the pages into the printer again. When printing a brochure or booklet, be sure to print on both sides of the paper. ***Hint: Reinserting the paper correctly may take a few attempts.***

You can also print on both sides by printing odd and even pages. To print odd and even, click the File tab, and then click the Print tab. At the Print tab Backstage view, click the down-pointing arrow at the right of the *Print All Pages* options in the *Settings* section, and then click the *Only Print Odd Pages* option at the bottom of the gallery. Click the Print button at the top of the gallery. After the odd pages are printed, flip the stack of pages over, and then click the *Only Print Even Pages* option. Click the Print button at the top of the gallery. Depending on the printer model, you might have to rotate and reorder the pages to print the other side of the stack.

Duplex printing
Printing on both sides of the paper. Some printers can print in duplex mode.

DTP POINTERS
Do not reverse the page order both in Word and in the printer's properties, or the two settings will cancel each other out.

Figure 6.14 Printing Using Manual Duplex

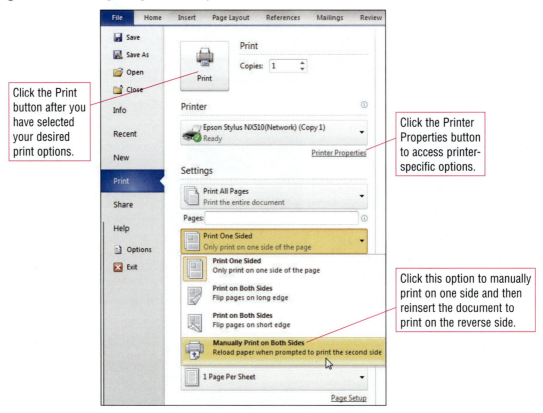

Click the Print button after you have selected your desired print options.

Click the Printer Properties button to access printer-specific options.

Click this option to manually print on one side and then reinsert the document to print on the reverse side.

In addition, you may change the printing order of the booklet pages by clicking the File tab and then clicking the Options button. At the Word Options dialog box with *Advanced* selected, add check marks next to options to print in reverse order or to print in front of or in back of a page as shown in Figure 6.15.

In Exercise 6.3, you will complete the brochure started in Exercise 6.2. As in the previous exercise, columns will be used to form the panels on the reverse side of the brochure. Refer to your dummy to see that panel 4 is the reverse side of panel 3, panel 5 is the reverse side of panel 2, and panel 6 is the reverse side of panel 1. As you progress through the exercise, remember to save your document often.

Figure 6.15 Changing Printing Options

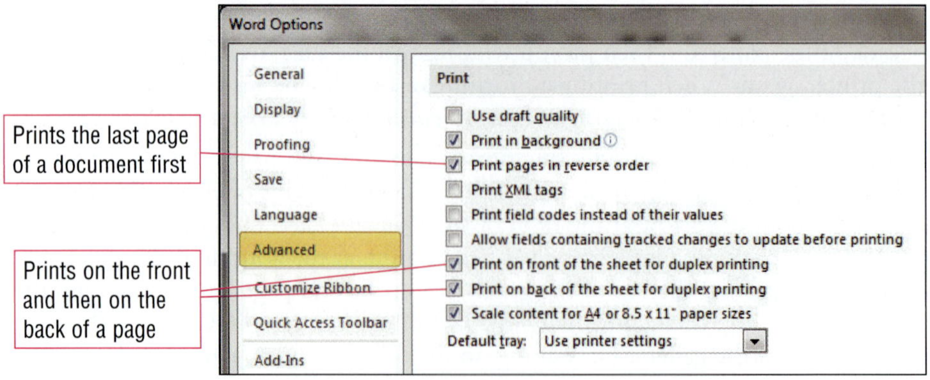

Prints the last page of a document first

Prints on the front and then on the back of a page

1. Open **C06-E02-Panels1,2,3.docx**.
2. Save the document with Save As and rename it **C06-E03-Safari**.
3. Create panels 4, 5, and 6 of the safari brochure shown in Figure 6.16 by completing the following steps:
   a. Press Ctrl + End to position the insertion point at the end of the page containing panels 1, 2, and 3, and then press Ctrl + Shift + Enter, or click the Page Break button in the Pages group on the Insert tab. *Hint: Columns should display because they were turned on earlier.*
   b. Complete steps similar to those used in Exercise 6.2 to format panels 4 and 5. (Columns should already be on.) Insert the following text files and photographs and then apply the following Picture Styles. *Hint: You could use the Format Painter to copy the bullets to panel text. Remember to insert a column break after formatting each panel. Resize the pictures to approximately 1.8" by 2.4".*

Text File	GraphicFile	Picture Style
Panel 4: **Safari4**	**Elephant**	Rotated, White
Panel 5: **Safari5**	**CapeBuffalo**	Beveled Matte, White

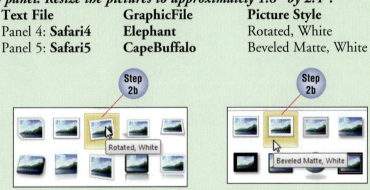

   c. Select the text in each panel and apply the same bullet as used in panels 1, 2, and 3.
   d. Apply the Heading 1 style to *Elephant* and *CapeBuffalo*.
   e. Adjust the headings if necessary so they align horizontally as shown in Figure 6.16.
4. Create panel 6 (cover) by completing the following steps:
   a. At the top of panel 6, press Enter six times. *Hint: Make sure you have selected the No Spacing style from the Quick Styles gallery.*
   b. Type **Out of Africa Safari at Kruger National Park**, and then press Enter six times.
   c. Select *Out of Africa . . .*, and apply the Title style from the Quick Styles gallery.
   d. Click the Text Box button in the Text group on the Insert tab, and then click Draw Text Box.
   e. Draw a text box below the title text that is approximately 1" in height and 1.75" in width.
   f. With the insertion point inside the text box, type **In search of the BIG**.
   g. Select the text *In search of the BIG* and change the font to 24-point Gloucester MT Extra Condensed (or a similar font) in *Green, Accent 4, Darker 25%* located in the fifth row and eighth column in the *Theme Colors* section of the Font Color palette. Arrange the text as shown in Figure 6.16.

   h. Right-align the text and remove the text box shape fill and the outline around the text box.

   i.   Draw another text box measuring approximately 2" in height and 1" in width.

   j.   With the insertion point inside the text box, type **5**.

   k.   Select *5*, and change the font to 100-point Papyrus in Brown, Accent 5 located in the first row and ninth column of the *Theme Colors* section.

   l.   Remove the text box fill and the outline around the text box.

   m. Position the text boxes as shown in Figure 6.16.

5. Copy the green animal graphic to the bottom of this page.

6. Add a reverse text effect to *AFRICA* in panel 6 as shown in Figure 6.16 by completing the following steps:

   a. Select *AFRICA*, and change the font color to *Green, Accent 4*.

   b. With *AFRICA* still selected, click the down arrow at the right of the Shading button in the Paragraph group on the Home tab, and then click *Brown, Accent 5* in the first row of the *Theme Colors* section.

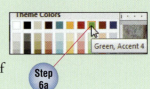

   c. Make any necessary adjustments in spacing so that the page looks similar to Figure 6.16.

7. Save the brochure with the same name **C06-E03-Safari**.

8. Print the first page of the brochure (you may want to print the brochure on parchment or beige-colored paper), reinsert the first page back in the printer, and then print the second page on the back of the first page or print using the manual duplex feature at the Print dialog box. ***Hint: Refer to the directions for duplex printing in the text preceding Exercise 6.3, if necessary.***

9. Close **C06-E03-Safari.docx**.

Formatting with Styles

Professional-looking documents generally require a great deal of formatting. Formatting within any document that uses a variety of headings, subheadings, and other design elements should remain consistent. Some documents, such as company newsletters, brochures, and manuals, may be created on a regular basis and require consistent formatting within the document as well as from issue to issue. You can save time and keystrokes by using Word's Styles feature to store repetitive formatting and to maintain consistent formatting throughout your document.

A ***style*** is a set of defined formatting instructions saved with a specific name in order to use the formatting instructions over and over. Because formatting instructions are contained within a style, a style may be edited, automatically updating any occurrence of that style within a document. For instance, if you applied a style to the bulleted text in all four panels of a brochure that specified an 18-point font size and then changed the font size to 16 points, all you would need to do is edit the formatting instructions in the style and all occurrences of the style would change.

Types of Styles

Word styles include character styles, paragraph styles, linked (paragraph and characters) styles, table styles, and list styles. At the *Styles* list box, you may see a paragraph symbol, a lowercase "a", and a combination of both characters next to each style that displays in the drop-down list. A ***paragraph style*** applies formatting instructions to the paragraph

Style

A group of defined formatting instructions that can be applied at one time to a whole document or to various parts of a document.

Paragraph style

A set of formatting instructions that applies to an entire paragraph.

Figure 6.16 Exercise 6.3

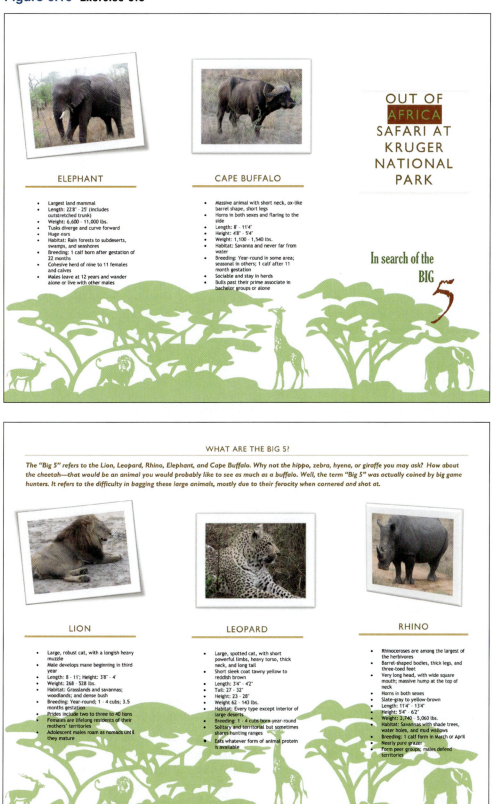

OUT OF
AFRICA
SAFARI AT
KRUGER
NATIONAL
PARK

In search of the
BIG 5

ELEPHANT

- Largest land mammal
- Length: 22'8" - 25' (includes outstretched trunk)
- Weight: 6,600 - 11,000 lbs.
- Tusks diverge and curve forward
- Huge ears
- Habitat: Rain forests to subdeserts, swamps, and seashores
- Breeding: 1 calf born after gestation of 22 months
- Cohesive herd of nine to 11 females and calves
- Males leave at 12 years and wander alone or live with other males

CAPE BUFFALO

- Massive animal with short neck, ox-like barrel shape, short legs
- Horns in both sexes and flaring to the side
- Length: 8' - 11'4"
- Height: 4'8" - 5'4"
- Weight: 1,100 - 1,540 lbs.
- Habitat: Savanna and never far from water
- Breeding: Year-round in some area; seasonal in others; 1 calf after 11 month gestation
- Sociable and stay in herds
- Bulls past their prime associate in bachelor groups or alone

WHAT ARE THE BIG 5?

The "Big 5" refers to the Lion, Leopard, Rhino, Elephant, and Cape Buffalo. Why not the hippo, zebra, hyena, or giraffe you may ask? How about the cheetah—that would be an animal you would probably like to see as much as a buffalo. Well, the term "Big 5" was actually coined by big game hunters. It refers to the difficulty in bagging these large animals, mostly due to their ferocity when cornered and shot at.

LION

- Large, robust cat, with a longish heavy muzzle
- Male develops mane beginning in third year
- Length: 8 - 11'; Height: 3'8" - 4'
- Weight: 268 - 528 lbs.
- Habitat: Grasslands and savannas; woodlands; and dense bush
- Breeding: Year-round; 1 - 4 cubs; 3.5 months gestation
- Prides include two to three to 40 lions
- Females are lifelong residents of their mothers' territories
- Adolescent males roam as nomads until they mature

LEOPARD

- Large, spotted cat, with short powerful limbs, heavy torso, thick neck, and long tail
- Short sleek coat tawny yellow to reddish brown
- Length: 3'4" - 4'2"
- Tail: 27 - 32"
- Height: 23 - 28"
- Weight 62 - 143 lbs.
- Habitat: Every type except interior of large deserts
- Breeding: 1 - 4 cubs born year-round
- Solitary and territorial but sometimes shares hunting ranges
- Eats whatever form of animal protein is available

RHINO

- Rhinoceroses are among the largest of the herbivores
- Barrel-shaped bodies, thick legs, and three-toed feet
- Very long head, with wide square mouth; massive hump at the top of neck
- Horns in both sexes
- Slate-gray to yellow-brown
- Length: 11'4" - 13'4"
- Height: 5'4" - 6'2"
- Weight: 3,740 - 5,060 lbs.
- Habitat: Savannas with shade trees, water holes, and mud wallows
- Breeding: 1 calf form in March or April
- Nearly pure grazer
- Form peer groups; males defend territories

Figure 6.17 Apply Styles Dialog Box

Click this down-pointing arrow to display a list of styles available in the current document.

Character style

A set of formatting instructions that applies to selected text only.

Table style

Style that is used in tables, such as borders, shading, alignment, and fonts.

List style

Style used to format bulleted or numbered lists.

that contains the insertion point or to selected text. A paragraph style may include formatting instructions such as text alignment, tab settings, line indents, line spacing, and borders and can include character formatting. A ***character style*** applies formatting to selected text within a paragraph. Character styles are useful for formatting single characters, technical symbols, special names, or phrases. Characters within a paragraph can have their own style even if a paragraph style is applied to the paragraph as a whole. A ***table style*** provides a consistent look to borders, shading, alignment, and fonts that are used in a table. ***List styles*** are used to format bulleted or numbered fonts.

To apply a style, first select the text to which you want to apply a style, and then on the Home tab, in the Styles group, click the style that you want. If you don't see the style that you want, click the More button to expand the Quick Styles gallery. If the style that you want does not appear in the gallery, press Ctrl + Shift + S to open the Apply Styles dialog box as shown in Figure 6.17. Under *Style Name*, type the name of the style you want.

Creating a New Quick Style

If you want to add a brand-new style or change a few of the styles in a Quick Styles set to reflect your document style preferences, complete the following steps:

1. Select the text that you want to create as a new style. For instance, suppose you want to apply bold and red to some text in your document.
2. On the Mini toolbar that appears above your selected text, click *Bold* and *Red* to format the text.
3. Right-click the selection, point to *Styles* on the shortcut menu, and then click *Save Selection as a New Quick Style*.
4. Give the style a name and then click OK. The named style that you created appears in the Quick Styles gallery with the name you gave it, ready for use whenever you want text to be bold and red.

Changing a Quick Style

In Word 2010, Quick Styles are predesigned styles that are designed to work together to create an attractive professional-looking document. The styles in the Quick Styles gallery are associated with the theme you have selected to use in your document and the Style Sets you chose to use in your document. You may want to experiment with selecting different themes and watching the changes in fonts, colors, and other attributes as you apply Quick Styles to your document. To modify a predesigned Quick Style, complete the following steps:

1. Select text that is styled with the attributes you want to change.
2. Format the selected text with the new attributes that you want.
3. On the Home tab, in the Styles group, right-click the style that you want to change.
4. Click *Update to Match Selection*. **Hint: If you changed the styles in a document and the styles are not updating the way you expected, click the Styles dialog box launcher, and then click Style Inspector to find out whether text was manually formatted instead of formatted by using styles.**

In addition, you may change a Quick Style by completing the following steps:

1. Right-click the Quick Style you wish to change, and then click *Modify* at the shortcut menu.
2. At the Modify Style dialog box, make the necessary changes.
3. Either give the modified style a new name (it will replace the original name), or save the style as originally named. Click OK.
4. Apply the modified style, or if it has been previously used in the document, all occurrences will be updated.

Choosing a Style Set

You can choose a set of styles that have been predesigned to work together for your entire document. All you have to do is choose the Style Set that is appropriate for the document that you are creating and then apply the styles from the convenient Quick Styles gallery while you create your document. You can also apply a different Style Set at any time. To choose a Style Set to apply to a blank document, complete the following steps:

1. Click the File tab, and then click New.
2. Double-click Blank document.
3. On the Home tab, in the Styles group, click the Change Styles button, and then point to Style Set.
4. Select a desired Quick Styles set, such as *Modern*. The Quick Styles gallery changes to reflect the Style Set that you selected. You can now use all the associated styles to build your document.

Changing a Style Set

Most of the time, you will not want to change the Style Sets listed when you click the Change Styles button in the Styles group on the Home tab. When you point to Style Sets after clicking the Change Styles button, you will see a list of styles with names such as Classic, Distinctive, Elegant, Fancy, Modern, and so forth. These style sets are predesigned to complement one another. However, under certain circumstances, you might want to change the attributes of a style in a Style Set.

After you have changed a Style Set, you can save the new Quick Style Set to the list of Style Sets in the gallery. To save the custom Quick Style Set, complete the following steps:

1. Create or modify the style in the Quick Style Set.
2. On the Home tab, in the Styles group, click Change Styles, and then point to *Style Set*.
3. Click *Save as Quick Style Set*.
4. In the Save Quick Style Set dialog box, type a name for your new Quick Style Set, and then click Save.

To view the new Quick Style Set, click the Change Styles button in the Styles group, and then point to *Style Set*. The new named Quick Style Set should display in the list so it can be applied to your document at any time.

Availability of Templates

Word bases a new blank document on the Normal template. By default, text that is typed is based on the **Normal style**. This means that when you start typing text, Word uses the font, font size, line spacing, text alignment, and other formatting instructions assigned to the Normal style, unless you specify other formatting instructions.

When you access a Blank Document, the Normal style is selected in the Quick Styles gallery displayed in the Styles group on the Home tab. All of the styles that are shown

◄ **DTP POINTERS**
Word 2010's Live Preview feature allows you to view different styles as you decide on the perfect one.

Change Styles

Normal style
A set of formatting instructions automatically applied to any text that is keyed unless other formatting instructions are specified.

Normal

Manage Styles

in the Quick Styles gallery are available for use in your Word document. These styles, as discussed earlier, are associated with the theme you have chosen. In addition to the Quick Styles shown in the gallery, a large selection of other built-in styles is available by clicking the Styles launcher at the bottom of the Quick Styles gallery. Click the Manage Styles button at the bottom of the drop-down list to import or export document styles and to manage system styles as shown in the Manage Styles dialog box in Figure 6.18.

Most of the Word built-in styles are available in any of its template documents. Some of these template documents also contain additional styles depending on the type of document being created. If you choose a different template document at the New tab Backstage view, the *Styles* list box will display the names of styles available for that particular template when you press Alt + Ctrl + Shift + S or click the Styles launcher.

Word contains some styles that are applied automatically to text when you use certain commands. For example, if you use the command to insert page numbers, Word applies a certain style to the page number text. Some other commands for which Word automatically applies a format include text alignment, tab settings, line indents, line spacing, borders, and, in some styles, character formatting.

When creating a brochure, in addition to using various style options, you will also need to understand the importance of how the page is folded to accommodate the brochure text and design elements. Controls useful in producing folded brochures are discussed in the next section.

Creating Booklets

Various types of booklets can be created in Word. The controls on these options, which include those that allow duplex printing and format headers and footers, are discussed in this section.

Figure 6.18 Manage Styles Dialog Box and Styles Task Pane

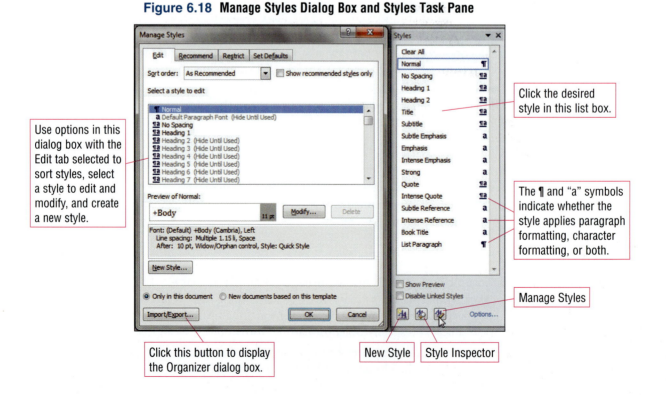

Use options in this dialog box with the Edit tab selected to sort styles, select a style to edit and modify, and create a new style.

Click the desired style in this list box.

The ¶ and "a" symbols indicate whether the style applies paragraph formatting, character formatting, or both.

Manage Styles

Click this button to display the Organizer dialog box.

New Style   Style Inspector

Creating a Folded Booklet

If you are interested in creating a folded booklet from scratch, start at a blank document and then, on the Page Layout tab, change the orientation to Landscape. Display the Page Setup dialog box, click the down-pointing arrow at the right of the *Multiple pages* list box, and then click *Book fold.* Change the margins as desired. Add text, graphics, headers or footers, and any other elements to your booklet. Print on both sides, fold the stack of sheets down the center, and staple them together in the center using a long-reach stapler.

Printing a Folded Booklet

When you select ***Book fold*** at the Page Setup dialog box, Word prints two pages on one side of the paper. When you fold the paper, it opens like a book. You would want to use this option when you are creating documents that have more than two pages, such as a menu, invitation, event program, or any other type of multiple-page document that uses a center fold. When planning the placement of your text and the order of the pages for printing, consider as an example that in an eight-page booklet, pages 8 and 1 are on the same side of the same sheet, as are pages 2 and 7, pages 6 and 3, and pages 4 and 5, as shown in Figure 6.19. It may take some trial and error when working with your printer, so try printing a dummy booklet first. You may click the Blank Page button in the Pages group in the Insert tab or press Ctrl + Enter to generate additional pages when using the Book fold feature.

Book fold
Word feature used to print two pages on one side of the paper.

Blank Page

Working with Headers and Footers

When using the book fold feature, your document will display with facing pages. In which case, the margins of the left page are a mirror image of those of the right page (i.e., the inside margins are the same width, and the outside margins are the same width). Besides increasing the ***gutter*** space to accommodate for binding, you will need to plan the placement of page numbering and other document information so that the text will display properly. The gutter position box at the Page Setup dialog box is not available when you use the mirror margins, 2 pages per sheet, or Book fold option. For those options, the gutter position is determined automatically.

A header consists of text or graphics that appear at the top of every page in a section. A footer appears at the bottom of every page. Headers and footers often contain page numbers, chapter titles, company logos, file names, author's name, or dates. To insert a header or footer into your document, you will need to start by accessing the Insert tab. On the Insert tab, click either the Header or Footer button in the Header & Footer group. You can create a different header or footer for the first page of a

Gutter
A gutter adds extra space to the side margin, top margin, or inside margin of a document that you plan to bind.

Header

Footer

Figure 6.19 Pages Arranged for Printing

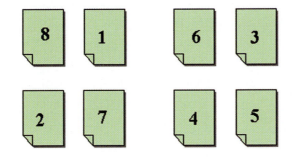

Figure 6.20 Predesigned Formats for Headers (Footers)

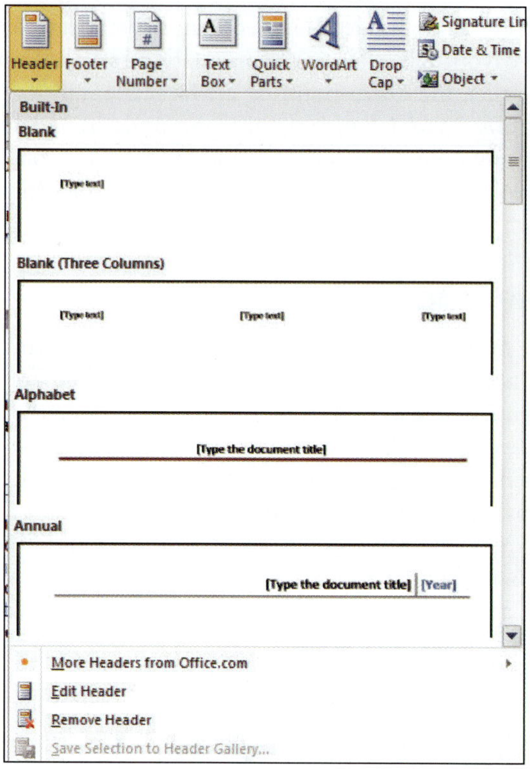

document or section, or create one header or footer for even-numbered pages and a different header or footer for odd-numbered pages.

The graphic or text that you insert in a header or footer is automatically left-aligned. To center an item, press Tab; to right-align an item, press Tab twice. When you click either the Header or Footer button, you will see many preformatted designs available to you at the drop-down lists as shown in Figure 6.20. In addition, distinctive designs for page numbering are available at the Building Blocks Organizer (Quick Parts).

Adding Page Numbering to a Booklet

Page Number

Any text, graphics, or fields that you add to a booklet may be entered into a header or footer to ensure that the items appear on every page of the document. If you add page numbering to a booklet in a header or footer, the numbering code will result in sequential numbering on each page. To turn on the numbering feature, click the Page Number button in the Header & Footer group on the Insert tab. You may choose from several options at the *Page Number* drop-down list to position the number at the top of the page or at the bottom of the page in many predesigned formats. Click the Header or Footer button to edit or remove this formatting.

1. Open a blank document to create a membership booklet similar to the one illustrated in Figure 6.21 by completing the following steps:
   a. Save the document as **C06-E04-GolfBookFold**.
   b. Click the Margins button in the Page Setup group in the Page Layout tab, click Custom Margins, change the top, bottom, right, and left margins to **0.5"**, and add **0.25"** to the gutter.
   c. Click the down-pointing arrow at the right of the *Multiple Pages* option in the *Pages* section, and then click *Book fold* from the drop-down list. *Hint: When you select* **Book fold***, the page changes automatically to* **Landscape.**
   d. Click the down-pointing arrow at the right of the *Sheets per booklet* option, click 8. Click OK.
   e. Press Ctrl + Enter seven times to generate a total of eight pages to your booklet.

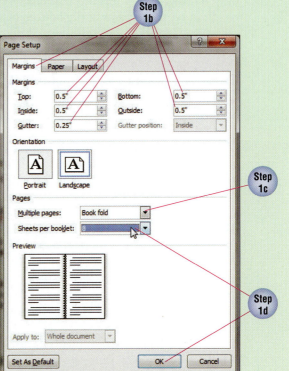

2. Position your insertion point in the first page and insert the photograph of the golfer as shown in Figure 6.21 by completing the following steps:
   a. Type **golfer** in the *Search for* text box at the Clip Art task pane. Insert the lady golfer image shown in Figure 6.21 or a similar one.
   b. Select the image, and size it to approximately 2.5 inches by 1.6 inches. Change the Wrap Text to *In Front of Text* and drag the image to a position similar to Figure 6.21.
   c. Select the image and then apply the *Beveled Matte, White* Picture Style located in the first row of the Picture Styles gallery.

   d. Insert the golf ball and club photograph as shown on the cover in Figure 6.21. At the Clip Art task pane, type **golf** in the *Search for* text box, insert the image, and then size the image to approximately 2.25 inches by 3.38 inches. *Hint: Substitute the image if necessary, but note that the image dimensions will vary from those specified above.* Change the Text Wrap to *Behind Text*, and then drag the image to a position similar to that shown in Figure 6.21.
   e. Select the image, click the Artistic Effects button in the Adjust group, and then click the *Texturizer* effect from the Artistic Effects gallery.

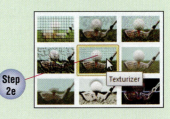

f. Select the image, click the Picture Styles More button, and then click the *Rotated, White* effect in the Picture Styles gallery.

Step 2f

3. Add the text at the bottom of the cover page by completing the following steps:
    a. Change the theme to the *Verve* theme.
    b. Drag and draw a text box that measures approximately 1.25 inches by 3.5 inches.
    c. Position the text box at the bottom of the cover page and type the following:
        Midwest Golf Club (Press Shift + Enter.)
        Women's 9-Hole Directory (Press Shift + Enter.)
        Summer 2012
    d. Select *Midwest Golf Club*, and click the Title style in the Styles gallery on the Home tab. Resize the text box if necessary.
    e. Select **Women's 9-Hold Directory** and change the font to 14-point Trebuchet MS with Kerning at 14 points.
    f. Select **Summer 2012** and change the font to 14-point Trebuchet MS in Small caps.
    g. Select **Summer 2012** and click the Text Effects button in the Font group, and apply the *Fill - White, Outline - Accent 1* effect.

Step 3g

    h. Select the text box, click the Shape Styles More button on the Drawing Tools Format tab, and then click the *Subtle Effect - Pink, Accent 1* effect in the Shape Styles gallery.

Step 3h

    i. Select all the text, and change the alignment to Align Text Right.
    j. Save the document again with the same name.
4. Position your insertion point at the top of page 2, press Ctrl + E, and type **Notes** in the top center of the page. *Hint: Turn on the Show/Hide feature, and position the insertion point before the Page Break code.*
5. Position your insertion point in page 3, and insert the **Welcome** file located in your *Chapter06* student data folder.

Step 6

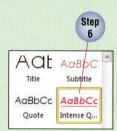

6. Select **Welcome to the 2012 golf season!** and apply the Intense Quote style in the Styles gallery.
7. Select the *Welcome* text beginning with *All scores are to be recorded…*, and click the Bullet button in the Paragraph group.
8. Click the Paragraph dialog box launcher to access the Paragraph dialog box and then remove the check mark next to the *Don't add space between paragraphs of the same style* option in the *Spacing* section. Click OK.

Step 8

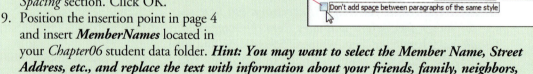

9. Position the insertion point in page 4 and insert *MemberNames* located in your *Chapter06* student data folder. *Hint: You may want to select the Member Name, Street Address, etc., and replace the text with information about your friends, family, neighbors, coworkers, etc.*
10. Insert the **MemberName** file located in your *Chapter06* student data folder in page 5 and 6.
11. Position your insertion point in page 7, and insert the **Schedule** file located in your *Chapter06* student data folder.

12. Apply the Title style to *Ladies 9-Hole Golf Schedule*, and apply the Intense Emphasis style to the schedule text.
13. Position your insertion point at the top of page 8, press the Enter key once, press Ctrl + E, and then type **More Notes**.
14. If the inserted text generated an additional page, press Ctrl + End, and then press the Backspace key to eliminate any additional pages (you should have eight pages in total for your booklet).
15. Add page numbering by completing the following steps:
    a. Position your insertion point at the beginning of your document (press Ctrl + Home).
    b. Click the Page Number button in the Header & Footer group in the Insert tab.
    c. Click the *Bottom of Page* option at the *Page Number* drop-down list.
    d. Click the *Plain Number 2* option in the *Simple* section of the Page Number gallery.
    e. Click to add a check mark in the check box next to the *Different First Page* option in the Options group in the Header & Footer Tools Design tab. Click the Close Header & Footer button.
16. Print the document by completing the following steps: *Hint: Make sure you have only 8 pages to your document!*
    a. Click the File tab, and then click the Print tab Backstage view.
    b. Click the down-pointing arrow at the right of the *Print One Sided* option in the *Settings* section, and then click the *Manually Print on Both Sides* option.
    c. Microsoft Office will print all of the pages that appear on one side of the paper and then prompt you to turn the stack over and feed the pages into the printer again. *Hint: You may have to experiment with reloading your pages properly.*
    d. Fold your pages to assemble your booklet.
17. Save and close **C06-E04-GolfBookFold.docx**.

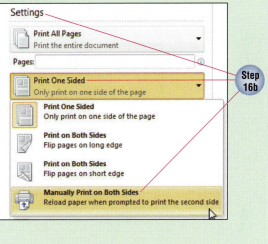

Step 16b

Creating a Brochure Using 2 Pages per Sheet

In earlier exercises, you used templates, tables, columns, and text boxes to create brochures folded in various sizes. Alternatively, you may use Word's 2 pages per sheet feature to format a brochure.

Word 2010 has a feature that makes creating single-fold brochures much easier. The *2 pages per sheet* feature divides each physical page (not the text) in half as shown in Figure 6.22, so that the printed page can be folded in half and used as a single-fold brochure or several pages can be folded and bound at the fold to create a booklet. Word displays and numbers each half page as a separate page. Any page formatting such as margins, paper size, and orientation can be applied to each half page. Headers and footers, page numbering, and page borders can also be inserted.

To use the 2 pages per sheet feature, select the Page Layout tab, click the Page Setup dialog box launcher button, click the down-pointing arrow at the right of

2 pages per sheet
A Word feature that divides each physical page (not the text) in half so that a printed page can be folded in half and used as a brochure or multiple pages can be folded into a booklet.

Figure 6.21 Exercise 6.4

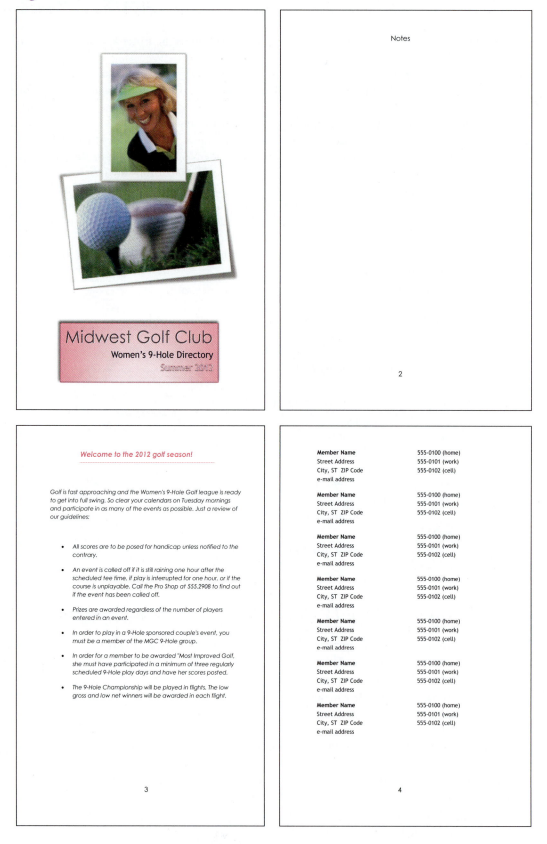

Figure 6.21 Exercise 6.4 (continued)

Member Name	555-0100 (home)
Street Address	555-0101 (work)
City, ST ZIP Code	555-0102 (cell)
e-mail address	

Member Name	555-0100 (home)
Street Address	555-0101 (work)
City, ST ZIP Code	555-0102 (cell)
e-mail address	

Member Name	555-0100 (home)
Street Address	555-0101 (work)
City, ST ZIP Code	555-0102 (cell)
e-mail address	

Member Name	555-0100 (home)
Street Address	555-0101 (work)
City, ST ZIP Code	555-0102 (cell)
e-mail address	

Member Name	555-0100 (home)
Street Address	555-0101 (work)
City, ST ZIP Code	555-0102 (cell)
e-mail address	

Member Name	555-0100 (home)
Street Address	555-0101 (work)
City, ST ZIP Code	555-0102 (cell)
e-mail address	

Member Name	555-0100 (home)
Street Address	555-0101 (work)
City, ST ZIP Code	555-0102 (cell)
e-mail address	

5

Member Name	555-0100 (home)
Street Address	555-0101 (work)
City, ST ZIP Code	555-0102 (cell)
e-mail address	

Member Name	555-0100 (home)
Street Address	555-0101 (work)
City, ST ZIP Code	555-0102 (cell)
e-mail address	

Member Name	555-0100 (home)
Street Address	555-0101 (work)
City, ST ZIP Code	555-0102 (cell)
e-mail address	

Member Name	555-0100 (home)
Street Address	555-0101 (work)
City, ST ZIP Code	555-0102 (cell)
e-mail address	

Member Name	555-0100 (home)
Street Address	555-0101 (work)
City, ST ZIP Code	555-0102 (cell)
e-mail address	

Member Name	555-0100 (home)
Street Address	555-0101 (work)
City, ST ZIP Code	555-0102 (cell)
e-mail address	

Member Name	555-0100 (home)
Street Address	555-0101 (work)
City, ST ZIP Code	555-0102 (cell)
e-mail address	

6

Ladies 9-Hole Golf Schedule

Tuesday	April 24	Opening Luncheon
Tuesday	May 1	Opening Scramble
Tuesday	May 8	9-Hole Event, Front
Tuesday	May 15	9-Hole Event, Back
Friday	May 18	9-Hole Couple's Golf
Wednesday	May 23	Women's Rally for the Cure
Tuesday	May 29	9-Hole Event, Front
Tuesday	June 5	9-Hole Event, Back
Tuesday	June 12	9-Hole Event, Crazy Days
Tuesday	June 19	9-Hole Event, Front
Tuesday	June 26	9-Hole Guest Day
Tuesday	July 3	9-Hole, Championship
Friday	July 13	9-Hole, Couples Golf
Tuesday	July 17	Closing Lunch

7

More Notes

8

Figure 6.22 2 Pages per Sheet

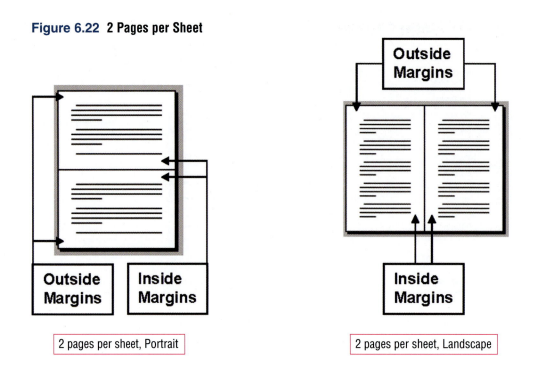

2 pages per sheet, Portrait   2 pages per sheet, Landscape

the *Multiple pages* list box, and then select *2 pages per sheet* at the drop-down list. In addition, select *Portrait* or *Landscape* in the *Orientation* section. Enter the desired margin values. Refer to Figure 6.22 to see where the outside and inside margins are located when Portrait or Landscape is selected.

Using Drop Caps as a Design Element

In publications such as magazines, newsletters, or brochures, a graphics feature called drop caps can be used to enhance the appearance of text. A ***drop cap*** is the first letter of the first word in a paragraph that is set in a larger font size and set into the paragraph. Drop caps identify the beginning of major sections or parts of a document.

Drop caps look best when set in a paragraph containing text set in a proportional font. The drop cap can be set in the same font as the paragraph text, or it can be set in a complementary font. For example, a drop cap can be set in a sans serif font while the paragraph text is set in a serif font. A drop cap can be one character or the entire first word of a paragraph. A special character may be used as the first character in a paragraph and then formatted as a drop cap to create an interesting effect. The examples in Figure 6.23 show some of the ways drop caps can be created and formatted. Practice restraint when using this design element or it can be distracting. However, remember that drop caps cannot be created in text boxes.

DTP POINTERS ▶

You cannot insert a drop cap into a text box.

Drop Cap

Although text boxes generally have replaced frames in the most recent versions of Word, the drop cap feature still uses a frame to enclose the text. A frame is similar to a text box except that it is inserted in the text layer rather than the drawing layer. You can customize the drop cap letter by selecting the letter within the frame, changing the font color and font style and adding special effects. You can also apply other formatting, such as borders and shading, to the frame itself. To insert drop caps, click the Drop Cap button in the Text group in the Insert tab.

Figure 6.23 Drop Cap Examples

A drop cap looks best when set in a paragraph containing text set in a proportional font. The drop cap can be set in the same font as the paragraph text or it can be set in a complementary font. For example, a drop cap can be set in a sans serif font while the paragraph text is set in a serif font. A drop cap can be one character or the entire first word of a paragraph. A special character may be used as the first character in a paragraph and then formatted as a drop cap to create a visually interesting effect. *(The drop cap is set in Curlz MT with a green font color and shadow effect applied; the body text is set in High Tower Text.)*

A drop cap looks best when set in a paragraph containing text set in a proportional font. The drop cap can be set in the same font as the paragraph text or it can be set in a complementary font. For example, a drop cap can be set in a sans serif font while the paragraph text is set in a serif font. A drop cap can be one character or the entire first word of a paragraph. A special character may be used as the first character in a paragraph and then formatted as a drop cap to create a visually interesting effect. *(The drop cap is set in Jokerman with a light blue font color; the body text is set in Comic Sans MS.)*

In publications such as magazines, newsletters, or brochures, a graphics feature called *drop caps* can be used to enhance the appearance of text. A drop cap is the first letter of the first word in a paragraph that is set in a larger font size and set into the paragraph. Drop caps identify the beginning of major sections or parts of a document. *(The drop cap is set in Mercurius Script MT with a plum font color; the body text is set in Book Antiqua.)*

In publications such as magazines, newsletters, or brochures, a graphics feature called *drop caps* can be used to enhance the appearance of text. A drop cap is the first letter of the first word in a paragraph that is set in a larger font size and set into the paragraph. Drop caps identify the beginning of major sections or parts of a document. *(The drop cap is from the Webdings character set; the body text is set in Verdana.)*

Copying Individual Styles from Other Documents and Templates

In Word 2010, the Manage Styles dialog box offers options for copying individual styles from an existing document or template to another document or template. To access the Organizer dialog box when you can copy styles to other documents, click the Import/Export button in the bottom left corner of the Manage Styles dialog box. The Organizer dialog box is shown in Figure 6.24.

Figure 6.24 Organizer Dialog Box

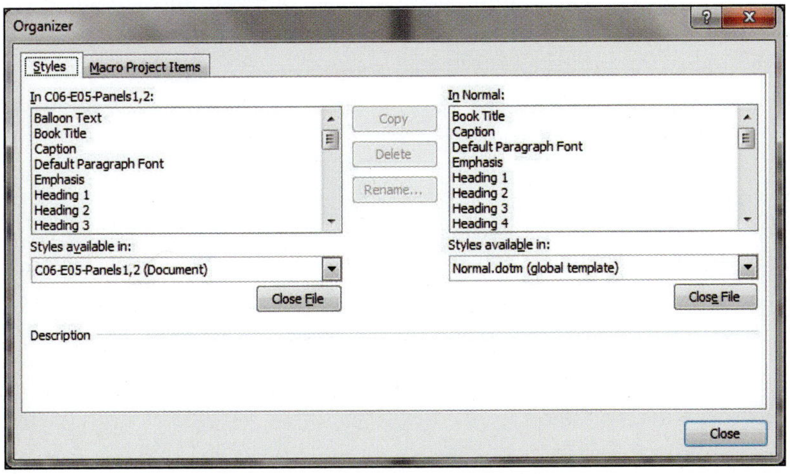

Using the Style Inspector

Style Inspector

If you changed the styles in a document and the styles are not updating the way you expected, click the Styles dialog box launcher, and then click Style Inspector to find out whether text was manually formatted instead of formatted by using styles. This feature may save you time in editing and locating errors in styles that you may have created or modified.

Exercise 6.5 Creating the Inside Panels of a Single-Fold Brochure Using Styles and a Drop Cap

1. Open **SingleFoldLandscape** located in the *SampleBrochures* folder in your *Chapter06* folder and then print the document on both sides of a sheet of paper. Use this as a dummy for Exercise 6.5.

2. At a blank document create the inside panels of a single-fold brochure as shown in Figure 6.25 by completing the following steps:
   a. Change the margins to **0.7**, change the page orientation to *Landscape*, click the down-pointing arrow at the right of the *Multiple pages* list box, and then select *2 pages per sheet*. Click OK.
   b. Verify that the theme is Office.
   c. With the insertion point located at the top of the document, insert the **HeartText** file located in your *Chapter06* folder.
   d. Select all the text in the document (Ctrl + A), and apply the No Spacing style.

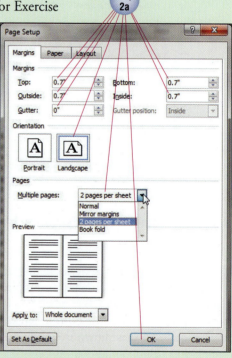

Step 2a

Step 2d

3. Format the drop cap paragraph as shown in Figure 6.25 by completing the following steps:
   a. Click the Show/Hide button on the Home tab to display nonprinting symbols.
   b. Select the first paragraph, and apply the Heading 1 style. Modify the Heading 1 style by changing the font to 14-point Lucinda Sans Unicode with bold, italics, and *Dark Blue, Text 2* font color from the *Theme Colors* section. Right-click on Heading 1 and then click *Update Heading 1 to Match Selection*.
   c. Position the insertion point anywhere in the first paragraph, and then click the Drop Cap button in the Text group on the Insert tab.

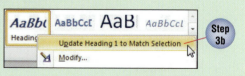

Step 3b

Step 3c

d. Click the Drop Cap Options button. At the Drop Cap dialog box, make sure *Dropped* is selected, change the font to *Harrington*, type **3** in the *Lines to drop* text box, and change the *Distance from text* setting to **0.1**. Click OK.

Step
3d

e. With the frame around the drop cap selected (blue sizing handles will display), change the font color to *Red, Accent 2* in the first row of the color palette, and remove italics.

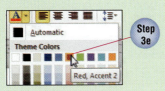

Step
3e

f. Apply a style, and then modify it by completing the following steps:

Step
3f1

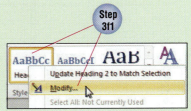

1) Select *Diabetes: The Latest News,* apply the Heading 2 style in the Quick Styles gallery, right-click on the Heading 2 style in the Styles gallery, and click *Modify.*

2) At the Modify Style dialog box, change the font size to 16-point Cambria, turn on bold, small caps, *Red, Accent 2*, and add **18 pt** Before each paragraph. *Hint: At the Modify Style dialog box, click Format in the bottom left corner to access the Font dialog box (to apply Small caps) and Paragraph to access the Paragraph dialog box (18 points Before).* At the Paragraph dialog box, select the Line and Page Breaks tab, and notice that the *Keep with next* option in the *Pagination* section has been selected. This will prevent the heading from being separated from the headings and paragraph that follows. Click OK twice. The modified Heading 2 style has replaced the previous Heading 2 style, which is saved with the document.

![Modify Style dialog box with Step 3f2 label pointing to Format menu options]

Step
3f2

3) Select *Tuesday, March 20, 2012,* and apply the Heading 3 style.
4) Right-click on the Heading 3 style, and then click *Modify*. At the Modify Style dialog box, change the font color to *Dark Blue, Text 2,* bold, and then change the Spacing Before to **0 pt** at the Paragraph dialog box (click the Format button, and then click *Paragraph*). Click OK twice.

5) Select *Katherine Dwyer, M.D.,* and then apply Heading 4.
6) Right-click on the Heading 4 style and then click *Modify*. At the Modify Style dialog box, change the font color to Black, turn off bold, turn on italics, and then change the *Spacing Before* to **0 pt** at the Paragraph dialog box (click the Format button and then *Paragraph*). Click OK twice.
7) Select the paragraph beginning *One of the best ways . . .,* change the font to 12-point Calibri, and add **12 pt** Before the paragraph. Right-click on the text, click Styles, and then click Save Selection as a New Quick Style.

8) At the Create New Style from Formatting dialog box, type **HeartBody** in the *Name* text box and then click OK.

9) Apply the Heading 2, Heading 3, Heading 4, and Heart Body styles to the remaining headings and paragraph as shown in Figure 6.25.

4. Position the insertion point before *All lectures* and type **9** pt in the *Before* text box at the Paragraph dialog box. Click OK.

5. Select from *All lectures:* until the end of the document and then change the font to 12-point Calibri in the *Dark Blue, Text 2* color in the first row of the *Theme Colors* section. Apply bold.

6. Insert tabs (press the Tab key) to align the lecture information (time and location) as displayed in Figure 6.25.

7. Position the insertion point before *The talk is . . .*, and type **9** pt in the *Before* text box at the Paragraph dialog box.

8. Select *FREE* and change the font color to *Red, Accent 2*. If the text in the last paragraph at the bottom of the first page wraps to the second page, adjust the *Spacing Before*.

9. Add the watermark image by completing the following steps:

    a. Click the Clip Art button in the Illustrations group in the Insert tab.

    b. At the Clip Art task pane, type **healthcare** in the *Search for* text box, and click Go. Select the medical image shown in Figure 6.25 or a similar image, and then click Insert.

    c. With the image selected, click the down-pointing arrow at the bottom of the Crop button in the Size group and then click *Crop to Shape* from the drop-down list. Click the heart shape in the *Basic Shapes* section of the Shapes gallery.

    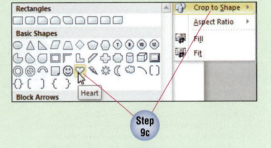

    d. Change the Wrap Text to *In Front of Text* and then size and position the image as shown in Figure 6.25. Make sure the heart displays on the left side of the brochure. ***Hint: The image will display on only one of the pages, and it will show as only half an image. Do not worry; it will print properly!***

    e. Select the image, click the Color button in the Adjust group, and then click the *Blue, Accent color 1 Light* thumbnail in the *Recolor* section.

    f. Click the Corrections button in the Adjust group and then select *Sharpen: 25%* in the *Sharpen and Soften* section.

    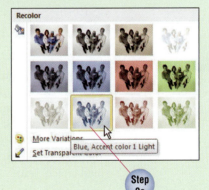

    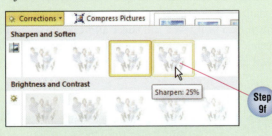

    h. Select the image and send it *Behind Text*.

10. Save the document as **C06-E05-Panels1,2**.

11. Save the document again with the same name, but save it in PDF format.

12. Print and then close **C06-E05-Panels1,2.docx**. Close **C06-E05-Panels1,2.pdf**.

Figure 6.25 Exercise 6.5

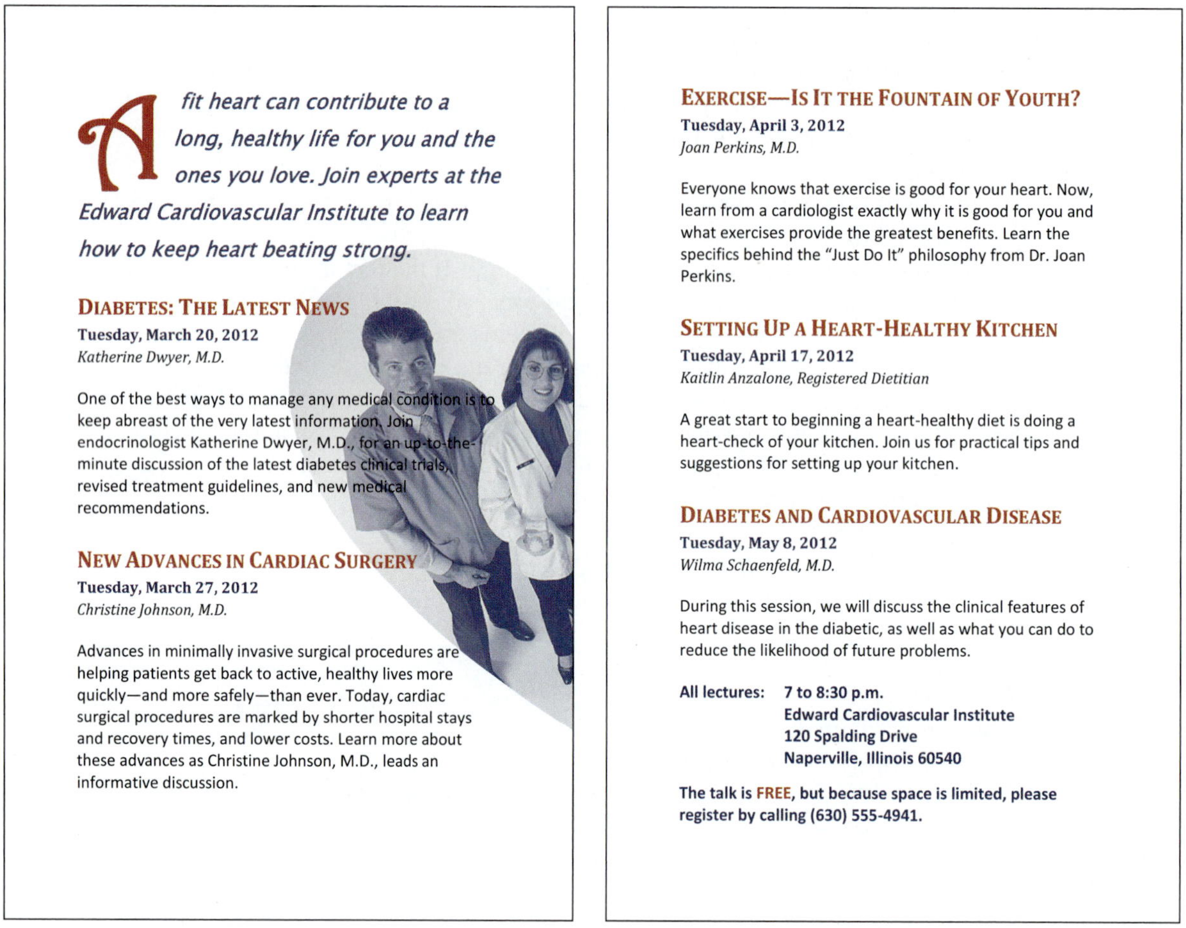

A fit heart can contribute to a long, healthy life for you and the ones you love. Join experts at the Edward Cardiovascular Institute to learn how to keep heart beating strong.

DIABETES: THE LATEST NEWS
Tuesday, March 20, 2012
Katherine Dwyer, M.D.

One of the best ways to manage any medical condition is to keep abreast of the very latest information. Join endocrinologist Katherine Dwyer, M.D., for an up-to-the-minute discussion of the latest diabetes clinical trials, revised treatment guidelines, and new medical recommendations.

NEW ADVANCES IN CARDIAC SURGERY
Tuesday, March 27, 2012
Christine Johnson, M.D.

Advances in minimally invasive surgical procedures are helping patients get back to active, healthy lives more quickly—and more safely—than ever. Today, cardiac surgical procedures are marked by shorter hospital stays and recovery times, and lower costs. Learn more about these advances as Christine Johnson, M.D., leads an informative discussion.

EXERCISE—IS IT THE FOUNTAIN OF YOUTH?
Tuesday, April 3, 2012
Joan Perkins, M.D.

Everyone knows that exercise is good for your heart. Now, learn from a cardiologist exactly why it is good for you and what exercises provide the greatest benefits. Learn the specifics behind the "Just Do It" philosophy from Dr. Joan Perkins.

SETTING UP A HEART-HEALTHY KITCHEN
Tuesday, April 17, 2012
Kaitlin Anzalone, Registered Dietitian

A great start to beginning a heart-healthy diet is doing a heart-check of your kitchen. Join us for practical tips and suggestions for setting up your kitchen.

DIABETES AND CARDIOVASCULAR DISEASE
Tuesday, May 8, 2012
Wilma Schaenfeld, M.D.

During this session, we will discuss the clinical features of heart disease in the diabetic, as well as what you can do to reduce the likelihood of future problems.

All lectures: 7 to 8:30 p.m.
    Edward Cardiovascular Institute
    120 Spalding Drive
    Naperville, Illinois 60540

The talk is **FREE**, but because space is limited, please register by calling (630) 555-4941.

In Exercise 6.6, you will create the back and cover (panels 3 and 4) of the heart brochure started in Exercise 6.5. To make this brochure self-mailing, the back of the brochure will be used for mailing purposes. To demonstrate another technique for creating this type of brochure, you will use a full sheet and text boxes to place text in specific locations on the page. This newly created material will be printed on the reverse side of Exercise 6.5. You will also save the brochure in PDF format and send it as an email attachment.

Exercise 6.6 Creating the Back (Panel 3) and Cover (Panel 4) of a Single-Fold Brochure

1. Open **HeartCoverandBack.docx** located in your *Chapter06* folder.
2. Save the document and name it **C06-E06-HeartBrochure**.
3. Format the cover and back as shown in Figure 6.26 by completing the following steps:
    a. Verify that the Office theme has been selected.
    b. Position your insertion point on *Spring 2012*, and then apply the Title style.

c. Change the Title style used in step 3b by completing the following steps:
1) Select *Spring 2012* and then click the Align Right Text (Ctrl + R) button in the Paragraph group on the Home tab.
2) Change the font to 24-point Calibri in small caps (Ctrl + Shift + K).
3) Click the down-pointing arrow at the right of the Borders button in the Paragraph group, and then click *Borders and Shading* at the drop-down list.
4) At the Borders and Shading dialog box, change the line color to *Red, Accent 2*; select *2¼ pt* in the *Width* section, click to add the line to the bottom of the preview box; and then click OK.

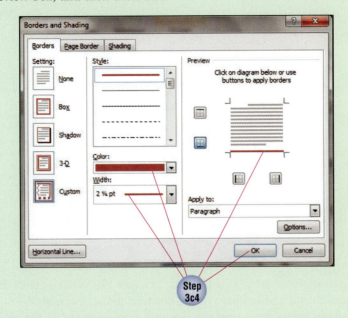

Step 3c4

5) Right-click *Spring 2012*, click Styles, and then click *Update Title to Match Selection*. **Hint: This updates the Title style to include the changes.**

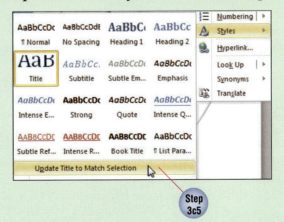

Step 3c5

d. Remove the text box outline and fill.
e. Select *Heart's*; change the font to 36-point Harrington in Red, Accent 2 in bold and small caps; and turn on Kerning at 14 pt. Click OK. Change the alignment to Align Right Text (Ctrl + R).

f.   Select *For your sake . . .*, change the font to 18-point Calibri in all caps and change the alignment to Align Text Right. ***Hint: Select*** **For your,** ***hold down the Ctrl key, and then select*** **sake . . ..**

4. Press Ctrl + Home to position the insertion point at the top of the page and then insert the same medical image used in Exercise 6.5. Substitute the image if necessary.

5. With the image selected, click the down-pointing arrow at the bottom of the Crop button in the Arrange group and then click *Crop to Shape* at the drop-down list. Click the heart shape in the third row of the *Basic Shapes* section.

6. With the image still selected, click the Picture Effects button in the Picture Styles group, click Shadow, and then click the *Inside Diagonal Top Right* effect in the *Inner* section.

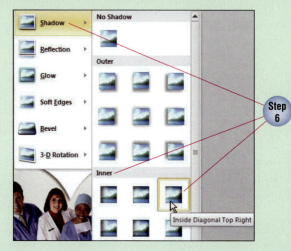

7. Size the image to approximately **3.3"** by **4.22"**, change the Wrap Text to the *In Front of Text* option, and then drag the image to the position shown in Figure 6.26. ***Hint: You may have to unlock the aspect ratio and the size will vary with the image selected.***

8. Insert the logo by completing the following steps:
    a. Press Ctrl + Home to position the insertion point at the top of the page, click the Picture button in the Insert tab, and then insert **EdwardCardioBW** from your *Chapter06* folder.
    b. Size the logo to approximately **.7"** by **1.88"**. ***Hint: You may have to unlock the aspect ratio.***
    c. Change the text wrap to *In Front of Text*, and then drag the image to the position shown in Figure 6.26.

9. Select *EDWARD CARDIOVASCULAR INSTITUTE* in the return address and change the font to 12-point Calibri, bold, in Dark Blue, Text 2 located in the *Standard Colors* section.

10. Save the document as **C06-E06-HeartBrochure**.

11. Reinsert Exercise 6.5 (**C06-E06-Panels1,2.docx**) into your printer, and then print **C06-E06-HeartBrochure.docx** on the back side.

12. Save the document again with the same name but save it in PDF format. Send the brochure to your college email address, and then open it using Adobe Reader®.

13. Close both documents.

Figure 6.26 **Exercise 6.6**

Chapter Summary

➤ Brochures and booklets may be used to inform, educate, promote, or sell. These documents may also be used to establish an organization's identity and image.

➤ A dummy is a mockup of a document used to visualize placement of text and objects to accommodate certain folds.

➤ The manner in which a brochure is folded determines the order in which the panels are set on the page. Folds create distinct sections in which to place blocks of text. The most common brochure fold is called a letter fold or single fold (portrait or landscape).

➤ A dummy can be created to help determine the location of information on the brochure page layout.

➤ Consistent elements are necessary to maintain continuity in a multiple-page brochure.

➤ The easiest method of creating the page layout for a letter-fold brochure is to use text boxes; the easiest method for a booklet is to use the book fold feature; and the easiest method for a single-fold brochure is to use the 2 pages per sheet feature. However, tables and columns may also be used to create the underlying structure of a brochure or pamphlet.

- You cannot insert a drop cap in a text box.
- Column formatting may be varied within the same document by using section breaks to separate the sections that will be formatted with different column settings.
- When you select Book fold at the Page Setup dialog box, Word prints two pages on one side of the paper. When you fold the paper, it opens like a book.
- When printing a booklet, be sure to print on both sides of the paper. This is known as duplex printing.
- A header consists of text or graphics that appear at the top of every page in a section.
- A footer appears at the bottom of every page. Headers and footers often contain page numbers, chapter titles, company logos, file names, author's name, or dates.
- Reverse text can be created in a document as a design element and usually refers to white text set against a solid black background. Reverse text can also be created with different colors for the text and the background, as well as shading.
- The front cover of a brochure sets the mood and tone for the whole brochure. The front cover title must attract attention and let the reader know what the brochure is about.
- Repetitive formatting that is used to maintain consistency in a single publication or among a series of documents may be applied to text by using a style.
- A style may be edited, and any occurrence of the style in the document is automatically updated to reflect the changes.
- Select predesigned styles at the Quick Styles gallery in the Home tab.
- Quick Styles are associated to the theme that has been selected.
- Display all available Word styles by clicking the Styles dialog box launcher.
- To clear all formatting to selected text, click the More button at the right of the Quick Styles gallery, and then click Clear Formatting, or apply the Normal style.
- Modified styles may be saved to the Quick Styles gallery as a replacement of the original style, or they may be saved with a new name. Styles are saved to the document where they are created.
- The Normal style from the Normal template is automatically applied to any text that is typed, unless you specify other formatting instructions.
- Word provides five types of styles—character, paragraph, linked (paragraph and character), table, and list. A character style applies formatting to selected text only. A paragraph style affects the paragraph that contains the insertion point or selected text. A linked style is a combination of a character style and a paragraph style. A table style provides a consistent look to borders, shading, alignment, and fonts that are being used in a table. A list style is used to format bulleted or numbered lists.
- A drop cap is a design element in which the first letter of the first word in a paragraph is formatted in a larger font size and set into the beginning of the paragraph.

Commands Review

FEATURE	RIBBON TAB, GROUP	BUTTON	KEYBOARD SHORTCUT
Apply Styles	Home, Styles		Ctrl + Shift + S
Blank Page	Insert, Pages		
Book fold	Page Layout, Page Setup		
Change Shape	Picture Tools Format, Crop, Crop to Shape		
Change Styles	Home, Styles		
Columns	Page Layout, Page Setup		
Drop cap	Insert, Text		
Footer	Insert, Header & Footer		
Format Painter	Home, Clipboard	Format Painter	Ctrl + Shift + C
Header	Insert, Header & Footer		
Manage Style	Home, Styles, Styles drop-down gallery		
Manual Duplex Printing	File tab, Print tab, Manually Print on Both Sides		Ctrl + P
New Style	Home, Styles, Styles drop-down gallery		
Normal Style	Home, Styles	AaBbCcD ¶ Normal	
Page Break	Insert, Pages	Breaks ▾	
Page Number	Insert, Header & Footer		
Style Inspector	Home, Styles, Styles drop-down gallery		
Styles	Home, Styles		Alt + Ctrl + Shift + S
Style Sets	Home, Styles		
2 pages per sheet	Page Layout, Page Setup		

Reviewing Key Points

A.	All styles	**I.**	Dummy	**Q.**	Panels
B.	Blank Page	**J.**	Duplex printing	**R.**	Paragraph dialog box
C.	Book fold	**K.**	Format Painter	**S.**	Paragraph style
D.	Character style	**L.**	Gate fold	**T.**	Parallel folds
E.	Clipboard	**M.**	Header and footer	**U.**	Table dialog box
F.	Columns	**N.**	Landscape	**V.**	Reverse text
G.	Crop to Shape	**O.**	Letter fold	**W.**	Style
H.	Drop cap	**P.**	Page Number	**X.**	2 pages per sheet

Completion: In the space at the left, provide the correct letter or letters from the above list that match each definition.

_____ 1. A mockup of a brochure.

_____ 2. This option at the Print tab Backstage view allows you to print the document on both sides of the paper and prompts you to reload the paper.

_____ 3. Folds in a brochure that all run in the same direction.

_____ 4. Use this dialog box to create columns of unequal width.

_____ 5. This feature divides a physical page in half and may be used to create single-fold brochures.

_____ 6. A set of formatting instructions saved with a name to be used repeatedly on different sections of text.

_____ 7. This Word feature prints two pages on one side of the paper so when you fold the paper, it opens like a book.

_____ 8. This is the name for the first letter of the first word in a paragraph that is formatted in a larger font size and is set into the paragraph.

_____ 9. This is the name for white text set against a black background.

_____ 10. Text or graphics that appear at either the top or bottom of every page.

_____ 11. This page orientation displays the page with the long side of the page on the top.

_____ 12. Use this feature to copy formatting from one area to another in a document.

_____ 13. This type of style applies formatting to selected text only.

_____ 14. The feature allows you to change the shape of an image.

_____ 15. Click this button to add a new page to a document.

Chapter *Assessments*

Assessment 6.1   Art Brochure

As a supportive member of the Newport Art League, use your desktop publishing skills to create a promotional brochure for the art league. Your target audience includes the general public, but more specifically artists, aspiring artists, art lovers, and those with a general interest in art. Your audience may also include both adults and children. Your purpose is to let your readers know what the art league has to offer. The content of your brochure will include information on annual art events, classes and workshops, membership, and volunteer opportunities.

In this assessment, you will create the back and cover panels of the Newport Art League's brochure. In the next assessment, you will create the back panels of the brochure. A sample solution of a complete brochure is provided in Figures 6.27; however, you are to create your own design (using text located in your *Chapter06* folder). Include the following specifications in your brochure design:

1. You may create a letter-fold (trifold), single-fold, or map-fold (use 8½ by 14-inch paper) brochure. You may create your brochure layout from scratch using text boxes, columns, tables, or 2 pages per sheet. Alternatively, you may use one of the brochure templates included in Word 2010, at Office.com, or at any other source for templates.

Figure 6.27 **Assessment 6.1 Sample Solution**

2. Include all of the information contained in the file **ArtText** located in your *Chapter06* folder.
3. Create a thumbnail sketch of your design and then create a dummy to guide you in the placement of text.
4. Select an appropriate theme, apply a Style Set if needed, use existing styles from the Styles gallery, or change the styles to fit your needs.
5. Use relevant graphics. A large selection of art-related graphics can be viewed by displaying the Clip Organizer and searching for clips with the keyword art. Viewing these graphics may serve as an inspiration for the design and color scheme of your brochure. Photographs tend to support sophisticated design.
6. Use a coordinated color scheme. Remember that you can customize text colors to match a color(s) in a clip art image, or you can customize the color(s) of a clip art image to match a specific text color or coordinate colors within another image. You may also use a customized Banner Shape as a watermark as shown in Figure 6.28.
7. Use appropriate typefaces. Make sure all text is legible. Turn on kerning for fonts over 14-points.
8. When creating the lines after Name, Address, City, State, ZIP, and Phone, create a table, and remove all the border lines except the bottom lines to the right of the label text.
9. Make any necessary adjustments to the spacing before and after paragraphs.
10. As you work, evaluate your design for the concepts of focus, balance, proportion, contrast, directional flow, consistency, and color.
11. Save the inside panels of the brochure, and name the file **C06-A01-Panels**.
12. Print and then close **C06-A01-Panels.docx**.

Figure 6.28 Assessment 6.2 Sample Solution

Assessment 6.2   Art Brochure

In this assessment, you will create the back panels of the brochure created in Assessment 6.1.

Include the following specifications:

1. Open **C06-A01-Panels.docx**. Save the document with Save As and name it **C06-A02-ArtBrochure**.
2. Refer to the dummy created in Assessment 6.1 to create the inside panels of the art league brochure. A sample solution is provided in Figure 6.28.
3. Apply any relevant styles created in Assessment 6.1.
4. Make any adjustments to the spacing or positioning of text.
5. Save the brochure document with the same name **C06-A02-ArtBrochure**.
6. Print the first page of the brochure and then print the second page on the back of the first page. Fold your brochure and check the placement of text and images in relation to the folds. Make any adjustments as necessary to produce a professionally finished product.
7. Print a copy of the **DocumentEvaluationChecklist** located in your *Chapter06* folder. Using the document evaluation checklist, evaluate your brochure design.
8. Close **C06-A02-ArtBrochure.docx**.

Assessment 6.3   Welcome to Beijing Travel Book

Assume you work at home as a virtual event planner. One of your clients has requested that you put together a helpful travel book for a conference that will be held in Beijing, China. The book will be printed at a commercial printer and spiral bound. The book, which measures 4.5 inches by 2.75 inches, will include commonly used Chinese phrases, new and famous sites, restaurants, shops, and emergency numbers. Figure 6.29 illustrates what the professionally printed book could look like. Include the following specifications in your design:

1. Open *Beijing* located in your *Chapter06* folder.
2. Type **Beijing** in the *Search for* text box at the Clip Art task pane and then insert the image in the cover cell.
3. Size and position the Beijing image as shown in Figure 6.30.

Figure 6.29 Sample Travel Book - Professionally Printed and Bound

Figure 6.30 **Assessment 6.3**

EMERGENCY

International SOS
"ya zhou guo ji jin ji jiu yuan zhong xin"
Clinic: 6462 5555
24-hour Alarm Center: 6464 5555
Tower C, BITIC Leasing Center
No. 1 North Street Xifusancun
Chaoyang District, Beijing

Being United Family Hospital and Clinics
"beijing he mu jia yi juan"
Tel: 6433 5555
No. 2 Jiangtai Road

Welcome to
Beijing 2012

SHOPS

Shard Box *"shen de ge gong yi pin diam"*
Jewelry, trinkets
09:00 – 19:00

Bai Gong Fang *"jing cheng bai gong fang"*
Silk carpet, art and craft, pearls
09:00 – 17:30

Bo Na Jade Articles Building
"bon na yu qi cheng"
Jade, pearls
08:00 – 18:00

PHRASES

Hello *"ni hao"*	Please *"qing"*
Good Bye *"jai jian"*	Thank you *"xie xie"*
Left *"zuo"*	Straight Ahead *"yi zhi zou"*
Right *"you"*	Please take me to *"qing dai wo qu"*
No *"bu"*	Stop *"ting che"*

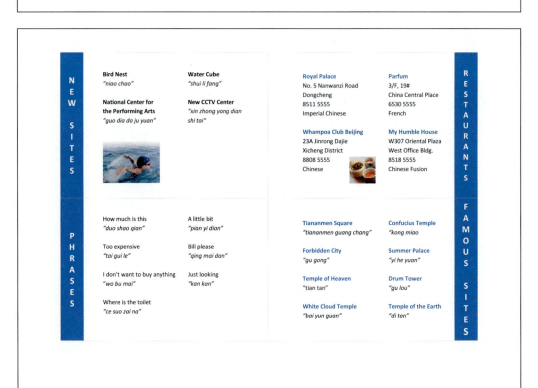

NEW SITES

Bird Nest
"niao chao"

**National Center for
the Performing Arts**
"guo dia da ju yuan"

Water Cube
"shui li fang"

New CCTV Center
*"xin zhong yang dian
shi tai"*

PHRASES

How much is this *"duo shao qian"*	A little bit *"pian yi dian"*
Too expensive *"tai gui le"*	Bill please *"qing mai dan"*
I don't want to buy anything *"wo bu mai"*	Just looking *"kan kan"*
Where is the toilet *"ce suo zai na"*	

RESTAURANTS

Royal Palace
No. 5 Nanwanzi Road
Dongcheng
8511 5555
Imperial Chinese

Whampoa Club Beijing
23A Jinrong Dajie
Xicheng District
8808 5555
Chinese

Parfum
3/F, 19#
China Central Place
6530 5555
French

My Humble House
W307 Oriental Plaza
West Office Bldg.
8518 5555
Chinese Fusion

FAMOUS SITES

Tiananmen Square *"tiananmen guang chang"*	**Confucius Temple** *"kong miao"*
Forbidden City *"gu gong"*	**Summer Palace** *"yi he yuan"*
Temple of Heaven *"tian tan"*	**Drum Tower** *"gu lou"*
White Cloud Temple *"bai yun guan"*	**Temple of the Earth** *"di tan"*

332   Chapter Six

4. Create text boxes to contain the text on the cover as shown in Figure 6.30.
5. The underlying structure of this document is a table; set left indentation settings to indent the text from the left edge of each cell. Set tabs to simulate columns for the text—press Ctrl + Tab to move your insertion point to the tab setting.
6. Type the text as shown in Figure 6.30 or if the text is difficult to see, open **BeijingText.docx** located in your *Chapter06* folder and copy and paste tyhe text or key from the document. The cell containing the *Phrases* vertical text has been formatted as an example for the rest of the vertical text. Type the text by typing a letter and then pressing Enter to advance to the next line. Apply a blue fill to the cells containing the vertical text.
7. Insert appropriate graphics to reinforce the visual appeal of the document.
8. Save the document as **C06-A03-WelcometoBeijing**.
9. Save the document again with the same name, and then save it in PDF format assuming that you will send the booklet to a commercial printer.
10. Print and then close **C06-A03-WelcometoBeijing.docx**. Close **C06-A03-WelcometoBeijing.pdf**.

Assessment 6.4   Group Project - Fundraiser Brochure with Chart

You are a member of a fund-raising committee for the Loaves & Fishes Food Pantry. With the help of the other members of your group, plan an event to raise money, and create a brochure that promotes the charity and advertises the event.

1. You may use the **LoavesandFishes.jpg** logo and the **PicnicinDecember.jpg** picture located in your *Chapter06* folder.
2. You may want to include a chart that illustrates the increase in the number of families served over the past three years. An example is shown in Figure 6.31. You may use Excel to create the chart or use Word to create a column chart type as shown in the sample solution. The **Loaves&FishesBagLogo.jpg** was used as a fill for the data. Make sure you resize the columns to accommodate the image as shown in Figure 6.31.
3. You may use the text in the sample document or if it is difficult to read, you may open **Loaves&FishesPicnicText.docx** located in your *Chapter06* folder, or research a similar organization on the Internet for facts, information, goals, and so on.
4. Open **DocumentEvaluationChecklist** located in your *Chapter06* folder, and print one copy.
5. Use the document evaluation checklist to analyze your brochure and make any additional adjustments if necessary. Label the exercise as **C06-A04-Fundraiser.docx**.
6. Print the completed form to the back of your brochure.

Figure 6.31 **Assessment 6.4 Sample Solution**

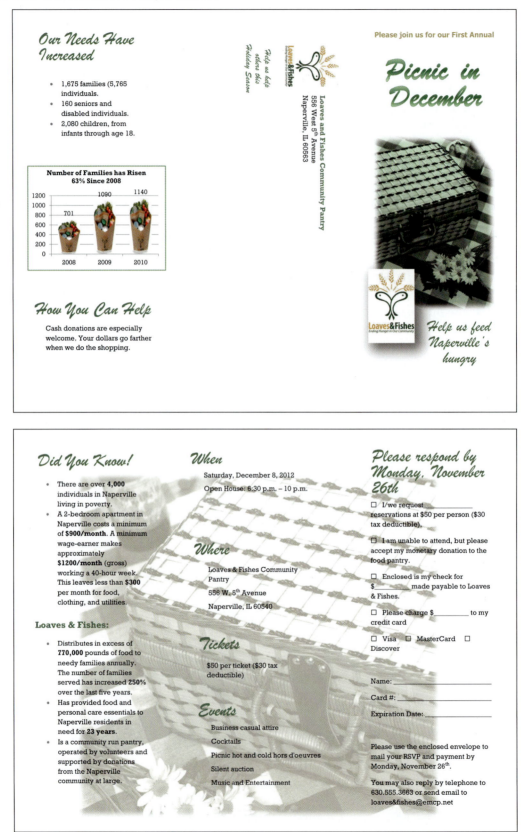

Chapter 7

CHAPTER07

Creating Specialty Promotional Documents

Performance Objectives

Upon successful completion of Chapter 7, you will be able to:

- Create specialty promotional documents.
- Review and apply design concepts.
- Create lines on which you can type.
- Create lines that align.
- Insert field codes.
- Create a data source and merge data.
- Create crop marks.

Desktop Publishing Terms

Data source	Mail merge	Merge fields
Field codes	Main document	Record

Word Features Used

Address Block	Leaders	Style Sets
Column breaks	Mail Merge wizard	Symbol
Crop marks	Main document	Tables
Data source	Page Border	Tabs
Field codes	Quick Styles	Themes
Header and footer	Section breaks	Update labels
Labels	Shapes	

By the time you reach this chapter, you will have been exposed to a number of different examples of desktop publishing applications. As you know, studying the work of others is a great way to pick up pointers on layout and design, as well as interesting uses of fonts, color, text, and graphics. In addition, you may access the Internet to find numerous sources for useful project ideas, tips, and resources. As mentioned in previous chapters, paper supply companies offer predesigned papers that are frequently available in catalogs; those catalogs may offer many helpful ideas for the layout and design of your documents, too.

Although this textbook typically presents one or two different approaches to creating a document, there are usually many other ways to achieve the same results. You must decide which approach is easiest for you to remember and apply. Mastering desktop publishing skills takes a lot of practice and experimentation. In this chapter, you will create specialty promotional documents such as tickets, subscription forms, gift certificates, merged postcards, bookmarks, name tags, business greeting cards, and invitations. Any one of the exercises presented in this chapter could be adapted to just about any other personal or business situation.

Creating Promotional Documents

In addition to flyers and announcements, other promotional documents include tickets, enrollment forms, gift certificates, postcards, bookmarks, name tags, invitations, and business greeting cards. They become promotional documents when a business or organization name is visible or an item or service is mentioned for sale in a document.

Whether creating tickets for a charitable event, discount coupons for a grocery store, bookmarks promoting reading at a public library, or coasters advertising a local restaurant, Word desktop publishing features combined with a little imagination can produce endless possibilities. Figure 7.1 illustrates other promotional documents created with the same basic design concepts and Word features used in most of the exercises in this chapter. Figure 7.2 illustrates many updated Word 2010 online templates promoting business interests.

Web pages on the Internet can also be considered promotional in nature. The vast exposure of the World Wide Web provides endless possibilities for advertising products, services, research, and data that may be presented on a company or corporation website.

Creating a Raffle Ticket Using Microsoft Online

The Office.com website includes a template for creating a raffle ticket using text boxes within a rectangular shape as shown in Figure 7.3. You may want to study how a template is created to apply similar techniques to your original designs. A formatted ticket is copied to create five tickets filling an 8½ by 11-inch sheet of paper. The raffle ticket template is accessed by clicking the File tab and then the New tab. At the New tab Backstage view,

Figure 7.1 Examples of Promotional Documents Created in Word

Bookmarks

Discount Coupon

Gift Certificate

Coaster

Ticket

Door Hanger

Figure 7.2 Examples of Word 2010 Online Templates That Promote Businesses

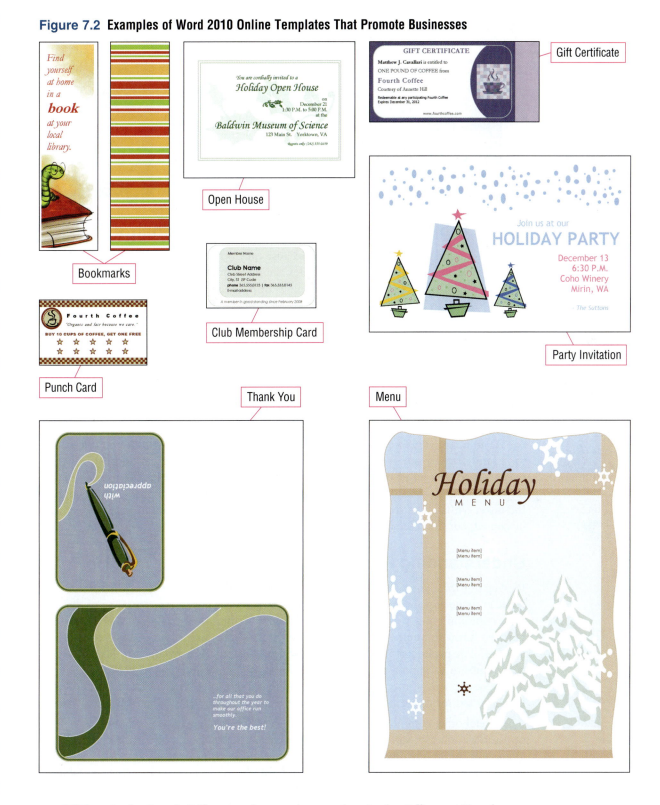

Bookmarks

Punch Card

Open House

Club Membership Card

Thank You

Menu

Gift Certificate

Party Invitation

type **Tickets** in the Search Office.com for template text box in the *Office.com Templates* section and then click the Start searching arrow or press Enter. Click the ticket template [*Raffle ticket (purple with stub, works with Avery 5371, 8371, 27871)*].

Figure 7.3 Office.com Ticket Template Formatted in Text Boxes

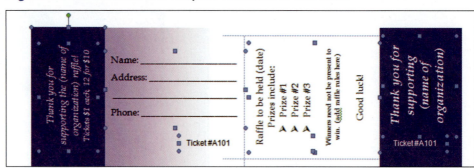

Using Tables to Create Promotional Documents

Tables are useful in desktop publishing because they offer options to format several objects consistently and predictably. Tables can give you precise control over layout. If your document needs to be separated by lines or has several areas that share a common border, tables can be a most efficient choice. However, tables require some planning before you use them in the layout of your document.

The Word table feature can be used to format tickets, and the Word *AutoNum* field codes can be used to number the tickets and stubs sequentially. You have probably worked with field codes before, although you may have not realized it. For instance, whenever you insert an automatic date, time, or page number, you are inserting *field codes* into your document. A specific field code can be inserted that will enable sequential numbering in tickets and stubs as shown in Figure 7.4.

As an active volunteer for Loaves & Fishes Food Pantry, you will create raffle tickets for a fundraiser in one of the chapter exercises. Each ticket will need a number printed twice—once on a ticket to serve as a claim ticket and once on a stub to be placed in a raffle. The tickets should be printed on 65-lb. uncoated cover stock, or a master copy of the ticket without the sequential numbering should be sent to a commercial printer to be copied, cut, numbered, and perforated.

Understanding Paper Types

Picking out the right paper for your project can be difficult. Paper types range from book to tissue paper. Each paper type has its own special characteristics. One of the most common types of paper is *bond*, which is used for a variety of applications, from business forms to home or office stationery. It is a strong sheet used in most copiers and printers. The paper cotton fiber content, which usually ranges from 25 to 50 percent, contributes to its popularity and good ink absorption. However, bond paper does have a tendency to jam printers easily. *Book* is another paper type that is commonly used. It is well suited for two-sided printing and is very durable as well as relatively inexpensive.

Several other common types of paper are available. *Cover* paper, also known as cardstock, is a heavy, stiff sheet which is durable and folds easily if in the direction of the grain. It is commonly used for folders, postcards, business cards, greeting cards, and book covers. *Index* paper is stiff, is inexpensive, and absorbs ink well, making it an acceptable choice for index cards and business reply cards. *Newsprint* paper is used almost exclusively for newspapers and is generally inexpensive and recyclable. *Offset* paper is used in offset printing because it is strong and resists tearing when used in large fast printers. *Tag* paper is dense and strong and is used for store tags. *Text* paper comes in many different colors and textures and is primarily used in applications such as announcements and brochures. *Specialty* papers include onionskin paper (also known as tissue paper) and rice paper.

Field codes

Command functions in Word that automatically create preformatted results.

DTP POINTERS ▶
Use graphics to help emphasize text.

DTP POINTERS ▶
View helpful information for choosing paper weight, size, and type by viewing www.desktopsupplies.com/paperexplained.html, or view desktoppub.about.com and type **paper** in the Search text box.

Figure 7.4 Inserting an AutoNum Field Code

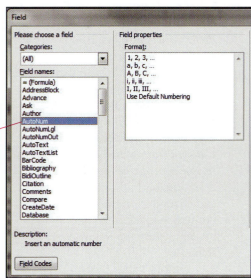

Click the Quick Parts button in the Text group on the Insert tab and then click Field.

At the Field dialog box, make sure *(All)* displays in the *Categories* section, select *AutoNum* in the *Field names* section, and then click OK.

The stiffness of paper depends mainly on the paper type. Additionally, the grain of paper may be listed on the packaging. The grain is simply the direction in which wood fibers in the paper are aligned. It is sometimes important to know the grain if you plan on folding the paper, because folding against the grain in a stiff sheet can cause the paper to crack. Stiff paper may often be scored so it is easier to fold.

*Note: Copy the **Chapter07** folder from the CD that accompanies this textbook to your storage medium and then make **Chapter07** the active folder. Remember to substitute graphics that may no longer be available.*

Exercise 7.1 Creating Tickets/Stubs with Sequential Numbering

1. At a blank document create a table for the tickets in Figure 7.5 by completing the following steps:
   a. Create a table with two columns and four rows.
   b. Select the entire table, right-click the table, and then at the shortcut menu, click *Table Properties*.
   c. At the Table Properties dialog box, select the Row tab, click in the check box at the left of *Specify height* to add a check mark, and then type **2"**. At the *Row height is* list box, make sure *At least* displays.

d. Select the Column tab, and type **4"** for the Column 1 *Preferred width*. Click the Next Column button.

e. At the Column tab, type **2.25"** for the Column 2 *Preferred width*. Click OK or press Enter. ***Hint: You may have to click the Next Column button twice to get to the appropriate column.***

f. Select the first column and change the right cell borderline to a dashed line by completing the following steps:

1) On the Table Tools Design tab, click the down arrow at the right of the Borders button in the Table Styles group, and then click *Borders and Shading* at the drop-down list.

2) At the Borders and Shading dialog box, click the Borders tab. Click the down-pointing arrow at the right of the *Apply to* list box and then make sure Cell is selected.

3) Click the right borderline in the Preview box to remove the line, click the third line (dashed line) from the top in the *Style* list box, and then click where the previous line displayed in the Preview box. In place of the single line, a dashed line should display. Click OK.

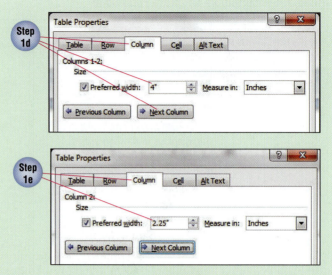

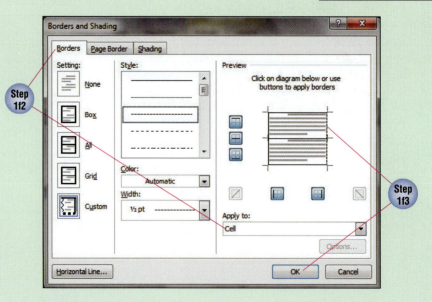

2. Save the document with Save As, and name it **C07-E01-Raffle**.
3. Insert the ticket and stub text by completing the following steps:
   a. Position the insertion point in the first cell in the first row and insert **Raffle** located in your *Chapter07* folder. Remove the hard return after *No*.
   b. Position the insertion point in the second cell in the first row and insert **Stub** located in your *Chapter07* folder. Remove the hard return after *No*.
4. Insert the Loaves & Fishes logo by completing the following steps:
   a. Position the insertion point in the first cell of the first row, and insert the logo graphic file, **Loaves&Fishes**, located in your *Chapter07* folder.
   b. Select the logo and then change the wrap text to *Tight*.
   c. Position and resize the logo as shown in Figure 7.5.
   d. Hold down the Ctrl key as you drag and drop a copy of the logo to the stub section of the ticket.
   e. Change the logo image into a watermark by selecting the image, clicking the Color button in the Picture Tools Format tab in the Adjust group, and then clicking the Washout thumbnail in the *Recolor* section.

   f. Position and size the logo as shown in Figure 7.5.
   g. Change the wrap text to *Behind Text*.
5. Insert sequential numbering by completing the following steps:
   a. Position the insertion point at the right of *No.* in the first cell in the first row and press the spacebar once. ***Hint: If too much space displays below* No., *delete the hard return below it.***
   b. Click the Quick Parts button in the Text group in the Insert tab, and then click *Field*.

   c. At the Field dialog box, make sure *(All)* displays in the *Categories* list box. In the *Field names* list box, click *AutoNum*. Click OK.
   d. Position the insertion point at the right of *No.* in the second cell in the first row (stub), press the spacebar once, and then insert the *AutoNum* field code.
6. Select the first row, and copy it to the Clipboard.
7. Position your insertion point in the next row, and press Ctrl + V to copy the content of the first row to the second row.
   a. Press F4 (repeat command) twice to create a total of four rows of tickets.
   b. Delete any empty rows that may appear on the next page.
8. Select the entire table and center it horizontally on the page by clicking the Properties button in the *Table* section of the Table Tools Layout tab and then clicking the *Center* option in the *Alignment* section of the Table tab in the Table Properties dialog box. Click OK.
9. View your tickets in Print tab Backstage view.
10. Save the document again as **C07-E01-Raffle**.
11. Print and then close **C07-E01-Raffle.docx**.

Figure 7.5 Exercise 7.1

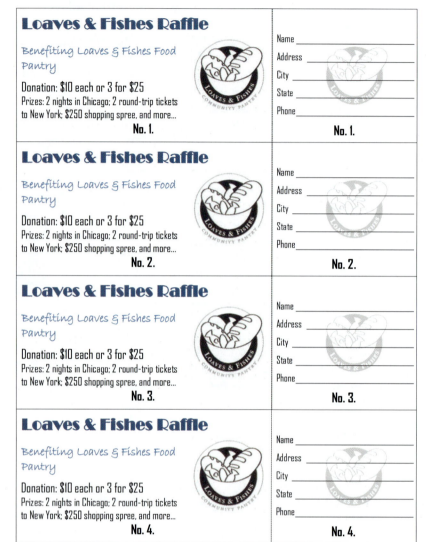

Creating and Aligning Lines on Which You Can Type

Have you ever opened a document, such as an application form, with the intention of typing on the lines that are provided only to find that your text pushes the line forward or you could not position the insertion point anywhere on the line to input your text? Several methods can be used to create lines on which you can type. Each of these methods will allow you to successfully place the insertion point on the line and type without typing over the line or pushing it to the right as you type.

Using the Underline Command and Tabs

The first method requires the use of the underline character and the Tab key for the creation of the line. To create a line for typing on by using the Tab key and Underline command, complete the following steps:

1. Set tab settings for the columns of text.
2. Press the Tab key to align the insertion point at the first tab setting.

3. Turn on underlining, and press the spacebar once to create a placeholder (you may want to turn on the Show/Hide ¶ feature so you can view the spacebar placeholder).
4. Press the Tab key to create the line.
5. Turn off underlining, and press the Enter key to move to the next line or the Tab key to move to the next column.

Figure 7.6 shows the tab settings and the use of the underline character and Tab key. To be sure it is working, move your insertion point to the position after the spacebar, and type some text. The text should appear typed above the line.

To type on the line that was created using the underline and tab method, it is important that the insertion point be placed after the placeholder. If the insertion point is placed on or before the placeholder, the line will be pushed to the right as you type.

Drawing a Line Using Shapes

The second method incorporates the use of the Line tool from the Shapes gallery. When a line or any other shape is placed within a document, it can be moved around the document by selecting the shape and pressing the arrow keys on the keyboard or selecting the object and dragging the move handle to the desired location. The shape will move in the selected direction along the lines of an invisible grid that exists within each document as discussed in earlier chapters. Each time an arrow is pressed, the shape will move in that direction to the next line of the grid. Often, the default spacing between the gridlines of a document is larger than desired for moving an object. In the next exercise, you will draw lines, adjust the grid settings to support accurate movement of the drawn lines, and align the lines within the form.

To type on the line that was created using the Shapes gallery, simply position the insertion point on the line and type. You may have to use the spacebar to advance the insertion point to the correct position. Remember to align the text on the left for each line.

Using Tables to Create Lines

The third method for creating lines that you can type on is to insert a table into your document and then add or remove borderlines to create the look of lines. Tables allow for easy alignment and placement of the elements of the form. Whether you are creating a document that will be printed or one that will be filled in on a computer, you may use a table as an underlining structure for organizing your text. Type your labels (text requesting input) in cells, and then remove all unnecessary borderlines as shown in Figure 7.7. If the form is to be completed online or in one of the Office programs, you may not need to display the text that the user inputs. However, still consider using tables to organize the layout of the form.

◀ **DTP POINTERS**
Press Ctrl + Tab to insert a tab inside a table cell.

Figure 7.7 Using a Table to Create Lines in a Form

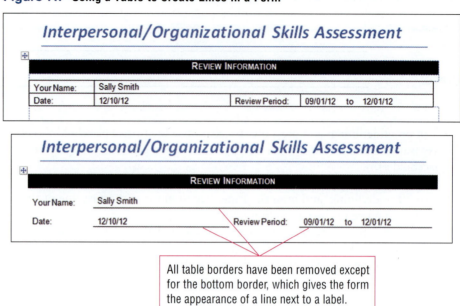

All table borders have been removed except for the bottom border, which gives the form the appearance of a line next to a label.

Inserting Field Codes and the Underlining Command

A fourth method that may be used for inserting text with a line is to add form fields to your document and to apply the underline command to the form field. When the user of the form inputs text, the underline command is activated as shown in Figure 7.8. More detailed information on form fields and content controls will be provided in Chapter 10.

Whether you are creating lines on which you can type or lines that are printed as hard copy, it is important that the lines always align properly. When using consistent tab settings to create lines, you will be assured that the lines will end at a specific point. When drawing lines using the Line Shape, you may use the Align button in the Arrange group on the Drawing Tools Format tab to adjust the vertical placement of the lines. You may also create lines that align by using tab leaders.

Using Tab Leaders to Create Lines That Align

To create lines that align, display the Tab dialog box, set tabs where you want the lines to begin, and then click the solid line leader (4) in the *Leader* section. Be sure to click *Set* before clicking OK. To use this method, create your settings at the Tab dialog box, type your label text, and then press Tab. A solid line should display from the tab setting to the right margin or to wherever you designated the leader to end.

In Exercise 7.2, you will use all three methods discussed previously for creating lines in a form. While you are working through the exercise, try to figure out which method is easiest to use. You may find that the table feature is the most precise and

Figure 7.8 Inserting Field Codes with Underlining

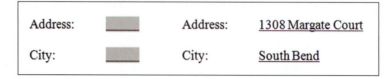

efficient. You would not typically use all three methods in one form. In Chapter 10, you will learn an additional method for creating lines in forms by using form fields in the Developer tab.

Exercise 7.2 Creating Lines for Typing

1. At a blank document create the form in Figure 7.9 by completing the following steps:
   a. Change the theme to Metro.
   b. Click the Font dialog box launcher, display the Advanced tab, and then click the *Proportional* option at the *Number spacing* drop-down list and the *Lining* option at the *Number forms* drop-down list. Click OK. ***Hint: This prevents the descenders in numbers from displaying below the lines.***
   c. Center and then type the following text and press the Enter key as noted:
      Best Sellers of the Western Region (Press Enter)
      March 14, 2012 (Press Enter)
      Conference Registration (Press Enter twice)
   d. Select *Best Sellers of the Western Region*, click the Text Effects button, and then click the *Gradient Fill - Green, Accent 1* effect.
   e. With *Best Sellers of the Western Region* still selected click the Grow Font button five times (20 points).
   f. Select *March 14, 2012,* click the Grow Font button two times, and apply bold.
   g. Select *Conference Registration,* click the Grow Font button three times, and apply bold, small caps (Ctrl + Shift + K) in Dark Red (first color in the *Standard Colors* section).
   h. Position the insertion point at the left margin a double space below *CONFERENCE REGISTRATION.*
   i. Display the Ruler and then create a left-aligned tab at 1 inch and a second left-aligned tab at 6.5 inches.
   j. Type **Name:** and then press the Tab key to align the insertion point at the first tab setting. This is where the underline will begin.
   k. Turn on underlining and press the spacebar one time. This creates a placeholder for the starting point of the line.
   l. Press the Tab key. A line is created between the insertion point and the last tab setting.
   m. Turn off underlining.
   n. Press the Enter key and type **Address:.**
   o. Press the Tab key to align the insertion point at the first tab setting.
   p. Turn on underlining, and press the spacebar one time to create the placeholder.
   q. Press the Tab key to create the line.
   r. Turn off underlining and then press Enter.

2. Use a table to create the City, State, and Zip lines by completing the following steps:
   a. Position the insertion point a default line space below the address line.
   b. Click the Table button in the Tables group in the Insert tab and then drag your cursor over the grid to create a table with one row and six columns.
   c. Select the table, click the down-arrow at the right of the Borders button in the Table Styles group in the Table Tools Design tab, and then click the *No Borders* option.
   d. Type **City:** in the first cell.
   e. Type **State:** in the third cell.
   f. Type **ZIP:** in the fifth cell.
   g. Resize the cells to accommodate the text by dragging the borderlines.

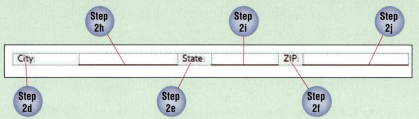

   h. Position the insertion point inside the second cell, click the down-arrow at the right of the Borders button and then click the *Bottom Border* option.
   i. Position the insertion point inside the fourth cell, and then click the Bottom Border button.
   j. Position the insertion point inside the sixth cell, and then click the Bottom Border button.

3. Create the Phone and Email lines by drawing a Line shape as shown in the following steps:
   a. Position the insertion point a double space below the above table.
   b. Type **Phone:** and press Enter.
   c. Type **Email:** and press Enter.
   d. Click the Line tool in the Shapes gallery. The cursor becomes a crosshair.
   e. Position the crosshair to the right of *Phone:* and visually align it with the left edge of the *Address:* line. This is where the line will begin.
   f. Drag to create a line approximately 2.5" long. ***Hint: Hold down the Shift key as you draw the line. This will guarantee a straight line.*** After the line is drawn, release the mouse button and the line will be selected. The line may appear in a green color.
   g. Select the line, and click the *Subtle Line - Dark 1* thumbnail in the Shape Styles gallery.
   h. Select the line and then press Ctrl + C to copy the line onto the Clipboard.

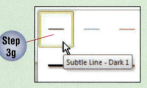

   i. Press Ctrl + V once to create one more line—you should have one for *Phone:* and one for *Email:*. The lines are staggered, and the last line is selected. ***Note: By copying and pasting the lines, the length of all the lines is the same.*** You can also duplicate lines by selecting the first line and then holding down the Ctrl key while pressing D on the keyboard. Drag the duplicated lines to position them properly.

4. Click the Align button in the Arrange group in the Drawing Tools Format tab, click the *Grid Settings* option at the bottom of the drop-down list, and then remove the check mark next to the *Snap objects to other objects* option in the *Object Snapping* section of the Drawing Grid. Click OK. ***Hint: This will allow you to adjust the position of the lines using the arrow keys in small increments without snapping to the grid at the default 0.13 setting.***

5. After the lines have been copied and placed within the form, press the Arrow buttons on your keyboard to position them as shown in Figure 7.9.

6. To adjust the line drawings, complete the following steps:
    a. Select the two drawn lines. ***Hint: Hold down the Shift key as you select each line drawing.***
    b. On the Drawing Tools Format tab, click the Align button in the Arrange group, and then click *Align Left* from the drop-down list. On the Ruler, point to the 1-inch tab setting. Click and hold down the mouse button on this tab setting. The vertical bar will show. You can use this bar to "eyeball" the horizontal alignment with the lines above.
    c. Align the lines horizontally (by using the Up Arrow key) with the guide words *Phone:* and *Email:*.
    d. Click anywhere within the form to deselect the lines.

7. Position the insertion point below the *Email* line, and then type the text shown in Figure 7.9.

8. Create the *Check one* text in a table. ***Hint: Make sure you remove the borderlines except for the first column and center the table horizontally.***

9. Select *Storyteller Books* in the check payable area, and change the font to 22-point Monotype Corsiva in Dark Red. Select *Storyteller Books* in the registration area, and change the font to 16-point Monotype Corsiva in Dark Red. Apply bold as indicated in Figure 7.9. Press Shift + Enter at the end of each line in the address.

10. Add the bookworm image shown in Figure 7.9 by completing the following steps:
    a. Position the insertion point at the bottom of the document. On the Insert tab, click the Clip Art button in the Illustrations group.
    b. At the Clip Art task pane, type **bookworm** in the *Search for* text box.
    c. Insert the image. Close the Clip Art task pane.
    d. Size and position the image as shown in Figure 7.9 rotate the image by clicking the Rotate button in the Arrange group on the Picture Tools Format tab, and then click *Flip Horizontal*. ***Hint: You are rotating the image so it faces the text.***
    e. Select the image, change the Wrap Text to *Square*, display the Picture Tools Format tab, and then click Drop Shadow Rectangle in the Picture Styles group.

11. Save the form as **C07-E02-LinesforTyping**.
12. Print **C07-E02-LinesforTyping.docx**.

13. Complete the form with your name and other information.
14. Save the form as **C07-E02-LinesforTypingCompleted**.
15. Print **C07-E02-LinesforTypingCompleted.docx**. *Hint: You may notice that the weight of the lines may not be consistent; therefore, it is a good idea to pick a method and use one method throughout the document. The three methods were used in this exercise for demonstration of the use of each method.*
16. Close **C07-E02-LinesforTyping.docx** and **C07-E02-LinesforTypingCompleted.docx**.

Figure 7.9 **Exercise 7.2**

Best Sellers of the Western Region

March 14, 2012

CONFERENCE REGISTRATION

Name: _____

Address: _____

City: _____ State: _____ ZIP: _____

Phone: _____

Email: _____

Registration deadline – February 22, 2012

Check one:

_____	$90	Participant from member institution
_____	$95	Participant from non-member institution
_____	$100	Institutional membership dues

Your check must accompany registration.

Make check payable to:

Storyteller Books

Mail registration to:

Storyteller Books
123 Main Street
Glen Ellyn, IL 60137

Figure 7.9 Exercise 7.2 (continued)

Best Sellers of the Western Region

March 14, 2012

CONFERENCE REGISTRATION

Name: Your name

Address: Your address

City: Your city   State: Your state   ZIP: Your zip

Phone: Your phone number

Email: Your Email address

Registration deadline – February 22, 2012

Check one:

X	$90	Participant from member institution
	$95	Participant from non-member institution
	$100	Institutional membership dues

Your check must accompany registration.

Make check payable to:

Storyteller Books

Mail registration to:

Storyteller Books
123 Main Street
Glen Ellyn, IL 60137

Creating Postcards to Promote Business

If you have a brief message to get across to prospective customers, postcards can be an appropriate means of delivering the message. Postcards are inexpensive to create and use. They can be used as appointment reminders, just-moved notes, return/reply cards, display cards, thank-you cards, or invitations. You can purchase predesigned, printed postcards with attractive borders and color combinations, in differing sizes and weights that meet U.S. Postal Service standards; and you can find blank, prestamped 3.5 by 5.5-inch postcards at any U.S. Postal Service location. Alternatively, you can use the Word Labels

Figure 7.10 Postcard Templates from Office.com Website

Chapter Seven

feature, which provides a predefined postcard sized at 4 by 6 inches. Two postcards will display on a standard-size sheet of paper when you use *Avery US Letter 5389 Postcards*.

Most postcards are created on 100- to 110-lb. uncoated cover stock paper. The paper weight or thickness should be strong enough to hold up in the mail. The front side of the postcard is used for your return address and the recipient's address along with an area reserved for the postage. On the reverse, you can create a headline and use a graphic, photo, or watermark to emphasize the message. You will need to leave room for your message and optional signature.

Figure 7.10 shows a few examples of postcards used in human resources, marketing, real estate, and other areas. The postcards include placeholder text that instructs you how to use the template. To locate these templates, click the File tab, and then click the New tab. Select a category, select a template, and then click the Download button. Each postcard may be designed and formatted to include promotional images and text by simply adding an appropriate photo, logo, or clip, along with a promotional statement, that reinforces the identity of the company or promotes a service or product in that organization. In addition, you may customize the postcards for mass mailing by using the Word Start Mail Merge feature.

Exercise 7.3   Creating Postcards Using the Labels Feature

1. At a blank document create the two postcards in Figure 7.11.
2. Insert the eye/world graphic shown in Figure 7.11, edit the image to determine the color formula used in the image, and then apply the color to text later in the exercise by completing the following steps:
   a. Click the Clip Art button and type **visions** in the *Search for* text box in the Clip Art task pane. Insert the image. ***Hint: If this image is no longer available, you may find it in your* Chapter07 *folder or substitute the image with another one.***

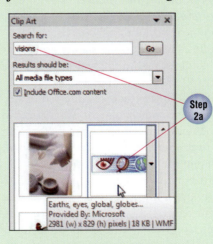

   b. Right-click the image and then click *Edit Picture* at the shortcut menu. At the prompt to convert the image to a Microsoft Office drawing object, click Yes.

c. Position the insertion point on the medium blue color in the image. Click the Shape Fill button in the Shape Styles group on the Drawing Tools Format tab and then click More Fill Colors. At the Colors dialog box, select the Custom tab, and then write down the existing color formula: Red 43, Green 122, and Blue 255. Click OK. ***Hint: If you cannot find this exact color, choose a similar one.***

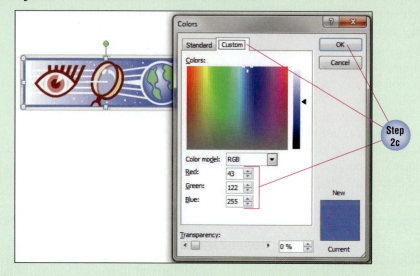

d. Close the document without saving.
3. At a blank document create two postcards by completing the following steps:
    a. Click the Labels button in the Create group in the Mailings tab.
    b. At the Envelopes and Labels dialog box, select the Labels tab.
    c. Click the Options button at the bottom of the Envelopes and Labels dialog box.
    d. At the Label Options dialog box, select *Avery US Letter* in the *Label vendors* list box, and then select *5389* in the *Product number* section. Click OK. ***Hint: You may select another postcard product number.***
    e. Click the New Document button.
    f. Click the View Gridlines button in the Tables group in the Table Tools Layout tab.
    g. With the insertion point located in the first postcard, press the spacebar once and then press Enter.
    h. Insert the same eye/world image that was inserted in step 2a.
    i. Select the eye/world image and change the Wrap Text to *Square*.
    j. Size and position the image similar to Figure 7.11. ***Hint: Drag a corner sizing handle to keep the image in proportion to how it was created.***
4. Insert the text by completing the following steps:
    a. Drag and draw a text box that measures approximately 2 by 3.5 inches.
    b. Position the insertion point in the text box and type **See the world a little clearer and a little brighter with regular eye examinations.**
    c. Select *See the world,* change the font to 24-point Bauhaus 93 in the blue font color in step 2c. ***Hint: See step 2c and type the Red, Green, and Blue settings at the Colors dialog box. Colors may vary.***
    d. Select the rest of the text, change the font to 24-point Harlow Solid Italic, and then change the color to *Olive Green, Accent 3*.

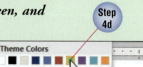

    e. Select all the text and change the horizontal alignment to *Center*.

Figure 7.11 Exercise 7.3

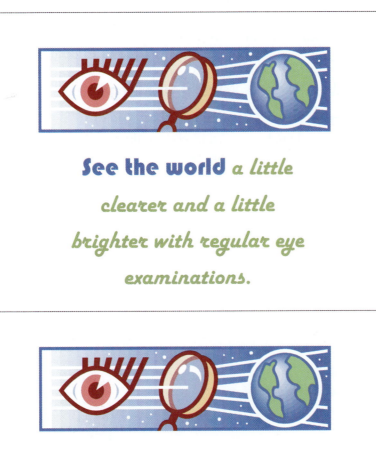

Merging Promotional Documents

Word includes a Mail Merge wizard you can use to create customized letters, email messages, envelopes, labels, directories, and normal Word documents. The wizard guides you through the merge process and presents six task panes. The six task panes include steps on selecting a document type to executing the final merge in customizing a document. The options in each task pane vary depending on the type of merge you are performing.

Mail merge is the process of combining variable information with standard text to create personalized documents. Generally, a merge takes two documents—the *main document*, which contains standard data such as the text of a form letter or the return address and picture on a postcard, with a *data source*, which contains variable data such as names and addresses. Special codes, located in the main document, known as *merge fields* direct Word to collect information from the data source and use it in the main document to create personalized documents. Use these Merge field names if they represent the data you are creating. Variable information in a data source document is saved as a record. A *record* contains all of the information for one unit (e.g., a person, family, customer, client, or business). A set of fields (first name, last name, address) makes one record, and a series of records makes a data source document.

Using the Mail Merge Wizard to Merge to a Postcard (Label)

The Mail Merge wizard can be accessed by clicking the Start Mail Merge button in the Start Mail Merge group on the Mailings tab as shown in Figure 7.12. Click the *Step by Step Mail Merge Wizard* selection at the bottom of the Start Mail Merge drop-down list to access the Mail Merge task pane as shown in Figure 7.13. Alternatively, you

Figure 7.12 Step by Step Mail Merge Wizard   **Figure 7.13 Mail Merge Task Pane**

Mail merge

The process of combining variable information with standard text to create personalized documents.

Main document

A form that receives the data.

Data source

Contains variable data such as names and addresses.

Merge fields

Special codes in the main document that direct Word to collect information from the data source and use it in the main document to create personalized documents.

Record

Contains all of the information for one unit (person, family, or business).

Start Mail Merge

DTP POINTERS

The United States Postal Service recommends typing addresses in ALL CAPS with no punctuation. See www.usps.com.

may click the merge-related buttons on the Mailings tab to perform a merge. Before completing the merge, Word can automatically check for errors in the merge. The mail merge process involves the following six steps:

1. Identify the type of document (letter, email message, envelope, label, or directory).
2. Specify whether you want to use the current document, start from a template, or start from an existing document.
3. Specify whether you are using an existing list, using an Outlook contact list, or typing a new list.
4. Prepare the main document using items in this task pane.
5. Preview the merged document.
6. Complete the merge and send it to the printer.

Preparing Labels Using the Mail Merge Wizard

Create mailing labels for records in a data source document in much the same way that you create envelopes. Use the Mail Merge wizard to guide you through the steps for preparing mailing labels. However, you may also use the Merge buttons on the Mailing tab instead of the Wizard. The postcard in Exercise 7.4 is defined as a label, which is formatted in a table; therefore, you will use the Table Tools Design tab and the Table Tools Layout tab to make adjustments to the postcard that is merged with a data source in this exercise. Information for Exercise 7.4 is provided in Figure 7.14, which follows the exercise.

Exercise 7.4   Creating a Data Source, Main Document, and Merged Postcards

1. At a blank document merge a data source to formatted postcards, as shown in Figure 7.15, by completing the following steps:
   a. Click the Start Mail Merge button in the Start Mail Merge group in the Mailings tab.
   b. At the Start Mail Merge drop-down list, click *Step by Step Mail Merge Wizard.*
   c. At the first Mail Merge task pane, make sure *Labels* is selected in the *Select document type* section of the task pane, and then click <u>Next: Starting document</u> located at the bottom of the task pane.
   d. At the second Mail Merge task pane, make sure *Change document layout* is selected in the *Select starting document* section of the task pane and then click <u>Label options</u>.

e.	At the Label Options dialog box, select *Avery US Letter* in the *Label vendors* list box, and then select *5389* in the *Product number* section. Click OK.

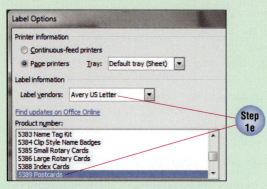

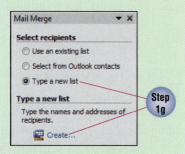

Step 1e

Step 1g

f.	Click <u>Next: Select recipients</u> at the bottom of the task pane.
g.	At the third Mail Merge task pane, click *Type a new list* in the *Select recipients* section. Click *Create.*
h.	At the New Address List dialog box, enter the information for the first patient as provided in Figure 7.14 by completing the following steps:

1)	Click in the *Title* text box, type **Mrs.**, and then press the Tab key (press Shift + Tab to move to the previous field).

2)	Type **Peggy** and then press Tab.

3)	Type **McSherry** and then press Tab twice.

4)	Type **3055 Kinzie Court** and then press Tab twice.

Step 1h1   Step 1h2   Step 1h3   Step 1h4

5)	Type **Wheaton** and then press Tab.
6)	Type **IL** and then press Tab.
7)	Type **60187**.
8)	Click the New Entry button to begin another record.
9)	With the insertion point positioned in the *Title* field, complete steps similar to those in steps 1h1 through 1h7 to enter the information for the three other patients shown in Figure 7.14.

i.	After entering all of the information for the last patient in Figure 7.14 (Margo Godfrey), click OK.

2.	At the Save Address List dialog box, save the data source and name it **NaperGrovePatientList**. Make sure your data source is saved in the folder you desire and then click Save. *Hint: Word saves this document as a database file with the .mdb extension. By default, Word stores the database file in the* **My Data Sources** *folder.*

3.	At the Mail Merge Recipients dialog box, verify that all four entries are correct and then click OK.

Step 3

4. Click <u>Next: Arrange your labels</u>.
5. At the fourth Mail Merge task pane, create the return address and message on the postcard as shown in Figure 7.14 by completing the following steps. ***Hint: Click the View Gridlines button in the Tables group in the Table Layout tab to display the light blue gridlines.***
   a. With the insertion point positioned in the upper left corner of the first postcard, change the theme to Flow.
   b. At the Paragraph dialog box, remove any spacing before or after and make sure single spacing is selected.
   c. With the insertion point positioned in the first postcard, press the spacebar once, press Enter, and then type the following text:
      Naper Grove Vision Care (Press Enter.)
      5018 Fairview Avenue (Press Enter.)
      Downers Grove, IL 60515 (Press Enter twice.)
      Just a friendly reminder! (Press Enter twice.)
      Please call our office now for your (Press Enter.)
      appointment (630) 555-3932. (Press Enter twice.)
   d. Select *Naper Grove Vision Care;* change the font to 16-point Calibri in bold, small caps; turn on kerning at 14 points; and then change the font color to the formula: Red 43, Green 122, Blue 255.
   e. Select the address and verify that the font is 11-point Constantia in Black.
   f. Select *Just a friendly reminder!* and change the font to 16-point Harlow Solid Italic in the *Lime, Accent 6* color.
   g. Select *It's time . . . 555-3932* and verify that the font is 11-point Constantia in Black.
6. Position the insertion point a double space below the text in step 5g and insert the Address block by completing the following steps:
   a. On the Page Layout tab, type **2.8"** in the *Left Indent* text box in the Paragraph group.
   b. At step 4 of the Mail Merge task pane, click *Address block* in the *Arrange your labels* section.
   c. Accept the default settings at the Insert Address Block dialog box. Click OK.
   d. Click the Update all labels button in the *Replicate labels* section. ***Note: A copy of the first postcard should display in the second postcard.***
   e. The Address block should display as shown here. Click <u>Next: Preview your labels</u>.
7. At the fifth Mail Merge task pane, look over the postcards that display in the document window to make sure the information was merged properly. If you want to see the postcards for the other recipients, click the double arrow buttons in the *Preview your labels* section.
8. Click <u>Next: Complete the merge</u>.

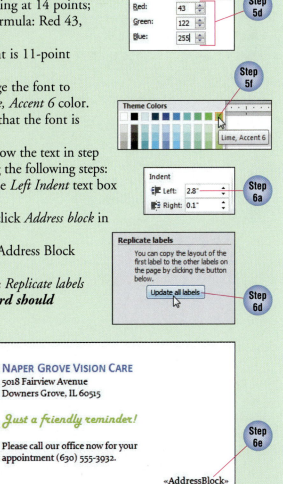

9. At the sixth Mail Merge task pane, click Edit individual letters in the *Merge* section.
10. At the Merge to New Document dialog box, make sure *All* is selected and then click the OK button.
11. Save the merged postcards as **C07-E04-Merged**.
12. Insert **C07-E03-Postcard.docx** (two sheets) into the printer, and then print **C04-E04-Merged.docx**. *Hint: You will be printing on the reverse side of the postcards.*
13. Close **C07-E04-Merged.docx**.
14. At the Sixth Mail Merge task pane, save the main document as **C04-E04-MainDoc**, and then close the main document.

Figure 7.14 Information for Data Source Fields

Title	=	Mrs.	*Title*	=	Mr.
First Name	=	Peggy	*First Name*	=	Eric
Last Name	=	McSherry	*Last Name*	=	Gohlke
Address Line 1	=	3055 Kinzie Court	*Address Line 1*	=	3090 North Orchard
Address Line 2	=		*Address Line 2*	=	
City	=	Wheaton	*City*	=	Downers Grove
State	=	IL	*State*	=	IL
ZIP Code	=	60187	*ZIP Code*	=	60515
Title	=	Mrs.	*Title*	=	Ms.
First Name	=	Kathleen	*First Name*	=	Margo
Last Name	=	Sinnamon	*Last Name*	=	Godfrey
Address Line 1	=	Apt. 14A	*Address Line 1*	=	Apt. 105B
Address Line 2	=	409 Highland Drive	*Address Line 2*	=	993 Sandpiper Lane
City	=	Downers Grove	*City*	=	Westmont
State	=	IL	*State*	=	IL
ZIP Code	=	60515	*ZIP Code*	=	60599

Creating Invitations and Cards

You may use the 2 pages per sheet feature to format a card such as the one you will create in Exercise 7.5; however, you may also use an alternate method—changing the top margin to 6 inches and inserting the text in overlapping text boxes. Keep in mind that you may even use tables for formatting most cards, such as holiday cards, business or personal invitations, seminar or open house announcements, personal notes, and birth announcements. A page border may be added to both pages or to just one. This option is conducive to creating cards in varying sizes and layouts. Also consider folding a half-sheet in half again and printing on cardstock.

Figure 7.15 Exercise 7.4

NAPER GROVE VISION CARE
5018 Fairview Avenue
Downers Grove, IL 60515

Just a friendly reminder!

Please call our office now for your
appointment (630) 555-3932.

Mrs. Peggy McSherry
3055 Kinzie Court
Wheaton, IL 60187

NAPER GROVE VISION CARE
5018 Fairview Avenue
Downers Grove, IL 60515

Just a friendly reminder!

Please call our office now for your
appointment (630) 555-3932.e

Mr. Eric Gohlke
3090 North Orchard
Downers Grove, IL 60515

NAPER GROVE VISION CARE
5018 Fairview Avenue
Downers Grove, IL 60515

Just a friendly reminder!

Please call our office now for your
appointment (630) 555-3932.

Mrs. Kathleen Sinnamon
Apt. 14A
409 Highland Drive
Downers Grove, IL 60515

NAPER GROVE VISION CARE
5018 Fairview Avenue
Downers Grove, IL 60515

Just a friendly reminder!

Please call our office now for your
appointment (630) 555-3932.

Ms. Margo Godfrey
Apt. 105B
993 Sandpiper Lane
Westmont, IL 60599

Figure 7.16 illustrates the result of dividing a standard-size sheet of paper into four cells using a table, which is then folded to accommodate text and graphics. Each of the four panels (cells) in Figure 7.16 has been identified with a panel number and marked with instructions for rotating text and graphics.

Another method may be used to produce two invitations or cards on a single sheet of landscaped paper divided into four sections. Using this method, you may type, format, and print the text on one side of a sheet of paper, and then reinsert the paper into your printer and print text and/or graphics on the reverse side. The final step is to cut the paper in half and fold the top to meet the bottom as shown in Figure 7.17. Word provides an option to print two half-sheet pages printed in landscape or portrait orientation on the same sheet.

Figure 7.16 Guide for Creating Cards in Portrait Orientation

Figure 7.17 Guide for Creating Cards in Landscape Orientation

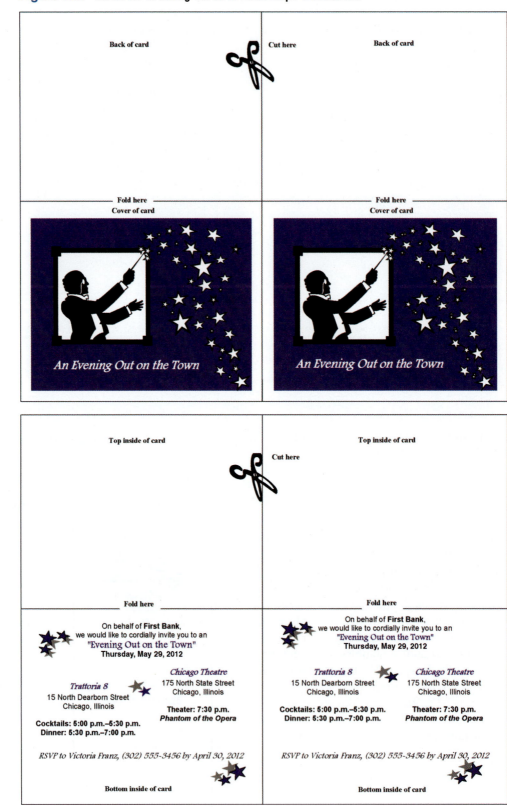

Planning and Designing Cards

In planning and designing your cards, consider focus, balance, consistency, proportion, contrast, and directional flow. Because you are working in a small area, remember to allow plenty of white space around design elements. If you are using a graphic image for focus, be sure that the image relates to the subject of the card. Promote consistency through the use of color, possibly picking out one or two colors from the graphic image used in your card and including the company logo, if one is available, to promote consistency among company documents. Select one or two fonts that match the tone of the document.

Your choice of paper is also important—consider using a heavier weight paper, such as 60- or 65-lb. uncoated cover stock paper. Packaged cardstock such as Greeting Card (glossy or matte finish) or Premium Inkjet Heavyweight may be used to produce near store-quality cards. Also consider using marbleized paper or parchment paper for invitations and other types of cards. The envelope size used with the HP Greeting Card paper package measures 5¾ by 8¾ inches. To print a custom-size envelope, type the desired dimensions at the Envelope Size dialog box as shown in Figure 7.18. Refer to your printer documentation to determine the correct way to load envelopes for your specific printer. If you have a long list of recipients, consider creating a master copy of your card and taking it to a commercial printer to have it reproduced and machine folded. For a mass mailing of an invitation or a holiday card, consider creating a data source consisting of names and addresses, and then merging this information onto envelopes or mailing labels.

Any card you may create from scratch, with templates from Word, or from the Office.com website, may be customized to promote your company's identity or show continuity with other company documents. Figure 7.19 illustrates card templates that were customized by adding the company's name; text was edited to fit the context of the card. When printing these cards for business purposes, you should use good-quality cardstock with envelopes that match. When printing the envelopes, you may want to add a design element from the card to reinforce a complete and professional look. Card templates can be found by using *greeting cards* or *holidays* as the search string.

DTP POINTERS
Promote consistency among company documents by inserting a logo and using colors found in the logo.

Figure 7.18 Creating a Custom-Sized Envelope

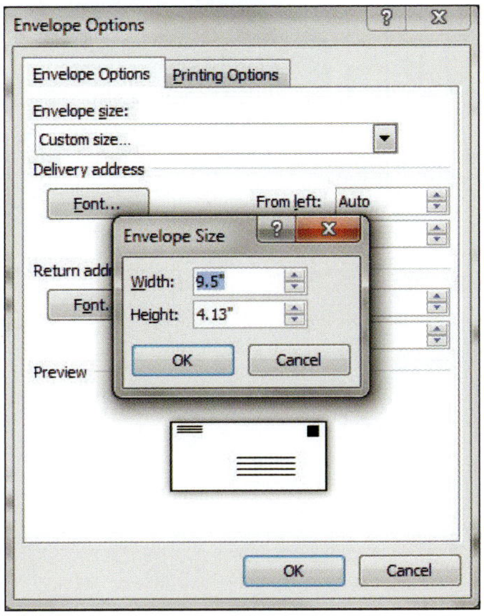

Figure 7.19 **Customized Card Templates from Office.com**

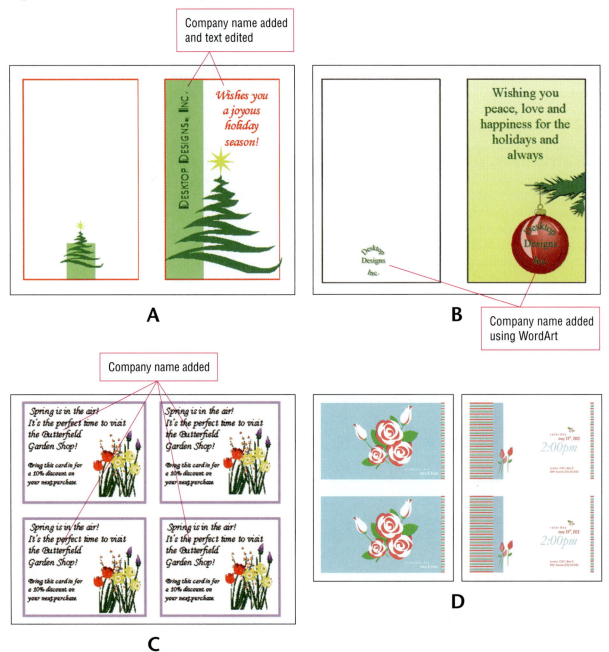

1. At a blank document, create the cover and back of the card shown in Figure 7.20 by completing the following steps:

   a. Change the margins to Top **6"**, Left **0.7"**, Bottom **0.7"**, and Right **0.7"**.

   b. Insert the border on the cover by clicking the Picture button in the Illustrations group on the Insert tab and then insert **border** located in your *Chapter07* folder.

   c. Select the border, click the Rotate button in the Arrange group in the Picture Tools Format tab, and then click the *Rotate Left 90°* option.

   d. With the image still selected, click the Size launcher in the Size group, and then remove the check mark at the left of the *Lock aspect ratio* option in the *Scale* section of the Layout dialog box. Type **6.6"** in the *Absolute* text box in the *Height* section and **4.2"** in the *Absolute* text box in the *Width* section. Click OK.

   e. With the border selected, click the Position button in the Arrange group in the Picture Tools Format tab, and then click the *Position in Bottom Center with Square* Text Wrapping option. Select the border again and change the Wrap Text to Behind Text.

2. Create the photo image in the center of the card by completing the following steps:

   a. Insert each of the telephone images shown in Figure 7.20 or similar images. At the Clip Art task pane, type **telephone** in the *Search for* text box, and then click Go.

   b. Resize each of the images so they measure approximately **1.2"** in height and **1.8"** in width.

   c. Change the Wrap Text for each image to *Tight* and then drag the photos to the center of the border as shown in Figure 7.20.

   d. Click to select each image while holding down the Shift key and then group the images together.

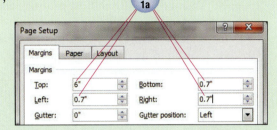

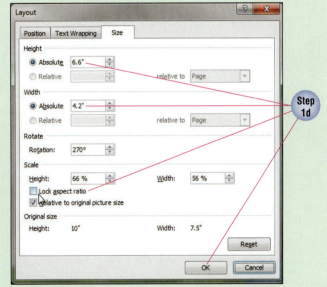

3. Create the text boxes located on the border by completing the following steps:

a. Drag and draw a text box that measures **0.8"** in height and **2.87"** in width.

b. Change the theme to Composite.

c. Position the insertion point inside the text box and type **Sharing, Inc.**.

d. Select *Sharing, Inc.*, click the Text Effects button in the Font group, select the *Gradient Fill - Lime, Accent 1* effect, and then change the font size to 32-point Calibri. Center the text horizontally.

e. Click the Shape Outline button, and then click *No Outline*.

f. Click the Shape Fill button, and click the *Lime, Accent 1, Lighter 60%* color.

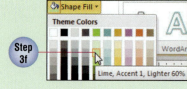

g. Click the Shape Fill button, click Gradient, click More Gradients at the bottom of the drop-down list, click the *Gradient Fill* option in the *Fill* section and type **66%** in the *Position* text box. Click Close.

h. Drag the text box to a position similar to Figure 7.20.

i. Drag a copy of the text box and position it as shown in Figure 7.20. Change the text to *Phonathon 2012*. Resize the text box to accommodate the text.

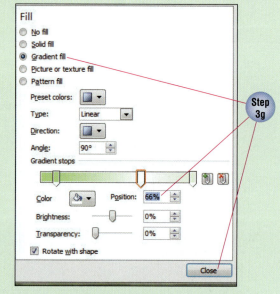

j. Select each object while holding down the Shift key, click the Group button in the Arrange group, and then click Group.

4. Create the WordArt logo on the back of the cover by completing the following steps:

a. Create the WordArt logo in the Header & Footer pane by clicking the Header button in the Text group and then clicking the *Edit Header* option near the bottom of the Header gallery.

b. Click the WordArt button in the Text group in the Insert tab, and click the *Fill - Teal, Accent 2, Warm Matte Bevel* design in the WordArt gallery.

c. Select *Your text here* and type **Desktop Designs**.

d. Click the Text Effects button in the WordArt Styles group, click the *Transform* option at the bottom of the drop-down list, and then click the *Triangle Up* option in the first row of the *Warp* section.

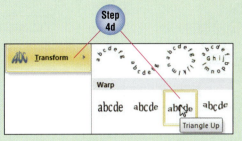

Step 4d

e. Rotate the WordArt image by clicking the Rotate button, and then click Rotate Left 90° twice.

f. Click one of the corner sizing handles and drag it inward to reduce the size of the WordArt object until it is similar to Figure 7.20. ***Hint: Hold down the Ctrl key and Shift key as you drag the corner sizing handle. Close the Header pane.***

g. Position the logo similar to Figure 7.20. ***Hint: If the WordArt object is difficult to move, change the wrap to*** **In Front of Text.**

5. Save the cover and back of the card and name the document **C07-E05-Cover**.

6. Print and then close **C07-E05-Cover.docx**.

7. Open **Sharing** located in your *Chapter07* folder.

8. Insert the family image shown in Figure 7.20 or a similar image. At the Clip Art task pane, type **family** in the *Search for* text box and then click Go. Close the task pane.

9. Select the image, change the Wrap Text to Square, and crop the bottom (gray area) of the image.

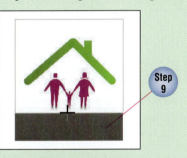

Step 9

10. Position the image as shown in Figure 7.20. Group all the objects.

11. Save this text as the inside document and name it **C07-E05-InsideText**.

12. Place the printed cover into your printer. ***Hint: Be careful to position it correctly so the inside document will print on the reverse side of the cover.***

13. Print and then close **C07-E05-InsideText.docx**.

14. **Optional:** Experiment with the 2 pages per sheet feature. In earlier versions of Word, this feature was unstable; however, in Word 2010 this feature appears to be working properly. Access the 2 pages feature by clicking the Page Setup dialog box launcher in the Page Layout tab. At the Layout tab, click the down-pointing arrow at the right of Multiple Pages in the *Pages* section. Click the *2 pages per sheet* option from the drop-down list. Recreate each of the pages from Exercise 7.5. Press Ctrl + Enter or click the Blank Page button in the Pages group in the Insert tab to generate a new page. Save your document as **C07-E05-2PagesPerSheet.docx**. Print pages 1 and 2 reinsert the page into your printer, and then print pages 3 and 4 on the back side of the page. Close the document.

Figure 7.20 Exercise 7.5

Cover

Inside

Back

Inside

Creating and Printing a Promotional Poster

In Exercise 7.6, you will create a promotional document for a golf club. The document will be formatted in the usual manner, but it will be printed as a poster measuring approximately 15 inches by 19 inches.

Printing a Promotional Poster

The directions for printing are given using an Epson inkjet printer. You will need to follow the directions for printing this exercise based on the printer options for your specific printer. Some experimentation may be necessary. Figure 7.21 shows the Epson Properties dialog box where you may access the appropriate poster size for printing. To access this dialog box, open your document in Word, click the File tab, and then click the Print tab. At the Print tab Backstage view, click the Printer Properties button located directly below the name of your printer in the *Settings* section. Select the appropriate tab that contains options for printing poster-sized documents. Select an option that accommodates a poster with four sheets (2 × 2). Also, select the desired orientation for your poster, and then click OK.

DTP POINTERS
Do not let your graphic overpower the message.

Figure 7.21 Creating and Printing a Promotional Poster

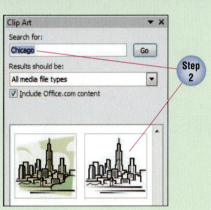

Trimming the Poster

After you have printed the four sheets, you will need to trim the pages along the lines indicated on each page. Then, you may tape the pages together for the finished poster. Alternatively, you may fold the inside marked borders and then tape them—this will provide more support for the taped area.

◀ **DTP POINTERS**
Use no more than two to three fonts for the poster and make sure they are legible.

Exercise 7.6 Creating a Poster

1. Open **Poster** located in your *Chapter07* folder.
2. Position the insertion point at the top of the document and insert the Chicago skyline graphic by typing **Chicago** in the *Search for* text box at the Clip Art task pane. Close the task pane.
3. Size the image to measure approximately **4.5"** by **5"**.
4. Change the Wrap Text to *Square* and then drag the clip to a position similar to that shown in Figure 7.22.
5. Create a text box that measures approximately **0.8"** by **3"** and then type **Sweet Home** in the text box.
6. Select *Sweet Home* and change the font to 36-point Bauhaus 93 in Red.
7. Remove the shape fill and the text box outline and then drag the text box to a position similar to Figure 7.22.

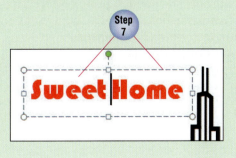

8. Drag and drop a copy of the text box to a position similar to Figure 7.22. Select *Sweet Home,* and replace it with **Chicago**.

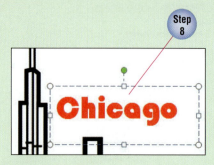

9. Change the theme to Slipstream.
10. Select the text in the text box below the Chicago skyline, change the font to 18-point Calibri, and center the text horizontally.
11. Select *Midwest Golf Club Ladies 9-Hole Guest Day*, click the Text Effects button, click the *Gradient Fill - Blue, Accent 1, Outline - White* effect, and then change the font size to 26 points. Turn on *Kerning* at 14 points and change the *Spacing* to *Expanded* by 0.5 points at the Font dialog box, Advanced tab.
12. Save the document and name it **C07-E06-Poster**.

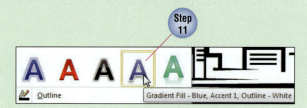

13. Print the document by completing the following steps. ***Hint: These steps may vary depending on your printer.***
    a. Click the File tab and then click the Print tab.
    b. Click Printer Properties in the *Printer* section below the name of your printer.

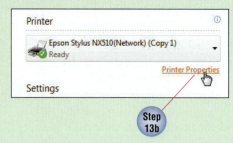

    c. Select the tab that provides an option to print a poster with four pages, select that option, and then click OK. Select an option similar to *Poster 2x2 (4 sheets)*.
    d. Click OK to close the Print dialog box.
14. Trim and then tape the pages together.
15. Make sure you return your printer settings back to the default settings.

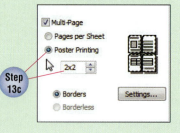

Figure 7.22 Exercise 7.6

Prints document on four pages

Sweet Home

Chicago

Midwest Golf Club
Ladies 9-Hole Guest Day

June 14, 2012

7:30 a.m.– Light breakfast
8:20 a.m. – To the links
11:30 a.m. – A Taste of Chicago

Wear a "Chicago" costume…your favorite Chicago hot
spot…famous Chicagoan…sports figures…
be creative and win the prize!

Inserting Word Crop Marks

You can structure a document by using crop marks as guides for trimming unwanted areas of your document. Word 2010 includes an option to turn on crop marks, but the feature only inserts crop marks at the margin settings and they do not print. To insert Word crop marks, click the File tab, click the Options button, select the Advanced tab, and then click to add a check mark at the *Show crop marks* option in the *Show document content* section (see Figure 7.23). The crop marks will display at the margin setting; you may want to adjust the margins.

Figure 7.23 Inserting Word Crop Marks

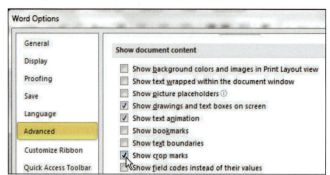

Creating Crop Marks Using Tabs

Additional crop marks can be added by creating tab settings at designated areas along the top and bottom of the document. When creating the bookmarks in Exercise 7.7, turn on the crop marks feature in Word, create tab settings in the Header & Footer pane (the crop marks automatically display on each additional page), insert symbols that resemble crop marks, and then make sure the crop marks align properly so that the user can cut or score the bookmarks accurately.

Printing Crop Marks

The crop marks in Word display only on the screen and do not print. If you create your own crop marks in the Header & Footer pane, they will print and serve as a guide for trimming. You may want to print the bookmarks on cardstock and then laminate them before trimming.

Exercise 7.7 Creating Bookmarks with Crop Marks

1. Open **Bookmark** located in your *Chapter07* folder.
2. Click the File tab, Options button, select the Advanced tab, and then click to add a check mark at *Show crop marks in the Show document content* section. Click OK.

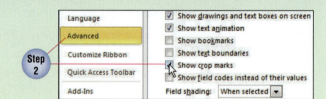

3. Create the crop marks as shown in Figure 7.24 by completing the following steps:
   a. Click the Header button in the Header & Footer group in the Insert tab and then click Edit Header.
   b. Click the Text Box button in the Text group in the Insert tab and then draw a text box that measures approximately 0.3 inch by 9 inches at the top of the Header pane. Remove the shape outline around the text box.

c. Display the Ruler, position the insertion point inside the text box, and then create center tabs at 2", 4.4", and at 6.8". ***Hint: Hold down the Alt key as you click on the Ruler to set the tabs; turn off the Drawing grid feature.***

Step 3c

d. Press Tab (2").
e. Click the Symbol button in the Symbols group on the Insert tab, click More Symbols, select the SimSun font at the *Font* list box, type **2534** in the Character Code box. The symbol resembles an upside down T. Click Insert and then Close.

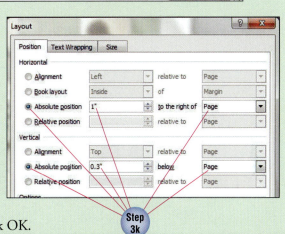

Step 3e

f. Press Tab (4.4").
g. Insert the same symbol as the one inserted in step 3e.
h. Press Tab (6.8").
i. Insert the same symbol as the one inserted in step 3e.
j. Select the text box, click the Position button in the Arrange group in the Drawing Tools Format tab, and then click More Layout Options.
k. At the Layout dialog box, change the *Absolute* position to **1"** to the right of *Page* in the *Horizontal* section. Change the *Absolute* position to **0.3"** below *Page* in the *Vertical* section. Click OK.

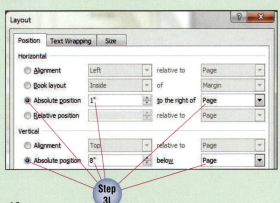

Step 3k

l. Select the text box containing the crop marks and while holding down the Ctrl key and the Shift key, drag and drop a copy below the bookmarks on the first page. The text box should be positioned at **1"** to the right of *Page* and **8"** below *Page*. Close the Header & Footer pane.

Step 3l

4. Save the document in PDF format, and name it **C07-E07-Bookmarks**. ***Hint: You may want to laminate the bookmarks and then cut them using the crop marks as guides.***
5. Print and then close **C07-E07-Bookmarks.pdf**.
6. Click the File tab, click Options, select the Advanced tab, and then remove the check mark next to the *Show crop marks* option in the *Show document* section. Click OK.

Figure 7.24 Exercise 7.7

Chapter Seven

Figure 7.25 Shipping Label Templates

Using Shipping Labels to Promote Corporate Identity

The Office.com Templates website includes several shipping labels formatted attractively with business names, logos, and color. Two examples of these labels are shown in Figure 7.25. You can easily adapt these templates to fit your needs by replacing the placeholder text, adding a logo, and changing the colors to reinforce consistency with your other documents. The shipping labels can be accessed by clicking the File tab and then the New tab. Click the Labels category, click the Mailing and Shipping category, and then click the Business category. Select the desired shipping label template and then click Download.

Chapter Summary

➤ Promotional documents may be formatted using templates or created from scratch using tables, text boxes, 2 pages per sheet, or book fold underlying designs.

➤ Press Ctrl + Tab to insert a Tab command in a table cell.

➤ Press the Tab key to advance from one cell to the next in a table.

➤ Insert an automatic numbering command to a ticket document by adding an AutoNum field code.

➤ You can create lines that you can type on by designing your document using tables, inserting fields, drawing a line shape, or drawing lines using the Underline command and tab settings.

➤ The table feature is one of the most efficient tools for designing and creating forms.

➤ The Labels feature formats documents so that they can be printed on designated label sheets.

➤ Field codes are used to format date, time, and page numbers automatically.

➤ Mail merge is the process of combining variable information with standard text to create personalized documents.

➤ Word includes a Mail Merge wizard that can be used to create different documents that include letters, email messages, envelopes, labels, and directories, all with personalized information.

- The Step by Step Mail Merge wizard guides the user through six steps for merging documents and presents a Mail Merge task pane for each step. Alternatively, you can use the Merge buttons on the Mailing tab.

- The data source and the main document may be merged to a new document or to the printer.

- A data source document and a main document are needed to perform a merge. A data source document contains the variable information. The main document contains the standard text along with identifiers showing where variable information is to be inserted.

- A record contains all of the information for one unit (person, family, customer, or client).

- Merge fields are special codes in the main document that direct Word to collect information from the data source and use it in the main document to create personalized documents.

- A main document can be edited in the normal manner. A data source document can be edited using the Mail Merge wizard or with buttons on the Mailings tab.

- A data source can be edited at the Mail Merge Recipients dialog box.

- The Auto Check for Errors button can be clicked in the Preview Results group on the Mailings tab to report each error in a merge as it occurs.

- The second Mail Merge task pane includes an option to use the current document, to change the document layout, or to start from an existing document.

- The third Mail Merge task pane includes an option to select recipients for the merge from an existing list, from an Outlook contact list, or from a new list that you create.

- The Address block hyperlink inserts a formatted address field into your main document.

- The replicate label feature in the Mail Merge task pane copies the layout of the first label to the other labels on the page. You must click the Update all labels button in the *Replicate labels* section to activate this command.

- Any formatting codes to be applied to the merged document should be inserted in the main document.

- The More items hyperlink in the *Arrange your labels* section of the fourth step in a merge includes other merge fields.

- Word includes a crop mark feature that adds crop marks to the corners of a document based on the margin settings. These marks do not print.

- Crop marks to assist in trimming a document can be created by setting tabs at the Header and Footer pane and inserting cropping symbols.

- A poster may be printed by accessing your specific printer Properties dialog box and selecting an option to print the poster on four sheets of paper or more. The number of pages selected will determine the size of the overall poster.

Commands Review

FEATURE	RIBBON TAB, GROUP	BUTTON
Address Block	Mailings, Write & Insert Fields	Address block...
Align	Page Layout, Arrange	Align ▾
Auto Check for Errors	Mailings, Preview Results	Auto Check for Errors

FEATURE	RIBBON TAB, GROUP	BUTTON
AutoNum	Insert, Text	▭ Field...
Borders	Table Tools Design, Table Styles	⊞ Borders ▾
Labels	Mailings, Create	
Page Border	Page Layout, Page Borders	
Start Mail Merge	Mailings, Start Mail Merge	
Symbol	Insert, Symbol	Ω
Table Properties	Table Tools Layout, Table	
View Gridlines	Table Tools Layout, Table	
WordArt	Insert, WordArt	A

Reviewing *Key Points*

A. Address Block
B. AutoNum
C. AutoText
D. Book fold
E. Ctrl + Tab
F. Field

G. Merge fields
H. Page Setup
I. Printer
J. Properties
K. Record
L. Replicate

M. Start Mail Merge
N. Tab
O. Table
P. 2 pages per sheet

Completion: In the space at the left, provide the correct letter or letters from the above list that match each definition.

_____ 1. The data source and the main document can be merged to a new document or to this.

_____ 2. This merge feature inserts a formatted address field into the main document.

_____ 3. This label feature in the Mail Merge task pane copies the layout of the first label to the other labels on the page.

_____ 4. Use this feature to create a line on which you can type.

_____ 5. This feature divides a physical page in half and may be used to create single-fold brochures.

_____ 6. This form field allows you to add automatic numbering to a ticket document.

_____ 7. *FirstName*, *JobTitle*, and *Address1* are examples of this type of code.

_____ 8. The *2 pages per sheet* option is accessed at this dialog box.

_____ 9. This contains all of the information for one unit (person, family, customer, or client).

_____ 10. Press these keys to add a tab within a table.

_____ 11. Click this button on the Mailings tab to begin the merging process.

_____ 12. This Word feature provides a framework for creating forms.

Chapter Assessments

Assessment 7.1   Creating a Promotional Gift Certificate

Gift certificates are excellent promotional documents that can be used for generating further purchases or used as rain checks, mini-awards, "runner-up" or prizes. As an employee at Butterfield Gardens, create a gift certificate that may be purchased by customers and used for in-store shopping.

1. At a Word document screen, create a gift certificate similar to Figure 7.26 by completing the following steps. (Type text from Figure 7.26.)
   a. Change all of the margins to 0.65 inch.
   b. Create a table with two columns and one row.
   c. Center the table horizontally.
   d. Change the default cell margins to 0.1 inch.
   e. Change the Row height to **2.65"**, change the Column 1 width to **4.75"**, and the Column 2 width to **2.25"**.
   f. Add a border around the outside of the table.
   g. Choose a theme and select appropriate fonts.
   h. Adjust the line spacing to accommodate the text properly. The sample uses single spacing with 0 points before and after.
   i. With the insertion point located in the first cell, type **Gift Certificate**. Press Enter twice.
   j. Select *Gift Certificate,* and then select a font similar to that shown in Figure 7.26 (the sample uses 36-point French Script MS).
   k. Set left tabs at 0.5 inch, 1.75 inches, 2.75 inches and 4.3 inches.
   l. Type the text in the first cell as shown in Figure 7.26. Press the spacebar once after typing a text label; click the Underline button on the Home tab, press the space bar again and then press Ctrl + Tab to move to the next tab and to create the underline. Turn off the underline feature and then press Enter twice.
   m. Type **Butterfield Gardens** and the address text as shown in Figure 7.26.
2. Insert a tree image similar to the one shown in Figure 7.26 or include the Butterfield Gardens Logo (BGLogo) located in your *Chapter07* folder. Type **apple tree** in the *Search for* text box at the Clip Art task pane. Size and position the tree image similar to Figure 7.26.
3. Create two more certificates by copying and pasting the table. ***Hint: Insert one hard return between each certificate.***
4. Save the document and name it **C07-A01-Certifcate**.
5. Print and then close **C07-A01-Certificate.docx**.

Figure 7.26 Assessment 7.1

Gift Certificate

Butterfield Gardens
29 W 036 Butterfield Road
Warrenville, IL 60555
(630) 555-1062

http://www.emcp.net/butterfield

Date _____

This certificate entitles _____

To _____ Dollars $ _____

Presented by _____

Authorized signature _____

Gift Certificate

Butterfield Gardens
29 W 036 Butterfield Road
Warrenville, IL 60555
(630) 555-1062

http://www.emcp.net/butterfield

Date _____

This certificate entitles _____

To _____ Dollars $ _____

Presented by _____

Authorized signature _____

Gift Certificate

Butterfield Gardens
29 W 036 Butterfield Road
Warrenville, IL 60555
(630) 555-1062

http://www.emcp.net/butterfield

Date _____

This certificate entitles _____

To _____ Dollars $ _____

Presented by _____

Authorized signature _____

Assessment 7.2 Creating Name Tags

An appropriate name badge (tag) shows your name, your title, and the company or organization with which you are affiliated. The individual's name should be easy to read and the most dominant element on the name tag. Remembering a person's name is one of the biggest compliments you can pay to that person. Name badges can definitely reduce the embarrassment of forgetting someone's name. An alternative to choosing labels for name badges is to purchase name-tag holders and insert a business card or name badge printed on heavier weight paper inside the holder. The holder is a clear plastic sleeve with a clip or pin on the reverse. Holders are usually available through mail-order paper companies or office supply companies. You will create name tags in this assessment and insert field codes for merging to a data source.

1. On the Mailings tab, click the Start Mail Merge button, and then click *Step by Step Mail Merge Wizard* or use the Merge buttons on the Mailings tab.
2. At the first step of the wizard, select *Labels*.
3. At the second step of the wizard, click Label options, and then select any product name for a name tag or name badge.
4. At the third step, select the recipients, **FloralDataSource**, located in your *Chapter07* folder.
5. At the fourth step, arrange the label by including the following:
   a. Make sure the table gridlines display.
   b. Position the insertion point in the first cell and type the text shown in Figure 7.27.
   c. Format the text similar to Figure 7.27.
   d. Insert the field codes as shown in Figure 7.27 by clicking *More items* in the *Arrange your labels* section.
   e. At the Insert Merge Fields dialog box, select and then insert the appropriate fields.
   f. Apply shading around the *First Name, Last Name,* and *Job Title* fields.
   g. Click the Update all labels button in the *Replicate labels* section.
6. Preview the labels at the fifth step and then complete the merge.
7. Save and then print **C07-A02-NameTags.docx**.

Figure 7.27 Assessment 7.2

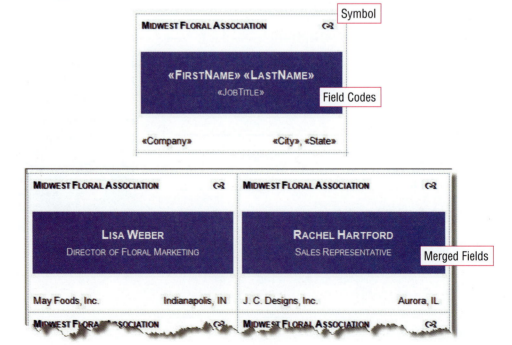

Assessment 7.3   Folded Bank Invitation

As an employee at First Bank, one of your responsibilities is to create an invitation for an "Evening out on the Town" to be sent to several important bank clients. Use the Word table feature and create the invitation in either landscape or portrait orientation to produce two on one sheet of paper. If you can find an appropriate template, you may use a template and customize it to include the following specifications:

1. Add graphics, watermarks, lines, borders, symbols, or other enhancements to your document. Use the following text:

   On behalf of First Bank, we cordially invite you to an
   "Evening Out on the Town" Thursday, May 24, 2012
   Trattoria 8
   15 North Dearborn Street
   Chicago, Illinois
   Dinner: 5:30 p.m.–7 p.m.
   Chicago Theater
   175 North State Street
   Chicago, Illinois
   Theater: 7:30 p.m.
   Phantom of the Opera
   RSVP to Victoria Franz, (302) 555-3456 by May 1, 2012

2. Include the following specifications:
   a. Consider your audience in creating an appropriate design.
   b. Prepare a thumbnail sketch.
   c. Use an appropriate font and vary the type size and typestyle.
   d. Change the character spacing in at least one occurrence.
   e. Use horizontal and vertical lines, or an appropriate graphic image, graphic border, or symbols to add interest and impact.
   f. Use special characters where needed—en or em dashes, bullets, and so on.
   g. Change the leading (spacing between the lines) if necessary.
3. Save the document and name it **C07-A03-Bank**.
4. Print and then close **C07-A03-Bank.docx**.
5. Evaluate your invitation with the **DocumentAnalysisGuide** located in your *Chapter07* folder.

Figure 7.28 Assessment 7.3 Sample Solution

Assessment 7.4   Integrated Application Form

In this exercise, you will create a scholarship application form using a Word table. You will insert information from an Excel worksheet into the Word table. Because of the Excel automatic calculating features, you will see that integrating Excel into the Word form makes it easier to make the computations.

1. Create the scholarship application form shown in Figure 7.29A by inserting a table and using the cells as placeholders for the information. Save the document as **C07-A04-ScholarshipApplicationForm**. *Hint: See the illustration below for help in visualizing how a table can be used to set up the form—non-printing gridlines, borderlines, labels, and so on. The settings do not have to be exactly as shown.*

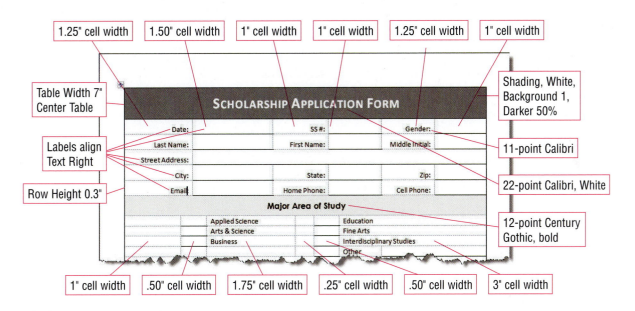

2. Start Excel and open **CommunityServiceHours.xlsx** located in your *Chapter07* folder. Alphabetize the categories by selecting the "Government" through "Day camp" cells and then clicking the Sort & Filter button in the Editing group on the Home tab. At the drop-down list, click *Sort A to Z*. If the Sort Warning dialog box appears, click the Continue with the current selection button and then click Sort.
3. Add borders to the bottom of each fill-in category and a double border to the "Total" cell.
4. Add the AutoSum formula to the right of the "Total" cell by positioning the insertion point in the cell and then clicking the AutoSum button in the Editing group on the Home tab. To add the cell references to the formula, click and drag cells B2:B8. Release the *left* mouse button and then click again the AutoSum button.
5. Copy cells A1:B9 to the Clipboard.
6. Click **C07-A04-ScholarshipApplicationForm** in the Taskbar to open Word. Position the insertion point in the left cell that is below the *Eligibility requirements* paragraph and click the down-pointing arrow on the Paste button in the Clipboard group on the Home tab. At the drop-down list, click *Paste Special, Microsoft Office Excel Worksheet Object*, and then click OK.
7. This inserts the Excel worksheet as an object, allowing you to utilize the Excel features while in Word. Double-click in the object and add the numbers shown in Figure 7.29B. The "Total" column should automatically recalculate. Click outside the object, and you will return to the Word editing functions. Click the Align Center button in the Alignment group in the Table Tools Layout tab.

Figure 7.29 Assessment 7.4 Integrated Application Form Sample Solution

SCHOLARSHIP APPLICATION FORM

Date: _____   SS #: _____   Gender: _____

Last Name: _____   First Name: _____   Middle Initial: _____

Street Address: _____

City: _____   State: _____   Zip: _____

Email: _____   Home Phone: _____   Cell Phone: _____

Major Area of Study

_____ Applied Science   _____ Education
_____ Arts & Science   _____ Fine Arts
_____ Business   _____ Interdisciplinary Studies
          _____ Other _____

H. S. Class Standing	Intended Student Status
_____ Junior	_____ Full-time (2 hours or more)
_____ Senior	_____ ¾-time (9 – 11 hours)
_____ Graduate	_____ ½-time (6 – 8 hours)

Eligibility requirements include a minimum of 40 hours of community service throughout your four years four years of high school. Fill in the number of hours you have volunteered in each category.

Thank you for your application. Please return to Kelly Cabana, 22 Parrot Way, St. Paul, MN 55102.

A

8. Enter the remaining text and symbols as shown in Figure 7.29B. *Hint: You can press the Tab key to move from one cell to the next to complete the form. Optional: Key your own name and address.*
9. Insert an appropriate graphic or photograph.
10. Save the document and name it **C07-A04-ScholarshipApplicationFormCompleted**.
11. Print and then close **C07-A04-ScholarshipApplicationFormCompleted.docx**.
12. Close **CommunityServiceHours.xlsx** and then exit Excel.

SCHOLARSHIP APPLICATION FORM

Date: June 7, 2012   SS #: 555-55-5555   Gender: Female

Last Name: Gibson   First Name: Allison   Middle Initial: E.

Street Address: 231 Marietta Avenue

City: Atlanta   State: GA   Zip: 30312

Email: agibson@emcp.net   Home Phone: 404.555.1234   Cell Phone: 404.555.4321

Major Area of Study

_____ Applied Science	_____ Education	
_____ Arts & Science	_____ Fine Arts	
__X__ Business	_____ Interdisciplinary Studies	
	_____ Other	_____

H. S. Class Standing   Intended Student Status

_____ Junior	__X__ Full-time (2 hours or more)
__X__ Senior	_____ ¾-time (9 – 11 hours)
_____ Graduate	_____ ½-time (6 – 8 hours)

Eligibility requirements include a minimum of 40 hours of community service throughout your four years four years of high school. Fill in the number of hours you have volunteered in each category.

Community Service	
Church activity	32
Day camp	4
Fund-raising	22
Government	
High school	12
Homeless shelter	4
Other	
Total	74

Thank you for your application. Please return to Kelly Cabana, 22 Parrot Way, St. Paul, MN 55102.

B

Assessment 7.5   Promotional Document Group Project

1. Form groups of three or four students. Assign necessary group tasks to accomplish creating a promotional document of your own design, one based on a sample document you have found, or a template located on the Internet. Use any of the Word features you have learned so far in addition to at least one integrated feature from one of the other Office programs. If you are using a sample document, first evaluate the document for good layout and design, a clear and

concise message, and proper use of other desktop publishing concepts as outlined in the **Document Analysis Guide**. Some possible promotional documents include the following examples:

- Invitation to a new store opening
- Introduction of a new course at your local community college
- Invitation to a class reunion
- Business greeting card or company party invitation
- Postcard as a follow-up or one promoting a new business (coffee shop, party planner, attorney's office, computer services as shown in Figure 7.30.)
- Membership card
- Ticket with a company or organization name or logo
- Form requesting information for membership
- Document used by a service company promoting e-Bill—paying your account balance online
- Postcard advertising a sample sale
- Poster advertising services at a travel agency

2. Create the document using a size other than 8½ by 11-inch paper, or print the document with multiple pages as a poster.
3. Save the completed document and name it **C07-A05-Promotional**.
4. Print and then close **C07-A05-Promotional.docx**. (Attach the original document if one was used.)
5. Discuss the approach used to create this document with the rest of the class. Each member should participate in the presentation.

Figure 7.30 Assessment 7.5 Sample Solution

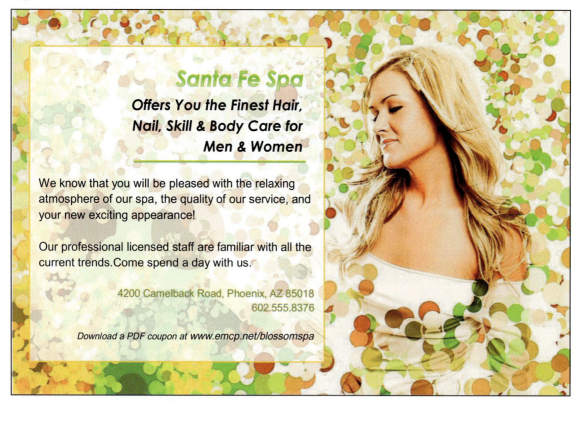

Chapter 8

CHAPTER08

Creating Basic Elements of a Newsletter

Performance Objectives

Upon successful completion of Chapter 8, you will be able to:

- Create newsletters from scratch.
- Review and apply design concepts.
- Use columns in newsletters.
- Create, modify, and apply styles.
- Improve the readability of newsletters.
- Adjust tracking and leading.
- Use Windows Photo Gallery.
- Use Windows Fax and Scan.

Desktop Publishing Terms

Byline
Em space
Folio
Headline
Leading

Logo
MHTML
Nameplate
Orphan
Subhead

Subtitle
Tombstoning
Widow

Word Features Used

Balanced and unbalanced
   columns
Character spacing
Column break
Columns

Line spacing
Mail Merge
Newspaper columns
Paragraph indent
Save as Template

Section break
Styles
Widow/Orphan control
Windows Fax and Scan

Designing a newsletter may appear to be a simple task, but newsletters are more complex than they appear. Newsletters can be the ultimate test of your desktop publishing skills. Remember that your goal is to get the message across. Design is important because it increases the overall appeal of your newsletter, but content is still the most crucial consideration. Whether your purpose for creating a newsletter is to develop better communication within a company or to develop awareness of a product or service, your newsletter must give the appearance of being well planned, orderly, and consistent. To establish consistency from one issue of a newsletter to the next, you must plan your document carefully.

Creating Basic Elements of a Newsletter

Successful newsletters contain consistent elements in every issue. Basic newsletter elements divide the newsletter into organized sections to help the reader understand the text, as well as to entice the reader to continue reading. Basic elements usually include

Figure 8.1 Basic Newsletter Elements

- *Nameplate:* The nameplate, or banner, consists of the newsletter's title and is usually located on the front page. Nameplates can include the company logo, a unique typeface, or a graphic image to help create or reinforce an organization's identity.

- *Logo:* A name, symbol, trademark, or graphic image used to create or reinforce an organization's identity. Often this symbol is used in the nameplate (banner) of a newsletter.

- *Subtitle:* A subtitle is a short phrase describing the purpose or audience of the newsletter. A subtitle can also be called a tagline. The information in the subtitle is usually located below the nameplate near the folio.

- *Folio:* A folio is the publication information, including the volume number, issue number, and the current date of the newsletter. The folio usually appears near the nameplate, but it can also be displayed at the bottom or side of a page. In desktop publishing, folio can also mean page number.

- *Headlines:* Headlines are titles to articles and are frequently created to attract the reader's attention. The headline can be set in 22- to 72-point type or larger and is generally typed in a sans serif typeface.

- *Subheads:* Subheads, or subheadings, are secondary headings that provide the transition from headlines to body copy. Subheads may also be referred to as section headings because they can also break up the text into organized sections. Subheads are usually bolded and sometimes typed in larger type sizes. There may be more space above a subhead than below.

- *Byline:* The byline identifies the author of an article.

- *Body Copy:* The main part of the newsletter is the body copy or text.

- *Graphic Image:* Graphic images are added to newsletters to help stimulate ideas and add interest to the document. They provide visual clues and visual relief from text-intensive copy.

the items described in Figure 8.1; Figure 8.2 shows their location on a newsletter page. Additional newsletter enhancements and elements are presented in Chapter 9.

Planning a Newsletter

Before creating a newsletter, consider the target audience and the objective for providing the information. Is the goal of the newsletter to sell, inform, explain, or announce? What is the purpose of the newsletter? Companies and organizations often use newsletters to convey a sense of pride and teamwork among employees or members. When planning a company newsletter, consider the following suggestions:

- If a scanner is available, use pictures of different people from your organization in each issue.

- Provide contributor forms requesting information from employees.

- Keep the focus of the newsletter on issues of interest to the majority of employees.

Figure 8.2 Identifying Basic Elements in a Newsletter Page

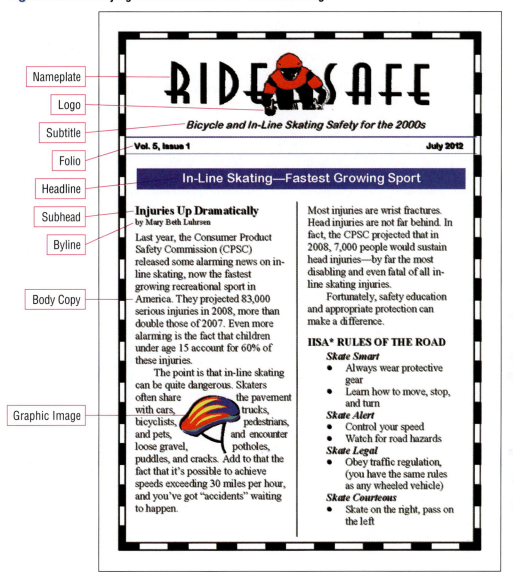

Nameplate
Logo
Subtitle
Folio
Headline
Subhead
Byline
Body Copy
Graphic Image

RIDE SAFE

Bicycle and In-Line Skating Safety for the 2000s

Vol. 5, Issue 1   July 2012

In-Line Skating—Fastest Growing Sport

Injuries Up Dramatically
by Mary Beth Luhrsen

Last year, the Consumer Product Safety Commission (CPSC) released some alarming news on in-line skating, now the fastest growing recreational sport in America. They projected 83,000 serious injuries in 2008, more than double those of 2007. Even more alarming is the fact that children under age 15 account for 60% of these injuries.

The point is that in-line skating can be quite dangerous. Skaters often share the pavement with cars, trucks, bicyclists, pedestrians, and pets, and encounter loose gravel, potholes, puddles, and cracks. Add to that the fact that it's possible to achieve speeds exceeding 30 miles per hour, and you've got "accidents" waiting to happen.

Most injuries are wrist fractures. Head injuries are not far behind. In fact, the CPSC projected that in 2008, 7,000 people would sustain head injuries—by far the most disabling and even fatal of all in-line skating injuries.

Fortunately, safety education and appropriate protection can make a difference.

IISA* RULES OF THE ROAD
Skate Smart
- Always wear protective gear
- Learn how to move, stop, and turn

Skate Alert
- Control your speed
- Watch for road hazards

Skate Legal
- Obey traffic regulation, (you have the same rules as any wheeled vehicle)

Skate Courteous
- Skate on the right, pass on the left

- Make sure you include articles of interest to varying levels of employment.
- Hand out regular surveys to evaluate newsletter relevancy.

If the aim of your newsletter is to promote a product, the focal point may be a graphic image or photograph of the product rather than more general company news. Your aim can also influence the selection of typefaces, type sizes, visual elements, and the placement of elements. Also consider the following questions when planning the newsletter: What is the image you want to project? How often will the newsletter appear? What is your budget? How much time can you devote to its creation? What items are likely to be repeated from issue to issue? And, will your newsletter accommodate ads, photographs, or clip art? After answering these questions, you are ready to begin designing the newsletter.

DTP POINTERS
Look at as many publications as you can to get design ideas.

Designing a Newsletter

Desktop publishing concepts and guidelines discussed in previous chapters provide you with good starting points for your newsletter. These guidelines emphasize the use of consistency, balance, proportion, contrast, white space, focus, directional flow, and color. If you are designing a newsletter for a company or organization, make sure the design coordinates with its design identity by using the same logo, typefaces, type sizes, column arrangements, and color choices that are used in other correspondence.

One of the biggest challenges in creating a newsletter is balancing change with consistency. A newsletter is a document that is typically reproduced on a regular basis, whether monthly, bimonthly, or quarterly. With each issue, new ideas can be presented, new text created, and new graphics or photos used. However, for your newsletter to be effective, each issue must also maintain a consistent appearance. Consistency contributes to your publication's identity and gives your readers a feeling of familiarity.

Consistent newsletter features and elements may include the following: size of margins; column layout; nameplate formatting and location, logos, color, ruled lines, and formatting of headlines, subheads, and body text. Later in the chapter, you will create styles to automate the process of formatting consistent elements.

Focus and balance can be achieved in a newsletter through the design and size of the nameplate, the arrangement of text on the page, the use of graphic images or scanned photographs, or the careful use of lines, borders, and backgrounds. When using graphic images or photos, use restraint and consider the appropriateness of the image. A single, large illustration is usually preferred over many small images scattered throughout the document. Size graphic images or photos according to their relative importance to the content. Headlines and subheads can serve as secondary focal points as well as provide balance to the total document.

White space around a headline creates contrast and attracts the reader's eyes to the headline. Surround text with white space if you want the text to stand out. If you want to draw attention to the nameplate or headline of the newsletter, you may want to choose a bold typestyle and a larger type size. Another option is to use WordArt to emphasize the nameplate title. Use sufficient white space throughout your newsletter to break up gray areas of text and to offer the reader visual relief.

Good directional flow can be achieved by using ruled lines that lead the reader's eyes through the document. Graphic elements, placed strategically throughout a newsletter, can provide a pattern for the reader's eyes to follow.

In Figure 8.2, focus, balance, contrast, and directional flow were achieved through the placement of graphic images at the top and bottom of the document, the blue shaded text box with reverse text, and bolded headings. If you decide to use color in a newsletter, do so sparingly. Establish focus and directional flow with color to highlight key information or elements in your publication.

Creating a Newsletter Page Layout

Typically, page layout begins with choosing the size and orientation of the paper and determining the margins desired for the newsletter. Next, decisions on the number, length, and width of columns become imperative. Typefaces, type sizes, and typestyles must also be considered, as well as graphic images, ruled lines, and shading and coloring.

DTP POINTERS ▶
Newsletter design should be consistent from issue to issue.

DTP POINTERS ▶
Use no more than one or two images per page if possible.

DTP POINTERS ▶
Use graphic accents with discretion.

DTP POINTERS ▶
Be generous with your margins: Do not crowd text.

Choosing Paper Size and Type

The first considerations in designing a newsletter page layout are the paper size and type. The number of copies needed and the equipment available for creating, printing, and distributing the newsletter can affect this decision. Most newsletters are created on standard 8½ by 11-inch paper, although some are printed on larger sheets such as 8½ by 14 inches. The most economical choice for printing is the standard 8½ by 11-inch paper, and it is easier to hold and read, cheaper to mail, and fits easily in standard file folders.

Paper weight is determined by the cost, the quality desired, and the graphics or photographs included. The heavier the stock, the more expensive the paper. In addition, pure white paper is more difficult to read because of glare. If possible, investigate other, more subtle colors. Another option is to purchase predesigned newsletter paper from a paper supply company. These papers come in many colors and designs. Several have different blocks of color created on a page to help separate and organize your text.

Creating Margins for Newsletters

After considering the paper size and type, determine the margins of your newsletter pages. The margin size is linked to the number of columns needed, the formality desired, the visual elements used, the amount of text available, and the type of binding. Keep your margins consistent throughout your newsletter. Listed here are a few generalizations about margins in newsletters:

Margins

- A wide right margin is considered formal. This approach positions the text at the left side of the page—the side where most readers tend to look first. If the justification is set at full, the newsletter will appear even more formal.

- A wide left margin is less formal. A table of contents or marginal subheads can be placed in the left margin giving the newsletter an airy, open appearance.

- Equal margins tend to create an informal look.

If you plan to create a multiple-paged newsletter with facing pages, you may want to use Word's mirror margin feature, which accommodates wider inside or outside margins. Figures 8.3 and 8.4 illustrate mirror margins in a newsletter. Often, the inside

◀ **DTP POINTERS**
Place page numbers on the outside edges when using mirror margins.

Figure 8.3 Outside Mirror Margins on Facing Pages of a Newsletter

Binding or fold

| Page 2 | Dancing | Art & Theater | Page 3 |

Art Happenings

Dancing lessons will be available at the Elite Dance Studio beginning March 1. Sign up early to guarantee that you will get the class you've been waiting for. Ballroom dancing and modern dance are popular classes.

Classes will be limited to twenty dancers. Come alone or sign up with a friend.

View artwork of open campus faculty—drawings, paintings, photographs, jewelry, and computer animation. Discuss available classes with faculty.

Theater
"Phantom of the Opera" will be playing

Outside mirror margins

Figure 8.4 Inside Mirror Margins on Facing Pages with Gutter Space

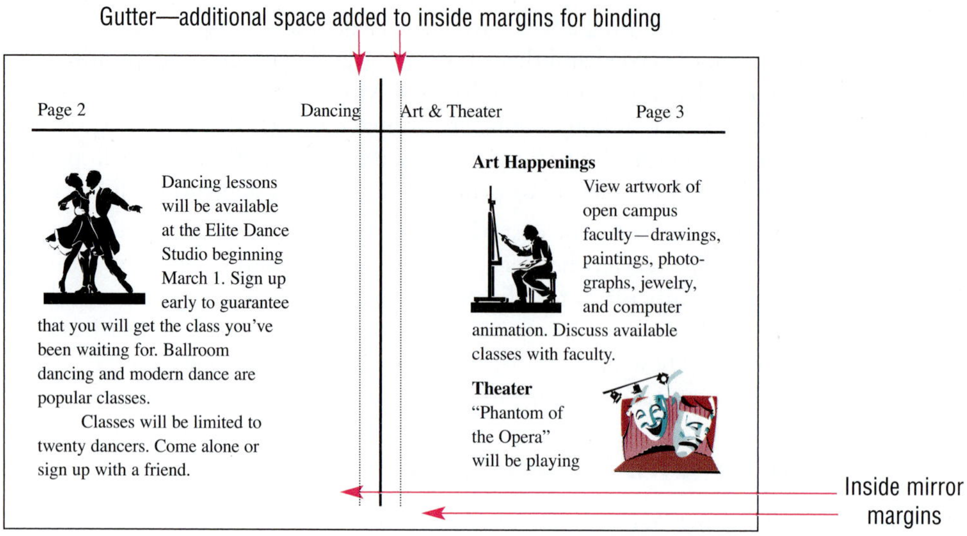

Gutter—additional space added to inside margins for binding

Page 2   Dancing | Art & Theater   Page 3

Dancing lessons will be available at the Elite Dance Studio beginning March 1. Sign up early to guarantee that you will get the class you've been waiting for. Ballroom dancing and modern dance are popular classes.

    Classes will be limited to twenty dancers. Come alone or sign up with a friend.

Art Happenings

View artwork of open campus faculty—drawings, paintings, photographs, jewelry, and computer animation. Discuss available classes with faculty.

Theater
"Phantom of the Opera" will be playing

Inside mirror margins

margin is wider than the outside margin; however, this may depend on the amount of space the binding takes up. To create facing pages with mirror margins, click the Margins button in the Page Setup group on the Page Layout tab, and then click *Custom Margins* at the bottom of the drop-down list. At the Page Setup dialog box, select the Margin tab, and then click the down-pointing arrow at the right of Multiple pages in the *Pages* section. At the drop-down list, click *Mirror margins*. If you plan to include page numbering, position the numbers on the outside edges of each page.

Also, consider increasing the gutter space to accommodate the binding on a multiple-paged newsletter. To add gutter space on facing pages, add the extra space to the inside edges; on regular pages, add space to the left edges. To add gutters, display the Page Setup dialog box with the Margins tab selected, and then select or type a gutter width at the *Gutter* option. Gutters do not change the margins but rather add extra space to the margins. However, gutters make the printing area of your page narrower. Gutter space may be added to the left side of your page, to the left and right sides if the mirrored margin feature is chosen, or to the top of a sheet.

DTP POINTERS
Use extra wide gutters or margins to counteract dense text.

Creating Newspaper Columns for Newsletters

When preparing newsletters, an important consideration is the readability of the document. The line length of text can enhance or detract from the readability of text. Setting the text in columns can make it easier for your audience to read the text. You will use columns to format the newsletter created throughout this chapter; however, keep in mind that you can also use linked text boxes to position text within a newsletter—this method is used in most of the newsletter templates and will be introduced in Chapter 9.

Newspaper columns in a newsletter promote the smooth flow of text and guide the reader's eyes. As discussed earlier, the Newspaper Columns feature allows text to flow from column to column in the document. To work with columns, Print Layout view should be selected. When the first column on the page is filled with text, the insertion point moves to the top of the next column on the same page in a snaking effect. When the last column on the page is filled, the insertion point moves to the beginning of the first column on the next page.

DTP POINTERS
Columns added to newsletters improve readability.

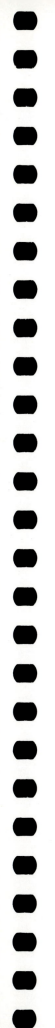

Figure 8.5 Columns Dialog Box

Inserts two columns, of which the left column is half as wide as the right

Adds a vertical line between columns

Amount of space between columns

Width of uneven columns

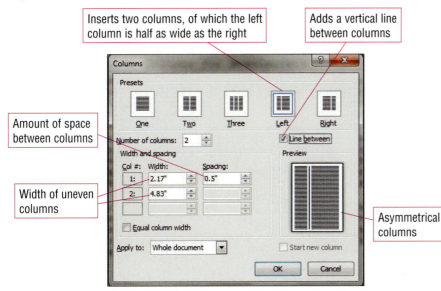

Asymmetrical columns

Newspaper columns can be created by clicking the Columns button in the Page Setup group on the Page Layout tab. At the drop-down list, select *One, Two, Three, Left, Right,* or *More Columns*. The *Left* and *Right* options enable columns of unequal width in an asymmetrical layout. Clicking the *More Columns* option displays the Columns dialog box as shown in Figure 8.5, where you can customize the widths of the columns and the white space between the columns.

Columns

Using Balanced and Unbalanced Columns

Word automatically lines up (balances) the last line of text at the bottom of each column. On the last page of a newsletter, the text is often not balanced between columns. Text in the first column may flow to the bottom of the page, while the text in the second column may end far short of the bottom of the page. Columns can be balanced by inserting a section break at the end of the text by completing the following steps:

1. Position the insertion point at the end of the text in the last column of the section you want to balance.
2. Display the Page Layout tab, and then click the Breaks button.
3. At the *Breaks* drop-down list, click *Continuous* in the *Section Breaks* section. Figure 8.6 shows the last page of a document containing unbalanced columns and a page where the columns have been balanced. If you want to force a new page to start after the balanced columns, click after the continuous break, and then insert a manual page break.

Breaks

Determining the Number of Columns

The number of columns used in newsletters may vary from one column to four or more columns. The size of the paper used, the font and type size selected, the content and amount of text available, and many other design considerations affect this decision.

One-column newsletters are easy to produce because the articles simply follow each other. If you do not have much time to work on your newsletter, this format is the one to use. The one-column format is the simplest to design and work with because it allows you to make changes and additions easily. You will want to use a large type size—usually 11 or 12 points—to accommodate the long line length of a one-column design. Be sure to use

Figure 8.6 Unbalanced and Balanced Columns

Unbalanced Columns   Balanced Columns

wide margins with this column layout. Also, keep in mind that an asymmetrically designed page is more interesting to look at than a symmetrical one, as shown in Figure 8.7.

The two-column newspaper format is the most frequently used selection for newsletters. It gives a formal look, especially if used with justified text. Generally, use type sizes between 10 and 11 points when using a two-column layout. Be careful to avoid *tombstoning*, which occurs when headings display side by side in adjacent columns. Using an asymmetrical design in which one column is wider than the other and adding graphic enhancements will make this classic two-column format more interesting.

A three-column format is successful if you avoid using too much text on the page. This popular format is more flexible for adding interesting design elements. You may use a smaller type size (9 to 11 points) and fit more information on a page. Placing headings, text, or graphics across one, two, or three columns can create a distinctive flow. Often, one column is reserved for a table of contents, marginal subheads, or a masthead (publication information), thus allowing for more white space in the document and more visual interest.

A four-column design gives you even more flexibility than the three-column layout; however, more time may be spent in putting this newsletter layout together. Leaving one column fairly empty with a great deal of white space to offset more text-intensive columns is a visually appealing solution. This format gives you many opportunities to display headings, graphics, and other design elements across one or more columns. You will need to use a small type size for your text—9 to 10 points. Also, consider printing on larger-sized paper when using this layout.

Using Varying Numbers of Columns in a Newsletter

Section breaks can be used to vary the page layout within a single newsletter. For instance, you can use a section break to separate a one-column nameplate from text that can be created in three columns, as shown in Figure 8.8. There are three methods for inserting section breaks in documents. One method uses selecting break options at the *Break* drop-down list. Another method automatically inserts a section break if you select the option *This point forward* in the *Apply to* section of the Columns dialog box. In the third method, select the text first, and then apply column formatting. To move the insertion point between columns, use the mouse or press Alt + Up Arrow to move the insertion point to the top of the previous column, or press Alt + Down Arrow to move the insertion point to the top of the next column.

Tombstoning
When headings display side by side in adjacent columns.

Figure 8.7 Symmetrical and Asymmetrical Designs in Newsletters

Symmetrical Design   Asymmetrical Design

In addition, when formatting text into columns, Word automatically breaks the columns to fit the page. If a column breaks in an undesirable location, you can insert a column break in the document to control where the columns end and begin on the page. To insert a column break, position the insertion point where you want the new column to begin, and then press Ctrl + Shift + Enter, or click the Breaks button on the Page Layout tab and chose Column from the Page Breaks section.

Figure 8.8 Section Breaks in Newsletters

One column
(section break) →

Two columns
(section break) →

← Three columns
(section break)

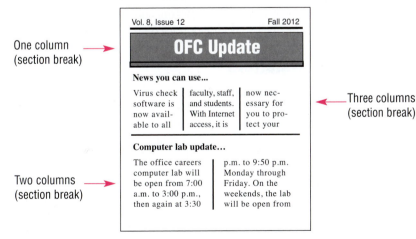

Changing the Number of Columns

Select

To change the number of columns for an entire newsletter, press Ctrl + A, or click the Select button in the Editing group on the Home tab, and then click *Select All* from the drop-down list. To change the number of columns for a portion of a document, select the affected text only; to change the number of columns in several existing sections, select the multiple sections. After selecting the text you want to change, click the Columns button, and select the number of columns desired. If you want to remove columns in your newsletter, click in the section or select multiple sections you want to change, click the Columns button, and then click *One*.

Changing Column Width

If your newsletter is divided into sections, click in the section you want to change, and then drag the column marker on the horizontal Ruler. If an adjacent column is hampering your efforts to change a column width, reduce the width of the adjacent column first. If the column widths are equal, all of the columns will change. If the column widths are unequal, only the column you are adjusting changes. To specify exact measurements for column widths, hold down the Alt key as you drag the column marker on the Ruler or access the Columns dialog box and type exact measurements in the text boxes provided.

Adding Vertical Lines between Columns

Position the insertion point in the section where you want to add a vertical line, access the Columns dialog box, click to add a check mark in the *Line between* check box as shown in Figure 8.5, and then close the dialog box.

Adding Borders and Horizontal Lines to Newsletter Pages

Page Borders

You can add page borders, paragraph borders, borders around images, borders around text boxes, and horizontal lines between paragraphs to change the appearance of your newsletters. To add a page border, click the Page Borders button in the Page Background group on the Page Layout tab. At the Borders and Shading dialog box, select the Page Border tab, and then select a particular line Style, Color, and Width, or select a predesigned Art border. To create a border around a paragraph of text, select the Borders tab, and then select options to change the line style, color, or width. Make sure *Paragraph* displays in the *Apply to* list box. You may also click the Horizontal Line button in the bottom left corner to access the Horizontal Line dialog box as shown in Figure 8.9.

Horizontal Line

Additionally, you may add a line for design by clicking the Shapes button in the Illustrations group, select a desired line in the *Lines* section, and then draw a line in your document. You can customize the line by clicking options on the Drawing Tools Format tab.

Using Styles in Newsletters

Styles are especially valuable for saving time, effort, and keystrokes in creating newsletters. Newsletters are typically one of the most frequently created desktop publishing documents, and they contain elements that must remain consistent from page to page as well as from issue to issue. Styles reinforce consistency in documents by saving repetitive formatting instructions with a name so they can be applied over and over.

In addition to predesigned system styles included in many Word templates or wizards, you have the option to create your own customized styles either based on system styles or created from scratch. Throughout the creation of the newsletter in Figure 8.10, you will use various predesigned system styles and customize them to certain specifications as well as create your own styles based on existing styles.

Figure 8.9 Horizontal Line Dialog Box

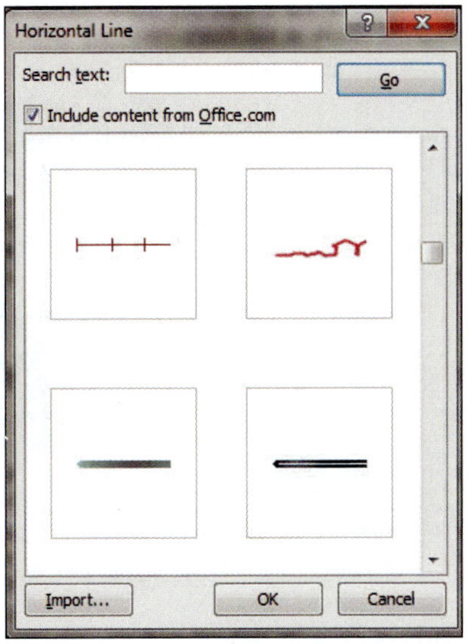

Adjusting Leading in Newsletters

While creating newsletters, you may find areas where adjustments should be made to increase or decrease white space between lines. This may occur when creating a nameplate, headline, subhead, or body text. Insufficient leading—vertical line spacing measured from the baseline of one line of text to the baseline of the next line of text— makes the text difficult to read; extra leading makes a page look less gray. However, too much leading or too little leading can make it difficult to find the beginning of the next line. You can adjust the leading by adding or removing points before or after lines of text, changing font sizes; selecting *At least, Exactly,* or *Multiple* options; and specifying point or line increments that adjust the spacing between the lines.

You may also alter paragraph spacing by clicking the Change Styles button in the Styles group. At the drop-down list, click the *Paragraph Spacing* option, and then select a desired paragraph setting *(No Paragraph Spacing, Compact, Tight, Open, Relaxed, Double)* from the *Built-In* list.

Large type size may require an adjustment from the normal leading. For instance, if a headline contains two lines both typed at 30 points, the space between the two lines may be too wide. Reducing the leading will improve the appearance of the heading. Consider the following guidelines when determining leading:

- Large type requires more leading.
- Longer lines need more leading to make them easier to read.
- Sans serif type requires more leading because it does not have serifs that guide the eyes along the line.
- Styles apply line spacing consistently in newsletters.

Creating Your Own Newsletter

A thumbnail sketch is an excellent way to experiment with different layouts and designs. Look at the work of others for hints and suggestions on different layouts. Creating a thumbnail is like "thinking" on paper.

◀ **DTP POINTERS**
When the line length increases, line spacing (leading) should also increase.

Figure 8.10 Loaves and Fishes Newsletter with Elements and Styles Marked

Logo

Folio

Headline

Byline

Drop cap

Body

Em space

Subtitle

Nameplate

Graphic

Quick Parts Building Block (Tiles Quote)

Creating a Nameplate

Throughout this chapter, you will build the newsletter shown in Figure 8.10. Each exercise involves creating a style for a specific newsletter element. Each exercise builds on the previous one, finally resulting in a completed newsletter with embedded styles and saved as a template to help you create the next issue.

Creating a nameplate for your newsletter will be the first step in building the Loaves and Fishes newsletter. A *nameplate* or banner is the first thing that captures the reader's eyes; it provides immediate identification of the newsletter. A nameplate is the artwork (graphic, logo, scanned image, or cropped image) and/or type that includes the name of the publication and is usually placed at the top of the first page of a newsletter. The choice of fonts, type sizes, and the designs of the name are important because the reader sees them repeatedly.

The nameplate in Exercise 8.1 consists of the organization's logo, the organization's name, and the newsletter name in the same colors as those used in the logo. A *logo* is a name, symbol, or trademark designed for easy recognition. Loaves and Fishes use two different logo designs in most of its publications. The Loaves and Fishes logos may display in black and white or in green and gold. Most nameplates remain unchanged from issue to issue; therefore, saving them as a style is not necessary. But the nameplate should be saved to a newsletter template. Figure 8.11 illustrates several examples of nameplates. Examine them for the use and different location of elements. Looking at the work of others can help you develop your own skills in design and layout.

Figure 8.10 Loaves and Fishes Newsletter with Elements and Styles Marked *(continued)*

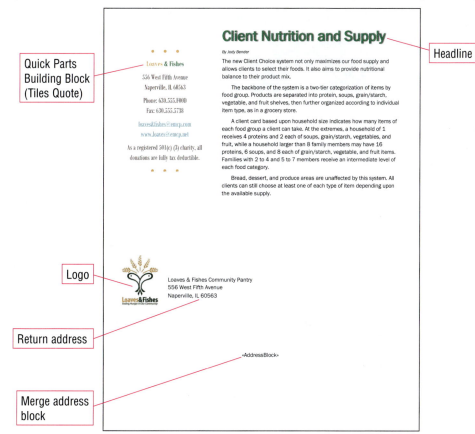

Quick Parts
Building Block
(Tiles Quote)

Headline

Logo

Return address

Merge address
block

*Note: Copy the **Chapter08** folder from the CD that accompanies this textbook to your storage medium and then make **Chapter08** the active folder. Remember to substitute graphics that may no longer be available.*

Figure 8.11 Sample Nameplates

Nameplate with reversed
text, gradient fill, and a
symbol

Nameplate with
layered text

Nameplate with
WordArt

Figure 8.11 Sample Nameplates (continued)

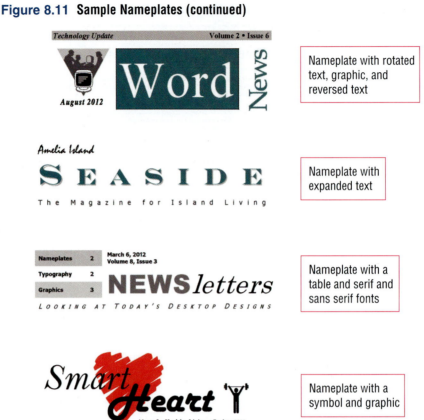

Nameplate with rotated text, graphic, and reversed text

Nameplate with expanded text

Nameplate with a table and serif and sans serif fonts

Nameplate with a symbol and graphic

Exercise 8.1   Creating a Nameplate for a Newsletter

1. Create the nameplate shown in Figure 8.10 by completing the following steps:
    a. Open a blank document, and then save the document as **C08-E01-Nameplate**.
    b. Change the margins to 0.5 inches (Narrow).
    c. Change the theme to Decatur, that is located in the *From Office.com* section.
    d. At the top of the document, press the Enter key 10 times, press Ctrl + Home to position the insertion point at the top of the document, and then insert the picture, **Loaves&FishesColor.jpg** logo, located in your *Chapter08* folder.
    e. Select the logo and change the *Wrap Text* to *Square*.
    f. Size the logo at **1.8"** in the *Shape Height* text box and **1.16"** in the *Shape Width* text box.

    g. Select the logo, and then position the logo as shown in Figure 8.10.
    h. Drag and draw a text box to the right of the logo that measures approximately 1 inch in height and 5.5 inches in width.
    i. Select the text box and type **1.1"** in the *Shape Height* text box and **5.6"** in the *Shape Width* text box in the Size group on the Drawing Tools Format tab.
    j. Position your insertion point inside the text box, change the alignment to Align Text Right, and then type **Loaves&Fishes**.

k. Select *Loaves*, and change the font to 72-point Haettenschweiler in the *Gold, Accent 5* color in the *Theme Colors* section in the Font Color drop-down gallery.

l. Select *&Fishes* and change the font to 72-point Haettenschweiler. Click the down arrow at the right of the Font Color button, click More Colors, display the Custom tab, and type **56** in *Red* text box, **140** in the *Green* text box, and **78** in the *Blue* text box in the *RGB Color Model* section. Click OK.

m. Select *Loaves&Fishes,* click the Font dialog box launcher, click the Advanced tab, expand the letter spacing by 1 pt., and then turn on kerning at 14 points. Click OK.

n. Drag the text box containing *Loaves&Fishes* to a position similar to Figure 8.10, and change the Shape Fill to *No Fill* and the Shape Outline to *No Outline*.

o. Select the & (ampersand), and change the font to 72-point Eras Bold ITC.

p. Drag and draw a text box that measures approximately 1 inch in height and 5 inches in width.

q. Select the text box and type **0.7"** in the *Shape Height* text box and **5"** in the *Shape Width* text box in the Size group on the Drawing Tools Format tab.

r. Position your insertion point inside the text box, change the alignment to Align Text Right, and then type **Food for Thought**.

s. Select *Food for Thought*, change the font to 36-point Bell MT in italics, and turn on kerning at 14 points.

t. Remove the text box fill and outline and then drag the text box containing *Food for Thought* to a position similar to Figure 8.10.

2. Save the document again as **C08-E01-Nameplate.docx**.

3. Close **C08-E01-Nameplate.docx**. Keep this file open if you are going to work on Exercise 8.2. ***Note: You only need to print when you are finished with the entire newsletter.***

Creating a Folio

The *folio* will consist of publishing information that will change from issue to issue, such as the volume number, issue number, and date. However, the formatting applied to the folio will remain consistent with each issue. Frequently, the folio is preceded or followed by a graphic line that sets the folio information apart from the rest of the nameplate. The folio may appear at the top of the nameplate or be placed below the nameplate as shown in the Loaves & Fishes newsletter. Reverse text may be used to add emphasis and interest—use a thick font or apply bold to make the font stand out against the shaded background. The Loaves & Fishes logo also includes the pantry's slogan, which reinforces the mission of the organization.

Folio

A newsletter element consisting of publishing information that will change from issue to issue, such as the volume number, issue number, and date.

1. Open **C08-E01-Nameplate.docx** and then create the folio for the newsletter in Figure 8.10 by completing the following steps:
   a. Save the file as **C08-E02-Folio** and then drag and draw a text box below the text box containing *Food for Thought* that measures approximately 0.3 inches in height and 7.5 inches in width.

   b. Select the text box and type **0.37"** in the *Shape Height* text box and **7.5"** in the *Shape Width* text box in the Size group on the Drawing Tools Format tab.
   c. Position your insertion point inside the text box, and type **Ending Hunger in Our Community**.

   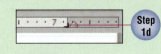

   d. With the insert point still located inside the text box, insert a Right tab at 7.2 inches.
   e. Press Tab, and then type **Summer/Fall 2012**.
   f. Select *Ending Hunger in Our Community* and *Summer/Fall 2012,* and change the font to 12-point Franklin Gothic Book in bold and italics.

   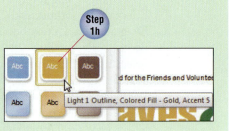

   g. With the insertion point positioned on the text in step 1f, click the Paragraph dialog box launcher, and then type **2 pt** in the *Before* text box and **10 pt** in the *After* text box in the *Spacing* section. Click OK.
   h. Select the text box, click the More button in the Shape Styles group, and then click the *Light 1 Outline, Colored Fill - Gold, Accent 5* effect in the Shape Styles gallery. The text should display in white automatically.

   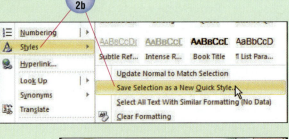

   i. Position the text box similar to Figure 8.10.
2. Create a style from existing text by completing the following steps:
   a. Position the insertion point anywhere in the folio text.
   b. Right-click the selection, point to Styles, and then click *Save Selection as a New Quick Style.*
   c. At the Create New Style from Formatting dialog box, type **Folio** in the *Name* text box and then click OK. **Hint: The Folio style is added to the list of styles in this document.**

3. Save the document, and name it **C08-E02-Folio**. (You may want to save this exercise and the following Loaves & Fishes newsletter exercises under one file name.)
4. Close **C08-E02-Folio.docx**. Keep this file open if you are going to work on Exercise 8.3. *Note: You only need to print when you are finished with the entire newsletter.*

Creating a Subtitle

As the third step in building a newsletter, you will create a *subtitle*. The text in the subtitle will remain consistent from issue to issue, so creating a style is not necessary. A subtitle emphasizes the purpose of the newsletter and identifies the intended audience. It is usually typed in a sans serif typeface in 14 to 24 points, and kerning should be turned on.

Exercise 8.3 Creating a Subtitle in a Newsletter

1. Open **C08-E02-Folio.docx**.
2. Save the document, and name it **C08-E03-Subtitle**.
3. Format the subtitle by completing the following steps:
   a. Drag and draw a text box above the text box containing *Loaves&Fishes* that measures approximately 0.3 inches in height and 5.25 inches in width.
   b. Select the text box and type **0.3"** in the *Shape Height* text box and **5.25"** in the *Shape Width* text box in the Size group on the Drawing Tools Format tab.

   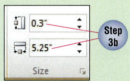

   c. Position your insertion point inside the text box, change the font to 10-point Franklin Gothic Book.
   d. Type **Published for the Friends and Volunteers of Loaves & Fishes Community Pantry**.
   e. Select the text and change the alignment to Align Text Right.
   f. Remove the text box fill and outline and then drag the text box containing the Subtitle text to a position similar to Figure 8.10. *Hint: Make sure the ending characters in each of the text boxes align vertically near the right margin.*
4. Group all the nameplate elements into one unit by completing the following steps:
   a. While holding down the Shift key, click to select each of the elements created up to this point.

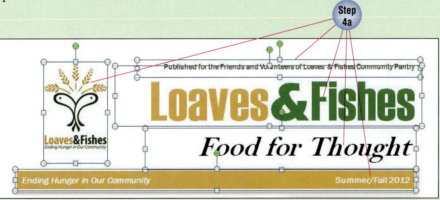

   b. Click the down arrow at the right of the Group button, and then click Group.
5. Save the document again with the same name, **C08-E03-Subtitle**.
6. Close **C08-E03-Subtitle.docx**. Keep this file open if you are going to work on Exercise 8.4.
   Note: You only need to print when you are finished with the entire newsletter.

Creating a Headline

After completing the folio, nameplate, and subtitle, you will now create a headline in Exercise 8.4. *Headlines* organize text and help readers decide whether they want to read the article. To set the headline apart from the text, use a larger type size, a heavier weight, and a different typeface than the body. When determining a type size for a headline, start with 18 points and increase the size until you find an appropriate one. As a rule, choose a sans serif typeface for a headline; however, this is not a hard-and-fast rule. Because the headline consists of text that will change with each issue of the newsletter, consider creating a style to format the headline.

Headlines of more than one line often improve in readability and appearance if leading is reduced. The leading in a headline should be about the same size as the type used. Using all caps (sparingly) or small caps substantially reduces leading automatically because capital letters lack descenders. Headlines and subheads should have more space above than below. This indicates that the heading goes with the text that follows rather than the text that precedes the heading.

Because headlines may be used several times in a newsletter, you will need to create a style to reinforce consistency and promote efficiency in formatting the document.

Exercise 8.4 Creating a Headline Style for a Newsletter

1. Open **C08-E03-Subtitle.docx**.
2. Save the document and name it **C08-E04-Headline**.
3. Create a section break between the folio and the headline by completing the following steps:
   a. Position the insertion point on the paragraph symbol below the Folio.
   b. Click the down-pointing arrow at the right of the Break button in the Page Setup group in the Page Layout tab.
   c. At the drop-down list, select *Continuous*.
4. Turn on the columns feature by completing the following steps:
   a. With the insertion point still positioned at the paragraph symbol below the Folio, click the down-pointing arrow below the Columns button on the Page Layout tab.
   b. At the drop-down list, click *More Columns*.

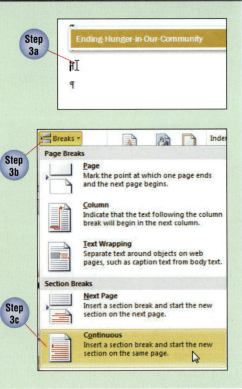

Step 3a

Ending Hunger-in-Our-Community

Step 3b

Breaks ▾   Inde

Page Breaks

Page
Mark the point at which one page ends and the next page begins.

Column
Indicate that the text following the column break will begin in the next column.

Text Wrapping
Separate text around objects on web pages, such as caption text from body text.

Section Breaks

Next Page
Insert a section break and start the new section on the next page.

Step 3c

Continuous
Insert a section break and start the new section on the same page.

c. At the Columns dialog box, select *Right* in the *Presets* section.

d. Type **0.4"** in the *Spacing* text box in the *Width and spacing* section.

e. Click the down-pointing arrow at the right of the *Apply to* list box and select *This point forward*. Click OK.

5. Create the headline by completing the following steps:

a. Change the font to 28-point Franklin Gothic Book, and apply bold.

c. Change the font color to the green color used in the Banner (Red 56, Green 140, and Blue 78).

d. Type **New Era in Client Choice**.

e. Select *New Era in Client Choice*, turn on kerning at 14 points, click the Text Effects button, click Shadow, and then click the Offset Right option in the *Outer* section.

f. Position your insertion point anywhere in the headline, click the Paragraph dialog box launcher, type **12 pt** in the *Before* text box and **0 pt** in the *After* text box in the *Spacing* section. Click OK.

6. Create a style from existing text by completing the following steps:

a. Position the insertion point anywhere in the headline text, point to *Styles*, and then click *Save Selection as a New Quick Style*.

b. At the Create New Style from Formatting dialog box, type **Headline** in the *Name* text box and then click OK. **Hint: The Headline style is added to the list of styles saved with this document.**

7. Save the document again with the same name **C08-E04-Headline**.

8. Close **C08-E04-Headline.docx**. Keep this file open if you are going to work on Exercise 8.5. *Note: You only need to print at the end of the entire newsletter.*

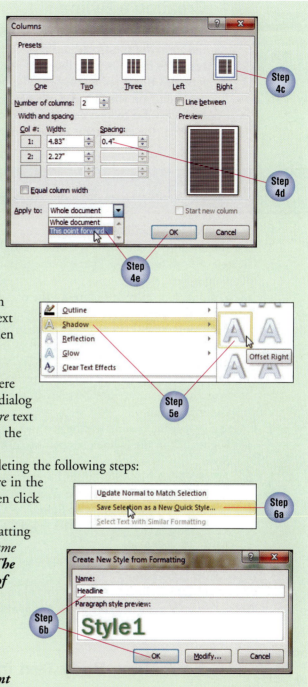

Creating a Byline

The next step in building the newsletter is to create the byline. The **byline** identifies the author of the article and is often typed in italic using the same typeface as the body text. The byline may be the same size as the body typeface, but it may also be set in a type size 1 or 2 points smaller. The byline may appear below the headline or subhead, depending on which is the title of the article, or it may appear as the first line of the body text if it follows a headline or subhead that spans two or more columns. Place the byline at the left margin or right-aligned in a column.

Exercise 8.5 Creating a Byline Style in a Newsletter

1. Open **C08-E04-Headline.docx**.
2. Save the document, and name it **C08-E05-Byline**.
3. Create a style to format the byline in the newsletter in Figure 8.10 by completing the following steps:
   a. Position your insertion point on the paragraph symbol below the Headline text.
   b. Type **By Jody Bender**. Turn on the Show/Hide feature and press Enter once if a paragraph symbol (Enter) does not appear after the byline.
   c. Select the byline *By Jody Bender,* and change the font to 8-point Franklin Gothic Book in italics.
   d. Display the Page Layout tab and type **0 pt** in the *Before* text box and **6 pt** in the *After* text box in the *Spacing* section in the Paragraph group.

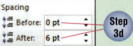

4. Create a style from existing text by completing the following steps:
   a. Right click in the byline text, point to *Styles*, and then click *Save Selection as a New Quick Style*.
   b. At the Create New Style from Formatting dialog box, type **Byline** in the *Name* text box and then click OK. (The Byline style is added to the list of styles saved with this document.)
5. Save the document again with the same name, **C08-E05-Byline**.
6. Close **C08-E05-Byline.docx**. Keep this file open if you are going to work on Exercise 8.6. *Note: You only need to print when the newsletter is complete.*

Formatting Body Text in a Newsletter

In this chapter you will format the body text for the newsletter you are building. You will also change the font and type size, and create em spaces for paragraph indentations. Before doing so, take a look at some of the formatting options that apply to body text.

Applying the Widow/Orphan Feature

The Widow/Orphan control feature is on by default. This feature prevents the first and last lines of paragraphs from being separated across pages. A **widow** is a single line of a paragraph or heading that is pushed to the top of the next page. A single line of text (whether part of a paragraph or heading) appearing by itself at the end of a page is called an **orphan**. This option is located in the Paragraph dialog box at the Line and Page Breaks tab.

Even with this feature on, you should still watch for subheads that are inappropriately separated from text at the end of a column or page. If a heading displays inappropriately, insert a column break. To insert a column break, position the insertion point where you want a new column to begin, and then press Ctrl + Shift + Enter, or click the Breaks button in the Page Setup group on the Page Layout tab.

Breaks

Align Left

Align Right

Center

Aligning Text in Paragraphs in Newsletters

The type of alignment you choose for a newsletter influences the tone of your publication. Text within a paragraph can be aligned in a variety of ways: at both the left and right margins (justified); at the left or right; or on the center of the text body, causing both the left and right margins to be ragged.

Justified text is common in publications such as textbooks, newspapers, newsletters, and magazines. It is more formal than left-aligned text. For justified text to convey a professional appearance, the line length must be appropriate. If the line length is too short, the words and/or characters in a paragraph may be widely spaced, causing "rivers" of white space. Remedying this situation requires increasing the line length, changing to a smaller type size, and/or hyphenating long words. Text aligned at the left is the easiest to read. This alignment has become popular with designers for publications of all kinds. Center alignment should be used on small amounts of text.

Justify

Indenting Paragraphs with Em Spaces

In typesetting, tabs are generally measured by em spaces rather than inch measurements. An **em space** is a space as wide as the point size of the type. For example, if the type size is 12 points, an em space is 12 points wide. Usually, you will want to indent newsletter text one or two em spaces.

Em space
A space as wide as the point size of the type.

Em space indentations can be created in two ways. One way to create an em space is to type an increment at the *Left* or *Right Indent* text boxes in the Paragraph group on the Page Layout tab. Alternatively, you can create an em space at the Tabs dialog box. In Exercise 8.6, you will change the default tab setting to 0.25 inch to create two em space indentations for each paragraph preceded with a tab code (0.25 inch is approximately 24 points, or 2 em spaces for text typed in 12-point type size). Be sure to use em spaces for any paragraph indentations used in newsletters. Also, use em spaces for spacing around bullets and any other indented text in newsletters.

Generally, the first paragraph after a headline or subhead is not indented even though all remaining paragraphs will have an em space paragraph indentation. In Figure 8.10, notice the paragraph formatting in the newsletter.

Exercise 8.6   Creating a Body Text Style in a Newsletter

1. Open **C08-E05-Byline.docx**.
2. Save the document, and name it **C08-C06-Body**.
3. Position the insertion point on the paragraph symbol below the byline text. Insert the text file **ClientChoice** located in your *Chapter08* folder.
4. Format the body text by completing the following steps:
   a. Click to place the insertion point at the beginning of the text *Saturday, September 13th* by pressing Ctrl + Shift + End, and then verify that the font is 11-point Franklin Gothic Book.

b. With the text still selected, click the Paragraph dialog box launcher to access the Paragraph dialog box. To change the paragraph indentions to an em space, click the Tabs button at the bottom left corner of the Paragraph dialog box.

c. At the Tabs dialog box, type **0.25"** in the *Tab stop position* text box, make sure *Left* is selected in the *Alignment* section, and then click the Set button.

d. Click OK to close the Tabs dialog box.

e. Position your insertion point in front of each of the paragraphs following the first paragraph, and then press the Tab key.

5. Create a style to format the body text by completing the following steps:

a. Position the insertion point in one of the paragraphs in the body of the newsletter except the first paragraph.

b. Right-click the selection, point to *Styles*, and then click *Save Selection as a New Quick Style*.

c. At the Create New Style from Formatting dialog box, type **Body** in the *Name* text box, and then click OK. ***Hint: The Body style is added to the list of styles saved with this document.***

6. Add a drop cap to the first paragraph by completing the following steps:

a. Position the insertion point in *Saturday* in the first paragraph.

b. Click the down-pointing arrow below the Drop Cap button in the Text group in the Insert tab, and click the *Dropped* option from the drop-down list.

c. Click the Drop Cap button again, click *Drop Cap Options* at the bottom of the drop-down list, and change the font to Bell MT in the *Options* section. Click OK.

7. Save the document again with the same name, **C08-E06-Body**.

8. Close **C08-E06-Body.docx**. Keep this file open if you are going to work on Exercise 8.7. *Note: You only need to print when the newsletter is complete.*

Creating Subheads for Newsletters

At times, a subhead may appear right after a headline; however, one does not appear in the case of this chapter's newsletter. **Subheads**, or **subheadings**, organize text and expand on headlines, giving readers more information or clues about the text. In addition, subheads also provide contrast to text-intensive body copy. Marginal subheads are sometimes placed in the left margin or in a narrow column to the left of the body text, providing an airy, open appearance. Subheads can be set in a larger type size, different typeface, or heavier weight than the text. They can be centered, aligned left, aligned right, and formatted in shaded boxes.

Inserting and Editing Graphic Images in Newsletters

Clip art added to a newsletter should support or expand points made in the text. Use clip art so that it will give the newsletter the appearance of being well planned, inviting, and consistent. Besides using the button on the Picture Tools Format tab to customize a picture, you may also modify clip art by ungrouping it using Word as a picture editor or by using Microsoft Office Picture Manager or Windows Paint. You can also scan images by using Microsoft Fax and Scan.

Figure 8.12 Using Microsoft Office Picture Manager to Remove Red Eye

Using Microsoft Office Picture Manager

Microsoft Picture Manager is installed with all Office suites and can be used on individual images. With the tools in Microsoft Picture Manager, you can customize images by changing colors, improving brightness and contrast, straightening, cropping, and removing red eye as shown in Figure 8.12.

Use the following instructions to start Picture Manager:

1. From the Start menu, click or point to All Programs.
2. Open the Microsoft Office folder.
3. Open the Microsoft Office 2010 Tools folder.
4. Click Microsoft Picture Manager.

Using Windows Paint for Images

Paint is a feature in Windows 7 that you can use to create drawings on a blank drawing area or in existing pictures. Many of the tools you use in Paint are found in the ribbon, which is near the top of the Paint window as shown in Figure 8.13.

Figure 8.13 Using Windows Paint for Images

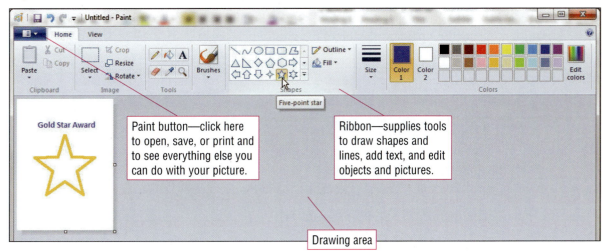

Figure 8.14 Using Windows Fax and Scan

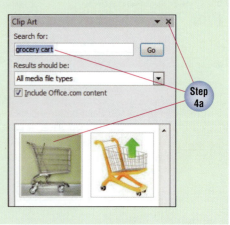

Using Windows Fax and Scan

In addition, you may want to scan predesigned company logos (with permission) or photographs that relate to the subject of your newsletter using Windows Fax and Scan, which is optimized for scanning, viewing, and storing text documents as shown in Figure 8.14.

Exercise 8.7 Inserting Graphic Images into a Newsletter

1. Open **C08-E06-Body.docx**.
2. Save the document, and name it **C08-E07-Graphics**.
3. Position the insertion point at the top of the second column at the beginning of the text.
4. Insert the photograph of a grocery cart as shown in Figure 8.10 by completing the following steps:
   a. Click the Clip Art button in the Illustrations group and type **grocery cart** in the *Search for* text box. Insert the image shown in Figure 8.10 or insert a similar image if this one is not available. Close the Clip Art task pane.
   b. Size the image to 2.14 inches in height and width.
   c. Select the image, change the *Wrap Text* to *Square*, and position the image similar to Figure 8.10.

d. With the image selected, click the down-pointing arrow at the right of the Rotate button in the Arrange group in the Picture Tools Format tab. At the drop-down list, click *Flip Horizontal*. **Note: You always want your graphic to face the text.**

e. Apply the *Soft Edge Rectangle* Picture Style located in the first row of the Picture Styles gallery in the Picture Tools Format tab.

f. Position the insertion point at the beginning of the paragraph located below the image, type **18 pt** in the *Before* text box in the *Spacing* section in the Paragraph group in the Page Layout tab.

5. Insert the AutoText entry located in the bottom right corner of the newsletter by completing the following steps:

a. Position the insertion point below the paragraph in the second column.

b. Click the Quick Parts button in the Text group in the Insert tab, and then click the *Building Blocks Organizer* option.

c. Click the *Tiles Quote* text box object in the Building Block Gallery, and then click Insert. **Hint: Click the Name column title to sort the building blocks alphabetically. The text box object will display in the first column at the left margin.**

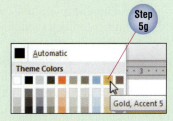

d. Select the object, and change the *Wrap Text* to *Square*.

e. Size and position the image as in Figure 8.10.

f. Select the placeholder text and type the following:

> Our Vision (**Press Enter.**)
> Ending Hunger in Our Community (**Press Enter.**)
> Our Mission (**Press Enter.**)
> **Loaves & Fishes provides food and leadership in the community by uniting and mobilizing resources to empower people to be self-sufficient.**
> *Hint: Resize the text box object if necessary.*

g. Select the three dots at the top of the text, hold down the Ctrl key and select the three dots at the bottom of the text, click the Font Color button on the Home tab, and then click the *Gold, Accent 5* color in the *Theme Colors* section.

h. Select *Our Vision*, hold down the Ctrl key and select *Our Mission*, and then change the font color to the green used earlier in the newsletter (Red 56, Green 140, and Blue 78).

i. Select *Loaves*, change the font color to the gold color, and apply bold.

j. Select *& Fishes*, change the font color to the green color, and apply bold.

6. Save the document with the same name, **C08-E07-Graphics**.

7. View your newsletter in Print tab Backstage view.

8. Keep this file open if you are going to work on Exercise 8.8. **Note: You only need to print when the newsletter is complete.**

Figure 8.15 Creating Round Labels to Bind a Folded Newsletter

Mailing a Newsletter

In Exercise 8 you will format the back of the newsletter you created in this chapter, merge to a data source, and then fold the newsletter to send it through the mail. Even though the USPS allows some staples in mail, it is better not to use staples to close your mail pieces. It can slow down sorting and delivery; the mail piece may not be handled automatically and cost more to process. As an alternative, you may want to fold the newsletter in half and attach a label to bind the halves together. Figure 8.15 illustrates the Avery US Letters - 8293 High Visibility Round Label definition that measures 1.5 inches by 1.5 inches.

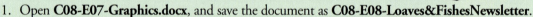

Exercise 8.8 Changing the Newsletter Layout and Merging to a Data Source

1. Open **C08-E07-Graphics.docx**, and save the document as **C08-E08-Loaves&FishesNewsletter**.
2. Press Ctrl + End to position the insertion point at the bottom of the page, and click the Page Break button in the Pages group in the Insert tab. *Hint: If the hard returns at the bottom of the first page automatically generate another page, you will not need to insert a page break.*
3. Click the Breaks button in the Page Setup group in the Page Layout tab, and then click *Continuous* in the *Section Break* section.
4. Change the column layout by completing the following steps:
   a. Click the Columns button in the Page Setup group, and click More Columns.
   b. Click *Left* in the *Presets* section.
   c. Type **0.4** in the *Spacing* text box in the *Width and spacing* section.
   d. Click the down-pointing arrow at the right of the *Apply to* list box and select *This point forward*. Click OK.

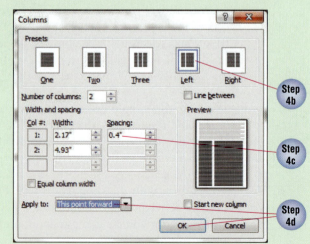

5. Insert a Quick Parts entry in the left column by completing the following steps:
    a. Position the insertion point in the left column of this page, click the Quick Parts button in the Text group on the Insert tab, click the Building Blocks Organizer option, click the Tiles Quote text box object in the Building Block Organizer, and then click Insert.
    b. Change the *Wrap Text* to *Square*, and then drag the object to a position similar to Figure 8.10.
    c. Type the following text:
        Loaves & Fishes (Press Enter.)
        556 West Fifth Avenue
        (Press Shift + Enter.)
        Naperville, IL 60563 (Press Enter.)
        Phone: 630.555.FOOD
        (Press Shift + Enter.)
        Fax: 630.555.5738 (Press Enter.)
        loaves&fishes@emcp.com
        (Press Shift + Enter.)
        www.loaves@emcp.net
        (Press Enter.)
        As a registered 501(c)(3) charity, all donations are fully tax deductible.
        Hint: If the (c) changes automatically to a copyright symbol, backspace to delete the symbol, and then retype (c).

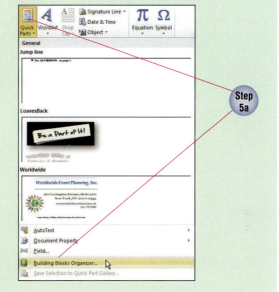

        d. Apply the green and gold font colors and bold as shown in Figure 8.10.
6. Create the text in the next column by completing the following steps:
    a. Position the insertion point below the *Tiles Quote* text box object, and then press Ctrl + Shift + Enter to the insertion point to the next column.
    b. At the top of the column, type **Client Nutrition and Supply**, and then press Enter.
    c. Position the insertion point in *Client Nutrition and Supply*, and then click the Headline style in the Styles gallery.
    d. Insert the **NutritionandSupply** file located in your *Chapter08* folder.
    e. Select *By Jody Bender*, and apply the Byline style in the Styles gallery.
    f. Select the article text, and apply the Body style in the Styles gallery.
7. Create the mailing text by completing the following steps:
    a. Position the insertion point at the end of the nutrition and supply text.
    b. Click the Breaks button in the Page Setup group in the Page Layout tab, and then click *Continuous* in the *Section Break* section.

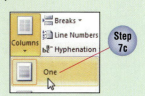

    c. Click the Columns button in the Page Setup group, and then click *One* at the drop-down list.
    d. Insert the **Loaves&FishesColor** logo located in your *Chapter08* folder.
    e. Change the *Wrap Text* to *Square*, and then size and position the logo as shown in Figure 8.10.
    f. Drag and draw a text box for the Loaves & Fishes return address as shown in Figure 8.10.
    g. Refer to Figure 8.10 for the return address text or see step 5c and position the text box to the right of the logo. Remove the Shape Fill and Shape Outline.

h. Drag and draw another text box for the merged mailing addresses in a location similar to Figure 8.10. Remove the Shape Fill and Shape Outline.

8. Insert the merge codes by completing the following steps:

a. Position the insertion point inside the mailing address text box, and then click the Start Mail Merge button in the Start Mail Merge group in the Mailings tab.

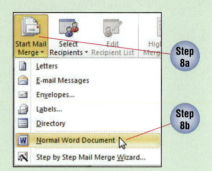

b. Click *Normal Word Document* from the drop-down list. ***Hint: Make sure the insertion point is positioned inside the mailing address text box.***

c. Click the Select Recipients button, and click *Use Existing List.*

d. Browse and open the **NaperGrovePatients.mdb** file in your *Chapter08* folder.

e. Click the Address Block button in the Write & Insert Fields group.

f. Accept all the defaults at the Insert Address Block dialog box, and then click OK.

g. Select the Address Block merge code in the newsletter, and then type **0 pt** in the *After* text box in the *Spacing* section in the Paragraph group in the Page Layout tab. ***Hint: This will result in single spacing the addresses.***

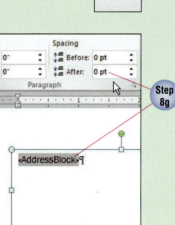

h. Click the Finish & Merge button in the Finish group.

i. Click *Edit Individual Documents* and then click *All* in the *Merge records* section of the Merge to New Document dialog box. Click OK.

9. Print only the merged newsletter addressed to *Rachel Weber* and then close the merged newsletters without saving them.

10. Save the main document as **C08-E08-Loaves&FishesNewsletter.docx**.

11. ***Optional:*** Create a circular label to be used when the newsletter is folded in half and sent through the mail. At a new blank document, access the Mailing labels and chose the Avery US Letters - 8293 High Visibility Round Labels and insert the **LoavesandFishes** black and white circular logo located in your *Chapter08* folder. Save the label as **C08-E08-MailingLabel**. Print and then attach the label to the folded newsletter.

Saving the Newsletter as a Template

To save time in creating future issues of your newsletter, save your newsletter as a template. To do this, delete all text, pictures, and objects that will not stay the same for future issues. Likewise, leave the nameplate and all text, pictures, symbols, and so on, that will remain (or use the same style) in each issue of your newsletter. For example, to save the Loaves & Fishes newsletter as a template, leave the following items and delete the rest:

- Folio (The month and volume/issue numbers will change, but the titles will remain—use the folio text as placeholder text.)
- Nameplate
- Subtitle
- Headline (The headline text will change, but the position and formatting will remain—use the headline text as placeholder text.)
- Byline (The byline text will change, but the position and formatting will remain—use the byline text as placeholder text.)
- Body text (The body text will change, but the formatting will remain—leave a paragraph as placeholder text.)

Exercise 8.9 Saving a Newsletter as a Template

1. Open **C08-E08-Loaves&FishesNewsletter.docx**, and complete the following steps to save it as a template (see Figure 8.16).
2. Typically you would delete all text and newsletter elements that will change with each issue (refer to the bulleted items in the preceding list). However, this can affect the placement of graphic placeholders in the document. Therefore, do not delete the paragraphs of text; instead, use them as placeholders for any new text you may insert for the next issue of the newsletter. Select the existing text and replace it with your new text.
3. Click the File tab and then click the Save As option.
4. At the Save As dialog box, select Word Template at the *Save as type* list box, type **C08-E09-Loaves&FishesNewsletterTemplate** in the *File name* text box, click Save, and then close the dialog box. ***Note: Consult your instructor if you should save this template to your hard drive or to another drive.***
5. To use the template, click the File tab and then click the New tab.
6. At the New tab Backstage view, click *New from existing* in the *Available Templates* section, browse to locate **C08-E09-Loaves&FishesNewsletterTemplate.dotx**, and then click Create New.
7. Select and replace text that needs to be updated. Delete any placeholder text when necessary.

Figure 8.16 Exercise 8.9

Chapter *Summary*

➤ Newsletter elements divide the newsletter into organized sections to help the reader understand the text. Basic newsletter elements include a nameplate, subtitle, folio, headline, subhead, byline, and body copy.

➤ The nameplate, or banner, consists of the newsletter's title and is usually located on the front page.

➤ A subtitle is a short phrase describing the purpose or audience of the newsletter.

➤ A folio is the publication information, including the volume number, issue number, and the current date of the newsletter.

➤ Headlines are titles to articles and are frequently created to attract the reader's attention.

➤ Subheads, or subheadings, are secondary headings that provide the transition from headlines to body copy.

➤ The byline identifies the author of an article.

➤ The main part of the newsletter is the body copy or text.

➤ If you plan to create a multiple-paged newsletter with facing pages, you may want to use the Word mirror margin feature, which accommodates wider inside or outside margins.

➤ Graphic images are added to newsletters to help stimulate ideas and add interest to the document.

➤ To speed up scrolling in your document and/or reduce the size of your document, you may replace the graphic at the document screen with a picture placeholder, reduce the image resolution, or discard unwanted cropped parts of an image.

➤ Focus and balance can be achieved in a newsletter through the design and size of the nameplate, through the use of graphic images, and through careful use of lines, borders, and backgrounds.

- The margin size for a newsletter is linked to the number of columns needed, the formality desired, the visual elements used, and the amount of text available. Keep margins consistent in a newsletter.
- The line length of text in a newsletter can enhance or detract from the readability of the text.
- Section breaks are used to vary the page layout within a single newsletter.
- Setting text in columns may improve the readability of newsletters.
- The Word default leading is equal to approximately 120 percent of the type size used.
- Tombstoning occurs when headings display side by side in adjacent columns.
- The last page of columns can be balanced by inserting a continuous section break at the end of the text.
- Indent paragraphs in a newsletter with em spaces (approximately 24 pt or 0.25 inch).
- Change the leading between lines of type by clicking options at the Paragraph Spacing Built-In drop-down list. You can access these options by clicking the Change Styles button in the Styles group in the Home tab.
- Styles assist in maintaining consistency in recurring elements.
- When formatting instructions contained within a style are changed, all of the text to which the style has been applied is automatically updated.
- Styles are created for a particular document and are saved with the document.
- Use the Microsoft Office Picture Manager program to edit images by removing red eye, changing colors, improving brightness and contrast, straightening, and cropping.
- To establish consistency from one issue to the next and to save time, you can save your newsletter as a template.

Commands Review

FEATURE	RIBBON TAB, GROUP	BUTTON	KEYBOARD SHORTCUT
Align Text Left	Home, Paragraph		Ctrl + L
Align Text Right	Home, Paragraph		Ctrl + R
Apply Styles	Home, Styles, More		Ctrl + Shift + S
Center	Home, Paragraph		Ctrl + E
Character spacing	Home, Font dialog box launcher, Advanced tab		Ctrl + D
Column Break	Page Layout, Page Setup	Breaks	
Columns	Page Layout, Page Setup		
Compress Pictures	Picture Tools Format, Adjust	Compress Pictures	
Continuous Break	Page Layout, Page Setup	Breaks	
Horizontal Line	Home, Paragraph		

FEATURE	RIBBON TAB, GROUP	BUTTON	KEYBOARD SHORTCUT
Justify	Home, Paragraph		Ctrl + J
Line Spacing	Home, Paragraph		
Margins	Page Layout, Page Setup		
Microsoft Office Picture Manager	Start, All Programs, Microsoft Office, Microsoft Office 2010 Tools, Microsoft Office Picture Manager		
Page Break	Insert, Pages		
Windows Fax and Scan	Start, All Programs, Windows Fax and Scan		
Windows Paint	Start, All Programs, Accessories, Paint		

Reviewing Key Points

True or False: Select the correct answer by circling T or F.

1. A folio provides information that describes the purpose of the newsletter and/or the intended audience of the newsletter.

    T   F

2. Column formatting affects the entire document unless your document is divided into sections.

    T   F

3. The last page of columns can be balanced by inserting a column break at the end of the text.

    T   F

4. Tombstoning occurs when headings display side by side in adjacent columns.

    T   F

5. To speed up scrolling in your document, you may replace the graphic at the document screen with a picture placeholder, compress the picture, or remove cropped areas from the image.

    T   F

6. If a headline contains two lines both typed in 36 points, the default spacing between the two lines (leading) should be increased to improve readability.

    T   F

7. After a style has been created, the only way to change the style is to rename it and create it again.

    T   F

Assessment 8.3 Merging in a Newsletter

In this assessment, you will open a Word document and then use the Mail Merge Wizard to merge an Access database. You will print two copies of the Naper Grove newsletter created in Assessment 8.2 and then print the document in Figure 8.18 on the back of the newsletter after merging a data source to the address section of the page. To create the merge, complete the following steps:

1. Print two copies of the Naper Grove newsletter, **C08-A02-Eyes.docx**.
2. Open **NGAddressMain** from your *Chapter08* folder.
3. Display the Mailings tab, click the Start Mail Merge button down arrow, and then click the *Step by Step Mail Merge Wizard* option.
4. At the first wizard step at the Mail Merge task pane, make sure *Letters* is selected in the *Select document type* section, and then click the <u>Next: Starting document</u> hyperlink located at the bottom of the task pane.
5. At the second wizard step, make sure *Use the current document* is selected in the *Select starting document* section, and then click the <u>Next: Select recipients</u> hyperlink.

Figure 8.18 Assessment 8.3 Sample Solution

6. At the third wizard step, click *Use an existing list* in the *Select recipients* section, and then click the <u>Browse</u> hyperlink in the *Use an existing list* section. Select the Access database named **NaperGrovePatients** located in your *Chapter08* folder.

7. At the Mail Merge Recipients dialog box, make sure all of the records are selected (a check box should display next to each row), and then click OK.

8. Click the <u>Next: Write your letter</u> hyperlink located at the bottom of the Mail Merge task pane.

9. Position your insertion point inside the text box that displays at the right of the clip art at the bottom of the page, and then click the <u>Address block</u> hyperlink.

10. At the Insert Address Block dialog box, make sure the address elements include First name, Last name, Address, City, State, Zip, and then click OK.

11. At the fourth wizard step, click the <u>Next: Preview your letters</u> hyperlink.

12. At the fifth wizard step, click the <u>Next: Complete the merge</u> hyperlink.

13. At the sixth wizard step, click the <u>Edit individual letters</u> hyperlink located in the *Merge* section.

14. At the Merge to New Document dialog box, make sure *All* is selected, and then click OK.

15. Save the merged letters and name the document **C08-A03-NGAddresses**.

16. Print the first and last merged letter to the back of each of the two copies of **C08-A02-Eyes.docx**.

17. At the next wizard step, save the edited main document with the same name, **C08-NGAddressMain**.

18. Close **C08-NGAddressMain.docx**.

19. Close **C08-A03-NGAddresses**, and then fold each newsletter with the address displaying on the outside—ready to mail.

Assessment 8.4   Recreating a Newsletter

As a group project, assign tasks for each of the members of your group to evaluate the newsletter in this exercise, discuss the necessary changes, and then recreate the document. Open and then print a copy of **ButterfieldGardens** located in your *Chapter08* folder. Assume you received this newsletter in the mail as a marketing promotional document. The newsletter looks relatively neat and organized, but with closer inspection, you notice there are a few errors in spelling, formatting, and layout and design. Recreate the newsletter according to the following specifications, using your own ideas for an interesting newsletter layout and design:

1. Prepare a thumbnail sketch of your design.

2. Recreate the nameplate or create a nameplate (logo, subtitle, folio) of your own for this company; consider using WordArt in your nameplate design. ***Hint: The Butterfield Gardens logo is located in your Chapter08 folder.***

3. Create a different layout and design for the newsletter using newspaper columns. Use more than one column in an asymmetrical design or consider using a template from the Microsoft Office.com templates website.

4. Correct all spelling and formatting errors. ***Hint: There are several errors in the data file.***

5. Use any graphics or scanned images that support your design. Consider using a graphic or photo from the Internet.

6. Consider inserting a SmartArt object, shape, chart, or Quick Parts.

7. Use any newsletter elements and enhancements that will improve the effectiveness and appeal of this newsletter. ***Hint: Remember to kern character pairs and condense or expand characters.***

8. Save your publication, and name it **C08-A04-Butterfield**.

9. Print and then close **C08-A04-Butterfield.docx**. Attach the thumbnail sketch to the back of the newsletter. ***Hint: Use your own ideas for the newsletter.***

Chapter 9

Using Design Elements to Enhance Newsletters

Performance Objectives

Upon successful completion of Chapter 9, you will be able to:

- Define and create design elements that enhance newsletters.
- Create headers and footers.
- Insert a table of contents into a newsletter.
- Create a masthead.
- Insert Quick Parts for sidebars and pull quotes.

- Define and create kickers and end signs.
- Insert a jump line.
- Add captions to pictures.
- Save a newsletter in HTML, and view it in an Internet browser.

Desktop Publishing Terms

Caption	HTML	Scanner
Copyfitting	Jump line	Screening
End sign	Kicker	Sidebar
Footer	Masthead	Spot color
Header	Pull quote	Table of contents

Word Features Used

Borders and Shading	Linking text boxes	Quick Parts
Building Blocks	Newspaper columns	Styles
Caption dialog box	Page Numbering	Symbols
Character spacing	Paragraph spacing	Templates
Headers and footers	Picture	Text boxes
Line spacing	Print 2 pages per sheet	Web Page Preview

Chapter 8 introduced you to the basic elements of a newsletter. Additional elements can be used to enhance the visual impact of a newsletter and to provide the reader with clues to the newsletter content. Newsletter-enhancing elements such as a table of contents, headers/footers, mastheads, pull quotes, kickers, sidebars, captions, ruled lines, jump lines, graphics, illustrations, photos, and end signs are discussed in this chapter.

Adding Visually Enhancing Elements to a Newsletter

The most effective newsletters contain an appealing blend of text and visual elements. As illustrated in Figure 9.1, visual elements such as a table of contents, pull quote, kicker, and sidebar can be used as focal points to tempt the intended audience into reading more than just the nameplate. Visual elements such as headings, subheads, table of contents, headers/footers, ruled lines, jump lines, and end signs can be used to indicate the directional flow of information in the document. Visual elements such as headings, subheads, headers/footers, pull quotes, sidebars, and page borders can be used to provide balance, proportion, and contrast in a newsletter. All of these elements, if used in a consistent format and manner, can create unity within a single newsletter and among different issues of a newsletter.

Formatting a Newsletter Using Columns, Text Boxes, and Tables

The majority of newsletters are formatted in a two- or three-column page layout. As discussed in Chapter 8, columns may be equal in width, providing a symmetrical design, or they may be unequal in width, providing an asymmetrical design. There are three ways to create the appearance of columns in a newsletter page layout—newspaper columns, text boxes, or tables. Your challenge is to determine which method will work best to achieve the desired results in your newsletter.

Figure 9.1 **Visually Enhancing Elements in a Newsletter**

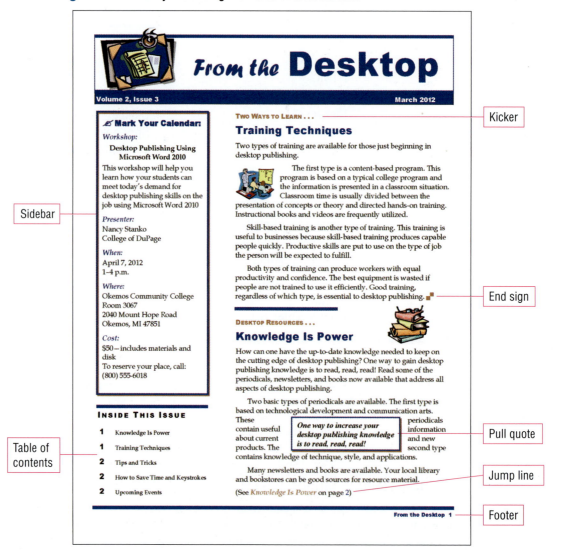

Using the Columns feature may seem like an obvious choice, especially when creating newsletters similar to those displayed and created in Chapter 8. However, placing text within text boxes or tables allows you to more easily change the position or shape (height and width) of an article, as is so often required when trying to copyfit text in a newsletter. For example, in the newsletter in Figure 9.1, a text box with a shadow border was used to create the sidebar (a Quick Parts sidebar could have been used, too); a table with a top border was used to create the table of contents (a Quick Parts table of contents could have been used). The second column was created by placing each article within a separate table. The dark blue line was drawn using a Line Shape to act as a visual separator between the two articles (tables). In this case, tables were the preferred method because of the graphic and pull quote that were contained in the articles. In a table, text will wrap around a graphic or text box, whereas text will not wrap around these elements if the original text is also contained within a text box. As compared to text boxes, however, tables are not as easy to position and may produce unpredictable results when inserting text boxes within the table.

As another example, look at Figure 9.6, shown later in this chapter. To accommodate the "Bicycle Safety" article (on page 1) and the text wrapping around the pull quote, the Columns feature was used to format the page into two uneven columns. All of the remaining articles and features are contained in text boxes. When using any of these methods to format a newsletter, pay special attention to the alignment of these elements in relation to the columns you are trying to create visually.

Using Templates from the Microsoft Office Online Templates Web Page

The Microsoft Office.com web page includes several newsletter templates, but this number may vary because templates are occasionally added to the collection. Figure 9.2 illustrates a list of templates available to you when you click *Newsletters* in the *Templates* section of the New Document dialog box. If you preview the templates in Word, you will find that most of the newsletters were created using linked text boxes. The text box method is efficient when you need to make adjustments for copyfitting an entire page or document. The size of each text box can be increased or decreased to fit more or less text, and the location of the boxes can be easily changed by dragging them to accommodate other elements in the newsletter.

The newsletter templates illustrated in Figure 9.2 are formatted using styles that reinforce consistency within the newsletter. In addition, the basic design and colors used in each newsletter stay consistent from page to page. As you can see in Figure 9.3, each newsletter includes many preformatted design elements such as banners, table of contents, pull quotes, picture captions, headers and footers, sidebars, and a placeholder for the recipient's address.

Creating Headers and Footers

Headers and/or footers are commonly used in newsletters, manuscripts, textbooks, reports, and other publications. The term *header* refers to text that is repeated at the top of every page. Alternately, the term *footer* refers to text that repeats at the bottom of every page. Headers and footers may be created from scratch at the Header & Footer pane using options on the Header & Footer Tools Design tab, or they may be inserted into a document by choosing Header or Footer Built-Ins or Quick Parts (also known as Building Blocks), which offer a variety of preformatted layout designs, text formatting, and content controls.

Header
Text repeated at the top of every page.

Footer
Text repeated at the bottom of every page.

Figure 9.2 Newsletter Templates at the New Tab Backstage View

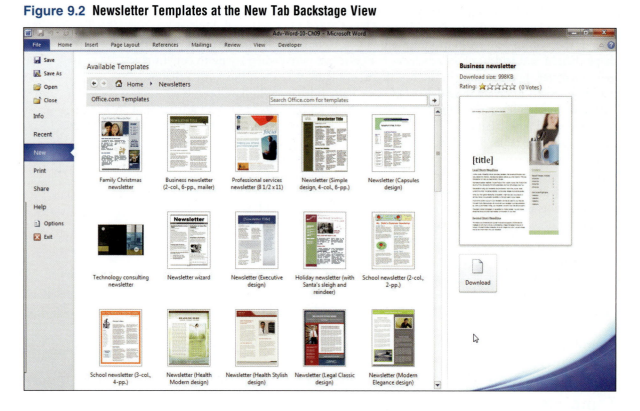

To create a header or footer at the Header & Footer pane, click either the Header or Footer button in the Header & Footer group on the Insert tab, and then click Edit Header or Edit Footer. Type the desired header text in the header pane. If you are creating a footer, click the Go to Footer button in the Navigation group on the Header & Footer Tools Design tab. Select various options to customize your header or footer, and then click the Close button.

Figure 9.3 Viewing Design Elements in Word Newsletter Templates

Business newsletter created in text boxes, in a 2-column layout, with 6 pages and a mailer

Email newsletter created in a table using Web Layout view

Business Newsletter

Business Email Newsletter

Business Email Newsletter

Business email newsletter created in a 2-column table, uneven layout with a narrow column on the left with background color and a wide column on the right with no background color, with hyperlinks

Holiday newsletter created in text boxes in a 2-column layout with a dots theme; includes a header, pull quote, and 6 pages

Holiday Newsletter with Poinsettia

Newsletter Template with Simple Theme

Newsletter template using text boxes

Newsletter template wizard using text boxes in a 2-column layout

Newsletter Wizard—Requires 2002 or Later

Newsletter template wizard using text boxes in a 4-column layout with 4 pages

Newsletter Template Wizard with Accessory Theme

Figure 9.4 Examples of Headers and Footers

TRAINING NEWS _____

Header Example

FINANCIAL SPOTLIGHT   NOVEMBER 2012
_____

Header Example

▽ ·· ***Winners wear helmets!***
  Header Example

Footer Example   ✈
_____
Page 2   ***Fly with Sunshine Air***

Footer Example
┌──┐
│ **Community News**   **3** │
└──┘

Footer Example
_____
                                                               3

In Figure 9.4, a thick blue horizontal line, the name of the newsletter, and the page number are included in a footer created manually in the footer pane. In a newsletter, it is common to place information such as a page number, a slogan, the name of the newsletter, the issue or date of the newsletter (field codes), and the name of the organization producing the newsletter in a header or footer as illustrated in the header and footer examples in Figure 9.4.

Because a header or footer is commonly repeated on every page starting with the second page, it provides the perfect place to reinforce the identity of a company or an organization. For example, including the company or organization name, a very small version of the nameplate, or a logo in a header or footer can increase a reader's awareness of your identity. In Figure 9.4, the Ride Safe header (the third header example) includes both the company logo and slogan, while the Community News footer includes the newsletter name and the page number.

Inserting Predesigned Headers and Footers

Building Blocks are accessed at both the Header or Footer Built-In galleries (click either the Header or Footer button on the Insert tab). Quick Parts (also known as Building Blocks), which are accessed by clicking the Quick Parts button, offer a variety of formatting and layout ideas. After a header or footer Building Block is customized to fit your needs, it will be saved to the document in which it was created. You also have the option to save it as a new Building Block added to the Building Blocks Organizer, where it will be available for use in other documents. To insert a header or footer Building Block, click the Header or Footer button on the Insert tab, and then select a sample from the Built-In galleries as shown in Figure 9.5.

DTP POINTERS ▶
Use a header or footer to reinforce company or organizational identity.

Figure 9.5 Inserting a Header or Footer Building Block

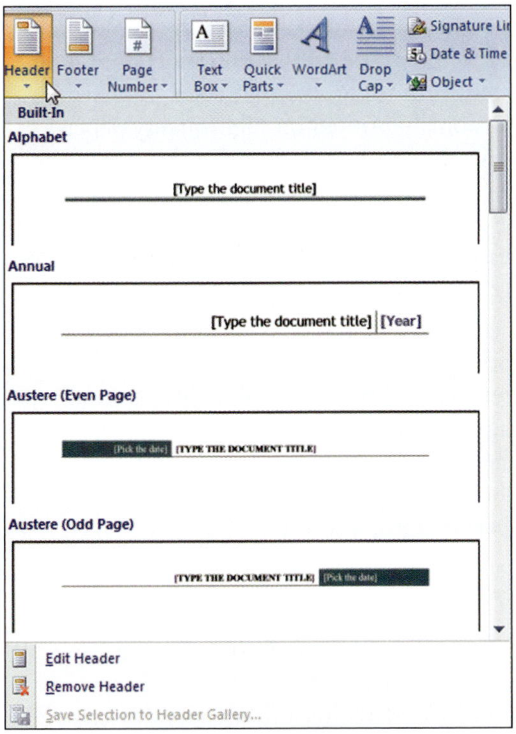

Header Building Blocks

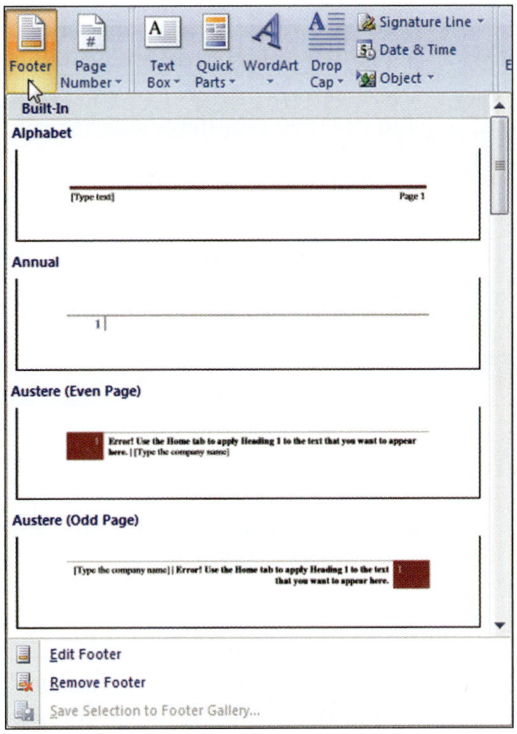

Footer Building Blocks

Placing Headers/Footers on Different Pages

By default, Word will insert a header and/or footer on every page in the document. You can create different headers and footers in a document. For example, you can do the following:

- Create a unique header or footer on the first page.
- Omit a header or footer on the first page.
- Create different headers or footers for odd and even pages.
- Create different headers or footers for sections in a document.

A different header or footer can be created on the first page of a document. To do this, position the insertion point anywhere in the first page, and then click to add a check mark in the *Different First Page* check box on the Header & Footer Tools Design tab. If you are creating a footer, click the Go to Footer button. The Header & Footer pane will be labeled First Page Header (or Footer). Type the text for the header or footer that will print on all but the first page, and then choose Close Header and Footer.

The ability to place different headers and footers on odd and even pages is useful when numbering pages in a multiple-paged newsletter. Odd page numbers can be placed on the right side of the page, and even page numbers can be placed on the left side of the page. For example, in a four-page newsletter, a footer can be created that includes right-aligned page numbering that will appear on the odd pages only. Alternately, another footer can be created that contains left-aligned page numbering that will appear on even pages only. To turn this feature on, display the Header & Footer Tools Design tab, and add a check mark next to *Different Odd & Even Pages* in the Options group.

Go to Header

Go to Footer

◀ **DTP POINTERS**
Consistent formatting of a header/footer helps to establish unity in a publication.

Using Spot Color

Spot color refers to using one other color, in addition to black, as an accent color in a publication. Using spot color can make a black-and-white publication more appealing. If you have a color printer, you can see the results of using a second color immediately. You can then take the newsletter to be professionally printed on high-quality paper. Using color always adds to the cost of a publication, so be sure to price this out in the planning stages of your document. The more colors used in a publication, the more expensive it is to produce. Spot color can be applied to such elements as graphic lines, graphic images, borders, background fill, headings, special characters, and end signs.

If your logo or organizational seal contains a particular color, use that color as a unifying element throughout your publication. You can also apply spot color to the background in a reverse text box or to a drop cap. Variations of a spot color can be obtained by ***screening***, or producing a lighter shade of the same color. Just as an all black-and-white page may appear gray, using too much spot color can change the whole "color" of the document, defeating the purpose of using spot color for emphasis, contrast, and/or directional flow. Refer to the two newsletter samples in Figure 9.6 to see how spot color can add to the visual appeal of a publication.

Using the Transparent Color Tool

The image used in the nameplate in Figure 9.6 was scanned professionally and copied to your student files in a file format that was compatible with Word 2010. Because of the bitmap file format in which it was saved, you cannot alter this image in Microsoft

Figure 9.6 Newsletter with and without Spot Color

With Spot Color   Without Spot Color

Word Picture (you cannot right-click on the image and click *Edit Picture*). However, you can alter the image by clicking the Set Transparent Color tool. This tool is accessible by clicking the Color button in the Adjust group in the Picture Tools Format tab as shown in Figure 9.7A. Remove the color from the image, making it transparent as shown in Figure 9.7B, and then add the color Red by clicking the Shading button in the Paragraph group in the Home tab as shown in Figure 9.7C. To make more sophisticated changes to a bitmap image, use a photo-editing program.

In the chapter exercises, you will build a two-page newsletter and add visual enhancements as you proceed. In addition, you will use copyfitting techniques and add spot color to the newsletter throughout the range of exercises. In Exercise 9.1, you will create a header and footer that will begin on the second page of the newsletter. You will also create a blank different first page header/footer so that the header and footer text will not print on the first page.

Note: Copy the **Chapter09** *folder from the CD that accompanies this textbook to your storage medium and then make* **Chapter08** *the active folder. Remember to substitute graphics that may no longer be available.*

Figure 9.7 **Using the Set Transparent Color Tool to Change Color in a Bitmapped Image**

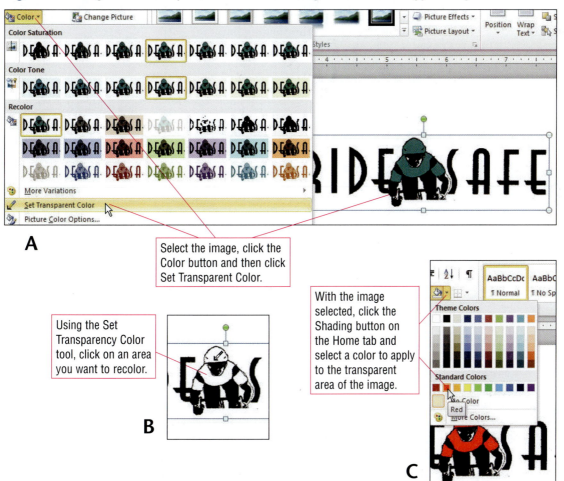

Exercise 9.1 Creating a Header and Footer in a Newsletter

1. Add a header and footer to the beginning stages of a newsletter, as shown on the second page of the Ride Safe newsletter in Figure 9.8, by completing the following steps:
   a. Open **NewsletterBanner** located in your *Chapter09* folder.
   b. Save the document with Save As and name it **C09-E01-Header&Footer**.
   c. Change the zoom to 75% and turn on the display of nonprinting characters.
   d. Select the month and year in the folio and type the current month and year.
   e. Select one of the dotted lines in the banner, click the Clipboard dialog box launcher button to display the Clipboard task pane, and then click the Copy button. (This line will be pasted into the header later.)

2. Change the spot color in the Ride Safe logo in the banner by completing the following steps:
   a. Select the Urban theme.
   b. Select the Ride Safe logo (cyclist with dark teal shirt and Ride Safe text) and then click the Color button in the Adjust group in the Picture Tools Format tab.
   c. Click the *Set Transparent Color* tool below the *Recolor* section, and then position the Set Transparent Color tool on the dark teal shirt in the logo, and then click. **Hint: The dark teal shirt should become transparent.**
   d. Click the down arrow at the right of the Shading button in the Paragraph group in the Home tab, and then select the *Teal, Accent 2, Lighter 40%* color.

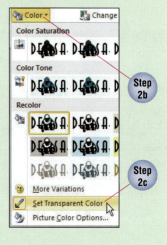

Step 2b

Step 2c

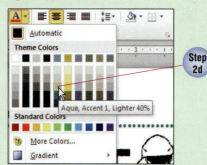

Step 2d

3. Create two uneven columns using the Columns feature by completing the following steps (These columns are being set up for some steps in future exercises and to avoid potential problems.):
   a. Press Ctrl + End to position the insertion point below the newsletter banner, and click the Columns button in the Page Setup group on the Page Layout tab.
   b. At the drop-down column list, select More Columns. At the Columns dialog box, select *Left* in the *Presets* section, change the spacing between the columns to **0.4"**, and then select *This point forward* in the *Apply to* list box. Click OK.

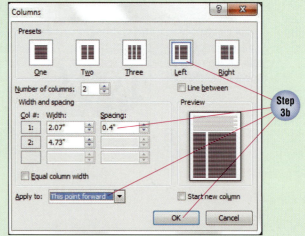

Step 3b

c. On the Page Layout tab, click the Breaks button, and then click *Column* from the drop-down list or press Ctrl + Shift + Enter.

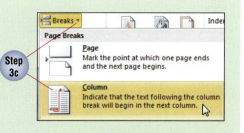

Step 3c

d. With the insertion point at the top of the second column, repeat the previous step to insert one more column break. This will produce a second page, which is necessary to produce the header and footer.

e. Press Ctrl + Home to position the insertion point at the beginning of the document.

4. Create a different first page header/footer by completing the following steps:

   a. Click the Header button in the Header & Footer group in the Insert tab, and then click Edit Header.

   b. On the Header & Footer Tools Design tab, add a check mark next to *Different First Page* in the Options group. **Step 4b** ***Hint: First Page Header – Section 1 should display in the header.***

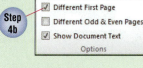

5. Create the header for the rest of the newsletter by completing the following steps:

   a. Click the Next button in the Navigation group. The header pane should be labeled Header – Section 2.

   b. Click the Link to Previous button to turn off this feature. ***Hint: If a prompt displays asking you to delete this header/footer and connect to the header/footer in the previous section, click No. You should not see the Same as Previous option displayed in the upper right corner of the header.***

Step 5a

Step 5b

   c. Click the Picture button in the Insert group.

   d. At the Insert Picture dialog box, browse to find the **Ridesf2teal** file located in your *Chapter09* folder, and then insert the file. ***Hint: This is a BMP (bitmapped) graphic file.***

6. Format the picture by completing the following steps:

   a. Click the Size dialog box launcher in the Picture Tools Format tab.

   b. Change the *Height* and *Width* options in the *Scale* section to **35%**. Click OK.

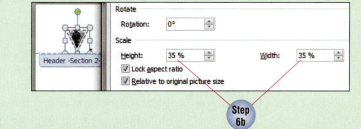

Step 6b

   c. Click once to the right of the image to deselect it.

7. Drag and draw a text box to the right of the Ride Safe logo that will accommodate the dotted line and slogan shown on page 2 of the newsletter in Figure 9.8. The text box should measure approximately **0.4"** by **6.75"**.

8. At the Drawing Tools Format tab, make the following changes:

   a. Click the Shape Outline button, and then select No Outline.

   b. Click the Position button in the Arrange group, and then click More Layout Options.

c. At the Layout tab, change the horizontal *Absolute position* option to **1.1"** and the *to the right of* option to *Page*, and change the vertical *Absolute position* option to **0.7"** and the *below* option to *Page*. Click OK.

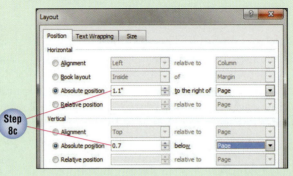

d. Click the Format Shape dialog box launcher at the bottom right corner of the Shape Styles group.

e. Click the Text Box option at the Format Shape dialog box.

f. Change the *Left* and *Right* margins in the *Internal margin* section to **0"**. Click Close.

9. Insert the dotted line and slogan by completing the following steps:

a. Click once inside the text box to position the insertion point.

b. Display the Clipboard task pane and click once on the dotted line item to insert it inside the text box. The line length will be adjusted in the following steps. Close the task pane.

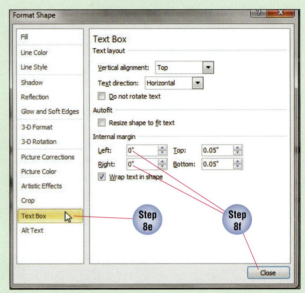

c. Position the insertion point in the middle of the dotted line, and then press Delete until the paragraph symbol displays at the end of the dotted line within the text box. Continue pressing the Delete key until there is approximately enough space at the end of the line to type the slogan within the text box.

d. Position the insertion point at the end of the dotted line, and then type **Winners wear helmets!** (If some of the text disappears, delete more of the dotted line until the entire slogan is visible.)

e. Select the slogan, and change the font to 11-point Tempus Sans ITC, bold, in Black.

f. With the text selected, display the Font dialog box and then select the Advanced tab. Click the down-pointing arrow in the *Position* list box, and select *Raised*. Make sure 3 pt displays in the *By* text box. (This raises the slogan to be in alignment with the dotted line.) Click OK.

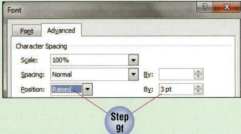

g. If the slogan wraps to the next line, delete more of the dotted line until the slogan fits in the text box. If you delete more than necessary, copy and paste more dots.

10. Create the footer that will begin on the second page by completing the following steps:
    a. Click the Go to Footer button in the Header & Footer group.
    b. If the *Same as Previous* option displays in the footer, click the Link to Previous button in the Navigation group to turn off this feature.
    c. Click the Page Number button in the Header & Footer group.
    d. Select *Bottom of Page*.
    e. Select *Dots* from the drop-down list.
    f. Click the Close Header and Footer button.
11. View the newsletter in Print tab Backstage view. Make sure no header or footer text displays on page 1 and the header and footer text correctly displays on page 2.
12. Save **C09-E01-Header&Footer**.
13. Close **C09-E01-Header&Footer.docx**, or keep the document open to continue with Exercise 9.2. *Hint: You may need to adjust the bottom margin if the footer does not print properly.*

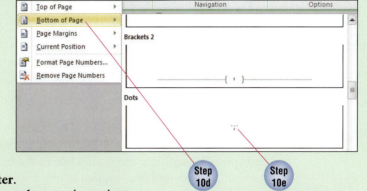

Figure 9.8 Exercise 9.1

Volume 5, Issue 2 · April 2012

RIDE SAFE

· Bicycle and In-Line Skating Safety for the New Millennium ·

Winners wear helmets!

Page 1   Page 2

Figure 9.9 Examples of Building Block Sidebars

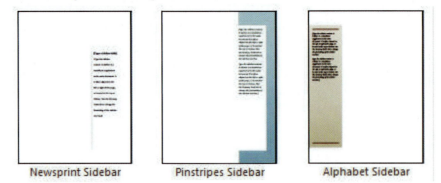

Newsprint Sidebar   Pinstripes Sidebar   Alphabet Sidebar

Look at **C09-E01-Header&Footer.docx** in the Print tab Backstage view and notice how the triangular logo in the header repeats the image of the bicyclist in the nameplate. In addition, the dotted line in the header on page 2 is consistent in style and color with the dotted lines located within the nameplate on page 1. The typeface used for the slogan is a youthful-looking typeface that reinforces the youthful message. The footer repeats the round bullet symbols found in the nameplate, the header, and the end signs, which will later be used within the body copy to indicate the end of an article. As you can see, headers and footers can provide a visual connection between the separate pages in a multiple-paged publication.

Creating Sidebars in a Newsletter

A *sidebar* is a block of information or a related story that is set off from the body text in some type of a graphics box. A sidebar can also include a photograph or a graphic image along with the text. Frequently, the sidebar contains a shaded or screened background. A screened (lighter) version of the main color used in a newsletter can serve as the background screen. The sidebar can be set in any position relative to the body text. In Word, sidebars can easily be created by using a text box and inserting text or by inserting predesigned built-in Text Boxes or Quick Parts. Examples of sidebars are shown in Figure 9.9.

In Exercise 9.2, you will create a sidebar using a text box and then position the text box at the left margin to set up the boundaries for the first column. The newsletter page layout will include two columns based on an underlying three-column grid. In later exercises, you will add more visually enhancing elements to the same newsletter.

Exercise 9.2 Inserting a Sidebar into a Newsletter

1. Insert a sidebar (containing the "In the Helmet Habit" feature) in the newsletter from Exercise 9.1, as shown in Figure 9.10, by completing the following steps:
    a. Open **C09-E01-Header&Footer.docx**, save the document with Save As, and name it **C09-E02-Sidebar**.
    b. Make sure the Urban theme has been selected.
    c. Change the zoom to 75%, and then turn on the display of nonprinting characters.
    d. Turn on kerning at 14 points.

e. Position the insertion point to the left of the first column break in the first column on page 1.

f. Drag and draw a text box that is approximately the same size and in the same position as the sidebar (see "In the Helmet Habit") shown in Figure 9.10.

g. Position the insertion point in the text box, and then insert **HelmetHabitText** located in your *Chapter09* folder. Do not be concerned if all of the text is not visible at this point.

h. Make sure the font size of the sidebar text is 10 points.

i. Change the height of the text box to **4.6"** and the width to **2.2"**.

j. Select the text box, click the Position button in the Arrange group, and then click More Layout Options.

k. At the Position tab, change the *Alignment* option in the *Horizontal* section to *Left* and the *relative to* option to *Margin*. In the *Vertical* section, change the *Absolute position* option to **3.3"** and the *below* option to *Page*. Click OK.

l. With the text box still selected, click the More button in the Shape Styles group, and then click the *Subtle Effect - Teal, Accent 2* effect.

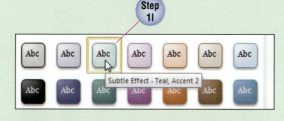

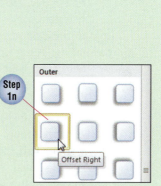

m. With the text box still selected, click the Shape Effects button in the Shape Styles group, and then click the *Shadow* option from the drop-down list.

n. Click the *Offset Right* shadow effect in the *Outer* section.

2. Format the text inside the sidebar by completing the following steps:

a. Position the insertion point at the beginning of the title *In the Helmet Habit*, and then press Enter.

b. Select *In the*, and then change the font to 12-point Times New Roman Bold Italic and the color to Teal, Accent 2.

c. Position the insertion point after *In the*, delete the space, and then press Enter.

d. Select *Helmet Habit*; change the font to 14-point Impact in Teal, Accent 2; and then expand the character spacing by 1.2 points. Click OK.

e. Position the insertion point within *In the*, display the Paragraph dialog box, and then change the *Line spacing* option to *Exactly* and the *At* option to 10 pt. Click OK.

f. Position the insertion point within the words *Helmet Habit*, and change the *After* setting to 6 pt.

3. For use in future issues, create styles for the sidebar heading by completing the following steps:

a. Position the insertion point within *In the* and click the Styles More button on the Home tab.

Step 3b

b. At the Styles gallery, click Save Selection as a New Quick Style.

c. At the Create New Style from Formatting dialog box, type **Sidebar Heading-1** in the *Name* text box. Click OK.

Step 3c

d. Position the insertion point anywhere within *Helmet Habit*, follow the preceding two steps, and name this style **Sidebar Heading-2**.

4. Position the insertion point after *. . . anyone!"* in the last line of the article text, press Delete to eliminate the extra hard return, and change the spacing *After* the paragraph to **6 pt**.

5. Insert the skater image by completing the following steps:

a. Deselect the text box and make sure your insertion point is not located in the text box containing the sidebar text.

b. Display the Clip Art task pane, type the keyword **in-line skating**, and then click Go. *Hint: Substitute the clip art if necessary or desired.*

Step 5b

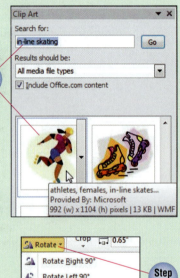

c. Click the image to insert the image into your newsletter. Do not be concerned if parts of your newsletter move out of place. Adjustments will be made in the next step.

6. Format the skater image by completing the following steps:

a. Select the skater image, click the Wrap Text button on the Picture Tools Format tab, and then click *In Front of Text*.

b. With the image selected, click the Rotate button in the Arrange group, and then click *Flip Horizontal*.

Step 6b

c. Use the corner sizing handles to reduce the size of the image so that it is similar to the skater image shown in Figure 9.10.

d. Click and drag the image so that it is overlapping the upper right corner of the sidebar text box as shown in Figure 9.10.

7. Save **C09-E02-Sidebar**.

8. Keep the document open if you are going to continue with the next exercise; otherwise, close **C09-E02-Sidebar.docx**. *Hint: This newsletter continues to build throughout the remaining chapter exercises. You only need to print when the newsletter is complete—after Exercise 9.9.*

Figure 9.10 Exercise 9.2, Page 1

Volume 5, Issue 2 • March 2012

RIDE SAFE

• Bicycle and In-Line Skating Safety for the New Millennium •

In the
Helmet Habit

"I don't quite know why my daughter, Kate, fell from her bike last July. Maybe she hit a small rock or just lost her balance. We found Kate lying on the ground. She was bleeding and had several cuts and bruises on her face and forehead. We called the paramedics and she began to lose consciousness just as they arrived. At the emergency room, we found out that Kate had a broken nose, a missing tooth, and four other loose teeth. Fortunately, for all of us, Kate was wearing a bicycle helmet. Without even asking, three different doctors have told us that the helmet probably saved Kate's life. Bicycle accidents can happen to anyone!"

Karen Brust
Boston, Massachusetts

Creating a Newsletter Table of Contents

A *table of contents* is optional in a one- or two-page newsletter. However, in multiple-paged newsletters, a table of contents is an important and necessary element. A table of contents lists the names of articles and features in the newsletter, along with their page numbers. The information in the table of contents greatly influences whether the reader moves beyond the front page. Consequently, the table of contents needs to stand out from the surrounding information. It must also be legible and easy to follow.

Table of contents
A list of articles and features and their page numbers.

Figure 9.11 Examples of Tables of Contents

A table of contents is usually located on the front page of a newsletter. It is often placed in the lower left or right corner of the page. It can, however, be placed closer to the top of the page on either side or even within an asymmetrically designed nameplate. If a newsletter is designed to be a self-mailer, the table of contents can be placed in the mailing section so the reader is invited into the newsletter before it is even opened. Figure 9.11 shows several examples of tables of contents.

The table of contents in Figure 9.12 is located in the lower left corner. The teal border, bullets, bold title, and numbers make the table of contents easily identifiable while adding visual interest to the page. The table of contents, along with the shadow box, also adds weight to the left side of the page and balance to the page as a whole.

There are many ways to format a table of contents to make it easy to find and visually interesting. As illustrated in Figure 9.12, a table of contents can easily be made by inserting text in a text box and then adding various borders, screened backgrounds, fonts, graphics, lines, reverse text, and special characters. You can also use paragraph borders and shading to highlight text in a table of contents.

Exercise 9.3   Inserting a Table of Contents in a Newsletter

1. Open **C09-E02-Sidebar.docx**.
2. Save the document with Save As and name it **C09-E03-TableofContents**.
3. Insert the table of contents text in a text box by completing the following steps:
   a. Draw a text box that is approximately the same size and in the same position as the table of contents text box shown in Figure 9.12.
   b. Position the insertion point in the text box, and insert the file **TableofContentsText** located in your *Chapter09* folder.
   c. Display the Drawing Tools Format tab, and then change the shape outline color to Teal, Accent 2.
   d. Change the line weight to **1½ pt**.
   e. Change the text box height to **1.9"** and the width to **2.2"**.

f. Click the Position button in the Arrange group, click the *More Layout Options* option, and then at the Position tab, change the *Alignment* option in the *Horizontal* section to *Left* and the *relative to* option to *Margin*. In the *Vertical* section, change the *Absolute position* option to **7.63"** and the *below* option to *Margin*. Click OK.

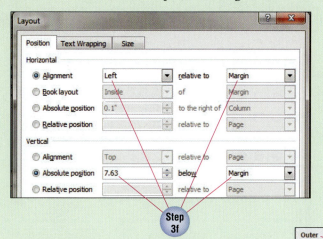

g. Click the Shape Effects button, click *Shadow* from the drop-down list, and then click the *Offset Right* effect in the *Outer* section.

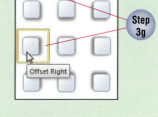

4. Format the table of contents title by completing the following steps:
   a. Select *In This Issue:*, apply the Subtle Reference style, and then change the font to 12-pt. Impact, *Expanded* by **1.2 pt**, and change the spacing *After* the paragraph to **8 pt**.

   b. Select the remaining text below the title and change the font to 11-point Times New Roman. ***Hint: Do not be concerned if some of the text is not visible at this point.***
   c. With the text still selected, change the spacing *After* the paragraph to **2 pt**.
   d. Change the *Line Spacing* option to Exactly and the *At* option to **12 pt**.

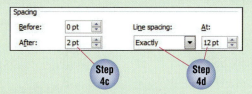

   e. With the text below the title still selecyed, click the down-pointing arrow at the right of the Bullets button in the Paragraph group on the Home tab, and then click the *Define New Bullet* option at the bottom of the Bullet Library.

f. At the Define New Bullet dialog box, click the Symbol button, choose the Wingdings font, and then select the last (round) bullet from the left in the eighth row (Wingdings: 159). Click OK to close the Symbol dialog box. *Hint: Type 159 in the Character code text box in the Symbol dialog box.*

Step 4f

g. With the text below the title still selected, click the down-pointing arrow at the right of the Bullets button, click Define New Bullet, click the Font button, and then change the bullet color to Teal, Accent 2. Click OK in both open dialog boxes.

h. Change the bullet position by clicking the Paragraph dialog box launcher button in the Paragraph group, and then at the Paragraph dialog box, change the *Left Indentation* setting to **0"** and the *Special Hanging* setting **By 0.3"**. Click OK.

Step 4h

i. Select each page number in the table of contents text box and change the font to Impact.

5. For use in future issues, create a style for the bulleted items in the table of contents by completing the following steps:

   a. Position the insertion point anywhere within the first bulleted item.

   b. Click the Styles More button, and then click the *Save Selection in a New Quick Style* option.

   c. At the Create New Style from Formatting dialog box, type **ToC Bullets** in the *Name* text box. Click OK.

Step 5c

6. Save **C09-E03-TableofContents**.

7. Keep the document open if you are going to continue with the next exercise; otherwise, close **C09-E03-TableofContents.docx**. *Hint: This newsletter continues to build throughout the remaining chapter exercises. You only need to print when the newsletter is complete—after Exercise 9.9.*

Figure 9.12 Exercise 9.3, Page 1

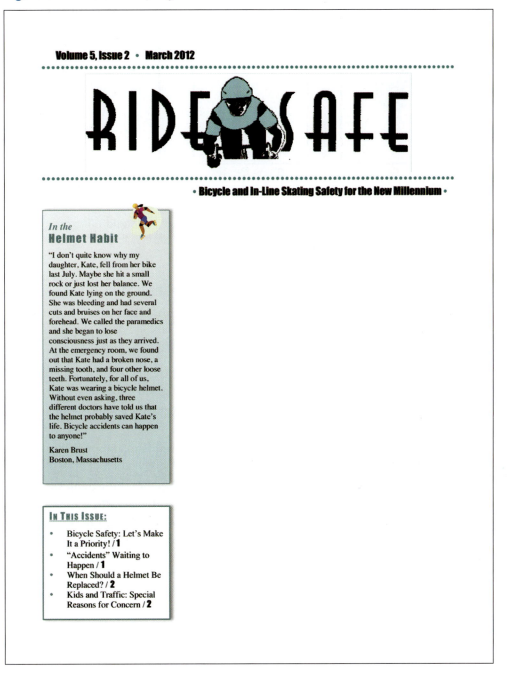

Creating Pull Quotes

A pull quote, as illustrated in Figure 9.13, acts as a focal point, helps to break up lengthy blocks of text, and provides visual contrast. A *pull quote* (also called a pullout or callout) is a direct phrase, summarizing statement, or important point associated with the body copy of a newsletter. Using pull quotes is an excellent way to draw readers into an article.

Pull quote

A short, direct phrase, statement, or important point formatted to stand out from the rest of the body copy.

Figure 9.13 Examples of Various Pull Quote Building Blocks

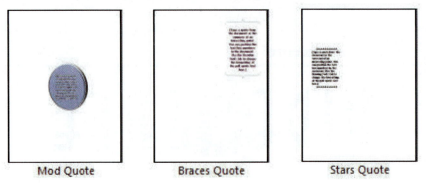

Mod Quote   Braces Quote   Stars Quote

Effective pull quotes are interesting, brief, and formatted to stand out from the rest of the body copy. Keep in mind the following tips when creating pull quotes for a newsletter:

- Include relevant and interesting text in a pull quote. Edit any direct quotes so they will not be taken out of context when read individually as a pull quote.

- Keep pull quotes brief—approximately 10 to 15 words and never longer than a few lines.

- Choose a font or font style that contrasts with the font used for the article text.

- Increase the type size.

- Vary the typestyle by bolding and/or italicizing the pull quote text.

- Set off the pull quote from the rest of the body text with ruled lines or a graphics box.

- Use at least one element in your pull quote design that establishes a visual connection with the rest of your newsletter.

- Be consistent. Use the same format for other pull quotes throughout the newsletter and throughout future issues of the same newsletter.

Figure 9.13 shows some different ways that pull quote formatting can be customized to attract the reader's attention. The oval and round rectangle were created using shapes. Various background fills were used including solid fill, textured fill, and gradient fill. The pull quote Building Block examples shown in Figure 9.13 are located in the Text Box Built-In gallery. Besides these predesigned pull quotes, you can create your own designs customizing text boxes or shapes.

In Exercise 9.4, you will insert the first newsletter article, format the article heading and article text, and create a pull quote. Because these particular elements may be repeated throughout the newsletter, you will then create styles for these elements.

DTP POINTERS
Pull quotes should be brief and interesting, and stand out from the rest of the text.

DTP POINTERS
Create styles for repetitive formatting.

Exercise 9.4 Creating Styles and a Pull Quote in a Newsletter

1. Open **C09-E03-TableofContents.docx**.
2. Save the document with Save As, and name it **C09-E04-PullQuote**.
3. Position the insertion point to the left of the column break in the second column, and then insert **BicycleSafetyText** located in your *Chapter09* folder.
4. Select the article heading *Bicycle Safety: Let's Make It a Priority!*, and make the following changes:
   a. Change the font to 18-point Impact, change the color to the teal color used earlier, and apply small caps (Ctrl + Shift + K). Make sure the Urban theme has been selected.
   b. Expand the character spacing by **1.2 pt**.
   c. Change the spacing after the paragraph to 6 points.
5. Create a style for future article headings by completing the following steps:
   a. Position the insertion point in the article heading.
   b. Click the Styles More button and then click Save Selection in a New Quick Style.
   c. At the Create New Style from Formatting dialog box, type **Article Head** in the *Name* text box. Click OK.

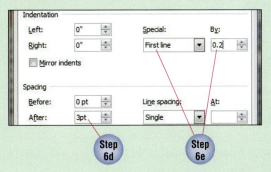

6. Format the article text by completing the following steps:
   a. Position the insertion point at the beginning of the line *Did you know . . .*, and select all of the article text.
   b. Change the font to 11-point Times New Roman.
   c. Click the Paragraph dialog box launcher button.
   d. At the Paragraph dialog box, change the spacing *After* the paragraph to **3 pt**.
   e. In the *Indentation* section, click the down-pointing arrow to the right of the *Special* option, select *First line*, and then change the *By* option to **0.2"** to indent the first line of each paragraph. Click OK.

7. With the article text still selected, create a style, and name it **Article Text**.

8. Create a style for the first paragraph of the article that eliminates the first line indentation by completing the following steps:
   a. Position the insertion point within the first paragraph of article text.
   b. Display the Paragraph dialog box, make sure the Indents and Spacing tab is selected, and then change the *Special* option to (*none*) in the *Indentation* section. Click OK.

Step 8b

   c. Create a style, name it **1st Paragraph**, and then press Enter.
9. Create a pull quote by completing the following steps:
   a. Click the Text Box button in the Insert tab, and then select the *Mod Quote* pull quote design from the Text Box Built-In gallery.

Step 9a

   b. Select the pull quote and then change the Shape Style to the *Light 1 Outline, Colored Fill - Teal, Accent 2* style.

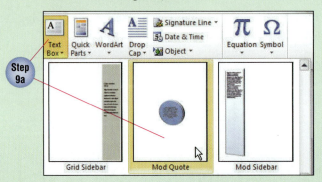
Step 9b

Light 1 Outline, Colored Fill - Teal, Accent 2

   c. Change the size of the pull quote by dragging the middle sizing handles until the pull quote measures approximately **2"** by **2.4"**.
   d. Position the insertion point in the pull quote, select the placeholder text, change the font to 9-point Georgia, bold, no italics and then type **"Over 500,000 trips a year are made to emergency rooms for bicycle-related injuries."** *Hint: You could select the text from the body text and paste it into the pull quote.*
   e. Drag the pull quote to a position similar to that shown in Figure 9.14.
10. In the last paragraph, select and bold *The bottom line?*. Then select and italicize the last sentence, *Bicycle safety is something we all need to make a priority!*.
11. Save **C09-E04-PullQuote**.
12. Keep the document open if you are going to continue with the next exercise; otherwise, close **C09-E04-PullQuote.docx**. *Hint: This newsletter continues to build throughout the remaining chapter exercises. You only need to print when the newsletter is complete— after Exercise 9.9.*

Figure 9.14 Exercise 9.4, Page 1

Volume 5, Issue 2 • March 2012

RIDE SAFE

• Bicycle and In-Line Skating Safety for the New Millennium •

In the
Helmet Habit

"I don't quite know why my daughter, Kate, fell from her bike last July. Maybe she hit a small rock or just lost her balance. We found Kate lying on the ground. She was bleeding and had several cuts and bruises on her face and forehead. We called the paramedics and she began to lose consciousness just as they arrived. At the emergency room, we found out that Kate had a broken nose, a missing tooth, and four other loose teeth. Fortunately, for all of us, Kate was wearing a bicycle helmet. Without even asking, three different doctors have told us that the helmet probably saved Kate's life. Bicycle accidents can happen to anyone!"

Karen Brust
Boston, Massachusetts

IN THIS ISSUE:

- Bicycle Safety: Let's Make It a Priority! / **1**
- "Accidents" Waiting to Happen / **1**
- When Should a Helmet Be Replaced? / **2**
- Kids and Traffic: Special Reasons for Concern / **2**

BICYCLE SAFETY: LET'S MAKE IT A PRIORITY!

Did you know that each year over 1,200 people die and thousands more are seriously injured in bicycle accidents? According to the American Academy of Pediatrics, more than 500,000 emergency room visits annually in the U.S. are attributed to bicycle accidents.

Surprisingly, most of these accidents, especially those involving children, occur on quiet residential streets. Most do not involve cars. And many could be prevented with proper training and safety equipment.

Think about it. Before we're allowed to drive a car, we have to be a certain age and go through extensive training and testing. Yet many of us—children in particular—ride the very same roads on a bicycle with little or no training at all. Kids are especially vulnerable because of their undeveloped peripheral vision (about two-thirds that of adults), poor speed judgment, and lack of a sense of danger. At Ride Safe, we believe bicycle safety education is crucial to our well-being and to that of our children.

The bottom line? *Bicycle safety is something we all need to make a priority!*

"Over 500,000 trips a year are made to emergency rooms for bicycle-related injuries."

Creating Kickers and End Signs

Additional elements, such as kickers and end signs, can also be used in a newsletter. A *kicker* is a brief sentence or phrase that is a lead-in to an article. Generally, it is set in a size smaller than the headline but larger than the body text. It is often stylistically distinct from both the headline and the body text. Kickers can be placed above or below the headline or article heading. In Figure 9.1, a kicker is placed above the first article heading and serves as a lead-in to the first article.

Kicker

A lead-in phrase or sentence that precedes the beginning of an article.

Symbols or special characters used to indicate the end of a section of text, such as the end of an article, are known as *end signs*. In Figure 9.1, an end sign follows the last paragraph in the first article. The end sign is the same color as the accent color in the newsletter to contribute to the unified appearance of this newsletter. The end sign in the Ride Safe newsletter, shown in Figure 9.15, mimics the dots in the nameplate, and the footer and the colors coordinate with the newsletter color scheme. Appropriate special characters or combinations of these characters—such as ℜ, ◎, ❀, ❖, ✪, and ✗, from the Wingdings and Webdings font selections—may be used as end signs.

In Exercise 9.5, you will add a kicker and an end sign to the Ride Safe newsletter you prepared in Exercise 9.4.

Exercise 9.5 — Creating a Kicker and an End Sign in a Newsletter

1. Open **C09-04-PullQuote.docx**.
2. Save the document with Save As, and name it **C09-E05-EndSign**.
3. Create the kicker by completing the following steps:
   a. Position the insertion point at the beginning of the first paragraph below the article heading.
   b. Type **Protect your child!**, and then press Enter.
   c. Select *Protect your child!*, and then change the font to 14-point Times New Roman bold italic.
4. Create a style for the kicker formatting by completing the following steps:
   a. Position the insertion point anywhere within the kicker.
   b. Create a style, and name it **Kicker**.
5. Create the end sign by completing the following steps:
   a. Position the insertion point after the paragraph mark at the end of the first article, and press the Tab key three times. ***Hint: Make sure italic formatting is turned off.***
   b. Click the Symbol button in the Symbols group in the Insert tab.
   c. Click More Symbols at the bottom of the drop-down gallery, and then select the Special Characters tab.
   d. Double-click the Em Dash selection and then select the Symbols tab.
   e. Change the *Font* option to *Wingdings 2* and double-click the ninth (round) bullet from the left in the eighth row (Wingdings 2: 152).
   f. Click the Special Characters tab again, double-click the Em Dash selection, and then click Close.
   g. Select the end sign and change the font to 11-point Impact. Select the round bullet, and change the color to Teal, Accent 2 (using the Urban theme).
6. Save **C09-E05-EndSign**.
7. Keep the document open if you are going to continue with the next exercise; otherwise, close **C09-E05-EndSign.docx**. ***Hint: This newsletter continues to build throughout the remaining chapter exercises. You only need to print when the newsletter is complete—after Exercise 9.9.***

Step 4b

Create New Style from Formatting

Name:
Kicker

Paragraph style preview:

Style1

OK   Modify...   Cancel

Figure 9.15 Exercise 9.5, Page 1

Volume 5, Issue 2 • March 2012

RIDE SAFE

• Bicycle and In-Line Skating Safety for the New Millennium •

BICYCLE SAFETY: LET'S MAKE IT A PRIORITY!

Protect your child!

Did you know that each year over 1,200 people die and thousands more are seriously injured in bicycle accidents? According to the American Academy of Pediatrics, more than 500,000 emergency room visits annually in the U.S. are attributed to bicycle accidents.

"Over 500,000 trips a year are made to emergency rooms for bicycle-related injuries."

Surprisingly, most of these accidents, especially those involving children, occur on quiet residential streets. Most do not involve cars. And many could be prevented with proper training and safety equipment.

Think about it. Before we're allowed to drive a car, we have to be a certain age and go through extensive training and testing. Yet many of us—children in particular—ride the very same roads on a bicycle with little or no training at all. Kids are especially vulnerable because of their undeveloped peripheral vision (about two-thirds that of adults), poor speed judgment, and lack of a sense of danger. At Ride Safe, we believe bicycle safety education is crucial to our well-being and to that of our children.

The bottom line? *Bicycle safety is something we all need to make a priority!* —●—

In the Helmet Habit

"I don't quite know why my daughter, Kate, fell from her bike last July. Maybe she hit a small rock or just lost her balance. We found Kate lying on the ground. She was bleeding and had several cuts and bruises on her face and forehead. We called the paramedics and she began to lose consciousness just as they arrived. At the emergency room, we found out that Kate had a broken nose, a missing tooth, and four other loose teeth. Fortunately, for all of us, Kate was wearing a bicycle helmet. Without even asking, three different doctors have told us that the helmet probably saved Kate's life. Bicycle accidents can happen to anyone!"

Karen Brust
Boston, Massachusetts

IN THIS ISSUE:

Using Linked Text Boxes in Newsletters

Newsletters routinely contain articles that start on one page and continue on another page. The text box linking feature makes it easier to create articles that are continued on subsequent pages. This feature allows text to flow from one text box to another even if the text boxes are not adjacent or on the same page. Any text box can be linked with any other text box. You need at least two text boxes to create a link; however, any number of text boxes can be used to create a chain of linked text boxes. For example, if your article starts on page 1, is continued on page 2, and then finishes on page 4, you can create a chain of three linked text boxes that will contain the article text. When the first text box is filled, the text automatically flows into the second text box, and then into the third text box in the chain. This is especially useful in editing and positioning an article that is continued on another page. If you add or delete text in one of the text boxes, the remaining text of the article in the other text boxes adjusts to the change also.

Furthermore, you can establish more than one chain of linked text boxes in a document. For example, you can create a chain of linked text boxes for an article that begins on page 1, and then continues on pages 3 and 4. For a different article in the same newsletter, which begins on page 2 and continues on page 4, you can create another chain of linked text boxes.

Creating the Link

To link text boxes, you must first create two or more text boxes. For example, if you have an article that begins on page 1 and is to be continued on page 2 of a newsletter, create a text box on page 1, and then create another text box on page 2. Size the text boxes to fit appropriately within the allotted column width, and then position the text boxes as desired. If necessary, additional size and position adjustments can be made after the text is added to the text boxes. To create a link between the two text boxes, complete these steps:

Create Link

1. Click the text box that is to be the first text box in the chain of linked text boxes.
2. On the Drawing Tools Format tab, click the Create Link button in the Text group. The mouse will display as a small upright pitcher. (You can also right-click on the text box and then click *Create Text Box Link* from the shortcut menu.)
3. Position the pitcher in the text box to be linked as shown in Figure 9.16. The pitcher appears tipped with letters spilling out of it when it is over a text box that can receive the link. Click once to complete the link.
4. To create a link from the second text box to a third text box, click the second text box, and then repeat steps 2 and 3. Repeat these steps to add more links to the chain.

Break Link

5. To break the chain of linked text boxes, click the Break Link button in the Text group on the Text Box Tools Format tab.

Figure 9.16 Linking Text Boxes

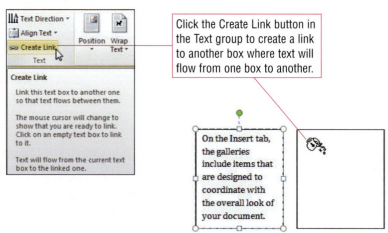

Click the Create Link button in the Text group to create a link to another box where text will flow from one box to another.

Creating Jump Lines

Featuring the beginning of several articles on the front page of a newsletter increases the chances of attracting readers. Also, some articles may just be too lengthy to fit on one page. You must, therefore, provide a way for your readers to know where to find the remainder of an article. A *jump line* in a newsletter is used to indicate that an article or feature continues on another page.

As an aid in the directional flow of information in a document, a jump line must be distinguishable from surrounding text so the reader can easily find it. A jump line is commonly set in small italic type, approximately 2 points smaller than the body copy type. As an option, jump lines can also be enclosed in parentheses.

Jump line

Text informing the reader that an article continues on another page or is being continued from another page.

Exercise 9.6   Creating Linked Text Boxes and a Jump Line in a Newsletter

1. Open **C09-C05-EndSign.docx**.
2. Save the document with Save As and name it **C09-E06-JumpLine**.
3. Insert linked text boxes by completing the following steps:
   a. Turn on the Show/Hide feature and then scroll to the bottom of page 1.
   b. Drag and draw a text box below the column break to hold the beginning of the second article. Adjustments will be made to the size and position of the text box in future steps as shown in Figure 9.17.
   c. Click to place the insertion point at the top of the first column on page 2, and then draw a text box to hold the remaining article text. Using the horizontal Ruler as a guide, limit the width of the text box to the column width in column 2. Adjustments will be made to the size and position of this text box in an upcoming exercise.
4. Create a link between the two text boxes so that text will automatically flow from one text box to another by completing the following steps:

   a. Select the first text box, and click the Create Link button on the Drawing Tools Format tab.
   b. Position the mouse, which now displays as an upright pitcher, in the second text box until it displays as a pouring pitcher, and then click once to complete the link.

   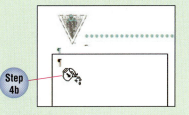

   c. Remove the shape outline in the first text box that is linked (at the bottom of page 1, second column).
   d. In the Size group, change the *Height* option of the text box to **1.6"**, and change the *Width* option to **4.7"**.
   e. Drag the text box to a position similar to that shown in Figure 9.17.
   f. Change the text box internal margins to **0"**.

   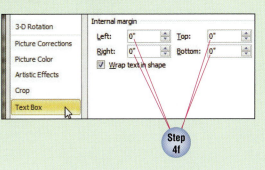

   g. Click once inside the first text box to position the insertion point, and insert the file **AccidentText** located in your *Chapte09* folder.

h. Check the text box on page 2 and make sure the remaining article text is visible. If not, use the sizing handles to enlarge the box.

i. Position the insertion point anywhere in the title *"Accidents" Waiting to Happen*, and then apply the Article Head style. ***Hint: If the Article Head style does not display in the Quick Styles gallery, click the Styles More button or press Alt + Ctrl + Shift + S to display the Styles list box.***

5. Format the article text by completing the following steps:

a. Position the insertion point at the beginning of the line *The majority of bicycle-car "accidents"...*, hold down the Shift key, and press Ctrl + End to select all of the article text in both text boxes. ***Hint: The text in the second text box will not be highlighted even though it is really selected.***

b. With the text selected, apply the Article Text style from either the Quick Styles gallery or the *Styles* drop-down list.

c. Position the insertion point anywhere in the first paragraph, and apply the 1st Paragraph style.

6. Create a jump line by completing the following steps:

a. Position the insertion point at the end of the first paragraph and press Enter twice.

b. Change the paragraph alignment to *Align Text Right*.

c. Access the Symbol dialog box, change the font to *Wingdings 3*, insert the second (triangle) symbol from the left in the sixth row (Wingdings 3: 113), and then click Close.

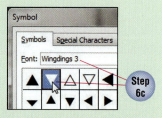

Step 6c

d. Press the spacebar once, type **See ACCIDENTS on page 2**. If the beginning of the second paragraph is visible below the jump line, press Enter to force this text to appear at the beginning of the linked text box on page 2.

e. Select *See*, and apply italics.

f. Select *ACCIDENTS*, and apply bold.

g. Select *on page 2*, and apply italics.

h. Select the entire jump line, and change the font to 10-point Times New Roman.

i. Make sure the *After* option in the *Spacing* section is set to **3 pt**.

Step 6i

7. Create a Quick Parts entry of the formatted jump line by completing the following steps. ***Note: A Quick Parts entry is created here instead of a style because the jump line contains mixed formatting and text that can be used in other jump lines.***

a. Select the entire jump line, including the triangle symbol.

b. Click the Quick Parts button in the Insert tab, and then click Save Selection to Quick Part Gallery.

Step 7b

c. At the Create New Building Block dialog box, type **jump line** in the *Name* text box, and then click OK.

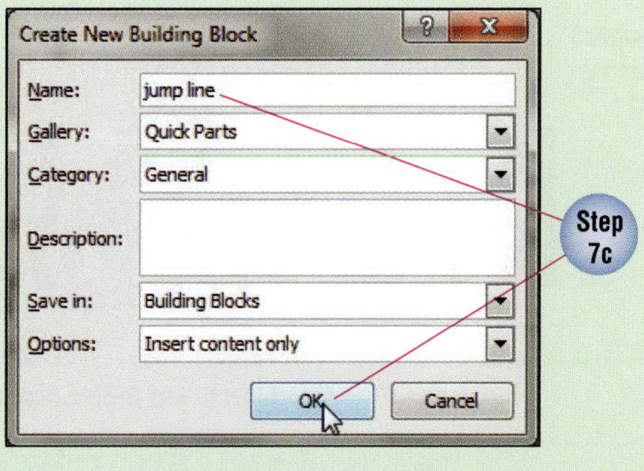

Create New Building Block

Name:	jump line
Gallery:	Quick Parts
Category:	General
Description:	
Save in:	Building Blocks
Options:	Insert content only

OK   Cancel

Step 7c

8. Insert the image of the man riding a bicycle by completing the following steps:
    a. Position the insertion point to the left of the column break.
    b. Display the Clip Art task pane, type the keyword **bicycle** or **cyclist** in the *Search for* text box, or choose a different image if necessary. Insert the image. Close the task pane.

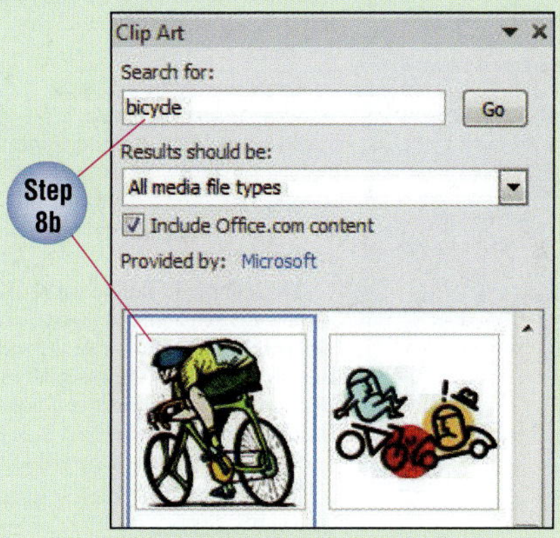

Clip Art

Search for:
bicycle   Go

Results should be:
All media file types
☑ Include Office.com content
Provided by: Microsoft

Step 8b

c. Select the image, and change the *Text Wrap* to *In Front of Text*.
d. Size and position the image as shown in Figure 9.17.
e. Select the image, click the Color button in the Adjust group, and then click the *Teal, Accent color 2 Dark* effect in the *Recolor* section.

Teal, Accent color 2 Dark

Step 8e

9. Save **C09-E06-JumpLine**.
10. Keep the document open if you are going to continue with the next exercise; otherwise, close **C09-E06-JumpLine.docx**. *Hint: This newsletter continues to build throughout the remaining chapter exercises. You only need to print when the newsletter is complete—after Exercise 9.9.*

Figure 9.17 Exercise 9.6, Page 1

Volume 5, Issue 2 • March 2012

RIDE SAFE

• Bicycle and In-Line Skating Safety for the New Millennium •

In the Helmet Habit

"I don't quite know why my daughter, Kate, fell from her bike last July. Maybe she hit a small rock or just lost her balance. We found Kate lying on the ground. She was bleeding and had several cuts and bruises on her face and forehead. We called the paramedics and she began to lose consciousness just as they arrived. At the emergency room, we found out that Kate had a broken nose, a missing tooth, and four other loose teeth. Fortunately, for all of us, Kate was wearing a bicycle helmet. Without even asking, three different doctors have told us that the helmet probably saved Kate's life. Bicycle accidents can happen to anyone!"

Karen Brust
Boston, Massachusetts

IN THIS ISSUE:

*   Bicycle Safety: Let's Make It a Priority! / **1**
*   "Accidents" Waiting to Happen / **1**
*   When Should a Helmet Be Replaced? / **2**
*   Kids and Traffic: Special Reasons for Concern / **2**

BICYCLE SAFETY: LET'S MAKE IT A PRIORITY!

Protect your child!

Did you know that each year over 1,200 people die and thousands more are seriously injured in bicycle accidents? According to the American Academy of Pediatrics, more than 500,000 emergency room visits annually in the U.S. are attributed to bicycle accidents.

Surprisingly, most of these accidents, especially those involving children, occur on quiet residential streets. Most do not involve cars. And many could be prevented with proper training and safety equipment.

"Over 500,000 trips a year are made to emergency rooms for bicycle-related injuries."

Think about it. Before we're allowed to drive a car, we have to be a certain age and go through extensive training and testing. Yet many of us—children in particular—ride the very same roads on a bicycle with little or no training at all. Kids are especially vulnerable because of their undeveloped peripheral vision (about two-thirds that of adults), poor speed judgment, and lack of a sense of danger. At Ride Safe, we believe bicycle safety education is crucial to our well-being and to that of our children.

The bottom line? *Bicycle safety is something we all need to make a priority!* ——•——

"ACCIDENTS" WAITING TO HAPPEN

The majority of bicycle-car "accidents" are not really accidents, but avoidable collisions. Most result from the bicyclist's failure to use proper riding techniques in a hazardous situation. Ironically, when asked, most children injured in traffic could describe the actual law they broke.

▼ *See ACCIDENTS on page 2*

Scanner

Equipment that converts a photograph, drawing, or text into a compatible digital file format that can be retrieved in specific programs.

Using Scanned Images in a Newsletter

Non-computer-generated images, such as photographs, illustrations, and diagrams, can be included in a newsletter through the use of a scanner and compatible scanner software. A *scanner* and its associated software convert a photograph, drawing, or text into a compatible digital file format that can be retrieved into Word. You may also use a digital camera and compatible digital camera software to convert photographs into compatible file formats that may be inserted into Word. See Chapter 5 for a brief discussion of this process.

One important factor to keep in mind is that you must get permission to use artwork, photos, or illustrations before you can legally scan them into a document. This includes artwork from the Web, even though you do not see the traditional copyright symbol. You may type the keywords **free graphics** or **free clip art** in a Web search engine to find a large selection of graphics that you are free to use. When you purchase clip art and stock photography, you generally buy the right to use it and even modify it, but you may not resell the images themselves as hard copy or computer images. When purchasing these items, read the copyright information provided in the front of the accompanying documentation.

If you want to include a photograph in a newsletter and a scanner is not available, you can insert a placeholder, such as a text box, in your newsletter. You can then print your newsletter, paste a photograph into the area reserved by the text box, and have a commercial printer duplicate your newsletter.

When trying to determine if your photographs should be scanned professionally, keep the following two points in mind:

- If you do not need high-quality output, using images scanned from a desk model scanner is acceptable.
- If you need high-quality output, use a service bureau to have your photos professionally scanned into your newsletter.

DTP POINTERS
Find out about copyright restrictions on any images you want to scan and request permission, if necessary.

Using Captions

Think of all the times you pick up a newspaper, newsletter, or magazine. How often do you look at a photograph and immediately read the accompanying explanation? Many graphic images can stand on their own; however, most photographs, illustrations, and charts need to be explained to the reader. Remember that your reader's eyes are automatically drawn to images or elements that stand out on the page. Adding an explanation to your image or photo quickly gives your reader an idea of what is going on, as shown in the sample captions in Figure 9.18. It may even entice your reader to

Figure 9.18 Caption Examples

Figure A Cape Town, South Africa

Safari at Lion Sands

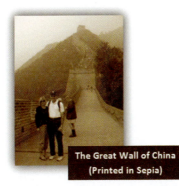

The Great Wall of China
(Printed in Sepia)

One Person Paying				
Enter the following amounts			Total	
Meal cost before tax	$16.27		Meal	$16.27
Tip percentage	18%		Tax	$1.43
Tax on the meal	$1.43		Subtotal	$17.70
			Tip	$2.93
			Total	$20.63

Table 1 Using a Tip Calculator

read the corresponding article. Descriptions or explanations that accompany graphic images, illustrations, or photographs are referred to as ***captions***.

Captions should explain their associated images while at the same time establish a connection to the body copy. Make the caption text different from the body text by bolding and decreasing the type size slightly. Legibility is still the key. Keep captions as short as possible, but make sure you explain those items that readers will see and wonder about. Also, be consistent throughout your document.

Elements, such as a Word picture, Word table, Excel worksheet, PowerPoint presentation, PowerPoint slide or graph, and so on, can be labeled and numbered using captions. (See Word Help or a Word reference manual for more information on this feature.) This type of captioning is very useful when creating detailed reports or publications such as a year-end financial statement, technical instructional manual, or research analysis. If elements do not have to be numbered, such as photographs in a newsletter, the easiest way to create a caption is to position the insertion point below the element and then type and format the desired caption.

Using the Picture Caption Feature

To create a picture caption, right-click on the graphic, choose *Insert Caption*, or select the graphic and click the Insert Caption button on the References tab. The Caption dialog box opens. At the Caption dialog box, look in the *Caption* box and notice that numbering has been automatically inserted. Click after the numbering, and type a descriptive caption if desired as shown in Figure 9.19.

Customizing Captions

At the Caption dialog box, you can exclude a label from a caption, change the Position of the caption from *Below selected item* or from *Above selected item*, delete a label, create a new label, change the numbering style, or add an AutoCaption. However, you do not have to use the Insert Caption feature to create captions. You can simply type the desired text in a text box or shape and then apply the Caption paragraph style to it; however the captions will not be automatically numbered.

Figure 9.19 **Caption Dialog Box**

Select the image, click the Insert Caption button, and then type the caption text in the Caption text box.

Exercise 9.7 Inserting a Caption for a Picture in a Newsletter

1. Open **C09-E06-JumpLine.docx**.
2. Save the document with Save As, and name it **C09-E07-Picture**.
3. Insert a text box that will contain the title by completing the following steps:
   a. Press Ctrl + End to position the insertion point at the top of page 2, and then press Ctrl + Shift + Enter to position the insertion point at the top of the right column.
   b. Drag and draw a text box at the top of the second column that measures **0.5"** inch by **4.5"**. *Note: You may have to resize the linked text box in the first column on the second page.*
   c. Remove the shape outline from the text box.
   d. Click once in the text box in the right column to position the insertion point.
   e. Type **Who Says Helmets Aren't Cool?** (Insert the arrow symbols at the front and end of the heading using the Wingdings font, the tenth and eleventh symbols from the left in the eleventh row—Wingdings: 201 and 202.)

   f. Drag and position the text box as shown in Figure 9.20.
   g. If the text box in column 1 and the text box just inserted in column 2 overlap each other, reduce the width of the text box in the first column so that it is approximately the same width as the column width. Use the horizontal Ruler as a guide.
   h. Apply the Article Head style to *Who Says Helmets Aren't Cool?* Center the text horizontally.
4. Insert a picture by completing the following steps:
   a. With the insertion point located at the top left corner of page 2, insert a photograph similar to the picture displayed in Figure 9.20. *Hint: Type* **cyclist** *in the* **Search** *for text box.*
   b. Change the *Wrap Text* to *In Front of Text*.
   c. Select the picture, and size it to approximately **2.5"** inches in height by **4.5"** in width. *Hint: You will need to increase the size of your picture and then crop any unnecessary areas of the picture to size it to measure 2.5" by 4.5".*

   d. Click the Compress Picture button in the Adjust group, click to add a check mark at the left of the *Delete cropped areas of the pictures* option in the *Compression options* section, and then click OK.

   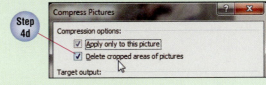

   e. Add a picture border or Picture Style (Simple Frame, White, or your choice).
   f. Position the image as shown in Figure 9.20.

5. Create a picture caption by completing the following steps:
   a. Select the picture, right-click, and then select *Insert Caption*.
   b. At the Caption dialog box, make sure *Figure 1* displays in the *Caption* text box, and then click OK.
   c. With the insertion point inside the caption text box and to the right of *Figure 1*, insert the file **PictureText** located in your *Chapter09* folder.

Step 5a

6. Select the text that you just inserted and verify that the font is 10-point Times New Roman, bold, and italic. Also, click after *Figure 1* and add a colon and two spaces.
7. Save **C09-E07-Picture**.
8. Keep the document open if you are going to continue with the next exercise; otherwise, close **C09-E07-Picture.docx**. *Hint: This newsletter continues to build throughout the remaining chapter exercises. You only need to print when the newsletter is complete—after Exercise 9.9.*

Figure 9.20 Exercise 9.7, Page 2

Figure 9.21 **Examples of Masthead Designs**

From the ▭▭▭ **Desktop**

Editor:	**Martha Ridoux**

Design and Layout:
Grace Shevick

Contributing Authors:
Jonathan Dwyer
Nancy Shipley
Christine Johnson

Published Monthly by:
DTP Training, Inc.
4550 North Wabash St.
Chicago, IL 60155
312 555-6840
Fax: 312 555-9366
http://www.emcp.net/dtp

©Copyright 2012 by:
DTP Training, Inc.
All rights reserved.

From the ▭▭▭ **Desktop**

Editor:
Martha Ridoux

Design and Layout:
Grace Shevick

Authors:
Jonathan Dwyer
Nancy Shipley
Christine Johnson

Published Monthly by:
DTP Training, Inc.
4550 North Wabash St.
Chicago, IL 60155
312 555-6840
Fax: 312 555-9366
http://www.emcp.net/dtp

©**Copyright 2012 by:**
DTP Training, Inc.
All rights reserved.

Creating a Newsletter Masthead

The ***masthead*** is a newsletter element that contains the publication information of the newsletter. A masthead (see Figure 9.21) usually contains the following items:

- Company or organization (producing the newsletter) name and address
- Newsletter publication schedule, such as weekly, monthly, or biannually
- Names of those contributing to the production of the newsletter, such as editor, authors, and graphic designers
- Copyright information
- A list of persons contributing to the production of a newsletter and other general publication information

The masthead may also contain a small logo, seal, or other graphic identifier. Although a masthead is commonly located on the back page of a newsletter, you will sometimes find it on the first page. Wherever you decide to place the masthead, be consistent from issue to issue in the masthead design, layout, and location.

Masthead
A newsletter element that contains the publication information of the newsletter.

◄**DTP POINTERS**
Be consistent in the design, layout, and placement of the masthead from issue to issue.

1. Open **C09-E07-Picture.docx**.
2. Save the document with Save As and name it **C09-E08-Masthead**.
3. Insert a predesigned quote text box to hold the masthead text by completing the following steps:
   a. Position the insertion point at the beginning of the second page of the newsletter.
   b. Click the Text Box button in the Insert tab and click *Tiles Quote* at the drop-down gallery.

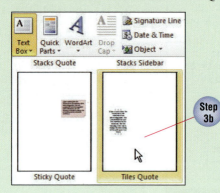

   c. Drag the text box to the bottom left corner of page 2 to a location similar to that shown in Figure 9.22.
   d. Size the text box to measure 3.4" in height and 2.2" in width.
   e. With the text box selected, apply the *Subtle Effect – Teal, Accent 2* effect in the Shape Styles gallery.

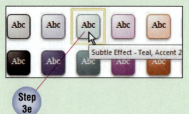

   f. Click once inside the text box to position the insertion point and then insert the file **MastheadText** located in your *Chapter09* folder.
   g. Delete the Enter after the last line of text and before the bottom three dots in the quote text box design.
4. Save **C09-E08-Masthead**.
5. Keep the document open if you are going to continue with the next exercise; otherwise, close **C09-E08-Masthead.docx**. *Hint: This newsletter continues to build throughout the remaining chapter exercises. You only need to print when the newsletter is complete— after Exercise 9.9.*

Figure 9.22 Exercise 9.8, Page 2

WHO SAYS HELMETS AREN'T COOL?

Research indicates that 60% of all U.S. bicycle-car collisions occur among bicyclists between the ages of 8 and 12. Children are permitted to travel with only "*look both ways before you cross the street*" and "*make sure you stop at all stop signs*" warnings. Obviously, these "warnings" are not enough.

Figure 1: Certainly not the children of Silverton, Oregon! One of the biggest reasons children don't wear bicycle helmets is because their friends don't wear them. By getting all the children in your school or neighborhood to order bicycle helmets at the same time, you can help turn this peer pressure from negative to positive. Suddenly, wearing a bicycle helmet becomes the "cool" thing to do. With your support, your kids can be "cool," too!

Winners wear helmets!

Ride Safe

Editor:
Brandon Keith
Design and Layout:
Cassie Lizbeth
Authors:
Chris Urban
Justine Youssef
Amanda Knicker
Published quarterly by:
Ride Safe, Inc.
P.O. Box 888
Warrenville, IL 60555
800-555-RIDE
Fax: 630-555-9068
© Copyright 2012 by:
Ride Safe, Inc.
All rights reserved.

2

Using Additional Enhancements for Starting Paragraphs

In Chapter 6, you learned about the drop cap feature. This design element is often used to indicate the beginning paragraph of a new article. Other types of paragraph enhancements can also be included in a newsletter. The following is a short list of paragraph enhancements—you may think of many more:

- Set the first few words of the beginning paragraph in all caps.
- Set the first line of the beginning paragraph in all caps.
- Set the first word of the beginning paragraph in small caps.

- Set the first line of the beginning paragraph in color.
- Use a larger type size with more leading in the first line of the beginning paragraph.

Understanding Copyfitting

Publications such as magazines and newsletters contain information that varies from issue to issue. Though there is structure in how the articles or stories are laid out on the page (such as the unequal two-column format in the Ride Safe newsletter), there may be times when more or less text is needed to fill the page. Making varying amounts of text or typographical enhancements fit in a fixed amount of space is referred to as *copyfitting*.

Copyfitting Suggestions

Many copyfitting techniques have been used in the exercises throughout this textbook. Some copyfitting suggestions include the following:

To create more space:

- Reduce the margins.
- Change the alignment.
- Change the typeface, typestyle, or size, but limit body type size to a minimum of 9 points, preferably 10 or 11 points.
- Reduce the spacing before and after paragraphs (or hard returns) to reduce the spacing around the nameplate, headlines, subheads, frames, or text boxes.
- Reduce the spacing between paragraphs.
- Turn on hyphenation.
- Condense the spacing between characters.
- Reduce the leading (line spacing) in the body copy.
- Remove a sidebar, pull quote, kicker, or end sign.
- Edit the text, including rewriting and eliminating sections.

To fill extra space:

- Increase the margins.
- Change the alignment.
- Change font size, but limit body type size to a maximum of 12 points.
- Increase the spacing between paragraphs.
- Adjust the character spacing.
- Increase the leading (line spacing) in the body copy.
- Increase the spacing around the nameplate, headlines, subheads, text boxes, or graphic images.
- Add a sidebar, pull quote, kicker, end sign, graphic lines, clip art, photo, etc.
- Add text.

Be consistent when making any copyfitting adjustments. For example, if you increase the white space after a headline, increase the white space after all headlines. Alternatively, if you decrease the type size of the body copy in an article, decrease the point size of all body copy in all articles. Adjustments are less noticeable when done uniformly. Also, adjustments often can be very small. For instance, rather than reducing type size by a whole point, try reducing it by 0.25 or 0.5 point.

Chapter Nine

In the Ride Safe newsletter created in the previous exercises, adjustments were made to the typeface, type size, typestyle, spacing above and below the article headings, spacing between paragraphs, spacing within the paragraphs (leading), and size and position of text boxes. In the next exercise, you will position the linked text box and add two more articles to the second page of the Ride Safe newsletter. You will also apply styles and insert a clip art image. These articles are selected and adjusted to "fit" into the remaining space.

Exercise 9.9 Adding Articles, Applying Styles, and Using Copyfitting Techniques

1. Add two articles and complete the "continued" article on the second page of the newsletter from Exercise 9.8, as shown in Figure 9.23, by completing the following steps (Make your own minor adjustments if necessary to fit the articles in their respective locations.):
   a. Open **C09-E08-Masthead.docx**.
   b. Save the document with Save As, and name it **C09-E09-Newsletter**.
   c. To make room for the article "The Light Bulb Test" at the beginning of page 2, click and drag the linked text box located on page 2 that contains the remaining text from the "Accidents" article to just above the Ride Safe pull quote, as shown in Figure 9.23. This text box will be formatted in future steps.
   d. Position the insertion point at the top of page 2, and then drag and draw a text box to hold the article, "The Light Bulb Test."
   e. Remove the shape outline and shape fill.
   f. Change the size of the text box to **3.65"** in height and **2.4"** in width.
   g. Drag the text box to a position similar to Figure 9.23.
   h. Change the internal margins of the text box to **0"**.
   i. Click once inside the text box to position the insertion point, and then insert the file **LightBulbText** located in your *Chapter09* folder.

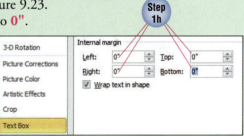

   j. Position the insertion point in the heading *The Light Bulb Test*, and apply the Article Head style.
2. Insert the light bulb image by completing the following steps:
   a. Position the insertion point between *Light* and *Bulb* in the heading, and press the spacebar one time.
   b. With the insertion point positioned between the two spaces, display the Clip Art task pane, type the keywords **light bulb** in the *Search for* text box, and select a similar image.
   c. Insert the light bulb image, which will be quite large, and it will appear that your article text has disappeared. This will be corrected in the next step.
   d. Select the light bulb image, and size it similar to the image shown in Figure 9.23. Make sure the light bulb is small enough so that your article heading fits on one line, and the article text fits within the text box.

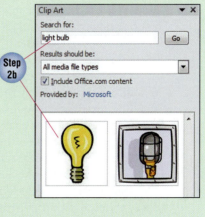

e. Position the insertion point in the first paragraph, and apply the 1st Paragraph style.

f. Position the insertion point in the second paragraph, and apply the Article Text style.

3. Create the end sign at the end of the article by completing the following steps:

a. On page 1, select the end sign at the end of the first article, and then click Copy.

b. Position the insertion point at the end of the article "The Light Bulb Test," press the spacebar three times, and then click the Paste button.

4. Select the linked text box that contains the remaining text from the "Accidents" article and make the following changes at the Drawing Tools Format tab:

a. Remove the shape outline and shape fill.

b. Change the size of the text box to **2"** in height and **2.4"** in width.

c. Drag the text box to a position similar to that shown in Figure 9.23.

d. Change the internal text box margins to **0"**.

5. Insert and format the "continued" jump line at the beginning of the text in the linked text box by completing the following steps:

a. Position the insertion point at the beginning of the text in the linked text box.

b. Click the Quick Parts button in the Text group in the Insert tab and then click *jump line* located in the *General* section of the *Quick Parts* drop-down list.

c. Delete the word *See*.

d. Select the word *on*, and type **from**.

e. Select the number *2*, and type **1**.

6. Insert the line above the jump line by completing the following steps:

a. Position the insertion point in the jump line, display the Page Layout tab, and then click the Page Borders button in the Page Background group.

b. At the Borders and Shading dialog box, select the Borders tab, and then click to add a 1-pt. black line at the top of the diagram in the *Preview* section. Make sure no borders display on the remaining sides of the diagram. Click OK.

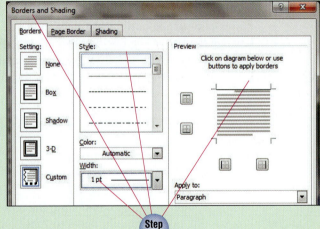

7. Copy and paste the end sign from the article "The Light Bulb Test" to the end of this article. (Drag the masthead text box downward slightly if necessary.)

8. Save **C09-E09-Newsletter**.

9. Insert an article in the remaining space in the second column by completing the following steps:

a. Drag and draw a text box to hold the article "When Should a Helmet Be Replaced?" that is approximately the same size and in the same location as shown in Figure 9.23.

b. Remove the shape outline and shape fill.

c. Change the text box height to **4.1"** and the width to **4.5"**.

d. Drag the box to a position similar to that shown in Figure 9.23.

e. Change the internal margins to **0"**.

f. Click once inside the text box to position the insertion point, and insert the file **ReplaceHelmetText** located in your *Chapter09* folder.

10. Apply styles to the article text just inserted by completing the following steps:

a. Position the insertion point in the title *When Should a Helmet Be Replaced?*, and then apply the Article Head style.

b. Select all of the paragraph text and apply the 1st Paragraph style.

11. Insert the bullet and emphasize the text at the beginning of each paragraph by completing the following steps:

a. Select the article text.

b. Click the Bullets button in the Paragraph group in the Home tab.

c. Click the Decrease Indent button in the Paragraph group to move the bullets to the edge of the text box.

d. Select the first sentence in each bulleted paragraph and change the font to 11-point Impact. ***Hint: Hold down the Ctrl key as you selected each beginning sentence and then apply bold or use the Format Painter.***

12. Scroll through the newsletter, and make any copyfitting adjustments that may be necessary.

13. Save **C09-E09-Newsletter.docx**.

14. View the document in Print tab Backstage view.

15. Print both pages of the Ride Safe newsletter using duplex printing by clicking the *Manually Print on Both Sides* option in the *Settings* section.

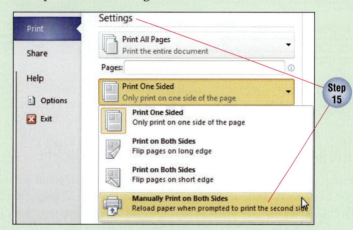

16. Print both pages again, but this time print them on one sheet of paper by completing the following steps:

a. Click the File tab, and then click the Print tab.

b. Click the down-pointing arrow at the right of the *1 Page Per Sheet* option at the bottom of the drop-down list in the *Settings* section.

c. Click the *2 Pages Per Sheet* at the drop-down list. Click the Print button. ***Hint: Make sure the first page prints on the left side of the paper and the second page prints on the right side of the paper—click the File tab, and then click the Options button. Click the Advanced button, and then clear the check mark in the check box next to* Print pages in reverse order *in the* Print *section. Click OK. Alternatively, turn off the* Reverse Order *option at your Printer Properties dialog box, but do not do both. By turning off the feature at both locations, you will actually turn on the feature.***

d. Return the print options to the default settings.

Figure 9.23 **Exercise 9.9, Pages 1 and 2**

Alternative Approaches to Saving a Newsletter

Saving a newsletter as a template reinforces consistency and promotes uniformity from issue to issue. If your newsletter includes a customized page-layout, modified styles, and placeholders, you may want to save the document as a template. If you are concerned about the cost of printing and distributing a newsletter, you can post your newsletter on a website or send it to your customers via email. If there is a possibility that your customers may not have Word, you can save your newsletter in PDF format and send it via email.

Saving Your Newsletter as a Template

To save time when creating future issues of your newsletter, save it as a template document. To save it as a template, delete all text, text boxes, pictures, objects, and so on, that will not stay the same for future issues. Likewise, leave all text, pictures, symbols, text boxes, and headers and footers that will remain the same in each issue of your newsletter. All styles created for the newsletter will remain with the template. For example, to save the Ride Safe newsletter as a template, leave the following items and delete the rest:

- Folio
- Nameplate
- Headers and footers
- Sidebar with the title because this will be a feature article every month (delete the sidebar article text only)

- Table of contents and heading (delete the table of contents text only)
- Masthead
- Remaining text boxes (delete the articles within each text box; the text boxes will most likely need to be reformatted each time you create a new issue of your newsletter, but they serve as a basic framework for future issues.)

After you have deleted the text and elements that will change every month, add placeholder text if desired, and then save the newsletter with Save As. At the Save As dialog box, click the down-pointing arrow at the right of the *Save as type* list box and select *Word Template* as the file type. Double-click the template folder in which you want to save your newsletter template (consult your instructor as to where to save your template—to your hard drive or to the DTP Templates folder), type a name for your newsletter template, and then click Save.

Sending a Newsletter as an Email Attachment

Imagine that you are the owner of a small business and would like to inform your customers of new products, upcoming sales or special promotions, and articles that may be of interest to them. You are thinking of preparing a monthly newsletter; however, you do not want the added expense of duplicating the newsletter and the cost of postage necessary to send the document. In addition, you do not have a website for your business so the prospect of posting the newsletter online is not viable. You would like to send the newsletter to your customers via email; however, you cannot be certain that all of your customers will have access to Microsoft Word. What can you do to ensure that your customers can read the newsletter when it is sent to them as an email attachment? See Figure 9.24 for an example of an email newsletter.

◀ DTP POINTERS
Email newsletters should be brief— typically no more than 1000 words in length.

Figure 9.24 Email Newsletter

HTML
Hypertext Markup Language is a formatting and organizational language ideal for displaying text, simple graphics, and hyperlinks on the Internet.

MHTML
A file format that creates a single file out of a web page that might ordinarily require support files—also known as .mht or Single File Web Page.

You may use Word 2010 to save your newsletter in PDF format and then send it as an email attachment. The PDF file format captures all of the elements of a printed document as an electronic image that you can view, print, and forward.

Viewing a Newsletter on the Web

You can save a newsletter formatted in Word in a web format such as ***HTML*** or ***MHTML*** that allows you to view the document in a web browser. If the newsletter is formatted in a table, the structure of the newsletter will stay in place when it is viewed on the Web.

Figure 9.25 Saving a Document in HTML Format

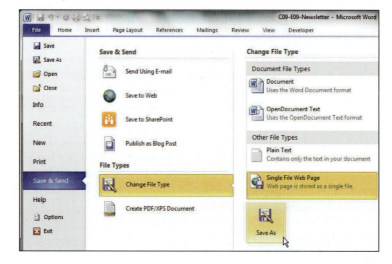

Figure 9.26 Adding the Web Page Preview Button to the Quick Access Toolbar

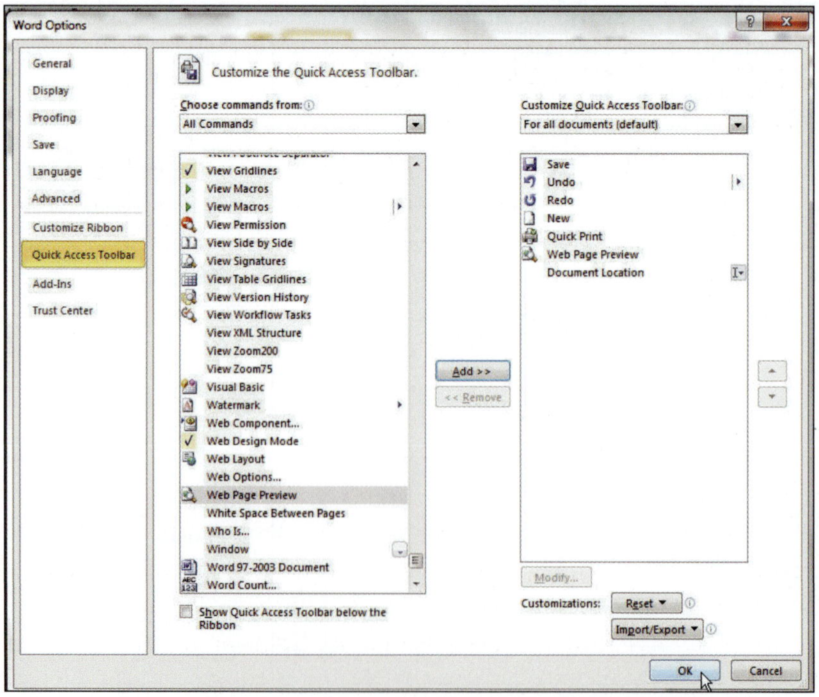

To save a newsletter in HTML, click the File tab and then the Save & Send tab. At the Save & Send Backstage view, click the *Change File Type* option in the *File Types* section, click the *Single File Web Page* option, and then click the Save As button as shown in Figure 9.25. At the Save As dialog box, type the *File name*, specify where you want to save document, enter a page title at the Enter Text prompt, click OK, and then click Save.

To view the newsletter in a web browser, add the Web Page Preview button to the Quick Access toolbar by clicking the Customize Quick Access Toolbar button at the end of the Quick Access Toolbar, click the *More Commands* option, click the down-pointing arrow at the right of the *Choose commands from* section, click All Commands, click the Web Page Preview button from the drop-down list, click Add, and then click OK as shown in Figure 9.26. Open the newsletter in Word and then click the Web Page Preview button to view the document as it would display on a web page in your chosen browser.

◄ **DTP POINTERS**
Create a newsletter in a table format for better viewing on a Web page.

Chapter *Summary*

➤ Elements can be added to a newsletter to enhance the visual impact, including table of contents, headers and/or footers, masthead, pull quotes, kickers, sidebars, captions, ruled lines, jump lines, page borders, and end signs.

➤ Use spot color—a color in addition to black—in a newsletter as an accent to such features as graphic lines, graphic images, borders, backgrounds, headings, and end signs.

➤ Headers and footers are commonly used in newsletters. Headers/footers can be placed on specific pages, only odd pages, or only even pages, and they can include page numbering, a slogan, a logo, or a horizontal ruled line.

➤ A sidebar is set off from the body text in a text box and can include a photograph or graphic image along with text.

➤ A sidebar may be created from scratch using a text box and adding enhancements to the text box or you may insert a predesigned sidebar found in the Text Box Built-In gallery or Building Blocks Organizer.

➤ In multiple-paged newsletters, a table of contents is an important element and is generally located on the front page in the lower left or right corner.

➤ A pull quote acts as a focal point, helps to break up lengthy blocks of text, and provides visual contrast.

➤ A pull quote may be created from scratch or you may insert a predesigned pull quote (Building Block) from the Text Box Built-In gallery or from the Building Blocks Organizer.

➤ A masthead is a repeating element that usually contains the company address, newsletter publication schedule, names of those contributing to the production, and copyright information. It is generally located on the back page of a newsletter.

➤ A kicker is typically set in a smaller type size than the headline but larger than the body text and is placed above or below the headline or article heading.

➤ Symbols or special characters used to indicate the end of a section of text are called end signs.

➤ In a newsletter, jump lines indicate a continuation of an article or feature on another page, which enables the newsletter to feature the beginning of several articles on the front page.

➤ Graphic images, illustrations, charts, diagrams, and photographs can add focus, balance, proportion, contrast, directional flow, and consistency to a newsletter.

➤ Non-computer-generated images such as photographs and illustrations can be scanned and inserted in a newsletter.

➤ Captions may be added to images to establish a connection to the body copy. Bold caption text and set it in a smaller point size to make it different from the body text.

➤ Predesigned Word captions may be added to an image, table, or graphic or you may create your own design from scratch using a text box.

➤ Copyfitting refers to making varying amounts of text or typographical enhancements fit in a fixed amount of space.

➤ Newsletters may be formatted in columns, tables, or text boxes.

➤ To continue an article created on one page of a newsletter to another page, use linked text boxes and jump lines.

➤ Newsletters may be saved in HTML, added to a web page, and then viewed in Web Page Preview.

➤ A newsletter may be saved and then sent as an email attachment. If the recipient does not have Word, the newsletter may be saved in PDF file format, then opened and viewed by using Adobe Reader. You cannot edit a PDF file in Word; however, you can edit a PDF file using Adobe Acrobat.

➤ Newsletters are often saved as templates to save time when creating future issues of the newsletter.

➤ Multiple pages can be printed on a single sheet of paper by selecting the *Pages per sheet* option in the *Settings* section of the Print tab Backstage view.

➤ All styles created for the newsletter remain with the newsletter document or template.

➤ Formatting a newsletter in a table structure holds the newsletter design elements in place when viewed in a web page.

Commands Review

FEATURE	RIBBON TAB, GROUP	BUTTON	KEYBOARD SHORTCUT
Break Link	Drawing Tools Format, Text	Break Link	
Captions	References, Captions or Right-click, Insert Caption		
Column Break	Page Layout, Page Setup	Breaks	Ctrl + Shift + Enter
Columns	Page Layout, Page Setup		
Different First Page	Header & Footer Tools Design, Options	Different First Page	
Footer	Insert, Header & Footer		
Go to Footer	Header & Footer Tools Design, Navigation		
Go to Header	Header & Footer Tools Design, Navigation		
Header	Insert, Header & Footer		
Link Text Boxes	Drawing Tools Format, Text	Create Link	

FEATURE	RIBBON TAB, GROUP	BUTTON	KEYBOARD SHORTCUT
Link to Previous	Header & Footer Tools Design, Navigation	Link to Previous	
Next Section	Header & Footer Tools Design, Navigation	Next	
Page Numbers	Header & Footer Tools Design, Header & Footer		
Previous	Header & Footer Tools Design, Navigation	Previous	
Quick Parts	Insert, Text		
Style list box	Home, Styles More		Alt + Ctrl + Shift + S
Symbol	Insert, Symbols	Ω	
Web Page Preview	Quick Access Toolbar		

Reviewing *Key Points*

A.	Caption	F.	Jump line	K.	Sidebar
B.	Copyfitting	G.	Kicker	L.	Spot color
C.	End sign	H.	Masthead	M.	Printer
D.	Footer	I.	Pull quote		
E.	Header	J.	Scanner		

Completion: In the space at the left, provide the correct letter or letters from the above list that match each definition.

_____ 1. A repeating element that can add consistency among newsletter issues and that contains the company address, newsletter publication schedule, names of those contributing to the production of the newsletter, and copyright information.

_____ 2. This feature describes or explains a graphic image, table, illustration, or photograph.

_____ 3. Text that is repeated at the top of every page.

_____ 4. A block of information or a related story that is set off from the body text in a graphic box.

_____ 5. A color in a newsletter, other than black, used as an accent.

_____ 6. A brief direct phrase, summarizing statement, or important point associated with the body copy of a newsletter.

_____ 7. A symbol or special character used to indicate the end of a section of text.

_____ 8. A feature that is used to indicate that an article or feature continues on another page.

_____ 9. A brief sentence or phrase that is a lead-in to an article.

_____ 10. This device converts a photograph, drawing, or text into a compatible digital file format.

Short Answer: On a blank sheet of paper, provide the correct answer for each question.

1. List at least three tips to consider when creating a pull quote.
2. Why is it important to have some knowledge of graphic file formats?
3. List at least four copyfitting ideas to create more space in a document.
4. What is the purpose of linking text boxes, and why is this feature advantageous in a newsletter?
5. List at least three paragraph enhancements that can be included in a newsletter.

Chapter Assessments

Assessment 9.1   Evaluating Newsletters

Find two newsletters from different sources. Review the newsletters for the following items. Label those items that you find in each newsletter, scan the newsletter with the items labeled, and send it to your instructor as an email attachment. (Consult your instructor if a scanner or email is not available.)

Caption	Jump line	Spot color
End sign	Kicker	Subheads
Folio	Masthead	Subtitle
Footer	Nameplate	Table of contents
Header	Pull quote	
Headlines	Sidebar	

Optional: Write a summary explaining which of the two newsletters is the most appealing and why.

Assessment 9.2   Using a Word Newsletter Template

In this assessment, you will incorporate your copyfitting skills and your knowledge of working with Word templates to create a business newsletter based on a Word template. A model solution is shown in Figure 9.27.

1. Open **CapeTownMeetingText.docx** located in your *Chapter09* folder.
2. Make sure **NewsletterTemplate.dotx** has been copied to your *Chapter09* folder so that you can copy the styles saved in the **CapeTownMeetingText.docx** to this template.
3. Copy the styles saved in the **CapeTownMeetingText.docx** file to the **NewsletterTemplate.dotx** by completing the following steps:

    a. Make sure the **CapeTownMeetingText.docx** file is open, click the Styles window launcher button at the lower right corner of the Styles group, and then click the Manage Styles button at the bottom of the Styles task pane.

    b. Click the Import/Export button located in the lower left corner of the dialog box.

    c. At the Organizer dialog box with the Styles tab selected, make sure **CapeTownMeetingText.docx** displays with a list of all the styles saved to this document in the left section of the dialog box.

    d. Click the Close File button in the lower right corner of the Organizer dialog box—the button should change to the Open File button. Click the Open File button and browse to locate *NewsletterTemplate*.dotx. located in your *Chapter09* folder. Click Open.

    e. Click the *Banner1* style in the list box at the left, and then click the Copy button. This should copy the style to the **NewsletterTemplate.dotx** file.

Figure 9.27 Assessment 9.2 Sample Solution

f. Continue copying the following styles from **CapeTownMeetingText.docx** to **NewsletterTemplate.dotx**:

    Banner2

    Body1

    Mission

    Subtitle1

    TableofContents

    Title1, Title2, and Title3

g. Click the Close button to close the Organizer dialog box, and then save the changes to **NewsletterTemplate.dotx**.

4. Open **NewsletterTemplate.dotx**, save the document as a Word document file and name it **C09-A02-McAfeeNetworkNewsletter**.

5. Copy and paste the text in the **CapeTownMeetingText.docx** file to the placeholder text in the **C09-A02-McAfeeNetworkNewsletter.docx**. You will need to do a considerable amount of copyfitting and reformatting of text. The placeholder objects may not accommodate your text and graphics properly, so your skills in desktop publishing with Word will be helpful. Replace the graphics as needed. *Hint: Change the view to View Side by Side, and then copy and paste between the two documents at one screen.*

6. Apply all appropriate styles to the text.

7. Draw a text box in the mailing area of the newsletter (bottom of second page) to accommodate names and addresses for a merge.

8. Display the Mailings tab, and then create a data source for merging to the mailings section of the newsletter. Create your own data source by asking at least four students in your class to provide their names and addresses for use in your merge. You may use the Mail Merge Wizard or the merge command button on the Mailings tab to complete your merge.

9. Save the newsletter again with the same name **C09-A02-McAfeeNetworkNewsletter.docx**.
10. Print and then close **C09-A02-McAfeeNetworkNewsletter.docx**. Close the **CapeTownMeetingText.docx** file.

Assessment 9.3   Saving a Newsletter in HTML

In this assessment you will open a Word newsletter template that was created in a table format. You will save the newsletter in HTML format and then view the document in Web Page Preview. This will give you an idea of what the newsletter will look like when it is uploaded to a web page. Create the newsletter by completing the following steps:

1. Open **WebPageTemplate.dotx** located in your *Chapter09* folder. ***Hint: This template may also be found in the New tab Backstage view in the Newsletter category.***
2. Scroll through the template to understand how the template was created, and read the placeholder text for helpful hints.
3. Save the document in HTML by completing the following steps:
    a. Click the File tab and then click the Save & Send tab.
    b. At File tab Backstage view, click the *Change File Type* option in the *File Types* section, click the *Single File Web Page* option in the *Other File Types* section, and then click Save As.
    c. At the Save As dialog box, type **C09-A03-WebPageNewsletter** in the *File name* text box, and then click the Save button.
4. Add the Web Page Preview button to the Quick Access toolbar by completing the following steps:
    a. Click the Customize Quick Access Toolbar button at the end of the Quick Access Toolbar, and then click the *More Commands* option from the drop-down list.
    b. Click the down-pointing arrow at the right of the *Choose commands from* section, and then click All Commands from the drop-down list and then click the Web Page Preview button from the list.
    c. Click the Add button to add the Web Page Preview button to the current list of Quick Access buttons as shown at the right of the Add button. Click OK.
5. Click the Web Page Preview button in the Quick Access Toolbar.
6. View the document in your Internet browser.
7. Press the Print Screen key on your keyboard and capture a picture of the newsletter in your browser. ***Hint: As an alternate to Steps 7 and 8, click the Screenshot button on the Insert tab and then click the Screen Clipping option. Use Word to paste a copy of the screen capture in the document.***
8. Open a blank document and then click the Paste button to paste a copy of the screen capture.
9. Save the document as **C09-A03-NewsletterCapture.docx**. Print and then close **C09-A03-NewsletterCapture.docx**. Close the Internet browser window.
10. Close **C09-A03-WebPageNewsletter**.

Optional: Replace the placeholder text in the newsletter with your own text. Customize the graphics and other design elements in the newsletter to complement your message.

Assessment 9.4   Inserting an Excel Worksheet into a Newsletter

Open **C09-E09-Newsletter.docx**, which you created in Exercises 9.1 through 9.9, and then format and embed a worksheet created in Excel as shown in Figure 9.28. Include the following specifications:

1. Save **C09-E09-Newsletter.docx** with Save As, and name it **C09-A04-RSIntegrated**.
2. Minimize Word, and then open Excel 2010.
3. At the Excel screen, open **RideSafeProducts.xlsx** located in your *Chapter09* folder.
4. Enhance the Excel table by completing the following steps:
    a. Select the Urban theme.
    b. Select cell A1, which contains *Ride Safe Products – 2012* (a thick black border should display around the cell), display the Home tab, click the Fill Color button in the Font group, and then click *Teal, Accent 2* in the top row of the color palette.
    c. With cell A1 still selected, click the drop down arrow at the right of the More Borders button in the Font group and then click *More Borders* at the bottom of the drop-down list. Select the Border tab, select the sixth line style in the right column in the *Line Style* list box, select Orange in the *Standard Colors* section of the

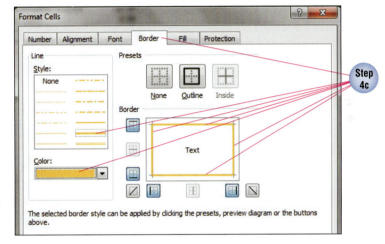

Color box, and then click Outline to add the borders in the preview diagram. Click OK.
    d. Select *Ride Safe Products - 2012*, change the font to 22-point Forte, and change the color to White.
    e. Select cells A2:C2 and change the font to 11-point Impact in Orange.
    f. Select cells A3:C11 and change the font to 10-point Franklin Gothic Book.
    g. Select cell A13, click the Format button in the Cells group, click *Row Height* at the drop-down list, and then change the row height to **28**.
    h. Select the text in cell A13, and then change the font to 8-point Franklin Gothic Book Italic.
    i. Position the insertion point in cell A13, click the Wrap Text button in the Alignment group.
    j. Select cells C3:C11, click the Number Format button in the Number group (General), and then click *Currency*.
    k. Select cells A1:C13 and apply the same thick orange border as in step 4c.

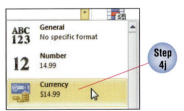

5. Save the Excel spreadsheet as **RideSafeProductsFormatted**.
6. Copy cells A1:C13 to the Clipboard.
7. Minimize Excel, and maximize Word.
8. Delete the last article text in the text box at the bottom of **C09-E09-Newsletter.docx**.

9. With the insertion point located inside the text box, click the down arrow on the Paste button in the Clipboard group on the Home tab. At the drop-down list, click *Paste Special*. Click the *Microsoft Office Excel Worksheet* option in the Paste Special dialog box, and then click OK. Adjust the size and position of the text box if necessary. ***Hint: When you view the Excel worksheet in the document screen, you will see a gray box. However, when you view the newsletter at the Print tab, you will see the Excel worksheet. It should print properly.***

10. Save, print, and then close **C09-A04-RSIntegrated.docx**.

11. Close **RideSafeProductsFormatted.xlsx**, and then close Excel.

Figure 9.28 Assessment 9.4 Integrated Sample Solution

Assessment 9.5   Researching on the Internet

In this assessment, work with another student in your class by opening
ButterfieldGardens.docx in your *Chapter09* folder and adding a second page
to the newsletter. You may use the Internet to find interesting articles about
gardening.

1. You may select a Word newsletter template, or you may design this
   newsletter from scratch. You may use the Columns feature and/or incorporate linked text boxes
   or use a table. You may also borrow design elements from Publisher and copy and paste them
   into your newsletter. Be creative and remember to use plenty of white space. Use the Butterfield
   Gardens logo provided in the *Chapter09* folder.
2. Insert several appropriate photographs or clip art images to enhance your document.
3. The newsletter must be at least two pages in length.
4. You may use the Internet to find interesting articles about gardening. Use a search engine to aid
   in your search. Type **gardening** in the *Search* text box at www.google.com, www.bing.com, or
   any other search engine of your own choosing.
5. The **ButterfieldGardens.docx** file contains proofreading errors and formatting inconsistencies.
   Correct all of the errors, and create styles to aid in reinforcing consistency.
6. Save your document, and name it **C09-A05-Butterfield**.
7. Print your newsletter back to back, and then close **C09-A05-Butterfield.docx**.
8. In class, edit each other's newsletters by completing the following steps:
   a. Independently choose an editor's name for yourself and do not share it with the rest of the
       class. (This is your chance to be famous!)
   b. Your instructor will collect all of the newsletters and randomly distribute a newsletter to
       each class participant.
   c. Sign your individual editor's "name" on the back of the newsletter and make editorial
       comments addressing such items as target audience, visual appeal, overall layout and design,
       font selection, graphic image selection, focus, balance, proportion, contrast, directional
       flow, consistency, and use of color.
   d. Exchange the newsletters so that you have an opportunity to write editor's comments on
       the back of each newsletter, identified by your individual editor's name only.
   e. Review the editor's comments on the back of your own newsletter, and revise your
       newsletter while keeping your editorial staff's comments in mind.
9. Save and name the revised version of your newsletter **C09-A05-Revised.docx**.
10. Print and then close **C09-A05-Revised.docx**.
11. Evaluate your revised newsletter with the document evaluation checklist
    (**DocumentEvaluationChecklist**) located in your *Chapter09* folder.

Performance Assessments

UNIT02

Preparing Promotion Documents and Newsletters

ASSESSING PROFICIENCIES

In this unit, you have learned to apply the design concepts to create flyers, brochures, newsletters, and many other business and personal documents.

*Note: Before completing the computer exercises, copy the **Unit02** folder from the CD that accompanies this textbook to your storage medium and then make **Unit02** the active folder. If necessary, substitute any graphics that are not available with similar graphics.*

Background Information for Assessments

Assume you are working for a well-known certified public accounting firm named Winston & McKenzie, CPA. A relatively new department in your firm, Executive Search Services Department, offers other companies assistance in searching for individuals to fill executive positions. You have been asked to prepare various promotional materials that will be used to inform other partners (owners), staff members, and clients of the scope of this department.

First, you will create a fact sheet (similar formatting to a flyer) highlighting the services of the Executive Search Services Department and the qualifications of its consultants. Second, you will prepare a self-mailing brochure that lists the services of the Executive Search Services Department, the benefits to the reader, the way to obtain more information, and a mailing label section. Third, you will create a newsletter highlighting the offerings of a local nonprofit organization for which you, as a representative of your company, are an active volunteer.

Think about the audience of an accounting firm in general, and then think more specifically about the audience that might use Executive Search Services. Before you begin, print **FactSheetText**, **W&McKText1**, **W&McKText2**, and **W&McKText3** located in your *Unit02* folder. Read the text in these documents to familiarize yourself with the services offered by this company. Include some consistent elements in all of the documents. Use a logo, a graphic image, a special character, text boxes, ruled lines, borders, fill, or color to create unity among the documents. Incorporate design concepts of focus, balance, proportion, contrast, directional flow, color, and appropriate use of white space. Figure U2.1 illustrates a sample document.

Assessment U2.1   Fact Sheet

Using the text in **FactSheetText**, create a fact sheet highlighting the services offered by Winston & McKenzie's Executive Search Services Department according to the following specifications (see Figure U2.1):

1. Create a thumbnail sketch of your proposed page layout and design. You will need to experiment with the layout and design.
2. Create styles for repetitive formatting, such as for bulleted text or headings.
3. Design a simple logo using WordArt, Clip Art, SmartArt, and/or Shapes or any other Word features.

4. Vary the fonts, type sizes, typestyles, and text effects to emphasize the relative importance of items.
5. Use bullets to list the services offered. You decide on the character to use as a bullet.
6. You may use any relevant picture, symbols, borders, colors, and so on, in your fact sheet. You decide on the position, size, shading, border/fill, spacing, alignment, and so forth. *(Hint: Photographs tend to look more professional than clip art.)*
7. Save the document and name it **U2-PA01-Facts**.

Figure U2.1 Performance Assessment U2-1 Sample Solution

About Executive Search Services...

Winston & McKenzie Executive Search consultants are both highly qualified and highly professional. Many have advanced degrees in personnel administration, psychology, organization development, marketing, and communications. This interdisciplinary dynamism within Winston & McKenzie, coupled with the insight and vision of your management team, turn the problem of finding a new executive into an opportunity to plan and act strategically.

YOU SELECT THE SERVICES THAT MEET YOUR NEEDS...

- Defining the position
- Handling internal candidates
- Generating candidates
- Assessing candidates
- Conducting interviews
- Testing candidates
- Performing reference and background checks
- Assisting with employment offers

For more information about Executive Search...
Please call Janet Rankins at (317) 555-6342 or Bill Bush at (317) 555-8989.

Winston & McKenzie Executive Search Services – Working with you and for you in selecting the right management team.

WINSTON & McKENZIE, CPA
Executive Search

WINSTON & MCKENZIE, CPA EXECUTIVE SEARCH

8. Print and then close **U2-PA01-Facts.docx**.
9. Print a copy of **DocumentEvaluationChecklist** located in your *Unit02* folder. Use the checklist to evaluate your fact sheet. Hand in both items.

Assessment U2.2   Facts Brochure

Using the text in **W&McKText1**, **W&McKText2**, and **W&McKText3** located in your *Unit02* folder, create a brochure according to the following specifications (see Figure U2.2). *(Reminder: Save periodically as you work through this assessment.)*

1. Create a dummy of the brochure layout so you know exactly which panel will be used for each section of text. Use **W&McKText1** as the text in panel 1, **W&McKText2** as the text in panel 2, and **W&McKText3** as the text in panel 3. (Panel 3 is actually the information request side of a card the reader can send to the company for more information. The mailing address side, which is panel 4, will be created in step 5.)
2. Prepare a thumbnail sketch of your proposed layout and design.
3. Include the following formatting:
   a. Change the paper orientation to landscape.
   b. Change the top and bottom margins to 0.5 inch, and the left and right margins to 0.45 inch.
   c. Turn on kerning at 14 points.
4. Create the inside panels of the brochure according to the following specifications:
   a. Use the Columns feature to divide the page into panels, use text boxes to format the panels, or select an Office.com template.
   b. Choose appropriate typeface, type size, and text effects selections that best reflect the mood or tone of this document and the company or business it represents. Insert column breaks to begin each new panel if columns are used.
   c. Consider using a drop cap, SmartArt, shape, watermark, or any other Word feature that creates focus.
   d. Create any styles that will save you time and keystrokes, such as styles for headings, body text, and bulleted items or apply any appropriate Quick Styles.
   e. Itemize any lists with bullets. You decide on the bullet symbol, size, color, spacing, and so forth.
   f. Use text boxes to specifically position text if necessary or to highlight text in a unique way.
   g. Include ruled lines. Choose a line style, thickness, placement, color, and so on.
5. To make the brochure self-mailing, create the mailing address side of the request for information (created in panel 3) by completing the following steps in panel 4:
   a. Insert the mailing address into a text box, then use the Text Direction feature to rotate the mailing address 90 degrees. You decide on an appropriate font, type size, and color. Type the following address:

   Winston & McKenzie, CPA
   Executive Search Services
   4600 North Meridian Street
   Indianapolis, IN 46240

   b. Use the mouse to size and position the text box containing the mailing address to an appropriate mailing address position.

c. Create a vertical dotted line representing a cutting line or perforated line at the right edge of panel 4. Draw the line from the top of the page to the bottom of the page. Pay attention to the placement of this dotted line. If the reader were to cut the reply/request card on this line, are the items on the reverse side of the card (panel 3) placed appropriately? If not, make adjustments.

6. Create the cover of the brochure by completing the following steps in panel 6:

a. Type **You Can't Afford to Make the Wrong Hiring Decision!** as the title of the brochure.

b. Use any appropriate graphic image that is available. A large selection of graphics is available by searching for clips using the keyword **business**. You may also consider creating your own logo on the front cover of the brochure. You decide on the position, size, and border/fill, if any.

c. Decide on an appropriate location and include the company name, address, and the following phone and fax numbers:

Phone: (317) 555-8900
Fax: (317) 555-8901
Email: winmk@emcp.net
Web: www.emcp.net/winmck

7. Save the brochure, and name it **U2-PA02-Brochure**.

8. Print and then close **U2-PA02-Brochure.docx**.

9. Print a copy of **DocumentEvaluationChecklist**. Use the checklist to evaluate your brochure. Make any changes, if necessary. Hand in both items.

Optional: To save on mailing costs, you must send out postcards to prospective clients. Rewrite and shorten the text in **W&McKText1** so it highlights the pertinent points, but fits onto a 4 by 6-inch postcard. Include the company's name, address, phone, and fax numbers. Alternatively, save the brochure as a PDF and send it to your clients as an email attachment.

Assessment U2.3   Volunteer Newsletter

Create a newsletter highlighting the offerings at the Loaves & Fishes Community Pantry, a local nonprofit organization for which you, as a representative of your company, are an active volunteer. Prepare the newsletter as an email attachment to be sent to all the donors and contributors of the organization. Include the following specifications:

1. Locate an email newsletter template on www.microsoft.com, or create the newsletter from scratch.

2. Insert the following text files located in your *Unit02* folder.

DonationsNeeded.docx
VolunteerOpportunities.docx
DietaryChanges.docx
HealthChoices.docx

3. Insert the Loaves & Fishes logo, **Loaves&FishesColor**.

4. Insert an appropriate image in at least one of the articles. You may want to configure the image into a Shape.

5. Save the document as **U2-PA03-LoavesFishesNewsletter**.

6. Print **U2-PA03-LoavesFishesNewsletter.docx**.

7. Save the document again as a PDF.

8. Send the newsletter, **U2-PA03-LoavesFishesNewsletter.pdf**, as an email attachment to your instructor. Close both versions of the newsletter.

You Can't Afford
to Make the
Wrong Hiring
Decision!

WINSTON & MCKENZIE, CPA
Executive Search

Winston & McKenzie, CPA
Executive Search Services
4600 North Meridian Street
Indianapolis, IN 46240

Phone: 317.555.8900
Fax: 317.555.8901
Email: winmck@emcp.net
Web: www.emcp.net/winmck

Winston & McKenzie, CPA
Executive Search Services
4600 North Meridian Street
Indianapolis, IN 46240

Identifying, Assessing, and Hiring Senior Officers

Your executive management team is critical to your institution's success. However, selecting the right individuals is not easy. Hiring the wrong candidates can cost your institution as much as two times their salary in wasted recruiting and training expenses, lost productivity, and lowered morale.

Winston & McKenzie, CPA, can help you make more effective staffing decisions. We do more than simply take job specs over the phone and send you a stack of résumés. We work with you to initially evaluate the position to determine whether it should be filled, altered, or eliminated. Once the decision to fill a position is made, we can conduct the entire search, parts of the process, or simply coach you through the process. Your needs determine our level of involvement.

Our search consultants utilize Winston & McKenzie's full range of specialized financial institution resources to enhance your search.

You Select the Services that Meet Your Needs

✓ Defining the position
✓ Handling internal candidates
✓ Generating candidates
✓ Assessing candidates
✓ Conducting interviews
✓ Testing candidates
✓ Reference & background checks
✓ Assisting with employment offers

I Would Like More Information...

on how Winston & McKenzie can help my institution find and hire the right management team.

For more information about our Executive Search Services please call:

Janet Rankins at (317) 555-6342
E-Mail: winmck@emcp.net

Visit our website at:

www.emcp.net/winmck

or complete the information request card below.

Name: _____
Institution: _____
Address: _____
City: _____
State: _____
ZIP _____
Email: _____
Telephone: _____
Cell: _____

Assessment U2.4   Portfolio Cover and Section Pages

1. Create cover and section pages for your portfolio (hard copy or electronic copy) with the following specifications:
   a. Ask your instructor if you should prepare a printed copy of your portfolio or if an electronic file is preferred. The electronic file may be saved as a PDF and emailed to your instructor.
   b. You may use the Cover Page feature on the Insert tab, or you may want to create your cover page and table of contents from scratch using at least one graphic element such as SmartArt, Shape, WordArt, a watermark, ruled lines, a graphic image, or a scanned image.
   c. Consider balance, focus, contrast, directional flow, and proportion when creating the cover.

Figure U2.3 **Performance Assessment U2.4 Sample Solution**

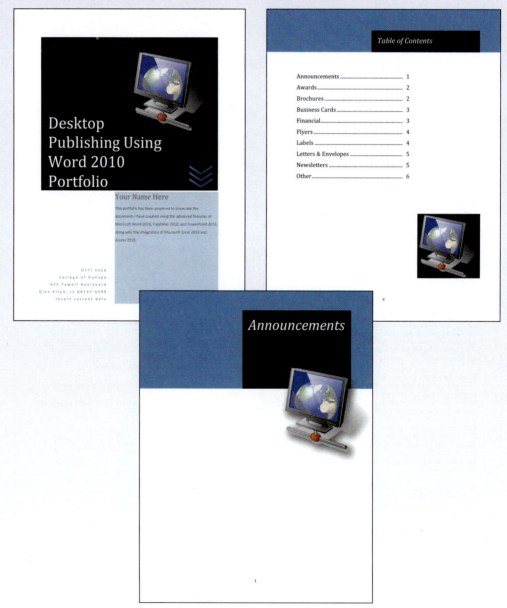

d. Use a consistent design element from your cover to create the section pages that will introduce various categories for your desktop documents. For instance, create a section for promotional documents or newsletters.

2. Save the completed cover, and name it **U2-PA04-Cover&Sections**. *Hint: Figure U2.4 is a sample document. You may use your own design ideas to complete this assessment.*

3. Print and then close **U2-PA04-Cover&Sections.docx**.

Optional: Create another cover for your portfolio. Assume that you are applying for a government position or for a job in a comedy gallery, and try to convey a tone that is appropriate to your purpose.

Assessment U2.5   Homeowner's Flyer

As an officer in your homeowner's association, you are responsible for preparing an announcement for an upcoming homeowner's meeting. Include the following specifications:

1. Use the advanced features of Word 2010 to create a document similar to the one shown in Figure U2.4.
2. Insert the text as shown in Figure U2.4.
3. You may print the document on standard-sized paper, or you may print it as a poster (printer dependent).
4. Save the document as **U2-PA05-Meeting**.
5. Close **U2-PA05-Meeting.docx**.

DTP CHALLENGE

Assessment U2.6   Creating a Virtual Office Resource Guide

Take your skills to the next level by completing this more challenging assessment.

1. Create a resource guide for a virtual office. Research information on helpful websites, commercial printers, computer repair companies, office supply companies, airports, limousine or taxi companies, local conference centers (hotels with conference room availability), restaurants for business meetings, community clubs or organizations for entrepreneurs, community college virtual office courses, temporary office employment companies, and any other resources you think would be valuable to a person operating a company from home.
2. Format the resource information in either a manual or booklet format.
3. Allow enough space to add additional resources to your document in the future. *Hint: Using a table may be helpful.*
4. Use appropriate graphics, fonts, tables, footers, and so on.
5. Use styles to reinforce consistency in the design.
6. Save the document as **U2-CA06-VirtualResourceGuide**.
7. Print and then close **U2-CA06-VirtualResourceGuide.docx**.

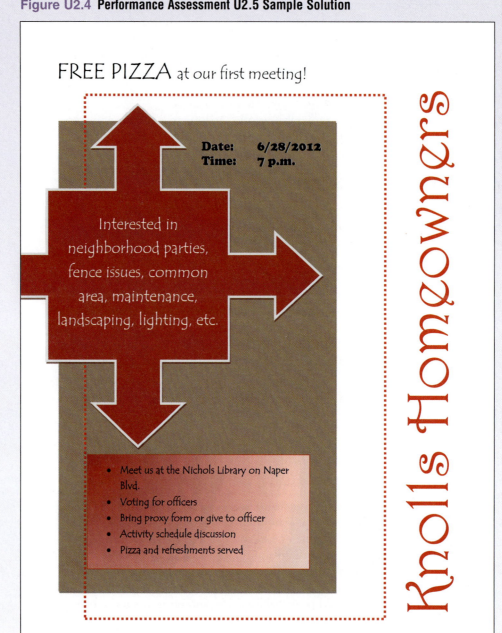

Unit 3

Producing Web Pages, Microsoft Publisher Documents, and PowerPoint Presentations

Chapter 10

CHAPTER10

Creating Web Pages and Forms

Performance Objectives

Upon successful completion of Chapter 10, you will be able to:

- Create a web home page with bookmarks and hyperlinks.
- Apply basic desktop publishing concepts to the layout and design of a Web page.
- Use Document Location to access the Internet or other files.
- Create forms using form fields and content controls.
- Create forms using Legacy Tools.
- Save and protect a form as a template.
- Create a web form.

Desktop Publishing Terms

Bookmark	Internet	Uniform Resource Locator
Content control	Internet Service Provider (ISP)	(URL)
Form	Intranet	Web page
Hyperlink	Legacy form fields	World Wide Web (www)
Hypertext Transfer Protocol (HTTP)	Round-trip	

Word Features Used

ActiveX Controls	Document Location	Restrict Editing
Blank web page template	Fill Effects	Split Cells
Bookmarks	Form fields	Tables
Building Block Gallery	Graphics	Templates
Bullets	Heading styles	Themes
Clip art	Horizontal lines	Web Layout view
Content controls	Hyperlinks	Web Page Preview
Design Mode	Legacy Tools	
Developer tab	Properties	

In this chapter, Word is used to create web pages. Web pages provide promotional information for products, resources, or services offered by a company or an organization. Increasingly, businesses, organizations, and individuals are accessing the Internet to conduct research, publish product or catalog information, communicate, and market products globally. In addition, companies are using intranets to efficiently share information among employees.

Users access the Internet for several purposes: to communicate using email, to subscribe to newsgroups, to transfer files, to socialize with other users, and to access virtually any kind of information imaginable.

What is a **Web page**? A Web page is a computer file containing information in the form of text or graphics along with commands in a language called Hypertext Markup Language (HTML). When one of these pages is placed on a server, which is a computer hooked up to the Internet, it receives an address that other users will type to call up the page.

Using Word for Creating Web Pages

Word 2010 can save documents as web pages by converting them to HTML (HyperText Markup Language), a type of file format that can be published on the Web. A web browser such as Microsoft Internet Explorer can read the HTML code and display the text and graphics in the web page. Although Word 2010 is a viable program for creating web pages, professional web designers may choose to use applications such as Microsoft Expression Web or Adobe Dreamweaver, especially if the website will have several pages and complex linking requirements.

A web page created in Word is basically the same as a regular document in terms of typing, formatting, and layout. However, a few Word features such as passwords, Word headers and footers, and columns do not transfer when you save in a Web Page format. Most Word documents are created in table formats if used in web pages. The table structure provides good boundary lines for text and images. When creating a web page in Word, use the Web Layout view, and then view the finished page using Web Page Preview.

Understanding Internet and Intranet Terminology

The **Internet** is a worldwide network of commercial, educational, governmental, and personal computers connected together for the purpose of sharing information. The **World Wide Web (www)** is the most commonly used application on the Internet and is a set of standards and protocols used to access information available on the Internet. An **intranet** is an "internal Internet" within an organization that uses the same Web technology and tools as the Internet and is also used to share information. Intranets are often only accessible to the employees within an organization. An intranet may provide employees with online access to reference material, job postings, phone and address lists, company policies and procedures, enrollment in and updates on benefit plans, company newsletters, and other human resource information.

Throughout this chapter, you will simulate creating web pages for both the Internet and an organization's intranet. These web pages will be saved as HTML files to a flash drive or hard drive. You will view each web page on the Internet Explorer screen in read-only view.

Accessing Web Addresses

The **Uniform Resource Locator**, referred to as the **URL**, is used to identify locations on the Internet. It is the address that you type to call up a web page or site. A typical URL is http://www.microsoft.com. The first part of the URL, http://, identifies the protocol. The letters *http* stand for **Hypertext Transfer Protocol**, which is one of the protocols or languages used to transfer data within the World Wide Web. The colon and slashes separate the protocol from the server name. The server name is the second component of the URL. For example, in http://www.microsoft.com, the server name is identified as www.microsoft. The last part of the URL specifies the domain to which the server belongs—for example, .com refers to "commercial," .edu refers to "educational," .gov refers to "government," and .mil refers to "military." If the protocol displays with an *s* in the acronym https://, the website is thought to be secured.

If you know the URL for a specific website and want to visit that site, type the URL in the *URL address* text box on your browser page or, as you will learn later in this chapter, you will be able to create a hyperlink from your Word-created web page to different URLs on the Internet.

Type the URL exactly as written, including any colons (:) or slashes (/). Web pages are constantly changing. If a particular web page asked for in an exercise is no longer available, you will need to substitute a different one. The home page is the starting point for viewing any website. At the home page, you can "branch off" to other pages within the website or jump to other websites. You do this with hyperlinks that are embedded in the web pages. A **hyperlink** is colored and underlined text or a graphic that you click to go to a file, a location in a file, an HTML page on the World Wide Web, or an HTML page on an intranet. Move the mouse pointer on a hyperlink, and the mouse pointer becomes a hand. This is one method for determining if something is a hyperlink. Most pages contain a variety of hyperlinks. Using these links, you can zero in on the exact information for which you are searching.

> **Hyperlink**
> Text or a graphic in a Web page that will connect you to other pages or websites in different locations.

Accessing Web Addresses Using the Word Document Location Text Box

Besides accessing specific websites from your favorite browser, you may also add a text box to your Quick Access toolbar that allows you to access the sites from within Word. To add the *Document Location* box to the Quick Access toolbar, where you can easily access other websites and destinations, complete the following steps:

1. Click the down-pointing arrow at the right of the Quick Access Toolbar and then click More Commands.
2. With the Quick Access toolbar selected in the left pane, click the down-pointing arrow at the right of the *Choose commands from* list box, and then click *All Commands*.
3. Click *Document Location*, and then click Add as shown in Figure 10.1. You completed similar steps in Chapter 9 when you added the Web Page Preview button to the Quick Access toolbar.

Figure 10.1 Customizing the Quick Access Toolbar for Web Access

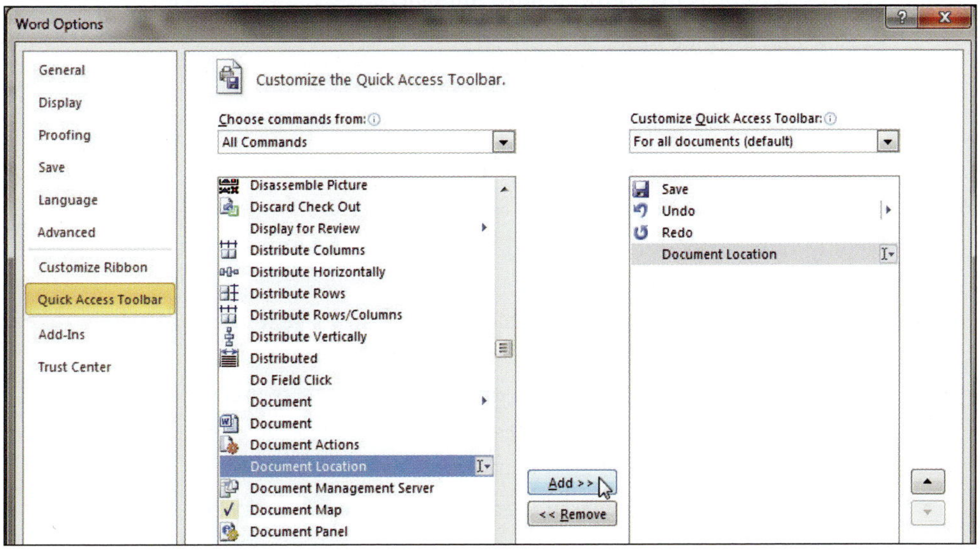

Figure 10.2 Using the Document Location Text Box

Type the URL or document location desired and then press Enter.

After the *Document Location* text box has been added to the Quick Access toolbar, it will display as shown in Figure 10.2, where you can type a URL in the Location box or click the down-pointing arrow next to it to access other files or websites from the drop-down list and then press Enter to connect to the desired destination.

Previewing in Web Layout View and Web Page Preview

To begin building from a blank web page, start a new document in Word and then switch to Web Layout view from the View tab or the view buttons in the bottom right corner of the screen. This will allow you to view the page very nearly as it will be when displayed on a web page.

However, if you need more realism, you may want to access Web Page Preview to examine the page in an actual web browser. Click the Web Page Preview button to open the current Word document in your favorite browser.

Planning and Designing a Web Page

You can build a website yourself or hire a freelancer or Web access provider. Some advertising consultants develop websites for a fee. However, you can easily create your own web pages.

Using Design Tips

Where do you start? Planning is a basic desktop publishing concept that applies to web pages as well as any other documents created in Word. During the planning stage of your Web page, consider the following web page design tips:

- Determine the goal of your website.
- Identify and focus on your intended audience.
- Review and critique other sites.
- Check your links on a regular basis (sites change often).
- Do not make your audience scroll sideways.
- Do not identify your site as a home page—obviously, it is.
- Do not overuse italics or bold.
- Determine elements to be emphasized and used. Keep the design simple. Use white space effectively.
- Be consistent with hyperlinks so that visitors know where they are, where they came from, and where they can go.
- Create a storyboard (a progression of web pages or links used to reinforce a theme or goal).
- Do not use annoying animated graphics that do not stop.
- Always check your web page in a browser for spacing, proportion, readability, line length, and so on.

DTP POINTERS ▶
Remember that just because your web page looks good in one browser doesn't mean that it will look good in all browsers.

DTP POINTERS ▶
Too many graphics or large graphics can slow down your Web page.

- Make sure your page fits within a standard browser window (800 × 600). Set monitor resolution at 96 pixels per inch.
- Do not use large graphics that take forever to download.
- Use graphics that relate to the content. Graphics should not distract from the message.
- Use clean and clear navigation so it is easy to maneuver within a website.
- Maintain a consistent color scheme (consider using predesigned themes in Word).
- Keep the background simple, making sure the text can be seen clearly. Make sure there is enough contrast between the text and background.
- Avoid small text and all caps.
- For bulleted text, avoid using a single bullet. Do not use more than two levels of bullets.
- Use consistent wording in bulleted text.
- Keep graphs simple. The most effective graphs are pie charts with three or four slices and column charts with three or four columns.
- Remember that a web page is the first impression you are giving the world about your product, information, or yourself. A poor web page can be worse for your business than having none at all.
- Maintain your website and keep it current.

◄ **DTP POINTERS**
Use a company logo to reinforce company recognition.

Planning Your Web Page

Consider using a thumbnail sketch and a storyboard to organize your page layout before actually creating it. Include space for text, photographs, graphics, headlines, divider lines, and so on. Instead of including everything on one huge web front page, use hyperlinks to other pages.

Remember that the website front door is its home page. This page should contain the elements to achieve the goals an organization (or individual) has set for the website. Understand what your goals are before you design the site. Are you creating a website on an intranet to share information among employees or a web page on the Internet to market a product or service? Know your budget before starting. There are things you can do on any budget, but some things (such as videos and animation) may cost more than you can afford.

Some Web designers suggest that you create a nameplate or banner to display a logo and company name in an interesting way. Include your company logo to reinforce your company's identity. The site should also include alternative ways to reach the company such as an address, telephone number, email address, and fax number.

Graphics are probably the simplest way to make your web page look better. Be sure to choose a graphic that is appropriate to the subject of the page. Animation, video, and scrolling words are eye-catching devices to entice your audience to return to your website. They can take a while to load. You may want to avoid using a graphic that takes longer than 15 to 20 seconds to load.

◄ **DTP POINTERS**
Create a folder to save your web page.

Tables in Web Page Design

Tables provide the framework for a web page. You can exercise some control over where text, pictures, and white space display in a web page by using cells in a table. Empty cells are often used to visually separate table information. When inserting pictures inside a cell, make sure the text wrap has been set to *In Line With Text* so that you can use the alignment buttons on the Table Tools Format tab.

Web Layout

Figure 10.3 Viewing a Table Structure In Web Layout View

Caring4Pets Animal Clinic		6340 Main Street Lisle, IL 60532 Caring4Pets@emcp.net Office Phone: 630.555.9876 Office Fax: 630.555.8871

You are the most important person in your pet's life; our goal is to support you in keeping your pets happy and healthy.

GENERAL INFORMATION	Business Hours:	
SERVICES		
STAFF MEMBERS	Monday:	7:30 a.m. – 7 p.m.
	Tuesday:	7:30 a.m. – 7 p.m.
CAT CARE INFO	Wednesday:	7:30 a.m. – 7 p.m.
DOG CARE INFO	Thursday:	7:30 a.m. – 7 p.m.
OTHER PETS	Friday:	7:30 a.m. – 7 p.m.
CLIENT SERVICE SURVEY	Saturday:	8 a.m. – 2:30 p.m.
	Sunday:	Closed

ANIMALS TREATED	Travel Directions:
Cats, Dogs, Exotics	View MapQuest Map

In Web Layout view, the table in your document will display with light blue gridlines as shown in Figure 10.3.

In Exercise 10.1, you will visit a website by typing the URL in the *Document Location* text box that you added to the Quick Access toolbar. This opens the Internet Explorer program window and also displays the home page for the website. The Internet Explorer program window contains many features similar to the Word window. As you view each of the websites listed in the exercise, pay attention to the layout and design of each home page.

Note: Before completing computer exercises, copy the* Chapter10 *folder from the CD that accompanies this textbook to your storage medium and then make* Chapter10 *the active folder. Substitute any graphics that are not available. Use similar graphics.

Exercise 10.1 Customizing the Quick Access Toolbar and Viewing Web Pages

1. Make sure you are connected to the Internet.
2. Add the *Document Location* text box and the Web Page Preview button (if it was not added in Chapter 9) to the Quick Access toolbar by completing the following steps:
   a. Click the down-pointing arrow at the right of the Quick Access toolbar, and then click More Commands.
   b. With Quick Access Toolbar selected in the left pane, click the down-pointing arrow at the right of the *Choose commands from* list box, and then click All Commands.
   c. Scroll down the list on the left, click Document Location and then click Add.

d. Click Web Page Preview, click Add, and then click OK to close the dialog box.
3. Explore several locations on the Internet from within Word by completing the following steps:
   a. Position your insertion point in the *Document Location* text box located on the Quick Access toolbar.
   b. Type **www.emcp.com**, and then press Enter.
   c. The home page will display similar to the one shown below. Notice that the layout is fairly simple but easy to understand and use. Each sample page illustrates a link to one of the three divisions of the publishing company. When a division is selected, you may click one of two links at the bottom of the screen to either visit the site or to learn more about the division. The overall look of the page is simple and free of clutter.

d. Close the web page by clicking the Close button in the upper right corner.
   e. Next, view **http://egov.cityofchicago.org**. Scroll down the home page, studying the layout and design elements.
   f. While at the Internet Explorer screen, type **www.nps.gov/yell** in the *URL address* text box and then press Enter. The Yellowstone National Park home page should display.
   g. Click the hyperlink <u>Support Your Park</u>, click the printer friendly button if printing is required by your instructor, and then click the Print button on the Internet Explorer toolbar.
   h. Close the Yellowstone website.

Creating a Web Home Page

DTP POINTERS ▶

Choose a design and theme that match the content of your Web page.

Now that you have spent some time viewing several website home pages, you may have a few ideas on how to design an appealing home page. Word includes many options that will allow you to customize your Web page by adding color, interesting fonts, eye-catching graphics and photos, and consistent styles.

Saving a Word Document as a Web Page

To save a web page, save as you would normally save a document, but set the file type at the Save As dialog box (or change the file type at the Save & Send Backstage view) to one of the following Web formats:

Round-trip

Convert an HTML file back to a Word document.

- Use Single File Web Page (MHT) when you are planning to send the web page via email. This format is also easy to download and manipulate.

- Use the standard Web Page format (HTML) when you are planning to **round-trip** the page between Word and a web browser. That is, if you save a Word document in HTML, you can later reopen the HTML file and convert it back to a Word document. This format is not recommended for emailing the page to others.

- Use the Web Page, Filtered format (HTML) when you need the resulting file to be plain HTML. Use this format if you intend to integrate the page into a larger website that was created with Dreamweaver or Expression. Do not use this format if you plan to edit the page in Word in the future.

Creating Hyperlinks in a Web Home Page

The websites you visited in Exercise 10.1 included hyperlinks to connect you to other pages or websites in different locations. The reader of your document can jump to a location in that document, a different Word document, or a file created in a different program such as an Excel spreadsheet. The destination document or file can be on your hard drive, on your organization's network (intranet), or on the Internet, such as a page on the Web. You can create hyperlinks from selected text or graphic objects—such as buttons and pictures. By default, the hyperlink text displays in blue and is underlined. When you return to the document after following a hyperlink, the hyperlink text color changes to dark red. You do not have to be on the Internet to use hyperlinks in Word documents.

Hyperlink

You can create a hyperlink in your own home page. To do this, first select the text you want specified as the hyperlink. On the Insert tab, click the Hyperlink button in the Links group. At the Insert Hyperlink dialog box, such as that shown in Figure 10.4, do one of the following:

- Type the web URL to which you want the text to link in the *URL address* text box.

- Use the folder list under the *Look In* text box to browse for a file.

- Select where to link your hyperlink—*Existing File or Web Page, Place in This Document, Create New Document,* or *Email address*.

- Add a screen tip or a bookmark.

If an email address is typed in the Internet format, yourname@servername.com (it is usually typed at the end of a web page), Word will automatically create a hyperlink to your default Internet mail program. In addition, you can create hyperlinks to bookmarks in a document, as described later. You can also create a hyperlink from another section in the document to the bookmark or from any other document to the bookmark.

Figure 10.4 Insert Hyperlink Dialog Box

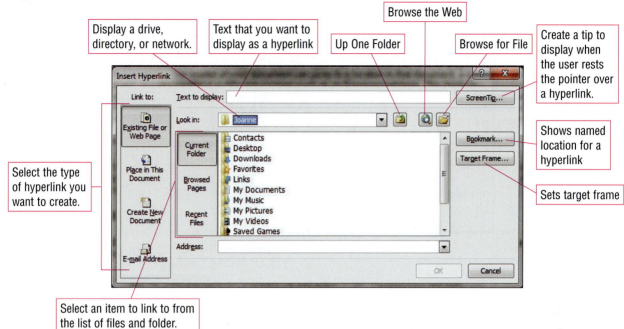

Display a drive, directory, or network.

Text that you want to display as a hyperlink

Browse the Web

Up One Folder

Browse for File

Create a tip to display when the user rests the pointer over a hyperlink.

Select the type of hyperlink you want to create.

Shows named location for a hyperlink

Sets target frame

Select an item to link to from the list of files and folder.

Editing or Deleting a Hyperlink

To edit an existing link, right-click the hyperlink and then choose *Edit Hyperlink, Select Hyperlink, Open Hyperlink, Copy Hyperlink,* or *Remove Hyperlink.*

Bookmark

Creating Bookmarks

A ***bookmark*** can be used to move your cursor to another location within the same document. It creates a link within the same page. You must first create a bookmark and then connect it to another location within your page by creating a hyperlink to it. Create a bookmark from the top of a page to a location within the page by completing the following steps:

1. Position the insertion point at the location you would like to make a bookmark, or select (highlight) text within your document such as *Top of Page*. The text can also be headings.
2. On the Insert tab, click the Bookmark button in the Links group.
3. In the *Bookmark name* text box, type a name for the bookmark. Do not include spaces in the name as shown in Figure 10.5.
4. Click the Add button. You can go to a specific bookmark by creating a hyperlink to it as discussed in the previous section or you can click the Bookmark button on the Insert tab, click the name of the bookmark, and then click Go To.

Adding Bullets and Lines to a Web Page

Bullets can be added to your document lists by clicking the Bullets button on the Home tab. You can also change regular bullets to special graphical bullets for your web page. Select the bulleted list in your document. Click the down-pointing arrow at the right of the Bullets button, view the Bullet selections in the Bullet Library, and then click Define New Bullet. At the Define New Bullet dialog box, click *Picture*. Scroll through the options shown in Figure 10.6, make a choice, and then click OK twice.

Figure 10.5 Bookmark Dialog Box

Figure 10.6 Picture Bullet Dialog Box

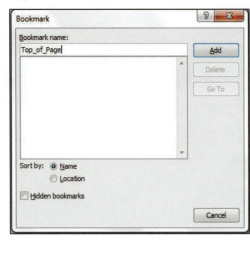

You can use horizontal lines to separate sections of a web page. On the Layout tab, click the Page Borders button in the Page Background group, and then click the Horizontal Line button in the bottom left corner. At the Horizontal Line dialog box, scroll through the line options, click the desired line type, and then click OK. Figure 10.7 shows a horizontal line added to the web page.

In this chapter, you will be saving your web pages to your *Chapter10* folder. For a home page to be available on the Web, however, you must have access to a web server. Consult your instructor if you are a student. Large businesses usually have their own server, and you should contact the Information Systems department of the company to arrange for space on the server to store your HTML documents (web pages). An option

Figure 10.7 Horizontal Line Dialog Box

for an individual is to rent space from an ***Internet Service Provider (ISP)***, a company that sells access to the Internet. The ISP you use to access the Web will also arrange to store your web page.

Using Other Office Components in Web Pages

You can create web pages using each of the applications in Office 2010. Excel web pages may be helpful when you want to use the worksheet formatting, calculation, and data analysis capabilities, for example, in creating electronic order forms, demographic information, testing or survey information, or a cost comparison. The Save As dialog box looks similar to the Word Save As dialog box. You will have an option to save the worksheet in HTML or with the XML format, which is a flexible format recommended if the page will be published and if the data are meant to be manipulated or acted on by other programs and scripts. Keep in mind that PowerPoint and Access may also be used in a website. All of these Office documents may be customized to reinforce a uniform web page design by using consistent themes, logos, fonts, colors, and images.

Adding Background Color to a Web Page

You can add background colors and textures to make your document more visually appealing to read online. The backgrounds will be visible on the screen in Word, at Web Page Preview, and in your browser. They will not display when the page is printed, unless your printer has an option to print background printing. To add a background color to your web page, click the Page Color button in the Page Background group on the Page Layout tab. Select a desired color, gradient, texture, or picture background fill.

DTP POINTERS
Enhance your document with a background.

Page Color

Printing a Background from Your Browser

To print a background or theme in Microsoft Internet Explorer, click Tools, and then Internet Options at the Microsoft Internet Explorer window. At the Advanced tab as shown in Figure 10.8, scroll down to *Printing* and click in the *Print background colors and images* check box to turn on this feature. Click the OK button to close the dialog box. When you print from Explorer, your background and theme colors will print.

DTP POINTERS
Backgrounds can print from your browser.

Figure 10.8 **Printing a Web Page Background**

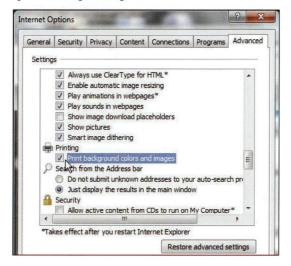

1. At a blank document, change the view to Web Layout, and then insert a table with 1 column and 7 rows.

2. Position the insertion point in the first row and then split the cell by completing the following steps:

   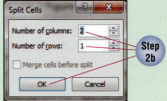

   a. Click the Split Cells button in the Merge group in the Table Tools Layout tab.
   b. At the Split Cells dialog box, type **2** in the *Number of columns* text box and **1** in the *Number of rows* text box. Click OK.

3. Position the insertion point in the first cell, and then insert a clip art image (or photograph) of your own choosing. Size similar to Figure 10.9.

4. Select the image and make sure the *In Line with Text* option in the Wrap Text is chosen.

5. With the image selected, click the Position button in the Alignment group in the Table Tools Layout tab, and then click the *Align Center* option.

6. With the image selected, click the *Simple Frame, White* option in the Picture Styles gallery in the Picture Tools Format tab.

7. Position the insertion point in the second cell in the first row, and insert your name by completing the following steps:

   a. Change the theme to Executive.
   b. Click the WordArt button in the Text group in the Insert tab; select a WordArt style, text effect, and font size, and then type your name.
   c. Select the WordArt object, change the Wrap Text to *In Front of Text*, and then move the WordArt text to the right of the picture image. Resize, recolor, and adjust it if necessary.

8. Click the Page Color button in the Page Layout tab, and then select a Color or Fill Effect that complements the image that you selected for your page.

9. Position the insertion point in the row below your image, press Enter once, click the Center Align button, and then type a sentence about yourself or type a favorite quote. Press the Enter key twice. Apply a desired Quick Style. ***Hint: You may want to modify the desired Quick Style spacing Before or After settings. You may need to reapply the Center command after applying the style.***

10. Position the insertion point on the Enter below the statement or quote in Step 9. Click the Page Borders button in the Page Background group in the Page Layout tab, select the Borders tab, click the Horizontal Line button in the bottom left corner, and then select a desired line style and click OK.

    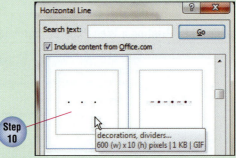

11. Position the insertion point in the row below your personal statement or quote. Type **Experience | Education | Contact**, and then press Enter. ***Hint: The | is the shift of the backslash key.***

12. Select *Experience | Education | Contact*, and apply a desired Quick Style. Make sure the line is centered horizontally. ***Hint: You can change the font color if you prefer at the Change Styles Colors drop-down gallery.***

13. Save the document by completing the following steps:
    a. Click the File tab, and then click the Save & Send tab.

b. At the Save & Send tab Backstage view, click the Change File Type button, and then click the Single File Web Page button. Click Save As.

c. At the Save As dialog box, type **C10-E02-MyWebPage** in the *File name* text box. Click the Change Title button, type **My Web Page** in the *Page title* text box, and then click OK. At the Save As dialog box, click Save. *Hint: If you get a message about some features not supported by Web browsers, click Continue.*

14. Position the insertion point in the row below *Experience...,* type **Professional Experience**, press Enter, and then apply another style of your choosing to the text.

15. Type information about your professional experience, and press Enter for each item in the list. *Hint: Figure 10.9 is sample text.* Press Enter twice after the last item.

16. Select the list and add bullets. *Hint: Try using Picture bullets.*

17. Insert another horizontal line to match the one inserted in Step 10.

18. Position your insertion point in the row below *Professional Experience*, type **Educational Background**, press Enter, and then apply a Quick Style.

19. Type information about your educational background and then press the Enter key twice.

20. Apply the same bullets as used in step 16.

21. Insert the same horizontal line by copying and pasting the line from the Office clipboard.

22. Type **Contact** in the next row, press Enter, and then apply another Quick Style. Type your contact information. *Hint: Press Ctrl + Tab to insert default tabs within the cell. Align the contact information using tabs not spaces.*

23. Insert hyperlinks to employers, colleges, and so on, where appropriate, by completing the following steps:

a. Select *Gateway* if you chose to use the text from the sample document; otherwise, type your own text in the *Professional Experience* section and then click the Hyperlink button in the Insert tab.

b. Click Existing File or Web Page in the *Link to* section of the Insert Hyperlink dialog box.

c. Type **www.gateway.com** in the *Address* text box or type your own company URL address.

d. Click the ScreenTip button in the upper right corner of the Insert Hyperlink dialog box.

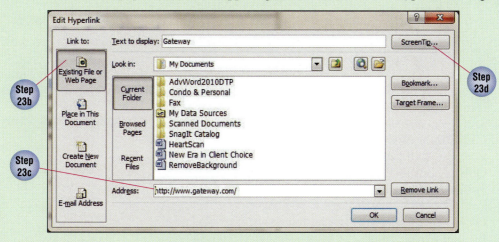

e. Type **Gateway** in the *ScreenTip text* text box. Click OK twice. *Hint: Test the link by holding down the Ctrl key and clicking the hyperlink.*

f. Continue creating hyperlinks to employers, colleges, and so forth, by following steps similar to steps 24a–24e. *Hint: American Cancer Society website is www.cancer.org.,*

University of Southern California website is www.usc.edu., and College of DuPage website is www.cod.edu.

24. Insert a bookmark to link from the bottom of the page to the top of the page by completing the following steps:
    a. Select the image at the top of your page. Click the Bookmark button on the Insert tab.
    b. At the Bookmark dialog box, type **Top_of_Page** in the *Bookmark name* text box and then click Add. ***Hint: You cannot name a bookmark with any spaces.***
    c. Position the insertion point in the last row, type **Top of Page**, and center it horizontally.
25. Hyperlink the headings/bookmarks by completing the following steps:
    a. Select *Experience* at the top of your page (do not include the space after the word) and then click the Hyperlink button in the Insert tab.
    b. Select *Place in This Document* in the *Link to* section.
    c. Click on the heading name, *Professional Experience*, and then click OK.

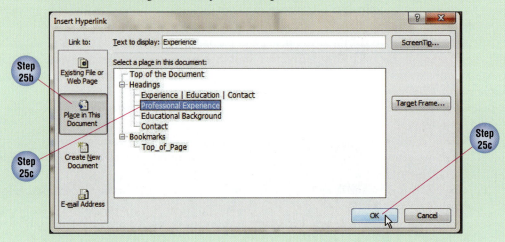

    d. Follow the procedure above to hyperlink the headings *Educational Background* and *Contact*.
    e. Select the text at the bottom of your document, *Top of Page*, click the Hyperlink button, and then click Bookmark at the Insert Hyperlink dialog box.
    f. Click the bookmark name, *Top_of_Page*, and then click OK.
26. Remove all the borderlines in the table by selecting the table, clicking the Borders button in the Table Styles group in the Table Tools Design tab, and then clicking the *No Border* option from the drop-down list.
27. Save the document again with the same name, **C10-E02-MyWebPage**.
28. Click the Web Page Preview button on the Quick Access toolbar. ***Hint: You added this button in Exercise 10.1.***
29. Print **C10-E02-MyWebPage** at Web Page Preview by clicking the Print button on the Internet Explorer toolbar. Close the browser window when you are finished. ***Hint: Make sure the background color prints; see the section in this chapter on printing backgrounds.***
30. Close **C10-E02-MyWebPage.html**.

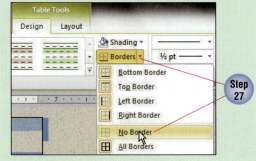

Figure 10.9 **Exercise 10.2**

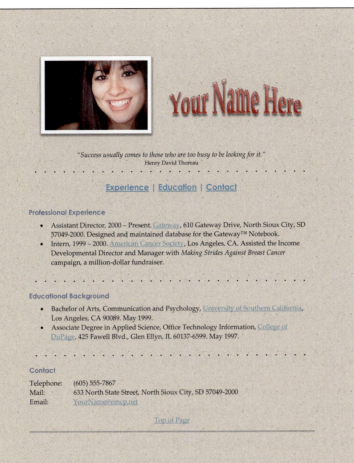

Form

A protected document that includes user-defined areas where information is entered.

Creating a Form Using Content Controls and Legacy Tools

In Word 2010, a *form* is a protected document that includes user-defined areas where information is entered into each designated area of the document. The forms you create in Word can be either printed or completed on paper or a filled-out form. Two kinds of fields can actually be entered into forms created in Word—the Word 2010 form fields known as content controls and the Legacy form fields that are carryovers from earlier versions of Word.

Content controls are locations within the form document where either text is entered or information is selected from a drop-down box, a check box, or a date picker. If you decide to insert content controls into your form, keep in mind that you can add instructional text in a content control. To do this, type the instructional text, select the text, and then click the Text button in the Controls group on the Developer tab.

Legacy form fields also provide areas where text can be entered, a check box can be checked, and a choice can be made from a list of drop-down options. There are only three types of Legacy form fields—Text Form Field, Checkbox Form Field, and Drop-down Form Field. Three additional tools are available, but they serve other purposes—Insert a Frame, Form Field Shading, and Reset Form Fields. Word 2010 contains options on the

Content control

Locations within a form where either text is entered or information is selected from a drop-down box, a check box, or a date picker.

Legacy form fields

Areas in a form where you can enter text, check a check box, or make a choice from a list of drop-down options.

Figure 10.10 Show Developer Tab on the Ribbon

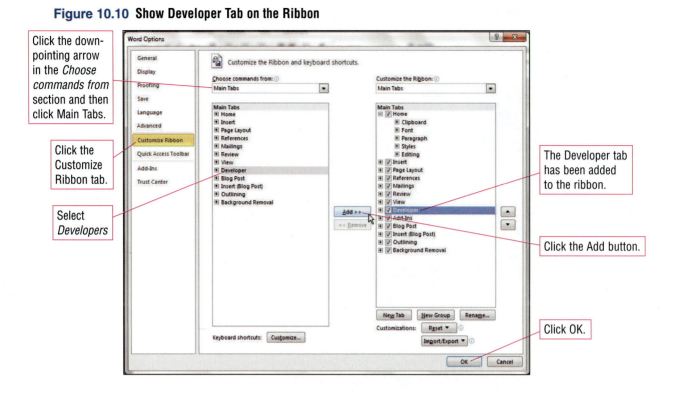

Click the down-pointing arrow in the *Choose commands from* section and then click Main Tabs.

Click the Customize Ribbon tab.

Select *Developers*

The Developer tab has been added to the ribbon.

Click the Add button.

Click OK.

Developer tab where you can insert content controls and access the Legacy Tools button, where you can select options from a palette of Legacy tools and ActiveX Controls.

Displaying the Developer Tab

Figure 10.10 displays the Developer tab with options that may be used to customize a form. To display the Developer tab at the Word Options dialog box as shown in Figure 10.11, complete the following steps:

1. Click the File tab.
2. Click Options.
3. Click Customize Ribbon.
4. Under Customize the Ribbon, click Main Tabs.
5. In the list, select the *Developer* check box, and then click OK.

Designing the Form First

When designing your form, consider first where the fixed text should be placed on the page. Consider typing the label followed by a colon and then the placeholder text for the fill-in data. This will help you visualize the layout of the form. As an alternative, you may want to use tabs to align the input data. Your form may give the appearance of being

Figure 10.11 Developer Tab

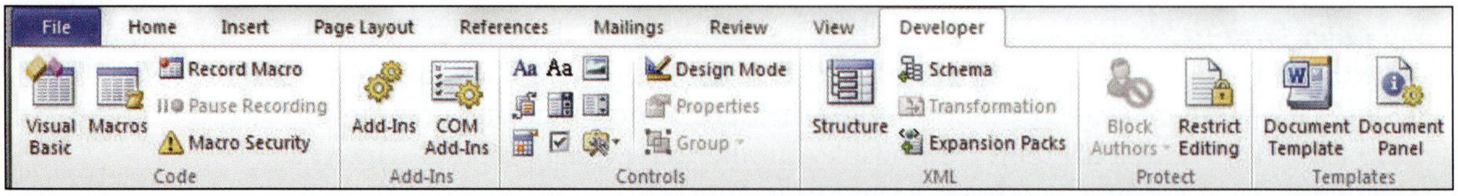

Figure 10.12 Visualizing the Layout of a Form

```
┌─────────────────────────────────────────────────────────────────┐
│ Name: XXXXXXXXXXXXXXXXXXXXXXXXXXXXXXXXXXXXXXXXXX                  │
│                                                                   │
│ Address: XXXXXXXXXXXXXXXXXXXXXXXXXXXXXXXXXXXXXXXX                 │
│                                                                   │
│ City: XXXXXXXXXXXXXXXXXXXXXXXXXXXXXX State: XX Zip: XXXXX-XXXX     │
│                                                                   │
│ (Using a Word Document)                                           │
│                                                                   │
│                                                                   │
│ Name:          XXXXXXXXXXXXXXXXXXXXXXXXXXXXXXXXXXXXXXXXXX         │
│                                                                   │
│ Address:       XXXXXXXXXXXXXXXXXXXXXXXXXXXXXXXXXXXXXXXXX          │
│                                                                   │
│ City:          XXXXXXXXXXXXXXXXXXXXXXXX State: XX Zip: XXXXX-XXXX │
│                                                                   │
│ (Using Tabs)                                                      │
│                                                                   │
│                                                                   │
│  ┌──────────────┬──────────────────────────────────────────────┐ │
│  │ Name:        │                                              │ │
│  ├──────────────┤                                              │ │
│  │ Address:     │                                              │ │
│  ├──────────────┼───────────────┬────────────┬──────┬─────────┤ │
│  │ City:        │               │ State:     │      │ Zip:    │ │
│  └──────────────┴───────────────┴────────────┴──────┴─────────┘ │
│                                                                   │
│ (Using a Table)                                                   │
└─────────────────────────────────────────────────────────────────┘
```

tidy. Use a table as the underlining structure for the labels and fill-in data as shown in Figure 10.12. The table may be the best solution for organizing the information.

After determining the basic layout of your form, consider arranging the fields in logical groups, using labels that are easy to understand, placing fields in expected order, varying the types of fields, and leaving enough space for user input.

When Should You Use Content Control and/or Legacy Tools?

The new content controls have great new capabilities, but they also have a few drawbacks. Use content controls if the user will be using Word 2010 or Word 2007 (controls do not work with earlier versions). You can combine both types of fields in a single form, but be aware that the fields work very differently; for instance, you may use the Tab key to advance from one field to the next, but you must use the mouse and click to activate other controls. You may want to stick to one field type if you only want to save the data or if the form will be filled out by people using earlier versions of Word.

A few advantages for using content controls include the following:

- More content controls are available than Legacy Tools.
- The document does not have to be protected for the form to function properly if completed in Word.
- Content controls can be set so that they cannot be deleted.
- Content controls are useful in connecting to XML data sources.

A few disadvantages include the following:

- A macro cannot be linked to a control.
- Predefined number formats are not available.
- Content controls cannot perform calculations.
- The length of an entry cannot be limited.
- Most importantly, an earlier version of Word (before 2007) cannot be used to fill in the form.

Adding Protection to Your Form

Restrict Editing

If you want users to enter information in the form template but not edit the template itself, then it is important to protect the template. To do this, click the Restrict Editing button in the Protect group on the Developer tab. This displays the Restrict Formatting and Editing task pane as shown in Figure 10.13. At this task pane, click in the *Allow only this type of editing in the document* check box to insert a check mark. Click the down-pointing arrow at the right side of the option box in the *Editing restrictions* section, and then click *Filling in forms* at the drop-down list. Click the Yes, Start Enforcing Protection button in the task pane. You will be prompted to type a password; however, it is not necessary to add one to the protected template. If you do not want the password, simply click OK without typing a password.

A Legacy form will not work properly unless it is protected. When unprotected, the form treats the fields as static text, and you cannot enter anything into them. On a protected form, you can click in a field or press the Tab key to move from field to field, or Shift + Tab will move you to a previous field.

In Exercise 10.3, you will create a real estate client information form that contains fields for text, such as *First Name:,* and so on, and create fields that contain drop-down lists, dates, and check boxes. You will be inserting content control only in this form. You will save the form as a protected template, open it, and then complete the form in Word. The Tab key will not advance you from one content control to the next; you will need to click to enter text in each field. You will also need to click inside the check box that corresponds with your desired response. The form you will create is shown in Figure10.14.

Figure 10.13 **Protecting a Form Template**

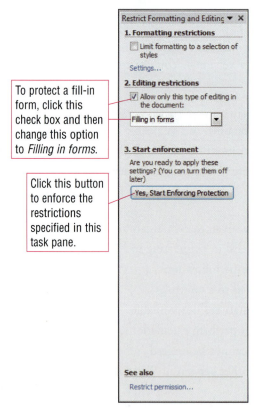

To protect a fill-in form, click this check box and then change this option to *Filling in forms.*

Click this button to enforce the restrictions specified in this task pane.

If you want to edit the form later, you will need to unprotect the form. To unprotect the document, open it and then click the Restrict Editing button in the Protect group on the Developer tab. At the Restrict Formatting and Editing task pane, click the Stop Protection button at the bottom of the task pane.

Exercise 10.3   Creating a Form with Content Controls

1. At a blank document, open **MidwestRealEstateFormTemplate** located in your *Chapter10* folder.
2. Select *Real Estate Client Information* in the second row (the banner text is typed in the first row), change the font to 12-point Verdana in bold, and center horizontally.
3. With the text still selected, click the Shading button in the Table Styles group in the Table Tools Design tab, and then click Black, Text 1, which adds a black background behind the text and automatically changes the text color to White.
4. Add content controls to the form by completing the following steps:
   a. Display the Developer tab and then click the Design Mode button to turn it on.
   b. Position the insertion point to the right of *Date:*, press the spacebar once if necessary, and then click the Date Picker content control in the Controls group. ***Hint: The date field will display a calendar. When Design Mode is off and the field is clicked.***

   c. Position the insertion point to the right of *Name:* and then click the Rich Text Content Control. ***Hint: The Rich Text Content Control allows the user to apply bold, apply italics, and type multiple paragraphs; the Plain Text Content Control limits the user and does not allow the user to apply formatting to the text.***
   d. Add text content controls for the following labels:
      Spouse's name:
      Address:
      Phone:
      Cell:
      Email:
   e. Position the insertion point to the left of *Home email* and insert a check box. Click the Check Box Content Control button in the Controls group in the Developer tab. Make sure the Check Box Content Control is centered and the font size is set at 12-points.

   f. Insert Check Box Content Controls at the left of the remaining labels in the *Preferred method of communication* section. Add a Rich Text Content Control after the *Other* label.

g. Position the insertion point in the row below the *Best time to call* section, and insert Rich Text Content Controls into both of the cells in this section.

h. Position the insertion point in the cell at the right of *Housing preference* and then click the Drop-Down Content Control button in the Controls group. ***Hint: Make sure the Design Mode is turned on.***

i. Select the Drop-Down List content control, and then click the Properties in the Controls group of the Developer tab.

j. At the Content Control Properties dialog box, type **Housing preference** in the *Title* and *Tag* text boxes. Click the Add button, type **Own**, click OK, click the Add button again, type **Rent**, click OK again, click Add once more, type **Lease**, and then again click OK. At the Content Control Properties dialog box, click OK.

k. Insert the following controls to the labels listed here and add the following drop-down lists:

Label:	Type of control:	Type this text and add to list:
Number of bedrooms:	Drop-Down Content Control	2, 3, 4, 5, 6 +
Number of stories:	Drop-Down Content Control	Ranch, Bi-level, Tri-level, 2-story
Number of baths:	Drop-Down Content Control	2, 3, 4, 5, 6 +
Number of garages:	Drop-Down Content Control	1, 2, 3, 4
How many square feet?	Rich Text Content Control	
Finished basement?	Drop-Down Content Control	Yes, No
Price range in thousands:	Drop-Down Content Control	100 - 220
		220 - 350
		350 - 500
		500 - 650
		650 - 800
		800 +
Formal living room	Drop-Down Content Control	Yes, No
Formal dining room	Drop-Down Content Control	Yes, No

5. In the *Housing financial information* section, insert Check Box Content Controls at the right of *Do you have a prequalified letter?*. Type **Yes** in the cell at the right of the first check box; type **No** in the cell at the right of the second check box. ***Hint: Make sure that the check boxes are formatted in 12-points and that they are centered horizontally.***

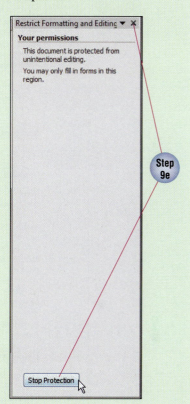

6. Position the insertion point to the right of *Type of financing:*, and add another Rich Text Content Control.
7. Position the insertion point to the right of *Mortgate:*, and add a Rich Text Content Control.
8. Click the Design Mode button in the Controls group in the Developer tab to turn it off.
9. Protect the form by completing the following steps:
   a. Click the Restrict Editing button in the Protect group on the Developer tab.
   b. At the Restrict Formatting and Editing task pane, click in the *Allow only this type of editing in the document* check box to insert a check mark.
   c. Click the down-pointing arrow at the right side of the option box in the *Editing restrictions* section and then click *Filling in forms* at the drop-down list.
   d. Click the Yes, Start Enforcing Protection button in the task pane. You will be prompted to type a password; however, it is not necessary to add one to the protected template. If you do not want the password, simply click OK without typing a password. Close the Restrict Formatting and Editing task pane.
   e. **Optional:** If you want to edit your protected template, display the Developer tab, click the Restrict Editing button in the Protect group, and then click the Stop Protection button at the bottom of the Restrict Formatting and Editing task pane. Close the task pane. Click the Design Mode button in the Controls group to turn this feature on, and then add any desired controls or remove any unwanted controls.
10. Save the form with Save As, and name it **C10-E03-RealEstateForm**.
11. Close **C10-E03-RealEstateForm.dotx**.
12. Open **C10-E03-RealEstateForm.dotx** and fill in all the data fields with relevant information. ***Hint: You will need to click inside each content control to fill in the data.***
13. Print the completed form and then close it.

Figure 10.14 **Exercise 10.3**

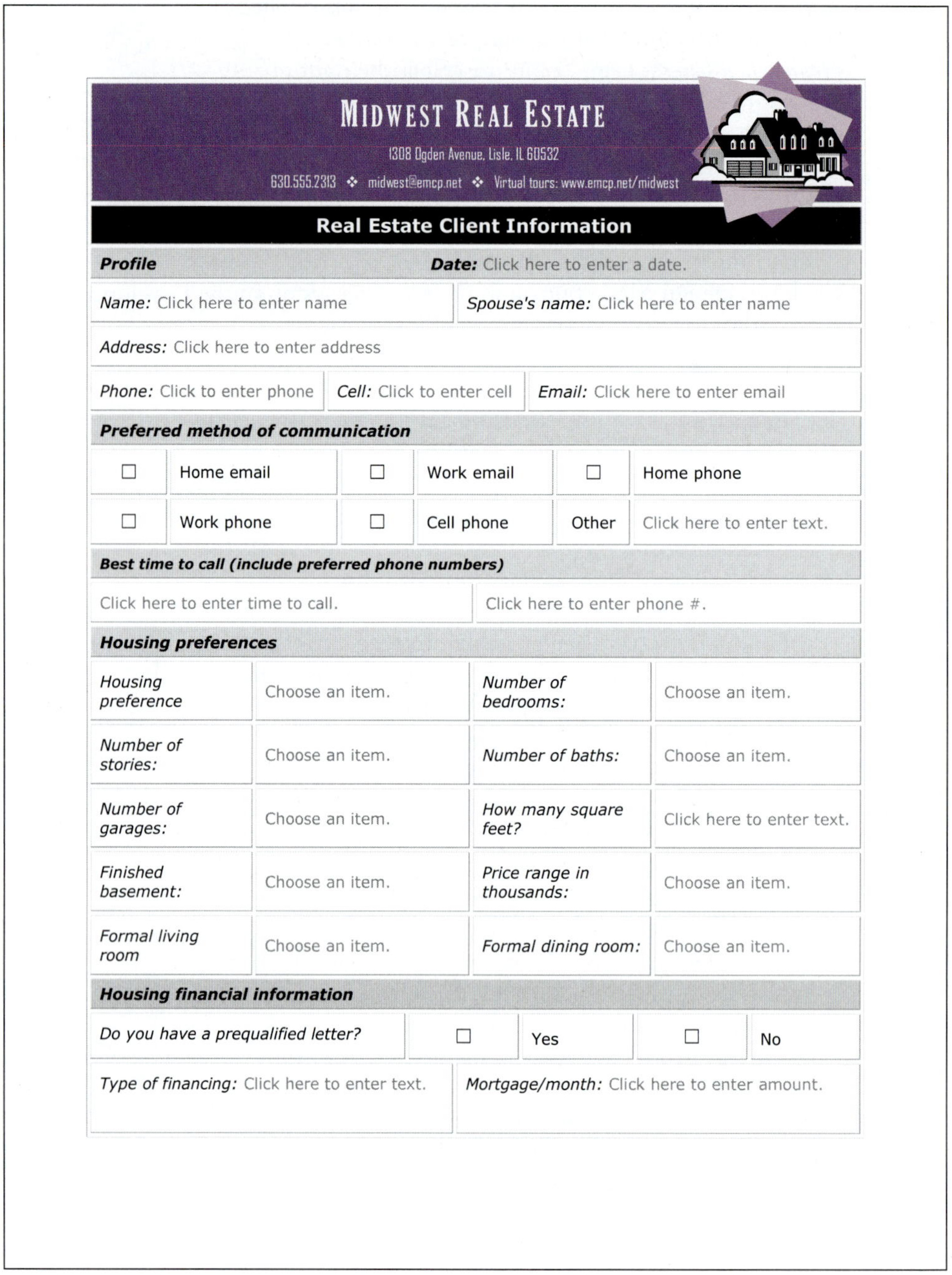

MIDWEST REAL ESTATE

1308 Ogden Avenue, Lisle, IL 60532

630.555.2313 ❖ midwest@emcp.net ❖ Virtual tours: www.emcp.net/midwest

Real Estate Client Information

Profile		Date: Click here to enter a date.	
Name: Click here to enter name		Spouse's name: Click here to enter name	
Address: Click here to enter address			
Phone: Click to enter phone	Cell: Click to enter cell	Email: Click here to enter email	

Preferred method of communication

☐	Home email	☐	Work email	☐	Home phone
☐	Work phone	☐	Cell phone	Other	Click here to enter text.

Best time to call (include preferred phone numbers)

Click here to enter time to call.	Click here to enter phone #.

Housing preferences

Housing preference	Choose an item.	Number of bedrooms:	Choose an item.
Number of stories:	Choose an item.	Number of baths:	Choose an item.
Number of garages:	Choose an item.	How many square feet?	Click here to enter text.
Finished basement:	Choose an item.	Price range in thousands:	Choose an item.
Formal living room	Choose an item.	Formal dining room:	Choose an item.

Housing financial information

Do you have a prequalified letter?	☐	Yes	☐	No
Type of financing: Click here to enter text.		Mortgage/month: Click here to enter amount.		

Determining Which Form Fields or Content Controls to Use

Content controls work only in Word 2010 documents and templates. You can apply formatting styles to them, and you can prevent them from being edited or deleted. There are nine content controls, and they are summarized in Figure 10.15.

Figure 10.15 Content Controls

Rich Text	Aa	Holds text that can optionally be formatted by the user (bold, italics, etc.).
Plain Text	Aa	Holds plain text that the user cannot format.
Picture		Holds a picture that the user inserts.
Building Blocks Gallery		Inserts a placeholder from which the user can select a building block from the gallery.
Combo Box		Displays a list of values that the user can select; the user can add other values.
Drop-Down List		Displays a list of values; the user cannot add more values.
Date Picker		Displays a calendar from which the user can pick a date.
Check Box	☑	Displays a check box that the user can click to add a check mark.
Legacy Tools		Displays a gallery of Legacy Tools and ActiveX Controls.

Legacy form fields are the field types that were available in earlier versions of Word. You can continue to use them in Word 2010, and you must use them for forms saved in the Word 97–2003 formats. Figure 10.16 explains each of the form fields. Hopefully, this will help you decide which form fields will fit your needs.

Figure 10.16 Legacy Form Fields

Text Form Field	ab|	Holds text.
Check Box Form Field	☑	Creates an on/off check box.
Drop-Down Form Field		Displays a list of values from which the user can choose.
Insert Frame		Creates a frame that holds static content.
Form Field Shading	a	Toggles form field shading on and off.
Reset Form Fields		Clears all entries in fields.

Figure 10.17 Saving Templates to *My templates* at the New Tab Backstage View

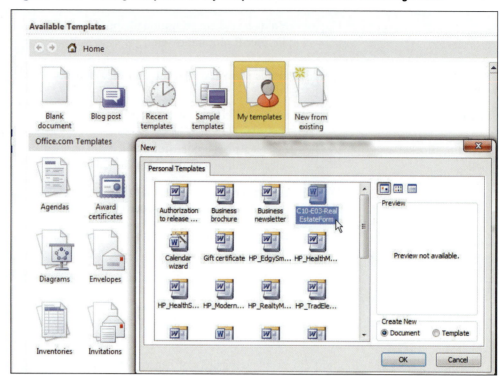

Filling in a Form

To fill in a form, open the protected form template document by clicking the File tab and then clicking the New tab. At the New tab Backstage view, click *My templates…* in the *Available Templates* section. At the New dialog box, click the desired template in the Personal templates gallery as shown in Figure 10.17, make sure *Document* is selected in the *Create New* section, and then click OK. If instructed to save your template to your storage device, open it from this device, and then save it as a document based on the template.

When you open the form template document, the insertion point is automatically inserted in the first data field. Type the information in the data field, and then press the Tab key to move to the next field or press Shift + Tab to move to the previous field. Clicking the content control placeholder may work better for forms created using content controls. To insert a check mark in a check box, press the spacebar or click in the field with the mouse.

Editing a Protected Form

If you want to edit your protected template, do the following:
1. Display the Developer tab.
2. Click the Restrict Editing button in the Protect group.
3. Click the Stop Protection button at the bottom of the Restrict Formatting and Editing task pane as shown in Figure 10.18.
4. Close the task pane.
5. Click the Design Mode button in the Controls group to turn this feature on, and then add any desired controls or remove any unwanted controls.

Figure 10.18 Editing a Protected Form

Figure 10.19 Printing Data Only

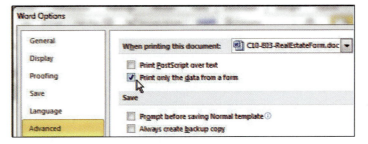

Printing a Form

After filling in a form, you can print the form in the normal manner. However, you also have the option to print just the data (not the entire form) or print the form and not the fill-in data. To print just the data in a form, display the Word Options dialog box, click the *Advanced* tab, and then click the *Print only the data from a form* in the *When printing this document* section as shown in Figure 10.19.

In Exercise 10.4, you will create a table as the underlying structure of a form and then insert Legacy form fields and send the form as an email attachment. When the user receives the email with form fields (use Legacy fields), they will see the fields embedded in the email. When the user replies to the email, the fields will be editable. Do not save the file in PDF format, because the user will not be able to fill in the form.

Exercise 10.4 Creating an Evaluation Form

1. Open **ConsultingBanner** located in your *Chapter10* folder.
2. Save the document as a template and name it **C10-E04-ConferenceEvaluation**. *Hint: Make sure the* **Save as type** *is a* **Word Template.**
3. Click Ctrl + End to move the insertion point below the banner.
4. Select the Technic theme.

5. Create a table as the structure for the form by completing the following steps:

   a. Click the Table button in the Insert tab, and then click Insert Table. At the Insert Table dialog box, type **3** in the *Number of columns* and **20** in the *Number of rows*. Click OK.

   b. With the insertion point inside the table, display the Table Tools Design tab, and then select *Light Shading – Accent 1* from the Table Styles gallery.

   c. Click the Properties button in the Table Tools Layout tab.

   d. At the Table Properties dialog box, select the Table tab, and click Center in the *Alignment* section.

   e. Select the Column tab and change the width of column 1 to approximately **0.5"**, column 2 to **3.2"**, and column 3 to **3.2"**. Click OK. *Hint: Click the Next Column button to move from one column setting to the next.*

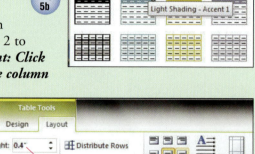

   f. Position the insertion point in column 2, row 1, turn on bold, and then type **Questions**. Press Tab, make sure bold is on, and then type **Evaluation**. Change the row height to 0.4", and center the text vertically and horizontally in each cell in this row.

   g. Select column 1, and click the Align Text Right button in the Paragraph group on the Home tab.

   h. Select column 2, except for the first row and click the Align Text Left button. Select column 3, except for the first row and click the Center button.

   i. Position the insertion point in column 1, row 2, and type **1**. Press the Tab key. Type **The conference was interesting**.

   j. Continue typing the number of the questions in the first column and the questions in the second column until you reach the heading *Topic*. Refer to Figure 10.20 for the text.

   k. After question 5, select the next row and merge the cells.

   l. Change the alignment to Align Text Left, type **Topic**, and then press Enter.

   m. Press Ctrl + Tab to move the insertion point to the default tab.

6. Create a drop-down list by completing the following steps:

   a. Click the Design Mode button on the Developer tab to turn on this feature.

   b. Click the Legacy Tools button and then click the Drop-Down Form Field button.

   c. Select the gray form field and then click Properties.

   d. At the Drop-Down Form Field Options dialog box, type **Getting Organized** and click Add; type **How Far Is Too Far?** and click Add; type **Communicate with Confidence** and click Add. Click OK.

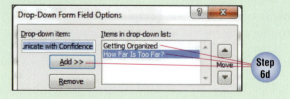

7. Continue typing the numbers and questions for 6–8. Refer to Figure 10.20 for the text.

8. After question 8, select the next row and merge the cells.

9. Change the alignment to Align Text Left, type **Facilities**, and then press Enter.

10. Continue typing the numbers and questions for 9–12. Refer to Figure 10.20 for the text.

11. After question 12, select the next row and merge the cells.

12. Change the alignment to Align Text Left, type **Additional Comments**, and then press Enter.

13. Continue typing the numbers and questions for 13–15. Refer to Figure 10.20 for the text.

14. To insert the text areas for questions 13–15, complete the following steps:

    a. Position the insertion point in the third column of the seventeenth row (right of question 13), click the Legacy Tools button, and then click the Text Form Field button. Make sure the Design Mode button is recessed (turned on).

    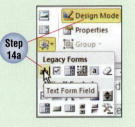

    b. Copy and paste the text area box to the eighteenth and nineteenth rows.

15. You are now ready to create the Evaluation column. Complete the following steps:

    a. Position the insertion point in the third column of the second row.

    b. Click the Legacy Tools button, click the Check Box Form Field button, and then press the spacebar once.

    c. Type **3** and then press the spacebar 10 times.

    d. Insert another Check Box Form Field, press the spacebar once, type **2**, and then press the spacebar 10 times.

    e. Insert another Check Box Form Field, press the spacebar once, type **1**, and then press the spacebar 10 times.

    f. Insert another Check Box Form Field, press the spacebar once, and then type **NA**.

    g. Select the cell containing the four option buttons, click Copy, and then paste this information to the rows shown in Figure 10.20.

16. Click the Design Mode button to turn off this feature.

17. Select each group of check boxes and text form fields (Questions 1-5), (Questions 6 - 8), (Questions 9 - 12), (Questions 13 - 15), and then click the Align Center button in the Alignment group in the Table Tools Layout tab for each group.

18. Remove all the border lines from the table.

19. Protect the form by completing the following steps:
    a. Click the Restrict Editing button in the Protect group in the Developer tab.
    b. At the Restrict Formatting and Editing task pane, click to add a check mark next to *Allow only this type of editing in the document.* From the drop-down list, select *Filling in forms.*
    c. Click Yes, Start Enforcing Protection.
    d. At the Start Enforcing Protection dialog box, do not insert a password. Click OK.
    e. Close the task pane.

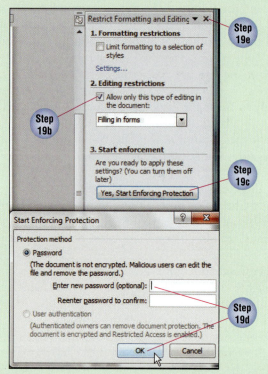

20. Save the document again with the same name, **C10-E04-ConferenceEvaluation**.
21. Close the form template.
22. Open **C10-E04-ConferenceEvaluation.dotx** and verify that the form fields are working properly. ***Hint: You may have to show "all files" to be able to see the template file.***
23. Print and then close **C10-E04-ConferenceEvaluation.dotx**.

Figure 10.20 **Exercise 10.4**

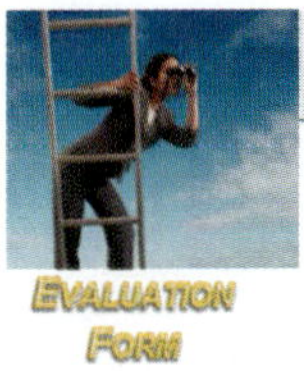

Cooper Consulting, Inc.

Conference: Pride and Professionalism

Please tell us what you think about the conference. Use the following scale:

3 Strongly Agree/Excellent   **2** Agree/Good   **1** Disagree/Needs Improvement   **NA**

	Questions	Evaluation			
1	The conference was interesting	☐ 3	☐ 2	☐ 1	☐ NA
2	The topics and subjects covered were relevant	☐ 3	☐ 2	☐ 1	☐ NA
3	I was energized or stimulated by the conference	☐ 3	☐ 2	☐ 1	☐ NA
4	I would recommend this format for future events	☐ 3	☐ 2	☐ 1	☐ NA
5	Overall quality of the conference	☐ 3	☐ 2	☐ 1	☐ NA
Topic					
	Getting Organized				
6	The presenter was well informed and interesting	☐ 3	☐ 2	☐ 1	☐ NA
7	I am interested in another presentation on this topic with more information	☐ 3	☐ 2	☐ 1	☐ NA
8	Overall quality of the presentation	☐ 3	☐ 2	☐ 1	☐ NA
Facilities					
9	The meeting events were well organized	☐ 3	☐ 2	☐ 1	☐ NA
10	The facilities were satisfactory	☐ 3	☐ 2	☐ 1	☐ NA
11	The meeting room arrangements were comfortable	☐ 3	☐ 2	☐ 1	☐ NA
12	The quality of the luncheon was good	☐ 3	☐ 2	☐ 1	☐ NA
Additional Comments					
13	What was the most useful thing you learned in this conference?				
14	What other topics are you interested in having presented?				
15	Comments and suggestions on this conference				

Creating Forms in a Web Page

You can use Word to create an interactive form that is used on the Web and that provides the user options to give input or answer questions. Users view and complete the form in a browser. Web forms use ActiveX Controls, which may require additional support files and server support.

DTP POINTERS
Users view and complete a Web form in their browser.

Inserting ActiveX Controls

DTP POINTERS

An Option button is used when you want to give the user only one option.

DTP POINTERS

A check box is used when you want to give the user more than one choice.

Along with inserting Legacy form fields, you may also access a set of ActiveX controls when you click the Legacy Tools button in the Controls group on the Developer tab. If you are designing a form where the user will be prompted to make a single choice from multiple options, such as Yes, No, or Maybe, you will want to add an Option button so that the user can select just one of them and the other options in the group will become deselected. To create Option buttons in your form, follow these steps:

1. Position the insertion point where you want the first Option button.
2. Turn on Design Mode.
3. On the Developer tab, in the Controls group, click Legacy Tools, and in the *ActiveX Controls* section, click the Option button.
4. With the Option button control selected, click Properties.
5. In the *Caption* box, type the text that should appear next to the button—or right-click on the Option button, click Option Button Object, click Edit, and then type the desired text.
6. In the *GroupName* box, type any name you like. The name must be the same for all buttons in the group.
7. Repeat these steps for additional Option buttons. Make sure you use the same name.
8. Close the Properties pane.
9. Turn off Design Mode.

ActiveX Security Issues

ActiveX controls are used in websites and other applications on your computer in the form of check boxes, text boxes, option buttons, and more. When inserting ActiveX Controls into the web form created in Exercise 10.5, a security dialog box may appear as shown in Figure 10.21. Ask your instructor whether you should enable the ActiveX. You should enable the ActiveX control only if you are sure it is from a trustworthy source.

Figure 10.21 ActiveX Controls Security Warning

Exercise 10.5   Creating a Web Page Survey Form

1. Create a web page form as shown in Figure 10.22 using a table and the ActiveX Controls by completing the following steps:
   a. Open **WebSurveyForm** located in your *Chapter10* folder.
   b. Save the form as **C10-E05-WebSurveyForm** in Single File Web Page format. *Hint: The document will display in Web Layout view.*
   c. Make sure the Technic theme is selected.
   d. Select *Web Page Survey* in the first cell (the form is created in a table) and apply the Title style. Select *Web Page Survey* and then click Align Center Left in the Alignment group in the Table Tools Layout tab.

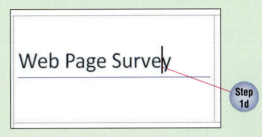

   e. Position your insertion point in the second cell in the first row and add a motion clip by typing **Web**, **Rotating**, or **Web animations** in the *Search for* text box in the Clip Art task pane. Size and position it as shown in Figure 10.22. *Hint: Substitute the image if it is no longer available. A motion clip displays with a yellow star in the bottom right corner in the Clip Art task pane. You could also insert a picture by clicking the Picture Content Control in the Controls group in the Developer tab. If you use the Picture Content Control, you may want to copy a desired clip art image or motion clip, paste it into the Insert Picture dialog box, and then insert the image.*

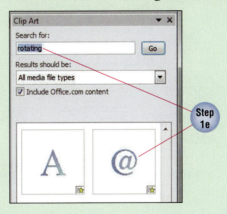

   f. Select the paragraph that begins *Please complete the following survey . . .* and apply the Subtitle style.
   g. Select *Which Web page will you evaluate?* and apply the Heading 2 style. Apply the Heading 2 style to the remaining headings: *What is the goal of the Web Page?, Who is the intended audience of the Web page?,* and *Design Elements.*
   h. Apply the Quote style to *List a few of the design...* text below the Design Elements heading and *Please include your name* text near the bottom of the page.
   i. Apply the Subtle Reference style to the *Top of Page | Email Results* text at the bottom of the page.

2. Add a gradient background color to the page by completing the following steps:

   a. Click the Page Color button in the Page Background group in the Page Layout tab.

   b. At the drop-down gallery, click Fill Effects.

   c. At the Fill Effects dialog box, select the Gradient tab.

   d. At the Gradient tab, click the *One color* option in the *Colors* section and then choose *Aqua, Accent 1* Theme color in the first row and fifth column of the Color 1 gallery.

   e. Move the slider toward *Light* to add white to the gradient.

   f. Select the *Horizontal* shading style. Click OK.

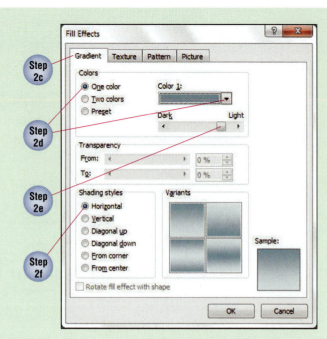

3. Display the Developer tab, turn on the *Design Mode* option, and then insert the following form fields:

   a. Position the insertion point in the first cell in the fourth row, and then click the Legacy Tools button.

   b. Click the Option button in the *ActiveX Controls* section.

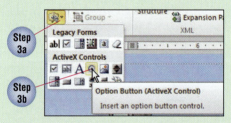

   c. Right-click on the Option button, click *OptionButton Object*, and then click *Edit*.

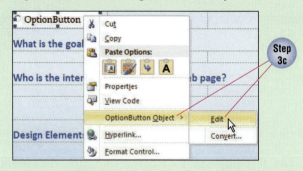

   d. Delete the placeholder text inside the Option control and type **target.com**.

   e. With the Option control selected, click Properties in the Controls group. ***Hint: You may need to deselect and then reselect the control.***

f. At the Alphabetic tab in the Properties box, click in the right column beside *GroupName* and type **goal1**. Click to the right of *Value* and type **True**. Close the Properties dialog box.

g. Position the insertion point in the second cell and add an option button as instructed in step 3f. Name the option control **coca-cola.com**. Type **goal1** at the right of *GroupName* and then type **False** at the right of *Value*.

h. Position the insertion point in the third cell and add an option button as instructed in step 3f. Name the option control **usps.com**. Again type **goal1** at the right of *GroupName* and type **False** at the right of *Value*.

i. Position the insertion point in the fourth cell and add an option button as instructed in step 3f. Name the option control **sandiegozoo.com**. Again type **goal1** at the right of *GroupName* and type **False** at the right of *Value*.

4. Position the insertion point in the row below *What is the goal of the Web Page?* and add Option controls by completing the following steps:

a. Insert an Option button in the first cell in the sixth row, name the control **Make money**, and change the *GroupName* to **goal2** and the *Value* to **True**.

b. Add Option buttons labeled as **Give information**, **Stroke an ego**, and **Provide a service**. Make sure you change the Properties settings for *GroupName* (goal2) and *Value(False)*.

5. Position the insertion point in the first cell of the row below *Who is the intended audience of the Web page?* and add Check Box controls by completing the following steps:

a. Insert a Check Box button in the ActiveX Controls in the first cell in the eighth row, name the control **7 years - 15 years** and change the *GroupName* to **goal3** and the *Value* to **True**.

b. Add Check Box buttons labeled as **16 - 21 years** and **Over 21 years**. Make sure you change the Properties settings for *GroupName* and verify the *Value* is set to False. Click the Close button at the Properties dialog box.

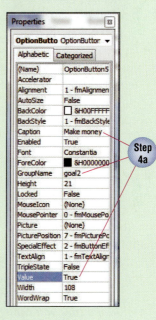

6. Position the insertion point in the ninth row. Click the Page Borders button in the Page Background group in the Page Layout tab, click the Horizontal Line button, and then select a graphical border that coordinates with the graphic and the styles used in the web page.

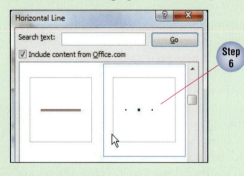

Step 6

7. To add more leading before the horizontal line, select the line, and type **18 pt** in the *Before* text box in the *Spacing* section in the Paragraph group in the Page Layout tab.

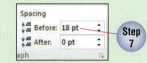

Step 7

8. Position the insertion point in the cell to the right of the text *List a few of the design elements . . .* and insert a Text Box control by completing the following steps:
   a. Click the Legacy Tools button and select the Text Box button in the Active X controls.
   b. With the Text Box control selected, click Properties.
   c. At the Properties dialog box, select **True** in the column (drop-down list) at the right of *EnterKeyBehavior*. Select **True** in the column (drop-down list) at the right of *MultiLine*. Select **True** in the column (drop-down list) at the right of *WordWrap*. Click the Close button at the Properties dialog box.
   d. Drag the sizing handles on the text box to expand the size of the box as shown in Figure 10.22.

9. Position the insertion point in the twelfth row to the left of *Please include your name.* and insert another Text Box control. Make the text box a little larger. Deselect the text box and press the Spacebar key once. ***Hint: Make sure you change the Properties to True at the EnterKeyBehavior and MultiLine options.***

10. Create a bookmark at the top of the page and then create a hyperlink to this bookmark from the *Top of Page* text at the bottom of the form.

11. Create a hyperlink to your instructor's email address.

12. Click the Design Mode button to turn off this feature. Make sure all border lines have been removed.

13. Save the Web page again as **C10-E05-WebSurveyForm** (in Single File Web Page format).

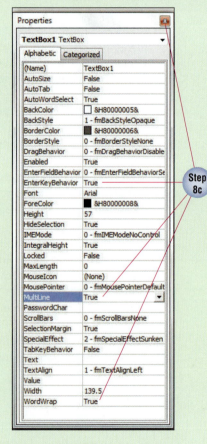

Step 8c

14. Preview the web page in Web Page Preview. *Hint: When you view your page in the Internet Explorer browser, a prompt may display restricting the web page from running scripts or ActiveX Controls. Select the option to Allow Blocked Content.*

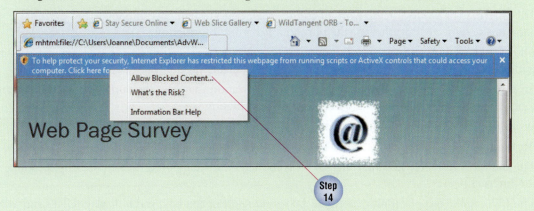

15. Complete the form, print, and then close **C10-E05-WebSurveyForm.mhtml**.

Figure 10.22 **Exercise 10.5**

Chapter Summary

➤ The Internet is a worldwide network of commercial, educational, governmental, and personal computers connected together for the purpose of sharing information.

➤ The World Wide Web (www) is the most commonly used application on the Internet and is a set of standards and protocols used to access information available on the Internet.

➤ An intranet is an "internal Internet" within an organization that uses the same web technology and tools as the Internet and is also used for sharing information.

➤ Word provides the ability to jump to the Internet from the Word document screen.

➤ An Internet Service Provider (ISP) sells access to the Internet.

➤ The Uniform Resource Locator, referred to as the URL, is the method used to identify locations on the Internet.

➤ The *URL address* text box is now called the *Document Location* text box, and it displays URLs and locations of an object, document, Web page, or other destination on the Internet or an intranet.

➤ Content controls can be inserted in a form with buttons in the Developer tab.

➤ The Developer tab can be displayed by clicking the Office button and then clicking Word Options. At the Word Options dialog box with the *Customize Ribbon* selected, select the *Developer* check box to display the Developer tab. Click OK.

➤ Home pages are the starting point for viewing websites. Home pages are also documents that describe a company, school, government, or individual and are created using a language called Hypertext Markup Language (HTML).

➤ Web pages should be planned and designed with a purpose in mind. Review other web pages on the Internet or an intranet for design ideas.

➤ Hyperlinks are colored and underlined text or a graphic that you click to go to a file, a location in a file, an HTML page on the Web, or an HTML page on an intranet.

➤ One method for creating a hyperlink is to select the text and then click the Hyperlink button in the Links group on the Insert tab.

➤ Bookmarks are created and used to move to another location within a document.

➤ Lines are added to a web page through the Clip Art task pane, from the Borders and Shading dialog box, or by accessing the Horizontal Line dialog box.

➤ A web page document can be previewed by adding the Web Page Preview button to the Quick Access Toolbar.

➤ Tables can be used to control the layout of a web page.

➤ Content controls can provide instructional text for users, and you can set controls to disappear when users type in their own text.

➤ A check box control is used when the user can select more than one choice at once.

➤ An option button control is used when the user should select only one option.

➤ Apply themes to your web page to control the Quick Styles that are available for convenient formatting and designing text in your web page.

➤ Options at the Restrict Formatting and Editing task pane can be used to protect a template.

➤ The Restrict Formatting and Editing task pane can be displayed by clicking the Restrict Editing button in the Protect group in the Developer tab.

➤ A form template can be edited by unprotecting the template, making desired changes, and then protecting the template.

➤ Instructional text can be added in a content control. To do this, type the instructional text, select the text, and then click the Text button in the Controls group on the Developer tab.

➤ The properties of the selected content control can be changed by clicking the Properties button in the Controls group on the Developer tab.

Commands *Review*

FEATURE	RIBBON TAB, GROUP	BUTTON	KEYBOARD SHORTCUT
Bookmark	Insert, Links		
Building Blocks Gallery	Developer, Controls		
Bullets	Home, Paragraph		
Date Picker	Developer, Controls		
Design Mode	Developer, Controls		
Document Location	File, Options, Quick Access Toolbar, All Commands		
Drop-Down List	Developer, Controls		
Horizontal Lines	Page Layout, Page Borders, Page Background		
Hyperlink	Insert, Links		
Legacy Tools	Developer, Controls		
Page Color	Page Background, Page Layout		
Picture Content Control	Developer, Controls		
Properties	Developer, Controls		
Restrict Editing	Developer, Protect		
Rich Text Content Control	Developer, Controls	Aa	
Web Page Preview	File, Options, Quick Access Toolbar		

Reviewing Key Points

Completion: On a blank sheet of paper, indicate the correct term, command, or number for each item.

1. List three reasons why users access the Internet.
2. The unabbreviated form of ISP.
3. A method used to identify locations on the Internet.
4. An "internal Internet" used to share information within an organization.
5. A feature that is used to move to another location within a document.
6. This Word feature may be used to control the layout of a web page.
7. A web page can be viewed at this Word preview screen.
8. A World Wide Web language that is abbreviated as HTML.
9. A button on the Developer tab that restricts how the form can be edited.
10. A task pane that displays when the Restrict Editing button on the Developer tab is clicked.
11. A button on the Developer tab that is used to insert a date content control.
12. This type of control can be used in a form if the person entering information needs to choose from a specific list of options.
13. Options at this dialog box can be used to customize a data content control.
14. A button on the Developer tab that must be activated before inserting form fields and content controls into a form.
15. The Legacy Tools button is located in this group on the Developer tab.

Chapter Assessments

Assessment 10.1   Real Estate Form and Excel Mortgage Calculator

In this assessment, you will open **C10-E03-RealEstateForm.dotx** and create a hyperlink from this form to an Excel spreadsheet. The spreadsheet includes automatic calculations for a mortgage loan (see Figure 10.23). Include the following specifications:

1. Open **C10-E03-RealEstateForm.dotx**, which was created in Exercise 10.3.
2. Unprotect the form by clicking the Restrict Editing button in the Developer tab. Click *Stop Protection* at the Restrict Formatting and Editing task pane.
3. Position the insertion point in the cell that contains the text *Housing financial information*, and then click the Split Cells button in the Merge group on the Table Tools Layout tab.
4. At the Split Cells dialog box, type **2** in the *Number of columns* text box and **1** in the *Number of rows* text box. Click OK.
5. Position the insertion point in the new cell to the right of *Housing financial information*, type **Loan Calculator**, and apply bold. Click the Hyperlink button on the Insert tab, and then create a hyperlink to the Excel file, **LoanCalculator1**, located in the *Chapter10* folder.
6. Protect the form again. Close the task pane.
7. Save the form with the hyperlink as **C10-A01-FormandCalculator**.
8. Close the form and then reopen it.
9. Press Ctrl and then click the hyperlink to access the Excel spreadsheet (loan calculator) located in the *Chapter10* folder.
10. Fill in the loan application for a loan of $200,000, at 6% interest rate, 30-year loan period, and use the current date.
11. Save the completed document as **C10-A01-FormatCalculatorExcel**.

Figure 10.23 Assessment 10.1

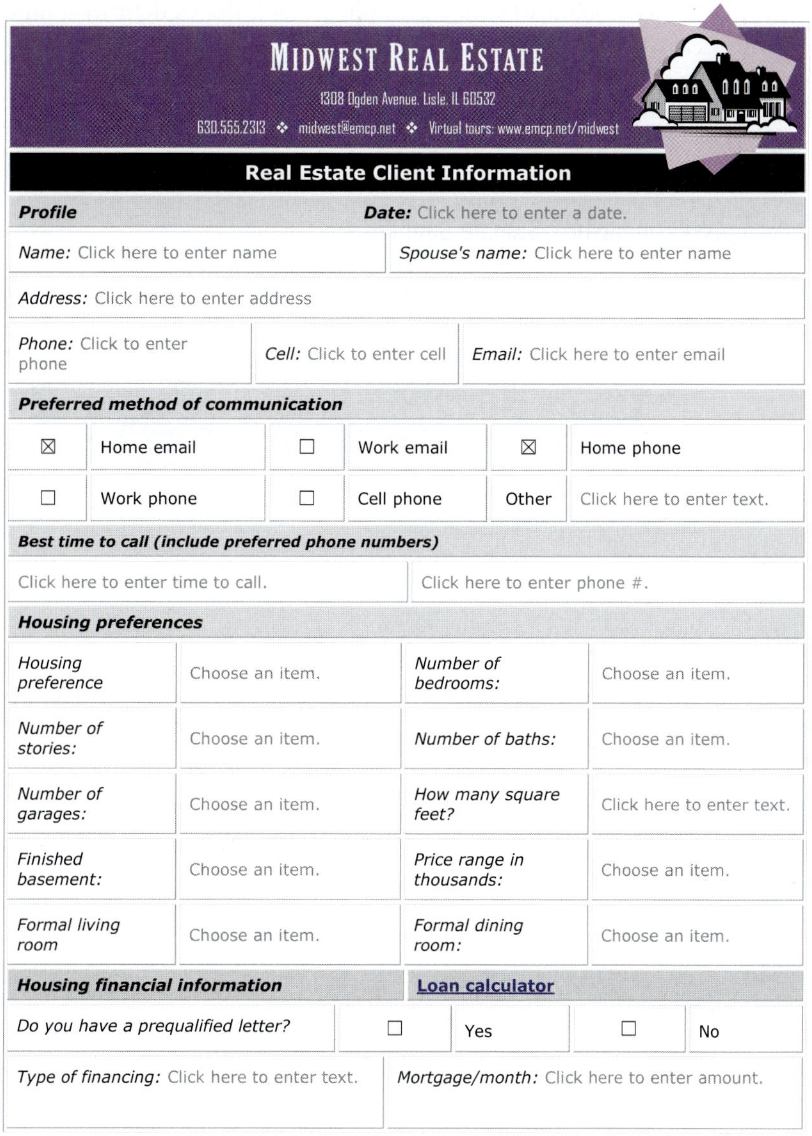

MIDWEST REAL ESTATE
1308 Ogden Avenue, Lisle, IL 60532

630.555.2313 ❖ midwest@emcp.net ❖ Virtual tours: www.emcp.net/midwest

Real Estate Client Information

Profile   **Date:** Click here to enter a date.

Name: Click here to enter name	*Spouse's name:* Click here to enter name

Address: Click here to enter address

Phone: Click to enter phone	*Cell:* Click to enter cell	*Email:* Click here to enter email

Preferred method of communication

☒	Home email	☐	Work email	☒	Home phone
☐	Work phone	☐	Cell phone	Other	Click here to enter text.

Best time to call (include preferred phone numbers)

Click here to enter time to call.	Click here to enter phone #.

Housing preferences

Housing preference	Choose an item.	Number of bedrooms:	Choose an item.
Number of stories:	Choose an item.	Number of baths:	Choose an item.
Number of garages:	Choose an item.	How many square feet?	Click here to enter text.
Finished basement:	Choose an item.	Price range in thousands:	Choose an item.
Formal living room	Choose an item.	Formal dining room:	Choose an item.

Housing financial information   **Loan calculator**

Do you have a prequalified letter?	☐	Yes	☐	No

Type of financing: Click here to enter text.	Mortgage/month: Click here to enter amount.

---

12. Print the first page of the loan calculation, print the real estate form, attach the documents, and then close both documents.

Assessment 10.2   Dental Insurance Form

Create a dental insurance form, such as that shown in Figure 10.24, and insert form fields and content controls where needed in the form. Include the following specifications:

1. Open **Dental** located in your *Chapter10* folder.
2. Insert an appropriate image in the first cell of the form. You may use a clip art image or a photograph of your choosing.

3. Insert content controls and Legacy form fields in the cells of the form.
4. When you are satisfied with the layout of the form, protect the document, and then save it as a template.
5. Send the template form to another student in your classroom and ask the student to complete the form. Ask the student user to evaluate the form for ease in competing it. Also create a hyperlink at the bottom of the form to send the form to your instructor's email.
6. Save the dental form as **C10-A02-Dental**.
7. Ask the student who completed your form to print it.

Figure 10.24 Assessment 10.2 Sample Solution

Long Island Dental Plan		
Enrollment Application Form		
Maxwell Laboratories, Inc.		**Date:** Click here to enter a date.

	Last Name	First Name and Middle Initial	
Applicant Information	Click here to enter text.	Click here to enter text.	
	Position/Job Title	Social Security Number	
	Click here to enter text.	- -	
	Street Address	Gender	Date of Birth (MM/DD/YYYY)
	Click here to enter text.	☐Male ☐ Female	
	City, State, Zip Code	Email Address	Marital Status
	Click here to enter text.	Click here to enter text.	Choose an item.
	Home Phone Number	Business Number	Cell Number
	- -	- -	- -
	Coverage Type	Dental Location Number	
	☐Single ☐Single + 1 ☐Family		

Create a hyperlink to your instructor's email address here.

Assessment 10.3 Integrated Merchandise Order Form

In this assessment, you will insert an Excel worksheet into a Word form template. Because of the Excel automatic calculating features, you will see that integrating Excel into the Word form makes it easier to make the computations.

1. Open **ApparelOrderForm** from your *Chapter10* folder.
2. Save the form as a template, and name it **C10-A03-ApparelOrderForm**.
3. Insert the Microsoft Excel 2010 spreadsheet with calculations below the email address by completing the following steps:
   a. Click the down arrow at the right of the Object button in the Text group in the Insert tab.
   b. At the drop-down list, select *Object*.
   c. At the Object dialog box, select the Create from File tab.
   d. At the Create from File tab, click Browse. Locate the *Chapter10* folder and double-click **ExcelApparelOrderForm**. Click OK. This inserts the Excel worksheet as an object, allowing you to use the Excel features while in Word.
   e. Save the form again as **C10-A03-ApparelOrderForm.dotx**.
4. Open **ApparelInputData**. Add the information above the Excel object to the order form.
5. Double-click inside the Excel object to access the Excel editing features. Enter the data from **ApparelInputData**.
6. Save the form and name it **C10-A03-CompletedApparelForm1**.
7. Follow these procedures to complete the second apparel form. Make sure you close the completed form and reopen the **C10-A03-ApparelOrderForm** to key the second form.
8. Save the second form and name it **C10-A03-CompletedApparelForm2**.
9. Print and then close the forms.
10. See the model answer in Figure 10.25.

Assessment 10.4 Creating a Web Page

As a group, assign individual tasks for each member of your group, and then design and create a web page on a topic of your group's choosing. Suggested topics include gardening, favorite sport or team, community project, volunteer project, hobby, or vacation spot. Look at other websites for ideas and layouts. Research your topic on the Internet and include at least three hyperlinks. Use appropriate graphics, borders, buttons, dividers, and background. Name your Web page **C10-A04-GroupWebPage**. *Optional:* Include a sound clip if you have sound available on your computer. Figure 10.26 is a sample solution.

Figure 10.25 Assessment 10.3 Sample Solution

Swimming Apparel Order Form

We will place our River Rats apparel order immediately following registration this year to ensure that the swimmers have their items for the summer swim season. Please note: All swimmers registered for summer swim will receive a complimentary team T-shirt.

Name:	Joseph Larabee
Address:	455 Ridgeland Circle
City:	Wheaton ST: IL ZIP: 60147
Phone:	603.555.1288
Child's Name: (for Sports Bag)	Jerrad

Order forms must be received by May 15 with registration. Please make checks payable to River Rats. If you have any questions, please call Kerry Swimmer at 555-8445 or email at kswimmer@emcp.net.

Item	Size				Quantity	Price	Total
	Small	Medium	Large	X-Large			
Team T-Shirt					0	$8	$0
Zip Hoodie Sweatshirt					0	$24	$0
Micro-Poly Full Zip Jacket		x			1	$37	$37
Micro-Poly Fully Lined Pants w/zipper on lower leg		x			1	$30	$30
Cotton Cheer Shorts					0	$10	$0
Plaid Flannel PJ Pant					0	$20	$0
Heavy Duty Sports Bag (w/child's name)					1	$32	$32
Total Number of Items Ordered					3		
Total Price							$99

Figure 10.26 Assessment 10.4 Sample Solution

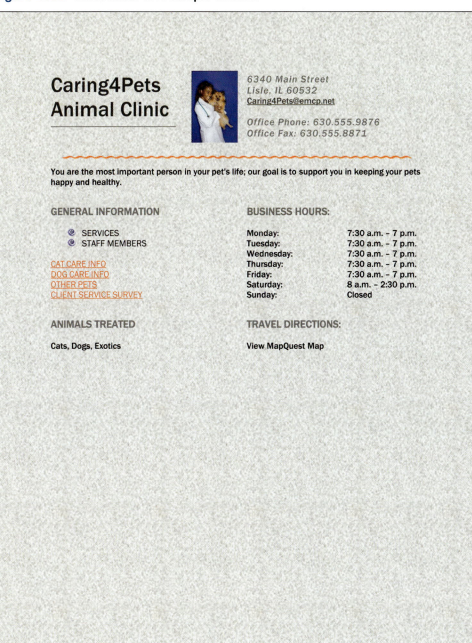

Chapter 11

CHAPTER11

Introducing Microsoft Publisher 2010

Performance Objectives

Upon successful completion of Chapter 11, you will be able to:

- Create a flyer with a coupon, trifold brochure, newsletter, flyer from scratch, merged postcard, flyer with pull-off tags, gift certificate, and poster.
- Determine when to use Word and when to use Publisher.
- Apply desktop publishing design concepts.

- Customize Publisher templates and create publications from scratch.
- Insert, Edit, and Update Business Information fields.
- Use Save As Picture and preformatted Building Blocks.
- Save publications in PDF format.
- Merge pictures and text using Catalog Merge.

Desktop Publishing Terms

Color Schemes	Linked picture	Ruler guides
Copyfitting	Logo	Scratch area
Embedded picture	Margin guides	Story
Grid guides	Master page	
Layout guides	Overflow	

Publisher Features Used

Building Blocks	Layout guides	Save as Picture
Catalog Pages (Merge)	Ligatures	Smart Tags
Color schemes	Master page	Text Fit
Connected text boxes	Pack and Go	Text overflow
Continued notice	Page numbers	Watermarks
Font schemes	Rotate or flip	
Hyphenation	Ruler guides	

Microsoft Publisher 2010 is a complete, easy-to-use desktop publishing program designed for small business users and individuals who want to create their own high-quality, professional-looking marketing materials and other business documents without the assistance of professional designers. Publisher consists of hundreds of customizable templates, flexible page layout guides, commercial printing options, and a full range of desktop publishing tools. With Publisher, you can create, design, and publish professional marketing and communication materials for print and email.

New and Improved Publisher 2010 Features

Publisher 2010 provides several new and improved capabilities to help you create a wide range of marketing materials, including the following:

- Hundreds of professionally designed templates—including new templates for popular brochures, newsletters, email, and other print publications
- Easy access to the Office.com online template gallery
- An updated user interface that includes the ribbon, Backstage view, and a cleaner workspace
- Improved design controls with visual layout guides and new object alignment technology
- New photo enhancements
- New Print and Preview screens with capabilities to view both sides of a page, multiple pages, page boundaries, and other pertinent print information
- Building blocks of content, style galleries, and font and color themes
- Sophisticated typography options such as true small caps, ligatures, and stylistic options
- Improved personalization of publications through Mail Merge, Email Merge, and Catalog Merge

Knowing When to Use Publisher, Word, or Microsoft Expression

If you are comfortable using Word to create professional-looking documents, use Word. Throughout Chapters 1 through 10, you have become familiar with many Word desktop publishing features, which make Word more than just a basic word processing program. Word has numerous templates, both within the program and online, that are similar to the types that Publisher contains. However, you may consider using Publisher if your publications require commercial printing. Publisher offers full support for commercial printing, including four-color separation, spot color processing, and automatic trapping for printing on an offset or digital press. Pantone Solid (spot colors) and Pantone Process colors are available to Publisher users who want to precisely match Pantone colors to colors used in business. However, you can work with Word from inside Publisher to edit a Publisher story, or you can pick a design set in Publisher and import a Word document.

Also, consider using Publisher if your document layouts need to be especially precise or complex. Publisher includes easy-to-use layout guides, Ruler guides, baseline guides, and Snap options to align objects to Ruler marks, guides, or other objects. Publisher includes hundreds of template options for common business publications and powerful design tasks, including color schemes, font schemes, and predesigned layouts and publication designs. Additional templates are available at the Office.com web page http://office.microsoft.com/templates.

Creating new websites and web publications is not available in Publisher 2010. However, users can still edit web publications created in earlier versions of Publisher. Users may create web pages using Microsoft Expression and supplement the design with interactive features available through Microsoft Silverlight.

Applying Design Concepts

Whether or not you create documents in Publisher using templates, you should understand and apply good design principles. You will still need to make critical

---

DTP POINTERS
Use Publisher if your publication requires a commercial printer.

DTP POINTERS
Publisher offers support for commercial printing, including color separation and spot color processing.

DTP POINTERS
Pick up design ideas from the works of others.

choices as to the type of publication that best conveys your message, a color scheme that reinforces the feel of your document, the identity of your target audience, and which design elements enrich your message and promote readability. Therefore, careful planning and organizing of content and design elements are as necessary when using Publisher as when using Word to create professional-looking documents.

Keep the overall look of your publication simple and use plenty of white space. Reinforce consistency by using consistent spacing, fonts, alignment, repetition, color, and decorative elements such as borders, drop caps, initial caps, and so on. Create interest in your publication by using strong contrast, alignment, and focus. Achieve balance and proportion and establish smooth directional flow in a document by organizing and positioning elements in such a way that the reader's eyes scan through the text and find particular words or images that you want to emphasize. As discussed earlier, color may create focus; however, it is also a powerful tool in communicating a message and portraying an image. The colors you choose should reflect the nature of the business you represent. If you use Publisher templates as the underlining structure of your customized document, many of the design decisions have been made for you; however, if you are customizing the template to fit your company design needs, you will want to apply the design concepts discussed in earlier chapters.

Getting Started with Publisher 2010

To start Publisher, click the Start button, point to All Programs, click Microsoft Office, and then click Microsoft Office Publisher 2010. When you first start Publisher, the New tab Backstage view will display. At the New tab Backstage view screen, you may choose installed templates, online templates, or a blank page in a specified size as shown in Figure 11.1.

Figure 11.1 New Tab Backstage View

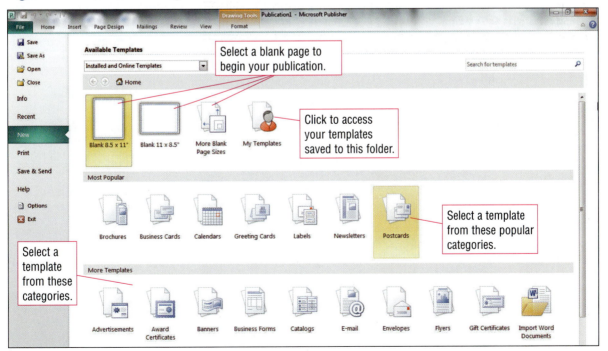

Choosing to Start from a Template

You may choose to start your publication from a blank document or from a template. Since Publisher 2010 provides hundreds of professionally designed templates that are frequently updated and new ones are constantly being added to the Microsoft Office.com template home page, you may want to start with one of these templates. After becoming familiar with the Publisher features, you may decide to start from scratch (blank page) and incorporate your own designs and ideas.

DTP POINTERS ▶

Use professionally designed templates for your publications, but customize them to fit your specific needs.

You may choose templates in the *My Templates* section, the *Most Popular* section, or the *More Templates* section. For instance, if you selected the *Newsletters* category, a plethora of newsletter templates with varying design elements displays. After selecting one of the newsletter designs, click the Download button located at the right of the newsletter thumbnails as shown in Figure 11.2. Depending on the template category selected, your desired template may display with the Download button in the bottom right corner or a Customize task pane may display with options to change the Color scheme, Font scheme, and other options. In which case, the Create button will display instead of the Download button.

Choosing to Start from Scratch

DTP POINTERS ▶

Pick up design ideas from the works of others.

If you choose to start your publication at a blank document, begin by clicking the *Blank 8.5 × 11"* category, the *Blank 11 × 8.5"* category, or click the *More Blank Page Sizes* category. If you click the *More Blank Page Sizes* category, blank pages in various sizes will display as shown in Figure 11.3. From the blank page sizes listed, select the one that best fits your needs. As you can see, Publisher offers a consistent user interface with the other Office programs. You may also choose commands on the ribbon to help

Figure 11.2 Newsletter Templates Category

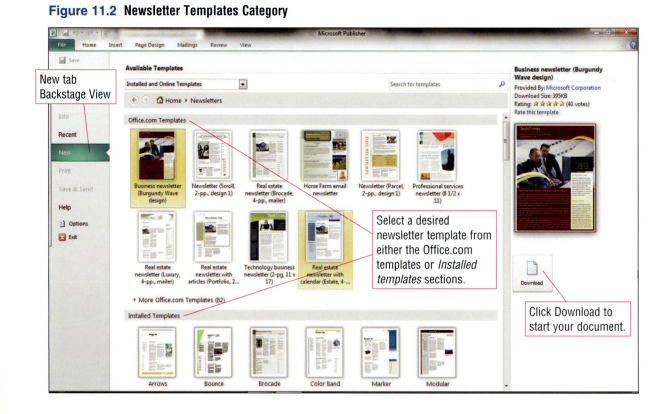

Figure 11.3 Selecting Blank Pages

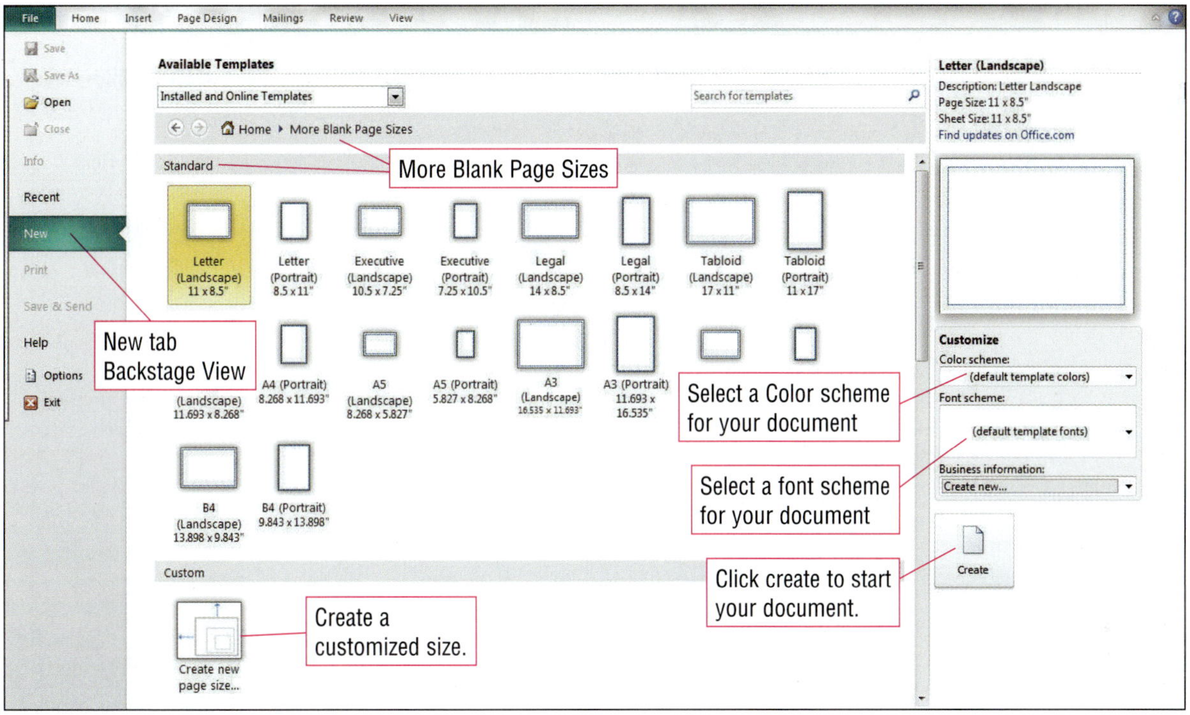

you create the document from scratch. When you insert various objects, contextual tabs will become available in the ribbon.

In Publisher, unlike Word, you must place all objects such as text, graphics, pictures, WordArt, and Shapes inside a frame before you can use them in your publication. When using Word, you simply begin typing your text at a blank document screen in a linear manner. However, with Publisher, text is considered an object and must be placed in a frame or text box. From the Text Box Tools Format tab or the Drawing Tools Format tab, there are buttons to customize text within the text box. You may also use commands on the Home tab to apply styles, change text alignment, change fonts, and apply other text enhancements. Figure 11.4 illustrates many of the basic commands that may be applied to text within a text box. You will create a publication from scratch later in this chapter in Exercise 11.6.

Customizing a Publisher Template

In Exercise 11.1, you will begin your publication from a Publisher flyer template. The template contains placeholder text, design objects, and graphics that hold formatting in place for your substitutions. You will be instructed to insert a Word file, AutoFit the text, replace the picture, delete a design object, and apply other formatting options to enhance your publication. You will also notice that certain text will automatically display in some of the text boxes. This is a result of the default text in the Business Information Set.

Figure 11.4 Microsoft Publisher Window with the Text Box Format Tab Displayed (Contextual Tab)

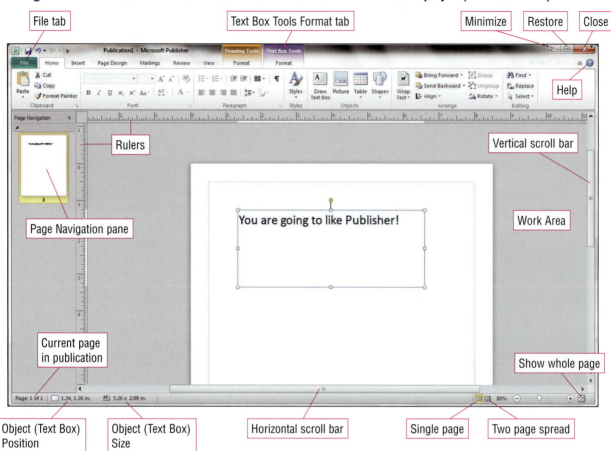

Working with Publisher Default Settings

The default settings for Publisher 2010 are located in the Normal style. The following settings are included:

- 10-point Calibri
- Black text color
- Kerning at 14 points
- Align Text Left
- Line spacing at 1.19sp
- Spacing after at 0.083"

Copyfitting

The process of adjusting the size and spacing of text to make it fit within a specific area of the page.

Text Fit

Copyfitting Text with Fit Text

The Text Fit feature automatically resizes text so that it will fit into the allotted space. To turn on the Text Fit feature, which is actually a ***copyfitting*** feature, complete the following steps:

1. Click in the text box.
2. Click the Text Fit button in the Text group in the Text Box Tools tab.
3. Do one of the following:
   a. To shrink or expand text to fit in the text box when you resize the box or type, click *Best Fit*.

Figure 11.5 Applying AutoFit Features to Text

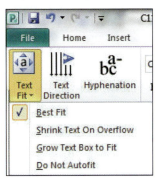

◄ DTP POINTERS
Press F9 to increase
the zoom to 100%.

Overflow

Text that does not fit
within a text box. The
text is hidden until it
can be flowed into a
new text box, or until
the text box with the
overflow resized to
accommodate the
text.

b. To have the text box expand to include the text, click *Grow Text Box to Fit*. To reduce the point size of text until there is no text in ***overflow***, click *Shrink Text On Overflow* (Figure 11.5). ***Overflow is text that does not fit within a text box. The text is hidden until it can be flowed into a new text box, or until the text box it overflows is resized to include it.***

c. To turn the Text Fit feature off so that the text stays the same size, click *Do Not Autofit*. With automatic copyfitting turned off, the font size remains the same whenever you resize the text box.

Changing Text Direction

Click the Text Direction button in the Text group in the Text Box Tools Format tab to change the orientation of the text to vertical. You will have more versatility in rotating your text if you create your text in WordArt where you can rotate text at 90 degrees to the right or left, flip vertically or horizontally, or rotate using the free rotate handle.

Using Hyphenation

Microsoft Publisher 2010 automatically hyphenates text as it is typed or pasted into text boxes. You can control where and how the hyphens appear in your text by using the Hyphenate dialog box. If the *Automatically hyphenate this story* check box is selected, the story will be automatically hyphenated based on grammatical rules and the distance of the hyphenation zone—the amount of space to leave between the end of the last word in a line and the right margin. To reduce the number of hyphens, make the hyphenation zone wider. To reduce the raggedness of the right margin, make the hyphenation zone narrower. If you have words that are long, you may want to control where the hyphens occur in the word. Press Ctrl + Shift + H or click the Hyphenation button in the Text group in the Text Box Tools Format tab.

Text Direction

Hyphenation

Consider the following guidelines:

* For a word that is always hyphenated and can be separated onto two lines, such as "two-thirds," press the hyphen key (-).

* For a word or number that is always hyphenated and can't be separated on two lines, such as "555-0123," press Ctrl+Shift+Hyphen (-).

* For a word that can be hyphenated, but only when it is necessary to split the word onto two lines, press Ctrl+Hyphen (-).

Changing Font Colors

You can change the color of text by selecting a color from your publication's color scheme or by selecting a new color, tint, or shade. For example, you can change the tint from deep green to light green by adding white, or you can change the shade from light green to dark green by adding black.

To apply a color from the Font Color palette, do the following:

1. Select the text that you want to change.
2. Click the down-pointing arrow at the right of the Font Color button in the Font group in the Text Box Tools tab or the Font Color button in the Font group in the Home tab.
3. Click the color that you want from the palette.

To apply a new color that is not in the color palette, do the following:

1. Select the text that you want to change.
2. Click the down-pointing arrow at the right of the Font Color button.
3. Click *More Colors*.
4. In the Colors dialog box, select the color that you want from the Standard tab, the Custom tab, or the PANTONE® tab.
5. Click OK. Publisher applies the color to the selected text and adds it to the Font Color and Fill Color palettes. **Note: PANTONE® Colors displayed here may not match PANTONE-identified standards. Consult current PANTONE Color Publications for accurate color. (PANTONE® and other Pantone, Inc. trademarks are the property of Pantone, Inc.© Pantone, Inc.)**

You can change the color of text and then fine-tune that color with tinting or shading. However, you cannot fill the color with patterns (such as a repeating horizontal or vertical line), textures (such a simulated wood grain), or gradients (such as a progression from light gray to a dark gray). To apply a tint or shade, do the following:

1. Select the text that you want to change.
2. Click the down-pointing arrow at the right of the Font Color button in the Text Box Tools tab.
3. Click *Fill Effects*.
4. Click the color that you want to use as the base color for the tint or shade in the *Base Color* list.
5. Under *Tint/Shade*, click the tint or shade that you want as shown in Figure 11.6.
6. Click OK. Publisher applies the tint or shade to the selected text and adds it to the Font Color and Fill Color palettes.

Ever see a color in your publication, an object, or a favorite picture and wish you knew what color it was so that you could apply it to other items in your publication? In Publisher you can grab the color from another object and paint it onto another object by using the Sample Font Color eyedropper tool at the bottom of the Font Color palette as shown in Figure 11.7. The color you grab will display in the *Recent Colors* section in the Font Color palette as shown in Figure 11.7. The Sample Font Color eyedropper tool is also available in other features such as the Shadow Effects, 3-D Effects, Shape Fill, and Shape Outline.

Sample Font
Color tool

Changes in the Font Dialog Box

You can specify how you want text to appear in your publication by selecting options in the Font dialog box as shown in Figure 11.8. The availability of some options depends on the languages and fonts that are installed and enabled for editing. Most of the

Figure 11.6 **Applying a Tint to Text**

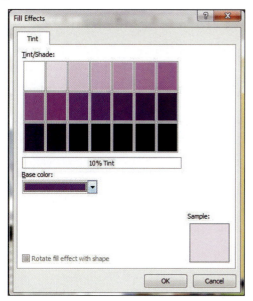

general options such as *Font*, *Font style*, and *Size* along with other text effects such as *Shadow*, *Outline*, and *Small caps* are similar to the same options available in the Word Font dialog box. The Shadow, Outline, Engrave, and Emboss effects are also located in the Effects group in the Text Box Tools Format tab.

Some fonts, such as Gabriola and Calibri, support a range of new features that enable you to transform ordinary text into fine typography. If the font you choose does not support the OpenType features this section will be unavailable. The following new typography features are available if the font you choose supports them:

- *Number style:* Tabular formatting that formats numbers so that each number uses the same number of pixels and will line up correctly in a table format. *Proportional* formatting formats numbers so that the number of pixels is proportional, for example a 0 may be wider than a 1. *Lining* and *Old-style* will either set the numbers to a baseline so that they are all the vertical position, or allow the numbers to have different positions as shown in this example.

Shadow

Outline

Engrave

Emboss

Number Style

Figure 11.7 **Using the Sample Font Color Eyedropper Tool**

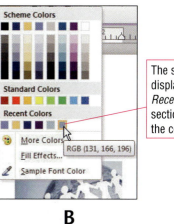

Click the Sample Font Color button at the bottom of the Font Color palette and then click the eyedropper tool on the color you want to grab.

The sample color displays in the *Recent Colors* section along with the color formula.

A   **B**

Figure 11.8 Font Dialog Box

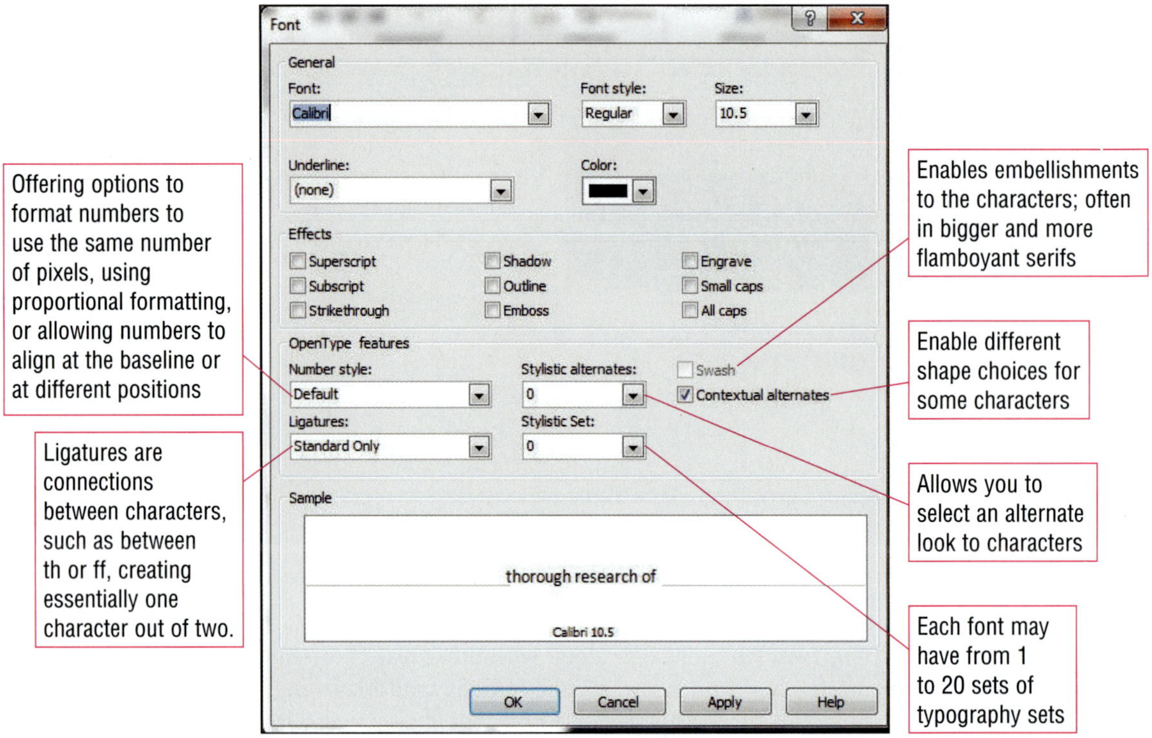

Offering options to format numbers to use the same number of pixels, using proportional formatting, or allowing numbers to align at the baseline or at different positions

Enables embellishments to the characters; often in bigger and more flamboyant serifs

Enable different shape choices for some characters

Ligatures are connections between characters, such as between th or ff, creating essentially one character out of two.

Allows you to select an alternate look to characters

Each font may have from 1 to 20 sets of typography sets

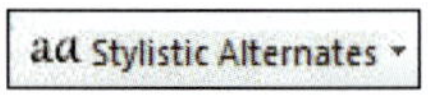

Stylistic Alternates

Ligatures

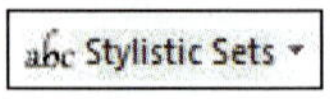

Stylistic Sets

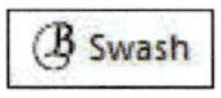

Swash

- *Stylistic alternates:* Allows you to select an alternate look for the look of the characters you have selected, if the font designer has created these alternates.
- *Ligatures:* Ligatures are connections between characters, such as between th or ff creating essentially one character out of two.
- *Stylistic Set:* Each font may have from 1 to 20 increasingly complex sets of typography styles for the selected font.
- *Contextual alternates:* This check box enables different shape choices for some characters depending on the context of the character and the design of the selected font; for example a "g" may have an open or closed loop on the bottom stroke of the character.
- *Swash:* This check-box enables embellishments to the characters, often in the form of bigger and more flamboyant serifs.

Using Publisher Features for Editing

The preset designs in Publisher can be a big help in getting you started with creating a new publication. However, when you want to customize any of these designs or save them for ease in applying, you may find the Smart Tags, Styles, and Business Information Sets helpful as well.

Working with Smart Tags

As with Word 2010, Smart Tags (Paste Options) will accompany text that has been copied and pasted or represented as placeholder text. When you mouse over the text, you will be provided with options to *Edit Business Information, Save to Business Information Set, Update from Business Information Set,* or *Convert to Plain Text.*

Applying Styles

As discussed in earlier chapters, styles are used to efficiently apply consistent formatting to text within a document. Styles also reinforce consistency among various documents where consistent designs are needed. To apply styles in Publisher, position the insertion on or select the text you want to apply style formatting to, and then click the down-pointing arrow below the Styles button in the Home tab. From the drop-down list, select a style with the desired formatting. If you start your document from a template, you will see a list of all the styles saved to the template. Keep in mind that you can also import styles from other documents, create styles from scratch, create styles by example, or modify an existing style.

Styles

Using Business Information Sets

Business Information sets are customized groups of information about either an individual or an organization that can be used to quickly fill in appropriate places in publications, such as business cards and flyers. The Business Information set can include components such as an individual's name, job position or title, organization name, address, phone and fax numbers, email address, tagline or motto, and logo. You can create as many different Business Information sets as you want. The data in each Business Information set is stored on the hard drive of the particular computer you are using.

When you create a publication, the Business Information set that you have used most recently is used to populate the new publication by automatically inserting the business information in place of the standard placeholder text that displays in the template. If you have not yet created any Business Information sets, the user's and organization's names are inserted from the information that you provided when the 2010 Microsoft Office system was installed.

Business Information

If you want to set up information that you can reuse in your publications, enter this information about your organization or personal information at the Business Information set. At the File tab Backstage view, click the Info tab, and then click the Edit Business Information button. In addition, you can click the Business Information button in the Text group in the Insert tab.

Figure 11.9 Create New Business Information Set Dialog Box

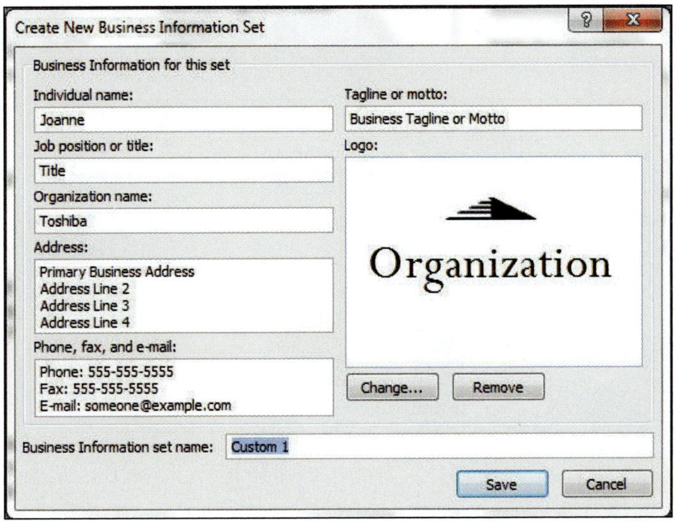

At the Create New Business Information Set dialog box, type all pertinent information, and then click Save as shown in Figure 11.9 You may even replace the logo placeholder with your own logo. Anytime you open a template with a logo placeholder, your own logo will display instead of the sample one. Click the Change button if you want to change the logo image. Remember that you can go back and change this information whenever you like. Click the Update Publication button to incorporate your changes. In addition, you may insert Business Information placeholders anywhere in your document by clicking the Business Information button in the Text group in the Insert tab, and then click the field you want to add to your publication.

Deleting Business Information Sets

In a classroom or lab situation, make sure you delete the Business Information Set that you created after each exercise. Print the publication, proofread it carefully, and then delete the Business Information Set you created. Otherwise, the next template that you use or the next Business Information field that you insert into your publication will show placeholder text from the previous set. Alternatively, simply type over the previous placeholder text with your new text.

*Note: Before completing the computer exercises, copy the **Chapter11** folder from the CD that accompanies this textbook to your storage medium and then make **Chapter11** the active folder. Substitute any graphics that are no longer available. Insert a similar image.*

Exercise 11.1   Creating a Flyer Using a Flyer Template

1. Open Publisher.
2. The New tab Backstage view should display, click the File tab if necessary to access the New tab.
3. At the New tab Backstage view, click the *Flyers* category in the *More Templates* section.

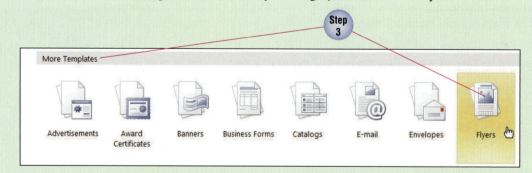

4. At the Available Templates screen, click the *All Marketing* category in the *Marketing* section.

5. Click the *Eclipse* flyer template in the *More Installed Templates Informational* section. The Eclipse template will display at the right in the Customize task pane.

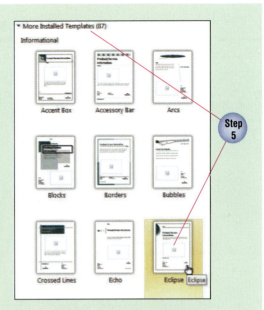

Step 5

6. Customize the Eclipse template by completing the following steps:

   a. At the Customize task pane, click the down-pointing arrow at the right of the *Color scheme* list box, and select the *Teal* color scheme from the drop-down gallery.

   b. Click the down-pointing arrow at the right of the *Font scheme* list box, and select the *Equity* font scheme from the drop-down list.

   c. *Create new...* should display in the *Business Information* list box. Click the down-pointing arrow at the right of the *Business information* list box and click *Create new....* The Create New Business Information Set dialog box should display. Type the text in the dialog box as shown below. The tagline should read **May your home be filled FOREVER with love and MUSIC.** Insert the **Forever Music Logo** located in your *Chapter11* folder by clicking the Add Logo button and then browsing for the logo in your Chapter 11 student data files. Type **Music** in the *Business information set name* text box. Click Save. **Hint: If you need to edit the Business Set after you created it, click the File tab and then click Edit Business Information. Click Delete at the Business Information dialog box if you want to delete a previous information set. Click Yes to delete the set and then click Close or New.**

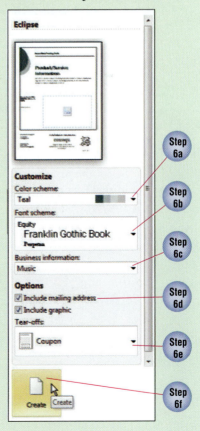

Step 6c

   d. Click to add a check mark at the options to *Include mailing address* and *Include graphic*.

   e. Click the down-pointing arrow at the right of the *Tear-offs* list box, and select Coupon.

   f. Click the Create button at the bottom of the *Customize* section.

7. Save the flyer and name it **C11-E01-Music**.
8. Click the first page thumbnail in the Page Navigation pane at the left of the template.
9. Press the F9 key or click the Zoom In button to zoom to 100%.
10. Replace the placeholder text by completing the following steps:
    a. Select the placeholder text at the top of the flyer *Forever Music Teaching Studio* and then type **Michael Costanza**.
    b. Mouse over *Michael Costanza*. When the Smart Tag button displays, click the down-pointing arrow, and then select *Convert to Plain Text*.

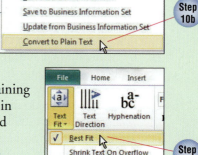

    c. With the insertion point located in the text box containing *Product/Service Information*, click the Text Fit button in the Text group in the Text Box Tools Format tab, and then click *Best Fit*.
    d. Select the placeholder text *Product/Service Information*, turn on bold, type **Forever Music**, press Enter, and then type **Teaching Studio**.
    e. Select *Forever Music Teaching Studio*, and change the font to Bodoni MT Condensed.
    f. With the text still selected, click the Paragraph dialog box launcher in the Paragraph group in the Home tab, and then type **0.8sp** in the *Between lines* text box in the *Line spacing* section. Click OK.

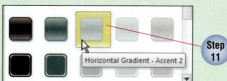

11. Add a gradient fill to the text frame containing *Forever Music…* by selecting the text box, clicking the More button at the Shape Style gallery in the Shape Style group in the Drawing Tools Format tab, and then clicking *Horizontal Gradient - Accent 2* in the seventh row and in the third column.

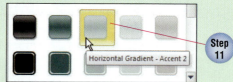

12. Replace the placeholder text below *Forever Music…* by completing the following steps:
    a. Select the placeholder text *Place text here that introduces…*, click the Insert File button in the Text group in the Insert tab, and then select **Lessons** (Word file) located in the *Chapter11* folder.
    b. Press Ctrl + A to select all of the text in the text box, click the Styles button in the Home tab, and then apply the Body Text style. Change the font size to 14 points.

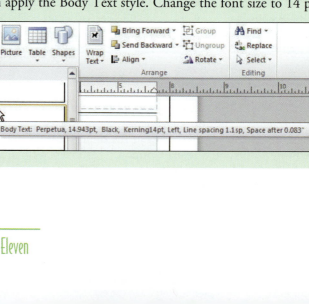

c. With the text selected, turn off the automatic hyphenation by clicking the Hyphenation button in the Text group in the Text Box Tools Format tab. Remove the check mark at the *Automatically hyphenate the story* option. Click OK.

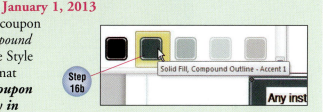

d. Remove the text box fill by clicking the Shape Fill button in the Shape Styles group in the Drawing Tools Format tab and then click *No Fill*.

13. Select the *Tagline* placeholder text, *May your home be filled FOREVER with love and MUSIC*, and apply the *Organizational Name 2* style. Select *FOREVER* and then *MUSIC*, and apply bold.

14. Select the telephone placeholder and type **812.555.9843**.

15. Make sure the company name, primary business address, phone, fax, and email are all correct. If an error exists, click the Business Information button in the Text group in the Insert tab, click Edit Business Information, click Edit, make the necessary changes, click Save, and then click Update Publication. Resize the logo if necessary.

16. Customize the coupon object by completing the following steps:

a. Type the following text in place of the *Coupon* placeholder text:

Name of Item or Service:	**Any instrument lesson**
Percentage Discount	**50% Off**
Organization Name:	**Forever Music Teaching Studio**
Describe your location...	**Downtown Bloomington**
Tel: 555-555-5555	**Tel: 812.555.9843**
Expiration Date:	**January 1, 2013**

b. Click the text box containing the coupon text and apply the *Solid Fill, Compound Outline - Accent 1* fill in the Shape Style gallery in the Drawing Tools Format tab. *Hint: When you select the coupon text box, black x's should display in the sizing handles.*

17. Add a picture to the center of the flyer by completing the following steps:

a. Right-click the picture placeholder in the middle of the flyer and then click *Delete Object* from the drop-down list.

b. Click the Clip Art button in the Illustrations group in the Insert tab, then type the keyword **grand piano** in the *Search for* text box, and then click Go. Click once to insert the image; the image should be similar to the one shown in Figure 11.10. *Hint: Insert the grand piano image without the gold star in the corner of the image - the gold star indicates a motion clip.*

c. Size and position the image similar to Figure 11.10.

18. Click to select the computer image in the coupon. When black sizing handles with Xs appear, insert the same piano image from the Clip Art task pane. Close the task pane. Make sure the size and position of the image is similar to Figure 11.10.

19. Click the second page thumbnail in the Page Navigation pane at the left of the document screen and then insert the **Forever Music logo**. Position the logo below the return address.

20. Save and then print **C11-E01-Music**. *Hint: Print the second page on the back of the flyer.* You will merge later in the chapter.

21. Ask your instructor if you should delete the Business Information Set named Music. To delete the set, complete the following steps:
   a. Click the Business Information button in the Text group in the Insert tab.
   b. Click Edit Business Information.
   c. Click Delete at the Business Information dialog box. Click Yes to delete the set and then click Close.
   d. Close **C11-E01-Music.pub**.

Figure 11.10 Exercise 11.1

Working with Font and Color Schemes

Font schemes and color schemes are professionally predesigned combinations of fonts and colors chosen to complement the overall look of the template document.

Applying Font Schemes

These schemes are generally saved within each Publisher template. If you are not satisfied with the look of the font choices in the template, you have the option to select a different combination of fonts, create your own personalized font scheme, or turn on or off font scheme options to update custom text styles, override applied text settings, and adjust font sizes.

To access these features, click the Font button in the Schemes group in the Page Design tab. From the drop-down list select a desired font scheme. If you cannot find a scheme that matches your company branding or does not support your design, click the *Create a New Font Scheme* option at the bottom of the list as shown in Figure 11.11. Create a new font scheme that enhances the look you are trying to achieve. Keep in mind that you can always override the Font scheme choices and select a desired font, font size, and font style at the Font dialog box or by choosing options in the Font group in the Home tab.

Applying Color Schemes

Publisher 2010 provides a gallery of professionally designed *color schemes* as shown in Figure 11.12. You can select one of the color schemes, customize a selected scheme, or

Fonts

Color Schemes
A predefined set of harmonized colors that you can apply to text and objects. Text and objects with an applied scheme color will change automatically when you switch to a new color scheme or modify the current color scheme.

Figure 11.11 Built-In Fonts

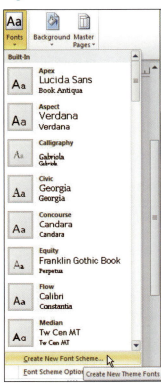

Figure 11.12 Color Schemes Gallery

Figure 11.13 **Create New Color Scheme**

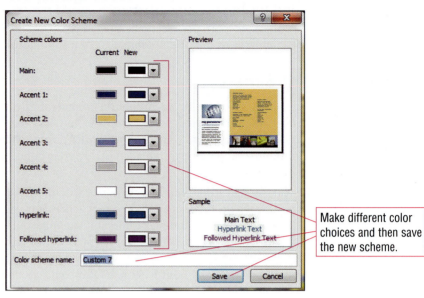

Make different color choices and then save the new scheme.

create a new custom color scheme. To create and save a custom color scheme, complete the following:

1. Click the More arrow at the color schemes gallery in the Schemes group in the Page Design tab.
2. Click the Create new color scheme button at the bottom of the gallery.
3. In the Create New Color Scheme dialog box, under New, click the arrow next to each color that you want to change, and then select a new color as shown in Figure 11.13.
4. To see more color choices, click More Colors.
5. Type a name for your custom color scheme, and then click Save.

All objects in your publication that were filled with scheme colors are now filled with the colors in your custom color scheme. Your custom color scheme is now the default color scheme. The colors that you selected also appear as the scheme colors in either the Font Color or Fill Color.

Layout Guides and Ruler Guides

Layout guides

Layout guides create a grid that is used to arrange text, pictures, and other objects.

Layout guides create a framework or grid for aligning text boxes, columns, graphics, headings, and other objects used in a publication. Layout guides include margin guides (boundaries), grid guides (such as column and row guides), baseline guides, and ruler guides.

Working with Layout Guides

You can customize layout guides by clicking the Guides button in the Layout group in the Page Design tab, clicking the Grid and Baseline Guides option, and then selecting settings at the Layout Guides dialog box as shown in Figure 11.14.

To select from a gallery of predesigned guides, click the Guides button in the Layout group in the Page Design tab. At the Built-In Ruler Guides gallery as shown in Figure 11.15, select a predesigned layout grid or add new horizontal and/or vertical ruler guides to your current page layout.

Guides

Figure 11.14 Layout Guides Dialog Box

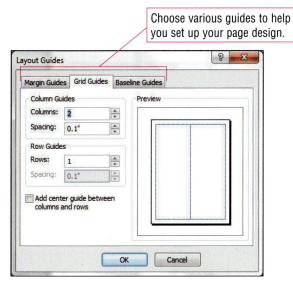

Choose various guides to help you set up your page design.

Figure 11.15 Built-In Ruler Guides Gallery

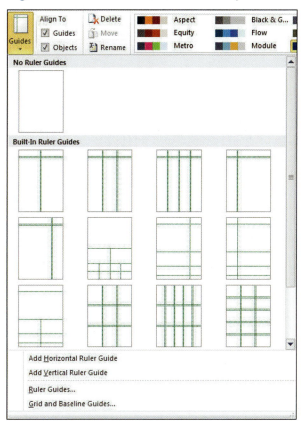

Working with Ruler Guides

Ruler guides display as green dotted lines and are usually created at the master page as shown in Figure 11.16. Ruler guides are useful when you want to align several objects or position an object at an exact location on the page. At the Built-In Ruler Guides gallery, click the *Add Horizontal Ruler Guide* or *Add Vertical Ruler Guide* options at the bottom of the gallery. Hold down the Shift key and then drag the double-pointed arrow with the two vertical or horizontal bars to create a new position for the guide. Hold down the Ctrl key as you drag the double-pointed arrow to create additional ruler guides. Click the Ruler Guides option to access the Ruler Guides dialog box as shown in Figure 11.17. Click options to Set, Clear, or Clear All vertical or horizontal ruler guides.

Align objects to rulers, guides, or other objects by clicking to add a check mark at the *Align To Guides* option and *Objects* option in the Layout group in the Page Design tab. When you move an object near another object, ruler, or guide, you will feel the object being pulled to the nearest guide. To view Rulers, Guides, Boundaries, Baselines, Page Navigation, *Scratch Area*, Fields, and the Graphics Manager, display the View tab and check these options in the Show group.

Working with Margin Guides

Use *margin guides* to set the amount of white space that you want around the edges of a publication. This selection reveals or hides the page boundaries that help guide placement of objects such as shapes, pictures, and text boxes. These margin guides do not appear when you print your publication, but they help you lay out the page.

> **Ruler guides**
> Ruler guides are useful to measure or align objects.

> **Scratch area**
> The gray area that appears outside the publication page. The scratch area is useful for holding objects.

> **Margin guides**
> Use margin guides to set the amount of white space that you want around the edges of a page.

Figure 11.16 Layout Guides (Margin, Grid, and Baseline), and Ruler Guides (Vertical and Horizontal) for a Brochure

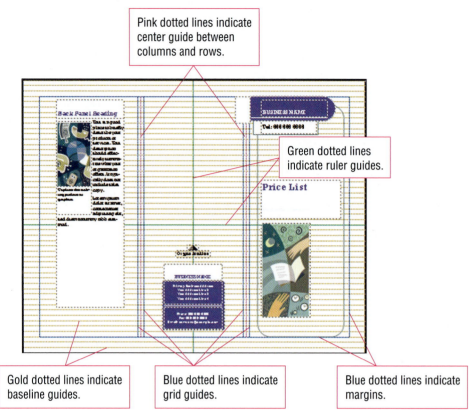

Pink dotted lines indicate center guide between columns and rows.

Green dotted lines indicate ruler guides.

Gold dotted lines indicate baseline guides.

Blue dotted lines indicate grid guides.

Blue dotted lines indicate margins.

Figure 11.17 Ruler Guides Dialog Box

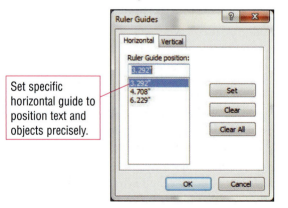

Set specific horizontal guide to position text and objects precisely.

DTP POINTERS ▶

If you have elements that you want to print to the edge of the page, extend the objects by at least 0.125 inches. This is considered a bleed where the element extends off the publication page.

Grid guides

Grid guides are useful in visualizing where columns are inserted in a publication. Grid guides also display the where rows are added to a document.

Working with Grid Guides

Use *grid guides* to set the number of columns and rows that you want on a master page. Any objects or grids set on a Master page show on all pages but cannot be edited on the regular page. At the Layout Guides dialog box, you can enter the number of columns that you want between the left and right margin guides and adjust the amount of space that you want between each column. You can also enter the number of rows that you want between the top and bottom margin guides and enter the amount of space that you want between each row.

Figure 11.18 New Alignment Technology

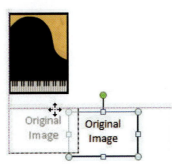

Use the ***baseline guides*** to align the baselines of your text. You can enter the amount of space that you want between horizontal baseline guides. The number that you enter is used as the line spacing amount for the paragraphs that you have set to align to the baseline guides.

Using New Object Alignment Technology

When you move objects in your publication you will notice dotted pink vertical and horizontal lines as you drag the object near other objects. The new object alignment technology provides visual layout guidance while keeping you in control of the final placement of the image or object. Figure 11.18 shows the pink lines as the text box is moved close to the graphic.

Working with a Master Page

Every page in a publication has a foreground and background layer. The foreground is where you insert text and design objects. The background layer is known as the ***master page***. Any objects placed in the master page will appear on every page. For instance, if you place a watermark on a master page of a three-page publication, the watermark will display on all three pages. Typically, a page-numbering code will be inserted in a master page so that all of the pages in the publication will be numbered consecutively. In addition, layout guides and rulers may be added to the master page. However, in Publisher 2010 you may use multiple master pages in a single publication. This allows you to create different master pages for different aspects of a publication.

To view a master page(s), click the View tab and then click the Master Page button, or press Ctrl + M. Master pages are identified by names such as Master Page (A) or Master Page (B). You can also create a two-page master, which is used when you create a publication that displays in a two-page spread. A two-page master allows you to put page numbering on the left for an even page and on the right for an odd page. Click the Master Page button in the View tab. The master pages will display in the Page Navigation pane at the left of the document as shown in Figure 11.19.

Master Page

Creating a Logo from Scratch

In advertising, a ***logo*** is a special design used as a trademark for a company or product. A logo can help a business make a big impression because a logo embellishes the company name and reinforces company identification. Create simple, but distinctive, logos in Publisher with WordArt effects, drawn objects, clip art, and the wise use of color and fonts as illustrated in the creation of a logo in Figure 11.20. When grouping an

Figure 11.19 Master Page at the Page Navigation Pane

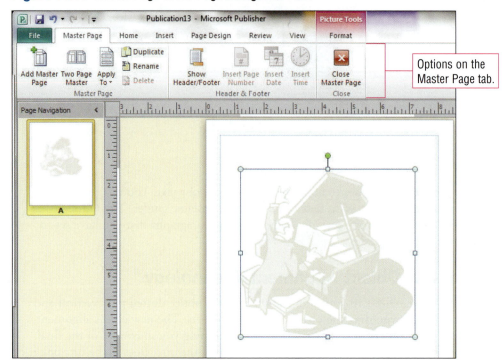

appropriate clip art with the name of the company, look for a special visual relationship between the two elements. Many Publisher features can be used to position objects precisely to create a logo. The logo can be used for standard business documents, such as a letterhead or business forms, and for promotional items, such as a shopping bag or a company give-away, including pens, t-shirts, caps, mouse pads, and more.

When you create branding for your business, you can store it and use it again in subsequent publications. If you create logos, lists of services, success stories, maps to a business location, testimonials, and pictures that you plan to reuse in your future publications, add these items to the Business Information Set or Page Parts Gallery.

Saving a Logo in Publisher

One of the most useful features in Publisher 2010 is the *Save as Picture* option. You may group objects together and save the entire selection as a picture. With this feature, you may create mastheads, logos, and other designs and save them in a file format for use on Web pages or print and reuse them within other publications. To use the Save as Picture feature, complete the following steps:

Figure 11.20 Grouping Objects to Create a Logo

Original
Image

Teal color scheme
applied and image
recolored RGB (51,102, 102)
Accent color 1 Dark

WordArt
Gradient Fill—
Blue, Shadow,
Wave

Grouped object
as a logo

Chapter Eleven

Figure 11.21 Saving a Picture

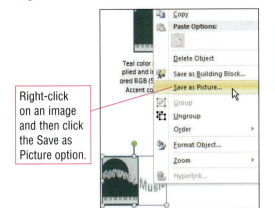

Right-click on an image and then click the Save as Picture option.

Figure 11.22 Creating a New Building Block (Page Parts Gallery)

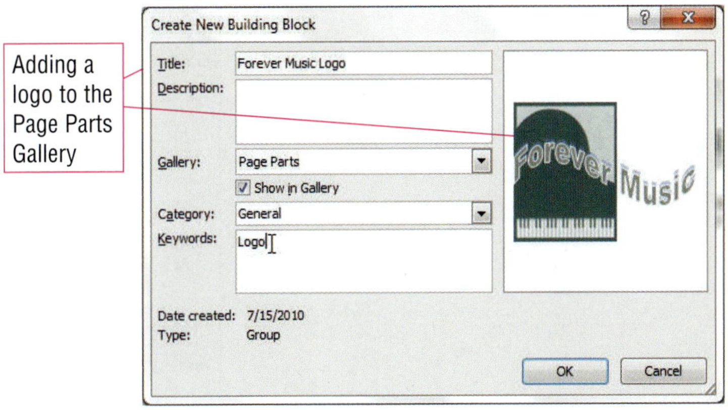

Adding a logo to the Page Parts Gallery

1. Select your objects and group them together.
2. Right-click on the grouped object and then choose *Save as Picture* from the shortcut menu as shown in Figure 11.21.
3. Choose a desired file format in the *Save as type* list box at the Save As dialog box.

You can also save your logo to the Page Parts Gallery or to the Business Information Sets as shown in Figure 11.22 and Figure 11.23.

Inserting WordArt

WordArt is a gallery of text styles that you can add to your publications to create decorative effects, such as shadowed or mirrored (reflected) text. You can use WordArt to add special text effects to your document. For example, you can stretch a title, skew text, make text fit a preset shape, or apply a gradient fill. This WordArt becomes an object that you can move or position in your document to add decoration or emphasis. You can modify or add to the text in an existing WordArt object whenever you want. To insert WordArt, complete the following:

WordArt

1. Select the Insert tab.
2. In the Text group, select the WordArt pull-down menu.

Figure 11.23 Inserting a Logo into a Business Information Set

Adding a logo to the Business Information Set.

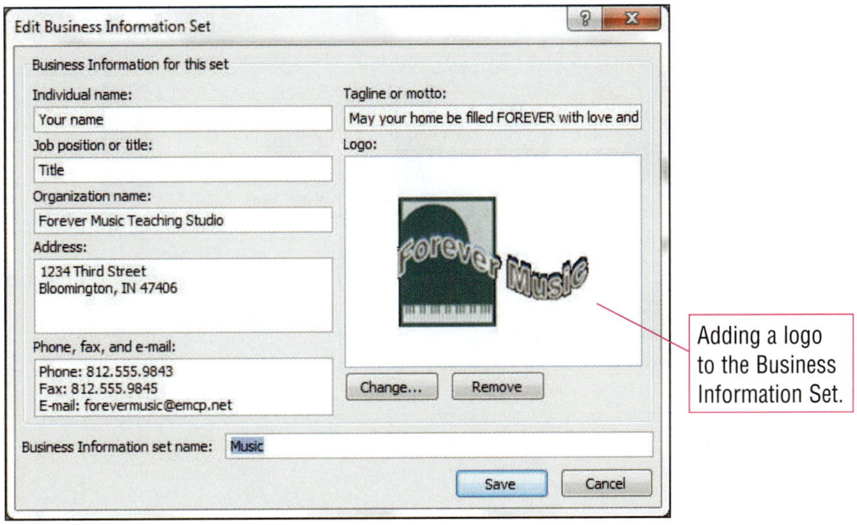

Figure 11.24 WordArt Gallery

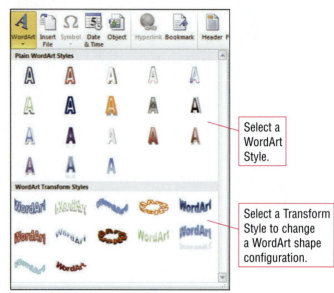

Select a WordArt Style.

Select a Transform Style to change a WordArt shape configuration.

3. Select from either the Plain WordArt Styles or WordArt Transform Style galleries as shown in Figure 11.24.
4. Type your text in the *Edit WordArt* text box, select the font and font size, and apply bold or italics, and click OK.

Exercise 11.2 Creating a Brochure Using a Publisher Template

1. Open Publisher.
2. At the New tab Backstage view, click the Brochures category in the *Most Popular* section.
3. Click Brochures under the Office.com Templates section and then click the *Informational brochure (Business design)* template in the *Office.com Templates* section and then click Download.

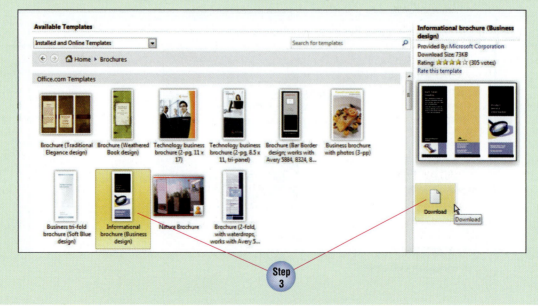

Step 3

4. Click the page 1 thumbnail in the Page Navigation task pane to display page 1.

5. Click the Color Scheme More button in the Scheme group in the Page Design tab, and then click the Create New Color Scheme button at the bottom of the gallery.

6. At the Create New Color Scheme dialog box, click the down-pointing arrow at the right of *Followed hyperlink* in the *Scheme colors* section, and then click the *Orange* color in the second row. Change the Color scheme name to **My Scheme** and then click Save.

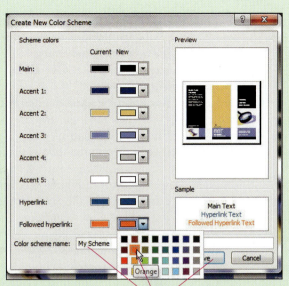

Step 6

7. Click the Guides button in the Layout group in the Page Design tab. At the drop-down list, click the *3 Columns with Heading* layout in *the Built-In Ruler Guides* section.

8. Click to select the *Product/Service Information* placeholder text in the cover panel in page 1, and type **Worldwide Event Planning**.

9. Press Ctrl + A to select *Worldwide Event Planning* and then click the Text Fit button in the Text group in the Text Box Tools Format tab. Click *Best Fit* from the drop-down list.

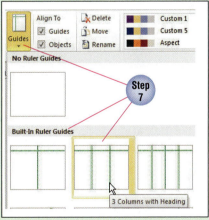

Step 7

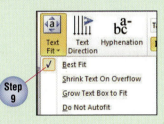

Step 9

10. With *Worldwide Event Planning* still selected click the Shadow button in the Effects group in the Text Box Tools Format tab.

11. Select the picture placeholder (magnifying glass) in the same panel, click the Clip Art button in the Illustrations group in the Insert tab, and then type **globe hands** in the *Search for* text box. Insert the image as shown in Figure 11.25 or a similar image if this one is no longer available. Close the Clip Art task pane.

12. Turn off Auto Fit. Select the *Organization Name* placeholder below the image, press F9 to zoom in, and then type **Worldwide Events Planning, Inc.**. Change the font size to 10 points.

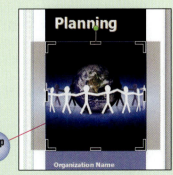

Step 12

13. Select the tagline placeholder text in the brochure cover panel and then type **Corporate Meetings | Weddings | Holiday Parties | Group Tours | Cultural Events**. Position the insertion point in the text and add 3 points before. *Hint: Click the Line Spacing button in the Paragraph group on the Home tab, click Line Spacing Options, and then type 3 in the Before Paragraphs text box.*

14. Select the telephone placeholder text and type **555.769.9999**. Change the font to 10-point Tahoma. ***Hint: Resize the text box if necessary.***

15. Save the document and name it **C11-E02-BrochurePage1.pub**.

16. Select the Organization logo placeholder in the middle panel, right-click the logo, and then click Delete Object from the shortcut menu.

Step 16

17. Create a logo by completing the following steps:
    a. Click the Clip Art button, search for another globe image as shown in Figure 11.25, insert the image and drag it to the Scratch Area surrounding the brochure (light gray area). Resize the image similar to Figure 11.25. Close the Clip Art task pane. ***Hint: Type*** globe blue men ***in the clip art search text box.***

    b. Click the WordArt button in the Text group, click the *Gradient Fill – Blue, Curved* style in the *WordArt Transform Styles* section.

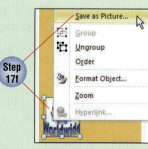

Step 17b

    c. At the Edit WordArt Text dialog box, type **Worldwide**, click OK, and then resize and drag the WordArt below the image.

    d. Hold down the Shift key, click the image, and then click the WordArt object. Click the Group button in the Arrange group.

Step 17d

    e. Right-click the image and then click Save As Picture.

    f. At the Save As dialog box, type **WorldwideLogo** in the *File name* text box. Make sure PNG Portable Network Graphics Format displays in the *Save as type* list box. Click Save. Save the logo to your *Chapter11* folder.

Step 17f

18. Drag the new logo to the location where the original logo displayed. As you drag the image, watch the vertical alignment bar snap the logo to the other objects on the page (address building block). See Figure 11.25.

19. Replace the Primary Business Address, Phone, Fax, and Email placeholder text with the text shown:

    421 Lexington Avenue, Suite 500
    New York, NY 10170-0555
    Phone: 555.769.9999
    Fax: 555.769.9888
    Email: worldwide@emcp.net

Step 18

20. Select the Back Panel Heading placeholder text on panel 1 and then type **We are organized….**

21. Click the placeholder text in the text box below *We are organized* and then insert **OrganizedText.docx** (Word file). Hint: The text will not display against the black fill in the text box. When you apply the style in the next step, the text will display in white against the black fill.

22. Press Ctrl + A to select the text, click the Styles button on the Home tab, and then apply the *Body Text 4* style.
23. If necessary, resize the text box containing the organized text.
24. Select the caption placeholder text and type **Our event planners are CSEP or CMP certified planners.** Position the caption as shown in Figure 11.25.
25. Select the key image below the caption text box, click the Clip Art button, type **planners** in the *Search for* text box, and then insert a picture similar to Figure 11.25. Resize and position the image as shown in Figure 11.25. Close the task pane.
26. Save the publication with the same name, **C11-E02-BrochurePage1**.
27. Keep the publication open to continue working on the brochure in Exercise 3.

Step 25

Figure 11.25 Exercise 11.2

Figure 11.26 Using the Design Checker

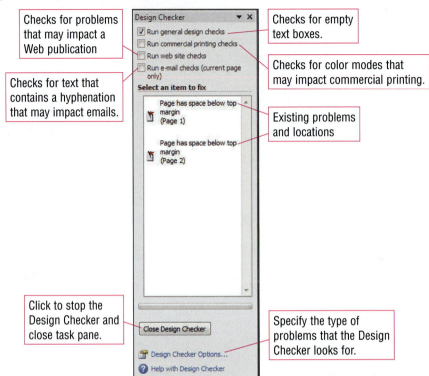

Checks for problems that may impact a Web publication

Checks for text that contains a hyphenation that may impact emails.

Checks for empty text boxes.

Checks for color modes that may impact commercial printing.

Existing problems and locations

Click to stop the Design Checker and close task pane.

Specify the type of problems that the Design Checker looks for.

Using the Design Checker

Run Design Checker

The Design Checker reviews your publication for a variety of design and layout problems, identifies potential problems, and provides the location of the problem and options to fix the problem. For example, if your message has many high-quality photos or it has bitmapped text, the Design Checker indicates that the file size may be too large for some recipients' mailboxes. To use the Design Checker, click the File tab, and then click the Info tab. At the Info Backstage view, click the Run Design Checker button. As shown in Figure 11.26, at the Design Checker pane, click options to customize how the checker will review your document.

Exercise 11.3 Creating a Brochure Using a Publisher Template

1. Open **C11-E02-BrochurePage1.pub**.
2. Format the left panel on page 2 by completing the following steps:
   a. Click page 2 thumbnail in the Page Navigation pane.
   b. Select the pushpin placeholder graphic, click the Clip Art button, type **worldwide** or **around the world** in the *Search for* text box, and then insert the image similar to Figure 11.27. *Hint: Select a similar image if the image is no longer available.* Close the task pane.
   c. Select the Main Inside Heading placeholder text and then type **Why pick Worldwide?**.

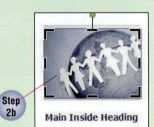

Step 2b

Main Inside Heading

d. Select the placeholder text in the text box below *Why pick Worldwide?* and insert the **KeyFactor.docx** file located in your *Chapter11* folder.

e. Select the text in step 2d (Ctrl + A), click the Styles button, and then apply the *Body Text* style and bold. Resize the text box if the overflow button displays.

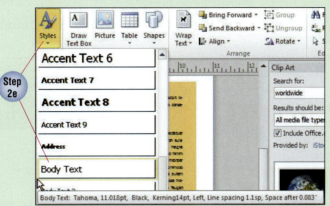

f. Select the text in the text box in Step 2e, click the drop-down arrow at the right of the Font Color button in the Font group in the Home tab, and then click the Sample Font Color eyedropper tool. ***Hint: Press Ctrl + A to select the text.***

g. Drag the eyedropper tool to the blue area surrounding the globe in the image in Step 2b and then click. ***Hint: The blue color from the image will automatically change the text color in the selected text box.***

3. Select the first *Secondary Heading* placeholder text in the middle panel and then type **Corporate Events**.

4. Select the placeholder text in the text box below *Corporate Events* and then insert **CorporateEvents.docx** located in your *Chapter11* folder.

5. Select the *Secondary Heading* placeholder below the Secondary Heading in Step 3 and then type **Personal Events**.

6. Select the placeholder text below *Personal Events* and then insert **PersonalEvents.docx**.

7. Select the next Secondary Heading placeholder and then type **Special Events**.

8. Select the placeholder text below *Special Events,* and insert **SpecialEvents.docx**. ***Hint: Did you notice that the text wrapped to a linked text box? The two side-by-side text boxes give the appearance of two columns of text. Avoid an orphan heading.***

9. Make any necessary adjustments so that the panel displays similar to Figure 11.27.
10. Right-click the text box object at the bottom of the page and then click *Delete Object* from the shortcut menu.
11. Right-click the bulb graphic at the bottom of the page and then click *Delete Object* from the shortcut menu.
12. Click the Picture button in the Illustrations group in the Insert tab, and insert the **EventGraphic.jpg** located in the *Chapter11* folder.
13. Select the image, increase the size, and then drag it to the bottom of the page as shown in Figure 11.27. ***Hint: Notice the vertical and horizontal guides as you drag the image to the bottom of the page.***

Step 13

14. Save the document and name it **C11-E03-EventPlanners**.
15. ***Optional:*** Apply a Page Background, and change the Color Scheme by completing the following steps:
    a. Click the Background button in the Page Background group in the Page Design tab, and click the *Accent 3 Horizontal Gradient* option in the *Gradient Background* section.

Step 15a

    b. Click the Undo button in the Quick Access toolbar. ***Hint: The blue gradient background color will use a lot of ink. You may want to use the background color if you send the publication to a professional printer and if your budget allows the additional cost.***

c. Change the Color Scheme by clicking the Schemes More button in the Page Design tab.

d. Click the *Pebbles* color scheme in the *Built-In (classic)* section.

e. View the changes to the overall look of the publication.

f. Click the Undo button on the Quick Access Toolbar.

16. Run the Design Checker by clicking the File tab and then clicking the Info tab. At the Info Backstage view, click the Run Design Checker button. At the Design Checker pane, click to add check marks at the left of the *Run general design checks* option and the *Run commercial printing checks* option. Review the items to fix. It is okay to ignore these particular suggestions. Click the Close Design Checker button.

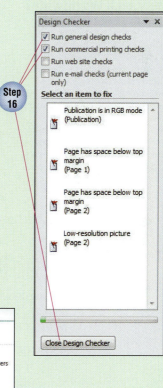

17. Save the pamphlet in PDF format by clicking the File tab and then the Save & Send tab. At the Save & Send Backstage view, click Create PDF/XPS Document in the *File Types* section, and then click the Create PDF/XPS button. At the Publish as PDF or XPS dialog box, change the location to your *Chapter11* folder on your storage device and then click the Publish button.

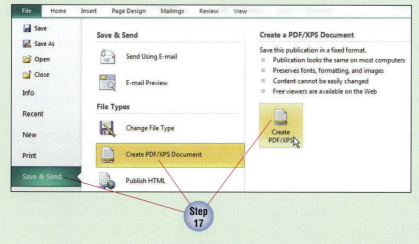

18. Print and then close **C11-E03-Eventplanners.pub**. Close C11-E03-Eventplanner.pdf.

Figure 11.27 Exercise 11.3

Why pick Worldwide?

A key factor to the success of Worldwide Event Planning, Inc. is its thorough research of all its vendors and suppliers. Its dedicated research also involves reading up on issues of customs and etiquette in unfamiliar markets. Worldwide conducts research; creates an event design; finds a suitable site; arranges food, décor, and entertainment; and plans transportation to and from the event.

Corporate Events

Our team of event planners provide coordination, execution, and management of corporate events from start to finish. Worldwide offers services for the following corporate events:

Global Conferences
Networking Events
Fundraisers
Holiday Parties
Office Events
Marketing Events
Trade Shows

Personal Events

Our mission is to assist every client in creating memorable events with a personal touch.

Family Reunions
Birthdays
Bridal Showers & Engagements
Anniversaries
Weddings
Graduations
Travel Arrangements & Tours

Special Events

Coordinating and managing the details of a special event can be daunting. Our professional staff will plan, coordinate, and execute your special event to perfection.

We offer services for the following special events:

Theatre/Concert Events
Parades
Political Events
Fundraisers
Fashion Shows
Sporting Events
Cruises
Cultural Events

Inserting Building Blocks

Building blocks are reusable pieces of content such as business information, headings, calendars, borders, and advertisements that are stored in galleries. Publisher 2010 has a variety of build-in building blocks for you to choose from.

To insert a build-in building block, do the following:

Page Parts

Calendars

Borders & Accents

1. If your publication is multi-paged, select the page where you want to insert the building block in the Page Navigation pane.
2. Click the desired building block gallery in the Building Blocks group in the Insert tab.
3. Scroll to find a building block, or click the More <gallery name> to open the Building Block Library dialog box.
4. Click the building block that you want to insert. Figure 11.28 illustrates the Page Parts building block gallery. Figure 11.29 illustrates the Calendars building block gallery. Figure 11.30 illustrates the Borders & Accents gallery and Figure 11.31 illustrates the Advertisements building block gallery.

You can also access the Building Blocks Library by clicking the Show Building Block Library button at the bottom of the Building Block group.

Figure 11.28 Page Parts Building Block Gallery

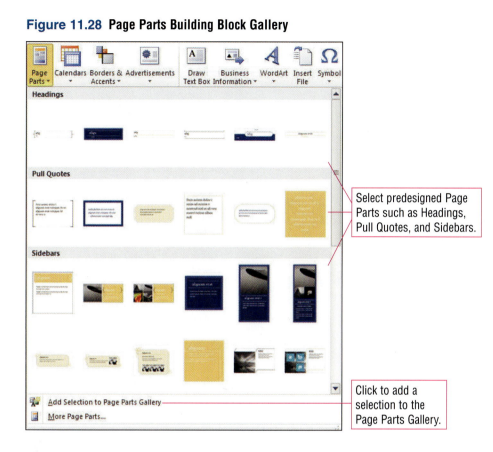

Select predesigned Page Parts such as Headings, Pull Quotes, and Sidebars.

Click to add a selection to the Page Parts Gallery.

Figure 11.29 Calendars Building Block Gallery

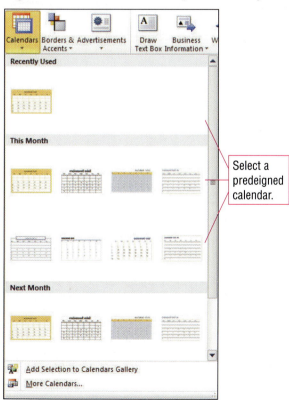

Select a predeigned calendar.

Figure 11.30 Borders & Accents Building Blocks Gallery

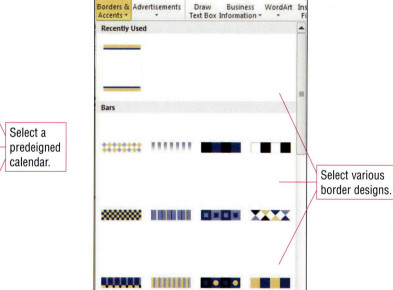

Select various border designs.

Figure 11.31 **Advertisements Building Block Gallery**

Advertisements

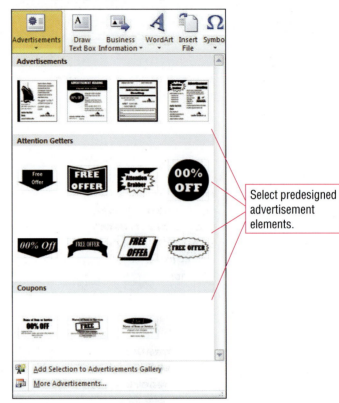

Figure 11.31 **Advertisements Building Block Gallery**

Select predesigned advertisement elements.

Working with Pictures and Shapes

Using buttons on the Insert tab, you can insert a picture, picture placeholder, or clip art. You can then modify the picture with picture styles, shadow effects, and captions. Using the drawing tools, you can create lines and basic shapes, as well as custom shapes that include balloons, arrows, stars, and many more elements that will add interest to your publication.

Inserting a Picture

Picture Placeholder

To insert a picture, click the Picture Placeholder button in the Illustrations group. The picture placeholder inserts an empty picture frame that is used to reserve space for pictures you want to add later. You can insert a picture into the picture frame by clicking the picture icon and then clicking either the Picture button or the Clip Art button to insert your desired image.

Picture

When you insert an image, the Picture Tools Format contextual tab appears with options to change the image brightness and contrast; recolor; apply a picture style; change the picture border, shape, caption, shadow, wrap, crop; and more.

Inserting a Caption

Clip art

Publisher includes a caption library with numerous picture caption designs. Insert an image, select the image, and then click the Caption button in the Picture Styles group in the Picture Tools Format tab. Select a caption from the caption library as shown in Figure 11.32.

Figure 11.32 Inserting a Caption

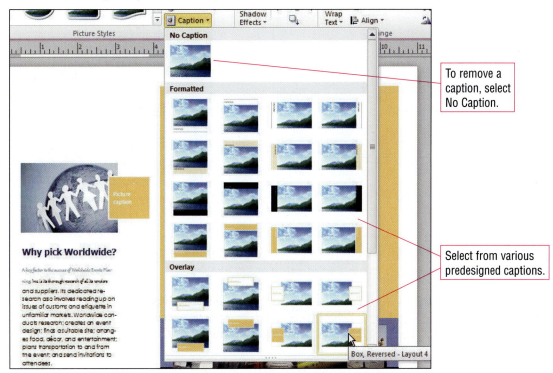

To remove a caption, select No Caption.

Select from various predesigned captions.

Inserting a Shape

To insert a shape, click the Shape button in the Illustrations group and then select a desired shape from the Shape gallery. Customize the border, fill, shape style, and other options at the Drawing Tools Format tab.

Shapes

Creating a Watermark

You can create a watermark in the master page that will subsequently display on every page of your publication. Otherwise, you may insert an image in the foreground layer, click the Recolor button in the Picture Tools Format tab, select a color variation (adjust the *Brightness* or *Contrast* if necessary), and then click the Send Backward button in the Arrange group. If the watermark does not display, you may have to change the text box fill to *No Fill.*

Embedded picture
A picture that is stored within a publication rather than being linked to a source file outside of the publication.

Viewing the Graphics Manager

The Graphics Manager task pane helps you to efficiently manage all the pictures that you have inserted into your publication, such as **embedded pictures** or **linked pictures**. Click the check box at the left of the *Graphics Manager* option in the Show group in the View tab.

Linked picture
A picture that links to a high-resolution image file that is stored outside of the publication file.

Working with Text

In Exercise 11.4, you will customize a newsletter template by inserting connected text boxes, page numbering in a master page, a watermark, and design gallery objects. The following information should help you become familiar with these Publisher features.

Figure 11.33 Columns Dialog Box

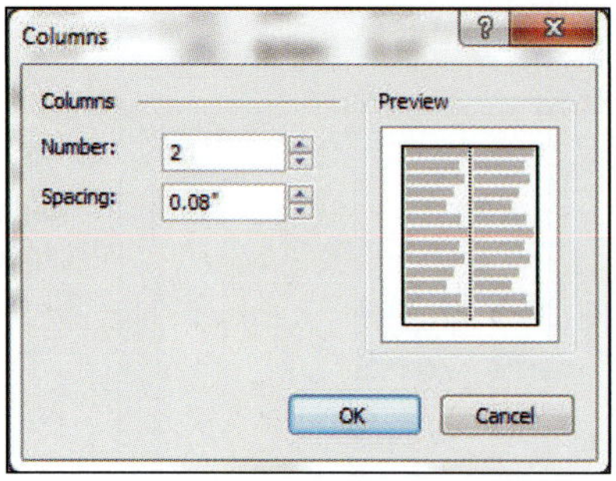

Figure 11.34 Drop Cap Gallery

Inserting Columns

To insert columns in Publisher, you must create a text box and then complete the following steps:

1. Right-click the text box that you want to change, and then click *Format Text Box.*
2. In the Format Text Box dialog box, click the Text Box tab, and then click Columns.
3. In the Columns dialog box as shown in Figure 11.33, type or select the number of columns you want in the *Number* box, and then type or select the spacing value between the columns, which is known as the gutter. Enter the amount of space you want to use between the columns in the *Spacing* box. You can also insert columns by clicking the Columns button in the Alignment group in the Text Box Tools Format tab.

If you want to add a line between the columns, complete the following:

1. Right-click the text box, click *Format Text Box,* and then click the Colors and Lines tab.
2. Under Preview, click the button for the center vertical line. Make sure no other buttons are selected so that the options you select for the line affect only the center vertical line.
3. Under *Line,* select the options you want for the center line, and then click OK.

Drop Caps

A drop cap is a formatting style that is often used to mark the opening paragraph of a publication. To create a drop cap, complete the following:

1. Click anywhere in the paragraph you want to change.
2. Click the Drop Cap button in the Text Box Tools Format tab, and then select the drop cap format you want. Figure 11.34 shows the Drop Cap gallery.

Drop Cap

You can customize your drop cap choice by changing the font, font color, font style, position, and size. When you create a custom drop cap, the custom style is added to the available drop caps list and you can use this style to create other drop caps in the current publication.

Working with Text in Overflow

If you have inserted or typed more text than your text box can hold, Publisher displays a message asking if you want Publisher to flow the text automatically or if you want to

Figure 11.35 Text in Overflow

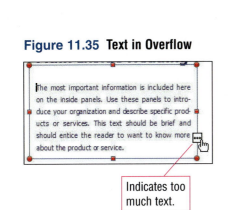

Indicates too much text.

Figure 11.36 Text Fit Options for Overflow

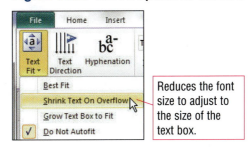

Reduces the font size to adjust to the size of the text box.

connect the text boxes yourself. If Publisher flows the text automatically, it will create text boxes as needed and then flow the text into the text boxes. However, if you decide to connect the text boxes yourself, the *Text in Overflow* indicator will display near the bottom of your text box as shown in Figure 11.35.

To accommodate the overflow text, you can click the Text Fit button in the Text Box Tools Format tab, and then click *Best Fit* or *Shrink Text On Overflow* as shown in Figure 11.36; you can resize the text box, or you can create another text box and connect the text boxes.

Using Connected Text Boxes

Text boxes are generally used in creating newsletters and many other publications in Publisher. Layout guides may be set up in a column format and then used to assist in sizing and positioning the text boxes for consistent-looking columns. For text to flow from one text box to the next, you must use the connected text box feature. Publisher 2010 refers to connected text boxes in a series as a ***story***. To create a chain of connected text boxes, complete the following steps:

1. Create as many text boxes as you think you may need.
2. Select the first text box in the series.
3. Click the Create Link button in the Text Box Tools Format tab. The pointer becomes an upright pitcher when you move it over the page.
4. Position the pointer (pitcher) over an empty text box and the pitcher tilts, as shown in Figure 11.37.
5. Click the empty text box to make the connection to the original text box.

Text boxes that are connected will display a right-pointing arrow and a left-pointing arrow to help you advance from one box to the other. To help a reader follow a story that may begin on one page and continue to another page, you may want to add a *Continued notice* at the bottom of the text box informing the reader where to find the rest of the story.

Story
Connected text boxes in a series.

◀ **DTP POINTERS**
Connected text boxes reinforce continuity and consistency.

Figure 11.37 "Pouring" Text into a Connected Text Box

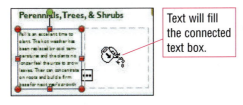

Text will fill the connected text box.

Figure 11.38 Adding a Continued Notice

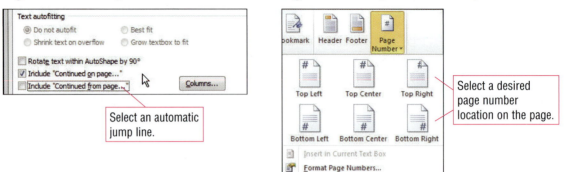

Select an automatic jump line.

Figure 11.39 Page Number Gallery

Select a desired page number location on the page.

Adding a Continued Notice

When you connect text boxes, text that does not fit into the first text box flows into the next connected text box. A chain of connected text boxes can span numerous pages. To add a *Continued notice* to a text box, complete the following steps:

1. Select the text box where you want to place a *Continued notice* and click the Text Box Tools Format tab.
2. Click the Format Text Box Dialog Box Launcher in the Text group.
3. Click the Text Box tab. In the *Text autofitting* section, click to add a check mark in the *Include "Continued on page…"* check box, or click the *Include "Continued from page…"* check box to add a check mark as shown in Figure 11.38, and then click OK.

Inserting Page Numbering

Page Number

Insert Page Number

Page numbering may be added to a publication in the foreground layer or in the Master Page layer. To insert page numbers, click the Page Number button in the Insert tab. At the Page Number gallery, select options to position the number in the current text box, show or remove the page number from the first page, or change the format of the numbers as shown in Figure 11.39.

To insert a page number in the Master Page layer, click the Insert Page Number button in the Master Page tab. If you are using more than one master page, you will want to place page numbering on each master page, whether it is a single page or a two-page spread. You can also set up headers and footers on a master page and insert the page numbering code, date, and time within them.

Exercise 11.4   Creating a Newsletter from a Publisher Template

1. Open Publisher.
2. At the New tab Backstage view, click the *Newsletters* category in the *Most Popular* section.

3. Select the Summer newsletter template and customize it by completing the following steps:
   a. Click the *Summer* thumbnail in the *More Installed Templates* section.
   b. Select the *Field* Color scheme.
   c. Select the *Solstice (Gill Sans MT)* Font scheme.
   d. Click the down-pointing arrow at the right of the *Business information* list box and then click Create New.
   e. Type the information shown in the Create New Business Information Set dialog box shown at the right. Add the Butterfield Gardens logo (BGLOGO) by clicking the Add Logo button or if a logo already exists, click the Change button. The Butterfield Gardens logo is located in the *Chapter11* folder. Type **Butterfield** in the *Business Information set name* text box. Click Save when you are finished typing the text.
   f. Make sure *Butterfield* displays in the *Business information* list box in the Customize task pane.
   g. Select *One page spread* in the *Options Page size* section.
   h. Click Create.

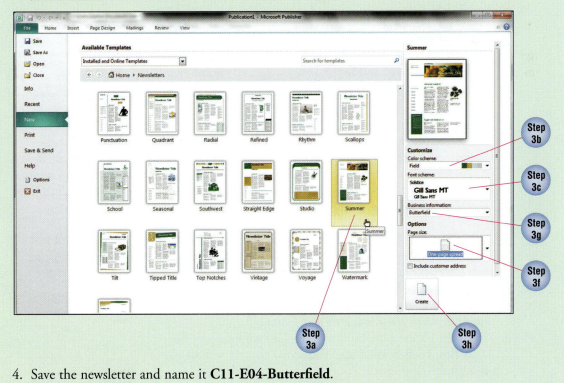

4. Save the newsletter and name it **C11-E04-Butterfield**.

5. At the Page Navigation task pane, click the page 2 thumbnail, hold down the Shift key, and then click the page 3 thumbnail. Click the Delete button in the Pages group in the Page Design tab. At the Microsoft prompt asking if you will delete objects, click Yes.

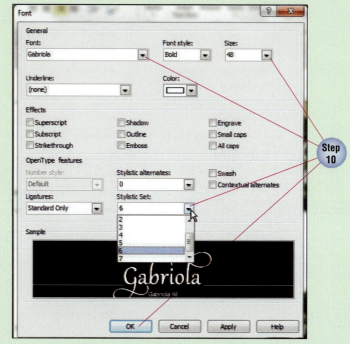

6. Display the first page, press F9, click the *Newsletter Date* placeholder, and then type **August 2012**.

7. Click the *Volume* and *Issue* placeholder and then type **Volume 2, Issue 8**.

8. Select the *Business Name* placeholder (Butterfield Gardens) and then type **The people who care.**

9. Click the *Newsletter Title* placeholder and then type **Butterfield Gardens**.

10. Select *Butterfield Gardens*, click the Font dialog box launcher button, change the font to 48-point Gabriola, and select **6** from the *Stylistic Set* drop-down list. Click OK.

11. Click the *Lead Story Headline* placeholder and then type **Winterizing Your Yard**.

12. The article text that you will insert will not fit into the connected text boxes on page 1; therefore, you will need to continue your story on page 2. To do this, complete the following steps:

   a. Click *page 2* on the Page Navigation task pane. ***Hint: Did you notice that the text you added to the Business Information Set automatically appears in the placeholders in the template?***

   b. Select the text box at the right of *The people who care.* near the top of the page, change the zoom to a percentage that allows you to clearly see the text, and then drag the bottom center resizing handle downward to the horizontal line above the *Back Page Story Headline* placeholder to increase the height of the text box. Drag the top middle sizing handle upward to the blue layout guide (margin guide). ***Hint: You will see the resizing handle snap to the layout guide as you approach it.***

   c. Click the *page 1* thumbnail and then click to select the third connected text box (click below the flower graphic to select the text box, not the flower) under the heading *Winterizing Your Yard*. ***Hint: When you click to select a specific connected text box, you will see Go to Previous Text Box or Go to Next Text Box hyperlinks near the top or bottom of the selected text box. Use these hyperlinks to move between the connected text frames.***

   d. Click the Create Link button in the Linking group in the Text Box Tools Format tab. The arrow pointer will display as a pitcher.

e. Click *page 2* on the Page Navigation task pane, position the pouring pitcher into the text box at the top of the page and at the right of *The people who care.*, and then click once. The text box should now be linked to the text boxes on the first page. ***Hint: The Go to Previous Text Box icon should display near the top of this box.***

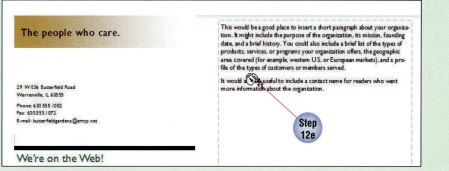

f. Click the Go to Previous Text Box button at the top of the connected text box on page 2.
g. Position your insertion point in the first connected text box under *Winterizing Your Yard* and insert the **Winterizing** text file located in the *Chapter11* folder.
h. With the insertion point positioned anywhere in the article, press Ctrl + A, and then apply the Body Text 4 style.
i. If you look at the linked text box on page 2, you will see an overflow symbol near the bottom of the text box. This symbol indicates that all the text does not fit in the text box, so to correct this situation, make sure all of the text is selected and then verify that the font size is 9-point Gill Sans MT. Click the Styles button in the Home tab, right-click the *Body Text 4* style, and then click *Update to match the selection*.
j. Display page 1, select the flower graphic (sizing handles with small Xs should display) near the *Winterizing Your Yard* article, click the Clip Art button, and type **gardening** in the *Search for* text box. Click Go and then insert a gardening image of your own choosing. Close the task pane.

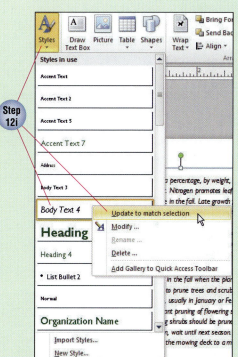

k. Select the image, click the Caption button in the Picture Styles group in the Picture Tools Format tab, and then click the *Box, Reversed - Layout 2* caption in the *Overlay* section.

l. Select the caption placeholder text and type **Think spring!**. Select *Think spring!*, click the down-pointing arrow at the right of the Character Spacing button in the Font group, and then click the *Loose* option at the bottom of the drop-down list.

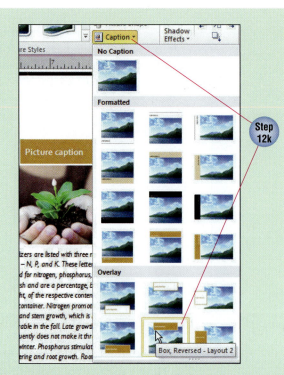

13. Add a jump line from the *Winterizing Your Yard* article on page 1 to the rest of the article on page 2 by completing the following steps:

a. Right-click the third connected text column on page 1 of the winterizing article, and then click *Format Text Box* at the shortcut menu.

b. At the Format Text Box dialog box, select the Text Box tab.

c. Click to add a check mark in the check box next to *Include "Continued on page..."* and then click OK.

d. Click the Go to Next Text Box hyperlink and with the insertion point positioned in the text box containing the rest of the article, right-click in the text box, click *Format Text Box*, and then select the Text Box tab.

e. Click to add a check mark in the check box next to *Include "Continued from page..."* and then click OK.

f. Click the <u>Go to Previous Text Box</u> and <u>Go to Next Text Box</u> hyperlinks to view the jump lines.

14. Click to select the first text box that contains the *Winterizing Your Yard* text, click the Drop Cap button in the Typography group in the Text Box Tools Format tab, and then click the *Drop Cap Style 7* style.

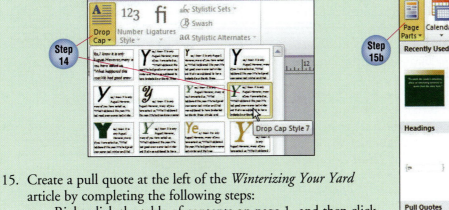

15. Create a pull quote at the left of the *Winterizing Your Yard* article by completing the following steps:
    a. Right-click the table of contents on page 1, and then click *Delete Object*.
    b. Click the Page Parts button in the *Building Blocks* section in the Insert tab.
    c. At the Page Parts gallery, click the *More Page Parts* option at the bottom of the gallery.
    d. At the Building Blocks gallery, click the All Pull Quotes category in the *Pull Quote* section.

e. Click the *Blocks* pull quote object in the *Pull Quotes* section, and then click Insert.

f. Size and then drag the pull quote object to the left of the *Winterizing* article as shown in Figure 11.40.

g. Select the first two sentences in the second paragraph of the *Winterizing Your Yard* article and then click the Copy button on the Standard toolbar.

h. Select the *Pull Quote* placeholder text and then click the Paste button. Center the text vertically, and then insert quotation marks around the quote. ***Hint: Center the text vertically by selecting the pull quote, and clicking the Align Center Left button in the Alignment group in the Text Box Tools Format tab.***

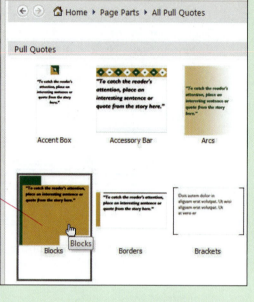

Step 15e

i. Select the pull quote text, and change the font to 8-point Gill San MT, bold.

Step 15h

16. Format the sidebar object located below the pull quote object by completing the following steps:

a. Select the bulleted text.

b. Type the following:

> **Winterizing includes good hydration, feeding, pruning, and disease control.**
> **Perennials, trees, and shrubs on sale.**
> **Taking care of birds.**

c. Add 6 points of space before *Special points of interest:*, select *Special points of interest* and change the font to 12.5-point Calisto MT, bold. Center the heading text.

Step 20a

17. Select the *Secondary Story Headline* placeholder and then type **Perennials, Trees, & Shrubs**.

18. Select the Story Text placeholder text below the Perennials headline and then insert the **Sale** text file located in the *Chapter11* folder.

19. Press Ctrl + A to select the entire article and then apply the *Accent Text 7* style.

20. Insert an advertisement object by completing the following steps:

a. Click the Advertisements button in the Building Blocks group in the Insert tab.

b. Click the Pointer object in the *Attention Getters* section.

Step 20b

c. Drag the Pointer object, and position it as shown in Figure 11.40. Select the placeholder text inside the Pointer object, and type **50% Off**.

d. Select the Shape Styles More button in the Shape Styles group, and then click the *Horizontal Gradient - Accent 2* style.

21. Save the newsletter with the same name, **C11-E04-Butterfield**.

22. Keep **C11-E04-Butterfield.pub** open if you are going to continue working on the second page of the newsletter in Exercise 11.5. Otherwise, print and then close **C11-04-Butterfield.pub**.

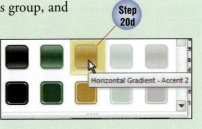

Step 20d

Horizontal Gradient - Accent 2

Figure 11.40 Exercise 11.4

August 2012
Volume 2, Issue 8

The people who care.

Butterfield Gardens

Winterizing Your Garden

"You are living in USDA Hardiness Zone 5. The average minimum temperature is minus 20 degrees Fahrenheit."

Y es, I know it is only August. However, many of you have asked us, "What happened this year. We had good snow cover last winter and that was supposed to have protected our plants (trees, shrubs, and perennials), but we lost some." Answering that question...and helping you avoid similar losses next year is the reason for this article.

You are living in USDA Hardiness Zone 5. The average minimum temperature is minus 20 degrees Fahrenheit. We tend to have some miserable winds out of the north and west during the winter creating wind chills as low as minus 80 degrees. This is very stressful on people and plants alike. Winterizing issues include hydration, feeding,

pruning, and disease control.

Hydration. We had a good spring for moisture. The summer has been extremely dry, as was last summer and fall. Lack of moisture was probably the largest single contributor to winter losses this past year. Two seasons of drought will be deadly for your plants; trees, shrubs, lawns, and perennials. Make sure that your plants go into the winter well watered. Many evergreen shrubs, including boxwood, rhododendron, holly, and bayberry, also appreciate some winter protection to prevent desiccation by our vicious winds. Wrap them loosely, with burlap and/or apply an anti-desiccant spray.

Feeding. After August 1, avoid

Think spring!

feeding plants with high nitrogen fertilizers. As you will remember, all fertilizers are listed with three numbers – N, P, and K. These letters stand for nitrogen, phosphorus, and potash and are a percentage, by weight, of the respective contents of the container. Nitrogen promotes leaf and stem growth, which is not desirable in the fall. Late growth frequently does not make it through

(Continued on page 2)

Special points of interest:

• Winterizing includes good hydration, feeding, pruning, and disease control.

• Perennials, trees, and shrubs on sale.

• Taking care of birds.

Perennials, Trees, & Shrubs

50% Off

Fall is an excellent time to plant. The hot weather has been replaced by cool temperatures and the plants no longer feel the urge to grow leaves. They can concentrate on roots and build a firm base for next year's growth

spurt. Cool weather also means that we do not need to be quite as careful with the watering schedule. The perennials go on sale September 1.The trees and shrubs go on sale October 1. Take advantage of this op-

portunity to add to the value of your property and the overall enjoyment of your yard or garden. Your family will thank you for your efforts next spring!

Figure 11.41 Save & Send Backstage View

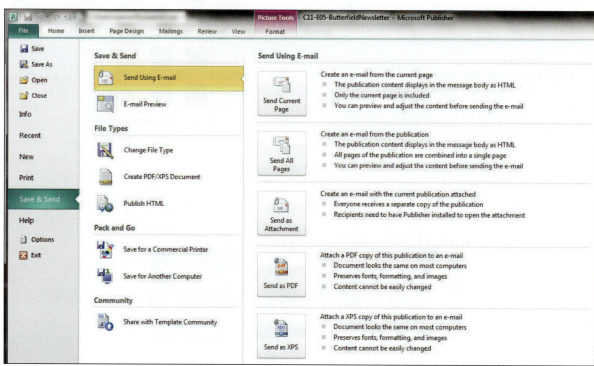

Using Publisher for Multiple Purposes

After your publication has been designed and created, you may print it, send it to a commercial printer, or send it through email.

Sending as an Email Message

You can send your newsletter as an email message or as an attachment to an email message to one or many recipients. If you want to send your newsletter to just a few recipients, you can simply send it as an email message. At the File tab Backstage view, click Save & Send, click Send Using Email, and then click Send Current Page, Send All Pages, Send as Attachment, Send as PDF, Send as XPS, or Email Preview as shown in Figure 11.41.

Use Mail Merge or Email Merge

If you want to send your newsletter to many recipients and you want to personalize it, you can perform a mail merge or an email merge. Just as when you perform a mail merge, when you perform an email merge, you must open a new or an existing publication and then click the Email Merge button in the Start group in the Mailings tab. From the drop-down list either choose *Email Merge* or *Step by Step Email Merge Wizard*.

To perform a mail merge, you must open a new or an existing publication and then click the Mail Merge button in the Start group in the Mailings tab. At the drop-down list either choose *Email Merge* and use the buttons on the Mailings tab or click the *Step by Step Mail Merge Wizard* as shown in Figure 11.42. You can use an existing list of contacts or type a new list.

Figure 11.42 Mail Merge Task Pane

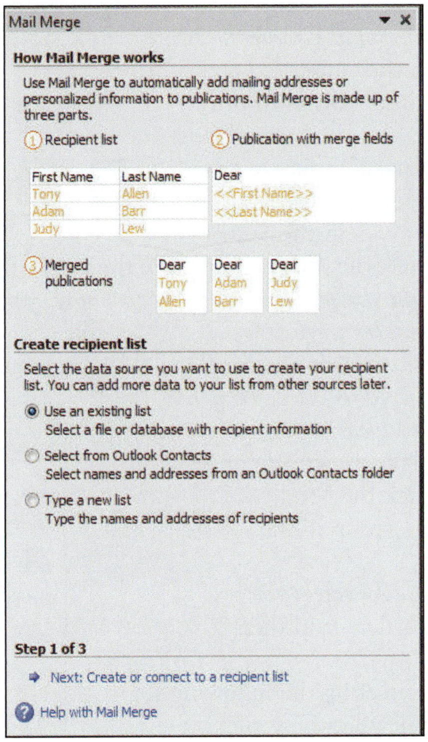

Mail Merge ▾ ✕

How Mail Merge works

Use Mail Merge to automatically add mailing addresses or personalized information to publications. Mail Merge is made up of three parts.

① Recipient list   ② Publication with merge fields

First Name	Last Name	Dear
Tony	Allen	<<First Name>>
Adam	Barr	<<Last Name>>
Judy	Lew	

③ Merged publications

Dear	Dear	Dear
Tony	Adam	Judy
Allen	Barr	Lew

Create recipient list

Select the data source you want to use to create your recipient list. You can add more data to your list from other sources later.

⦿ Use an existing list
  Select a file or database with recipient information

○ Select from Outlook Contacts
  Select names and addresses from an Outlook Contacts folder

○ Type a new list
  Type the names and addresses of recipients

Step 1 of 3

➡ Next: Create or connect to a recipient list

❓ Help with Mail Merge

Exercise 11.5 Creating a Newsletter from a Publisher Template

1. Open **C11-04-Butterfield.pub** and save it as **C11-E05-ButterfieldNewsletter**.
2. Click *page 2* in the Page Navigation task pane, and make sure all the placeholder text is complete with the information that you entered into the Business Information Set for Butterfield. If any of the information is missing, insert the text as shown in Figure 11.43.
3. Delete the placeholder object above the Butterfield logo.
4. Increase the size of the Butterfield logo as shown in Figure 11.43.
5. Edit the text box containing the web address by selecting the example *Web Address* placeholder text and then typing **www.emcp.net/butterfieldgardens**. *Hint: Retype* **We're on the Web!** *and resize the text box if necessary.*
6. Format the back story on page 2 by completing the following steps:
   a. Click to select the *Back Page Story Headline* placeholder text and then type **Fine Feathered Friends**.
   b. Select the corn graphic in the bottom left of the second page of the newsletter, click the Clip Art button, type **birds leaves** in the *Search for* text box, click Go and then insert the image. Close the task pane. *Hint: If the image is no longer available, choose a similar image.*

Step 6b

   c. Size and then position the image as shown in Figure 11.43.
   d. Select the *Caption* placeholder text and then type **Stop at Butterfield Gardens and see our selection of feeders, birdbaths, heaters, and quality bird food.** If necessary, ungroup the caption, and drag the middle sizing handle to make the caption larger to hold all of the text.

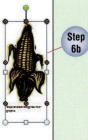

e. Add a fill color to the caption box by clicking the Shape Styles More button, and then clicking the *Diagonal Gradient - Accent 2* fill.

7. With the placeholder text selected in the connected text boxes below *Fine Feathered Friends*, insert **Birds** from the *Chapter11* folder.

8. Add a watermark to the text box on page 2 that contains the winterizing text by completing the following steps:

   a. Click the Clip Art button, type **bugs** in the *Search for* text box, and then click Go. Insert the image. Substitute the image if necessary. ***Note: Because you do not want to add the watermark to both pages, you will not want to create the watermark in the master page screen.***

   b. With the image selected, click the Recolor button in the Adjust group in the Picture Tools Format tab, and then click *RGB (102, 163, 133) Accent color 1 Light* in the *Light Variations* section.

   c. Size and position the watermark as shown in Figure 11.43.

   d. With the image still selected, click the Send Backward button in the Arrange group in the Picture Tools Format tab.

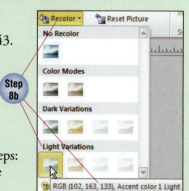

   e. If the image does not show through, select the text box containing the winterizing article, and then change the fill to *No Fill*.

9. Add a page number to page 2 by completing the following steps:

   a. Display the second page of the newsletter by clicking the page 2 thumbnail in the Page Navigation pane.

   b. Click the Page Number button in the Header & Footer group in the Insert tab.

   c. Make sure a check mark does not display next to the *Show Page Number on First Page* option and then click the Bottom Right thumbnail in the Page Number drop-down gallery.

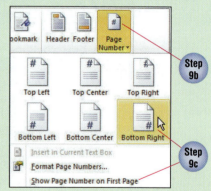

   d. The page number exists in a footer in the Master Page view. Click the Master Page button in the Views group in the View tab. Notice that Master Page A displays in the Page Navigation pane. With Master Page A selected in the Page Navigation pane, notice the page numbering code located in the footer. If additional pages are added to the newsletter, each page will be numbered consecutively.

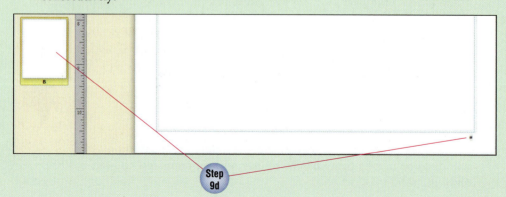

e. Click the Close Master Page button.

f. Click the *page 1 navigation* icon to view page 1—no page number should display. Click page 2 on the Page Navigation control to view page 2—2 should display. If 2 does not display in the lower right corner of page 2, click to select the last text box on the page and change the fill color to No Fill.

10. Save the newsletter with the same name **C11-E05-ButterfieldNewsletter**.

11. Print both pages of the newsletter using both sides of the paper.

12. Save the newsletter again, but this time in PDF format, and then view it using Adobe Reader® software.

13. Close **C11-E05-ButterfieldNewsletter.pub** and then close C11-E05-ButterfieldNewsletter.pdf.

Figure 11.43 Exercise 11.5

The people who care.

29 W 036 Butterfield Road
Warrenville, IL 60555

Phone: 630.555.1082
Fax: 630.555.1072
E-mail: butterfieldgardens@emcp.net

We're on the Web!

www.emcp.net/butterfieldgardens

Butterfield GARDENS

(Continued from page 1)

the winter. Phosphorus stimulates flowering and root growth. Root growth enables the plant to absorb necessary water and nutrients from the soil. Potash helps the plant absorb micronutrients in the soil and promotes nutritional health. The most important feeding you can do for your plants in the fall is with a fertilizer in the 10-16-20 or 10-10-10 range.

Pruning. Pruning is stressful in the fall when the plant is still actively growing. If you feel the need to prune trees and scrubs, wait until they are completely dormant, usually in January or February. There are exceptions to this. Dormant pruning of flowering shrubs cuts off next year's flowers. Flowering shrubs should be pruned within a month of flowering. If you can, wait until next season. Lawn pruning should be reduced by raising the mowing deck to a much greater height.

Disease. Proper management of the preceding issues reduces stress that would otherwise weaken the plants, leaving them susceptible to diseases. Fungal problems can be treated at this time, as can insect infestations. A horticultural oil spray can be used to smother any insects that would like to overwinter on your trees and shrubs. This can be applied at any time from now through March. Fungal problems can be treated with lime sulfur spray.

Fine Feathered Friends

When to feed birds. It is best to provide food all year long. February through August, when natural grasses and fruit bearing trees are not mature and birds are nesting and producing young, is very important. During the winter months, it is often difficult for birds and wildlife to find adequate food sources. The fall months are important because the feeding patterns are established for the winter.

What about water? Clean fresh water should be provided at all times. During winter months water sources are often frozen. A birdbath with a water heater will supply outdoor crea-

Stop at Butterfield Gardens and see our selection of feeders, birdbaths, heaters, and quality bird food.

tures with needed water. During the summer, drinking and bathing water is important. City (tap) water often contains chemicals that are not part of nature. Using a nutritionally fortified wild bird food is recommended.

How will birds find my feeders? Birds find food by sight. Place feeders in easily seen areas. Be patient and the birds will come. To have many birds on a frequent basis can take a year or two depending on your geographical area and the migration patterns of the birds. If you don't seem to be attracting birds, make sure you have the right food. If you purchase inexpensive

mixes containing a lot of milo, millet, and corn, you may not attract the more desirable songbirds. If you have a good food available, try tying a piece of tin foil on top of the feeder. A little glint from this foil will catch their eye.

How much will the birds eat? Songbirds have a very high metabolic rate and a body temperature of 109 degrees. They need to eat constantly in order to store up energy for cold winter periods and need to eat frequently in summer months to burn off heat. Some birds will consume more than their body weight on a daily basis.

2

Creating a Publication from Scratch

Publisher predesigned templates can be a big help in getting started with your new publication. However, if you want to create your own unique look, you may want to start with a blank publication. If you know how to work with frames (text boxes, picture frames, building blocks, etc.), you can create a document from scratch.

Starting from a Blank Publication

To create a blank publication, complete the following steps:

1. Start Publisher, click the File tab, and then click New.
2. To quickly create a standard 8.5 by 11 inch blank publication, click *Blank 8.5 x 11"* or *Blank 11 x 8.5"*.
3. Click More Blank Page Sizes.
4. Click the thumbnail that displays the design for the publication you want.
5. Click the *Color Scheme* or *Font Scheme* list arrow and make your choices.
6. Select other options such as size.
7. Click Create.

Setting Up the Page

Use guides to help you design your page. Click the Margins button to change the default margin setting. Click the Orientation button to change the page orientation to portrait or landscape. To change the page size, click the Size button in the Page Setup group in the Page Design tab. Click the Page button in the Pages group in the Insert tab to insert a blank page or a duplicate page.

Using Commercial Printing Tools

If you need printing options that you do not have on your desktop printer, you can send your publication to a commercial printer that can reproduce your work on an offset printing press or a high-quality digital printer. Publisher provides full support for commercial printing, including conversion to spot or process color with automatic color separation. Advanced tools such as trapping (overlapping the edges of different colors), graphic linking, and embedding fonts promote high-quality printing. To choose the desired commercial printing options, open your publication, click the File tab, and then click the Info tab (Figure 11.44). Click the Commercial Print Settings button in the *Commercial Print Information* section. Choose options for selecting color models, embedded fonts, and registration (trapping, overprinting, and spot color settings).

Changing Color Print Settings

If you print your publication to a high-quality digital color printer, you do not have to worry about color. Digital color printers accurately reproduce millions of colors. If you plan to send you publication to a commercial printer for offset printing, you have several color-model options.

Any Color Model (RGB)

If you print using a color desktop printer, you use the RGB (Red, Green, and Blue) color model. This model is the least expensive color model to use; however, it is also the most difficult to match colors between print jobs.

DTP POINTERS ▶
Use a commercial printer if you want to print a publication in larger quantities, print on special paper such as vellum or card stock, or use binding, trimming, and finishing options.

DTP POINTERS ▶
Consult with your commercial printer before and during the design process to save time and money later.

DTP POINTERS ▶
Before you start your project, describe your project and goals, and find out your commercial printer's requirements.

Figure 11.44 Commercial Print Settings

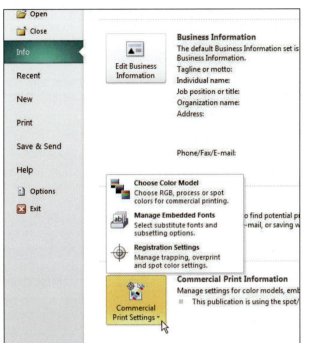

Single Color Model

If you print by using one color, everything in your publication is printed as a tint of a single ink, which is usually black.

Spot Color Model

If you print by using a spot color, everything in your publication is printed as a tint of a single ink—usually black—and a tint of one additional color, the spot color, which is the accent color. Publisher uses PANTONE® colors for spot colors.

Process Colors

If you use this model, your publication is printed in full color using varying percentages of cyan, magenta, yellow, and black (CMYK). Using process-color printing requires the press operator to line up the impression of one ink with the other, which is called registration. This makes process-color printing more expensive than spot-color printing.

Process Plus Spot Colors

This color model is the most expensive to print because it combines process-color printing with one or more spot-color inks.

Embedding Fonts

Embedding the fonts in your publication is one of the best ways to ensure that a font is always available, even if you move the publication to a new computer or take it to a commercial printing service. Publisher embeds TrueType fonts by default when you use the Pack and Go Wizard to prepare your publication to take to a commercial printing service. You do not need to select this in the Fonts dialog box before you run the wizard.

Figure 11.45 Using the Pack and Go Wizard

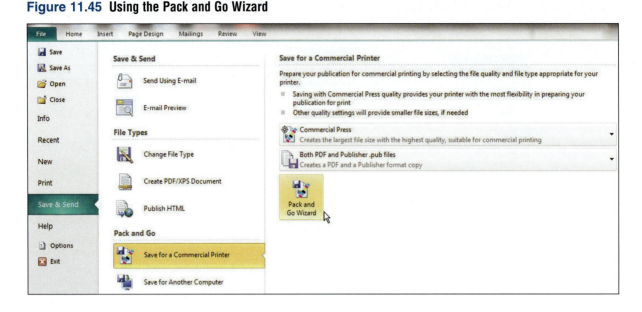

Managing Registration Settings

In commercial printing, the process of adding a slight overlap between adjacent areas of color to avoid gaps caused by registration errors is called trapping. Color trapping is necessary to compensate for poor color registration. Poor color registration occurs when the printing plates used to print each color are not aligned perfectly. Poor registration causes unintentional white slivers to appear between adjoining colors.

Using Pack and Go

The Pack and Go Wizard is accessed by clicking the Save & Send button in the File tab Backstage view as shown in Figure 11.45, and it is used to pack a publication and its linked files into a single file that you can take to a commercial printer to be printed. Pack and Go ensures that you have the files necessary to hand off the publication to a commercial printer by compacting all the information, embedding fonts, including linked graphics, print composites, and separation proofs. The Unpack.exe file will automatically unpack the Pack and Go file.

Exercise 11.6 Creating a Real Estate Flyer from Scratch

1. Open Publisher.
2. Click the *Blank 11 x 8.5"* thumbnail at the New tab Backstage view.
3. Click the More Schemes button in the Schemes group in the Page Design tab, and then click the *Field* color scheme.
4. Click the Borders & Accents button in the Building Blocks group in the Insert tab.
5. Click the *More Borders and Accents* option at the bottom of the Borders & Accents gallery.

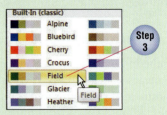

6. Click the *Open Border* thumbnail in the *Frames* section, and then click Insert.
7. Select the Open Border frame, click the Rotate button in the Arrange group in the Drawing Tools Format tab, and then click *Rotate Left 90°*.

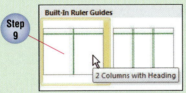

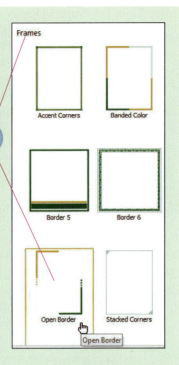

8. Drag the sizing handles in the frame to fit the margin guides.
9. Click the Guides button in the Layout group in the Page Design tab and then click the *2 Columns with Heading* thumbnail in the Built-In Ruler Guides gallery. These guides will help you visualize where the design elements will be placed on the page.

10. Click the Clip Art button in the Illustrations group in the Insert tab and then type **house** in the *Search for* text box of the Clip Art task pane. Complete a search for a home picture of your own choosing and then insert the image.
11. Drag the image to the upper left section of the publication, and then size it similar to the image in Figure 11.46. Crop the image if necessary. ***Hint: Use the guides to help position the image. Align the top of the image with the green guide line below the margin guide line.***
12. Click the Advertisements button in the Building Blocks group, click the *More Advertisements* option at the bottom of the Advertisements gallery, click the *Explosion 1* thumbnail in the *Office.com Building Blocks* section and then click Insert.

13. Drag and drop the explosion shape to the upper left corner of your house image. Select the shape so that the sizing handles with the little Xs display, click the Shape Styles More button, and then click the *Horizontal Gradient - Accent 1* color.

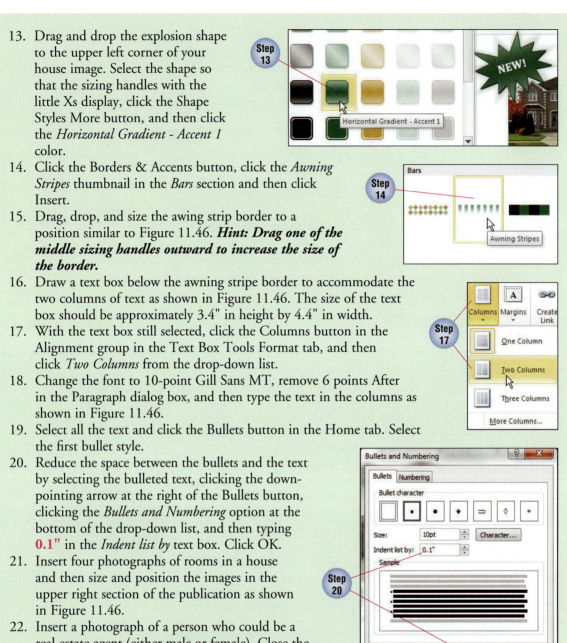

14. Click the Borders & Accents button, click the *Awning Stripes* thumbnail in the *Bars* section and then click Insert.

15. Drag, drop, and size the awing strip border to a position similar to Figure 11.46. **Hint: Drag one of the middle sizing handles outward to increase the size of the border.**

16. Draw a text box below the awning stripe border to accommodate the two columns of text as shown in Figure 11.46. The size of the text box should be approximately 3.4" in height by 4.4" in width.

17. With the text box still selected, click the Columns button in the Alignment group in the Text Box Tools Format tab, and then click *Two Columns* from the drop-down list.

18. Change the font to 10-point Gill Sans MT, remove 6 points After in the Paragraph dialog box, and then type the text in the columns as shown in Figure 11.46.

19. Select all the text and click the Bullets button in the Home tab. Select the first bullet style.

20. Reduce the space between the bullets and the text by selecting the bulleted text, clicking the down-pointing arrow at the right of the Bullets button, clicking the *Bullets and Numbering* option at the bottom of the drop-down list, and then typing **0.1"** in the *Indent list by* text box. Click OK.

21. Insert four photographs of rooms in a house and then size and position the images in the upper right section of the publication as shown in Figure 11.46.

22. Insert a photograph of a person who could be a real estate agent (either male or female). Close the Clip Art task pane. Customize the photograph by completing the following steps:

    a. Select the photograph and then click the Recolor button in the Adjust group in the Picture Tools Format tab.
    b. Select the *RGB (0, 102, 51), Accent color 1 Dark* color variation in the *Dark Variations* section.

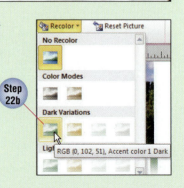

c. Add the caption as shown in Figure 11.46 by clicking the Caption button in the Picture Styles group in the Picture Tools Format tab, and then click the *Box, Reversed - Layout 4* caption style in the *Overlay* section.

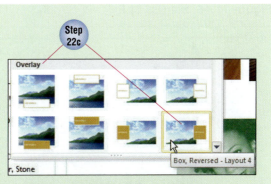

d. Resize the caption to hold the text as shown in Figure 11.46. Type **Call Micah 630.555.5674**, and choose an appropriate font and font size. ***Hint: To resize the caption to accommodate the text, ungroup the caption from the picture.***

23. Insert the logo, **RealEstateLogo.jpg**, located in your *Chaper11* folder. Position the logo as shown in Figure 11.46. Hint: The logo was created by grouping a clip art image with a text box.

24. Save the document and name it **C11-E06-RealEstate**. Print the document.

25. Prepare the publication to be sent to a commercial printer by completing the following steps:
    a. Click the File tab, and then click the Info tab.
    b. Click the Run the Design Checker button and review the suggestions given in the Design Checker task pane. Click the Close Design Checker button.
    c. Click the File tab, and then click the Save & Send tab.
    d. Click the *Save for a Commercial Printer* option in the *Pack and Go* section.
    e. Click the Pack and Go Wizard button in the *Save for a Commercial Printer* section.

    f. At the Pack and Go Wizard dialog box, click the *Other* option, click the Browse button, and browse to save the compressed file to your *Chapter11* folder. Click OK.
    g. Click the Next button.
    h. At the Pack and Go Font Embedding dialog box, click OK.
    i. At the Pack and Go Wizard dialog box, click OK to print a composite proof of the publication.
    j. Close **C11-E06-RealEstate.pub**.
    k. Locate the zipped (compressed file) in your *Chapter11* folder, and then double-click the file to unzip the file. Open the publication (Publisher file) and then click OK if the Load Fonts dialog box displays. View the document, and then close it.

Figure 11.46 Exercise 11.6

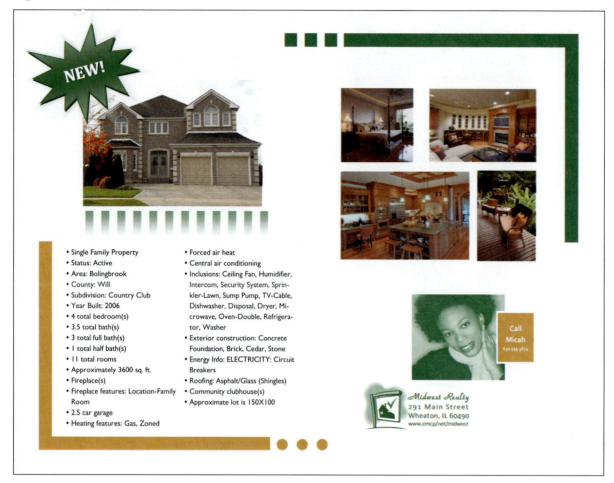

Using Catalog Merge

Using Publisher, you have the ability to connect to a data source, such as an Access database, an Excel spreadsheet, an Outlook Contact list, or even a Word table, and use the data to create a catalog of your products or services. You can use this feature to create directories, photo albums, or any other type of publication that displays one or more items on each page.

How Catalog Works

Catalog merge is similar to mail merge. There are basically three steps in the process:

1. Use a data source with record information (can even include picture file formats).
2. Merge a document with the catalog merge area and merge fields that are placeholders for record information.
3. Merged pages display multiple records per page as shown in Figure 11.47.

Planning Your Catalog

You may want to include a cover, table of contents, order forms, and pages for your merge fields, you can even include pictures of your items. You may start by using a Publisher template, or you may create your document from scratch and then save it as a

Figure 11.47 Catalog Merge Document

[Catalog merge document layout showing two product sections, each with the following placeholder text:]

Name of product or service

Describe the product, service, or event here. Include a brief description and any features.

Add the price, order number, and other properties.

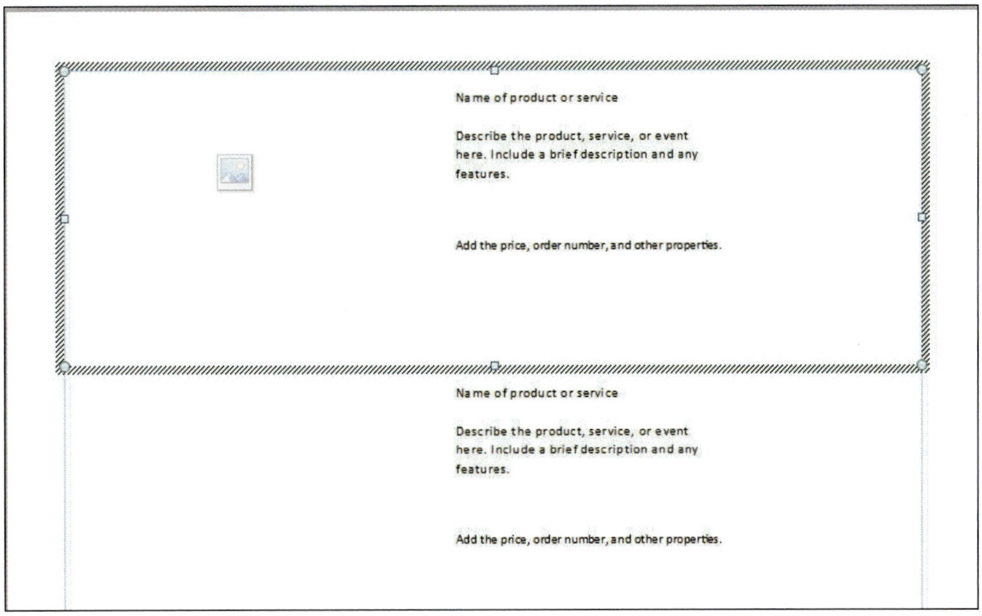

template for future use. If you plan to add the merged pages that you create to the end of an existing publication, make sure your catalog merge document (template) matches the existing publication in page size and type.

Inserting Text Data Fields

Carefully plan your data source so that you include everything you want in your catalog. The data fields that you include in your data source document must correspond with the merge fields that you insert into your catalog merge document. Make sure each row in your data source, or record, corresponds to the information for one item.

Inserting Picture Fields

When including pictures, you need to make sure that you insert any merge field that represents a picture file as a picture field by clicking the Picture Field button in the Insert group in the Catalog Tools Format tab. Do not include the actual picture or image in your data source. If you plan to save your picture files and your data source in the same folder, type the file name for the relevant picture, for example, myphoto.jpg. If the pictures files will be located in a different folder from the data source, type the path for the relevant picture.

Text Field

Picture Field

Creating a Catalog

Prepare a thumbnail sketch of your catalog illustrating where pictures and text fields should display. Determine if a cover is needed and then sketch that design as well. You may want to open a Publisher catalog template and study how the template was prepared before creating your document from scratch. You may use a Publisher template, but sometimes customizing complicated templates can be time consuming and challenging if numerous changes are needed.

After carefully planning your data source and deciding on what merge fields will be needed, open a blank document screen in Publisher, and complete the following steps:

Figure 11.48 Catalog Tools Format Tab

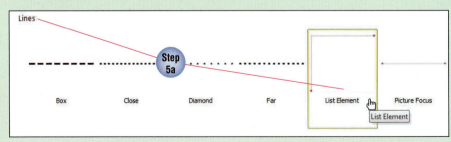

1. Click the Catalog Pages button in the Pages group in the Insert tab.
2. Click the second page thumbnail in the Page Navigation task pane.
3. Click the Add List button in the Start group in the Catalog Tools Format tab and either create a new data source or select an existing one. When the source is located, the buttons on the Catalog Tools Format tab will display as shown in Figure 11.48.
4. Select a desired layout. Size and position the *Catalog Merge Area* text box.
5. Click the first page thumbnail in the Page Navigation task pane.
6. Format the cover for your catalog.
7. Click the second page thumbnail.
8. Type the labels for your text in the *Catalog Merge Area* text box.
9. Position the insertion at the right of each label and insert an appropriate merge field.
10. Click the picture placeholder if one is available in the layout. Click the Picture Fields button, and then click the More Picture Options button. At the Insert Picture Field dialog box, click the Specify Folders button in the bottom left corner, and then select the location where your pictures are located. Click OK. Make sure your graphic files are located in the same folder as your data source.
11. Click the Preview Results button in the Preview Page group and then merge your document.

Exercise 11.7 Creating a Catalog

1. Open Publisher.
2. Click the *Blank 8.5" x 11"* thumbnail at the New tab Backstage view.
3. Click the Catalog Pages button in the Pages group in the Insert tab.
4. Click the page 1 thumbnail in the Page Navigation task pane.
5. Format the cover (page 1) by completing the following steps:
   a. Click the Borders and Accents button in the Building Blocks group, click the More Borders and Accents button, and then click the *List Element* border in the *Lines* section. Click Insert.

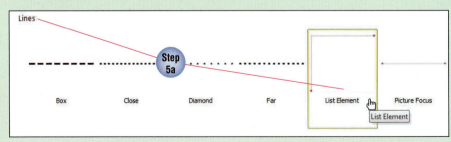

b. Drag the sizing handles of the border to fit the margin guides.

6. Click the WordArt button in the Text group in the Insert tab and then select the *Fill - Blue, Reflection Curved* effect in the *WordArt Transform Styles* section.

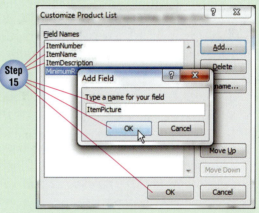

7. At the Edit WordArt Text dialog box, type: **Circle of Friends** press Enter, and type **2012 Holiday Fundraiser**. Click OK.

8. Drag the WordArt object to a position similar to Figure 11.49.

9. Click the Clip Art button in the Insert tab, type **hands** in the *Search for* text box. Insert an image similar to Figure 11.49. Size and the position the image as shown and apply a Picture Style of your own choosing.

10. Click the page 2 thumbnail in the Page Navigation task pane.

11. Click the Add List button in the Start group in the Catalog Tools Format tab.

12. Click Type New List.

13. At the New Product List dialog box, click the Customize Columns button.

14. At the Customize Product List dialog box, delete all the default Field Names.

15. Click the Add button and add the following Field Names: **ItemNumber**, **ItemName**, **ItemDescription**, **OpeningBid**, **MinimumRaise**, and **ItemPicture**. Click OK after each entry and then click OK to close the Customize Product List dialog box.

16. Type the text in the Catalog Merge Product List as shown here. Click OK.

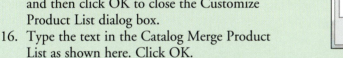

17. Save the data source to the *My Data Source* folder in your *Chapter11* folder. Notice that the graphic files have been saved to this folder as well. **_Hint: Add your initials to the file name that is already in the My Data Source folder._** Click OK at the Catalog Merge Product List dialog box.

18. Click the *4 entries, picture on left* layout.

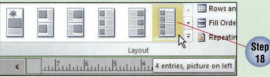

19. Type the labels for each of the Merge Fields as shown here:

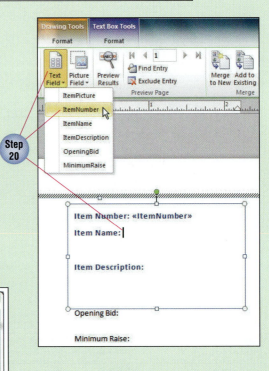

20. Position your insertion point at the right of the colon next to each of the data labels in the document (you may have to add a space), and then click the Text Fields button in the Insert group in the Catalog Tools Format tab. Select the appropriate merge field from the drop-down list. Insert each of the fields that match the labels in the document. Resize the text boxes if necessary.

21. Click the Picture placeholder at the left of the text fields in the document.

22. Click the Specify Folders button and then select the Data source folder from the list. Click OK. *Hint: The graphic files have been* ***saved in the*** **My Data Source** ***folder in your*** **Chapter11** ***folder.***

23. Click the Preview Results button.
24. Save the document as **C11-E07-CatalogMerge**.
25. Print and then close **C11-E07-CatalogMerge.pub**.

Figure 11.49 Exercise 11.7

Figure 11.49 **Exercise 11.7 (continued)**

Item Number: 101

Item Name: Holiday Welcome

Item Description: Wreath with $25 Suzette's gift certificate

Opening Bid: $100

Minimum Raise: $10

Item Number: 103

Item Name: Tree with Ornaments

Item Description: Tree with hand-painted ornaments

Opening Bid: $150

Minimum Raise: $20

Item Number: 104

Item Name: Picnic Basket

Item Description: Classic picnic basket with glasses, champagne, linen napkins, and plates

Opening Bid: $50

Minimum Raise: $5

Item Number: 102

Item Name: Floral Arrangement

Item Description: Fresh flower arrangement and gift certificate from Growing Things

Opening Bid: $75

Minimum Raise: $10

Chapter *Summary*

➤ Microsoft Publisher 2010 is a complete easy-to-use desktop publishing program designed for small business users and individuals who want to create their own high-quality, professional-looking marketing materials and other business documents without the assistance of professional designers.

➤ Publisher can be used for publications that require commercial printing. Publisher offers full support for commercial printing, including four-color separation and spot color processing.

➤ Publisher should be used if document layouts need to be especially precise or complex. Publisher includes easy-to-use layout guides, ruler guides, and alignment options to align objects to ruler marks, guides, or other objects.

➤ Begin your publication at the New tab Backstage view screen where you will find options to select templates or choose blank page sizes and recent publications from which you can base your document.

➤ Consistency can be reinforced by using design sets in Publisher and using styles for spacing, fonts, alignment, repetition, color, and decorative elements such as borders, drop caps, initial caps, and so on.

➤ A Business Information set inserts data stored on its page to placeholder text containing information about a company name, contact information, and logo.

➤ In Publisher, unlike Word, all objects such as text, graphics, pictures, WordArt, and Shapes must be placed inside a frame before you can use them in your publication.

➤ Font schemes make it quick and easy to pick fonts that look good together. To change all of the fonts in your publication, you may apply a new font scheme.

➤ Every page in a publication has a foreground and background layer. The foreground is where you insert text and design objects. The background layer is known as the master page.

➤ Any objects placed on the master page will appear on every page, such as page numbering.

➤ The layout guides create a framework or grid for margins, text boxes, columns, graphics, headings, and other objects used in a publication.

➤ Baseline guides are guides to which lines of text can be aligned to provide a uniform appearance between columns of text.

➤ Ruler guides display as green dotted lines and are created at the master page. Ruler guides are useful when you want to align several objects or position an object at an exact location on the page.

➤ Building Blocks contain a wide variety of predesigned objects to enhance your document, including logos, headlines, calendars, pull quotes, and attention-getters.

➤ In advertising, a logo is a special design used as a trademark for a company or product. A logo can help a business make a big impression since a logo embellishes the company name and reinforces company identification.

➤ The Text Fit feature includes options to automatically resizes text so that it will fit into the allotted space. Your choices include *Best Fit*, *Shrink Text On Overflow*, *Grow Text Box to Fit*, and *Do Not AutoFit*.

➤ One of the most useful features in Publisher 2010 is the new *Save as Picture* option. You may group objects together and save the entire selection as a picture.

➤ The Page Navigation Pane displays each page and allows you to navigate from one to the other.

➤ When text boxes are connected, text that does not fit into the first text box flows into the next connected text box.

➤ Publisher 2010 refers to connected text boxes in a series as a story.

➤ To help a reader follow a story that may begin on one page and continue to another page, a *Continued notice* can be added at the bottom of the text box informing the reader where to find the rest of the story and a *Continued from* notice at the top of the next text box.

- Page numbering may be added to a publication in the foreground layer or in the master page layer.
- Headers and footers can be created with automatic page numbers, current date and time display, and any text.
- A watermark can be created in the master page that will subsequently display on every page of a publication.
- Mail merge can be used to combine records from a data source with a Publisher publication to create multiple copies of the publication that are individually customized using the Mail Merge, Email Merge, or Catalog Merge.
- When sending a publication to a commercial printer, you can select a color model that best fits your printing needs.
- Publisher includes a Pack and Go Wizard for packing a publication for reproduction by a commercial printer.
- Design checker runs as part of the Pack and Go Wizard listing all occurrences of problems that it has detected in a document.
- You can use the catalog merge feature in Publisher to create directories, photo albums, or any other type of publication that displays one or more items on each page.
- The Publisher catalog merge can use a variety of data source formats. You can generate a data source in Publisher, use a data source in Excel, Word, Outlook, Access, and many other sources.
- The data fields that you include in your data source correspond to the merge fields that you insert into your catalog merge document (template).
- Format your catalog merge document by clicking the Catalog Pages button, selecting a catalog layout, typing labels for your text fields, clicking the Text Field button in the Insert group in the Catalog Tools Format tab, selecting text fields you want to insert, and then previewing your merge before printing it.
- Click the Picture Field button in the Insert group in the Catalog Tools Format tab to insert pictures in a catalog merge.
- If you want to include multiple catalog merges in a publication, you will need to create a new publication for the merged pages because there can only be one set of catalog pages per publication.

Commands Review

FEATURE	RIBBON TAB, GROUP	BUTTON
Advertisements	Insert tab, Building Blocks group	
Borders & Accents	Insert tab, Building Blocks group	
Business Information set	Insert tab, Text group	
Calendars	Insert tab, Building Blocks group	
Caption	Picture Tools Format tab, Picture Styles group	Caption
Color schemes	Page Design tab, Schemes	
Continued notice	Right-click text box, click *Format Text Box*, click *Text Box* tab, then click *Include "Continued on page…"* or *Include "Continued from page…"*	
Create Text Box Link	Text Box Tools Format tab, Linking group	

FEATURE	RIBBON TAB, GROUP	BUTTON
Drop Cap	Text Box Tools Format tab, Typography group	
Emboss	Text Box Tools Format tab, Effects group	A Emboss
Engrave	Text Box Tools Format tab, Effects group	A Engrave
Fonts	Page Design, Schemes group	Aa
Guides	Page Design tab, Layout group	
Hyphenation	Text Box Tools Format tab, Text group	a-bc
Ligatures	Text Box Tools Format tab, Typography group	fi
Number Style	Text Box Tools Format tab, Typography group	123
Master Page	Page Design tab, Page Background group	
Outline	Text Box Tools Format tab, Effects group	A Outline
Pack and Go Wizard	File tab, Save & Send tab, Save for a Commercial Printer section	
Page Parts	Insert tab, Building Blocks group	
Picture Field	Catalog Tools Format tab, Insert group	
Picture Placeholder	Insert tab, Illustrations group	
Run Design Checker	File tab, Info tab	
Sample Font Color	Home tab, Font tab	
Save as Picture	Right-click Picture, click Save as Picture	
Shadow	Text Box Tools Format tab, Effects group	A
Styles	Home tab, Styles	A
Stylistic Sets	Text Box Tools Format tab, Typography	abc Stylistic Sets ▾
Text Direction	Text Box Tools Format tab, Text group	
Text Field	Catalog Tools Format tab, Insert group	
Text Fit	Text Box Tools Format tab, Text group	
Watermark	Select picture, Picture Tools Format tab, Recolor, Adjust group	
WordArt	Insert tab, Text group	A

Reviewing Key Points

Completion: On a separate sheet of paper, indicate the correct term or command for each item.

1. Another name for the background layer in Publisher.
2. A Publisher feature that stores information about a business and then automatically inserts that information into placeholder text.
3. List four categories of building blocks that are available in Publisher.
4. Non-printable lines that help you align objects and layout design objects in your publication.
5. This feature allows you to group objects together and save them as a single picture.
6. This feature makes it quick and easy to pick fonts that look good together.
7. Click this button in the Text group in the Text Box Format tab to automatically resize text so that it will fit into an allotted space.
8. Click this button to connect one text to another.
9. Publisher includes this wizard for packing a publication for reproduction by a commercial printer.
10. A term that Publisher 2010 uses for connected text boxes in a series.
11. A special design used as a trademark for a company or product.
12. Predesigned color combinations that you can apply to the design objects in your publication.
13. This feature inserts an empty picture frame to reserve space for pictures you want to add later.
14. This features applies a text formatting style that capitalizes the first character in the opening paragraph of a publication.
15. This area of the Publisher screen displays each page as a thumbnail.
16. With this feature you create a publication and then combine the publication with information from a data source to generate merged pages with multiple records per page.
17. List three data sources you may use in a catalog merge.
18. The _____ _____ that you include in your data source correspond to the _____ _____ that you insert into your catalog merge template (document).
19. This tab will display on the ribbon when you click the Catalog Pages button in the Pages group in the Insert tab.
20. Click the _____ button to insert a picture from your data source.

Chapter Assessments

Assessment 11.1   Advertising a Real Estate Sale

1. Create a flyer in Publisher 2010 advertising the sale of a condominium on Kiawah Island in South Carolina by including the following specifications:
   a. Consider your target audience and the topic of the flyer in the layout and design of your document.
   b. Consider the amenities: 10-mile beach, tennis courts, swimming pools, golf courses, bicycle trails, and a natural environment in choosing images that will create focus in your flyer.
   c. Use colors that are bright and cheerful.
   d. Include an attention-getter building block.

e. Include a tear-off design object as shown in Figure 11.50. ***Hint: The tear-off object is available by clicking the Building Blocks dialog box launcher in the Insert tab, clicking the Business Information category, and then clicking the Phone Tear-Off thumbnail in the*** Contact Information *section. Click Insert.*

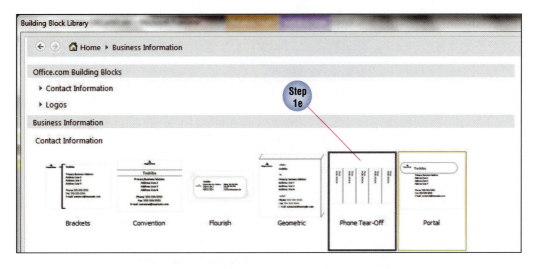

f. Include the text as shown in Figure 11.50.
2. Save the document as **C11-A01-Kiawah**.
3. Print and then close **C11-A01-Kiawah.pub**.

Assessment 11.2   Real Estate Postcard

1. As a realtor in Columbus, Ohio, you are eager to inform neighbors, friends, and prospective clients of a new marketing approach where clients may view a panoramic video of a home by visiting your company website. Create a postcard that promotes a virtual home tour and include the following specifications:
   - Use an appropriate postcard template or create the postcard from scratch.
   - Create multiple copies on a sheet.
   - Choose a font scheme.
   - Apply a *Ligature* and *Stylistic Set* to the real estate company name and address. ***Hint: Change the font to Gabriola.***
   - Choose a color scheme.
   - Include a logo, graphic, or picture.
   - Use the AutoFit Text feature in at least one text box.
   - Include the following information:
       Virtual Home Tour
       Call me for information on having a customized 360° Panoramic Video of your home placed on the Internet for buyers to view.
       Pleasantville Realty
       One Northbrook Lane
       Columbus, OH 43204
       Sarah Takamoto
       Phone: 513.555.3489
       Fax: 513.555.3488
       Email: pleasantvl@emcp.net
       www.emcp.net/pleasantvl
2. Save your publication and name it **C11-A02-Virtual**.
3. Print and then close **C11-A02-Virtual.pub**.

Figure 11.50 Assessment 11.1 Sample Solution

Assessment 11.3   Gift Certificate

1. Create a gift certificate for Butterfield Gardens and include the following specifications:
    a. Refer to the Butterfield newsletter created in Exercises 11.4 and 11.5 for facts about Butterfield Gardens such as address, phone number, fax number, and email address.
    b. Insert a certificate number, expiration date, and redemption value.
    c. Create multiple copies on a sheet.

d. Choose a color scheme that complements the newsletter created in Exercises 11.4 and 11.5.

e. Choose a font scheme that is interesting and appropriate for the document.

f. Include one graphic image, picture, and/or the Butterfield logo. The Butterfield logo is located in your *Chapter11* folder.

2. Save your publication and name it **C11-A03-GiftCertificate**.

3. Print and then close **C11-A03-GiftCertificate.pub**. *Hint: Print multiple gift certificates per page.*

Assessment 11.4   Integrating an Access Database

In this assessment, you will use the Publisher Mail Merge feature to merge data to the postcard created in Assessment 11.2. You will edit the Access database and use the filter feature to select only the addresses in Columbus, Ohio. Complete the following instructions:

1. Open **C11-A02-Virtual.pub**.

2. Click *page 2* in the Page Navigation task pane.

3. Select the *Recipient Address* placeholder text.

4. Click the Mailings tab, click Mail Merge, and then click *Mail Merge* from the drop-down list.

5. Click the Select Recipient button in the Mail Merge tab and then click Use Existing List.

6. At the Select Data Source dialog box, select **Ohio List** (Access file) located in the *Chapter11* folder. Click Open.

7. In the Mail Merge Recipients dialog box, you can select the recipients that you want to include in the merge. Click the arrow next to the ZIP column heading and then select *43204* from the drop-down list. Click OK.

8. At the Mailings tab, click the Address Block button in the Write & Insert Fields group. **Hint: Make sure the placeholder text is selected.**

9. Click OK at the Insert Address Block dialog box.

10. Click the Preview Results button in the Preview Results group in the Mailings tab, and then click the arrow buttons to view the merged recipients.

11. Click the Finish & Merge button and then click *Merge to New Publication* from the drop-down list.

12. Save the merged document as **C11-A04-Merge**.

13. Print Multiple pages per sheet as shown below.

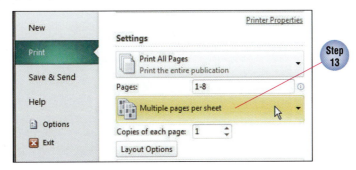

14. Save the main document as **C11-A04-MainDoc** and then close the document.

Assessment 11.5   Creating a Catalog Merge Document

Prepare a catalog merge publication on a topic of your own choosing. Include the following specifications:

1. Your catalog should include a cover.
2. Format the cover with interesting fonts, font colors, images, or any other design elements that reinforce the topic of the publication.
3. Create a data source, and include a picture field. Make sure the picture file names correspond to the images you have saved to a folder along with your data source file. Select pictures that complement the data and the topic of the catalog.
4. Select a layout that will accommodate all the data you want to include in your catalog.
5. Type appropriate labels for each of your merge fields, and format them with interesting fonts, font sizes, and other enhancements.
6. Save your catalog, and name it **C11-A05-Catalog**.
7. Merge to a new publication print, and then close **C11-A05-Catalog.pub**.
8. Save the main document as **C11-A5-MainDoc** and then close the document.

Assessment 11.6   Creating a Poster

1. Form a group and delegate tasks for each member of the group to create a poster based on a template you may download from the Office.com template website.
2. Complete a search for a poster template, and add text that your group has decided to use to advertise a business, workshop, class, or activity of their own choosing. Consider using a digital camera or cellphone camera and taking pictures of your college or classroom, your home or apartment for rent or sale, your community buildings and landscapes, or current travels for a travel poster. Use interesting and attention-getting fonts. Demonstrate your knowledge of the design concepts discussed throughout this textbook.
3. Save the document as **C11-A06-GroupPosterProject**, and then print it. *Hint: Trimming the pages may be necessary.*
4. Present the poster to the entire class, and discuss how your group prepared the document in Publisher 2010.

Chapter 12

CHAPTER12

Creating Presentations Using PowerPoint

Performance Objectives

Upon successful completion of Chapter 12, you will be able to:

- Plan, design, and create presentations.
- Create slides and add text and other objects.
- Insert pictures, clip art, WordArt, SmartArt, charts, and media clips.
- Apply themes; add and change slide layouts; rearrange, hide, and delete slides.

- Add transitions, custom animations, and sound.
- Save a presentation as a video.
- Print and run a presentation.

Desktop Publishing Terms

Animate	Motion paths	Theme
Build	Slide master	Transition
Effect	Storyboard	

PowerPoint Features Used

Animation	Media	Slide layouts
Animation Pane	Notes Master view	Slide library
Artistic Effects	Office.com Templates	Slide Master view
Clip Art	Outline/Slides pane	Slide Orientation
Handout Master view	Quick Styles	Slide Show view
Hyperlinks	Rehearse Timings	Slide Sorter view
Importing from Excel	Save & Send	SmartArt
Importing from Word	Screenshot	Themes

Getting Started with PowerPoint 2010

PowerPoint is a presentation graphics program you can use to organize and present information. With PowerPoint you can create visual aids for presentation and then print copies of the aids as well as run the presentation. PowerPoint 2010 introduces some fantastic new tools that you can use to effectively create, manage, and collaborate with others on your presentations; enhance your presentations with video, picture, and animations; and deliver and share presentations more efficiently. Some of these new features include using the New tab Backstage view, co-authoring presentations, organizing slides into sections, applying SmartArt graphic picture layouts, adding screenshots to slides, applying artistic textures and effects to pictures, using transitions

Figure 12.1 PowerPoint Window

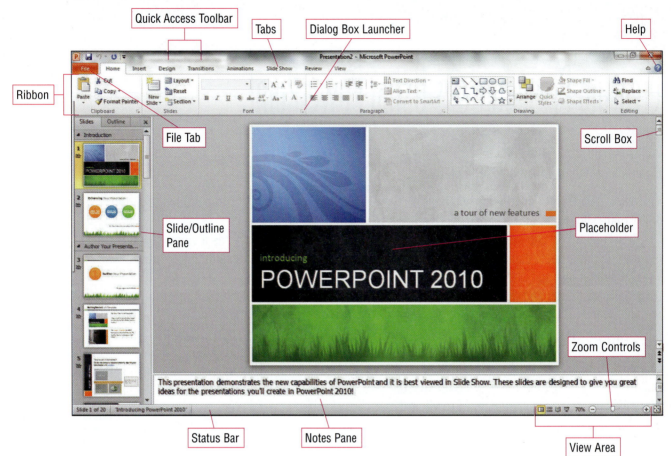

with 3-D motion graphic effects, turning your mouse into a laser pointer, and broadcasting your slide show.

DTP POINTERS ▶
Click the Question Mark button in the upper right corner for Help on new PowerPoint features or click the Help tab in the File tab Backstage view.

Preparing a presentation in PowerPoint generally involves following some basic steps:

1. Open PowerPoint.
2. Plan the presentation.
3. Design the presentation.
4. Create and edit slides.
5. Save, print, and run the presentation.
6. Close the presentation and then close PowerPoint.

Opening PowerPoint

To open PowerPoint 2010, click the Start button on the Windows Taskbar, point to *All Programs,* click *Microsoft Office,* and then click *Microsoft PowerPoint 2010.* The Microsoft PowerPoint window will display as shown in Figure 12.1.

When you start PowerPoint, it opens in Normal view, where you create and work on slides. By default, PowerPoint 2010 applies the Blank Presentation template, which appears in Figure 12.2. Blank Presentation is the simplest and most generic of the templates in PowerPoint 2010 and is a good template to use when you first start to work with PowerPoint.

Figure 12.2 Blank Presentation with Title Slide Layout

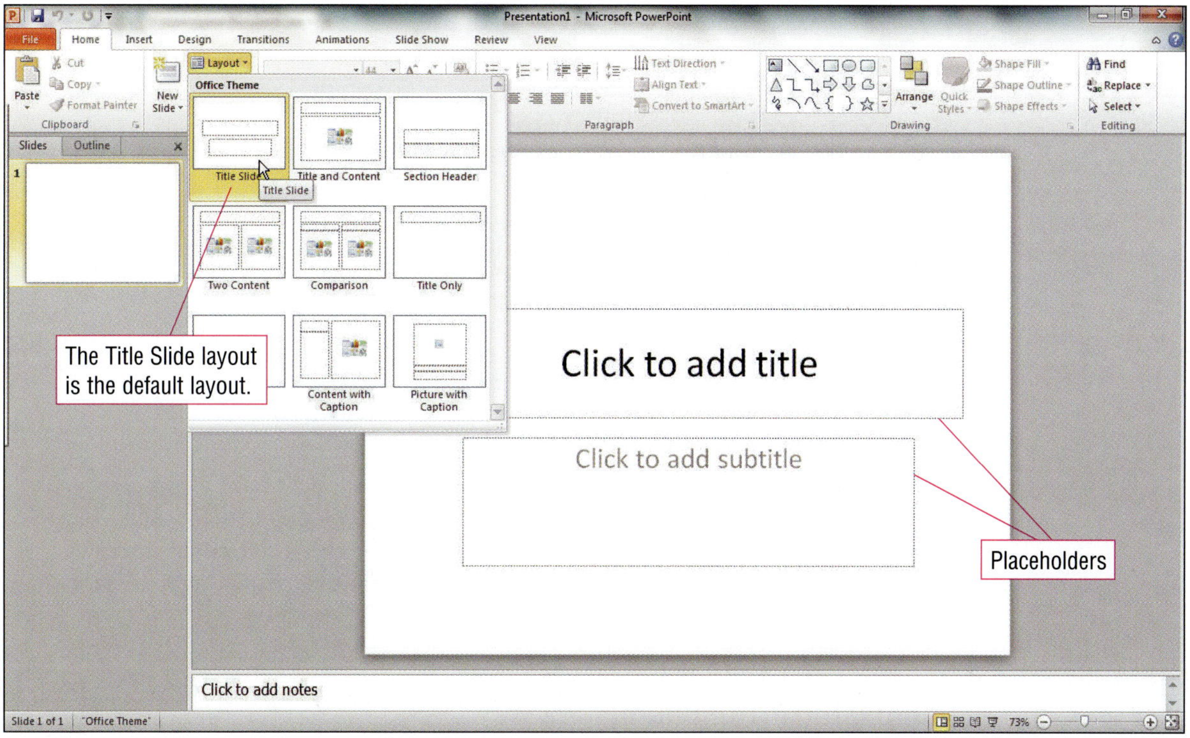

The Title Slide layout is the default layout.

Placeholders

To create a new presentation that is based on the Blank Presentation template, do the following:

1. Click the File tab.
2. Point to New, and under the *Available Templates and Themes* section, select Blank Presentation.
3. Click Create.

Working with Layouts

When you open a blank presentation in PowerPoint, the default layout called *Title Slide* appears, but there are other standard layouts that you can apply and use. Layouts define positioning and formatting for content that will later appear on a slide. To choose or change layouts, click the Layout button in the Slides group on the Home tab or right-click on the slide and then click *Layout* at the shortcut menu. Using either method, select the desired layout and proceed with customizing your slide.

Microsoft Office PowerPoint 2010 includes built-in, standard layouts, or you can create custom layouts that meet your specific organizational needs. People creating presentations in your organization can then use either the built-in layouts or your custom layouts to create their presentations.

A slide layout contains placeholders as shown in Figure 12.3. For text placeholders, click the placeholder, and then type the text. For other objects, click the icon in the placeholder and then work with the chosen object.

If you do not find a standard layout that suits your needs or the needs of presentation authors within your organization, you can create a custom layout. You can create reusable custom layouts that specify the number, size, and location of placeholders, background content, and optional slide and placeholder level properties. You can also

Figure 12.3 Slide Layout Placeholders

Slide Layout Placeholders	
Placeholder	**Description**
Add Title	Enter title text
Add Subtitle	Enter subtitle on Title Slide
Bulleted	Enter bulleted list
Insert Table	Inserts a table
Insert Chart	Inserts a chart
Insert SmartArt Graphic	Inserts a SmartArt object
Insert Picture from File	Inserts a picture from a chosen location
Clip Art	Inserts a picture from the Clip Art Task Pane
Insert Media Clip	Inserts a media file
Add Text	Enter text
Blank	No placeholders

distribute custom layouts as part of a template, so you no longer have to waste valuable time cutting and pasting your layouts onto new slides or deleting content on a slide that you want to use with new and different content. Use the Insert tab to insert a comprehensive collection of objects into your slides, including shapes, hyperlinks, headers and footers, and sounds.

Planning the Presentation

The planning process for a presentation is basically the same as for other documents you have created. In the planning stages, you must do the following:

DTP POINTERS
Good presentation skills include attention to message, visuals, and delivery.

DTP POINTERS
Introduce one concept per slide.

DTP POINTERS
Consistency is important in maintaining a uniform appearance.

DTP POINTERS
Be consistent when using color to present facts in a presentation.

- **Establish a purpose.** Do you want to inform, educate, sell, motivate, persuade, or entertain?
- **Evaluate your audience.** Who will listen to and watch your presentation?

  What is the age range? What are their educational and economic levels?

  What knowledge do they have of the topic beforehand? What image do you want to project to your audience?
- **Decide on content.** Decide on the content and organization of your message. Do not try to cover too many topics—this may strain the audience's attention or cause confusion. Identify the main point.
- **Determine the medium to be used to convey your message.** To help decide the type of medium to be used, consider such items as topic, equipment availability, location, lighting, audience size, and so on.
- **Show one idea per slide.** Each slide in a presentation should convey only one main idea. Too many ideas on a slide may confuse the audience and cause you to stray from the purpose of the slide.
- **Maintain a consistent design.** A consistent design and color scheme will create continuity and cohesiveness. Do not use too many colors or too many pictures or other graphic elements.
- **Keep slides easy to read and uncluttered.** Keep slides simple and easy to read. Keep words and others items such as bullets to a minimum. Limit the number of words per line and the number of lines to five or six. You may use bullets to assist in organizing information and adding white space to text. As an alternative, consider using SmartArt to graphically illustrate points that you want to make.

- **Determine printing needs.** Will you provide your audience with handouts? If so, will the handouts consist of a printout on both sides? An outline of the presentation? Notes on the printout for note taking?

Designing the Presentation

When choosing a design for the slides, consider your audience, topic, and method of delivery. You would not want to select a design with vibrant colors for an audience of conservative bankers. Nor would you use a design with dark colors or patterns if you plan to photocopy printouts—the contrast of colors and patterns may blur. In addition to design, consider the following items when determining layout:

- **Continuity.** Ensure consistency, avoid redundancy, and use forceful expressions in the design and layout. Repeat specific design elements such as company logos, color, font, and type of bullets used. Consistent elements help to connect one slide to the next and contribute to a cohesive presentation. Some of PowerPoint's design templates coordinate with Microsoft Publisher design sets and Word templates to provide continuation of design across various documents.

- **Legibility.** One typeface is fine; use two at the most. Instead of changing typefaces, try varying the type style, such as bold, italics, or any of the new text effects. Legibility is of utmost importance. Eighteen points is the minimum for an appropriate type size. You want everyone in the room to be able to read what you have taken the time to prepare. Choose a thicker font or apply bold to increase the readability of the text. When formatting headings, keep titles short if possible; long headings are harder to read. Kern and track if necessary. Use a sans serif typeface.

- **Color.** Use restraint with color to enhance the message, not detract from it. Colors must look good together. Studies on the psychology of color suggest that certain colors elicit certain feelings in an audience. For example, blue backgrounds promote a conservative approach to the information presented and provide general feelings of calmness, loyalty, and security. Yellow or white text against a dark blue or indigo background is a good combination. Black backgrounds are effective in financial presentations. Black also seems to show directness or forcefulness. Green backgrounds project an image of being direct, social, or intelligent. Green acts to stimulate interaction and is a good choice for use in training and educational presentations. Purple or magenta is appropriate in presentations that tend to entertain or represent less conservative or serious topics.

- **Create an outline.** An outline is a list of headings in the chronological order of the presentation. Follow basic outlining rules such as "Every A needs a B," meaning that you should have at least two supporting points for each main point. You may import outlines created in Word and formatted with heading styles into PowerPoint presentations.

- **Create a storyboard.** A *storyboard* is a visual example of the headings in the outline. When creating a storyboard, your information should not exceed what will fit on a 5 by 7-inch index card to avoid filling an entire 8½ by 11-inch sheet of paper. The goal is to limit the amount of information the audience must read so that they can focus on what is being said and visually presented. Write in phrases instead of sentences; you will be less inclined to read from your presentation. Phrases also work well in bulleted format.

- **Use graphics to illustrate your message.** Graphics break up text and stimulate interest in the message. One graphic for every two or three slides is sufficient. Also, consider using SmartArt, Shapes, and Charts to graphically illustrate a point.

◀ DTP POINTERS
Keep headings short in slides.

◀ DTP POINTERS
Using ALL CAPS does not leave room for further emphasis.

◀ DTP POINTERS
Remember that the audience must be able to read your slides from a distance. Generally speaking, a font size smaller than 18 might be too difficult for the audience to see.

Storyboard
A visual example of the headings in an outline.

- **Consider the medium.** In addition to careful planning and preparation for your presentation, consider the actual delivery of the presentation. Be sure that the medium you select fits the audience and available equipment.
- **Prepare fully.** Be ready for the unexpected. If you are providing the audience with handouts, know how many you will need. Have a backup plan for equipment failures or if you forget the materials. Bring additional extension cords and power strips. Be prepared for all logical possibilities. You can feel at ease in front of an audience by being fully prepared and practicing the presentation.

Designing with Themes

Office PowerPoint 2010 comes with many new themes. Themes simplify the process of creating professional presentations. The background, text, graphics, charts, and tables all change to reflect the theme that you select. You can apply the same theme to a Microsoft Office Word 2010 document or Microsoft Office Excel 2010 worksheet that you apply to your presentation. When you apply a theme to your presentation, the Quick Styles gallery and your SmartArt objects change to adapt to that particular theme. Theme colors, theme fonts, and theme effects reinforce consistency in your presentation.

Figure 12.4 illustrates a few new themes that you can apply to your presentation. To apply a theme to all slides, display the Design tab, and then click a desired theme in the Themes group. To apply a theme to only some slides, select the slides to which you want to apply a theme (press Ctrl when you click each one to select multiple slides). On the Design tab, in the Themes group, right-click a theme thumbnail, and then click *Apply to Selected Slides*.

You can customize the themes by clicking the Colors, Fonts, and Effects buttons in the Themes group and choosing options to change the theme to match your organization's branding or your personal preferences.

Figure 12.4 Themes

Applying Quick Styles

The Quick Styles feature in PowerPoint enables you to preview a number of styles before you select the one you want to apply to your presentation. Click to position the mouse cursor in your slide placeholder where you want to apply the new style and then click the Quick Styles button in the Drawing group on the Home tab. From the drop-down list, select a style you want to preview. To see additional styles, click More in the lower right corner of the styles examples; a gallery of style choices will appear as shown in Figure 12.5.

Applying a Template Design

Besides creating a presentation at a blank document screen and applying themes for consistency and focus, you may select a template. To start your presentation from a predesigned template design, click the File tab and then click the New tab. At the New tab Backstage view, select a template category from the *Available Templates and Themes* section or from the *Office. com Templates* section as shown in Figure 12.6.

Figure 12.5 **Quick Styles**

Quick Styles

Giving the Presentation

As the actual day for your presentation approaches, review the following points to make sure you are ready:

- Arrive early to check the equipment and then view the screen from your audience's perspective.

- Be prepared for technical problems—carry extra hard copies of your presentation to use as handouts if the equipment is faulty. Bring an extra power strip, extra bulb, and/or extension cord.

Figure 12.6 **Templates**

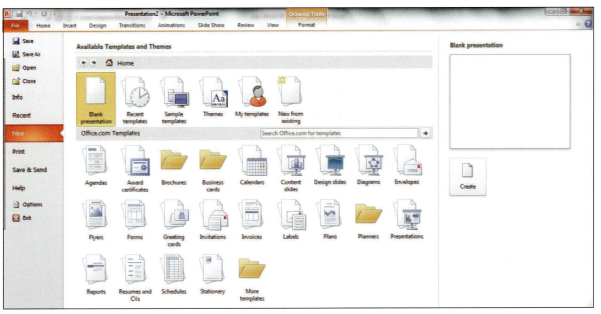

Set Up Slide Show

- Have your presentation ready—display the first slide with your name, topic name, and other pertinent information on the screen as your audience enters the room.

- Bring a pointing device, such as a laser pointer, or use your mouse as a laser pointer by viewing the presentation in Reading View or Slide Show View and then holding the Ctrl key down while pointing to objects on the slides. Change the color of the laser pointer by clicking the Set Up Slide Show button in the Set Up group in the Slide Show tab.

- Depending on the nature of your presentation, use your imagination to come up with a clever attention-getting device. For instance, if your presentation is on gardening, give each member of your audience an inexpensive package of seeds; if you are presenting information on taking a vacation to Belgium, pass out Belgian chocolates; if your presentation is on a new budget plan, mark one of your handouts with a star and offer a free lunch to the audience member holding that particular handout.

- Practice makes perfect—be sure you are proficient in using the equipment and the software.

- Remain poised and confident.

- Use good volume and speak at a moderate speed.

- Clearly identify each of the points, but do not read them from your slides.

- Do not over-entertain your audience—sounds can get annoying, too many graphics distracting, and too many slides boring.

- If your presentation is of a serious nature, do not use unnecessary sound, graphics, or animations. Choose your visual theme and colors carefully.

- Summarize your presentation and ask for questions if appropriate.

- Provide your audience with a handout to take with them—it reinforces follow-up and continued interest.

Running a Slide Show

You have several options in PowerPoint 2010 to run a slide show presentation. To run the presentation, you need to access the Slide Show option. To open Slide Show view, do either of the following:

- Click the Slide Show tab, and click a command in the Start Slide Show group. You can choose to start on the first slide or on the current slide.

- Click the Slide Show button in the lower right part of the PowerPoint window next to the Zoom slider.

Slide Show

To get out of Slide Show view, press Esc; right-click on the slide, and then click *End Show* from the shortcut menu; or mouse over the Slide Show toolbar in the bottom left corner of your slide presentation, click the Pause button, and then click *End Show* from the shortcut menu.

There are several methods for running a slide show in PowerPoint. You may run the slide show manually by clicking the mouse button, pressing the Spacebar, or pressing Enter. In addition, you can use the navigation commands on the shortcut menu to access slides. You may also advance slides automatically or set up a slide show to run continuously.

In Exercise 12.1, you will open a predesigned introductory PowerPoint 2010 slide presentation. This presentation will provide a good preview of the new features in PowerPoint 2010 before you actually create a presentation on your own in Exercise 12.2.

*Note: Before completing the computer exercises, copy the **Chapter12** folder from the CD that accompanies this textbook to your storage medium and then make **Chapter12** the active folder. Substitute any graphics that are no longer available. Insert a similar image.*

Exercise 12.1 Previewing New PowerPoint 2010 Features

1. Open PowerPoint.
2. Click the File tab and then click the New tab.
3. At the New tab Backstage view, click the *Sample templates* category in the *Available Templates and Themes* section.
4. Click the *Introducing PowerPoint 2010* thumbnail and then click Create.
5. Study the presentation screen. Notice the thumbnails in the Slide tab at the left of the screen, the Notes pane at the bottom of the screen, the SmartArt objects, the consistent design, and the appropriately sized text.
6. Click the Slide Show button in the View bar next to the Zoom controls at the bottom right corner of the presentation screen.
7. At the Slide Show view, click the left mouse to advance from one slide to the next. Read the content on each slide to learn more about the new 2010 PowerPoint features. Notice the animations and transitions assigned to each slide.
8. At the end of the show when the screen turns black, click the mouse to exit the show.
9. Click the File tab and then click Close.
10. Click the File tab and then click Exit if you are ready to exit PowerPoint. Otherwise, leave PowerPoint open.

Creating and Editing Presentations

Now that you have studied a professionally prepared presentation and are familiar with some of the many new PowerPoint 2010 features, you are ready to create your own presentation from scratch.

New Slide

📋 Layout ▾

Layout

Inserting a New Slide

Create a new slide in a presentation by clicking the New Slide button in the Slides group on the Home tab. This displays the New Slide gallery as shown in Figure 12.7. The layouts that display coordinate with the theme selected. The same layouts also display by clicking the Layout button in the Slides group. The new slide is added after the selected slide. In addition, you may choose options to duplicate a selected slide, create a slide from an outline, and reuse a slide at the bottom of the New Slide gallery.

You can also insert slides from other presentations. Open the presentation that you want to add slides to and make sure you are in Normal view. On the Home tab, in the Slides group, click the arrow next to the New Slide button and then click Reuse Slides. In the task pane that displays, browse to either a *slide library* or a presentation file that has the slides you want to use. Choose the *Keep source formatting* option if you want to keep the original slide's look. Click each slide that you want to insert into your presentation. A slide library is a Microsoft-shared resource that requires you to use PowerPoint 2010 and be connected to the Office SharePoint Server 2010. With the slide library, you can store slides in a shared location for others to access, track and review changes to slides, and locate the latest version of a slide.

Inserting and Customizing Objects

After you create a slide and select a desired slide layout, you may modify any of its objects on the slide layout or insert your own objects at a blank slide layout. The items in the following sections present new or out of the ordinary suggestions for changing objects.

Customizing Bullets

Add text to the bullet placeholder in your desired slide layout or add a bulleted list to a blank slide layout by clicking the Text Box button, drawing a text box, and then clicking the Bullets button to begin your bulleted list. To convert the existing bulleted or numbered

Figure 12.7 New Slide Gallery

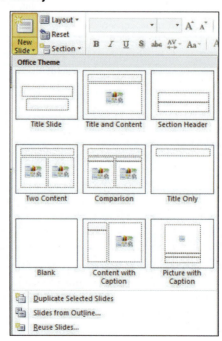

Figure 12.8 Converting a Bulleted List into a SmartArt Object

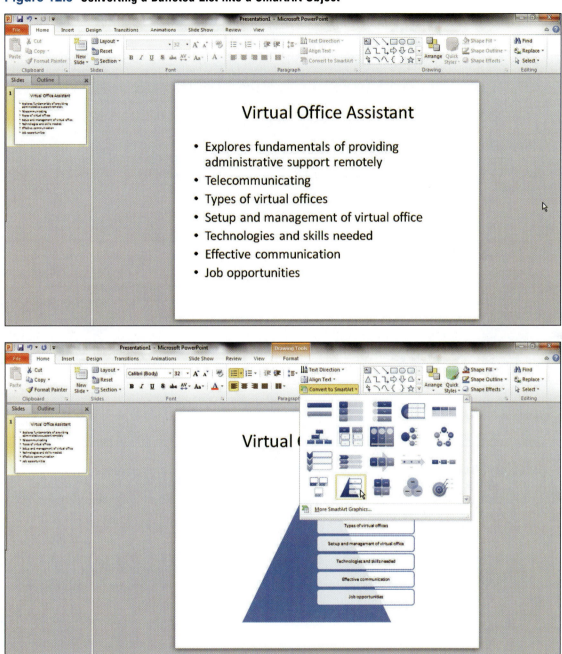

list to a SmartArt graphic, select the bulleted list and click the Convert to SmartArt Graphic button in the Paragraph group on the Home tab as shown in Figure 12.8.

To use a picture as a bullet, select the bulleted text if already typed, click the down-pointing arrow at the right of the Bullets button on the Home tab, click the Picture button on the Bulleted tab in the Bullets and Numbering dialog box, and then scroll to find a picture icon that you want to use as shown in Figure 12.9. If you are using a clip art image, search for the image, right-click the image and then click *Copy*, access the Picture Bullet dialog box, click the Import button, and then paste the image. Click OK to insert the image as a picture bullet.

Convert to SmartArt

Figure 12.9 Inserting Picture Bullets

1. Select the bulleted text.

2. Click the down-pointing arrow next to the Bullets button.

3. Click the Bullets and Numbering button to access the Bullets and Numbering dialog box.

4. Click the Picture button.

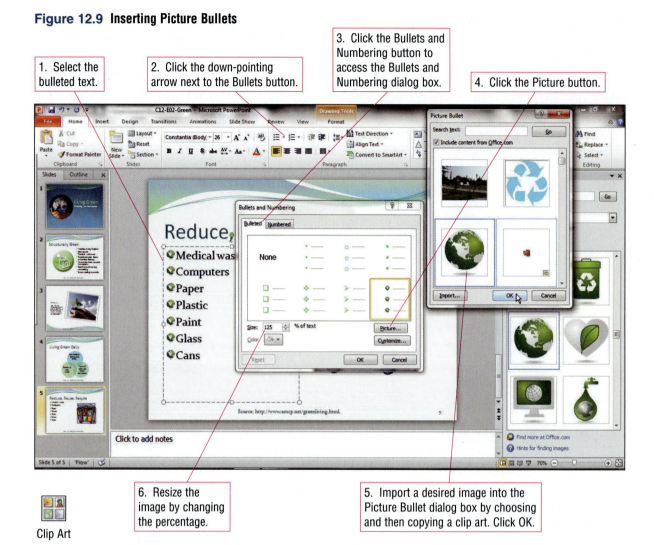

6. Resize the image by changing the percentage.

5. Import a desired image into the Picture Bullet dialog box by choosing and then copying a clip art. Click OK.

Clip Art

Insert Picture from File

Compress Pictures

Compress Pictures

DTP POINTERS
Use the Shift and Ctrl keys together to maintain a proportional object while you drag to resize the object.

DTP POINTERS
if you are emailing a picture, you can specify a lower picture resolution to reduce the file size

Inserting Pictures and Clip Art

To insert a clip art image or photograph, either click the Clip Art or Insert Picture from File content icons in your slide layout or click the Picture or Clip Art buttons on the Insert tab.

Compressing a Picture

Compressing a picture to reduce the size of the file changes the amount of detail retained in the source picture. This means that after compression, the picture can look different than before it was compressed. Because of this, you should compress the picture and save the file, before applying an artistic effect. You can redo the compression even after saving the file as long as you have not closed the program you are working in, if the compression plus the artistic effect is not the look you want.

Applying Artistic Effects

To add interesting artistic effects to images in your slides as shown in Figure 12.10, complete the following:

Figure 12.10 Artistic Effects

1. Click the picture that you want to apply an artistic effect to.
2. Under Picture Tools, on the Format tab, in the Adjust group, click Artistic Effects.
3. Click the artistic effect that you want. ***Hint: You can move your mouse pointer over any of the effects and use Live Preview to see what your picture will look like with that effect applied before you click the one that you want.***
4. To fine-tune the artistic effect, click *Artistic Effects Options*.

Other picture enhancements include Remove Background, Corrections, Color, Picture Styles, Picture Border, Picture Effects, and Picture Layouts. All of these features are similar to other Office program picture effects. Experiment with the features to understand their characteristics.

Use a Picture or Clip as a Slide Background

A picture was added to the slide shown in Figure 12.11. To add an image to an entire slide, click the slide that you want to add a background picture to. To select multiple slides, click the first slide, and then press and hold Ctrl while you click the other slides. Click the Background Styles button in the Background group in the Design tab and then click Format Background at the bottom of the drop-down gallery. At the Format Background dialog box, select the option button next to *Picture or texture fill*. Click either File or Clip Art in the *Insert from* section, and then select and insert the image. Click Close.

Inserting SmartArt

PowerPoint is perfect for displaying information visually. SmartArt converts simple text into attention-getting shapes and colors that enhance your message (see Figure 12.12). You can create moving, animated SmartArt graphics to provide additional emphasis or show your information in phases. You can animate your entire SmartArt graphic or only an individual shape in your SmartArt graphic. Animation will be discussed later in the chapter.

Artistic Effects

Background Styles

◄ DTP POINTERS
Add a background picture to emphasize a point or to show conclusion to the presentation.

SmartArt

Figure 12.11 Picture Background

Adding a Header and Footer

Header & Footer

Headers and footers display text, slide or page numbers, and dates you may want at the top or bottom of single slides or all slides. To insert headers and footers, display the Insert tab, and then click the Header & Footer button in the Text group. In addition, header and footer information may be typed at the slide master where it may be positioned, sized, and formatted.

Understanding Presentation Views

PowerPoint provides a variety of presentation viewing options. The view can be changed by clicking the various view buttons that are available on the View tab. The views include Normal, Slide Sorter, Notes Page, and Reading View (New!). You may also change the view of your presentation by clicking the Normal, Slide Sorter, Reading View, and Slide Show View buttons on the View bar in the bottom right corner of your presentation screen.

Figure 12.12 Adding SmartArt Objects to a PowerPoint Presentation

Normal View

Work in Normal view when working in the Outline pane, Slide pane, and Notes pane. You will use the Slides pane most often to add text, graphics, movies, and sounds.

Normal

Slide Sorter View

Slide Sorter view gives you a view of your slides in thumbnail form. This view makes it easy for you to sort and organize the sequence of your slides as you create your presentation, and then also as you prepare your presentation for printing. You can add sections in Slide Sorter view as well, and sort slides into different categories or sections.

Slide Sorter

Notes Page View

In the Notes pane, which is located at the bottom of the presentation screen, you can type notes that apply to the current slide. Later, you can print your notes and refer to them when you give your presentation. You can also print notes to give to your audience or include the notes in a presentation that you send to the audience or post on a Web page. Click the Notes Page button in the Presentation Views group in the View tab.

Notes Page

Reading View

This view is new to PowerPoint 2010 and it is a good view to use when you want to rehearse your presentation at a full screen but not in the Slide Show mode.

Reading View

Saving and Printing a Presentation

When sharing presentations, you may want to save your slides in the traditional manner with a PPTX extension, or as a PDF file viewed with Adobe Reader, or even as a video saved in a WMV format. In addition, you may also print a PowerPoint presentation in a variety of formats.

Saving a Presentation as a Template

To save a presentation as a template that can be used over and over, click the File tab and then click Save As. In the *File name* box, type a file name, or do nothing to accept the suggested file name. In the *Save as type* list, click *PowerPoint Template*, and then click Save.

Saving Presentations in PDF or XPS Formats

Office PowerPoint 2010 supports saving your presentations in PDF format that preserves document formatting and enables file sharing. The PDF format ensures that when the file is viewed online or printed, it retains exactly the format that you intended and that data in the file cannot be easily changed. The PDF format is also useful for documents that will be reproduced by using commercial printing methods. XPS is an electronic file format that also preserves document formatting and enables file sharing.

Figure 12.13 Saving a Presentation as a Video

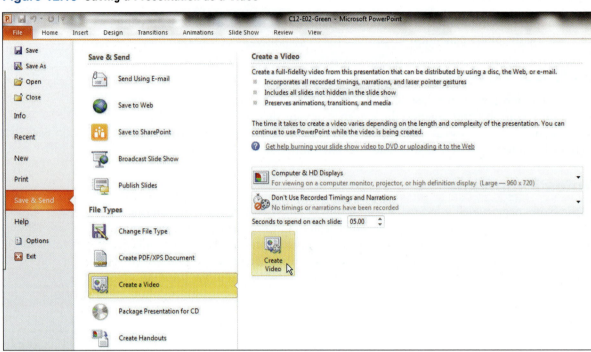

Saving a Presentation as a Video or Broadcast

You can save your presentation as a video file and then share it with others on a web site, DVD, or network. To save a presentation as a video, click the File tab, and then click Save & Send as shown in Figure 12.13. Click Create a Video. Click the Resolution list and choose one of the following:

- *Computer & HD Displays use 960 x 720*
- *Internet & DVD use 640 x 480*
- *Portable Devices use 320 x 240*

Click the Timing list arrow, and then click *Don't Use Recorded Timings and Narrations* or *Use Recorded Timings and Narrations*, and then specify a time. Click the Create Video button. Specify a name and location for the video and then click Save.

You can also broadcast a presentation over the Internet, but you will need a Windows Live ID. Click the File tab, click Save & Send, click Broadcast Slide Show, click the Broadcast Slide Show button, click Start Broadcast, enter your Windows Live ID, and then click Copy Link or Send in Email to share the broadcast link.

Printing a Presentation

A presentation may be printed in a variety of formats. You may print each slide on a separate piece of paper; print each slide at the top of a page, leaving the bottom of the page for notes; print all or a specific number of slides on a single piece of paper; or print the slide titles and topics in outline form. To print a presentation, click the File tab and then click Print. At the Print tab Backstage view, click the down-pointing arrow at the right of the *Print what* list box, and then click the desired printing format as shown in Figure 12.14.

Figure 12.14 Printing a Presentation

1. Click the File tab.

4. Click the Print button.

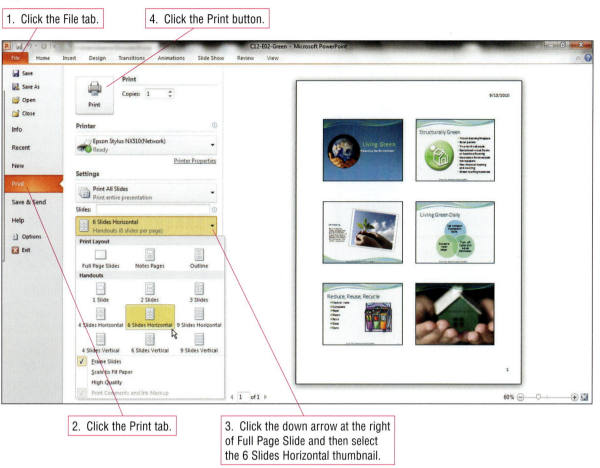

2. Click the Print tab.

3. Click the down arrow at the right of Full Page Slide and then select the 6 Slides Horizontal thumbnail.

Exercise 12.2 Creating, Saving, Running, and Printing a Presentation

1. Click the File tab, click the New tab, click *Blank presentation* in the *Available Templates and Themes* section, and then click Create.
2. Click the More button in the Themes group in the Design tab and then click the *Flow* theme.
3. Change one of the colors in the Flow theme by completing the following steps:

Step 2

a. Click the Colors button in the Themes group in the Design tab.
b. Click the Create New Theme Colors button at the bottom of the drop-down list.
c. At the Create New Theme Colors dialog box, click the down-pointing arrow next to *Accent 3* and then select *Green, Accent 5* at the color gallery.

d. Type **Environment** in the *Name* text box.

e. Click Save.

4. At the Title Slide (default first slide), click anywhere in the text *Click to add title* and then type **Living Green**. Click anywhere in the text *Click to add subtitle* and then type **Protecting the Environment**.

5. On the Insert tab, click the Clip Art button in the Images group, type **hands earth** in the *Search for* text box, and then select an image similar to the one in Figure 12.15. Size and position the image appropriately by holding down the Ctrl key and Shift key while dragging a corner sizing handle. Close the Clip Art task pane.

6. Select the earth image, click the More button in the Picture Styles group in the Picture Tools Format tab, and then click *Beveled Oval, Black* in the Picture Styles gallery.

7. Save the presentation as **C12-E02-Green**.

8. Click the New Slide button in the Slides group in the Home tab, and then click the *Two Content* thumbnail in the New Slide gallery.

9. On the second slide, type **Structurally Green** in the *Click to add title* placeholder.

10. Click in the right content area in the bulleted placeholder text, *Click to add text*, and then type the following text, pressing the Enter key at the end of each line, except the last item:

> **Wood-burning fireplace**
> **Solar panels**
> **2-by-6 wall studs**
> **Reclaimed-wood floors or bamboo flooring**
> **Insulation from recycled newspapers**
> **Geo-thermal heating and cooling**
> **Green roofing materials**

11. Click the Clip Art icon in the left side of the slide layout and insert a clip art image it by completing the following steps:

a. At the Clip Art pane, type **green house** in the *Search for* text box, and then select an image similar to the one shown in Figure 12.15. Size and position the image. Close the Clip Art task pane.

b. Select the image and click the Artistic Effects button in the Adjust group in the Picture Tools Format tab.

c. Click the *Paint Brush* thumbnail in the second row of the drop-down gallery.

12. Add another slide (Slide 3) and then select the *Picture with Caption* layout from the New Slide drop-down gallery. Insert the hands image as shown in Figure 12.15 by completing the following steps:

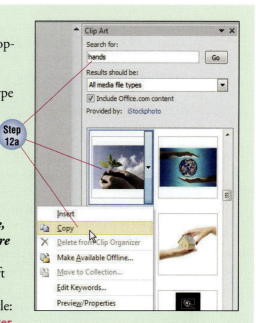

a. Click the Clip Art button on the Insert tab, type **hands** in the *Search for* text box, mouse over the image to access the down-pointing arrow at the right of the image, and then click *Copy*. Close the Clip Art task pane.

b. Right click the Picture placeholder box in Slide 3, and then click Paste Options, Paste. ***Hint: The picture should conform to the size, shape, and tilted direction of the slide Picture placeholder.***

13. Click *Click to add title* in the top text box to the left of the hands picture, type **Landscaping**, and then type the following text in the text box below the title: **Green landscaping includes collecting storm water for landscaping. Collecting food scraps and putting yard and plant clippings in the compost bin. Planting trees also aids the environment.**

14. Add another slide (Slide 4) and then select the *Title and Content* layout from the New Slide drop-down gallery.

15. Type **Living Green Daily** in the *Click to add title* placeholder in Slide 4.

16. Click the Insert SmartArt Graphic icon in the center of Slide 4.

17. At the Choose a SmartArt Graphic dialog box, click Relationship, and then click the Basic Venn graphic. Click OK.

18. Type the text inside each Venn circular shape as shown in Figure 12.15 (Slide 4).

19. Click the Change Colors button in the SmartArt Styles group in the SmartArt Tools Design tab and then click the *Colorful Range - Accent Colors 2 to 3* in the *Colorful* section.

20. Add another slide (Slide 5), select the *Two Content* layout, and then type the text as shown in Figure 12.15.

21. Insert a clip art image similar to the one shown in Figure 12.15. **Hint: Search for a Recycle image.**

22. Change the default bullets to Picture bullets in Slide 5 by completing the following steps:

a. Click the Clip Art button in the Images group on the Insert tab. Type **Recycle** in the *Search for* text box at the Clip Art task pane. Locate an earth image similar to the one shown in Figure 12.15.

b. Mouse over the image and then click *Copy.*

c. Close the Clip Art task pane.

d. Select the bulleted list in Slide 5.

e. Click the arrow next to the Bullets button in the Paragraph group in the Home tab.

f. Click Bullets and Numbering at the bottom of the drop-down gallery.

g. At the Bullets and Numbering dialog box, click the Picture button, click the Import button at the bottom of the drop-down gallery.

h. Right-click anywhere in the white area of the *Picture library* section of the Add Clips to Organizer and click *Paste.* Click Add.

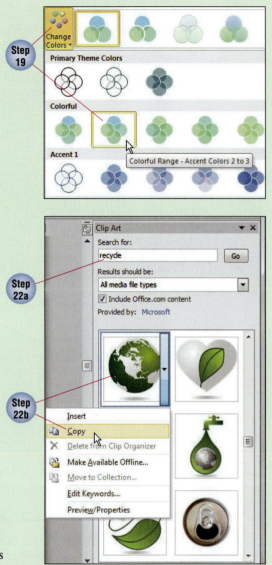

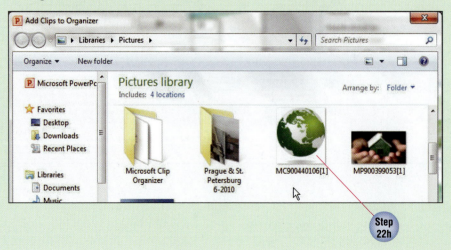

i. Select the image and then click OK.

j. With the bulleted list still selected, click the drop-down arrow next to the bullet option and click the Bullets and Numbering option at the bottom of the list. Increase the size of the bullet by typing **125** in the *Size % of the text* text box. Click OK.

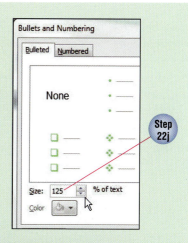

23. Add another slide (Slide 6), select the *Blank* layout, and then add a picture background by completing the following steps:

a. Click the Background Styles button in the Background group in the Design tab and then click Format Background at the bottom of the drop-down gallery.

b. At the Format Background dialog box, select the option next to *Picture or texture fill*. Click Clip Art in the *Insert from* section.

c. At the Select Picture dialog box, type **green house** in the *Search text* text box. Click Go.

d. Select the house/hands image as shown in Figure 12.15. Click OK and then click Close.

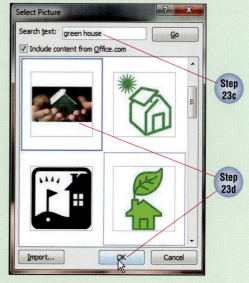

24. Add a footer to the presentation by completing the following steps:

a. Click the Header & Footer button in the Text group in the Insert tab.

b. At the Header and Footer dialog box, select the Slide tab.

c. Add a check mark at *Date and time* and select the *Update automatically* option.

d. Add a check mark at *Slide number*.

e. Add a check mark at *Footer* and then type **Source: http://www.emcp.net/greenliving. html**.

f. Add a check mark at *Don't Show on title slide*.

g. Click Apply to All.

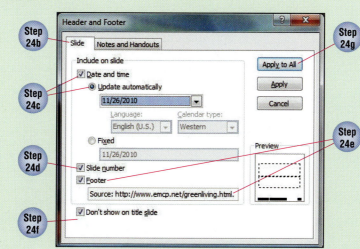

25. Click the Slide 1 thumbnail in the Slides tab that displays at the left of the PowerPoint screen.

26. Click in the Notes pane at the bottom of the screen and then type **Optional: Instructors ask your students to add three more slides to this presentation. Choose appropriate slide layouts and add text and graphics that reinforce the overall theme of this presentation.**

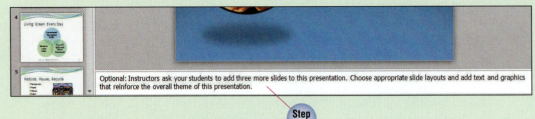

Step 26

27. Save the presentation again as **C12-E02-Green**. *Hint: PowerPoint will automatically insert the .pptx extension.*
28. Change the views by completing the following steps:
    a. Click the Slide Sorter button in the Presentation View group in the View tab.
    b. Click the Notes Page button.
    c. Click the Reading View button and click the spacebar to advance through Slides 1 through 6.
    d. Click the Slide Show button in the View bar at the bottom of the PowerPoint screen. Click the mouse to advance the slides.
    e. Click the Normal button.
    f. Click the Slide 1 thumbnail in the Slides tab.
29. Print all six slides on one page by completing the following steps:
    a. Click the File tab and then click the Print tab.
    b. Click the down-pointing arrow at the right of the Full Page Slides gallery in the *Settings* category and then click *6 Slides Horizontal* in the drop-down list.
    c. Click the Print button.
30. Close **C12-E02-Green.pptx**.

Figure 12.15 **Exercise 12.2**

In Exercise 12.2, you created a presentation by using a theme, selecting slide layouts, and typing text in slide placeholders. In Exercise 12.3, you will insert text from an outline created in Word, apply a template design, format the slides at Master Slide view, add transitions, and run the presentation automatically.

Reinforcing Consistency

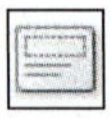

Slide Master

Slide master
The slide that stores information about the design template applied, including font styles, placeholder sizes and positions, background design, and color schemes.

DTP POINTERS
To display a logo on every slide in your presentation, add the logo to the Master Slide.

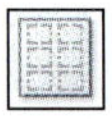

Handout Master

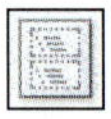

Notes Master

Each PowerPoint presentation comes with a set of masters: slide, notes, and handout. These master pages maintain consistency among the slides in a presentation.

Using a Slide Master

The ***slide master*** stores information about the design template applied, including font styles, placeholder sizes and positions, background design, and color schemes. A template file can contain one or more slide masters, depending on the complexity of your presentation, and each slide master can contain one or more standard or custom sets of layouts. Because slide masters affect your entire presentation, when you create and edit a slide master, you work in Slide Master view.

It is a good idea to create a slide master before, rather that after, you start to build individual slides. When you create the slide master first, all of the slides that you add to your presentation are based on that slide master. Figure 12.16 shows a single slide master that contains several optional layouts.

Using a Handout Master and a Notes Master

In addition to the slide master, you may use the handout master or the notes master. Depending on your presentation needs, you may customize your handouts or notes to accommodate your text, logo, graphics, charts, SmartArt, or other objects. Placing these objects within a master page reinforces consistency on each of the slides in the presentation and on all handouts and notes that you may use during your presentation.

Figure 12.16 Slide Master

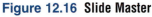

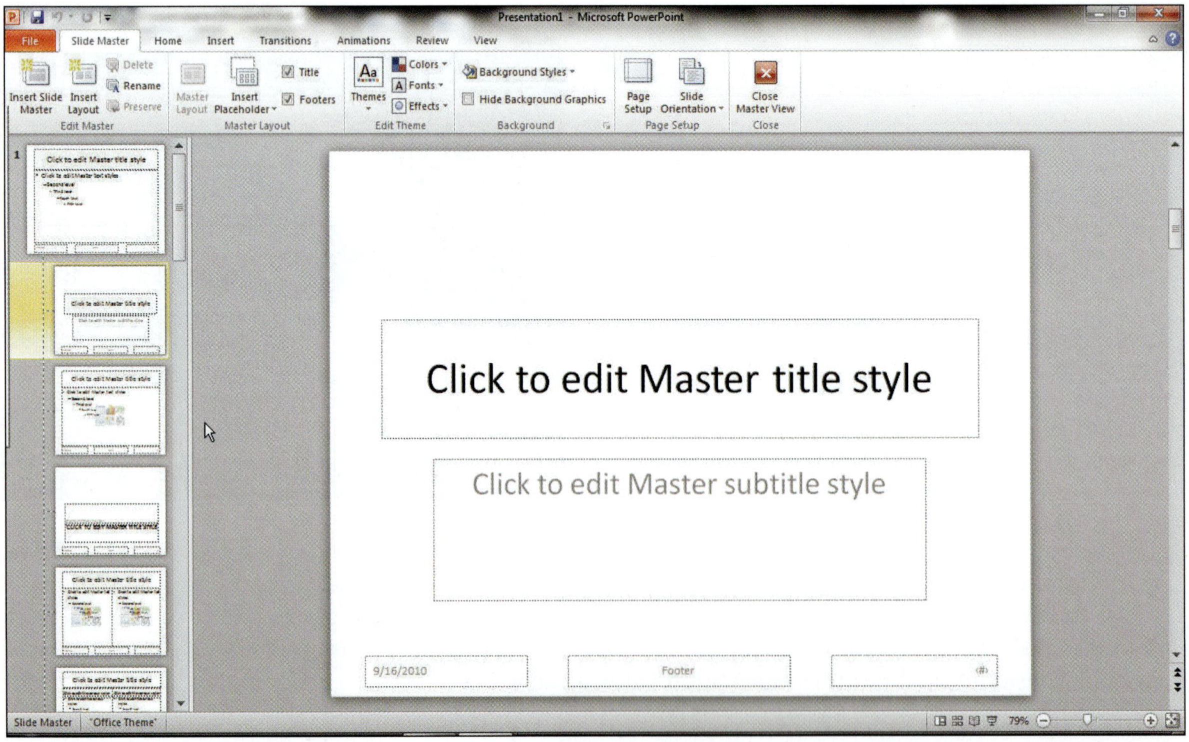

Working with Slides

Besides adding text to slides in normal view, you may also enter text in the outline pane, where it is easy to organize your ideas. You may also create an outline in Word and import it into a PowerPoint presentation. After your text is entered, you may want to apply transitions to the slides and then run the presentation automatically.

Adding Text to a Slide in Outline View

If you are creating a longer presentation with more slides or more text, consider using the Outline/Slides pane with the Outline tab selected as shown in Figure 12.17. Press the Tab key to move the insertion point to the next tab stop. This move changes the formatting, which is dependent on the design template you are using. Press Shift + Tab to go the previous tab stop and to change the formatting.

Organizing Slides

You may rearrange, delete, and add slides in the Slide Sorter view. To move a slide, select the slide and drag it to a new location. To delete a slide, select it and press the Delete key. To add a slide, position the insertion point (vertical line) to the left of the location where you want to add a slide and then click the New Slide button on the Home tab.

Additionally, you may use the mouse to move text with the Outline tab selected. Position the mouse pointer on the slide icon or bullet at the left side of the text until the arrow pointer turns into a four-headed arrow. Hold down the *left* mouse button, drag the arrow pointer (a thin horizontal line) to the desired location, and then release the mouse button. You may also select text and cut, copy, and paste text and objects by clicking these options in the Clipboard group on the Home tab.

Importing a Word Outline into PowerPoint

If you have an existing outline created in Word, you can import it into PowerPoint. PowerPoint will create new slides, except the Title Slide, based on the heading levels used in Word. Paragraphs formatted with the Heading 1 style become titles, Heading 2 styles become bulleted text, and so forth. If styles were not used, PowerPoint uses tabs or indents to place the text on slides. To import a Word outline to PowerPoint, display the Home tab, click the arrow next to New Slide in the Slides group, and then click Slides from Outline. Locate and double-click the file that contains the outline that you want to insert in your presentation. The file opens in PowerPoint.

Figure 12.17 **Adding Text in Outline View**

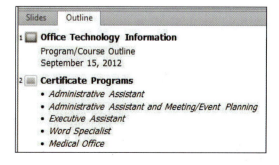

Figure 12.18 Adding Transitions

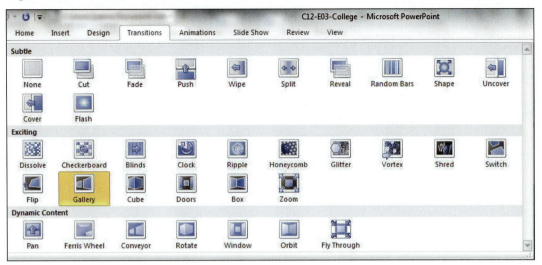

Adding Slide Transitions

Slide *transitions* are the animation-like effects that occur in Slide Show view when you move from one slide to the next. You can control the speed of each slide transition effect, and you can also add sound. Microsoft Office PowerPoint 2010 includes many different types of slide transitions as shown in Figure 12.18. To see more transition effects, click the More button.

To add a slide transition, display the Transitions tab and select a transition at the Transition gallery. Select the *After* check box. Enter the time (in seconds) before the presentation advances to the next slide and then click the option *Apply To All* if you want to apply the selected transition to all the slides in the presentation. You may also vary the amount of time by using the *Rehearse Timings* option in the Slide Show tab. In addition, you may click the arrow next to Sound, and then add a sound that you want from the list. The Duration setting specifies the length of the transition. Click the Preview button to view the transition before running the presentation.

Running a Slide Show Automatically

Slides in a slide show can be advanced automatically after a specific number of seconds. Open a presentation and make sure the first slide is selected or click the From Beginning button or From Current Slide button in the Start Slide Show group in the Slide Show tab. You may also set up your slide show by clicking the Set Up Slide Show button in the Slide Show tab. When you click Slide Show, the slides will advance automatically by the number of seconds designated.

Preview

From Beginning

From Current Slide

Set Up Slide Show

1. Make sure PowerPoint is open and then import an outline created in Word by completing the following steps:
   a. In PowerPoint, click the File tab, and then click New.
   b. At the New tab Backstage view, type **Technology at work** in the *Search Office.com for templates* search text box in the *Office.com Templates* section. Click the right-pointing start searching arrow.

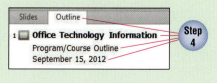

   c. Select the *Technology at work design template* in the *Office.com Templates* section.
   d. Click Download.

2. On the Home tab, click the down-pointing arrow at the right of the New Slide button, and then click *Slides from Outline*.

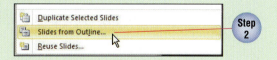

3. At the Insert Outline dialog box, select **CertificatePrograms.docx** located in the *Chapter12* folder, and then click Insert.

4. At the Outline/Slides pane, select the Outline tab, click immediately right of the *Slide 1* icon, type **Office Technology Information**, and then press Enter. Press Tab and then type **Program/Course Outline**. Press Enter, and then type **September 15, 2012**.

5. Change to Slide Sorter view and move Slide 6 (Professional Development) before Slide 3 (Virtual Office). To do this, position the arrow pointer on Slide 6, hold down the *left* mouse button, drag the arrow pointer (with a square attached) between Slides 2 and 3, and then release the mouse button. A vertical line will display between the two slides.

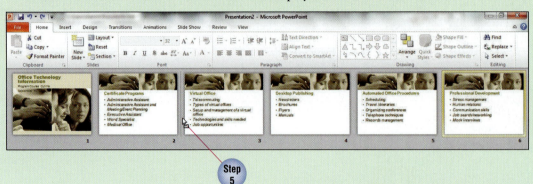

Step 5

6. Save the presentation with Save As and name it **C12-E03-College**. *Hint: At the prompt to save the presentation using an earlier version, click OK.*
7. Change the formatting at the Slide Master by completing the following steps:
   a. Display the View tab.
   b. Select Slides 2 through 6.
   c. Click the Slide Master button in the Master Views group.
   d. Add the college logo by clicking Insert and then click Picture.
   e. At the Picture dialog box, insert **CollegeLogo** located in the *Chapter12* folder.
   f. Position the logo in the lower right corner of the Slide Master as shown in Figure 12.19.

Click to edit Master title style

- Click to edit Master text styles
  - Second level
    - Third level
      - Fourth level
        » Fifth level

Step 7f

11/28/2010   Footer

   g. Click the Close Master View button on the Slide Master tab.

8. Add slide transitions to the slides while in Slide Sorter view by completing the following steps: *Hint: It is not recommended to apply a different transition to every slide; however, to familiarize you with the different transitions available in PowerPoint 2010, you are being asked to apply different transitions for each slide in this presentation.*
   a. Select Slide 1, display the Transitions tab, click the More button in the Transition to This Slide group, and then click the *Gallery* transition in the *Exciting* section at the Transitions gallery.

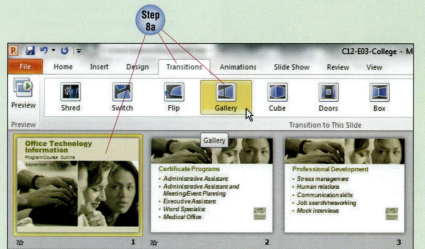

   b. Select Slide 2 and apply the *Flip* transition.
   c. Select Slide 3 and apply the *Zoom* transition.
   d. Select Slide 4 and apply the *Vortex* transition.
   e. Select Slide 5 and apply the *Ripple* transition.
   f. Select Slide 6 and apply the *Cube* transition.
9. Run the presentation by completing the following steps:
   a. Press Ctrl + A to select all the slides.
   b. On the Transition tab, deselect the option to run the presentation *On Mouse Click* in the Timing group. Click to add a check mark next to the *After* option and change the setting to 4 seconds.

   c. Click the first slide and then click the Slide Show button.
10. Save the presentation with the same name **C12-E03-College**.
11. Print the presentation in Notes Pages and then close **C12-E03-College.pptx**.

Figure 12.19 Exercise 12.3

Enhancing a Presentation

In Exercise 12.4, you will add standard and custom animations to text, objects, and clip art in a presentation. You will create builds to organize information and add interest to the slides.

Figure 12.20 Adding Sections to Presentations

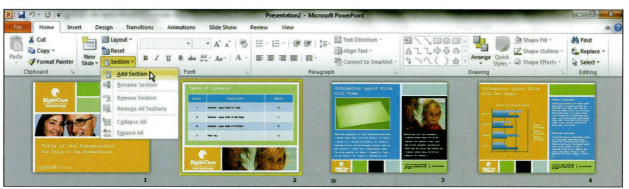

Inserting Sections in a Presentation

If you are working on a large presentation or collaborating on a presentation with others, you can organize your slides into sections that can make the process much easier. You can assign different sections to different people on your team and then when the sections are no longer needed, you can remove them and consolidate your team's efforts.

To create sections, display the Home tab, click the Section button, and then click *Add Section* as shown in Figure 12.20. To rename a section, click the section name to select it, click the Section button, click *Rename Section*, type a name, and then click OK. To collapse or expand a section, click the Collapse or Expand arrow In the section name. To remove a section, click the section name, click the Section button, click *Remove Section* or *Remove All Sections*.

Section

Running a Slide Show in Rehearsed Time

In the previous exercises, you practiced running a slide show manually by clicking the mouse button at each slide, and automatically by typing a specific increment of time for all of the slides. In Exercise 12.4, you will practice running the presentation in a continuous loop and ending the loop by pressing the Esc key.

To create timings through rehearsal, click the Slide Show tab, and click the Rehearse Timings button. As the slide show runs, rehearse your presentation by clicking or pressing Enter to go to the next transition or slide. Note the seconds as they display in the Recording toolbar as shown in Figure 12.21. When you are done, click Yes to accept the timings. To test the timings, start the slide show and note when the slides advance too quickly or too slowly. Review and edit the individual timings in Slide Sorter view.

Rehearse Timings

Figure 12.21 Setting Rehearsed Timings for Slides

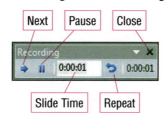

Running a Slide Show in a Continuous Loop

In a continuous-loop slide show, all of the slides are viewed over and over again until you stop the show. This feature is especially effective when presenting a new

Figure 12.22 Set Up Show Dialog Box

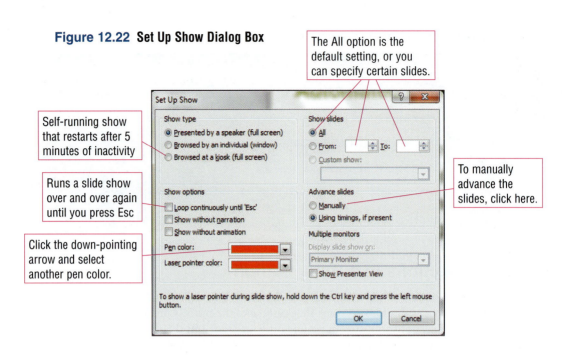

The All option is the default setting, or you can specify certain slides.

Self-running show that restarts after 5 minutes of inactivity

Runs a slide show over and over again until you press Esc

Click the down-pointing arrow and select another pen color.

To manually advance the slides, click here.

product or service at a trade show or at a new store opening. To run a presentation in a continuous loop, display the Slide Show tab and then click the Set Up Slide Show button in the Set Up group. At the Set Up Show dialog box, click the check box to the left of *Loop continuously until 'Esc'*, as shown in Figure 12.22, and then click OK.

Figure 12.23 Animation Gallery

Stopping a Presentation

To stop a presentation while it is being viewed in Slide Show, right-click anywhere in the presentation screen, and then click *End Show*. At the shortcut menu that displays, you will also see options to view the next or previous slide, to go to a specific slide, to make the screen black or white, to use a pointer or laser, to annotate a slide, or to access Help. You may also press Esc to stop a presentation.

Adding Standard Animation Effects

You can *animate* your slides by adding a special visual or sound effect to text or an object to add interest to your presentation. You can apply animation effects to text or objects on individual slides, to text and objects on the slide master, or to placeholders on custom slide layouts. For example, you can have your text bullet points fly in from the left, one paragraph at a time, or hear the sound of applause when a picture is uncovered.

To apply a standard animation effect to text or an object, select the object that you want to animate, click the More button in the Animation group in the Animations tab, and then select the animation effect that you want as shown in Figure 12.23. The movement of individual elements on a slide, such as *Fade*, *Wipe*, and *Fly In*, is known as an *effect*. This desired animation will affect all of the slides formatted if it is applied in the slide master.

Adding Custom Animation Effects to a Presentation

Apply custom animation to selected objects in a slide by clicking the Animation Pane button in the Advanced Animation group in the Animations tab. This displays the Animation Pane at the right side of the screen. Use options in this task pane to control the order in which objects appear on a slide, choose animation direction and speed, and specify how objects will appear in the slide as shown in Figure 12.24.

Figure 12.24 Custom Animation Task Pane

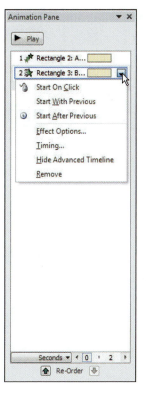

You can also apply custom animations to items on a slide, in a placeholder, or to a paragraph, including single bullets and list items. For example, you can apply a fly-in animation to all items on a slide or you can apply the animation to a single paragraph in a bulleted list. Use *Entrance*, *Emphasis*, or *Exit* options in addition to preset or custom *motion paths*, which are the paths that a specified object or text will follow as part of an animation sequence for a slide.

You can also apply more than one animation to an item, so you can make a bulleted item *Fly In* and then *Fly Out*. Most animation options include associated effects from which you can choose. Associated effects

---

Animate
To add a special visual or sound effect to text or an object.

Effect
Method of displaying movement in individual elements on a slide, such as Fly from Top, Spiral, and Swivel.

Animation Pane

DTP POINTERS
Add a build to bulleted items to focus attention on one item at a time.

DTP POINTERS
Do not overuse the animation feature.

DTP POINTERS
To remove an animation effect, click the item in the Animation Pane, and then click Remove.

Motion paths
The path that a specified object or text will follow as part of an animation sequence for a slide.

include options for playing a sound with an animation and text animations that you can apply to a letter, word, or paragraph (such as having a title fly in one word at a time instead of all at once, called a *build*). You can preview the animation of your text and objects for one slide or for your entire presentation.

Exercise 12.4 Inserting Animation Effects in a PowerPoint Presentation

1. Open PowerPoint 2010.
2. Click the File tab and then click New.
3. At the New tab Backstage view, type ocean in the *Search Office.com for template* search text box and then click the right-pointing arrow.

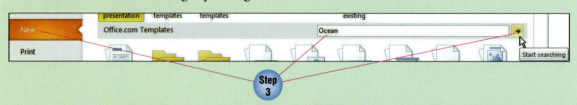

4. Select the *Ocean design template* and then click Download.

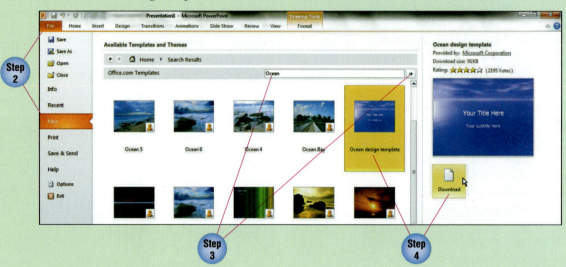

5. On the Home tab, click the arrow next to the New Slide button, and then click Reuse Slides from the drop-down gallery.

6. At the Reuse Slides task pane, click the Open a PowerPoint File hyperlink.
7. Select **Kiawah** located in the *Chapter12* folder. Click Open.

8. Right-click the first Kiawah slide in the Reuse Slides task pane and then click *Insert All Slides*.

9. If the first slide is blank, delete it by right-clicking on the slide thumbnail and then clicking *Delete Slide* from the shortcut menu.

10. Save the presentation using Save As and name it **C12-E04-Kiawah**.

11. Close the Reuse Slides task pane.

12. Select the Slide 2 thumbnail in the Slide pane and then click the Section button in Slides group in the Home tab and then click Add Section. ***Hint: A new section has been added to the slide presentation so that you can format Slide 1 differently from the remaining slides.***

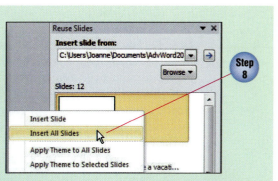

Step 8

13. Display Slide 1 in Normal view and then format Slide 1 by completing the following steps:

   a. With Slide 1 selected, click the Background Styles button in the Background group in the Design tab.

   b. Click Format Background at the drop-down gallery.

   c. Click the Fill button at the left of the Format Background dialog box.

   d. Click the *Picture or texture fill* option and then click the Clip Art button.

   e. At the Select Picture dialog box, type **beach chairs** in the *Search text* text box. Click Go.

   f. Select the beach photograph as shown in Figure 12.25 or a similar one and then click OK. Click Close.

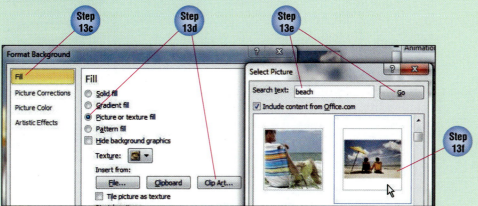

Step 13c   Step 13d   Step 13e   Step 13f

14. Animate the objects in Slide 1 by completing the following steps:

   a. Select the title, *Welcome to Kiawah Island, South Carolina*, click the More button in the Animation gallery in the Animations tab, and then click the *Grow & Turn* effect. ***Hint: The number 1 should display next to the* Welcome to Kiawah Island, South Carolina *text box.***

   b. Select the red crab image in the bottom left corner of Slide 1, click the More button in the Animation gallery, and then click the *Custom Path* effect in the *Motion Paths* section.

Step 14a

Step 14b

c. Drag the crosshairs along the bottom of the slide to the bottom right edge of Slide 1. Double-click the crosshairs to end the path.

d. Select the crab image again, click the Animation Pane button in the Advanced Animation group, click the down-pointing arrow at the right of the second animation listed in the Animation Pane, and then click *Timing*.

e. At the Custom Path dialog box, type **10 seconds** in the *Duration* list box, and then click OK.

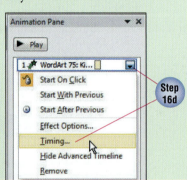
Step 14e

15. Add transitions to all of the slides in the presentation. Apply transitions of your own choosing.

16. Select the Slide 2 thumbnail in the Slide pane and then animate the objects in Slide 2 by completing the following steps:

    a. Select the picture title and then click the More button in the Animation group.

    b. At the Animation gallery, click the *Fly In* effect.

    c. With the title still selected, click the Effect Options button in the Animation group. Click the *From Bottom-Left* effect from the drop-down gallery.

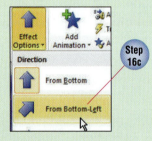
Step 16c

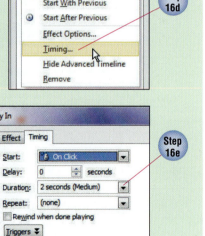
Step 16d

    d. With the text box still selected, click the down-pointing arrow at the right of the first animation listed in the Animation Pane, and then click *Timing*.

    e. At the Fly In dialog box, click the down-pointing arrow at the right of the *Duration* list box, and then click *2 seconds (Medium)*. Click OK.

    f. Select the sun image in the upper left corner, click the More button in the Animation group, and then click the *Lines* effect in the *Motion Paths* section.

    g. Drag the crosshairs downward toward the top of the child photograph.

    h. Select the text box containing the bulleted text.

    i. Apply the *Fade* effect in the *Entrance* section.

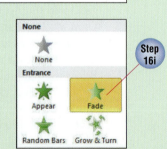
Step 16e

17. Click the Slide 3 thumbnail in the Slides tab at the left of the Normal slide screen. Format Slide 3 by completing the following steps:

    a. Select the title text box, and then apply the *Shape* effect.

    b. Select the text box containing the bulleted items and apply the *Wave* effect in the *Emphasis* section of the Animation gallery.

    c. Hold down the Shift key as you select each of the three photographs in Slide 3 and then apply the *Float out* effect in the *Exit* section of the Animation gallery.

    d. Click the Slide 4 thumbnail in the Slides tab.

Step 16i

18. Format Slide 4 as shown in Figure 12.25 by completing the following steps:

    a. With Slide 4 displayed in Normal view, select the title text box, apply the *Appear* effect, click the Show Additional Effect Options launcher button in the bottom right corner of the Animation group, and then select the *By word* option in the *Animate text* list box. Click OK.

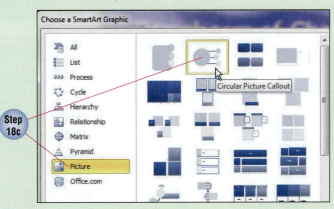

    b. Click the Insert SmartArt Graphic icon in the left side of the slide layout.

    c. At the Choose a SmartArt Graphic dialog box, click the Picture button, and then click the *Circular Picture Callout* layout. Click OK.

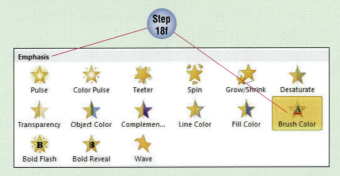

    d. Click the large circle picture placeholder and insert the **Plantation** graphic located in your *Chapter12* folder.

    e. Click each of the remaining smaller circle picture placeholders and insert the **Crane**, **Flowers**, and **Cooking** graphics located in your *Chapter12* folder.

    f. Select the text box containing the bulleted list, and then click the *Brush Color* effect in the *Emphasis* section of the Animation tab.

19. Click Slide 1 and then click the Slide Show button in the Status bar or display the Slide Show tab and then click the From Beginning button in the Start Slide Show group. ***Hint: Click the mouse to prompt slide for next animation or transition. Right-click Slide 4 during the presentation and click*** End Show ***if you want to stop the slide show.***

20. Save the presentation as **C12-E04-Kiawah**.

21. Leave **C12-E04-Kiawah.pptx** open if you intend to continue with Exercise 12.5. Otherwise, close **C12-E04-Kiawah.pptx**.

Figure 12.25 Exercise 12.4

Welcome to Kiawah Island, South Carolina

Why take a vacation on *Kiawah*?
- Ten miles of pristine, sun-swept beach
- Twenty-one miles from historic Charleston
- Environmentally sensitive planned island—natural beauty preserved

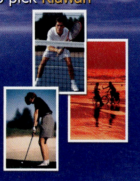

More reasons...to pick Kiawah
- Five championship golf courses
- Top tennis facilities, camps, and clinics
- Thirty miles of paved leisure trails
- Twenty-one acre Night Heron Park recreation

The charm of Charleston
- Visit the new South Carolina Aquarium
- Experience Southern cuisine
- Don't miss the Battery, Waterfront Park, and the Maritime Center

Integrating a Presentation

In Exercise 12.5, you will add slides that include a Word table, an Excel workbook, motion clips, and hyperlinks.

Using Screenshots

Screenshot

Screenshots, such as that shown in Figure 12.26, are useful for capturing snapshots of information that might change or expire. Screenshots are also helpful for copying from web pages and other sources whose formatting might not successfully transfer into the file by any other method. When you take a screenshot of something (for example, a web page), and the information changes at the source, the screenshot is not updated.

When you click the Screenshot button, you can insert the whole program window or use the Screen Clipping tool to select part of a window. For instance, you could access a web page, open PowerPoint, click the Screenshot button, click the Screen Clipping option, and then drag the crosshairs to select the area of the web page you want to capture.

Open program windows are displayed as thumbnails in the Available Windows gallery and when you pause your pointer over a thumbnail, a tooltip pops up with the program name and document title. To add the whole window, click the thumbnail in the Available Windows gallery.

DTP POINTERS
After you add the screenshot, you can use the tools on the Picture Tools tab to edit and enhance it.

Figure 12.26 Creating Screenshots

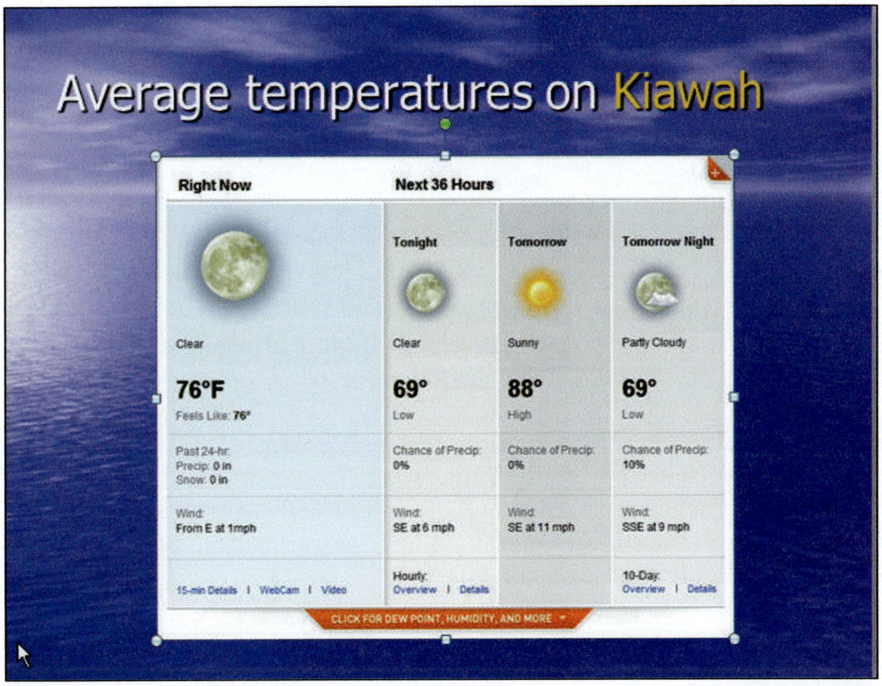

Adding Action Buttons

Action buttons are drawn objects placed on the slide that, when activated, will perform a specific action. For instance, an action button can advance to a specific slide, file, or location on the Web. To insert action buttons, display the Insert tab and then click the Action button in the Links group. At the Action Settings dialog box, select an option to create a hyperlink to the Next slide, Previous slide, and so on; to run a program, macro, or object action; or to play a sound.

Using Hyperlinks

You can enrich your presentation by inserting hyperlinks. A hyperlink can take you to a location within the same document, a different document, or a location on the Web. You can even use hyperlinks to advance to multimedia files, such as sounds or videos. To add a hyperlink, display the Insert tab and then click the Hyperlink button in the Links group.

Adding Media Clips and Sounds

To achieve a full multimedia effect, you can include media clips (movies and sounds) to your presentation. PowerPoint can play a clip automatically or you can play the clip on demand using the mouse. Use of these features requires your computer system to have a sound card and speakers. Media clips are inserted, resized, moved, and copied in the same way as any other image.

To add a movie or sound, display the Insert tab, click the Clip Art button, and then click the down arrow at the right of *Selected Media file types* in the *Results should be* list box and select *Movies*. Type a desired media clip topic and then click Go. In addition, you may change the slide layout and choose a layout that includes a clip art icon. You can also insert movies and sound files by clicking the Movie button and/or the Sound button in the *Media Clips* section on the Insert tab. At the Movie and Sound drop-down galleries, you can select options that match the desired result.

Additionally, you may save your presentation as a video and share it. To save the presentation as a video, click the File tab, click Save & Send, and then click Create a Video.

Exercise 12.5 (continued from Exercise 12.4)

1. Open **C12-E04-Kiawah.pptx**.
2. Save the presentation as **C12-E05-KiawahVacation**.
3. Click the Slide 5 thumbnail in the Slides tab at the left of the Normal screen.
4. Format Slide 5 with a Word table by completing the following steps:
   a. Open Microsoft Word.
   b. Open **KiawahTemperature.docx** located in the *Chapter12* folder.
   c. Select the table and then click Copy on the Home tab.
   d. Close the Word document and then exit Word.
   e. If PowerPoint is not displayed, click the button on the Taskbar representing PowerPoint.
   f. Make sure Slide 5 displays in the Slide pane.
   g. Click the down arrow at the bottom of the Paste button on the Home tab.
   h. At the Paste Options dialog box, click the second option, *Keep Source Formatting (K)*.
   i. Position the table similar to the one shown in Figure 12.27.
5. Format Slide 6 by completing the following steps:
   a. Read the instructions within this slide.
   b. Access www.bing.com/maps and then search for a map of Kiawah Island, South Carolina. Click the Screenshot button in the Image group in the Insert tab and then click the Screen Clipping button at the bottom of the drop-down menu. Close the www.bing.com/maps website and then size and position the map as shown in Figure 12.27. ***Hint: You may have to crop the screenshot so just the map shows. Your map may vary.***

Step 4g

Step 4h

Step 5b

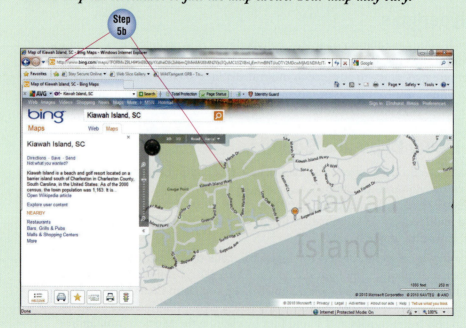

6. Format Slide 7 by completing the following steps:
   a. Display Slide 7 in the Slide pane.
   b. Insert a bitmap image by clicking the Insert Picture from File icon in the content frame in Slide 7.
   c. At the Insert Picture dialog box, locate the **CondoLayout** file in the *Chapter12* folder. Click Insert.
   d. Select the image and apply the *Bevel Rectangle* picture style. Size and position the image as shown in Figure 12.27. ***Hint: Resize the placeholder if necessary.***
   e. Select the image and apply the *Shrink and Turn* animation in the *Exit* section.

   Step 6d — Bevel Rectangle

7. Insert an Excel worksheet in Slide 8 by completing the following steps:
   a. Open Microsoft Excel.
   b. Open the worksheet named **VillaRentalRates** located in the *Chapter12* folder.
   c. Copy the worksheet to the Clipboard by selecting cells A1:B26 and then clicking *Copy*.
   d. Do not close the Excel workbook or exit Excel.
   e. Click the button on the Taskbar representing PowerPoint.
   f. Display Slide 8 in the Slide pane.
   g. Click the down-pointing arrow below the Paste button on the Home tab and then click *Paste Special*.
   h. In the Paste Special dialog box, make sure *Microsoft Office Excel Worksheet Object* is selected in the *As* list box, and then click OK.
   i. Resize and reposition the object if necessary to look similar to Figure 12.27.
   j. Select the Excel worksheet object in Slide 8 and apply the *Wheel* exit animation.
   k. Close **VillaRentalRates** and then close Excel.
8. Format Slide 9 by applying the Fade effect to the *Title* text box.
9. Insert an appropriate motion clip to Slide 9.
10. Save the presentation again with the same name **C12-E05-KiawahVacation**.
11. Run the presentation by clicking the Show Slide button on the View bar. ***Hint: The effects, transitions, and animations are advanced by clicking the*** left ***mouse button.***
12. Save, print the presentation with six slides per page, and then close **C12-05-Kiawah Vacation.pptx**.

Figure 12.27 Exercise 12.5 (continued on next page)

Figure 12.27 Exercise 12.5 (continued)

More reasons...to pick Kiawah

- Five championship golf courses
- Top tennis facilities, camps, and clinics
- Thirty miles of paved leisure trails
- Twenty-one acre Night Heron Park recreation

The charm of Charleston

- Visit the new South Carolina Aquarium
- Experience Southern cuisine
- Don't miss the Battery, Waterfront Park, and the Maritime Center

Average temperatures on Kiawah

January	59	July	89
February	61	August	89
March	67	September	84
April	76	October	77
May	82	November	69
June	86	December	61

Map of Kiawah

Parkside villa layout

- Park view
- Lagoon view
- Villa with dock
- 2 bedrooms/2 baths
- 3 bedrooms/3 baths
- 5 minute walk to beach

Rental rates

Contact us today

- Call Chase Sheehan Property Management Island Rental 843.555.8213
- www.emcp.net/kiawah
- kiawah@emcp.net
- Golf Vacations Sam Lantz 843.555.8214

Additional PowerPoint Features

Microsoft Office PowerPoint 2010 allows you to create a photo album using pictures on your hard disk or other storage media. PowerPoint 2010 also includes a feature that allows you to efficiently transport your presentation to another computer.

Creating a Photo Album

Creating a photo album in Microsoft Office PowerPoint 2010 from pictures on your hard disk or other storage media is a great way to share photographs or other illustrations. You can customize the album by using layout options such as frames of different shapes, and you can add captions to each picture. To create a photo album, complete the following steps:

1. On the Insert tab in the Illustrations group, click the Photo Album button.
2. Click the File/Disk button. In the Insert New Pictures dialog box, navigate to the folder on your hard disk containing the photos you want to include in the album. Select the images that you want to include in your album, and then click Insert.
3. In the Photo Album dialog box, the *Pictures in album* list includes the graphics you selected. You can select each picture in turn to view it. You can change the order in which the pictures will appear in the album by clicking the picture you want to move and then clicking the Move Up or Move Down button. You can also adjust the rotation, contrast, and brightness of each picture.
4. Under Album Layout, click the Picture layout arrow, and then in the list, select the desired layout.
5. Click the Frame shape arrow, and in the list, click Rounded Rectangle. Click Create.

PowerPoint creates a presentation called Photo Album that contains a title slide and a slide containing the pictures.

For interesting designs for your photo album, type **Album** in the *Search Office.com for templates* text box in the *Office.com Templates* section at the New tab Backstage view. Use a template as the starting point for your dynamic photo album presentation. Include footers with the locations and dates of your pictures.

Package a Presentation to a CD

The most efficient way to transport a PowerPoint presentation to another computer is to use the Package for CD feature. With this feature you can copy a presentation onto a CD or to a folder or network location and include all of the linked files, fonts, and PowerPoint Viewer program in case the destination computer does not have PowerPoint installed on it. To use the Package for CD feature, click the File tab, click the Save & Send tab, click *Package Presentation for CD* in the *File Types* section, and then click the Package for CD button. At the Package for CD dialog box, type a name for the CD and then click the Copy to CD button as shown in Figure 12.28.

Figure 12.28 Using the Package for CD Feature

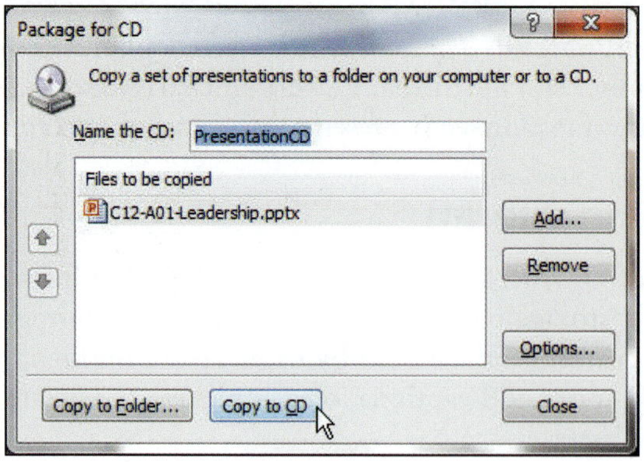

Chapter *Summary*

➤ A presentation communicates information using visual images to convey the message to an audience.

➤ When choosing a presentation design for slides, consider the audience, topic, and method of delivery.

➤ SmartArt graphics help you illustrate processes, concepts, hierarchies, and relationships in a visual, dynamic way.

➤ Theme colors, theme fonts, and theme effects reinforce consistency in your presentation.

➤ Layouts can be used to arrange objects and text on a slide. Layouts contain placeholders, which in turn hold text, such as titles and bulleted lists, and slide content such as SmartArt graphics, tables, charts, pictures, shapes, and clip art.

➤ The slide master stores information about the design template applied, including font styles, placeholder sizes and positions, background design, and color schemes.

➤ The PDF format ensures that when the file is viewed online or printed, it retains exactly the format that you intended and that data in the file cannot be easily changed.

➤ Creating a photo album in Microsoft Office PowerPoint 2010 from pictures on your digital camera or other storage media is a great way to share photographs or other illustrations.

➤ Rearrange slides within a presentation in Slide Sorter view or in Normal view with the Slides tab selected in the Outline/Slides pane.

➤ If you want changes made to a placeholder to affect all slides in a presentation, make the changes at the slide master.

➤ PowerPoint provides viewing options for presentations that include Normal view, Slide Sorter view, Notes Page, and Reading View.

➤ Slides in a slide show can be advanced manually or automatically at specific time intervals, or a slide show can be set up to run continuously.

➤ Transition refers to what action takes place as one slide is removed from the screen during a presentation and the next slide is displayed.

➤ Preparing a presentation using the Outline tab in the Outline/Slides pane helps to organize topics for each slide without the distractions of colorful designs, clip art, transitions, or sound. It is a good view to use when brainstorming the creation of a presentation.

➤ Sound effects and animation create impact in a slide show.

➤ PowerPoint's build technique displays important points one at a time on a slide.

- If you are creating a long presentation with many slides and text, use the Outline tab in the Outline/Slides pane to organize the topics for the slides.
- An outline can be created in PowerPoint, or an outline can be imported from another program, such as Microsoft Word.
- The background of a presentation should correlate to the visual medium that you are using. You may create a picture background that fills the entire slide.
- Presentations can be printed with each slide on a separate piece of paper; with each slide at the top of a page, leaving room for notes; with all or a specific number of slides on a single piece of paper; or with slide titles and topics in outline form.
- Adding tables and charts is an excellent way to show important information about relationships among groups of data.
- Sound and/or video effects that will play as the presentation runs can be added. You can configure a sound or video object to play continuously until the slide show is ended.
- A custom motion path can be created that lets you control where an object will move.
- Microsoft's Package for CD feature allows you to compress your presentation and run it from a computer that does not have PowerPoint loaded on it. It includes a mini-application called PowerPoint Viewer.

Commands Review

FEATURE	RIBBON TAB, GROUP	BUTTON, OPTION
Add Animation	Animations, Advanced Animation	
Animation Pane	Animations, Advanced Animation	Animation Pane
Background Styles	Design, Background	Background Styles ▾
Convert to SmartArt	Home, Paragraph	Convert to SmartArt ▾
Custom Slide Show	Slide Show, Start Slide Show	
Effect Options	Animations, Animation	
From Beginning	Slide Show, Start Slide Show	
Header & Footer	Insert, Text	
Hyperlink	Insert, Links	
Layout	Home, Slides	Layout ▾
New Slide	Home, Slides	
Normal View	View, Presentation Views or View toolbar at bottom of slide pane	

FEATURE	RIBBON TAB, GROUP	BUTTON, OPTION
Notes Page	View, Presentation View or View toolbar at bottom of slide pane	
Package a CD	File tab, Save & Send, Package Presentation for CD	
Photo Album	Insert, Illustrations	
Rehearse Timings	Slide Show, Set Up	
Screenshot	Insert, Images	
Section	Home, Slides	Section ▾
Setup Slide Show	Slide Show, Set Up	
Slide Master View	View, Master Views	
Slide Number	Insert, Text	
Slide Sorter View	View, Presentation Views or View toolbar at bottom of slide pane	
SmartArt	Insert, Illustrations	

Reviewing Key Points

True or False: Circle T or F for the following:

1. Slide animation refers to how one slide is removed from the screen and replaced with the next slide.

      T   F

2. If you want changes made to placeholders to affect all slides in a presentation, make the changes at the slide master.

      T   F

3. You can rearrange slides in Slide Sorter view.

      T   F

4. Click the Delete key to stop a presentation in a continuous loop.

      T   F

5. Press the Esc key on the keyboard to end a presentation without running all of the slides.

      T   F

6. Add a picture background to a slide by clicking the Insert Clip Art button on the Design tab.

       T   F

7. A slide layout format may contain a table placeholder.

       T   F

8. You can add rehearsed timings in Slide Sorter view.

       T   F

9. You can use the Laser pointer in Slide Show view.

       T   F

10. You can add a SmartArt object to a slide by selecting a content layout that includes an icon that links you to this feature or click the Convert button in the Design tab.

       T   F

11. You cannot add black or white to a slide to temporarily hide the slide content.

       T   F

12. You cannot customize the colors in a theme.

       T   F

13. You can change the speed of a transition and a build.

       T   F

14. PowerPoint's build technique displays important points one at a time on a slide.

       T   F

15. Use the Paste Special feature on the Insert tab to insert an Excel worksheet into a PowerPoint slide.

       T   F

Chapter Assessments

Assessment 12.1   Women into Leadership Presentation

Use the following text to create a slide show presentation on women into leadership. Figure 12.29 displays the first two slides from a sample presentation on this topic. Include the specifications listed below the text:

Women into Leadership

Leadership: Influence and Impact

Describe some characteristics you associate with the word LEADERSHIP.

What is leadership:

    Leadership is action, not position.

    Leadership is influence, not authority.

Leadership translates vision into reality.

Leadership inspires others to dream more, learn more, do more, and become more.

Leadership is getting people from where they are to where they have not been.

Paving Your Leadership Path

Take ownership of your career.

Have an action plan.

Get sponsorship from senior leaders—support and visibility.

Take advantage of the resources available.

Accept the challenge and reject the victim mentality.

How Do You Grow as a Leader?

Seek out stretch opportunities.

Find a mentor.

Know your strength and weaknesses.

Build your strengths.

Lead through others.

Quote - *(Access the Internet to find an appropriate quote for this last slide - search for Women in Leadership quote.)*

1. Create at least six slides.
2. Use an appropriate theme or template.
3. Insert at least one clip art image or photograph to reinforce the message in the slide.
4. Use at least one SmartArt object to emphasize an important point.
5. Use a search engine to find an appropriate quote for the last slide.
6. Add transitions and animations to the slides.
7. Insert slide numbers and the current date.
8. Save your presentation as **C12-A01-Leadership.pptx**.
9. Run your presentation for your class and prepare handouts for all the students in the classroom. Critique each other's presentations along with the professionalism of the delivery by using the **PresentationEvaluation.docx** available in your *Chapter12* folder.
10. Save the presentation as a video by clicking the File tab, Save & Send, Create a Video, and then the Create Video button. Save the video to your storage device, double-click the file to open it, and then view the video.
11. Close **C12-A01-Leadership.pptx** and then **C12-A01-Leadership.vmv**.

Figure 12.29 Assessment 12.1 Sample Solution

Figure 12.30 Assessment 12.2 Sample Solution

Assessment 12.2   Virtual Office Presentation

Use the Internet to research the virtual office concept. Create a presentation from your findings. Figure 12.30 displays the first two slides from a sample presentation on this topic. If your college provides a virtual office class, you may use information about this course offering. Include the following specifications:

1. Create at least six slides.
2. Use an appropriate theme or template.
3. Insert a least one clip art image or photograph to reinforce the message in the slide.
4. Use at least one SmartArt object to emphasize an important point.
5. Add transitions and animations to the slides.
6. Time the slides to change every five seconds or any time sequence of your choosing. Make the slide show a continuous on-screen presentation.
7. Save your presentation as **C12-A01-Virtual.pptx**.
8. Run your presentation for your class and prepare handouts for all the students in the classroom. Critique each other's presentations along with the professionalism of the delivery by using the **PresentationEvaluation.docx** form available in your *Chapter12* folder.
9. Close **C12-A02-Virtual.pptx**.

Assessment 12.3   Personalized Presentation

Prepare a PowerPoint presentation of your own choosing. Some suggestions for presentation topics include outlining your medical plan at work, planning an incredible international vacation, highlighting the advantages of attending a particular college or university, pursuing a career in real estate, highlighting your home town, or planning a vacation. Create an on-screen presentation in PowerPoint according to the following specifications:

1. Use a blank presentation screen, a design template, or a template from the Office.com Templates and customize it to complement your presentation. *Hint: Photographs make dramatic backgrounds.*
2. Use the Internet and a search engine to research a topic of your own choosing.
3. Use several slide layouts to vary the look of your presentation.
4. Apply an appropriate theme if you are starting at a blank presentation screen.
5. Add any appropriate clip art, animated clips, movies, or photographs.
6. Use a build effect for the bulleted items. You decide on the bullet symbol to be used.
7. Apply transition effects to your slides.
8. Time the slides to change every five seconds.

Figure 12.31 Assessment 12.4 Sample Solution

9. Make the slide show a continuous on-screen presentation.
10. Save the presentation and name it **C12-A03-MyPresentation**.
11. Run the presentation for your classmates.
12. Open and then print a copy of **PresentationEvaluation.docx** located in the *Chapter12* folder. Ask your audience to evaluate your presentation.
13. Print and then close **C12-A03-MyPresentation.pptx**. *Optional:* Add animation and sound effects to your presentation. Consider creating a short video or your own photographs using your digital camera. Insert the video and images into your presentation. Also, experiment with saving the presentation as a video file.

Assessment 12.4   Photo Album in PowerPoint

Create a photo album in PowerPoint 2010 and include the following specifications:

1. If you have access to a digital camera, take a series of photographs on a subject of your own choosing. *Hint: You may want to use the Compress Picture feature in the Adjust group on the Picture Tools Format tab to reduce the size of the photographs.*
2. You may use a theme or a template as the basic design of your presentation.
3. Insert a sound clip to your photo album.
4. Include slide transitions and slide animations in your presentation.
5. Save your album as **C12-A04-Album**.
6. Print and then close **C12-A04-Album**. Figure 12.31 shows a sample solution.

Assessment 12.5   Creating a Document in PowerPoint

1. Using PowerPoint 2010, prepare a certificate of completion or a flyer using a slide layout and theme. You may use a template or create the document at a blank publication screen.
2. Create the certificate for a coworker, an outstanding teacher, a supportive friend, or a generous volunteer; or create a flyer promoting a new business or class at your college.
3. Save the document as **C12-A05-Document**.
4. Print and then close **C12-A05-Document.pptx**. *Optional:* Create another slide in landscape orientation that relates to the document created in this assessment. Use the slide as a cover, print your flyer on the back side of the cover, and then fold it in half and use the slides as a single-fold brochure. Figure 12.32 displays a sample information sheet prepared in PowerPoint using a slide layout.

Figure 12.32 Assessment 12.5 Sample Solution

Assessment 12.6   Adding Visual Effects to Presentations

1. Open PowerPoint, click the File tab, and then click New.
2. At the New tab Backstage view, click the *PowerPoint presentations and slides* category in the *Office.com Templates* section.
3. Click the *Example Slide effects with instructions* category.
4. Click the *Static picture effects for PowerPoint slides* template and then click Download.
5. Run the presentation and then recreate two designs following the directions provided in these slides. You may want to print the slides to read the instrucions.
6. Save your slides as **C12-A06-Visual.pptx** and then print them. Close **C12-A06-Visual.pptx**.

Performance Assessments

Preparing Publications

ASSESSING PROFICIENCIES

In Unit 3 you learned how to create forms in Word that you could actually fill in without viewing the lines move around the screen, you were introduced to many desktop features in Publisher, and you learned how to create dynamic presentations in PowerPoint. The following assessments will test your proficiency in each of these areas.

Note: Before completing computer exercises, copy the **Unit03** *folder from the CD that accompanies this textbook and then make* **Unit03** *the active folder.*

Assessment U3.1   Creating a Fill-In Form using the Developer Tab

Create a tuition wavier dependency verification form similar to the one shown in Figure U3.1. The completed form is shown on the next page.

1. At a blank document, create a table as an underlining structure for the form.
2. Type the text as shown in the form in Figure U3.1. Apply appropriate styles to the text in the form.
3. Create a logo for Midwest College.
4. Display the Developer tab, click to turn on Design Mode in the Controls group, and then add Legacy Forms text fields next to each label in the form.

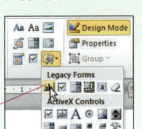

Step 4

5. Insert a date picker form field next to the date next to the signature line at the bottom of the form.
6. Insert check boxes in the *Choose One* section.
7. Click the Design Mode button to toggle it off.
8. Click the Restrict Editing button in the Protect group. Select the option to allow the user to fill in the form. A password is not necessary.
9. Save the form as a template and name it **U03-PA01-TuitionForm.dotx**.
10. Close the form.
11. Reopen the form and complete it.
12. Print and then close **U03-PA01-TuitionForm.dotx**.

TUITION WAIVER DEPENDENCY VERIFICATION

Midwest College

FORM FOR BENEFITED EMPLOYEES

Key all **highlighted** sections, print, sign/date hard copy, and return to Human Resources **OR** print blank form, print in all **highlighted** sections, sign/date, and return to Human Resources.

Employee Name: (type or print)	
Employee ID #:	

Choose One: (X)

☐	Administrator	☐	FT Faculty
☐	Benefited Classified	☐	Operating Engineer
☐	FOP	☐	Retiree

1. Spouse

Last Name:	
First Name:	
Spouse ID # OR	
Social Security Number:	

2. Dependant

Last Name:	
First Name:	
Relationship:	
Dependant ID # OR	
Social Security Number:	
Date of Birth (mm/dd/yyyy):	

3. Dependant

Last Name:	
First Name:	
Relationship:	
Dependant ID # OR	
Social Security Number:	
Date of Birth (mm/dd/yyyy):	

If you have additional eligible dependants, please complete and attach a second form.

I hereby certify that the above named dependant(s) are eligible to be a tax dependant on my United States Federal Tax Form 1040/1040A for the calendar year ended December 31, 2012.

Employee Signature   **Date** Click here to enter a date.

_____

Assessment U3.2   Creating a Heart Scan Flyer using Publisher

Use Publisher to create the heart scan flyer shown in Figure U3.2. Include the following specifications:

1. Open Publisher.
2. Study the strong vertical alignment of the flyer in Figure U3.2.
   At a blank document, draw text boxes to hold the text. Drag the boxes to position them appropriately.
3. Type the text shown in Figure U3.2 and format the text similarly. Remember to expand the text when necessary.

4. Insert a graphic that supports the subject of the flyer and apply a shadow effect.
5. Select a color scheme that complements the graphic. Add text color to add spot color to the document and reinforce the graphic.
6. Insert the **EdwardCardioBW.tif** file located in your *Unit03* folder.
7. Make any necessary adjustments in leading to make the text look similar to Figure U3.2.
8. Save the document and name it **U03-PA02-HeartScan**.
9. Print and then close **U03-PA02-HeartScan.pub**.

Figure U3.2 Assessment U3.2

ANNOUNCING

Ultra *Fast* Heart Scan

from the Edward Cardiovascular Institute

15 minutes, start to finish...

Take it during your lunch hour...
and be back in time for your 1 o'clock meeting.

Ultra Fast Heart Scan is the simple, non-invasive heart test you have heard about—the one that uses powerful electron beam tomography to detect coronary artery calcification at an early, treatable state. It's the only test in the western suburbs with this technology.

To schedule your appointment, call Monday–Friday, 8 a.m. to 5 p.m.

1-877-45-HEART

EDWARD
CARDIOVASCULAR INSTITUTE

Assessment U3.3   Creating a Flyer with Tear-Offs

Using Publisher 2010, create a flyer with tear-offs as shown in Figure U3.3 and include the following specifications:

1. Open Publisher.
2. Type the text shown in Figure U3.3. Key this text in the tear-offs:
   Julia Hatcher, Steppin' Out
   Phone: 952.555.3234
   www.emcp.net/steppinout
   Email: steppinout@emcp.net

   Use your own design ideas in creating the flyer. Figure U3.3 is a sample document.
3. Insert images of your own choosing.
4. Select a theme, fonts, and colors that complement your message.
5. Insert the tear-offs by clicking the Page Parts button in the Building Blocks group in the Insert tab.

Figure U3.3 **Assessment U3.3 Sample Solution**

6. Insert the attention-getter by clicking the Advertisement button in the Building Blocks group and then clicking the *More Advertisements* option at the bottom of drop-down gallery. ***Hint: The theme you select will influence the fonts available and the colors that appear on the building block objects.***
7. Save your document as **U3-PA03-Dance**.
8. Print and then close **U3-PA03-Dance.pub**.

Assessment U3.4   Redoing a Document

Find a printed document and redo the document using Publisher, Word, or PowerPoint. If possible, integrate the document using Access and/or Excel. Include the following:

1. If the document needs improvement, recreate the document to make it better.
2. Be sure to demonstrate the use of good design—review Chapter 1 if necessary.
3. Save the document as **U3-PA04-Redo**.
4. Print **U3-PA04-Redo** and then attach it to the original document.
5. Write a short summary of where you improved the document and how you went about reproducing it.
6. Close **U3-PA04-Redo**.

DTP CHALLENGE

Assessment U3.5   Creating a Social Networking Presentation

Take your skills to the next level by completing this more challenging assessment.

Are you up-to-date on current technology and communication trends? Research *Social and Professional Networking* on the Internet and then create a PowerPoint presentation highlighting each of these current trends. Some of the keywords you may want to research include *Facebook, Skype, LinkedIn, Jigsaw, Twitter, Blogging,* and *YouTube*. Include information on membership requirements, costs, pros and cons, and an explanation of each site.

Include the following specifications:

1. Create at least six slides.
2. Use the Internet to research the content.
3. Insert clip art, photographs, or SmartArt to enhance your presentation.
4. Vary your slide layouts.
5. Apply slide transitions and animations.
6. Save your presentation as **U3-CA05-OnlineNetworking**.
7. Print your presentation with 3 slides per page. This allows for an area to take notes at the right of the printed slides. ***Optional:*** Print enough copies for your instructor and all the students in your class.
8. Run your presentation using appropriate timed durations.
9. Close **U3-CA05-OnlineNetworking.pptx**.

Index